GREAT BOOKS

My Adventures with Homer,

Rousseau, Woolf, and Other

Indestructible Writers of

the Western World

DAVID DENBY

A TOUCHSTONE BOOK
Published by Simon & Schuster

TOUCHSTONE
Rockefeller Center
1230 Avenue of the Americas
New York, NY 10020

First Touchstone Edition 1997

TOUCHSTONE and colophon are registered trademarks
of Simon & Schuster Inc.

Designed by Leslie Phillips

Manufactured in the United States of America

10   9   8   7   6   5   4   3   2

The Library of Congress has cataloged the Simon & Schuster edition as follows:
Denby, David.
Great books : my adventures with Homer, Rousseau, Woolf, and
other indestructible writers of the Western world / David Denby.
p. cm.   Includes bibliographical references and index.
1. Civilization, Western—History—Sources—Study and teaching
(Higher)—United States.
2. Humanities—Study and teaching (Higher)—United States.
3. Literature—Study and teaching (Higher)—United States.
4. Denby, David—Books and reading.   I. Title.
CB245.D44   1996   909′.09812—dc20   96-18634   CIP
ISBN 0-684-80975-3
ISBN 0-684-83533-9 (Pbk)

Three of these chapters appeared in *The New Yorker* in slightly different
form: chapter 1 (as "Does Homer Have Legs?," September 6, 1993),
chapter 21 (as "Queen Lear," October 3, 1994), and chapter 27
(as "Jungle Fever," November 6, 1995). An earlier version of chapter 4
appeared in *Columbia College Today* as "Confronting the *Odyssey*"
(winter–spring 1994).

(continued on page 493)

Acknowledgments

This book would not have been conceived, written, or published without the encouragement and support of four exceptionally strong-willed persons: Kathy Robbins, literary agent; Alice Mayhew, editorial director of Simon & Schuster; Tina Brown, editor of *The New Yorker;* and the most formidable of all, Cathleen Schine, novelist, mother, friend, and wife.

I would like to thank the many students, teachers, and administrators I met at Columbia, both those named in the book (the teachers and administrators accurately, the students pseudonymously) and those unhappily omitted for lack of space. They all put up with my intrusions into the classroom and patiently answered questions in hallways, elevators, dorm rooms, offices, quadrangles, streets, and restaurants. I would particularly like to thank Kathryn Yatrakis, the associate dean of the college; Professor Eileen Gilooley, the administrative coordinator of the Literature Humanities and Contemporary Civilization courses; the former directors of those courses, Professor James Mirollo and Professor J. W. Smit, respectively; and, for general support, Professors Andrew Delbanco and Michael Rosenthal.

For this book about reading, I asked some of the best readers I could find (none connected with Columbia) to criticize individual chapters. I am especially grateful for the extraordinary efforts of Louis Menand, whose brilliance, logical sense, and sweet stubbornness have already become legendary among readers, friends, and students; and I am indebted as well to Adam Gopnik, Jonathan Lear, Mark Lilla, Judith Shulevitz, Henry Finder, Paul Berman, Nancy Franklin, Robert Caserio, and Penny House. My sense of gratitude to all of them leads me to insist that any remaining errors and misconceptions in the book are entirely my own responsibility.

I would also like to thank, at Simon & Schuster, Lisa Weisman and copy editors Fred Wiemer and Steve Messina; and at *New York* magazine, former editor Edward Kosner and current editor Kurt Andersen, who patiently tolerated my occasional absences; and Annys Shin, who did some necessary fact-checking.

In loving memory of

EZRA LAWRENCE DENBY

and

IDA HARKAVY DENBY

Contents

Introduction

In the fall of 1991, thirty years after entering Columbia University for the first time, I went back to school and sat with eighteen-year-olds and read the same books that they read. Not just any books. Together we read Homer, Plato, Sophocles, Augustine, Kant, Hegel, Marx, and Virginia Woolf. *Those* books. *Those* courses—the two required core-curriculum courses that I had first taken in 1961, innocently and unconsciously, as a freshman at Columbia College. No one in that era could possibly have imagined that in the following decades the courses would be alternately reviled as an iniquitous oppression and adored as a bulwark of the West.

One of the courses, Literature Humanities, or Lit Hum, as everyone calls it, is (and was) devoted to a standard selection of European literary masterpieces; the other, Contemporary Civilization, or C.C., offers a selection of philosophical and social-theory masterpieces. They are both "great books" courses, or, if you like, "Western civ" surveys, a list of heavyweight names assembled in chronological order like the marble busts in some imaginary pantheon of glory. Such courses were first devised, earlier in the century, at Columbia; they then spread to the University of Chicago, and in the 1940s to many other universities and colleges. They have since, putting it mildly, receded. At times, they have come close to extinction, though not at Columbia or Chicago.

Despite my explanations, my fellow students in 1991 may well have wondered what in the world I was doing there, sitting in uncomfortable oak-plank chairs with *them*. I was certainly a most unlikely student: forty-eight years old, the film critic of *New York* magazine, a husband and father, a settled man who was nevertheless unsettled in some way that may not have been any clearer to me than it was to them. Was it just knowledge I wanted? I had read many of the books before. Yet the students may have noticed that nothing in life seemed more important to me than reading those books and sitting in on those discussions.

11

This book is an account of my year as a second-time student. I have written it the way it happened to me, as a journey sometimes perilous, sometimes serene, and as an introduction to the great stories and momentous ideas I consumed with such hunger in middle age. An adventure book, then, and also a naïve book, an amateur's book—in other words, a folly. It couldn't have been anything else.

❖   ❖   ❖

The project began when my wife suggested that I put up or shut up. In 1989 or 1990, somewhere back there, Cathleen Schine and I were reading, with increasing amazement, the debate about the nature of higher education in this country. Merely reciting the clichés of the debate now induces a blue haze of exasperation and boredom: What role should the Western classics and a "Eurocentric" curriculum play in a country whose population was made up of people from many other places besides Europe—for instance, descendants of African slaves and American Indians? Should groups formerly without much power—women, as well as minorities—be asked to read through a curriculum dominated by works written by Dead White European Males?

The questions were not in themselves unreasonable, but it now seems hard to believe that anyone above sixteen could possibly have used, as a term of blame, the phrase "Dead White European Males." The words have already taken on a quaint period feel, as moldy as the love beads that I wore once, in the spring of 1968, and then flung into the back of a dresser drawer. Such complaints, which issued generally from the academic left, especially from a variety of feminist, Marxist, and African-American scholars, were answered in turn by conservatives with resoundingly grandiose notions of the importance of the Western tradition for American national morale. In their consecutive stints as chair of the National Endowment for the Humanities, William Bennett and Lynne V. Cheney said some good things about the centrality of the humanities in the life of an educated person. But the clear implication of their more polemical remarks was that if we ceased to read the right books, we could not keep Communism or relativism—or whatever threatened the Republic—at the gates. There were national, even geopolitical considerations at stake. Literature had become a matter of *policy*. I was depressed by this fate for literature, and by the assumptions that emerged from such conservative attacks on the academic left as Roger Kimball's *Tenured Radicals* (1990), in which literature appears as an ineffably noble but essentially static body of values that could, and should, be inoculated into every generation of American students. Passivity was not my ideal of a reader's response; nor could I understand how the works in question could ever have reached canonical status if they had produced nothing more vital in readers than grateful acceptance.

As I made my way through the debate, I began to suffer from an increasing sense of unreality. Thirty years earlier, I had enjoyed Lit Hum and C.C. a great deal, but then had largely forgotten them, as one forgets most college courses one takes. Exactly how the books for the courses had remained in my mind, as a residue of impressions and a framework of taste and sensibility, and even of action, I could not say. That was the mystery, wasn't it?—the mystery of education. Exactly how does it matter to us? The participants in the debate, however, seemed to know. They made extravagant claims for or against the books and the Western tradition the books embodied. At the same time, they discussed the books themselves—works of literature, philosophy, and political theory—in an unpleasantly featureless and abstract way that turned them into mere clubs and spears in an ideological war. Shakespeare an agent of colonialism? Rousseau part of the "hegemonic discourse"? The Greek classics a bulwark of democracy? Was it really literature and philosophy that people were discussing in such terms? One had the uncanny sense that at least some of the disputants hadn't bothered to read the books in question in more than twenty years. Could such classic works actually be as boring as the right—or as wicked as the left—was making them sound? The books themselves had been robbed of body and flavor. And in so many of the polemics, the act of reading itself had become hollowed out—emptied of its place in any reader's life, its stresses and pleasures, its boredom, its occasional euphoria. It had lost its special character of solitude and rapture.

Yet strange as the debate seemed to me, it had a galvanizing effect. For months, I was angry and even pained. I felt I had been cheated of something, and it didn't take long to realize why. If some of the disputants appeared to be far away from the books in question, I knew that I was far away from them, too. I had read, I had forgotten, and I felt the loss as I did the loss of an old friend who had faded away. I was filled with longing and curiosity. What was the actual experience of reading such books? What did one get out of them? What pleasure, what anger, what excitement and anguish? Most of all, what was *in* them? How could they cause such rage in women, African-Americans, radical academics, and such complacent triumphalism in conservative male politicians? What were we talking about here?

I worked myself into a high state of indignation, and Cathy, both a novelist and a reader, shared my view but grew tired of my outrage. There she sat in our apartment in New York, reading book after book, in bed, in the living room, at the chair by the living-room window. Often she read with a cat in her lap, the animal happily purring; its mistress, lost in her reading, scratched its head for hours. My wife was too kind, and perhaps too busy, to point out something that later seemed obvious: I had become something of a nonreader myself; or, let us say, a reader of journalism, public-affairs books, and essays on this or that. "If you're so upset about this," Cathy finally said, "why don't you take your Columbia courses again?"

Thus the revenge of the reader on the nonreader: why don't you read and stop complaining? Certainly the means to answer my questions lay at hand. Columbia was only a couple of miles from my apartment on the West Side of Manhattan. And the courses, though somewhat different in their selection of texts (see the reading lists on pages 21–24 and 465–466), had not changed much in conception.

Few people at Columbia, in 1961 or in the nineties, publicly called Lit Hum and C.C. "great books" courses, a term which smacked of leather-bound "sets" with gold-leaf edges and the hard sell of snobbish magazine and newspaper ads. The taint of consumerism and middlebrowism, as the college well knows, was never too far from lists of classics. The college tried to dispel that taint by the way it organized and taught the two courses. First of all, the readings were often difficult, especially for contemporary students. Here was the Western tradition with a vengeance, honored by custom and justified, the college insisted, by need. The implication of requiring the courses from everyone was clear enough: Whatever trade or profession, whatever glory or ignominy lay in store for the eighteen-year-old student, he or she should not undergo it without this fortification. These were the authors who most dramatically constituted "the West"; these were among the books that spoke most directly to what a human being was and could be. They should be part of everyone's culture.

Second, the courses were taught not by authorities or specialists holding forth in a lecture hall, but by a wide variety of faculty working entirely in small sections. The classes might be led by a senior professor who had taught the course for decades or by a fourth-year graduate student trying to make some money while working on her dissertation. And the instructors came from any one of a number of fields. The Department of English and Comparative Literature dominated Lit Hum, but teachers from Philosophy, Religion, Classics, French, German, Italian, Slavic Studies, and Middle East Languages and Cultures also took part. C.C. was taught by historians, but also by political scientists, philosophers, classicists, economists, anthropologists, an occasional sociologist or historian of religion. All were expected to partake in what the academic left has ridiculed as the "narrative" of Western culture. The charm, and some would say the strength, of the courses lay in their proud nonspecialization, their appeal to the old ideal of a student armed for selfhood and citizenship. The courses were situated as far as possible from the current vogues of "theory" and "contextualization" and such cutting-edge scholarly concerns as race, gender, and class. The student just jumped in; he read a series of great works. In contemporary academic terms, the courses were a scandal.

I was eager to jump myself, but many things intervened, and by the time I came back to the idea, a couple of years later, I realized that I was stumbling through a kind of crisis, a muddle that made the project perhaps even more necessary than I had thought before.

I have been a journalist all my life, a film critic since 1969, and I enjoy magazine writing very much. But by the early nineties I was beginning to be sick at heart, sick not of movies or movie criticism but of living my life inside what the French philosopher Guy Debord has called "the society of the spectacle"—that immense system of representations and simulacra, the thick atmosphere of information and imagery and attitudes that forms the mental condition and habits of almost any adult living in a media society in the late twentieth century. A member of the media, I was also tired of the media; I was more than uneasy in that vale of shadows, that frenetic but gloomy half-life filled with names, places, chatter, acts, cars racing, gunshots, experts talking, daytime couples accusing one another of infidelity, the sheer busyness of it all, the constant movement, the incredible activity and utter boredom, the low hum of *needs being satisfied*.

Not my needs, however. The media give information, but information, in the 1990s, has become transitory and unstable. Once in place, it immediately gets pulled apart, the fragments upgraded, the rest hustled off the stage. No one's information is ever quite adequate, which is one reason among many that Americans now seem half-mad with anxiety and restlessness. Like many others, I was jaded yet still hungry; I was cast into the modern state of living-in-the-media, a state of excitement needled with disgust. At the end of the century, the end (even!) of the millennium, the media threaten to take over altogether and push literature out of sight, and my disgust was tinged with intense emotions I couldn't quite pin down—nostalgia, regret, anger, even despair.

But it was no time for elegy.

I needed to start work on this book in part because I no longer knew what I knew. I felt that what I had read or understood was slipping away. I possessed information without knowledge, opinions without principles, instincts without beliefs. The foundations of the building were turning to sand while I sat in the upper balconies looking out at the sea. Feeling the wiggle, I knew I was in trouble. I sensed my identity had softened and merged into the atmosphere of representation, and I couldn't quite see where it ended and I began. My own memories were lapsing out into the fog of media life, the unlived life as spectator. Perhaps the professional movie critic, as he ages, undergoes a special anxiety, though I don't think so. We are all movie critics; I just happen to write down and publish my opinions. Everyone lives in the media.

Reading "the great books" may seem an odd solution to a "midlife crisis" or a crisis of identity, or whatever it was. Why not travel or hunt elephants? Chase teenage girls? Live in a monastery? These, I believe, are the traditional methods—for men, at least—of dealing with such problems. But if I wanted adventure, I wanted it in a way that made sense for me. Reading seriously, I thought, might be one way of ending my absorption in media life, a way of finding the edges again.

But why not just sit and read? Why go back to Columbia? Because I wanted to see how others were reading—or not reading. The students had grown up living in the media. What were they like? What had happened to teaching in the age of the culture debate, in a corner of the university far from the war yet obviously touched by the noise of battle? One way of dispelling the crudities and irrelevancies of the "culture wars" was to find out what actually went on in classrooms.

And I wanted to add my words to the debate from the ground up, beginning and ending in literature, never leaving the books themselves.

❖   ❖   ❖

For a full academic year, I read the books, observed the students and teachers, and hawkeyed myself. At the same time, except for a few short periods of leave, I went to movies and reviewed them, as I had for years, for *New York* magazine; I helped my wife get the children up in the morning and to bed at night, and lived, as normally as I could, as father and husband, taxpayer and partygoer, friend and enemy. The point, I thought, was not to give up my life but to live it fully and to see how the books fit into the way I lived.

I set some ground rules. I would read everything and take notes, but I would write only about the books that most engaged me. Extending piety to classics that one didn't respond to was an academic vice, and I had to avoid it. I would read for enjoyment and instruction, and when bored, I would say so. Second, I would rely on my own responses and the classroom material, and stay away from secondary sources. I knew I would find it impossible not to reread some critical classics—Erich Auerbach's *Mimesis*, for instance, a half-century-old masterpiece of commentary that could almost serve as a companion to Lit Hum. But I did not want to become so immersed in contemporary academic criticism that I would spend all my time understanding and debating the latest theorists rather than attending to Machiavelli. I decided to read only enough of the recent academic criticism to get a general idea of what the professors were up to.

As a practicing journalist and critic, I had learned to trust naïve responses—not to consider them inviolate or final, but to trust the initial charge of feeling. By necessity as well as temperament, a cultural journalist is usually an impressionist and an empiricist; he rarely cares *how* we know things as much as he cares *what* we know and what effect it has. Texture, color, and experience excite him; art, if he hasn't gone numb, ravishes his senses. But the context and social composition of art leave him cold or figure for him only as secondary matters. I trust I will not be accused of praising ignorance. But without feeling proud of what one lacks, one can make the most of the skills and knowledge that one has. Writing the book, I wanted to avoid the technology of criticism; I longed to commit the unspeakable sin (in academic circles) of belletrism—the sin of writing the book for the reader's pleasure and my own.

❖   ❖   ❖

I hope no one will read the book as a glorification of one particular university and an implicit put-down of other universities and colleges. It is not so intended. For there is no royal road to heaven but only the many roads large and small, the innumerable brambled paths and curving detours as well, a thousand steps and turns leading to education. Columbia is the setting of the book but not its subject. Anyone looking for institutional history or administrative detail will have to look elsewhere.* The general reader need know only that C.C. grew out of Columbia's War Issues course offered during the First World War and was considered from the beginning a defense of Western civilization; and that Lit Hum (or Humanities A, as it was initially called) emerged in 1937 from a General Honors course developed by teacher and editor John Erskine over a period of years. From the beginning, Lit Hum was intended to enshrine the literature of Christian Europe in a college increasingly populated by the children of Eastern or Southern European immigrants—the unwashed but not unwashable Jews and Italians who needed to be assimilated into the larger culture of the country. What an irony, then, that such courses are now attacked for *marginalizing* later generations of immigrants, or members of minority groups, or women. Was there anything of the original intention or effects still at work in the courses? It was one of the things I wondered about when I started.

* Gerald Graff, in his *Professing Literature: An Institutional History* (Chicago: University of Chicago Press, 1987; pp. 132–136) situates Columbia's core-curriculum courses within the history of American higher education. For greater detail, see Justus Buchler, "Reconstruction in the Liberal Arts," in *History of Columbia College on Morningside Heights*, edited by Dwight Miner (New York: Columbia University Press, 1954); Daniel Bell, *The Reforming of General Education* (New York: Columbia University Press, 1966); Lionel Trilling, "Some Notes for an Autobiographical Lecture," in *The Last Decade: Essays and Reviews, 1965–75* (New York: Harcourt Brace Jovanovich, 1979); and Timothy P. Cross, *An Oasis of Order: The Core Curriculum at Columbia College* (New York: Office of the Dean, Columbia College, 1995).

A few other disclaimers. I don't mean to imply that these are the only books that matter, or even that they are necessarily the best collection of Western classics for such courses. To some degree, the lists remain arbitrary. I believe that most people at Columbia who teach or administer Lit Hum or C.C. will admit that. Other universities have different lists that may be equally valid, and at times Columbia itself has had different books on its own lists (over 130 works, in varying combinations, have turned up on the Lit Hum list since 1937). With world enough and time, we would read everything, and such lists wouldn't be necessary at all. But anyone offering a course must choose, and certainly the lists are representative and therefore a fit subject for analysis. Second, Columbia is quite explicit about the preliminary nature of the enterprise: The Western tradition embodied in its core curriculum is not meant to exclude other traditions but merely to provide a base for undergraduates to stand on. A student generally takes the courses in the first two years of school. She then majors in history, or biology, or archaeology, or African-American studies. If she has literary interests, she may read the Metaphysical poets and the nineteenth-century British novelists; or the African-Americans Frederick Douglass, W. E. B. Du Bois, Richard Wright, Toni Morrison; or the Africans Ngũgĩ Wa Thiongo and Chinua Achebe; or such writers of the Islamic World as Naguib Mahfouz and Mahmoud Darwish. She does whatever it is that she does with her major, her reading, her identity, and her life. But first she starts out in a specific place, and it is worth asking whether that is a good place, a justified place, a necessary place.

A Note on Editions and Translations

Except where noted, I have used the editions and the translations that Columbia assigns to its students. (See the reading lists, pages 21–24, for details.)

A Note on Chronology

For the purposes of this book, I took the Lit Hum and C.C. courses together, something that students rarely do in the 1990s (the reading lists have become too long). Quickly enough, I discovered that the courses almost never stay in sync chronologically. Thus in November of the fall term, while C.C. jumps ahead to St. Augustine and the fourth century A.D., Lit Hum is still reading Plato, who wrote more than seven hundred years earlier. I was left with a compositional choice—either to arrange the books in simple chronological order or to keep them closer to the order in which I experienced them. I chose the latter strategy, though modifying it slightly so as to alternate, for variety, Lit Hum and C.C. authors and so as not to send the reader flying too violently from one era to another and then back again.

A Note on the Names of Teachers and Students

All the teachers appear under their own names. Columbia undergraduates, however, should not be press-ganged into my spiritual adventure at a vulnerable time in their lives. Therefore, I have assigned them pseudonyms. The students are real; the names are not.

A Note on How to Read This Book

I responded to the books as I read them, one after another, embedded in the two courses. But books this powerful cannot live comfortably in an arbitrary narrative; each book is also a mold-shattering world of its own. Therefore, the reader should feel free to read the chapters either consecutively, following my adventure over time, or in any order he wants, as interest or pleasure suggests.

Reading Lists

LITERATURE HUMANITIES

Homer	*Iliad* (Chicago; Lattimore, trans.)
	Odyssey (Harper; Lattimore, trans.)
Hymn to Demeter	*Homeric Hymns* (Johns Hopkins; Athanassakis, trans.)
Sappho	Translations by J. V. Cunningham and others
Aeschylus	*Oresteia* (Chicago; Lattimore, trans.)
Sophocles	*Oedipus the King* (Chicago; Grene, trans.)
	Antigone (Chicago; Grene, trans.)
Thucydides	*The History of the Peloponnesian War*; selections (Penguin; Warner, trans.)
Euripides	*Electra* (Chicago; Vermeule, trans.)
	The Bacchae (Chicago; Arrowsmith, trans.)
Aristophanes	*The Clouds* (Meridian; Arrowsmith, trans.)
Plato	*Symposium* (Hackett; Nehemas and Woodruff, trans.)
	Apology (Hackett; Grube, trans.)
	or
	The Republic (Hackett; Grube, trans.)
Aristotle	*The Nicomachean Ethics* (Oxford; Ross, trans.)
	The Poetics (Macmillan; Grube, trans.)
Virgil	*Aeneid* (Random House; Fitzgerald, trans.)
The Bible	The Old Testament: Genesis, Job (Meridian; King James or Revised Standard Version)

CONTEMPORARY CIVILIZATION

SECTION I: THE GREEK AND ROMAN WORLD

Thucydides	*The History of the Peloponnesian War*; selections (Penguin; Warner, trans.)
Plato	*The Republic* (Penguin; Lee, trans.)
Aristotle	*The Politics* (Penguin; Sinclair, trans.)
	The Nicomachean Ethics (Oxford; Ross, trans.)
Cicero	*On the Good Life* (Penguin; Grant, trans.)

SECTION II: THE SOURCES OF THE JUDEO-CHRISTIAN TRADITION

The Bible	The Old Testament: Genesis, Exodus, Isaiah
	The New Testament: Matthew, Acts, Romans, James, Revelation (Meridian; Revised Standard Version)

SECTION III: THE MIDDLE AGES

Augustine	*City of God*; selections (Penguin; Bettenson, trans.)
Aquinas	*Aquinas on Politics and Ethics* (Norton; Sigmund, trans.)
Pizan	*The Book of the City of Ladies* (Persea; Richards, trans.)

SECTION IV: RENAISSANCE AND REFORMATION

Machiavelli	*The Prince* (Modern Library; Ricci, trans.)
	The Discourses; selections (Modern Library; Dettmold, trans.)
Hillerbrand, ed.	*The Protestant Reformation* (Harper)
Calvin	*The Institutes* (Baker; Lane and Osborne, trans.)

SECTION V: THE NEW SCIENCE

Descartes	*Discourse on Method* (Hackett; Cress, trans.)
Galileo	*Discoveries and Opinions* (Anchor; Drake, trans.)

SECTION VI: NEW PHILOSOPHY AND THE POLITY

Hobbes	*Leviathan*; selections (Penguin)
Locke	*Second Treatise of Government* (Hackett)

SPRING SEMESTER

LITERATURE HUMANITIES

Bible	The New Testament: The Gospels (Meridian; King James or Revised Standard Version)

Augustine	*Confessions* (Penguin; Pine-Coffin, trans.)
Dante	*Inferno* (Bantam; Mandelbaum, trans.)
Boccaccio	*The Decameron*; selections (Penguin; G. H. McWilliam, trans.)
Montaigne	*Essays*; selections (Penguin; Screech, trans.)
Shakespeare	Play of choice
	King Lear (Penguin)
Milton	*Paradise Lost* (optional) (Macmillan)
Cervantes	*Don Quixote*; selections (Penguin; Cohen, trans.)
Descartes	*Discourse on Method* (Hackett; Cress, trans.)
	Meditations on the First Philosophy (Hackett; Cress, trans.)
Goethe	*Faust* (Part One) (Bantam; Salm, trans.)
Austen	*Pride and Prejudice* (Penguin)
Woolf	*To the Lighthouse* (Harbrace)
	A Room of One's Own (optional) (Harbrace)
	Instructor's Choice

CONTEMPORARY CIVILIZATION

SECTION I: THE ENLIGHTENMENT AND THE FRENCH REVOLUTION

Rousseau	*Discourse on the Origin of Inequality* (Hackett; Cress, trans.)
	The Social Contract (Hackett; Cress, trans.)
Hume	*An Enquiry Concerning the Principles of Morals* (Hackett)
Kant	*Foundations of the Metaphysics of Morals* (Macmillan; Beck, trans.)
	"What Is Enlightenment?" (Macmillan; Beck, trans.)
Madison et al.	*Federalist Papers*; selections (optional)

SECTION II: ECONOMY, SOCIETY, AND THE STATE

Smith	*The Wealth of Nations*; selections (University of Chicago)
Hegel	Introduction to *The Philosophy of History* (Hackett; Rauch, trans.)
	Appendix to *The Philosophy of Right* (optional) (Hackett; Rauch, trans.)
	"Lordship and Bondage" from *The Phenomenology of Mind* (optional) (Harper & Row; Baillie, trans.)
Marx	*The Marx-Engels Reader*; selections (Norton; Tucker, ed.)
Mill	*On Liberty* (Hackett)
Wollstonecraft	*Vindication of the Rights of Woman* (Penguin)

SECTION III: DARWIN, NIETZSCHE, FREUD

Darwin   *Darwin*; selections (Norton)
Nietzsche   *On the Genealogy of Morals* (Vintage;
                            Kaufmann, trans.)
Freud   *The Freud Reader*; selections (Norton; Gay, ed.)

SECTION IV: MODERNITY AND ITS DISCONTENTS
(Instructor Chooses at Least One Book from Both A and B)

A. Science and Revolution in the Twentieth Century
Weber   *From Max Weber: Essays in Sociology* (Oxford; Gerth
                            and Mills, trans.)
Gramsci   *The Modern Prince and Other Writings* (International;
                            Marx, trans.)
Arendt   *On Violence* (HBJ)
                        The Origins of Totalitarianism; selections (HBJ)
Lenin   *Imperialism* (International)
                        State and Revolution (International)
Habermas   *Transformation of the Public Sphere* (Beacon; Burger
                            and Lawrence, trans.)

B. The Ambiguities of Integration: Class, Race, and Gender
Beauvoir   *The Second Sex*; selections (Vintage; Parshley, trans.)
MacKinnon   *Feminism Unmodified* (Harvard)
Jagger & Strahl, eds.   *Feminist Frameworks* (McGraw-Hill)
Rawls   *A Theory of Justice* (Harvard)
Fanon   *The Wretched of the Earth* (Grove; Farrington, trans.)
Malcolm X   *Autobiography* (Grove)
West   *Prophesy Deliverance!* (Westminster)
Foucault   *Discipline and Punish* (Vintage, Sheridan, trans.)
                        Supreme Court Decisions

We seek knowledge only because we desire enjoyment, and it is impossible to conceive why a person who has neither desires nor fears would take the trouble to reason.

Rousseau,
Discourse on the Origin of Inequality

FIRST SEMESTER

Chapter *1*

HOMER I

- ~ The *Iliad*
- ~ Professor Edward Tayler tells us we will build a self
- ~ The college bookstore; my lost attention
- ~ Columbia students then and now
- ~ C.C. begins: Anders Stephanson and the hegemony of the western calendar
- ~ Professor Tayler teaches the *Iliad*
- ~ Achilles the hero*

I had forgotten. I had forgotten the extremity of its cruelty and tenderness, and, reading it now, turning the *Iliad* open anywhere in its 15,693 lines, I was shocked. A dying word, "shocked." Few people have been able to use it well since Claude Rains so famously said, "I'm shocked, *shocked* to find that gambling is going on here," as he pocketed his winnings in *Casablanca*. But it's the only word for excitement and alarm of this intensity. The brute vitality of the air, the magnificence of ships, wind, and fires; the raging battles, the plains charged with terrified horses, the beasts unstrung and falling; the warriors flung facedown in the dust; the ravaged longing for home and family and meadows and the rituals of peace, leading at last to an instant of reconciliation, when even two men who are bitter enemies fall into rapt admiration of each other's nobility and beauty—it is a war poem, and in the Richmond Lattimore translation it has an excruciating vividness, an obsessive observation of horror that causes almost disbelief.

> Idomeneus stabbed at the middle
> of his chest with the spear, and broke the bronze armour about
> him

---

* In his extraordinary translations of the *Iliad* and the *Odyssey*, which Columbia uses, Richmond Lattimore attempted to get back to the sound of the original Greek with such spellings as "Achilleus" and "Hektor." In quoting from Lattimore's translations, I have respected his spellings, while returning, in my own text, to the traditional "Achilles," "Hector," and so on.

which in time before had guarded his body from destruction.
He cried out then, a great cry, broken, the spear in him,
and fell, thunderously, and the spear in his heart was stuck fast
but the heart was panting still and beating to shake the butt end
of the spear.   (XIII, 438–44)

If I had seen that quaking spear in a shopping-mall scare movie, I would
have abandoned the sticky floors and headed for the door. Exploitation
and dehumanization! Teenagers never *read* anything—that's why they
love this grisly movie trash! Yet here is the image at the beginning of
Western literature, and in its most famous book.

The quivering spear was hair-raising, though there were even more
frightening images: eyeballs spitted on the ends of spears and held aloft
in triumph, a blade entering at the mouth "so that the brazen spearhead
smashed its way clean through below the brain in an upward stroke, and
the white bones splintered." Homer records these mutilations with an
apparent physical relish that suddenly gives way to bitter sorrow (this is
one way the images differ from those in horror movies) and to a yearning for ordinary life, a caress of nostalgia slipped into the mesmerizing
catastrophe before us. The exultant violence is shot through with the
most profound dismay. The Greeks, camped outside the walls of Troy,
are far from home, but home, and everything lovely, proper, and comforting that might happen there, is evoked in heartbreaking flashes.
There is the case of

Simoeisios in his stripling's beauty, whom once his mother
descending from Ida bore beside the banks of Simoeis
when she had followed her father and mother to tend the sheep-
        flocks.
Therefore they called him Simoeisios; but he could not
render again the care of his dear parents; he was short-lived,
beaten down beneath the spear of high-hearted Aias,
who struck him as he first came forward beside the nipple
of the right breast, and the bronze spearhead drove clean through
        the shoulder.
He dropped then to the ground in the dust, like some black
        poplar . . .   (IV, 472–82)

The nipple of the *right* breast. Homer in his terrifying exactness tells us
where the spear comes in and goes out, what limbs are severed; he tells
us that the dead will not return to rich soil, they will not take care of elderly parents, receive pleasure from their young wives. His explicitness
has a finality beyond all illusion. In the end, the war (promoted by the
gods) will consume almost all of them, Greeks and Trojans alike, sweeping on year after year, in battle after battle—a mystery in its irresistible

momentum, its profoundly absorbing moment-to-moment activity and overall meaninglessness. First one side drives forward, annihilates hundreds, and is on the edge of victory. Then, a few days later, inspired by some god's trick or phantasm—a prod to the sluggish brain of an exhausted warrior—the other side recovers, advances, and carries all before it. When the poem opens, this movement back and forth has been going on for more than nine years.

❖ ❖ ❖

The teacher, a small, compact man, about sixty, walked into the room, and wrote some initials on the board:

W A S P

D W M

W C

D G S I

While most of us tried to figure them out (I had no trouble with the first two, made a lame joke to myself about the third, and was stumped by the fourth), he turned, looking around the class, and said ardently, almost imploringly, "We've only got a year together. . . ." His tone was pleading and mournful, a lover who feared he might be thwarted. There was an alarming pause. A few students, embarrassed, looked down, and then he said: "This course has been under attack for thirty years. People have said"—pointing to the top set of initials—"the writers are all white Anglo-Saxon Protestants. It's not true, but it doesn't matter. They've said they were all Dead White Males; it's not true, but it doesn't matter. That it's all Western civilization. That's not quite true either—there are many Western civilizations—but it doesn't matter. The only thing that matters is this."

He looked at us, then turned back to the board, considering the initials "DGSI" carefully, respectfully, and rubbed his chin. "Don't Get Sucked In," he said at last. Another pause, and I noticed the girl sitting next to me, who has wild frizzed hair and a mass of acne on her chin and forehead, opening her mouth in panic. Others were smiling. They were freshmen—sorry, *first-year students*—and not literature majors necessarily, but a cross-section of students, and therefore future lawyers, accountants, teachers, businessmen, politicians, TV producers, doctors, poets, layabouts. They were taking Lit Hum, a required course that almost all students at Columbia take the first year of school. This may have been the first teacher the students had seen in college. He wasn't making it easy on them.

"Don't get sucked in by false ideas," he said. "You're not here for political reasons. You're here for very selfish reasons. You're here to build a self. You create a self, you don't inherit it. One way you create it is out of the past. Look, if you find the *Iliad* dull or invidious or a glorification of war, you're right. It's a poem in your mind; let it take shape in your mind. The women are honor gifts. They're war booty, like tripods. Less than tripods. If any male reading this poem treated women on campus as chattel, it would be very strange. I also trust you to read this and not go out and hack someone to pieces."

Ah, a hipster, I thought. He admitted the obvious charges in order to minimize them. And he said nothing about transcendental values, supreme masterpieces of the West, and the rest of that. *We're here for selfish reasons*. The voice was pleasant but odd—baritonal, steady, but with traces of mockery garlanding the short, definitive sentences. The intonations drooped, as if he were laying black crepe around his words. A hipster wit. He nearly droned, but there were little surprises—ideas insinuated into corners, a sudden expansion of feeling. He had sepulchral charm, like one of Shakespeare's solemnly antic clowns.

I remembered him well enough: Edward Tayler, professor of English. I had taken a course with him twenty-nine years earlier (he was a young assistant professor then), a course in seventeenth-century Metaphysical poetry, which was then part of the sequence required for English majors at Columbia, and I recalled being baffled as much as intrigued by his manner, which definitely tended toward the cryptic. He was obviously brilliant, but he liked to jump around, keep students off balance, hint and retreat; I learned a few things about Donne and Marvell, and left the class with a sigh of relief. In the interim, he had become famous as a teacher and was now the sonorously titled Lionel Trilling Professor in the Humanities—the moniker was derived from Columbia's most famous English literature professor, a great figure when I was there in the early sixties.

"The Hermeneutic Circle," Tayler was saying. "That's what Wilhelm Dilthey called it. You don't know what to do with the details unless you have a grip on the structure; and at the same time, you don't know what to do with the structure unless you know the details. It's true in life and in literature. The Hermeneutic Circle. It's a vicious circle. Look, we have only a year together. You have to read. There's nothing you'll do in your four years at Columbia that's more important for selfish reasons than reading the books of this course."

Could they become selves? From my position along the side of the classroom, I sneaked a look. At the moment they looked more like lumps, uncreated first-year students. The men sat with legs stretched all the way out, eyes down on their notes. Some wore caps turned backward. They were eighteen, maybe nineteen. In their T-shirts, jeans, and turned-around caps, they had a summer-camp thickness, like counselors just back from a hike with ten-year-olds. *Give me a beer.* The women, many of them also in T-shirts, their hair gathered at the back with a rubber band, were more directly attentive; they looked at Tayler, but they looked blankly.

Tayler handed out a sheet with some quotations. At the top of the page were some verses from the beginning of Genesis.

> And God said, Let there be light; and there was light.
> And God saw the light, that it was good: And God
> divided the light from the darkness. . . . And God said,
> Let there be a firmament in the midst of the waters,
> and let it divide the waters from the waters.

"You may not believe that God created the universe," Tayler said, mournful, sepulchral, "but, anyway, look what God is doing in this passage. He's setting up opposites. Which is something we do all the time in life. Moral opposites flow from binary opposites. There are people you touch, and people you don't touch. Every choice is an exclusion. How do you escape the binary bind? Look, St. Augustine, whom we'll read later, says that before the Fall there were no involuntary actions. Before the Fall, Adam never had an involuntary erection." Pause, pause . . . "If Adam and Eve wanted to do something, they did it. But you guys are screwed up; you're in trouble. There's a discrepancy between what you want to do and what you ought to do. You want to go out and have a beer with friends, and you have to force yourself through a series of battles. After the Fall, you fall into dualities."

There were other quotations on the sheet, including one from John Milton, but Tayler didn't say right then what their significance might be. He looked around. Was anyone getting it? Maybe. Was I? We would see. Then he turned all loverlike and earnest once more. And he said it again.

"Look, keep a finger on your psychic pulse as you go. This is a very selfish enterprise."

❖ ❖ ❖

By the time the action of the *Iliad* begins, the deed that set off the whole chain of events—a man making off with another man's wife—is barely mentioned by the participants. Homer, chanting his poetry to groups of listeners, must have expected everyone to know the outrageous old tale. Years earlier, Paris, a prince of Troy, visiting the house of the Greek king Menelaus, took away, with her full consent, Helen, the king's beautiful wife. Agamemnon, the brother of the cuckold, then put together a loose federation of kings and princes whose forces voyaged to Troy and laid siege to the city, intending to punish the proud inhabitants and reclaim Helen. But after more than nine years of warfare, the foolish act of sexual abandonment that set the whole cataclysm in motion has been largely forgotten. By this time, Helen, abashed, considers herself merely a slut (her embarrassed appearance on the walls of Troy is actually something of a letdown), and Paris, her second "husband," more a lover than a fighter, barely comes out to the battlefield. When he does come out, and he and Menelaus fight a duel, the gods muddy the outcome, and the war goes on. After nine years, the war itself is causing the war.

How can a book make one feel injured and exhilarated at the same time? What's shocking about the *Iliad* is that the cruelty and the nobility of it seem to grow out of each other, like the good and evil twins of some malign fantasy who together form a single unstable and frightening personality. After all, Western literature begins with a quarrel between two arrogant pirates over booty. At the beginning of the poem, the various tribes of the Greeks (whom Homer calls Achaeans—Greece wasn't a national identity in his time), the various tribes assembled before the walls of Troy are on the verge of disaster. Agamemnon, their leader, the most powerful of the kings, has kidnapped and taken as a mistress from a nearby city a young woman, the daughter of one of Apollo's priests; Apollo has angrily retaliated by bringing down a plague on the Greeks. A peevish, bullying king, unsteady in command, Agamemnon, under pressure from the other leaders, angrily gives the girl back to her father. But then, demanding compensation, he takes for himself the slave mistress of Achilles, his greatest warrior. The women are passed around like gold pieces or helmets. Achilles is so outraged by this bit of plundering within the ranks that he comes close to killing the king, a much older man. Restraining himself at the last minute, he retires from the combat and prays to his mother, the goddess Thetis, for the defeat of his own side; he then sits in his tent playing a lyre and "singing of men's fame" (i.e., his own) as his friends get cut up by the Trojans. What follows is a series of battles whose savagery remains without parallel in our literature.

It is almost too much, an extreme and bizarre work of literary art at the very beginning of Western literary art. One wants to rise to it, taking it full in the face, for the poem depicts life at its utmost, a nearly ceaseless activity of marshaling, deploying, advancing, and fleeing, spelled by peaceful periods so strenuous—the councils and feasts and games—that they hardly seem like relief at all. Reading the poem in its entirety is like fronting a storm that refuses to slacken or die. At first, I had to fight my way through it; I wasn't bored but I was rebellious, my attention a bucking horse unwilling to submit to the harness. It was too long, I thought, too brutal and repetitive and, for all its power as a portrait of war, strangely distant from us. Where was *Homer* in all this? He was everywhere, selecting and shaping the material, but he was nowhere as a palpable presence, a consciousness, and for the modern reader his absence was appalling. No one tells us how to react to the brutalities or to anything else. We are on our own. Movie-fed, I wasn't used to working so hard, and as I sat on my sofa at home, reading, my body, in daydreams, kept leaping away from the seat and into the bedroom, where I would sink into bed and turn on the TV, or to the kitchen, where I would open the fridge. Mentally, I would pull myself back, and eventually I settled down and read and read, though for a long time I remained out of balance and sore.

❖ ❖ ❖

Other men may have more active recollections—scoring a goal, kissing a girl at the homecoming game, all that autumn-air, pocket-flask, Scott Fitzgerald stuff—but my sweetest memory of college is on the nuzzling, sedate side. At the beginning of each semester, I would stand before the books required for my courses, prolonging the moment, like a kid looking through the store window at a bicycle he knows his parents will buy for him. I would soon possess these things, but the act of buying them could be put off. Why rush it? The required books for each course were laid out in shelves in the college bookstore. I would stare at them a long time, lifting them, turning through the pages, pretending I didn't really *need* this one or that, laying it down and then picking it up again. If no one was looking, I would even smell a few of them and feel the pages— I had a thing about the physical nature of books, and I was happy when I realized that my idol, the great literary critic Edmund Wilson, was obsessed with books as sensuous objects.

Obviously, it wasn't just learning that excited me but the *idea* of reading the big books, the promise of enlargement, the adventure of strangeness. Reading has within it a collector's passion, the desire to possess: I would swallow the whole store. Reality never entered into this. The difficulty or tedium of the books, the droning performance of the teacher— I might even have spent the entire previous semester in a self-absorbed funk, but I roused myself at the beginning of the new semester for the wonderful ritual of the bookstore. Each time I stood there, I saw myself serenely absorbing everything, though I was such an abominably slow reader, chewing until the flavor was nearly gone, that I never quite got around to completing the reading list of any course.

And so it has been ever since. Walking home from midtown Manhattan, I am drawn haplessly to a bookstore—Coliseum Books, at Broadway and Fifty-seventh, will do—where I will buy two or three books, which then, often enough, sit on my shelves for years, unread or partly read, until finally, trying to look something up, I will pull one or another out, bewildered that I have it. I like to *own* them: I had grown into a book-buyer but not always a book-reader; a boon to the book trade, perhaps, but not a boon to myself.

Reading, after eating and sex one of the most natural, central, and satisfying of all acts, had amazingly become a vexed experience. I read a great deal, sometimes I read all day long, but most of the stuff was journalism, essays, criticism, or novels that had been adapted into movies and that I needed to check out before writing my film reviews for *New York* magazine, or books by writers whom I never missed (Philip Roth, Saul Bellow, John le Carré) and whose work seems less like something new than a reacquaintance with trusted friends. But what did I *read*? I mean read seriously? Reading Marcel Proust's *Swann's Way* was a rapturous experience not likely to be succeeded by the rest of *Remembrance of Things Past*. At least, not in my present state of distraction. To read anything as densely, lusciously detailed as Proust, you have to set aside a special time, at least an hour of quiet, and though there were people I know who got up early to read Proust or even a decent new American novel, I can't get myself up early, and if I could, I would make coffee and read the *Times* in peace before the boys hit the kitchen. My wife, whose life was certainly as disrupted and jangled as mine, still read a great deal, book after book, sometimes plowing straight through an author's entire work. But I no longer had the concentration or the discipline for serious reading; I had lost the habit of just falling into something the way real readers do, devouring it on the bus, in the tub, at a lunch counter. Movies more than satisfied my desire for trash, but when I picked up a serious book, my concentration often wandered after twenty pages. I wanted to read it, but vagrant thoughts came charging in, and the words from the book got caught at a bottleneck leading to my attention. My rhythm had changed. I was a moviegoer, a magazine-reader, a CNN-watcher. Following a breaking story on CNN, I would watch updates at certain points of the day, and then pick up the story again when a car alarm woke me in the middle of the night, then catch the denouement in the morning. This business of being "informed" could be almost nightmarish: If you stayed with a story long enough, you began to feel as if you were a ball rolling over and over, or the hands of a clock coming back to the same point.

Going back to school would force me to read the whole shelf in the bookstore. By going back, I would not be searching for my youth—a ghoulish thought. Youth, I now saw, was the most overpraised time of life. You can't watch your own kids playing when you're young, or enjoy power, and the money you spend belongs to your parents. I dawdled and stumbled through the early part of my life and enjoyed the prerogatives of middle age, but I longed for . . . another *chance*, another time spent reading seriously, another shot at school. I was sick of not really knowing anything; I longed to submit myself to something larger than my career.

At the age of forty-eight, I stood in front of the shelves in Columbia's bookstore at 115th Street and Broadway, a larger and better-lit place than the store in my day, which was so tightly packed one never got away from that slightly sweet smell that new books have. I was absurdly excited. There they were, the books for the Lit Hum and C.C. courses: the two thick volumes of Homer; the elegant Penguin editions of Aeschylus and Hobbes, with their black borders and uniform typeface; the rather severe-looking academic editions of Plato and Locke, all business, with no designs on the cover or back, just the titles, and within, rows of virtuously austere type. They were as densely printed as lawbooks. I was thrilled by the possibility that they might be *difficult*. I would read; I would study; I would sit with teenagers.

❖   ❖   ❖

Can Achilles really be the first great hero of our literature? He seems a fool, an infantile narcissist. The first word of Western literature is *mēnin*—in old Greek, "rage" or "wrath." Homer means Achilles' rage, the kind of rage that has an element of divine fury in it and that destroys armies and breaks cities. But to us (though not to the early Greeks), Achilles' anger seems less divine than vain and egotistical. His war booty has been stolen by another man, and he sits sulking in his tent. Is the immense size of his anger not absurdly out of proportion to its cause? Yet Achilles dominates the poem even as he withdraws; his moody self-preoccupation is part of what makes him fascinating. He creates an aura, a vibration of specialness. We understand something of who he is from Marlon Brando's glamorously sullen performances in his youth. A greater destiny flows from Achilles' angry will than from the settled desires of simpler men.

He is very young, perhaps in his early twenties, fearless, tall, fleet-footed, strong, a compound of muscle and beauty with so powerful a sense of his own precedence that he is willing to let the war go badly when his honor is sullied. The Trojans, led by their stalwart, Hector, kill many Greeks and come close to burning the Greek ships and cutting off their retreat. Hoping to stem the tide, Achilles' tentmate and beloved friend Patroclus enters the battle. He dons Achilles' armor, and in that armor—as a substitute for Achilles—he is slain by Hector.

Achilles' withdrawal now comes to an end. Enraged, inconsolable, he prepares at last to enter the battle (we are deep into the poem, and we have not yet seen him fight), an event accompanied by a cataclysmic rending of the heavens and the seas. The sky darkens, the underworld nearly cracks open. Huge forces, unstoppable, move into place. Achilles begins to fight, expelling his anguish in a rampage. As Book XXI opens, he is driving the Trojans back toward Troy:

> But when they came to the crossing place of the fair-running river
> of whirling Xanthos, a stream whose father was Zeus the im-
> > mortal,
> there Achilleus split them and chased some back over the flat land
> toward the city, where the Achaians themselves had stampeded in
> > terror
> on the day before, when glorious Hektor was still in his fury.
> Along this ground they were streaming in flight; but Hera let fall
> a deep mist before them to stay them. Meanwhile the other half
> were crowded into the silvery whirls of the deep-running river
> and tumbled into it in huge clamour, and the steep-running water
> sounded, and the banks echoed hugely about them, as they out-
> > crying
> tried to swim this way and that, spun about in the eddies.
> As before the blast of a fire the locusts escaping
> into a river swarm in air, and the fire unwearied
> blazes from a sudden start, and the locusts huddle in water;
> so before Achilleus the murmuring waters of Xanthos
> the deep-whirling were filled with confusion of men and of horses.
>   But heaven-descended Achilleus left his spear there on the bank
> leaning against the tamarisks, and leapt in like some immortal,
> with only his sword, but his heart was bent on evil actions,
> and he struck in a circle around him. The shameful sound of their
> > groaning
> rose as they were struck with the sword, and the water was red-
> > dened
> with blood. As before a huge-gaping dolphin the other fishes
> escaping cram the corners of a deepwater harbour
> in fear, for he avidly eats up any he can catch;
> so the Trojans along the course of the terrible river
> shrank under the bluffs. He, when his hands grew weary with
> > killing,
> chose out and took twelve young men alive from the river
> to be vengeance for the death of Patroklos, the son of Menoitios.
> These, bewildered with fear like fawns, he led out of the water
> and bound their hands behind them with thongs well cut out of
> > leather,
> with the very belts they themselves wore on their ingirt tunics,
> and gave them to his companions to lead away to the hollow ships,
> then himself whirled back, still in a fury to kill men.   (XXI, 1–33)

Homer didn't have to tell his listeners that the leather thongs, tightening as they dried, would cut into the flesh of Achilles' Trojan captives. Nor did he have to explain why Achilles later kills a Trojan warrior, an acquaintance, who begs for mercy at his knees. But how is the American reader supposed to respond to this? He comes from a society that is nominally ethical. Our legal and administrative system, our presidential utterances, our popular culture, in which TV policemen rarely fail to care for the victims of crime, are swathed in concern. Since the society is in fact often indifferent to hardship, it is no surprise that irony and cynicism barnacle the national mood. By contrast, the Greek view was savage but offered without hypocrisy. Accepting death in battle as inevitable, the Greek and Trojan aristocrats of the *Iliad* experience the world not as pleasant or unpleasant, nor as good and evil, but as glorious or shameful. We might say that Homer offers a conception of life that is noble rather than ethical—except that such an opposition is finally misleading. For the Greeks, nobility has an ethical quality. You are not good or bad in the Christian sense. You are strong or weak; beautiful or ugly; conquering or vanquished; living or dead; favored by gods or cursed. Here were some of Tayler's "binary opposites," but skewed into matching pairs alien to us, in which nothing softened Homer's appraisal of quality.

Academic opponents of courses in the Western classics constantly urge readers to consider "the other"—the other cultures, odd or repugnant to Western tastes, which we have allegedly trampled or rendered marginal and also the others who are excluded or trivialized within our own culture: women, people of color, anyone who is nonwhite, nonmale, non-Western. But here, at the beginning of the written culture of the West (the *Iliad* dates from perhaps the eighth century B.C.), is something like "the other," the Greeks themselves, a race of noble savages stripping corpses of their armor and reciting their genealogies at one another during huge feasts or even on the field of battle. Kill, plunder, bathe, eat, offer sacrifices to the gods—what do we have to do with these ancient marauders of the eastern Mediterranean?

❖ ❖ ❖

They looked awfully pale for college students. From where I sat, on the steps of Low Library, watching them walk around the campus on the second day of school, there was hardly a suntan in sight. Didn't anyone go to the beach anymore? I knew this was a city campus, but we've just had three months of *summer*. They didn't look all that happy, either; they looked serious, even a bit gloomy, and tense. Opening-week anxieties perhaps. Also, the tuition was a fortune (about $23,000 including room and board), and even though many of them received aid, they probably needed more money. They had spent the summer working, that was it, and working indoors. No time for the beach. Anyway, Columbia students never did look too healthy. One could not call it a debonair campus (the glamorous go elsewhere). They were smart, though, and serious and ambitious, and isn't that what I liked about them?

In my day, back in the early sixties, the College was heavily populated with city Jews and Italian-Americans, bookish, sallow young men (like me) preoccupied with Sartre and Kafka, Beethoven and the Modern Jazz Quartet, young men in green corduroy jackets or pea coats, who smoked unfiltered cigarettes, Camels or Gitanes, in the Bogart imitation fashionable at the time. We weren't the only students, of course. In fact, we were a minority, my friends and I—English and history majors heading for careers in law, teaching, and journalism—but we had created our own snobbish version of Columbia, which centered on such famous writers (and fairly recent students) as Allen Ginsberg and Jack Kerouac, and such English teachers as Trilling, Frederick Dupee, and Steven Marcus. There were also the students I thought of as Ivy League boys—noble oarsmen, I called them—who had a haughty but depressed air, as if they were disappointed not to be at Princeton. I was prejudiced against them, not only because their manners were different from ours but because they were so often in good shape. Now most of the male students were in better physical shape than we had been; they almost all had some muscle tone (infra dig among intellectual students in 1961).

More important, the students weren't all male anymore; women had been admitted in 1982 and now made up half the college. And the size of the minority population had grown. Walking into another Lit Hum section (I was sampling different approaches), I had nodded to a few students, and then a few more, and suddenly realized that the class was utterly unlike the ones I had sat in thirty years earlier. Out of a class of twenty-two first-year students, there were exactly four white males. Four! The students were from Europe, India, Singapore. O America! They were from everywhere. But why was I so surprised? Did I *want* a predominance of white males in the class? I did not. Still, an old-grad memory bank had been jolted. If you are a man over forty, you simply do not realize, until you enter a classroom, how pluralistic American university education has become.

"John F. Kennedy was killed on November twenty-second, 1963," the teacher said. "Is that an objective statement?"

The other required great-books course—Contemporary Civilization, or C.C.—was also getting under way. As the students listened to this opening sally, they looked blank. They were mostly sophomores, and were not about to make fools of themselves. Was it a trick? "Let's see a show of hands," the teacher said. Most of the hands reluctantly went up.

"I can't say it's objective," said an Asian-American student, a boy with a gentle face and glasses. "I didn't see it; it happened before I was born."

"Well, all right. You mean you can't be sure it's *true*. But is it an objective *statement*?"

Most of the students murmured yes.

"But what about that year, 1963. In the Jewish calendar it was 5724 or whatever, and in the Chinese calendar it's something else. The date of the birth of Christ was decided by an ill-educated sixth-century monk. Christ was actually born in 4 B.C.E. Isn't 1963, by virtue of its being a year in the Christian calendar, an ideological date?"

A small, widening circle of puzzlement. Was he serious? The teacher was a history professor, a Swede named Anders Stephanson, and the students couldn't make him out yet. He was handsome, slender, about forty years old, with blond hair and blue eyes and a rather dazzling smile, and he wore faded jeans and, under a dark jacket, a white T-shirt. To my eyes, the T-shirt was a rakish touch, especially with the black jacket. A youthful biker-intellectual, then? No, I couldn't see him slopping beer on the table. When he talked, the rhythms and vocabulary were the purest advanced academese. The accent was almost British, the manner emphatic—boisterous yet stern in Brit academic style.

"Sure, you can come up with a different date on another calendar," one of the boys said at last. "But Kennedy died on the same day whatever calendar you use. The date is a convention."

"Ah, a *convention*. A convention. Right."

Only Stephanson, in his flagrant Swedish/Oxford accent, said, "Roight!"

"Roight! And that convention, for better or worse, is the way we establish the calendar. A whole series of hegemonic processes account for our telling time in that way. It's not the Chinese or the Jewish way. The books in this course, like the calendar, follow the material development of Western Europe, the domination of Europe. China in the thirteenth century may have been an advanced culture, much more advanced than Europe, but for various reasons, it didn't dominate the world, and its books aren't in this course."

Well, there it was. I had heard it, and on my first day in C.C. class. Nothing could be called objective, nothing could be taken as natural or universal, not even a date. Such was a principal conviction of the "cultural left," the academic insurgents eager to unseat the illusion of Westerners that their ideas and institutions amounted to a universal norm. In this first meeting of his C.C. section, in a small, tight room in Mathematics Hall, Stephanson was pulling out rugs the students hardly knew they were standing on. *Your most everyday assumptions are arbitrary—politically determined.*

He offered the upturned students the new academic dispensation. The C.C. reading list, however traditional (Plato, the Bible, Rousseau, Kant, Marx, etc.), was the result of an arbitrary process. That the books had survived for so long was proof not of their universality but of exactly the opposite—that they were part of a tradition that had triumphed *politically*. Stephanson didn't even call them "books"; he used the standard new-academic "texts," which has a deromanticized, disillusioned sound, the name of something *imposed*, official, like a president's speech, not the fruit of a writer's desire and a reader's pleasure. The texts, he said, "represent a condensation of a certain way of putting education before students and saying what is culture and what isn't. It isn't an innocent list."

When Stephanson said the books weren't "innocent," he emphasized the word heavily, an intense young barrister before the court. After attending Gothenburg University, in Sweden, he had done graduate work at New College, Oxford, and finally at Columbia, but Oxford appeared to be the determining stylistic influence. I was beginning to be charmed by the mock-Brit strenuousness.

This notion that lists were not innocent was central to attacks on "the canon." Such lists reeked of exclusion. "The teaching of literature *is* the teaching of values," Henry Louis Gates, Jr., the distinguished African-American scholar and critic, wrote in 1990. "Not inherently, no, but contingently, yes; it is—it has become—the teaching of an aesthetic and political order, in which no women or people of color were ever able to discover the reflection or representation of their images, or hear the resonances of their cultural voices." Gates was arguing not for the dissolution of the traditional canon but for its enlargement to include those missing voices. Many others went much further, however, into a kind of philosophical attack on the hierarchies of judgment that produced lists of classics in the first place. Such lists (and not just Columbia's core curriculum, of course) amounted to a unitary, or almost unitary, sensibility and set of values, which elected itself as central, even universal, in an endless process of self-confirmation, rather like a club that insisted on the superiority of its own members while refusing to see the qualities of anyone else. What was presented in this tradition as "universal" (so the argument went) actually represented no more than the experience and the drive to power of a limited group. Universality was not only a false claim, a mystique and an imposture; it was political in its intentions and effects. And "the canon," so far from being a mere anodyne collection of remarkable works, was a key element in the "hegemony" of white Euro-

American males, a disguised ideological spearhead of such Western modes, good and bad, as individualism, market capitalism, imperialism, racism, and sexism.

If Tayler, in his Lit Hum section, was saying, "These books will form you," Stephanson the C.C. teacher was saying, "These books have been *selected* to form you." Yet, as I sat there, I felt not dismay but something like a warming swell of pride. The idea was almost titillating: *we* were the object of this immense historical process that had been going on since the flowering of Greek literature.

"They are canonical works," he said, "in the sense that they lend themselves to constant reinterpretation," and this led into his explanation of the way the class would go. He would not tell us what to think; he would monitor the discussion and keep it on track. The students would take turns working up "presentations" of the individual authors.

"One never accepts the texts as they seem to be," he said. "One always *interrogates* them. There may be no 'objective' points of view, but there are serious readings."

We will be serious readers and muck about with the books. But how?

❖ ❖ ❖

"Think shape, how it's put together," Tayler was saying, "rather than what the characters feel or don't feel. The *Iliad* is not a simple glorification of war; something else is happening here. And the something else requires an epic reading."

Enough initials; this was the real thing, the nuts and bolts of literary analysis. He was working with the class on the structure of the huge poem, getting them to see large overall movements and then smaller movements and patterns within limited blocks, giving them a handle on the sprawling text, which suddenly began to seem not nearly so sprawling. Tayler could be called a historian of ideas, but when he dealt directly with the text, he used a method derived from the New Criticism, the method of literary analysis which flourished in American universities from the forties to the sixties and which insisted on the formal unity of a great work of art. In recent years, the New Criticism had actually become rather rare, another casualty of the changed ideology of university literary study. Tayler was attempting to do something now widely regarded as impossible or delusional or even secretly political—letting the text "speak for itself."

Tayler didn't just tell the students what he wanted, of course. Imploring and urging, he pulled it out of them, asking leading questions, dropping hints, asking them to read aloud passages that have no apparent connection, passages spaced far apart in the book. At times, the class stalled, and he retreated from his point, literally stepping backward and letting his head drop for a moment before approaching from another angle, like a guerrilla force making tentative forays through the jungle. Eventually, he would coax them out of hiding and surround them.

Cornered, a student spoke.

"Um, because Achilles calls this guy he's, y'know, about to kill, 'Friend'?"

The freshmen stumbled a lot, speaking in broken fragments. Some of them would start and then trail off or just stare blankly when Tayler called on them, and suddenly, even though I knew he wasn't going to call on me, my palms began to sweat and I looked down at my notebook, because I didn't always know the answer either, and school, *school,* came flooding back—a time when I often didn't know the answer. Even worse, he was the kind of teacher who kept a student on the spot, trying to rattle the kid's brain enough until the answer, lost in the bottom drawers of sloth and forgetfulness, suddenly fell out—something I always hated, because in that situation my brain would usually lock up. Fortunately, he seemed to understand that there was no point just waiting. When a student went into lockup, he would eventually move away to someone else, or he would take what the student had said, however minimal, and play with it, enlarging it so it made some kind of sense, and then weave it together with the three or four intelligible words that someone *else* had said; and soon these two half-mute students, still flushed with embarrassment, were described as *building* something together, or even as having a full-fledged "disagreement." Which was pretty funny, since neither of them was aware of having said much of anything. Sometimes, emboldened by Tayler's magic tricks, the students would begin talking and actually become the rabbits he had pulled out of the hat. He began as a con artist and ended up holding the class by its ears.

Why was structure so important? The class was a little ragged, but he kept working at it, jumping all over the poem. Would he tie together all the loose ends? Suspense gathered in the spaces between his summarizing remarks. He worked on, say, five books of the *Iliad* at a time, getting the students to see a recurring pattern of oaths, truces, duels, and feasts, and after an hour or so (the class met for two hours twice a week) they were beginning to do it without much prodding, finding the symmetries—"ring composition," he called it, in which chunks of structural elements returned in the poem but with the elements in reverse order. Then, suddenly, he went to the board, and drew something.

"What's this?"

"Cat," someone said, a student named Hurewitz.

"Yeah. And Hurewitz, what's this?"

"Rat," said Hurewitz.

"*Rat*? Hurewitz, *c'mon*!"

"Oh, um . . . pig!"

"Yeah. Pig. See, your cultural baggage is novels, movies, and TV; you're used to reading for character and psychological development. So you can recognize the cat. But if your cultural baggage doesn't let you see the squiggle on the tail, you're lost, you're still lapping milk instead of heading for the trough. This poem isn't a novel"—he crossed out the cat—"it's a piggy epic. In all these instances, I've been asking you to look at the squiggle on the tail—asking you to look at a mind that works differently. It's an epic, it works by circles and symmetries. Look, it's a poem about wrath, about a special kind of wrath. Achilles drops out and sits sulking in his tent for days. So what's all this other stuff doing there—the battles and the other heroes? We study all these minor heroes and these patterns because they exemplify different aspects of the heroic code. Then we understand what Achilles means, because he violates the code."

Smiles broke out, relief. The mystification was over—for the time being.

"Intellectual thumbscrews have been applied, and I'm sorry. I apologize for it. What I've been trying to do is to teach you how to read the older works of art. You have to read something from another culture. There's no psychology in this thing, no conflict between free will and determinism, no subjective and objective. It's an epic—all foreground. But it's not a random collection of battles; each part gets its emotional counterpart later. As soon as you get used to it, you can get rid of me, which will be a relief to you. You get rid of me, and you get you."

Suddenly, everyone looked up. How would that happen?

The formal approach, I could see, was Tayler's defense against banality. He mentioned the contemporary resistance to reading the *Iliad*. There had been a time in the late eighties at Columbia when the yearly prospect of reading the poem in Lit Hum had been greeted by dismay from some of the younger faculty. It was a poem that oppressed women and glorified war, and it had an infantile hero, and so on. I smiled to myself, because I had been thinking along the same lines, and without the benefit of any critical theory. Tayler didn't say so in so many words, but I gathered that his opinion was that any idiot could see those things, and you could see them while never seeing what the epic poem *was* about. By deconstructing it or appropriating it to some modern perception of class, power, gender—none of which much applied to Homer—you made the poem meaningless. The older classics, he implied, would not live if the books were turned into a mere inadequate version of the present.

I got that part, but I still didn't see how studying the poem formally was going to reveal the students to themselves. Did he mean it or was it just a conceit? Because if he did mean it, it was a tremendous promise— and a frightening one. Did they want to be mucked around with that openly—the girl just out of high school, with long straight hair and a serene way about her; the big guy from California with his legs sprawled out; the Korean boy who said little to anyone but was awfully polite? As for me, the last thing I wanted at eighteen was to be revealed to myself. And at forty-eight? Maybe it was too late.

◆   ◆   ◆

When the Greek and Trojan warriors in the *Iliad* fall, they go down heavily, slowly, like great trees, with all their lineages, stories, lands, and animals crashing down with them. The slaughter is huge but never impersonal. You feel each death freshly as a blow; you never go numb. Everything in the poem has a remarkable weight and consequence, even the warriors' boasts. The men address one another formally, recounting the family honors and triumphs—the spears taken from fallen enemies, the shields, helmets, and corselets, all taken "in the pride of their shining." Genteel modern taste forbids boasting (poor form, a winner never boasts), but the Homeric vaunting has a far different flavor from, say, two Mafia dons comparing turf. The shining helmets would not be so valuable if the men who wore them had not been of heroic quality. Glory is possible everywhere: It is the helmets in the *pride* of their shining.

Nor is Homer ever indifferent to the ceremonies attendant on behavior or possessions. He insists on the fitness of things. Calling this a "heroic code" doesn't capture the prescriptive and celebratory force of it. Feasting and acts of warfare and of sacrifice to the gods can be performed properly in only one way—superbly, with utmost effort and lavish skill and maximum exposure to failure. The act must risk, in the outward trajectory of its effort, the clear possibility of shame. When performed supremely well, it may be painful but never meaningless.

Again: Nothing could be further from our world. The absence of pity was only the first shock. The second came slowly and was perhaps more a frightened realization than a shock: The splendor of the *Iliad*, the magnificence of earth, air, and weather, and the clash of arms, would not be fully possible if the ethical component ruled the poem. Physical exultation blazes out, untrammeled. It is not a humanist work, and it can't be made into one (though many have tried).

When I understood this—and Tayler helped a great deal—I stopped fighting the poem. I relaxed; I began to enjoy it, though my attention still wandered away. Imps of distraction invaded my paradise. They came unbidden, summoned by some charge of energy in the poem that would draw from my unconscious a daydream or a series of daydreams—I was a warrior, forging mighty prose—and then suddenly I would snap out of it and five minutes had passed, a little pocket of time gone forever.

Surely my concentration was patchier than it once was. As a teenager, I lay on my bed in my parents' apartment, reading for hours, looking up only to study the pattern of woolen threads in a thick afghan lying at the foot. Green, brown, green, brown . . . and then back to Dickens or Tolstoy. Or I would sit on my bed in my dormitory room up at Columbia, with its pale green cement-block walls, the sound of traffic receding to nothing (for New Yorkers, traffic is like the ocean—white noise), and I would fall into a novel for hours. I can no longer *submit* to fiction in that way; I read and stop, read and stop, a train halted by obstacles on the track, bad weather, power failures. Everyone complains that young people, growing up on TV, movies, video games, and rap music, lack the patience for long, complex, written narratives, and yet as a child I had not watched all that much television, and I had also lost my patience in middle age. Have all the movies I've seen in the last thirty years broken the circuits, sending the lines helter-skelter? A gloomy idea, for, if it's true, my thoughts, such as they were, were doomed to incompleteness, haplessly shifting perspectives, manic intrusions. Snurfling gremlins were moving the furniture around. My thoughts were mediated.

But could movies really be the culprit? My moviegoing friends did not complain of poor concentration. More to the point, my life had grown much more complex. I was married to a clever and formidible woman, and there were two kids running around; I had multiple jobs and a lot more to think about than I had had at eighteen. A much larger experience was now casting up its echoes. Perhaps daydreaming was not simply wasted time but an elaboration, a sort of disguised commentary from the deep. Perhaps it was a relief from the ferocity of the poem, too.

❖ ❖ ❖

How can a man who stays out of the action through many days (and many thousands of lines), angrily keeping to his tent as friends and enemies die, remain the hero of an epic? The answer to this question suggests why the *Iliad*, for all its frightening strangeness, its violence and barbarity, will not easily yield its place or its predominance at the beginning of the Western tradition in literature.

The crux of the poem—certainly for the modern reader—comes in Book IX, well before Achilles reenters the war. As the Trojans wait at their night fires, ready to attack at dawn, the Greeks, now in serious trouble, send three ambassadors to Achilles with promises of gifts. The three warriors, including Odysseus, the wiliest of the kings, beg Achilles to give up his anger. This is what they offer: tripods, cauldrons, horses, gold, slave women, one of Agamemnon's daughters as a future bride, and even the return of Achilles' slave mistress, whom Agamemnon swears he has never touched. What more can Achilles ask for? According to the warrior code that they all live by, he should take the gifts and return to battle. His honor had been assaulted; now it has been satisfied.

Achilles' initial answer, a staggering Shakespearian speech of more than 120 lines (lines 308 to 429), composed in shifting planes of thought and emotion, sounds unlike anything else in the poem, for it shows a man struggling to say what has never been said, or even imagined, before that instant. If the other warriors all hold forth with the awareness of family traditions, honors, trophies, and plunder supporting their words, Achilles speaks only for himself.

> For as I detest the doorways of Death, I detest that man, who
> hides one thing in the depths of his heart, and speaks forth an-
>   other.
> But I will speak to you the way it seems best to me: neither
> do I think the son of Atreus, Agamemnon, will persuade me,
> nor the rest of the Danaans, since there was no gratitude given
> for fighting incessantly forever against your enemies.
> Fate is the same for the man who holds back, the same if he fights
>   hard.
> We are all held in a single honour, the brave with the weaklings.
> A man dies still if he has done nothing, as one who has done
>   much.
> Nothing is won for me, now that my heart has gone through its
>   afflictions
> in forever setting my life on the hazard of battle.
> For as to her unwinged young ones the mother bird brings back
> morsels, wherever she can find them, but as for herself it is
>   suffering,
> such was I, as I lay through the many nights unsleeping,
> such as I wore through the bloody days of the fighting,
> striving with warriors for the sake of these men's women.
>   (IX, 312–27)

>   Of possessions
> cattle and fat sheep are things to be had for the lifting,
> and tripods can be won, and the tawny high heads of horses,
> but a man's life cannot come back again, it cannot be lifted
> nor captured again by force, once it has crossed the teeth's barrier.
>   (IX, 405–9)

The hero turns out to be a hero after all. Achilles' rage and withdrawal, which had seemed almost infantile, a narcissistic wound at most—he's lost his war booty, his slave mistress, to Daddy—has had the remarkable effect of awakening this haughty young man to a new conception of war. Suddenly, he is groping toward an idea of honor that doesn't depend on the bartering of women and goods or on the opinions that men have of one another's prowess. "We are all held in a single honor. . . . A man dies still if he has done nothing, as one who has done much." For the greatest warrior in the world, that is a devastating admission. From our point of view, Achilles has jumped forward to a private or even spiritual sense of worth: Honor is a matter between a man and Zeus or between a man and himself, and in the end, no one can be compensated for the death of another; the worth of life is immeasurable. When you read this speech against the behavior and the speeches of the other heroes (as Tayler did with his class), you see that Achilles has come close to breaking with the honor/shame code of Homer's warrior society. He has made an attempt, not always successful, to reach consciousness itself, the consciousness that (for a modern reader) has been missing from the poem.

The first hero of consciousness can go only so far; his revolt is incomplete. After Patroclus is killed, Achilles' wrath turns into personal rage at Hector, Patroclus' slayer, and he goes on a rampage (as we've seen), killing everyone in sight; he pushes the Trojan army back into the city, and finally kills Hector, whose body he drags around the walls for days. At the funeral of Patroclus, he sacrifices the twelve young Trojans taken in the river, slitting their throats along with the sheep and cattle and piling the bodies high on the funeral pyre. Sleepless and unappeasable, he has gone mad with grief.

Now, in the complacent "humanist" reading of the *Iliad*, Achilles achieves completeness as a hero at the end of the poem. He gives Hector's body back to the great warrior's father—Priam, the king of Troy. In the scene of Priam's supplication of Achilles in Book XXIV ("I have gone through what no other mortal on earth has gone through; I put my lips to the hands of the man who has killed my children"), one of the most moving things in all literature, he attains compassion (so the reading goes), and is ready to die. Homer ends the poem with the burial of Hector, but we know that Achilles has chosen glory and an early death rather than a comfortable middle age in the safety of his father's land. His character improved, Achilles renounces cruelty and rejoins the community; he will die (after the action of the poem) as a hero fulfilled.

But this is too pat; it's Sunday-school stuff, or perhaps a Lit Hum reading from fifty years ago. If that were all the poem added up to— the maturing of an arrogant young man—one could more easily agree with the people ready to give the *Iliad* a rest. But it isn't so. Rage such as Achilles', once awakened, cannot be silenced, for it takes on a new cruelty, the cruelty of thought: The questions he asks about war and death remain unanswered in the poem because they cannot be answered. The *Iliad*, for all its vaunting glory, remains in tension with itself, questioning, and even subverting, its own ethos, and it leaves one profoundly uneasy. When I finished it, I felt relief and also a kind of awe. Could this be the same work castigated by some critics and teachers as a mere insensible celebration of war, a triumphalist school for modern imperialists and chauvinists eager to extend their hegemony over the physical and social world? Achilles knows he will attain immortal renown as a hero, yet he's the only one who takes the measure of death. One imagines him at the end of the poem as still unconsolable and unconsoling, still raging somewhere on the plains outside Troy. The written civilization of the West begins with a hero who both embodies and questions the nature of civilization as it was then constituted.

❖   ❖   ❖

A white male and a bourgeois, a man who was raised on the culture of the West, I am not an imperialist, exactly, but I write from within the walls of the imperium and enjoy its protections. Seen from the outside, by the cultural left, that is my identity. But only as seen from outside. For how could identity defined by race, gender, and class (the cultural left's inescapable trinity) account for the use that any of us makes of the cards we've been dealt? Or for the way we feel about our own experience? And so, when I finished the *Iliad*, a few things came back to me, and I recalled that at eighteen, as a freshmen reading both core-curriculum courses, I had been dismayed by Homer's war poem. A young man suffering the self-conscious torments of eighteen (and self-conscious torment was very much a fashionable style at Columbia in 1961), I measured the difference between myself and Homer's heroes and I was not happy about it. I was overawed by physical courage and by the poem's grandeur, which I experienced as a taunt.

In the interim, I had become a New York householder and father. I now enjoyed thick walls, fitted sheets, and Pellegrino water on the dinner table; and when I read the *Iliad* again, it troubled me in a different way. The poem's amoral magnificence, the unhoused splendor of air, feasts, and fire, resounded with the savage celebration of physical joy whose excesses—once the shock wore off—became almost completely intoxicating. Which left one, at the very least, with a considerably diminished satisfaction in fitted sheets and Pellegrino water. Middle-class life was no more than a pleasant compromise compared with

As when along the thundering beach the surf of the sea strikes
beat upon beat as the west wind drives it onward; far out
cresting first on the open water, it drives thereafter
to smash roaring along the dry land, and against the rock jut
bending breaks itself into crests spewing back the salt wash;
so thronged beat upon beat the Danaans' close battalions
steadily into battle, with each of the lords commanding
his own men. . . .   (IV, 422–29)

I do not mean to imply that the *Iliad*'s power can be measured by the distress it causes a single middle-class reader. A great work of art is likely to be challenging and even subversive of almost anyone's peace. Even the quiet final book of the *Iliad*, in which Priam travels through the Greek lines and asks for the body of his son, is filled with sorrow and threat and intimations of the catastrophe to come—the sacking of Troy, the slaughter of the remaining men, the carrying away of the women and children as slaves. Homer celebrated remorseless cruelty, and loathed the results of remorseless cruelty. The *Iliad* in its ambivalence about glory and death challenges most of our current ideas about what is right and wrong, what is true, what is heroic, and finally, what is human.

Chapter 2

SAPPHO

- Alma mater without tears; trying to sit on a classroom chair
- The "Hymn to Demeter"
- Sappho's fate and reputation
- A Sappho poem
- A slight alteration to, and improvement of, the Lit Hum "narrative"

I might as well admit it: I had no special memories of the Columbia campus. It was a city campus, and an ungracious one at that, without a coffee shop, a comfortable lounge, or any other place a student could slink off to; with no more than a worn patch of green and vagrant glimpse of flowering bush, and nothing gratuitously beautiful, luxurious, or absurd anywhere. And so, after my sophomore year, I had moved out of the dorms with friends and into an apartment on 112th Street between Broadway and Amsterdam, and I had escaped whenever possible into the city—to Carnegie Hall or folk clubs in the Village or to the movie-revival houses on the Upper West Side, whose sticky floors, broken seats, and mentholated urinals offered a flavor more congenial to student taste than the bland discomforts of the campus. Fred Astaire, the Marx Brothers, and Jean Renoir softened the austerities of Columbia life.

In 1897, the distinguished architectural firm of McKim, Mead & White had given the campus an integral design, but I had never encountered anyone who was passionate about the neo-Renaissance, red-brick buildings with limestone trim and pale green copper roofs that surrounded the large open space between Low Library to the north and the blockish, Herbert Hooverish Butler Library to the south. The space is impressive—any open space in Manhattan is impressive—and the campus climbs nobly to a high terrace at its northern end. Yet those reddish classroom and dorm buildings on its east and west borders, though handsome, are not, putting it ruthlessly, beautiful; nor are they old enough to be interesting. And Low itself, with its neo-Palladian dome, is impressive in its solemn aspirations but not in its dimensions or imagination. The dome has its fans, but I am not one of them. To me, it looks like a flying saucer sitting atop columns. When I think of college, I think of friends and teachers and of an intellectual atmosphere that so tasted of postwar New York you could bottle it.

I had spent much of my undergraduate classroom time in Hamilton Hall, near Amsterdam Avenue on the west side of the campus. Many of the Lit Hum and C.C. sections as well as other courses in the humanities were held in that building; it was the site, over the years, of student demonstrations and "occupations." Hamilton Hall! To undergraduates, it was as familiar as the inside of their bookbags. Entering it again, and expecting to feel not much of anything, I was suddenly stirred. Why? I wondered. The lobby was certainly nothing special. But it was the very featurelessness that moved me—the high-ceilinged, solemn, pristine blankness, the essence of Old American Academic, which offered neither charm nor greeting but only a readiness to be filled with something. Walking slowly up the long staircases (students went streaming past), I passed a small poster at the first landing for "the Lesbian Bisexual Gay Coalition Dance Extravaganza." On other days, there were signs for nostalgic post-Stalinist Communist action groups and heteros-against-sexism groups ("Confronting Sexism in Myself and Others: A Men's Workshop for Change"). The landings had become an ever-changing billboard for campus activism, for all the grievances, accusations, and self-accusations of the age. Was I a hetero against sexism? I supposed I was, but I couldn't imagine joining a group of men to discuss it. Would not women teach the men soon enough what "sexism" was?

The staircases emptied out and classes got underway. Voices were speaking in perhaps forty rooms in Hamilton Hall, though barely an echo could be heard within the stairwell. Maybe they said superb, maybe ordinary, things. Hamilton was now filled with teachers and students; I was back in college. I repeated this to myself, as a mantra. In a largely utilitarian, philistine, and media-dazed society, college was one of the few earnest places. Hamilton Hall enclosed within its solemnity the tenderest part of our national life.

But why were the classroom seats so hard? Solid planks of oak, joined at right angles, and stained a somber dark brown, they make not the slightest concession to the forty-eight-year-old's natural shape. I couldn't find a way to sit in these chairs. If I slumped, leaning against the slab that served as a back, my butt gradually slipped forward, my legs slid out, and my spine felt like a tightrope. If I then sat up straight to take notes— a flat tray for note-taking was appended from the chair on its right side—I would lean forward, putting my weight on the tray, and I feared I might pitch forward and hit the floor.

Tayler's room in Hamilton Hall had nothing but these punitive seating instruments; Stephanson's room, on the other hand, was not in

Hamilton but in Mathematics, another of the McKim, Mead & White buildings, but on the high terrace of the north campus, behind Low Library. The room was dominated by a seminar table with some heavy school chairs gathered around it. These chairs were a little more cozily shaped, with scooped contours. But I couldn't sit at the table with the other students. It was their class; I was an observer, not a usurper, so I sat along the walls, where there was another layer of chairs, eavesdropping on the languid talk before Stephanson arrived. The students in this class, and Tayler's, regarded me with curiosity; they nodded and then whispered to their friends. They seemed disconcerted when I asked them a personal question, as if I were a cop checking them out. A spy, perhaps. But for whom? I explained what I was doing, but my explanations always sounded odd and unconvincing to me and perhaps to them. A book project? Set in *school*? Perhaps they ignored the talk of a book project and took me as I really was—as a man who couldn't believe the size of his own appetite. I wanted to keep my mouth shut and just listen, but as classes got underway, I felt myself brimming over. This observer business was going to be hard.

❖ ❖ ❖

Dazed and exhausted by the *Iliad*, we paused in Lit Hum before turning to the *Odyssey* and gratefully read the "Hymn to Demeter" and some lyric poetry by Sappho—the work of two women wedged in between the gigantic epics. The Demeter hymn is a gentle work of 495 lines that nevertheless cuts right to the core of life. Demeter, the goddess of fertility and the harvest, has a beautiful daughter, Persephone, who is kidnapped (i.e., raped) and carried away by Hades, the brother of Zeus and lord of the underworld. Hades drags her down to his own kingdom. The heroic mother, now alone, and sore and unforgiving, hides at first among mortals in the Greek city of Eleusis. But after a period of grieving, she exercises her revenge: She causes famine on earth, which not only deprives men and women of their food but the gods of their sacrifices. If Persephone doesn't come back, men and women will die, and the gods will go unworshiped. Alarm gathers on Mount Olympus: After much sending of messengers to Eleusis and Hades and back, the gods decide that the stolen Persephone will spend one portion of the year (winter) in the underworld with Hades, at which time nothing will grow on earth, and the rest of the year with her mother, who gratefully blesses the fields with leaves and flowers and food. Hence the seasons, cold and warm, barren and fruitful; and hence, at the time of the harvest, the actual mystery cults at Eleusis. A mix of worship and saturnalia, half high mass, half Fort Lauderdale at spring break, the Eleusis rites were lawless events in which the celebrants mooned one another, held aloft large priapic constructions, made love, shouted obscene jokes, threw shit. Yes, the beautiful, serious Greeks did all these things, expelling their fear of empty fields and death in rites both holy and profane.

The hymn, filled with a mother's grief and love, is lovely and often funny, but it has mysterious corners. In her anguish at Eleusis, Demeter hires herself out as a kind of glorified wet nurse, tending a princely child whom she decides to raise as a god, tempering him in the fire at night when his parents are asleep. What is this doing there? Why is she toasting the male child? Tayler offered an anthropological and symbolic interpretation: The hymn conveys the pressure of a shift from an earlier matriarchy to the patriarchal organization of the nascent Greek city-states. The male child, tempered by fire (experience), will take over, in part because the goddess of the harvest has been pacified and has given up her dreadful powers. If you thought about it, a frightening portent lies within the hymn: If outraged women withdraw their blessing, life comes to a halt.

For the sake of harmony, Lit Hum assumes the author of the "Hymn to Demeter" is female. No one is absolutely sure. In 1961, when I first took the course, neither the hymn nor Sappho had a place on the Lit Hum list; they were both added in 1986, three years after women were first admitted to the college. Jane Austen had been added the year before, and Virginia Woolf was added four years later, in 1990. No one could quarrel with their place on the reading lists. But what about Sappho? Could her inclusion be considered a case of special pleading, a touch of the political truncheon cracking the old statues? Something had to go to make room for the new entrants, so the Latin writer Lucretius, whose eccentric epic *On the Nature of Things* I had remembered enjoying, had been booted off the list, and so had Dostoyevsky, and the exuberantly scatalogical, allegedly sexist Rabelais. Suspiciously, I read on.

> Love strikes me again, that makes the legs give way,
> That sweet-bitter, not-to-be-fought-with shape.

Reading Sappho is a tantalizing moment in Lit Hum, since her work survives principally in short fragments (such as the above) quoted by later writers or pulled out of ancient, crumbling papyri. One poem, which I have reproduced below, has survived complete, and so have a few longer fragments, about five hundred lines in all, but the rest has withered into dust. Sappho, deemed unworthy of preservation, or unworthy of presentation to the young, may not have been transferred, in the Middle Ages, to parchment, which lasts longer than papyri. Sappho wrote love lyrics, a genre ranked lower in the literary hierarchy than epic poetry or tragedy. Was a prejudice against women hidden in the generic preference? Even if she *were* copied, her work may have been lost at certain nodal points when literary survival was hanging in the balance—for instance, in the sacking of Byzantium in 1204, during the disgraceful Fourth Crusade. "When the palace is on fire," I heard one professor say, "you save the epic poems."

No one doubts that there was a great deal more, perhaps nine papyrus "books" of poems, and there's widespread agreement that it was major work. Sappho lived after Homer, around 600 B.C.—on Lesbos, of course—and became famous in the succeeding centuries. Her face was engraved on coins, her statue put up in great cities; Plato apparently called her "the tenth muse." But the work, maddeningly, is no longer *there*, only the evidence of high talent and high reputation.

Sappho occupies a problematic place in the course. Can there be any doubt that she was favored *as a woman* over other "lost" poets whose fragments might also be studied? As I thought about it, my resistance to the choice began to grow, and a burr of irritation sank into my enjoyment of Sappho (and she is, even in fragments, immensely enjoyable). She has been given something like preferential treatment, in the cause of an obvious demonstration—a rebuke to those who cannot imagine the existence of a major female poet in the classical world. We were celebrating the idea of a woman ruffling the preserve of Dead White Males rather than a graspable achievement.

But then consider the grim history of her reputation; and considering it, judge whether the demonstration might not be necessary. Revered in the fifth century B.C., Sappho was ridiculed in the next century and for a long time thereafter. For Sappho not only wrote about love, she wrote about love between women, and her sensuous lyrics caused a stir of uneasiness and disapproval. In the fourth century B.C., satirical Athenian playwrights mocked her as a prostitute, a suicide, sexually insatiable, and so on. More than two thousand years later, in the late nineteenth century, the mythmakers were still at it. Baudelaire, Verlaine, and Pierre Louÿs, celebrants of decadence, exploited her legend as a frenzied lesbian exotic, a woman of unending desire, a gorgon of eros. She became a figure in pornographic literary fantasies. The French, perhaps, merely used her for their own obsessions, but the ridicule she received from those fourth-century-B.C. Greeks might be considered more ugly, indeed the height of male hypocrisy, since the Greeks solemnly romanticized male homosexual relations. The Victorians dutifully cleaned her up, which was another kind of desecration.

As Josephine Balmer pointed out in her edition of Sappho's work,* Sappho the writer has often been judged as a *person*. Hostile commentators, mostly men, assume that in her intimate declarations she is merely writing about herself; they drop the usual analysis of literary per-

---

* *Sappho: Poems & Fragments* (Secaucus, N.J.: Meadowlands, 1984).

sona—the notion that a poet might be creating herself as a character. (They wouldn't write about a male poet that way.) Balmer obviously has a point. Sappho has been smeared, and successfully; an aura of scandal and abuse has attached itself to her fame. People who have never read her know only that she is some sort of wild dyke poet. And the smear was perpetrated by ignoring what she wrote.

From the evidence of the poems, Sappho enjoyed a high social position; she was married and had a daughter. Tayler, treating her briefly, described her as "highly educated, very smart, with perhaps five hundred years of poetic tradition behind her." Like Homer, she came out of an oral culture; the poems, though written down, were meant to be recited aloud. Imagine a salon of brilliant women, most of them married aristocrats, gathering for an evening's entertainment. There would be some music. Then Sappho would stand and sing. Her poems were about private emotions, longing, sex, marriage, parting, desire—as in this invocation to the love goddess, Aphrodite, for aid in the quest for a woman.

> Bright-throned, undying Aphrodite,
> God's child, manipulator, hear me!
> Destroy not with anguish and heartbreak,
>   Lady, my spirit,
>
> But come to me here if other times
> You ever my voice in the distance
> Have heard, and, leaving your father's house,
>   Have come, your golden
>
> Chariots yoked, your beautiful swift
> Sparrows, dense-winged, spiraling above
> The black earth, from th'heavenly aether
>   Through the middle air,
>
> And now here. You, of the Lucky Ones,
> With a smile on your undying face,
> Asked what now is the matter with me?
>   Why now do I call?
>
> What do I most wish for for myself
> In my mad heart? "Who is it I must
> Now win over for you? Who, Sappho,
>   Is unfair to you?
>
> "She who avoids will soon be seeking;
> Who gives back gifts will be giving hers;
> Who does not love will soon be in love,
>   If unwillingly."

Come once more! This hard-to-be-dealt-with
Anxiety loosen, and what my
Spirit would have let it have, yourself
  My fellow-soldier.
              (translated by J. V. Cunningham)

I am very happy someone made me read this poem. After Homer's excruciating immensities, Sappho's high spirits were an extraordinary relief. The poet presents herself as on the make for a woman, but caught
between desire and self-ridicule; insatiable, perhaps, but absurd, too.
Who won't come across for you *this* time, Sappho? Aphrodite, we
gather, has heard these demands before and has satisfied them before.
Yet the goddess will make the difference; she will make the woman Sappho loves turn to the poet even against her own will. Perhaps this element of persuasion is what has irritated readers, for behind the mock
invocation of the love goddess lies the ready assumption that the flame
will spread, that desire is catching (Aphrodite will touch us even if we
don't want to be touched), and the pursued will become the pursuer.
Sappho is both *in* the poem and, as a poet, controlling the character in
the poem, both an agent of desire and a fool of desire. The spirit of it, I
thought, was passionate and demanding and, at the same time, ironic
and playful.

Tayler's class, catching the tune, pointed to the way Sappho (in this
and other poems) adapted the Homeric imagery of warfare and conquest for an intimate purpose—how she riffed on Homer's heroic style.
Tayler then turned to the women in the class, teasing them about desire
a little ("Has this ever happened to you?"), then moved to the men, trying to get them to talk about love as Sappho characterized it—as "sweet-
bitter." A few of the women smiled and nodded, but the men remained
grumpily silent or spoke only a few grudging words, uncreated still, not
knowing whether to roll with the punch or take offense. I thought Tayler
went too far with one girl; she was young and heavy, and wrapped in
sleep, possibly even depressed, and he pulled a liberated-uncle number
on her, talking of sex. But he talked strangely about it; he said the students must embrace desire at some point if they were going to live, yet
they would find nothing but trouble when they did. Sweet-bitter.

Did the two women poets belong in the course? I'm not eager to make
a fetish of Columbia's reading list, which, after all, remains a fairly arbitrary selection that frequently changes. Other universities have other
lists. But let's not pretend that we're indifferent to the issue of who's on
such lists and why. Feminist and counterfeminist arguments clung to my
pleasure. In different ways, the triumphant patriarchy marked both authors. The old matriarchal order evoked in the "Hymn to Demeter" had

been extinguished with such thoroughness that anyone like Sappho who threatened the new patriarchal dispensation, even with lyric poems and self-mocking desire, had to be rudely put down. The two-millennia-long slandering of Sappho's reputation was a bleakly useful indication of why so few women before the seventeenth century created great works of literature, philosophy, painting, and music.

Competition between great writers is absurd. Still, I could not maintain that I had learned more about art or life thirty years earlier by reading Lucretius rather than Sappho, a poet who was ironic, funny, modern in spirit, entirely fresh. There wasn't much *of* her, but what there was, as Spencer Tracy said, speaking of another female genius, was "cherce." So I buried my earlier doubts: The meagerness of Sappho's surviving fragments was no argument for ignoring what we *do* have. Quite the contrary. Reading her between Homer's epics was both a literary and a sanity-restoring experience. Not just a spear through the chest but love makes the legs give way; *love* loosens limbs, too. We could no longer read Homer, and perhaps other writers in the course, in quite the same way. The Lit Hum "narrative" had been altered; the door had been pushed open, no more than a crack, but laughter and sanity had flooded in.

At the heart of the argument against "the canon," there was a logic that some outsiders found bizarre. Take the situation of women students. For thousands of years, as the history of Sappho's reputation suggests, women had been generally denied higher education as well as discouraged from heroic composition in literature, philosophy, painting, and so on. But if until, say, about the seventeenth century this infamous double prohibition had caused women in the West to produce little of superlative value—or little of superlative value which has survived—how could this disaster be used as an argument *against* women now studying the masterpieces of the past? For women had gained full access to the universities at last. Shouldn't they use it, in part, to study what earlier women were forced to study on their own or not at all? In *A Room of One's Own*, written in 1929, Virginia Woolf spoke again and again of how it would take not just financial independence but generations of education, and the work of many minor writers, to produce great literature by women. First, women needed to get into the libraries and universities; they needed a thorough grounding in the great work of the past. By suggesting that women were in some way "oppressed" by reading works that didn't "represent" them, wasn't the cultural left in effect proposing to deny women yet again, this time with the highest motives, access to the works that Woolf thought they needed to read? And wasn't the same underlying logic at work in the insistence that minorities newly admitted into the university should read work that "represented" them rather than the classic works their parents had no chance, or were forbidden, to read?

Columbia had not accepted that logic; it rejected the notion that the reading list of either Lit Hum or C.C. should represent the ethnic and gender composition of the students taking the courses. First of all, there was an obvious practical issue: In the modern American university, with its pluralistic student body, one would have to represent everybody, and the courses would become meaningless. But in any case representation wasn't the issue. In an opening-day C.C. section taught by Professor J. W. Smit—a Dutch-born history professor and the head of the C.C. program—the question of black writers and black representation had been raised, with some heat, by a black woman student. "Where were *my* people while all this was going on?" she asked. "We were *there*." And Smit, a large, affable man with a mellifluous voice, sighing slightly, had said: "They were *there*, but they weren't part of the influence on America. Has Chinese political thinking influenced American political thought? Our free-market economy led to, and molded, our individualistic thinking. African community organization has led to a very different way of thinking—the ideology of community-based organization. American civilization has come, as it were, too late after some of the other great civilizations to receive their influence."

Smit's argument for sticking to the classics, then, was historical *influence*. America's principal institutions—its political and economic system, its language, its jurisprudence, its notion of rights, its emphasis on individualism—were derived from England and Western Europe as filtered through the founding fathers and the early political, religious, and intellectual leaders. The C.C. reading list represented the evidence of history. It was not a course put together with reference to the accomplishments (or feelings) of blacks, Latinos, Asians, Native Americans, or the many others who had also played a large role in the actual building of the country, its railroads, cities, farms, and so on, anyone who had created its folk culture, its popular speech and humor and music rather than its legal and market institutions. That all such things were as important to Americans as Plato, or even more important, no one denied; but they formed a different kind of culture. First came the inheritance; then the development of the American soul.

The books remained, Smit said. "They are big whales governing our lives."

Whales? I pondered his metaphor. Whales dive to the bottom and then rise, blowing hard, swallowing hundreds of fish as they go. Great, devouring beasts, lords of the universe. In the nineteenth century, they bashed the harpoonists out of longboats with their tails. But whales were now everybody's easy prey; some species hovered near extinction. How could whales "govern"? They were mighty creatures but vulnerable, all too vulnerable. Was that what Smit meant? If the books were whales, a lot of people in American universities certainly wanted them dead on the beach.

The black woman student was far from satisfied, and with still more heat insisted, "The course is sort of sexist, sort of elitist. That bothers me. It leaves out other civilizations."

She was polite and she was brave. How many students would have the courage to confront the head of the C.C. program on the first day of the course? Smit had to answer her.

"Western civilization," he said, "has brought forth religious wars, slavery, Nazism and the Holocaust, but also the democratic political arrangements of the West. These books are both good and bad, dangerous and the essence of civilization. We teach them in a different way from the way we did fifteen years ago. A course like this *could* impose the values of the canonical books. Now we bring out the inconsistencies, the silences."

Silences may speak, if one notices them. "For instance," he went on, "there's a peculiar way of looking at gender in Plato and Aristotle. And the Bible certainly comes out of a patriarchal set of mind. The writers are expressing in an unconscious way the disposition of their time as well as their own disposition. They think differently from the way we do—but that's precisely the value of reading the books. That those who think so differently from us still have so much power is amazing. It's the same with race—which, by the way, as an idea, is a fairly recent invention. The way we think about race is basically an invention of the eighteenth and nineteenth centuries. That earlier writers were unaware of race, or that they express prejudices unconsciously, is of great use to us."

So Smit, giving the college's official view, turned canon-bashing inside out: Because the books were still powerful, you *had* to read them. Otherwise, you wouldn't know what you were talking about—you wouldn't know what you were fighting against, if a fight was what you wanted. It was finally a matter of language: If you didn't read the books, you would become a prisoner of your own clichés.

In part, Smit was free to make his case for an unchanged C.C. because the university, recognizing the force of such complaints as the black student's, had taken action outside the course. In 1988, Columbia admitted that the two great-books courses, as well as required courses in Western art and music, might induce a limited and complacent perspective in students. The College therefore decided to add what it called at the time "the extended core"—the further requirement that all undergraduates take two half-year courses in "major cultures," that is, non-Western cultures (say, Modernist Thought in the Arab World, or Latin American Literature). By 1991, the compromise struck many students that I spoke to as a fair one, though the rubric "extended core" rankled some minority students, who thought it had the sound of an afterthought. By the spring of 1992, the College had changed the name of the requirement to Cultures and Issues. Additional changes after I left, were contemplated,* but for the time, the college had adroitly satisfied both traditional and reformist constituencies, keeping its core curriculum but also requiring students to look across borders.

---

* By 1994, the Cultures and Issues requirement was arranged in pairs of half-year courses, such that a student might take, say, two courses in "major cultures" or a matched pair of courses—African history the first semester and African-American literature the second, or Asian humanities followed by modern Japanese history.

Chapter 3

PLATO I

~ The *Republic*; the Ring of Gyges and the purpose of C.C.
~ Professor Stephanson declaims in the open air
~ Plato builds his utopia from the ground up
~ Plato's education of the guardians
~ My son Max and the media: pleasure, pleasure, pleasure
~ Liberal and fundamentalist education
~ Does an education in the media society create "just" individuals?

I was daydreaming again.

Sitting at home one night in mid-September, and reading on the living-room sofa, the scene of my wandering attention, I had arrived at the early section of Plato's immense philosophical dialogue the *Republic* in which Plato's teacher and friend, Socrates, begins his discussion of justice. *Justice!* In the America of the 1990s, it seemed no more than a fond ideal. What did we know of justice? The criminal-justice system, overloaded, stymied, pulled apart by racial loyalties, was in a state of semicollapse. Social justice was, as an ideal, repudiated by a good part of the country—at least as anything attainable through conscious governmental action. The marketplace, which, in the conservative view, rewarded the virtuous and punished the lazy, had become, in the event, the most widely respected dispenser of justice. As a theoretical subject, justice gave off the sweet, dim odor of a college bull session. *What if God doesn't exist? What came before the Big Bang? What would perfect justice be? Pass the chips.* But college bull sessions were exactly what the forty-eight-year-old man wanted. So I read on.

Plato put something enticing in the early pages of the *Republic* (in what came to be known as Book II)—a temptation, an opening to freedom—and when reading it I began daydreaming again. The question on the table was this: Would anyone be law-abiding if he were not afraid of punishment? Would anyone pursue justice for its own sake? Or would he simply get away with whatever he could? As always, Plato's dialogue consists of a conversation with Socrates and some representative young

64

men of the Athenian aristocratic class. One of the fellows egging on
Socrates—Glaucon, a friend trying to get Socrates to make the best case
possible for justice—tells a strange and maliciously undermining story. It
is the myth of the Ring of Gyges. In the old kingdom of Lydia, a shepherd, Gyges (pronounced "*Guy*–jeez"), removes a gold ring from the
corpse of a giant. When sitting with the other shepherds, Gyges begins
playing with the ring, turning the jewel to the inside of his hand. Suddenly, he realizes that the shepherds are talking about him as if he
weren't there. With the jewel turned inside, the ring makes him invisible!
Glaucon continues:

> Having made his discovery he managed to get himself included in
> the party that was to report to the king, and when he arrived se-
> duced the queen, and with her help attacked and murdered the king
> and seized the throne.
>   Imagine now that two such rings existed and the just man put on
> one, the unjust the other. There is no one, it would commonly be
> supposed, who would have such iron strength of will as to stick to
> what is right and keep his hands from taking other people's prop-
> erty. . . . the just man would differ in no way from the unjust, but
> both would follow the same course. (Penguin; pp. 105–6)

   . . . Let's see, *lunch*, lunch at . . . at Le Cirque! Yes, head straight for
the kitchen, one of New York's proudest, and there remove Henry
Kissinger's *brochette de quenelles* as it was waiting to be served, and eat
it in the corner. . . . No, this was pathetic, it lacked virtuosity. Snatching
the morsels from his fork would be more like it, and then impeding his
arm as he lifted his glass to drink, my own lips meeting the glass for a
swallow. That was better, more like Harpo, who always wore the Ring
of Gyges. Sternly passing by Van Cleef & Arpels and the other Fifth Avenue diamond merchants (I have my own ring!), I steal a Lexus LS 400
from a midtown garage, drive it to Kennedy Airport, park, and snuggle
in an empty first-class seat to Zurich, where, disembarking, I sneak into
an unoccupied room at the Baur au Lac. In the morning, a quick gaze at
the lake. Would there be a black swan? But enough lollygagging. Off to
work. Back to the airport, head to Baghdad, where I find a knife in a
street bazaar, make my way to Saddam's headquarters, bypassing the
guards, and plunge the knife into the dictator's . . .
   No.
   Snapping out of it, I realized with a pang of disappointment that I
wouldn't do any of this. Well, maybe the bit with the *quenelles*. But even
if I were invisible, I could not kill Saddam Hussein, though I wouldn't
mind if someone else killed him. Glaucon, I thought, was wrong—at
least in my case. I would remain "just," though not necessarily out of

moral conviction. Long-maintained bourgeois habits of obedience to the law would probably keep me honest, nonviolent, and even faithful. I wouldn't want to sleep with any woman who would sleep with an invisible man. (Perhaps I was closer to Groucho than to Harpo.) All right, *once*, for a kick. But who was worth spying on? Certainly not Madonna, who had long ago made the whole world into voyeurs. What, then, was my adventure? One could commit provisional crimes—steal an Armani suit, become visible, wear the suit to a party, and then return it in the morning. One could steal from the rich! But that wasn't a lawless fantasy; it was a liberal fantasy. What then? To sneak off and take a nap whenever one wanted!

Not much of a fantasy life. The truth is, I thought that too many people in America acted as if they were already wearing the Ring of Gyges. The dream of total invisibility—the hope of getting away with murder— was one of the things hurting us. The first time I read the *Republic*, when I was eighteen, I might have taken the ring. But now I wanted peace and civil order and accountability. Anyway, I was too much a creature of the media; I needed visibility, not invisibility. I wanted to be seen.

Of course, the question of liberty and punishment would never go away. It wasn't just a schoolroom issue. And it was more of a question now than ever. If the Contemporary Civilization course—an introduction to political philosophy—had a single theme, it might be "What holds a civil society together? Is it fear? Or loyalty to an ideal? Honesty? An unseen and unsigned contract? Could a society exist if its members were not in some way committed to justice?" At the moment, the old schoolroom questions had a rather terrifying immediacy. America in the nineties seemed demoralized, and in ways that Plato would have understood: The shame associated with committing a crime and the fear of punishment had both nearly vanished; at the same time, no one seemed to much believe in America as a civil society anymore. The common notion of what the truth looked like and felt like—not an ideal but a shared agreement of what reality consisted of—had all but vanished under the pressure of race, class, and gender loyalties. The society worked well for some individuals and for some groups, and one fought for oneself or one's group. But the corollary of group partisanship was the sense of group victimization. Blacks felt victimized by whites, and whites by blacks; women by men, and men by women. A society in which everyone feels he's a victim can never come to the end of its grievances. Few people thought of the society as a system for mutual protection and benefit; few were committed to it as a whole. Was anything holding us together? In its way, the *Republic* addresses all these questions.

Plato would not have been satisfied with my practice of acting hon-

estly out of middle-class habit and timidity. In the *Republic*, he attempts
to prove, among a great many other things, that we can be made to see,
actually acknowledge, that our best and truest interests lie in behaving
justly. Socrates turns on the skeptics and cynics in his party who insist
that ethics is merely a matter of expediency or power in which the strong
do what they please. He offers a radical, pre-Christian morality: It is *always* wrong to harm others; it is better to be the victim than the perpetrator of injustice. And doing right will work out better for us in the end.
If we really understood our own interests, we would be *good*, rejecting
even the Ring of Gyges (if it were offered). We would choose to be
happy—happiness understood not as momentary pleasure but as that
state of contentment in which the elements of our nature remain in harmony. The just man was the happy man.

Reading this, I sighed deeply: Tell that to a kid trying to steal a car. Or
to a Wall Street predator.

The *Republic*, the first major text in the C.C. course, was written
around 375 B.C., at least 350 years after Homer composed his epics.
Frustrated by the practical life of politics, in which he had suffered many
defeats, Plato had established a school in Athens, the Academy, part of
whose purpose was to train a new generation of political leaders; the *Republic* can be considered as a kind of guidebook to their education. At
the same time, the book, in its very form, is a representation of the
drama of education. It is also the single most widely read work of philosophy in the West, and for immediately obvious reasons. Plato, an en-
trancing writer, had perfected the form of a dialogue, with its gracefully
sinuous plait of questions and answers, its anticipation of the readers'
objections, its courtesies that are really a form of sly mockery. Socrates
the great teacher seems to flatter his students and friends, praising them
extravagantly. Oh, yes, they're so wise, so clever, and his own powers are
so feeble, so terribly feeble! But he'd just like to ask them some small
question: What do they mean by such-and-such a word, such-and-such
an idea? And then *wham!* he catches them in some contradiction or confusion, and they're knocked sprawling.

Along with the Bible, Aristotle's *Nicomachean Ethics*, and Thucydides' *History of the Peloponnesian War,* the *Republic* was the only
book read in both core-curriculum courses, and it could be read in many
different ways, as a mass of social doctrine, a study of comparative
forms of government, a gigantic prose poem about perception and
knowledge, a treatise on art and ethics. It was an exceedingly rich and
complex book, and Professor Stephanson began his classes on it by out-
lining its structure and expounding its central notions, taking us through
it section by section. Which was an unusual way for him to proceed. As

I was to discover, he usually went straight to the heart of a work, developing a few points, and then embroiling the students with one another (when they were up to it).

I had become fond of his manner. He spoke the way a good many of the younger teachers spoke, in academic dialect, as if the dangerous subjectivity of language could be tamed by using standard terms, but he had energy and flair. He was buoyant and rascally; he invited the students to a kind of ongoing party at which only big ideas and big words would be allowed. Clinking raised glasses, we would all speak some racy new academic jargon. He wanted to tease and even ravish the students, not to lecture them, but with Plato he made an exception. We needed the frame, for certainly there were many oddities in the *Republic*.

His classroom in Mathematics Hall was closed for the day, so we sat outside, on the grass, in the pleasant patch of green in front of Mathematics, on the high terrace of the campus's northern end. The bees were buzzing around, flying from student to student, and nearby some jackhammers were buzzing, too, sending up the constant din of New York as it tore up its surface and attended to the busy fluids and cables below. How you had to fight to concentrate in this city! Even when situated indoors, the mere acts of reading and speaking had to push through a farrago of noise—buses accelerating, car alarms running though their cycle of nut-brain dismay, airplanes heading for La Guardia and Kennedy. In front of Mathematics, his sweater draped over his shoulders, Stephanson was even more stentorian than usual. He fairly shouted into the normal New York racket, and every once in a while the jackhammers would stop and people passing by would suddenly hear a professor hollering, in near-British, something like, "Aren't you, as college students, part of the guardian class? And as members of an elite, shouldn't you be ruling the others for their own benefit?"

In class, I did not daydream. I was all attention and took notes. Stephanson laid it out for us.

We can't study justice by looking at individuals, Socrates says, or by looking at our day-to-day life, with its incessant, nagging conflicts between people and interests. Instead, let's look at justice in its pure form. Let's set up an ideally just society—indeed, an ideal society, from top to bottom—and then, once we have examined justice on a grand scale, let us see whether there is a congruent form of justice in the individual. First the big picture, then the little picture.

As you may have guessed, Plato has little interest in what most of us would define as justice: equality before the law. What he's after is not a *legal* concept of justice at all but justice as a quality of being, in both states and individuals, an ethics for public and private use that is in essence right.

As I read the early parts of the *Republic*, I quickly decided that Plato—whatever he may say—would not have taken such pains to set up an ideal society only to establish an analogue with an individual. I simply didn't believe it. Plato must have had some larger critical intent—a longing, perhaps, to correct messily democratic Athens, with its factions and crowds and demagogues. In any case, one watches the game in fascination. Get out the constructor set, start from the ground up, take nothing for granted, and never mind practicality! Workers, farmers, craftsmen, doctors, musicians, artists, poets, armies of servants and slaves, all will be necessary in our society, and then we will need warriors to defend this rich civilization, warriors who are high-spirited but gentle to their fellow citizens—warriors who have been turned by education into *philosophers*. We will divide the warrior class, or guardians, into rulers, who actually lead, and auxiliaries, who help carry out the decisions.

At first, there's a waggish, let's-play spirit to all this. But when Plato turns to the education of the guardians, the good-humored play, the bantering arguments, sometimes heated, sometimes amiable, give way to a singleness of purpose that I found startling and rather sinister. Creating an ideally just society means controlling everyone from birth to maturation. The education of the guardians must be tightly monitored, Socrates says, beginning with the stories told to them as children, which shall contain nothing that would form their characters improperly. Thus the episodes in Homer of the gods misbehaving or even quarreling must be cast out. Tales of the gloomy afterlife must also be discarded. Our guardians must fight bravely, without fear of death. Plato would excise from the *Odyssey* a scene in which the souls of Penelope's dead suitors pass into Hades:

> And as when bats in the depth of an awful cave flitter
> and gibber, when one of them has fallen out of his place in
> the chain that the bats have formed by holding one on another;
> so, gibbering, they went their way together....   (XXIV, 6–9)

Too frightening, too depressing. Scenes of lamentation and hilarity must go, too. We cannot read of heroes weeping over fallen comrades or of the gods enjoying some malicious prank. We want to induce self-control and discourage all forms of indulgence and moral weakness.

In defense of Plato, it should be said that the Greeks had nothing equivalent to the Bible or the Koran as a mold of conduct; *Homer* was their mold of conduct, and students, memorizing and reciting long passages, took him very seriously indeed. During those speeches, the student was expected to give himself emotionally to what he was reciting, to "become" what he read. Still, there's no doubt that Plato's notions amount to a high-minded case for censorship. In the *Republic*, an unyielding "moral" account of the nature of reading and imitation wins out over art, for Plato seems literally to believe that we become what we read and therefore the art that the young are exposed to must be strictly limited. Plato had little interest in art as we conceive it in an advanced capitalist country at the end of the twentieth century—art as an autonomous activity enjoying its own powers and "rights."

For of course we surround our children with art of one sort or another; we drown them in entertainment, representation, simulacra, games, stories. We may try to control what they see, but most of us know that it's impossible. We bring them up a little differently here, and we have a different notion of how to create "just" individuals. Harmony is less our ideal than variety of choice. We hope that individuals will choose to be good, that they will reject the Ring of Gyges when it is offered. Since we aren't creating all that many just individuals, we are possibly wrong.

❖ ❖ ❖

Max, my older son, born in 1983, has a thick green carpet in his room, a tufted and matted shag that my wife and I inherited from the previous owners of our West End Avenue apartment in New York. I remember kneeling on that carpet when Max was six or seven. Wading through the green as we cleaned up Max's toys, we got to spend a lot of time thinking about the moral nature of his education. Pennies, rubber bands, paper clips, marbles, peanut shells, dirty socks, toy soldiers, wooden blocks, G.I. Joes, crayons—a sort of kiddies' bouillabaisse, a thickening stew of plastic and metallic stuff, gathered in the green. It was the landscape of the American child.

One day, the carpet was covered with hundreds of pieces of plastic, and I sat among them, overwhelmed. A friend of Max's had just been over, and the boys had dumped boxes of toys onto the floor. There were Legos, of course—the tiny plugged and stamped modular pieces that fit together in innumerable combinations—but also He-Man and Skeletor, the mobile, olive-green figures of the Teenage Mutant Ninja Turtles, odd figures from G.I. Joe, *Sesame Street*, and maybe two or three other toy groups I couldn't identify. On the floor were the plastic detritus of a half-dozen—what?—not toys exactly, but toy *systems*, many of them also available as television shows or movies or both, and linked as well to computer games, video-arcade games, comic books, regular children's books, clothes, and cereal boxes. Sometimes the characters from one comic book slid to another, so the books promoted one another laterally. Have I left anything out? Buttons? Stickers? Advertising jingles? The "interactive" future of CD-ROMs—every child his own moviemaker, choosing among clichéd elements to make his own action film or mistaken-identity comedy—had not yet arrived. We were still in the age of consumption. Total consumption: Each part of the toy system sells the other parts, and so the child is surrounded, almost to the limits of his horizon. Idly, I lifted one of the superheroes and broke off an arm.

Max was not merely a TV-watcher, as I was when I was his age in the early fifties. He was engulfed by the media—by television and to a lesser extent radio, but also by movies, video- and audiotapes, comics, activity books, computer games, Nintendo systems and the portable Game Boy as well as all the electronic games he occasionally visited in arcades. Pleasure, pleasure, pleasure! The media offer pleasure, with the electronic noises, like the taps on the bottom of a dancer's shoes, beep-beeping at the kid as he plays, reinforcing, warning, consoling, jeering. *Beep-boop-beep-boop!* The child plays, creating a narrative with the game, killing enemies, sinking ships, building cities, and the game comes back at him with an accompanying narrative, a guide to his response like the throbbing soundtracks of forties Hollywood movies, which told audiences how to feel. *Beep-boop-beep-boop!* No mere person could be so regular a companion. Cleaning up, I tossed a football into Max's toy closet, and one of the little dingbats, clobbered in a tender spot, squawked back at me, "*Fire when ready! Fire when ready!*" We are not alone.

Forty years ago, parents worried about the influence of comic books or perhaps television, and they often worried too much.* For nothing lasts in modern media. The games and TV shows cut the path of their own extinction, creating the restlessness in the child that he quickly turns against the games and shows themselves. Children go from one obsession to another, discarding—I don't know—Looney Tunes for *Superman* and *Superman* for *MacGyver* and *MacGyver* for *The Wonder Years* and *The Wonder Years* for Wolfenstein and Wolfenstein for Sim City and Sim City for Civilization and Civilization for Myst and Myst for Doom and Doom for Doom II. . . . Nothing lasts! The restlessness produced by each station of this Via Dolorosa annihilates the child's devotion, and he passes on. Finally, the child emerges at the other end of the media tunnel. He goes to school, develops interests, becomes a teacher, a banker, a lawyer, a failure; a lover and maybe a parent. He survives.

So individually, none of these things struck me then or now as harmful. But collectively, I'm not so sure. Even if the child's character is not formed by a single TV show, movie, video or computer game, the endless electronic assault obviously leaves its marks all over him. The media keep upping the ante on the kid, slyly pressing him to go further (more violence, more sex), egging him on, joking—go *further*!—creating and

* See Robert Warshow's much-anthologized essay, "Paul, the Horror Comics, and Dr. Wertham," for a balanced view from 1954.

satisfying new areas of the forbidden, so the child never develops at his own natural rhythm but longs to conform to the media's notion of where he should be. Even if the parent controls the child's experiences of the media, the children tell each other everything; they play the game the media have set them to play, teasing each other with ghoulish violence and bits of raunchy sex they have gleaned here and there. The media press in on all sides, bursting the parental walls.

The child survives, but along the way he becomes a kind of cynic; or rather he becomes an ironist, a knowing ironist of waste. He knows that everything in the media is transient, *disposable*. Everything on television is just for the moment—it's just *television*—and the kids pick up this derisive tone, the sense that nothing is truly serious. As they get older, David Letterman functions as their prince of irony: They learn from him that every part of their identity can be taken back; everything is a role, a put-on. And one wondered whether such children would attain the firmness and simplicity of character that Plato thought necessary in "just individuals."

❖   ❖   ❖

Was Plato playing with us? The social ideas of the *Republic* seemed a mixture of the authoritarian and the naïve. At times, there's a tinge of irony and mockery in some of the proposals, but the tone is elusive. We sense that we are being kidded, but we don't know exactly how. Plato refers elsewhere to "lawless desires" as if they were a constant of our nature, but in his discussion of education he *appears* to be supporting the notion that character is infinitely malleable by training; people will enact only the behavior that they have heard about. Thus heroes must hear no soothing music but only martial tunes. No hyperemotional Mahler for our guardians, no rock and roll either, just Sousa and the service anthems.

Of course, you couldn't dismiss Plato's notions out of hand. If we didn't believe that education formed character, we wouldn't fight over education so much. Everyone prefers her children to read and see some things more than others. But *what* things? And what information would we forbid our children? The notion of a controlled education has had a long history. Plato's notions of education resurface in the assumptions of fundamentalists of many types, who talk as if art *were* life, or at least has a direct influence on life. Salman Rushdie's novel *The Satanic Verses*, in which an insane character makes jokes about Allah, is an attack on all Islam. Kill the novelist! An American commercial movie—a thriller— which has a bad marriage in it is not a dramatization of a single, fictional marriage but an attack on the institution of marriage itself. Protect the institution of marriage!

In a liberal education, however, children hear many stories from many sources, and they hear about all sorts of behavior—wickedness and goodness and the many fascinating varieties in between—and we teach them what a narrative is and what its moral relation to life might be. Even William Bennett's popular anthology *The Book of Virtues* offers some negative examples—Lady Macbeth egging on her husband to kill, for instance. Children learn that life is not always fair, that virtue doesn't always triumph, but that virtue is virtue nonetheless. A liberal temperament, whether religious or not, assumes that the young can hear about evil and still be brought to embrace the good. In fact, they *must* hear about evil, or else they cannot love the good—or love it truly.

This notion was also at the heart of Columbia's core curriculum. On the opening day of Lit Hum, Professor Tayler had given us that piece of paper with quotations on it, and one of the quotations—which he did not immediately explain—was an extraordinary passage from John Milton's defense of free speech, *Areopagitica*. Tayler used the quotation for his own purpose, but it worked just as well for C.C.

> Assuredly we bring not innocence into the world, we bring impurity much rather: that which purifies us is trial, and trial is by what is contrary. . . . They are not skillful considerers of human things who imagine to remove sin by removing the matter of sin. For . . . it is a huge heap increasing under the very act of diminishing. . . . Good and evil we know in the field of this world grow up together almost inseparably. . . . It was from out of the rind of one apple tasted, that the knowledge of good and evil, as two twins cleaving together, leaped forth into this world. And perhaps this is that doom which Adam fell into of knowing good and evil, that is, of knowing good by evil.

You must be tempted or you cannot be good. You must sense what it is to wear the Ring of Gyges, or else your rejection of it means nothing. Children must hear of wickedness, or they could not choose virtue.

❖   ❖   ❖

I want to deliver the "great books" to my children, and all the minor books, too, the good minor novelists, the detective writers, travel writers, poets, journalists, historians, autobiographers—I want them to discover the great habit of reading everything, the raw appetite for print between covers, which I have almost lost myself and which I now mourn. But I am in danger of making myself and them crazy over the issue. After all, Max, who is now, as I finish this book, thirteen, does many things beside sit in front of screens. He goes to school, draws, skates around on his blades, plays basketball in the park, rides horseback at summer camp; he reads science-fiction novels, writes stories, hangs out with his friends, listens to Jimi Hendrix and the Beatles as well as Nirvana and Snoop Doggy Dogg. What more do I want of him? Leave the kid alone. I turned to books, as it happened, because I was timid and shy, an only child who spent a great deal of time alone in a New York apartment and needed company and solace. I was compulsive about reading; I wanted *too much* from reading.

Still.

A few years ago, when Max opened a book, he chewed his shirt and crumpled his shoelaces into a ball; then, sitting on the bed, he rolled backward, holding the book in the air, his legs and bottom up in the air, too; then he fell to his side and put his face down on the book as if he were examining some bugs in the grass. He seemed eager to come at the book from some angle, underneath it, from the side perhaps, or *behind* it; sometimes he would fall into a rage and throw the book down. As I watched this, my adoration of him only grew, but I also felt licked: The media, it turned out, fed his temperamental quirks just fine. He had no trouble, I told myself petulantly, sitting still for Billy Joel and cartoons, for war movies and wrestling, for video and computer games, and all the things that operated at his tempo. *They* knew how to keep him interested, and how to sell him products at the same time. It was time to fight back.

Entering the battle directly would have brought about defeat more rapidly than not entering it at all. So my wife and I got sneaky; we waited for our moment. A few years ago, Max loved Wolfenstein, the computer game in which the player gets to shoot Nazi SS guards by the dozens. (The game has had many successors in the point-and-shoot style, such as Doom and Dark Forces). The player wields a gun, which is seen at the bottom of the screen, and he proceeds through three-dimensional mazes, down corridors, through doorways, advancing from level to level, shooting and getting shot (a face, in a small picture, shows the wounds), passing through realms ever more difficult, until, finally, down one corridor moves an awkward, enraged figure, and—*bam!*—you shoot him and he falls over, spurting blood. He is dead. It is Adolf Hitler. The game ends.

Perhaps my son, wearing the Ring of Gyges, would not hesitate to shoot Saddam Hussein, since the game, I realized, is as close to wearing the ring as you can get. A grown-up friend brought Wolfenstein over and installed it on the computer before we could see how bloody it was, how crude, how easily it gave in to the child's (all right, the *male* child's) love of destruction. Both boys, Tommy, who is now nine, as well as Max, became immediately hooked, and a fight would have been bruising and self-defeating. So we do what we always do, we *extend*. We use the game to talk to them about World War II and even the Holocaust and then from there the Cold War and the Berlin Wall.

Outgunned by the media, parents are shamelessly pedagogical. After all, they are playing for the highest stakes: They are making souls. Without planning or talking about it, my wife and I set up a line of resistance, facing the anti-information, the unbroken, fast, tight, beeping rhythm of the media with our counterrhythm, our own talk, which is slow, factual, anecdotal, and open-ended. Before bed, we tell them stories, innumerable stories, of wickedness and virtue, sometimes two, three, or even four before they are satisfied. The media squeeze out of children many lovely things that would complete their natures; we try to put them back in, often with a sense of rage that the whole issue has almost been wrested from our hands.

We had never seriously considered prohibiting the screens outright. I knew there were parents who did that, heroes of parenting who read Jane Austen to the children when they turned seven, but I could never cut the children off from their media-devouring friends. *The Simpsons* alone was a complete world of manners and jokes that my wife and I shared with the boys, groaning like Marge whenever anyone asked any of us to do anything. Most video games are mesmerizing; I enjoyed them, too, and in case, as a movie critic I was in the worst moral position to take a stand against moviegoing and television. (When I argue with the boys, forcing them to reduce their TV habit, they are gracious enough not to harp on this all-too-obvious point.) I *believe* in pleasure, even in "immediate" pleasures, "shallow" pleasures. Pleasure is the route to understanding; you expand on what you love, going from one enthusiasm to the next, one book to the next, one piece of music to the next, and finally what you wind up with as the sum of these pleasures is your own soul.

But how would pleasure—which was the principle of our media society—lead children to "justice," and "happiness," in the sense that Plato meant? (We would call it a state of "contentment," but it's the same thing.) Too many questions! Plato had thrown so many balls in the air, I couldn't catch them all: the ideal society, education, happiness, authority! I would have to come back to this, for once again, in Lit Hum, Homer had begun singing (or chanting or whatever it was he did), and even though I was sure I had read enough Homer, I had to listen.

Chapter 4

HOMER II

- ~ Professor Tayler tells the students they are all Telemachus
- ~ The students try to read aloud without giving themselves away
- ~ A return to Tom's
- ~ The *Odyssey* as dark comedy: Eat or be eaten
- ~ I fall into banality and arrive at the moment of truth: Can one reject what has given one pleasure?
- ~ Professor Tayler rescues me from banality

"You are all Telemachus, aren't you?" Professor Tayler said to his class as we swung into the other great Homeric epic, the *Odyssey*. Telemachus? The son of Odysseus? Rumpled and sleepy, or all wound up, their eyes locked onto their notebooks, the women's faces oddly blurred, the men with that protectively doltish look, caps turned around backward, the students, I thought, were like Telemachus only in uncertainty. They were in hiding. Was that what Tayler meant?

After struggling through the firestorm of the *Iliad*, I began the *Odyssey* with a heavy heart—*more* animal sacrifices, *more* lengthy genealogies, *more* irritatingly frivolous gods. I had learned to love the *Iliad*, but did we really have to read *both* Homeric epics? My reading sofa had become a groaning bench. I remembered the poem, dimly: Penelope weaving, unweaving, weaving . . . all those years at the loom putting off suitors while Odysseus was out there at sea fornicating and pretending to get home. God, it's hearty stuff. The culture had made a cliché out of the *Odyssey* (thrilling cruise ships took people on an "odyssey" from Fort Lauderdale to San Juan, and back), and I thought I knew why: The poem was official and flavorless, a tiresome masterpiece. But I was eager to see what Tayler meant, and I lurched into it.

So once more, the familiar story. In the beginning, Telemachus does not know who he is. Ten years have passed since Troy fell, twenty years since Odysseus, one of the greatest Greek warriors, certainly the most devious and resourceful, left home to fight. Twenty years! In Ithaca, Telemachus sits at his father's palace, watching and fuming as the finest young men in the kingdom, suitors for the hand of his mother, Penelope, feast on the royal cattle and sheep. They've been at it for years, these most outrageous of hangers-on, eating, carousing, sleeping with the servants, and Telemachus feels they are feeding on *him*—eating his "substance," as he puts it; swallowing up his inheritance. A sore and angry boy, a late teenager, warlike in temperament but unsure of how far to assert himself, he has a teenager's blustering indignation and confusion; he longs to become his father's son and kill the suitors, but he doesn't know how. He has never seen Odysseus. "My mother says indeed I am his," he says bitterly. "I for my part do not know. Nobody really knows his own father." An unanswerable remark, though the poem suggests at least a partial answer: You know your father by coming into your own identity, becoming yourself. The *Odyssey* called teenagers to nothing less than the most heroic destiny: Who are you and what is your quality?

As I moved into the poem, I saw that, however Tayler taught it, the *Odyssey* would cause trouble for me. P.C. issues loomed ominously: The patriarchal order, in all its mingled tender beauty and ferocity, unfurled its standard. What was Tayler doing, challenging the students in that way, telling them they were all Telemachus? Here was an implacably aristocratic view of heredity: The man's qualities will show up in the fighting mettle of the boy. The very heart of the patriarchal order. Was Tayler going to lay this on his college freshmen? And the women, too?

At the same time as Telemachus sits at his humiliating table, Odysseus languishes in the caverns of a wooded island with Calypso, the nymph-goddess, who entertains and entraps him, refusing to allow him to leave. He has become a prisoner of her inexhaustible hospitality, "suffering griefs in the sea-washed island, the navel of all waters." Tayler seized on the name Calypso, making it a key to the gigantic poem. Looking like a tiger with a quivering animal in its jaws, he told us that Calypso, in the old Greek, means "cloak." So Odysseus is Calypsoed—cloaked, buried in the amniotic fluid ("the navel of all waters"), his identity hidden, his way home to his kingdom, his wife, his son, completely cut off.

As before, Tayler converted metaphoric and symbolic analysis into a direct challenge to the students. He wanted to find them out and hassle them. This was no place for a chastely analytical approach, and he bore in. When the poem begins, both father and boy are struggling to assert an identity that has been suppressed. Telemachus, eager for news of Odysseus, voyages out, visiting the other war heroes, who returned long ago; Odysseus, aided by his protector, the goddess Athena, finally breaks free of Calypso and attempts once again to get home. Each man tells stories, asserting his identity in an account, sometimes true, sometimes fanciful, of his origins and desires. The poem moves through an increasingly tense series of strategic disguises and revelations, what Tayler called "recognitions"—first simple identifications, then more profound recognitions of quality and nobility, and finally the most profound of all, the mutual recognition, in conversation, and in bed, of Odysseus and Penelope as husband and wife. All of which causes as much pain as pleasure. And he turned that doubleness against the students.

"In ancient Greek, one of the meanings of the word 'Odysseus,' " he said, "is 'to make trouble.' The corollary of that is the whole damn bunch of you are born for trouble. . . . Unless you want to stay buried in the navel of the sea."

He spoke in his gravelly, small-professor voice, with significant pauses, and he worked the most surprising changes out of silence. This overly intimate, liberated-uncle stuff suddenly gave way to the most bitter regret, the most plangent melancholy. Tayler egged the students on and mourned their future loss of innocence, their future unhappiness, at the same time. He called them to existence and told them they would be battered by it.

God knows they needed awakening. Though the students said they enjoyed the *Odyssey*, they still can't read it—read it aloud, that is. Asked to deliver a passage in class, they drone, men and women alike, running through the lines quickly and flatly, even the most emotional moments, as if reading the manual for a Mita copier.

> . . . now Telemachos
> folded his great father in his arms and lamented,
> shedding tears, and desire for mourning rose in both of them;
> and they cried shrill in a pulsing voice, even more than the outcry
> of birds, ospreys or vultures with hooked claws, whose children
> were stolen away by the men of the fields, before their wings grew
> strong; such was their pitiful cry and the tears their eyes
> wept.   (XVI, 213–19)

As they read, the students could have been saying, "Insert the paper into the tray appended at the left. . . ."

I wanted them to be beautiful and vibrant, and they were fainthearted and sluggish, asleep still. At that moment, the insistence on *speaking* in the *Odyssey* seemed almost a joke on the students' diffidence. When asked his name, Odysseus always tells a story about himself. In an oral culture, you have to be able to say who your parents are, how much land you've got, who you've killed, who you've been conquered by, what gods you have propitiated or outraged. You *are* this narrative of yourself. The students, however, have been produced not by an oral culture but by a languid aural and visual culture, in which everything is a role, everything *provisional*, and speech may be an opening to mockery or self-mockery. In an ironic looking-and-listening culture, almost no one can tell his own story. Public speech is not what we care about. In high school, few of the students were asked to memorize poetry; some of them may never before have read aloud in class.

In the first few weeks of school, I witnessed an embarrassing spectacle. A teacher, trying to warm things up on opening day, would go around the room, asking the students to give a short account of themselves. Reddening, their voices dropping sometimes to a whisper, they would turn their stories into questions.

"Um, I'm Joe Morrison? I come from Minnesota? A small town called Park Rapids? And ah, I think, I don't know yet, what my major is?"

They must *have* stories; they're just too guarded to speak them, too guarded to read aloud in a style that would give anything of themselves away. Lit Hum, I could see, was designed to break down their guardedness. There was a touch of Platonic character formation in the course. By asking the students to read classic texts, the course not only offered them an introduction to literary study, it forced them to attach a small part of themselves, and then perhaps a greater part, to Telemachus' fear or Achilles' anger or, later, when we got to *Pride and Prejudice* at the end of the year, to Elizabeth Bennet's high-spirited directness. Perhaps, through some process of transformation, they *would* become the stories they read, and finally become their own stories. This wasn't quite what Tayler said, but it seemed to be part of his plan.

The complicating factor in all this is that Odysseus usually lies. He washes ashore at the island of the Phaiakians, and after some hesitation and subterfuge, tells them his story, and he tells it straight. But then he goes home to Ithaca and lies brilliantly to everyone, disguising himself even before his wife, son, and father. Like all successful dissimulators, he mixes a good deal of truth into his fictions: He presents himself as a noble lord fallen to beggary, and recounts adventures and catastrophes close to his own but not quite his own. Only gradually, bringing these odd, unsettling simulacra closer and closer to the truth, does he reveal his identity.

"You can't tell the truth directly; there's no way of telling it directly," Tayler said to us, quoting the Emily Dickinson poem that begins "Tell all the truth but tell it slant." He was speaking personally, I realized, explaining his indirect, lunge-and-retreat method of teaching, in which he made a guerrilla raid on the subject, never blurting out what he wanted simply and plainly but jabbing the students until they blurted it out themselves. But telling the truth "slant" was central to his notion of Western art, too. The question of identity, it turned out, was hardly a simple matter in Homer: Merely asserting oneself was hardly enough. Even at the beginning of the literary tradition of the West, the self has masks, and remakes itself as a fiction, and not as a guiltless fiction either.

"Think double" was a favorite Taylerism. Everything in great literature, every act and word, might mean something apart from its obvious meaning, perhaps even its opposite.

❖ ❖ ❖

After struggling to stay focused on the *Iliad*, I read the *Odyssey*, to my amazement, without stopping, planted in my seat. My idea of it, dimmed by the aura of cliché surrounding the poem's reputation, was completely false. It was an astonishing work, every bit as demanding, as crazy, as wildly beautiful and finally ungovernable as the *Iliad*. I read with a widening pleasure that warmed me like sunshine. The *Odyssey* is an after-the-war poem, a plea for relief and gratification, and it turns, at times, into a sensual, even carnal, celebration.

> . . . when great Odysseus had bathed in the river and washed from
> his body
> the salt brine, which clung to his back and his broad shoulders,
> he scraped from his head the scurf of brine from the barren salt
> sea.
> But when he had bathed all, and anointed himself with olive oil,
> and put on the clothing this unwedded girl had given him,
> then Athene, daughter of Zeus, made him seem taller
> for the eye to behold, and thicker, and on his head she arranged
> the curling locks that hung down like hyacinthine petals.
>
> (VI, 224–31)

> . . . so Athene gilded with grace his head and his shoulders,
> and he went a little aside and sat by himself on the seashore,
> radiant in grace and good looks; and the girl admired him.
>
> (VI, 235–37)

MGM in its heyday could have done no more for Gable. The elderly Homer writes about sensations and domestic comforts, about physical happiness and relations between people. His heroes have gone from fighting the war to telling stories about it, from asserting identity on the battlefield to asserting it at the feast table and in bed. The body, abused, torn, sated only by killing and savage meat-and-wine feasts in the *Iliad*, now requires its normal daily tending and comfort. Odysseus needs a bath and needs to get back into his own bed; his elderly father, Laertes, who has left the palace in Ithaca in disgust, and now lives in the country on the floor of a hovel, needs a winding sheet to be buried in. We are all in need of a home, an enclosure, tightly wound around us, and friends.

And now comes the surprise, the source of the *Odyssey*'s amazing power. It turns out the poem is a huge black comedy. Just when the exhausted heroes most want rest and comfort and pleasure, they find terror and entrapment. The *Odyssey* is the most famous of the *Nostoi*, or homecoming poems—epics about the return of the heroes of the Trojan War. A disastrous return in many cases, as the men, punished by the gods for some crime or dereliction of worship, suffer catastrophic weather and shipwreck, or, landing home at last, die at the hands of treacherous wives. Hospitality may be vicious, the beginning of annihilation. The most celebrated and familiar parts of the *Odyssey*—the bizarre creatures and dangers, the giants and sirens and weird disasters—are far more interesting than mere sci-fi spectacle and threat. Homer seems to be working out the perversities of appetite. Men are devoured by their needs and the needs of others, by the destructive hunger, for instance, of the barbarous, one-eyed Polyphemus, chief of the "lawless, outrageous Cyclopes," a giant who horribly eats some of Odysseus' men, "like a lion reared in the hills, without leaving anything, / . . . entrails, flesh and the marrowy bones alike," and would have swallowed Odysseus himself had he not plunged a stake into the single orb of the sleeping creature.

In this poem, as Tayler said gleefully, "you either eat, or you are eaten, and if you eat, you had better eat the right thing and in the right place." Sensual pleasures—eating the lotus blossoms that bring peace or the cattle of the sun god, which brings punishment, or yielding to the island nymphs and sirens—can destroy you or sap your will to go home.

Yes, a cruel joke! The gigantic poem is built around an excruciating paradox: The temptation to rest, to fill your stomach is almost overwhelming, yet the instant you rest, you are in danger of losing consciousness or life itself. In the end, short of death or oblivion, there *is* no rest, a state of being that might be called the Western glory and the Western disease. That Homer cannot attain peace—that there's something demonic, unappeasable, and unreachably alien in the spirit of the *Odyssey* as well as in the *Iliad*—has not much figured in the epic's popular reputation as a hearty adventure sage. It was a finer, more exhilarating and challenging work than most people thought.

❖ ❖ ❖

Why was I ragging on the freshmen? They were new to college, and unsure of themselves in some way, so why get sore at them? For a few days, I was baffled, and then my mind began drifting back to myself as an eighteen-year-old, a somewhat shadowy young man in a green corduroy jacket, tense, self-conscious, and wary, a freshmen not at all happy living between the green-cement-block walls of a room in New Hall (as it was then called), a mortifyingly faceless dormitory at 114th Street and Broadway. At Columbia now, between classes, I walked around campus, looking for some trace of that person—the shadow—some corner or monument or patch of grass where life had happened to him, and I didn't see much of anything. Some evidence must remain, I thought: a cigarette ash, an old laundry ticket stuck beneath the seats in the reading room on the third floor of Butler Library, the hideaway right next to the periodicals room, the blessed refuge with its alcoves and its solemn smokers (a minority even then), and, best of all, its leather chairs, large, comfortable, a throne for reading—in all, it was the most gracious place I found at Columbia in the early sixties. And surely if one searched there, deep in the chairs, one would find a memory, a stain even. . . .

I usually got bored at about that point. My memories of myself were gone, or so faded I didn't care to pluck at them for fear they would dissolve altogether. So I would go where I knew I would find myself. With dread in my heart, I walked off campus, and approached the folkloric greasy spoon, Tom's Restaurant, at 112th and Broadway—Tom's, celebrated in the Suzanne Vega hit song, a restaurant whose nondescript facade occasionally serves as an exterior shot in *Seinfeld* and in whose unhappy depths I had once eaten a hundred meals or more. I stood outside, and the taste of the gravy ladled across the meatloaf or brisket and sometimes doubling as soup (with lima beans added) rose in my gorge, and for a long time I could not go in. I stared through the window— brown plastic booth seats, brown stools, the pink formica counter, and, pasted to the window, a stained menu: "Baked Macaroni 'A la Grecque' . . . $4.00." A la *Grecque*, no less! Nothing had changed, not even the prices.

My life as an undergraduate hadn't been much. Teachers, friends, books, music, movies, a few drunken parties, some pranks not worth telling, and a long, long delay before the serious love affair, which came, when it came, in my mid-twenties. After a while, I knew that I was mad at the students who had no story to tell because I had no story to tell, not of my earlier years anyway, or of my years at the college, when I read and listened and hibernated, waiting for something to happen, and became convinced that I had been reborn as the hero of Henry James's novella *The Beast in the Jungle*, a young man who prepares himself for some special fate, readying himself for years, and is killed by the knowledge that his special fate is to be one man of his time to whom nothing whatever was to happen. The beast hadn't sprung on me in quite that way. I had slowly escaped the jungle and come up to speed, but I was punished for my early nonexistence with a hole where memory should be, and I grieved over it.

❖ ❖ ❖

Few works of literature inspire as much dread as the last four books of the *Odyssey*. Homer, who earlier had seemed indifferent to the techniques of suspense, now delays and delays, and in the gaps of that suspended movement one's anxiety grows. After much subterfuge, and many shrewd and perverse half-true stories, Odysseus finally unmasks himself to his son and to his loyal swineherd (he doesn't want to tip his hand to Penelope yet), each scene of recognition engendering greater emotion than the previous one. But in the midst of relief, the unpleasant conviction grows that Odysseus will slaughter all the suitors. For it is vengeance he wants, not justice; the suitors haven't killed anyone or laid a hand on Penelope, but they all must die. Athena wills the slaughter, and Odysseus, who has gathered a few allies, wants it, too.

> And now Athene waved the aegis, that blights humanity,
> from high aloft on the roof, and all their wits were bewildered;
> and they stampeded about the hall, like a herd of cattle
> set upon and driven wild by the darting horse fly
> in the spring season, at the time when the days grow longer;
> but the other men, who were like hook-clawed, beak-bent vultures,
> descending from the mountains to pounce upon the lesser birds;
> and these on the plain, shrinking away from the clouds, speed off,
> but the vultures plunge on them and destroy them, nor is there any
> defense, nor any escape, and men are glad for the hunting;
> so these men, sweeping about the palace, struck down
> the suitors, one man after another; the floor was smoking
> with blood, and the horrible cries rose up as their heads were
>   broken.   (XXII, 297–309)

So the vultures from the earlier passage whose children were stolen away and who weep here descend on the lesser birds and destroy them. Was Homer offering a covert judgment of Odysseus, a man capable of weeping over his lost child and then killing weaker men? Probably not: "justice" was not a notion that Homer, writing some 375 years before Plato, was necessarily aware of. Homer's listeners would not have found anything wrong in Odysseus' slaughter of the suitors: he was liberating his homeland. By feeling as much horror as I did, I knew I was reading the poem anachronistically.

How could one not? Even if one wants to read the old books in their own terms, as Tayler demanded of us, how can one do that without suppressing natural responses? There is something unregenerate in Homer's civilization, and in ours, that can't simply be ignored: The cult of merciless force is also part of "the West." Just as I was cozying up to Homer and the Greeks as my brothers, seekers in sensual pleasure and comfort, the poem was forcing me to see them, again, as dangerous and savage, as much the "other" as my familiar—the other that was also part of us. Think double, Professor Tayler said.

As Tayler worked on the structure of the book, and the students began warming again to the task of reading for pattern and symbol and thematic transformation, I realized I had fallen into banality—just what Tayler hated. But I decided not to be ashamed of what was obvious. The trouble with Tayler's formalist approach to literature was that it left some of the juicier moral questions outside the net. He thought such questions too easily corrupted into contemporary cliché. But look, as Tayler would say, look! After Odysseus and his men kill the suitors, Odysseus forces the palace serving girls who had been sleeping with the suitors to bury the bodies of their lovers; and then when they are finished, Telemachus, at his father's orders, kills all the women. *Telemachus* kills them, a very young man and therefore (we would say) not capable of absolute judgment in sexual matters. In Homer's terms, of course, the women belong to Odysseus and Telemachus; the men's property has been sullied, and as Odysseus' heir, Telemachus has a right to exact punishment, and that's that. He's a man; he has rights over women.

> Now the thoughtful Telemachos began speaking among them:
> "I would not take away the lives of these creatures by any
> clean death, for they have showered abuse on the head of my
>   mother,
> and on my own head too, and they have slept with the suitors."
>   So he spoke, and taking the cable of a dark-prowed ship,
> fastened it to the tall pillar, and fetched it about the round-house;
> and like thrushes, who spread their wings, or pigeons, who have
> flown into a snare set up for them in a thicket, trying
> to find a resting place, but the sleep given them was hateful;
> so their heads were all in a line, and each had her neck caught
> fast in a noose, so that their death would be most pitiful.
> They struggled with their feet for a little, not for very long.
>   (XXII, 461–72)

O evil patriarchy! I was outraged. But the issue was not a simple one, for the *Odyssey* is a beautiful book, even these lines are beautiful as poetry, and what's cruel in the poem is inseparable from what's moving in it. The Homeric tenderness, held in check in the *Iliad*, bursts out fully in the *Odyssey*, and the reader enters the paradise of the patriarchal vision of life, in which young men long to assume the responsibilities of their fathers, and wives are faithful to the long-gone husbands, who, though unfaithful themselves, nevertheless long to return; the paradise in which hospitality is rendered to guests, slaves warm the beds of heroes, and servants remain loyal to masters. Everything abundant and splendid, fragrant and comfortable—in Western literature, one may have to jump all the way to Tolstoy's *War and Peace* to experience again so strong a love of the material and physical joys of life. And in that patriarchal vision of existence, ruthless violence and the treatment of women as property are as thoroughly imprinted as is Telemachus' maturing into manhood.

Suddenly, and early in the year, I had arrived at the moment of truth. And I realized, despite my dismay over the slaughter of the suitors and the servant girls, that I had to trust my pleasure. I was a movie critic, and I believed in pleasure, and if I rejected this book after enjoying it so much, I would now be rejecting myself and entering into a false relation to both life and art. The *Odyssey* partly depends on notions that have caused the suffering and self-suppression of half the world's population, and that was a contradiction I would have to live with. Turning politically against a book that one loved was a form of lying.

One can reject the injustices of the past without rejecting the flower of those sinful old civilizations—an obvious enough idea, though one that has grown increasingly rare in contemporary American universities, where the past seems under perpetual suspicion and even the art of the past is treated as if complicit in evil. Should Homer be dropped from college courses? No, he should not. Doing so would deprive students not only of the poetry, which flows in overwhelming waves, rendering the social view secondary, but of an experience they could not possibly get from a proper modern book—the heartrending impression of the sweetness of life and the misery of life intertwined. When I asked the women students about the serving girls, most of them seemed to understand that. They shrugged their shoulders and said something like, "That's the way women were treated then. You can't quarrel with history." It was early in the year, perhaps too early to question the syllabus. They were eager to read.

Despite my doubts about Tayler's method, I could see that in the end he was right: A book like the *Odyssey* can never be simply appropriated by one social view or the other; it's too complex, it bursts one's little critique (which in any case is only everyone else's little critique). The slaughter of the suitors and the serving girls is a morally disastrous moment in Western literature, but having said that, one also has to say that criticism of the *Odyssey* on feminist and moral grounds is largely beside the point. It would be hard to say the poem suffers *as art* from its patriarchal assumptions.

And the evidence is not so simple anyway. When Odysseus arrives at the palace, Penelope examines the broad-shouldered but raggedly dressed stranger, engaging him in long conversations. Or are they really *tests*? What an extraordinary woman she is—certainly no hapless weaver of her own insignificance but every bit Odysseus's equal in will and possibly in duplicity, too. Does she recognize her husband? Homer certainly doesn't say so, but the scenes can be read—and have been read by certain scholars—as implying that she knew it was Odysseus all along. In this view, she *refuses* to acknowledge him. It seems possible: Imagine the strength of her resistance to intimacy during the twenty years of her abstinence. Earlier she had said that she would prefer the gods let her die rather than "please the mind of an inferior husband." An amazing remark: She will not please *the mind* of an inferior husband. There speaks the first woman of Western literature, who is also the first serious woman of Western literature.

Accepting intimacy with her own peerless husband is no easy affair. Even after he stands before her in beautiful kingly robes and announces himself and grows angry at her stubbornness, she delays, testing, probing, pretending that she doesn't know him, that she has moved the bed he had long ago made for them. Odysseus had built the bed around an olive tree (its trunk was a bedpost) and therefore rooted it to the center of the earth. This bed, she says mischievously, this bed we will set up for the stranger outside the bedchamber. When Odysseus loses his temper—his earth-rooted bed can now be moved!—she knows the man before her can only be her husband.

Odysseus and Penelope return to "their old ritual" in the bed rooted to the center of the earth. It is the final recognition. "Odysseus passes the bed test," said Tayler, looking around at the students. "You've all got to pass the bed test." He was getting flirtatiously intimate again. It was really an outrageous thing to say to eighteen-year-olds, but he was determined to be tough with them. His way out of formalism—at least with first-year students—was to bring their reading back to the question of their own identity. He would bring them out of their sleeping and droning selves, but he would not make "identity" an easy matter for them. They would test it against the magnificence of this:

> And as when the land appears welcome to men who are swim-
>   ming,
> after Poseidon has smashed their strong-built ship on the open
> water, pounding it with the weight of wind and the heavy
> seas, and only a few escape the gray water landward
> by swimming, with a thick scurf of salt coated upon them,
> and gladly they set foot on the shore, escaping the evil;
> so welcome was her husband to her as she looked upon him,
> and she could not let him go from the embrace of her white arms.
> Now Dawn of the rosy fingers would have dawned on their
> weeping,
> had not the gray-eyed goddess Athene planned it otherwise.
> She held the long night back at the outward edge, she detained
> Dawn of the golden throne by the Ocean, and would not let her
> harness her fast-footed horses who bring the daylight to
> people:
> Lampos and Phaethon, the Dawn's horses, who carry her.
> Then resourceful Odysseus spoke to his wife, saying:
> "Dear wife, we have not yet come to the limit of all our
> trials. . . ."   (XXIII, 233–49)

Odysseus, one of the meanings of whose name is "trouble," cannot rest. He will soon go off to complete his adventures. Summing up, Tayler looked around and spoke slowly.

"You can go back to the amniotic sea," he said, "or you can make your surface shining and impenetrable, so no one knows you. Look at you guys, you think you can find unalloyed happiness. Some of you are hermetically sealed; some of you are going to be terrified if you are found out. Look, I don't know why you can't just have joy. But if you're going to be truly recognized, it has to involve trouble and pain. You can be Calypsoed or Odysseused, buried or troubled."

Some advice! Some advice to give the future leaders of the Western world, the hegemonic lawgivers, the triumphalist accountants of the white imperium!

"Some books have proven themselves central," said the professor, speaking in a purposefully bland voice. "They have elicited a variety of responses with regard to key questions of morality, selfhood, government. It's not as if they open a single door; they can be taught in many ways. And the core list isn't absolutely fixed. There's a ten-to-twenty-percent movement of texts each year."

His voice was pleasant, his manner reserved. Professor Haruo Shirane, of the Department of East Asian Studies and Japanese Literature, and the chair of the Standing Committee on the Core (a faculty group that met occasionally to review issues relating to the core courses), had agreed to meet some students in a dormitory lounge and listen to their comments and complaints. It was a surprisingly cold night in October, and a small group of students had gathered in the tenth-floor lounge of old Hartley Hall, one of the red-brick buildings on the side of the campus near Hamilton. Shirane began by giving the consensus view at the college about the core curriculum, and reviewing what the administration had decided back in 1988—to add some women authors but to keep Lit Hum and C.C. intact, and to keep intact as well the two required half-year courses, Music Humanities and Art Humanities, both introductory surveys solely concerned with the high arts of the West (classical music, the Parthenon, Raphael, St. Peter's, Picasso, Frank Lloyd Wright, and so on). As it held the line, the college added the requirement that students take courses in two other cultures, or one other and a contemporary social issue.* Shirane's neutral manner stated that he would explain but not sell the 1988 decisions; he implied that criticism of the core might be valid or at least plausible. He was finished, and he asked for comments.

* This arrangement was later amended into required matching pairs of courses (say, African history and African-American literature), as explained on p. 63.

There was a slight pause. A few people looked down, and then a white male student raised his hand and said, "If it's about major questions, why limit your analysis to the Western outlook? Why not the Upanishads or the Bhagavad-Gita?"

Shirane looked relieved. He had heard this one before. "The argument is," he said evenly, "that even in two courses of two semesters each you can't possibly do justice to those key Western texts. We don't want a smorgasbord. If we put in many traditions, you will come out with just a fuzzy idea of many questions and issues and nothing solid."

An African-American student, a woman, who had been standing throughout the meeting, leaning over slightly, now spoke with considerable emotion. "The underlying message of C.C. and Lit Hum," she said, swaying forward "is that these books, the culture of these white men, is supreme."

She was, I guessed, a junior, and she had glasses and earrings, with some hair falling away from a knot in the back and hanging loosely at the side of her face, and she leaned in toward Shirane, who nodded and said nothing; and so she looked around for a response, and there wasn't one, except from another black female student, who stood near her and nodded. The student who wanted to read the Upanishads filled the void. "You spend part of three years of course work," he said, "studying Western civilization. But a core education that focuses only on one part of the world's ideas is no longer a core."

Relieved again, Shirane returned to the practical issue: "The faculty is up to its necks just getting a grip on these Western texts; asking them to master the Eastern literature is perhaps too much."

Well, that was a pragmatic and candid remark. The Lit Hum and C.C. faculty came from many departments: Philosophers taught literary texts, and historians philosophical texts. You couldn't expect them to master Eastern classics as well. But now the second black student moved forward, and stood next to her friend. "The student body has changed," she said. "You've let women and people of color into the school, but the books in the core courses are all white."

Again Shirane nodded but made no answer, and as he looked around, I felt for the first time a twinge of annoyance. Was he going to defend the courses or not? If it was your job to pass on a certain conception of culture, I don't see how you could be bashful about it. Either risk being a square or get out of the game. He didn't even say what was obvious, which was that the courses had never been conceived as representative of the student body. Nor were the books distributed evenly into epochs or countries. Despite changes in the reading lists in recent years, the Greeks continued to dominate the first half of the year in Lit Hum. Except for Aquinas, Dante, Boccaccio, and Christine de Pizan, there was nothing in either course dating from the fall of Rome to the Renaissance. Although a few sections might read Frederick Douglass or W. E. B. Du Bois (individual instructors had, at the end of the year, some leeway in the choice of texts), C.C. did not require a single black author (unless one counted Augustine, who was born on the fringes of the Roman Empire, in North Africa). As Professor Smit, the head of the C.C. program, had said on opening day, the books were representative only of influence and supreme intellectual and creative power, though this latter notion, of course, had been much questioned. Were the seemingly consensual standards, the assumptions about life and art that had combined to elevate, say, Homer, the Bible, Shakespeare, and Tolstoy to the summit of Western literature—were these standards themselves a product of political and economic forces? Either defend the standards, I thought, or abdicate.

The tepid conversation had uncomfortably come to life. A young man, unshaven, with glasses resting on a sharp nose, began to speak angrily. He was clearly of Indian or Pakistani descent, though his accent was purest American—East Coast, I thought. He made some standard remarks about the value of absorbing something of what the West had accomplished. After all, you were going to live and work here, weren't you?

"But why make the courses about the Western world at all?" The first black woman said, not responding to his question. She was urgent now, the dam was breaking. She leaned in toward the center of the room.

"Why did I have to listen in Music Humanities to this Mozart?" She pronounced it *Moh*-zart, drawing out the first syllable contemptuously. "My problem with the core is that it upholds the premises of white supremacy and racism. It's a racist core. I was made to feel inferior as a child . . . what I learned as a child, the white person is a better person, a superior person, I am hearing here again in Lit Hum and C.C. Who is this Mozart, this Haydn, these superior white men? Are they the only ones whose culture matters? The message is that this is the superior culture. Why is Mozart better than some African drummer? There are all kinds of beautiful music I see excluded from Music Humanities. There are no women, no people of color."

"But it's not a matter of color," said the student of Indian descent. "These are classic works. Anyway, you *knew* Columbia had these courses," he said, speaking very nervously, in sudden bursts, as if he were eager to get out the words before forgetting them or changing his mind. "Why did you come here? Why not go to another school?"

That did it. She let out her breath sharply, almost in a gasp, and her voice rose in pitch. "You see, your reaction is 'Shouldn't I go somewhere else?' " she said. "But why not change this place?" And a few minutes later, as her charge of racism went unanswered the conversation drifted into other areas, she tore out of the room with an exasperated sigh.

I was too depressed by this exchange, and too jumbled in my emotions—she was admirable, she was furiously angry, and, I thought, disastrously wrong—to take in anything else that was said in the meeting. She
had stormed out before I could get her name, and I felt staggered by not
knowing her and by not understanding what had happened to her, what
had really happened to her at Columbia.

Chapter 5

PLATO II

~ Facing staleness as a movie critic
~ The *Republic* (continued): the source of modern totalitar-
ianism?
~ Defining another's best interests
~ The great myth of parents; passing on one's culture to
children
~ The theory of forms; inside Plato's cave

I was reading seriously, reading Homer, Plato, Aristotle, Sophocles, all
the Greeks. But I needed more time. Life got in the way—a good life, but
in the way. I had always known it would, but I was determined not to
rope off my school adventure, not to become a hermit, anything medieval or cloistered, but to remain a modern middle-class man, living my
life as normally as possible. As if I had any choice! There were days
when I wanted to be free just to study, to eat at any hour and sleep whenever I wanted to, unshaven and raw as an eighteen-year-old—and then
the little one, Thomas, would take my hand and lead me into his room
to show me something he had drawn, pulling me away from Plato, and
I was exasperated but grateful, because a child's hand is like nothing else
on earth.

The movies got in the way, too. At night, after dinner, I would rush to
a screening, and then on Friday, a day without classes, I would sit down
at home and try to put aside the philosophy and literature and write my
New York magazine review of Arnold Schwarzenegger's extraordinary
new work, *Headhunter 3: The Nightmare Returns*. And sometimes I
couldn't easily do it. "I'm stale," I would moan when I had trouble hitting the right keys. It was the movie critic's version of spiritual dryness—
the bleak desolation felt by religious people when they couldn't find their
way to God. I was stale, and not just because the movies were bad. That
they *were* bad, I had no doubt: too many love letters to the LAPD, too
much Macaulay Culkin sticking burrs into Joe Pesci's hide in *Home
Alone 6*, too many winsome Gen-X comedies, too many British films
called *Cocktails by the Lake* with all nine Redgraves wearing dinner

clothes. Cheers! Hollywood cynicism and the weariness of the other filmmaking countries had worn a hole in my ardor. A movie made without courage, without faith in the audience left me in a state of dull-eyed disgust, and most of them were made that way. Increasingly, they were made without storytelling craft as well. (For that, one turned to Dick Wolf's *Law & Order* on TV.) American movies had peaked in the early seventies. By the early nineties, after a long decline, Hollywood seemed intent on turning out no more than eight or ten pictures a year that could interest an adult. And the foreign cinema had become a mere shadow of itself, a mere *wraith* compared to the glory days of the sixties, when masterpieces arrived each year from Italy, France, Japan, and Eastern Europe. Good movies were still being made, but what we so confidently called in the sixties "the film culture"—film as a way of life, knowledge, and art—seemed an illusion at best. If movies had always been a battleground between commerce and art, commerce, as only a fool would deny, had won.

But to say something like that week after week was to embrace professional death. Working as a movie critic was a great life as long as you had something interesting to write about, even something provocatively bad, and you could put some juice in your talk. You were lucky enough to be paid to seek your pleasure, and because pleasure was holy, you had to struggle not to fall into cynicism. That was the danger, not bad movies. Many a smart film critic had been ruined by the wrong kind of sophistication. His will to fight shriveled, his quiver empty or filled with no greater shaft than a pathetic joke or two, the critic wound up displaying his superiority to the subject. He became a crank, a scold, a bore. Often enough, he missed the few good movies that *did* come along.

"Why are the acting and the filmmaking technique in Martin Scorsese's *Cape Fear* so jumpy?" I demanded in a lead sentence I wrote about this time. "The performers look as if their heads are being squeezed in a winepress." Maybe so, but I was doing a little squeezing myself. What *is* a winepress, anyway? Had I ever seen one? *Cape Fear* was a terrible movie, but I was reaching for the words. "Stay fresh!" I would command myself as I sat down to write, revving up like an athlete before a game. And on those bad days, when I was dry, locked in myself, and making winepress metaphors, I could see the danger all too clearly. "Arnold Schwarzenegger's *Headhunter 3* lacks the bitter tragic force of the *Iliad*." If I ever wrote a sentence as stupid as that, or even thought it, I would be finished (and also unemployable). No, I would not fall into the trap of allowing the classics to make the movies look small, or commit the vulgar error of becoming contemptuous of what gave me my livelihood. Disgust was one thing; turning into a fake, another.

After a few weeks of school, I pulled myself out of it. The Greek classics were not making the movies look small. Reading the Greek classics only made me more exasperated by bad movies and more avid for good ones. I would race from Sophocles to a new action movie and then back to Sophocles, and each was actually a relief from the other. Seeing *Headhunter 3* made me long not for Sophocles but for a great action movie. And when I realized that Sophocles was not hurting my feelings about movies, I would settle down and do my job. *Someone* had to review *Headhunter 3* (after all, it did have that great scene in which Arnold put his fist through the guy's stomach and carved his initials on his back). It might as well be me.

I was a student, and I was scared of falling behind. So I read compulsively, not just in the little office Columbia had given me in Hamilton Hall (on the eighth floor, under the green copper roof) but at home, late at night, or while Thomas was taking a bath; and I read in screening rooms or movie theaters before the movie, in restaurants and doctors' offices, in buses and on the subway, where I was surrounded by people engrossed in books by John Grisham, Robert Ludlum, and Michael Crichton. Sometimes I read standing up, the way a horse sleeps. Looking around me in the subway as I struggled to read Plato, I envied the people with the new Grisham. Reading for pleasure, with no thought of "improvement," they at least knew what they were doing. You could actually read John Grisham on the IRT express; the rushing noise and the rapid clicking of the wheels propelled you even faster through the plot. In these desperate bursts of reading, the effort, I realized, was more important to me than the result (which was negligible). I was carrying my Lit Hum and C.C. books around with me the way someone else might wear a talisman, to ward off evil.

❖　❖　❖

Stephanson, declaiming, had arrived at that point in the *Republic* that is most offensive and bizarre to modern taste—the notion that in the ideal state everyone would do what was appropriate to his predefined essential function. Remember that the point of the game is to contrive a state in which every element is in harmony, and therefore justice is possible. Harmony would lead to justice! So Plato assigned the functions: Artisans and farmers and businessmen would produce; the rulers, at the top, would govern for the benefit of all; the auxiliaries would carry out decisions. Women could do anything men could do; they would exercise naked with the men and share the duties of the guardians (if they were qualified). There was little need for laws because the rulers would act only in the interests of the society (Plato revised this absurdity in a later dialogue). In any case, the guardians would be forced to be honest. Forbidden to hold land or goods or plate, they would live in the barracks and eat at mess like common soldiers. Yes, they would have absolute power, but they would embrace austerity, probity, self-denial. Mixed in with this insistence on self-discipline, however, was a giddy touch of sensual fantasy—the heroes of battle would be allowed to "kiss" (a euphemism, I assume) anyone they wanted to, male or female, as a reward for bravery.

Despite the shafts of irony and the moments of play, Plato seemed quite serious. Sex would be arranged along the lines of domestic breeding of animals—that is, the superior strain would be selected for intercourse and childbearing, the inferior discouraged, in such a way as to produce the greater number of superior children. Since children belonged to the state, not to families, the less talented children of rulers would be demoted, the cleverest and strongest children of artisans and farmers raised into the guardian class. Everyone would agree to such violent dispersions of the family unit because the state itself would be one large family, a single organism in which men and women alike would sacrifice personal interest to the common good.

I give so much of the doctrinal side of the *Republic* because the book, to my amazement (obviously I had forgotten it), appeared to be the source of antidemocratic theory and a possible fountainhead of some of the worst follies of the twentieth century—eugenics, for instance, and collectivized agriculture, and so on. Hitler, Stalin, and Pol Pot may not have drawn directly on Plato, but they certainly had drawn on notions of utopia that Plato put into the air, and with these notions in mind, the dictators were unlikely to suffer the slightest moral doubt about censorship or indoctrination, or much difficulty in altering the status of whole classes of people or eliminating them altogether. Human beings were always such an impediment to perfection.

Rereading these texts in middle age, I had the sobering thought that ideas were not as harmless as they had seemed when working them up for an exam at eighteen. By that, I don't mean to imply that Plato would have approved of Stalin. Later in the *Republic*, he makes a detailed critique of tyrants and tyranny, and again and again he states as his purpose the desire to insure happiness for everyone. But if Plato was not responsible for Stalin, he had still written a great deal of foolishness. He was himself tempted by the Ring of Gyges: Utopian thought was a way of getting away with murder.

By the time Plato returns to the justice question, it seems almost a joke, since the entire created society is the epitome (in our eyes) of injustice. Plato's goal of harmony requires a degree of self-suppression that we would find intolerable. In the ideal state, Plato says, the just man would not steal anyone else's property, and he would do his own job and *only* his own job, without usurping anyone else's. For everyone fully deserved to be where he was, forever, and would accept his situation as proper. The different parts of the state would exist together in peace.

And so with the individual. Exactly as the ideal state, with its appropriate disposition of talents and responsibilities, embodies justice, the individual in whose psyche the forces of appetite, intellect, and spirit are held in balance would act justly. Each of his powers would attend to its own function and usurp no other; that is, such a man would not be a slave of appetite or desire, nor overly rational to the point of passivity, and so on. And in such a state of balance, he would act justly and therefore attain happiness, for the unjust man, always unsettled or afraid, could not be happy. Happiness was the goal, happiness the end.

Yes, but how do you get there? What could cause people to give up their desire, their ambitions? Even Plato must have known it was impossible. To insure that everyone stayed in place, Plato teasingly insisted on the inculcation of a kind of fairy tale, the "magnificent myth"—the myth, taught to everyone, that God fashioned men so that gold was put in the composition of the rulers; a lesser metal, brass, in the auxiliaries; and mere iron and bronze in the farmers and other workers. Everyone would know his intrinsic worth and would remain content to stay where he is. We would have an end to social envy.

In a democratic society, however, in which each person assumes he has the same metal in his internal composition as everyone else, and the shining of someone's outer garments (cars, houses, vacations) flashes in his eyes, there is no end to social envy; and envy, I am convinced, is one of the causes of our disorder. But what are we to do? Competition and free movement is the essence of the democratic ethos, so our situation is possibly intractable, even tragic, our chaos possibly unavoidable: We would always suffer the consequences of what we value most in our system. Plato's utopia is fascinating—and heartbreaking—as an example of the harmony our ideals have ruled out as impossible.

❖　❖　❖

At Columbia, reading the *Republic* as a source of vicious or hapless social doctrine was not, I gathered, considered the smart way of dealing with it. After all, everyone knew Plato was no lover of democracy. The Anglo-Austrian philosopher Karl Popper had *said* all that in his book, *The Open Society and Its Enemies*, written in a state of despair at the beginning of World War II, when fascism was tearing through Europe. No, the hip way of reading the *Republic* was to ignore or downplay the mass of communitarian and fascist notions, and to admire Plato's ability to sustain an internally coherent logical structure over so many wonderfully written pages.

Okay, I was impressed, and I sat and read for hours at a time, entranced by this fabulous nonsense. I was a reader of philosophy. But how, I had wondered, would a left-wing teacher like Stephanson deal with this wonderfully strange and rather authoritarian book, with its assumption of the necessity of hierarchy? When Stephanson, sitting outside Mathematics Hall, had needled the students about their status as guardians, there was a murmur of indignation. Some pretended not to understand what he meant; others took it as a personal attack, as if he had accused them of being stuck up or intolerant. In the next class, which was held in our normal room, the conversation continued.

"Look, we're sitting here discussing Plato on this campus which overlooks one of the worst urban ghettos in the world," said one of the boys hotly—the same boy, in fact, who had challenged Stephanson on the calendar question on the first day. "Harlem is down there. We're up here. That's what it means to be an elite."

His name was Rob Lilienthal, and he was doing, at Stephanson's request, a "presentation," expounding Plato for the rest of us, with occasional interruptions, questions, and amplifications from Stephanson. Tall, gangly, with a casual slab of hair combed across his forehead, Lilienthal was a second-year physics major, the son of a professor. He had an arrogant way about him that I found engaging, though the other students appeared to be turned off. He said things with a grin, as if they were self-evident. So here was a guardian type, and he was willing to admit it. Because he could admit it, he could also see what was painful about it.

The class came to a stop for a second as the jackhammers, still working outside, rattled in the distance somewhere. In American universities, the cultural left was insisting that courses such as C.C. were setting up white male students as a dominating ruling class and excluding other people from a sense of free enjoyment of *their* own powers. Certainly Plato could be cited as warranting the notion of a chosen and self-perpetuating elite, yet the students found this part of Plato offensive. Reading the work, in other words, had made them conscious of the delusions of elitism—so much so that they explicitly rejected the role of guardians for themselves. Stephanson's taunting of the students, I realized, had had the hidden intention of inoculating them against the temptations of superiority. So the left-academic conceit that students simply took over the views of the "hegemonic" discourse struck me as unlikely.

But what were Stephanson's own views? At this point, they were not at issue. Not directly, at any rate. First the students had to understand *Plato's* views. In these classes, he took the role of expounder, not critic; he forced the students to face what was in the text and define their relation to it.

When they were baffled, he set the context for them, explaining, for

instance, that Plato, obsessed with the decline of Athens after the Peloponnesian War—the long struggle against Sparta, which Athens had
lost—loathed the democratic regime that ran the city. Among other
things, Athens had put his teacher Socrates to death. "Plato," he said,
"had an aristocratic disdain for heterogeneity, the chaos of democratic
rule—bad men rising to the top, good men thrust aside. He wanted a society that would not degenerate into mob rule, a society in which
philosopher-kings presided over an organic order in which everyone
would agree that his best interest lay in being ruled.

"One point of the Socratic teasing out of the truth," Stephanson went
on, "is to get everyone to know his best interests. And everyone would
see the justice of this state if he were brought to see his true interests by
an interlocutor like Socrates, who by asking the right questions would
force him or her to abandon old prejudices."

A black woman, Vanessa, quiet until that point, suddenly raised her
hand. "How can he or anyone determine what my best interests are?"

"Socrates' questions," said Stephanson, "will tease out what deep
down inside your best interests are." She shook her head, puzzled, and
Lilienthal, hearing a pause, looked at her intently and said, "*You* may
not know what your best interests are; you may be passionate, say, and
make a mistake."

"Yeah," said Vanessa, "but how do you *know* I don't know what my
best interests are?"

"Well, someone has to know what the real truth is," said Stephanson,
rocking back and forth in his chair. Suddenly, he looked like a ship's
prow, bucking through the waves. I was surprised by his words. The *real*
truth? Did he believe in "essentials" after all? For the American cultural
left, Plato's notion of a universal form of truth was hopeless, a prime example of the sin of "essentialism" or "foundationalism." A truth posited
as universal, the mantra went, was no more than the ruling class's way
of defining truth to its own advantage. In the real world, every group
had its own consciousness of truth, which it tried to impose on everyone
else. Delegitimizing the Western tradition—with Plato at the core of the
core—was now considered necessary work for parts of the academic
left. It was a way of aiding the powerless.

Stephanson held the desk now with his hands, and sliced the waves. "I
think what you're saying," he said to Vanessa, "is that since everyone
has a different conception of what's right, there *is* no right. Roight? But
you could be wrong. Plato never says substantively what truth *is*, only
that it exists. If, by means of Socratic dialogue, we dig deep down, me by
means of questions, and you by means of answers, we reach down to the
latent ideas, we will in the end, agree. In essence, you are like me. By

means of draining out all the absurdities and contradictions in what you believe, you will realize you don't really think what you do now."

For the moment, he was taking the point of view of the text, expounding Plato in a teacherly way, but she didn't hear that, she heard only a white man—two white men, actually—telling her that he could know what her best interests were, and she repeated her question, a little more indignantly this time.

❖ ❖ ❖

Parents, I think, are held in the grip of a common fiction: Their children can possibly do anything and *know* anything; they can, each one of them, recapitulate the entire cultural life of men and women. In democratic America, few people would be foolish enough to speak this way aloud. Whatever else it is, child-rearing is a profoundly material activity. Excrement, laundry, feeding, clothes, schools, teeth, books, toys, bus trips—the holy material life of childhood! Consciously, a parent immersed in child-rearing knows that it's inhuman not to limit his demands on his children. May God let them stay healthy and have a good life! That's enough! But unconsciously, we think the sky's the limit. The child has the potential to go as far as possible in a certain direction. Every child a Joan of Arc, a Napoleon, a Michael Jordan, a great lover, a great sinner! That's *our* "magnificent myth," the precondition of all education in a democratic country. Each birth is the rebirth of the human race.

Believing in the myth is perhaps more necessary in America than anywhere else. For in a country in which the media set many of the values, derision can easily bully parents out of having standards at all for their children; and almost everything the children hear from the media or their friends turns "culture" and "learning" into a joke or a duty—at best an area of pious silence. In movies, dumb is in; the wisecracking heroes and heroines of old movies have been replaced by slobs, screwups, and idiot savants mysteriously blessed by God. For teenagers, knowing something (apart from computers) is rarely cool. The person who puts on airs is the eternal American figure of fun: In a TV sitcom, for instance, anyone who thinks she's special becomes a butt; once she's joshed out of it, and admits she's a goof like everyone else, then she's fine, but not until then. At many American schools, a teenager had better hide or make fun of his intellectual interests if he doesn't want to face a daily gauntlet of ridicule. Some black students, as many studies have shown, bully their friends out of studying hard, accusing them of "going white," as if achievement were a racial issue. Mediocrity defines what's normal and therefore what's human; excellence is an attack on all the others. It's the nightmare side of democracy, and truer and truer every year.

Can a child who plays only videos and watches TV and movies be happy? If he goes straight into computer games and from there disappears into cyberspatial intercourse, can he be happy? He will have pleasure, yes, but happiness in Plato's sense of living in harmony? For all my love of movies, I did not think movies and the media were enough, or I would not be going back to school and fretting over such questions.

As he grew older, my son Max became, in the technical sense, a reader. The real question is: Will he be a "reader" in the honorific sense, a reader who reads many good things at all levels? Will he have what used to be called "a reading life"? Back there when he was seven, as I sat on the floor, surrounded by the plastic menagerie, I thought, "What if he doesn't care about the stuff we love? What if he doesn't love our pictures, our music and books?" Dreary thoughts and pathetic questions, but no parent, however relaxed in his demands on his children, quite escapes the dread that they call up. We say we want our children to create their own culture, but secretly we suffer a narcissistic wound when the children reject the things that we love. An African-American friend of mine, about my age, confronted with a young black man in his office who insisted that "Ice-T is more of an artist than Charlie Parker," punched the blasphemer in the nose and lost his job. The young man wasn't his son, but it was the same thing.

❖ ❖ ❖

I thought of Vanessa's question about someone else telling her what her interests were, and of the African-American student who ran out of the core-curriculum meeting, and I came to understand what the real subject of the *Republic* is, the real obsession underlying all the talk of the ideal state and justice.

When I was fourteen, maybe fifteen, I saw two men arguing in the street. Standing close, they swore at each other, faces red and bulging, moving closer and closer, butting each other like a baseball manager and an umpire. In those days, men still wore hats, and as the men argued, the hat brims touched and parted and then touched again, like the beaks of two exotic birds in a courtship ritual. The sight was more ridiculous than frightening, but it put me into a melancholy tailspin. I carried my grief around for days. Why do people disagree about things—why do they disagree at all? They have the same appetites, the same needs. The objects that cause their emotions may be different in different parts of the world, but *the emotions are the same*. Fear, pleasure, sorrow, exaltation . . . a stubbed toe hurts as much in Moscow (it was the height of the Cold War) as in New York. And even if beliefs are different, everyone, or almost everyone, admires courage, fears death, loves his children, lusts after beautiful men or women or both, prefers pleasure to pain, comfort to squalor.

When Plato wrote the *Republic*, Greece was breaking up, just the way Yugoslavia and the Soviet Union have broken up in our time. So Plato wanted something that would hold things together. After all, the good life is knowable—why do people differ? The answer is that they have different *interests*, more or less property, and different loyalties. When people are divided in their interests, he reasoned, the state falls apart. To have unity—that is, true unity, in which all the parts work together as a functioning organism—you've got to have a certain kind of art and culture, a political system that convinces people it operates on their behalf, and rulers who know the truth.

But how did they know? By Book VI, Plato had launched into his theory of knowledge, the most remarkable section of the *Republic*. He sets up a hierarchical table of intellectual functions, in which the top section is occupied by what he calls "intelligence," or knowing the form of the good—the "good" defined as the source which gives the objects of knowledge their being. We are in the realm of pure form, pure ideals. For instance, there are many different kinds of dogs in the world, yet we recognize not only different species but something in common to all of them, and that is doghood, the essence of dog—the *idea* of dog, which exists eternally, before and after the life of any one dog. All individual dogs partake of this ideal. The same relationship holds between the idea of tableness and the different tables on which we variously eat, work, and store things, and between the idea of car and the Infiniti Q45 or Oldsmobile Cutlass Supreme that we want to drive.

Now, this makes a certain sense. We recognize a formal quality common to all dogs. They all operate on canine principles. They *have* something, the absence of which is undoggy. That part is fine. What is hard to accept is Plato's insistence that only the *idea* of dog is real, and that the particular dogs in the kennel and the front yards of our houses are no more than apparent—that is, they are imperfect copies of the unchanging and perfect original (by this measure, a painting of a dog would be a copy of a copy). According to Plato, only a philosopher, using the powers of dialectic, can perceive the good and the forms themselves.

Most of us, obviously, would not make the cut. The next level down in the table of intellectual functions, just below full understanding of the good, is "reason," or mathematical logic. For instance, the application of Euclid's theorems: knowledge susceptible to absolute proof. Everything else is of inferior value, and falls below a dividing line into the third realm, the realm of opinion. That's where most us live. We see the objects in the world, the imperfect copies, and we little realize that they are mere shadows. We see beautiful things without seeing beauty itself. We may think the Q45 or the little Dodge Neon is a perfect car, but we are deluded; it just partakes of the ideal form of automobile to a greater degree than the bulbously unappealing Chevrolet Caprice. In other words, sense impressions, textures, sensual appreciation all mean very little. As we are not seeing the real thing, observation has no more than an intermediate value. Plato, in his most famous trope, compares us to people imprisoned in a cave.

"I want you to go on to picture the enlightenment or ignorance of our human condition somewhat as follows. Imagine an underground chamber like a cave, with a long entrance open to the daylight and as wide as the cave. In this chamber are men who have been prisoners there since they were children, their legs and necks being so fastened that they can only look straight ahead of them and cannot turn their heads. Some way off, behind and higher up, a fire is burning, and between the fire and the prisoners and above them runs a road, in front of which a curtain-wall has been built, like the screen at puppet shows between the operators and their audience, above which they show their puppets."

"I see."

"Imagine further that there are men carrying all sorts of gear along behind the curtain-wall, projecting above it and including figures of men and animals made of wood and stone and all sorts of other materials, and that some of these men, as you would expect, are talking and some not."

"An odd picture and an odd sort of prisoner."

"They are drawn from life," I replied. "For, tell me, do you think our prisoners could see anything of themselves or their fellows except the shadows thrown by the fire on the wall of the cave opposite them?"

"How could they see anything else if they were prevented from moving their heads all their lives?"

"And would they see anything more of the objects carried along the road?"

"Of course not."

"Then if they were able to talk to each other, would they not assume that the shadows they saw were the real things?"

"Inevitably."

"And if the wall of their prison opposite them reflected sound, don't you think that they would suppose, whenever one of the passers-by on the road spoke, that the voice belonged to the shadow passing before them?"

"They would be bound to think so."

"And so in every way they would believe that the shadows of the objects we mentioned were the whole truth."

"Yes, inevitably." (Penguin; pp. 317–8)

Suppose one man is freed and climbs to the surface (a guardian type, trained in philosophy); he ascends through the separate realms of illusion, belief, reason, and intelligence, at last arriving at a vision of the good, i.e., the sun. Now he can see the real objects of the world, the forms themselves. If he has the courage, he will not remain among these radiant visions but will go below once more and, against all the strength of their resistance, try to convince his old friends, the cave people, that they live in a world of illusion. The heroism of the philosopher-king is that he *returns*. Noblesse oblige.

I found it comical that Plato, who places so high an emphasis on provable truth, depends, in his theory of forms, on sheer assertion. In the *Republic*, he never tells us what the good *is*, only that it's there. He and a few people like him can see it; the rest of us can't. Either you get it or you don't. But that's what all self-appointed elites say. Perceiving "the good," or, in our terms, "proper values," is a tautology, at least as a qualification for political leadership. We shall educate some people in philosophy in such a way that they shall be able to perceive the good; they shall perceive it, or claim to, and are therefore qualified to lead us. Everyone else not only lives in a state of illusion but would fight any attempt to dispel his ignorance. "Just whom is fooling *whom*?" as Joan Crawford, pulling herself up royally, is alleged to have said.

I couldn't get over a primitive suspicion that the theory of forms and Platonic idealism in general was a kind of elegant con game. How can we know that truth or the good exist apart from specific instances tested against time and experience? How can we know beauty except by the manifold instances of it? What defined Wille Mays's greatness as a base runner was the peculiar way, rounding second, he lowered his left shoulder toward the ground, picking up speed like a motorcyclist leaning into a curve, not the resemblance of his style to some imagined perfect form of baserunning. Ty Cobb ran the bases differently, and so does Rickey Henderson.

Scientific and mathematical work, however, is a different affair, and Stephanson, in his last class on the *Republic*, emphasized Plato's importance in setting up demonstrable proof—what could be proved absolutely—as one of the highest goods. "The real with a capital *R*," he said, plowing through the waters, the bow rising and falling. "The real has been paradigmatic to our whole conception of science. It spins, later, into rationalism. We could say the real are axioms on which scientific research could be conducted universally. Piercing the vale, going beyond the world of appearances is our scientific method. Seeing the essence of multiform phenomena. The principles of rocket propulsion are the same in China as in the USA. Plato initiates the insistence on absolute progress, the establishment of universals."

"But how do you know?" said one of the women students indignantly. Earlier in the year, she had been quiet, a short-haired Latina who spoke English without an accent. "How do you know when you've seen the good? How do we know if someone has *ever* seen it?" Women, it appeared, rejected Platonic idealism with greater fervor than men. Women had grown tired of men telling them what was essential.

Stephanson did not quite answer her question, perhaps because there was no answer. Instead, he went back to the necessity of demonstrable proof. "Look," he said, "Plato established the primacy of a certain kind of theoretical working through of a problem, whether the work is empirically based or not. He's right, you know. There is a distinction between opinion and knowledge."

❖   ❖   ❖

One value of core-curriculum courses, I thought, might be that they made explicit the roots of things that we already know. Or half-know. Students arrive at college with general notions of things, perhaps dimly apprehended from the media culture, and the courses tell them—what? How they know what they know. Plato, for instance, was a prime source in the West for that intellectual tradition of valuing the "higher" in life. Until recently—let's say until the last four hundred years or so—educated people have emphasized the afterlife rather than the present; the soul rather than the belly; the ineffable rather than the known; ideals rather than practical achievement; innate ideas rather than observation; form rather than materials; self-control rather than self-exploration; virtue as a state of being rather than a habit of practical activity. A case could be made for the value of each of the first terms, but (many of us would now say) not a superior case. The "lower" often has more vitality than the "higher."

We no longer placed unique value on "the higher" and many of us had abandoned the search for "absolute truth." We were all in the cave, the media cave, sifting through representations, and choosing the ones we liked. We were free to embrace many partial truths; we were able to embrace virtue only after rejecting wickedness—in the nonfundamentalist world, we especially insisted on that freedom. But doing so, we had seriously weakened the sense of community and the respect for superior intellectual authority that Plato thought was necessary for a successful state. We had no absolute and simple way of establishing any idea or opinion as better than any other. The case for "the good" had to be made each time from the beginning. It could be made, but only tortuously and individually, not as a category. We did not practice obedience to philosophical masters. Instead, every man for himself, every group for itself, every ethnic sensibility with its own art.

And the entire notion of transcendent aesthetic experience had come under attack, and was widely considered a shuck—not a liberation but a boring imposition at best, a form of colonization at worst. In the core-curriculum meeting, the African-American woman insisted she had been reenslaved by Columbia's requirement that she listen to a little Mozart. A fair number of black students spoke the way she did. She was outraged.

She made me think again of Max in the media cave, taking his cues from the rubble on his bedroom carpet and from the media. Max had become, like his friends, an ironist of waste and impermanence and of identities tried on and discarded, and among his ironies was to dress, at eleven, as a gangsta rapper, with boxer shorts pulled high, baggy corduroy trousers, chain wallet, long hair, and knit cap. "Whass*up*?" he would shout into the phone when one of his friends called. A child of the media, he imitated African-American street culture; they all did, he and his friends, privileged white middle-class kids, gleefully shouting the words of the songs at one another. Max didn't intend the imitation as a joke or a put-down, of course. He was quite serious about it as style. But it was a style *he didn't necessarily mean to keep*. It was a style for now and for tomorrow, but perhaps not for the day after that. He was an ironist. As a very young white male, and therefore a person in a relative situation of power, he did not feel lessened by wearing someone else's clothes. He was free to accept or reject an identity, whereas the black college student thought she was playing for keeps. But was she? Would immersion in Western culture destroy her, lessen her, change her identity? I would have to observe, and listen, and think about that again.

I wanted to force my sons out of the cave. In the cave, they could know pleasure but not what Plato meant by happiness. They must read, they must learn, they must reject simple pleasures for more complex ones. They must engage at least part of the culture of the past on its own terms, without letting the media tease and jolly the past out of existence. They must experience life and be seen, and all without the Ring of Gyges. They may return if they want, but definitely they must leave. Not to become leaders but to become men.

Chapter 6

SOPHOCLES

- Professor James Shapiro's Lit Hum section
- *Oedipus the King:* I develop a peculiar cough
- Professor Shapiro asks many questions
- Rebecca tries to make it all come out right; the students reject fate
- Blindness as a consequence of success

Professor Tayler always worked from a plan in his head. His method as a teacher was to get the students to fill in the plan and to read the books in his way, and as much as I loved watching him, I knew after one or two classes that I wanted to see a looser approach as well, a teacher who would allow the students to run free now and then.

On a tip from a sophomore, I had wandered into the section taught by James Shapiro at its second meeting, when the class was just getting into the *Iliad*. Shapiro had entered on that day and thrown his books down on the table with the words, "All right, sports fans, who's new here?" A young English professor, he was was tall and blond, a genial, informal type, with exposed arms swinging loosely. He wore a short-sleeved purple shirt, open at the neck, and sneakers, and he carried a gym bag. "The Giants win, the Jets lose!" he announced a few days later. Who was this, the Coach?

In that second meeting with his class, Coach was still getting to know everyone, and he moved around the seminar table and then around the outer ring of students sitting in chairs against the walls, asking them where they were from, what they were majoring in. A pal, he offered a warming touch of high school. He was easing them into undergraduate study. And what a mix they were! (This was the class I had mentioned earlier, which had only a few white males.) There was a lone black student, Henry, from Baltimore; women from Lebanon and Italy; a small, shy young woman from Singapore, who had been taught by British ex-colonials and who had read, it quickly became clear, more English and American literature than most of the American students.

"The *Iliad*! The *Iliad*!" Suddenly, Shapiro's voice rang out. "The *Iliad*! Did you like it?"

Did they *like* it? Did he mean the question seriously? Would they answer it seriously? I would have been too timid and pious at eighteen to admit out loud that I didn't like one of the books in Lit Hum. Getting no clear answer, he said, "What did you find strange about it?" Then they began to speak, tentatively at first, phrasing their remarks as questions. ("It was too repetitive?") They found the poem very strange indeed, strange and cruel, static and distant, and the gods exasperated them, the randy and lawless Greek gods, who argue and fornicate and intervene maliciously in the affairs of men. One girl, Rebecca, who was all balled up, her hands twisting, her face flushing red when she spoke, stumbled over the question of free will. How can people be free if the gods know what is coming—if the gods are busy arranging things?

Well, this was what I had wanted. Shapiro nodded gravely and let them go on. Sitting down, he was no longer loose and gangly. He hunched over the desk, suddenly looking smaller and more concentrated. He had an extraordinary solemnity now and a stare that was friendly but unflinching. He played the students off against one another, not always answering their questions but asking new questions himself. Tension mounted in the unanswered pauses.

"In war," a new voice was saying, and loudly, "in war, there's no right or wrong, only winning." It was the lone black student, Henry. He hadn't said a word earlier in the class, but now he was shouting, and shouting happily. The discussion had turned to Hector, the mighty Trojan hero who loves his wife and son, occasionally feels fear, and in general shows more in the way of ordinary human composition than Achilles or any of the Greeks. But Henry was laughing at Hector (and, I guessed, at the sensitivities of the other students). "Hector's humanity gets in his way," he said.

Cynical, but at least it was a view. And when Henry made a statement, he didn't turn it into a question like some of the others. He was *telling* us something. He was tall, very dark, and wore black clothes and black-framed glasses, and his hair was flat on top in a wedge cut. When he spoke, he moved his arms and shoulders, pushing the words into the air. He was excited. He relished Achilles' predominance, the violence of the poem. I winced a little. But why shouldn't he relish the violence of the poem? You were supposed to relish it—and be dismayed by it at the same time. He wasn't dismayed, but at least he was in touch with half of Homer's spirit. A student to watch.

❖ ❖ ❖

It was some weeks later, in October, the most pleasant of New York seasons, and we had finished Homer and Sappho in Shapiro's class and were now reading the Greek dramatists, starting with Aeschylus, whose fearsome trilogy, the *Oresteia*, I had admired without really enjoying. Sophocles came next, then Euripides and Aristophanes. Shapiro's section met on the sixth floor of old Hamilton Hall, and before the *Oedipus* class, some of the students, waiting for Shapiro to arrive, had raised the large window and had gone out on the stone balcony, tilting their faces toward the sun for a minute. They had accepted me in their number, at least provisionally, and I went out and joined them. Shapiro's method—asking them what they *thought*—led to a spirit of openness, and they chattered about the course and about not getting much sleep, and a few asked me about the new movies.

The movies? I tried, but I couldn't do it. What I wanted to talk about was the alarming things I had learned from reading *Oedipus the King* again. There was something peculiarly frightening, even menacing, in this most famous and familiar of Greek tragedies, though I couldn't say that to the students. They wouldn't have understood what I was getting at. Nor could I have understood it, or said it, in 1961. Back then, I had frozen up and said nothing in class. *Oedipus* was an appalling work.

> King, you yourself
> have seen our city reeling like a wreck
> already; it can scarcely lift its prow
> out of the depths, out of the bloody surf.
> A blight is on the fruitful plants of the earth,
> a blight is on the cattle in the fields,
> a blight is on our women that no children
> are born to them; a God that carries fire,
> a deadly pestilence, is on our town,
> strikes us and spares not, and the house of Cadmus
> is emptied of its people while black Death
> grows rich in groaning and in lamentation. (23–30)

So speaks a priest on behalf of the citizen of Thebes. He speaks not just of a nightmare, but of a recurring nightmare: the ancient Greek city of Thebes had gone through a similar torment twenty years earlier. That time, Thebes was held in painful thrall by the Sphinx, "the hooked, taloned maid," a monstrous creature with a woman's head, a lion's body, and a serpent's tail. The Sphinx waited at the city's gates, posed a riddle, and devoured anyone who failed to answer it. The riddle goes like this: "What is it that walks on four legs in the morning, on two at midday, and on three in the evening?" What, indeed? I would have made an easy meal for the Sphinx. But an outsider, Oedipus, a man appearing from nowhere, came up with the answer ("Man, for he crawls in infancy, walks erect in maturity, and uses a staff in old age") and saved the city from the beast, who hurled herself from the rocks. Oedipus then assumed the throne, which was vacant. Laius, the king, had recently been mysteriously slain while on a journey, and the Thebans, preoccupied with the Sphinx, had ignored the crime. In a kind of legal appropriation of the royal line, Oedipus both claimed the throne and married Laius's widowed queen, Jocasta—in all, a strange, abrupt, and mysterious beginning to a kingship that has, in the event, lasted for many successful years.

As we first see him, Oedipus is a figure of power and command, with no interest in charming anyone. This new disaster in Thebes must be ended. *He will take steps.* Oedipus's brother-in-law, Creon, returns with word from Apollo's oracle: The still-unsolved murder of the old king, Laius, has placed a curse over the city. When the murderer is expelled or killed, the curse will be lifted. So now Oedipus knows what he must do. Intelligent yet overbearing, with a triumphantly self-dramatizing sense of his own powers, as if he alone could take responsibility for the city, Oedipus curses the unknown murderer, banishing him from Thebes. As Oedipus sets about finding the criminal, I noticed, as I read at home, that I had begun coughing—a dry, barking hack that came from nowhere. I felt an irritation at the sound, the way one does when someone at the back of the elevator tries to suppress a cough and it comes out anyway, and one hears him coughing and failing to suppress the cough at the same time.

This tremor of anxiety was a bit strange. After all, I had read Sophocles' play before. I knew all about the myth of Oedipus (it was one of the few myths I could remember); everyone knows about Oedipus. But Sophocles' play is a structure of dread, a pattern of suspicions aroused, allayed, aroused again, then satisfied beyond possible doubt, and the working out of the pattern created not only dramatic irony—the audience knows what Oedipus does not know—but a sense of the irony at the heart of life. What we would avoid, we become; what we loathe, we are. That's the part I couldn't really tell eighteen-year-old men and women. I don't think anyone else could explain it either. Some things have to be experienced without preparation, like the searing cold air on a bad winter day, taken with every breath.

The story of *Oedipus the King* flows out of two interlocking prophecies from Apollo's oracle. Long ago, just before Laius and Jocasta had a son, the oracle insisted the child would kill his father. Laius, in a panic, had dispatched the infant to die on a wooded hillside. Years later, Oedipus, a foundling raised by the king of a neighboring city (Corinth), hears from the oracle that he is destined to kill his father and marry his mother. He panics, too, and flees Corinth (he doesn't know the king there is not his real father). In sum: A father hears he will be killed by his

son and therefore rids himself of the son; a foundling hears he will kill
his father and sleep with his mother and therefore flees from the man
and woman he takes to be his parents. Working it out now, forging
ahead into the dark terror, Oedipus relates an incident from his past to
Jocasta. At a crossroads,

> I was encountered by
> a herald and a carriage with a man in it,
> just as you tell me. He that led the way
> and the old man himself wanted to thrust me
> out of the road by force. I became angry
> and struck the coachman who was pushing me.
> When the old man saw this he watched his moment,
> and as I passed he struck me from his carriage,
> full on the head with his two pointed goad.
> But he was paid in full and presently
> my stick had struck him backwards from the car
> and he rolled out of it. And then I killed them
> all. If it happened there was any tie
> of kinship twixt this man and Laius,
> who is then now more miserable than I,
> what man on earth so hated by the Gods,
> since neither citizen nor foreigner
> may welcome me at home or even greet me,
> but drive me out of doors? And it is I,
> I and no other have so cursed myself,
> And I pollute the bed of him I killed
> by the hands that killed him. Was I not born evil?
> Am I not utterly unclean?   (802–23)

And then I killed them all. Just like that. *Killed them all.* An enormous
anger at the behest of an enormous will.

And now, what does he do? A powerful man must *know*. A president,
a company head, a chief engineer or magazine editor wants to know all
the possible plots and conspiracies in the air, anything that could undermine him. Oedipus is great because he goes on even though what he
finds out will undermine him. Ignorance is destructive, and knowledge is
destructive, too—the ultimate bind for both the man of action and the
intellectual. And I sat there coughing nervously, even though I certainly
remembered the end. The chorus—horrified citizens—recoils and pla-
cates, searching for a haven somewhere, and Jocasta tries to stop Oedipus from going on. "I beg you," she says to Oedipus, "do not hunt this
out—I beg you, if you have any care for your own life." Her desperate
remarks have an almost comic haplessness. She *knows*. God, does she
know. But she tries to turn aside from despair. Earlier, ridiculing the

prophecies, she had said, "As to your mother's marriage bed,—don't fear it. Before this, in dreams too, as well as oracles, many a man has lain with his own mother." Yes, that is certainly reassuring.

It is a terrifying play. Yet Shapiro had arrived in an uproarious mood: Tragedy brought out a combative gaiety in the Coach. He settled in, and fired a series of rhetorical questions at the students, trying to get them to name their anxieties. Franz Kafka said that he wanted works of literature that would affect us as "a catastrophe," works that would break up "the frozen sea" within us; Shapiro was hacking away at the frozen adolescent sea. He began with the fairy-tale aspects of the myth—the baby abandoned, the foundling raised as a prince in another great city.

"Whose mother told her she was found?" Shapiro shouted cheerfully at the class. "Anyone found in a basket under a bridge?" A quiet girl with glasses raised her hand. "Somewhere in Queens?" she said, with a rising intonation, as if there could be a wrong answer.

For an instant, Shapiro looked stunned. He had not expected a literal response. But he quickly recovered, and resumed his attack, hacking away. "Each one of you, I hate to say, is not legitimate. Your parents are not your parents. However, I have information about where they can be found. Anyone interested in following this up . . ."

They laughed, a little nervously I thought, and he asked them more menacing questions, a whole quiverful in fact, leaning over the conference table and staring at them individually.

"If you discovered you were illegitimate, would you not be the person you thought you were? Would you rather meet your twin than your natural mother? [Would I *what*?] What's so terrible about killing your father? What's so bad about sleeping with your mom? Is this an essential fantasy that we all have? Is it something that all men want unconsciously? Is that it?"—turning to the women again—"Do you find yourself unconsciously attracted to guys who remind you of your father?"

Some of them looked disgusted. They cannot answer these questions, except with jokes or elaborate reasonableness. "To find out who you are is a struggle you have to go through all your life," said one woman, Susan, with considerable dignity, as if she were going to restore order to these shambling proceedings. It was a fine remark, but it was an answer to a different set of questions. What she was speaking of is not the kind of self-recognition that Oedipus or any other hero of Greek tragedy undergoes.

They were fending off the play, and I couldn't quite blame them. Greek tragedy is a horrifying literature. You fear disaster, mess, unspeakable acts of rage? You think that family life is a secure haven for the victorious and the brave? The world is even worse than you think, and the family a bed of treachery.

The servant who took Laius' infant baby away is summoned, and the story is pieced together by that master detective Oedipus, the impacable bloodhound sniffing out the tracks he has made himself. *He* is the baby left to die; and he is the man fated to murder his father and sleep with his mother. Finally, he storms off and enters the palace, following Jocasta, who had earlier fled in despair; and in a state of ghastly foreboding we listen to the chorus's lamentations, until at last the character known simply as the Second Messenger comes out and makes his famous report:

> The worst of what was done,
> you cannot know. You did not see the sight.
> Yet in so far as I remember it
> you'll hear the end of our unlucky queen.
> When she came raging into the house she went
> straight to her marriage bed, tearing her hair
> with both her hands, and crying upon Laius
> long dead—Do you remember, Laius,
> that night long past which bred a child for us
> to send you to your death and leave
> a mother making children with her son?
> And then she groaned and cursed the bed in which
> she brought forth husband by her husband, children
> by her own child, an infamous double bond.
> How after that she died I do not know,—
> for Oedipus distracted us from seeing.
> He burst upon us shouting and we looked
> to him as he paced frantically around,
> begging us always: Give me a sword, I say,
> to find this wife no wife, this mother's womb,
> this field of double sowing whence I sprang
> and where I sowed my children! As he raved
> some god showed him the way—none of us there.
> Bellowing terribly and led by some
> invisible guide he rushed on the two doors,—
> wrenching the hollow bolts out of their sockets,
> he charged inside. There, there, he saw his wife
> hanging, the twisted rope around her neck.
> When he saw her, he cried out fearfully
> and cut the dangling noose. Then, as she lay,
> poor woman, on the ground, what happened after,
> was terrible to see. He tore the brooches—
> the gold chased brooches fastening her robe—
> away from her and lifting them up high

dashed them on his own eyeballs, shrieking out
such things as: they will never see the crime
I have committed or had done upon me!
Dark eyes, now in the days to come look on
forbidden faces, do not recognize
those whom you long for—with such imprecations
he struck his eyes again and yet again
with the brooches. And the bleeding eyeballs gushed
and stained his beard—no sluggish oozing drops
but a black rain and bloody hail poured down.

So it has broken—and not on one head
but troubles mixed for husband and for wife.
The fortune of the days gone by was true
good fortune—but today groans and destruction
and death and shame—of all ills can be named
not one is missing.   (1237–1286)

How odd that even at the point of catastrophe Sophocles writes with a passion for ruthless definition—"the bed in which she brought forth husband by her husband, children by her own child. . . ." Sophocles' style, as Professor Tayler pointed out in *his* class on the play, was marked by rhetorical exactitude, balanced antithesis, and a habit of splitting one element into two, or combining two into one, a verbal figure that mirrored the splits and joinings of the characters. Did this furious exactness, I wondered, bring a kind of solace to Sophocles and his audience—the last remnant of control in the maelstrom? A pleasure in knowing exactly what something in its horror really *was*? Classicism, it turned out, was not a style devoted to "serenity" but to making art out of the uncontrollable.

And what kind of people were these Greeks anyway, sitting together in huge audiences watching tragedies at public festivals? Plays like *Oedipus the King* were popular entertainment: Sophocles was not some obscure bitter poet who attained recognition only after his death. He was beloved in his own time, a great prizewinner, the author of over a hundred plays (most of them lost). The audience must have seen these plays with pleasure, for if they were paralyzed with fear they would not have come back. They must have been strengthened in some way. In our time, the powerful has devolved into shock—into the remake of *Cape Fear.* We are hooked on shock; the Greeks were caught by heroism.

For all its wild calamitousness, the messenger's speech is a gravely beautiful affair. Oedipus' courage makes it so. He pulls off the brooches holding up Jocasta's robe, and if we stretch a bit, we can imagine that he looks at the naked body of his wife and mother and then strikes out his eyes, as if punishing himself for lustful thoughts. When he emerges, blinded, and the chorus says he were better dead, he insists that on the contrary it is better to live with the truth. "What I have done here was done best—don't tell me otherwise, do not give me further counsel." Oedipus' imperious temper returns; he implies that death might be the easy way out. And I was coughing and coughing, even as I was caught in admiration of Oedipus.

❖ ❖ ❖

"He didn't *know* he was killing his father."

In Shapiro's second class on *Oedipus*, Rebecca, the woman who got red when she spoke and who twisted her hands together, was talking of the king. She was a liberal Jewish girl from the Midwest, strenuous in her sense of fairness, a morally armed and fortified reader. Her hair was pulled away tautly from her face and held at the back by a small red band, and occasionally, when just listening, she would suddenly remove the band, pitching her hair forward, her head down, as if bowing before some jealous god. Then she would put her hands in the hair, fingers spread out, and pull the hair taut again, refastening the band at the back. She was a teacher's dream—Shapiro's dream, anyway, I could see that—because she experienced books in an intensely personal way. She might say foolish things, but she didn't hold back.

And now she was trying to make it come out right, and saying, in effect, that Oedipus couldn't be held responsible for the death of his father. For Rebecca, and for students in other classes I heard discussing the play, Oedipus was a mere victim of Apollo's malicious plan. For them, Oedipus was not free *not* to kill his father and marry his mother; the interlocking fulfilled prophecies, they thought, rendered the play morally invalid. True Americans, they were used to the claims of victimization but had trouble comprehending a man who is destroyed partly through his own greatness.

"By blinding himself," Rebecca continued, "he's taking away the opportunity of ever knowing that *it's not his fault*." A curious remark; she made it, flushing dark red, with some heat, as if Oedipus had been perverse. But the Greeks didn't necessarily think that Oedipus was innocent, and Oedipus himself makes no effort to exonerate himself (not in this play, at any rate). That the gods had chosen him to suffer meant, for the Greeks, that he was in some way guilty: Oedipus was the kind of man who would do what he was fated to do. (The gods weren't quite as arbitrary as Rebecca thought.) And Sophocles gives him freedom enough: Even though fated to kill his father, he acts freely from one moment to the next, choosing to kill the irascible old man and his party at the crossroads. Years later he could have postponed the investigation.

Listening to Rebecca, I felt the urge to cough again: I had developed a furious itch somewhere low in my throat.

The play was a long way from us. The whole sickly, self-pitying side of modern life, especially American life, with its feel-good therapies, its euphemisms, its self-transformation movements, its support groups and women's movements and men's movements, its insistent cry of victimization, as if everyone were a victim, as if *life* made you a victim—all of this was calculated, consciously or not, to avoid precisely the moment of knowing who you are and what you have done and what you are responsible for. . . . It was very far from us. The therapies and living strategies that had turned "know thyself" into "absolve thyself"—no, it was "pump thyself"—and perhaps the generally well-ordered homes of the Columbia students as well, had left the students unprepared for Oedipus' fierce assumption of personal accountability. They were American teenagers, and that kind of tragedy—not entirely your fault but not quite an accident either—was not yet part of their understanding of how life worked. They localized and dismissed it as "fate," a trick played on human beings by old dead gods. In real life, they intimated, you could ace out the world once you figured out how it worked. Or barring that, you could *work things out*. American life, the students thought, was not fair, but it could be improved through reason and compassion. The play, on the other hand, was beyond reason and compassion.

Like my sons, Max and Tommy, they were children of the media, and I got the sense that for them an identity was provisional; everything could be *taken back*. The media had tricked them out of facing what young people in all societies have not wanted to face—that you make certain choices that you can't go back on, that identity itself is a kind of fate. You were one person and not another person. They had a fate, these students, each one of them.

Yet in her own way, Rebecca had put her finger on what is so extraordinarily troubling. *He didn't know what he had done.* When she spoke, I suddenly knew why the muscles were tightening in the bottom of my throat.

Oedipus is peremptory but neither corrupt nor criminal. He's not merely insensible either, like Nicholas II, the last czar of Russia, who believed to the end that the people of his country loved him, and who, upon hearing his death sentence from the Bolsheviks, exclaimed, "What, what?" Poor czar! "I don't get your question," George Bush said in the second presidential debate of 1992 to the black woman who asked him if the national debt had affected him *personally*. Oedipus *got* the question; he got all the questions. Smart and tough, and never literal-minded, he knows how to read riddles, and he's flexible enough—an outsider has to be flexible—to share power, at least nominally, with his wife and her brother Creon. The play is upsetting, among other reasons, because it suggests you can be smart and tough and you can still kill your father and sleep with your mother. Irrational forces control the universe, and the irrational controls human desire. Intelligent people are no more protected than stupid ones from committing appalling acts. Cough, cough.

I had got caught up in this in a more personal way than I had expected. Blindness, not fate, is the organizing metaphor of *Oedipus*. Blindness first metaphorical and then literal in a powerful and successful middle-aged man; blindness cutting him off from knowledge despite his very drive for knowledge. *That* was the thing rasping at my unconscious as I was reading, the sense that the drive for success and dominance—*my* drive—by its very nature contains within it the danger of insensibility. In the very act of succeeding at anything, you must cut yourself off from some vital part of yourself. And that part could destroy you. How could an eighteen-year-old know that?

The powerful man worries about what he doesn't know, about the information that could hurt him, never realizing that his success has already hurt him. I thought of the powerful people I knew: my mother, now dead; magazine editors, a corporation president, an investment banker, any of a number of movie directors; some famous critics and university professors—yes, especially them, the professors. At a panel discussion, they would complain of the exclusion of minorities and women from the culture of the past in a thick-textured jargon whose precise function was to exclude anyone whose mind worked differently from theirs. They were great at seeing everyone's power needs but their own. I had rarely met a powerful person who knew himself. Or herself. Women were no different in this regard. How could they see everything and remain what they were? For you cannot have complete self-recognition and continue to be a public man or woman, an authority, a lawgiver, a benefactor. Blindness was *necessary* to the powerful, who fight an upheld mirror as if it were the devil himself; they know that self-recognition can destroy them. "You're killing me with this stuff!" my mother used to wail when I tried, however gently, to tell her in her retirement a few things about her effect on the people around her. In a way, I *was* killing her: I was reminding her that she was no longer powerful enough not to care how she spoke to people.

Oedipus is a hero because he longs to know the truth even after he suspects that it will finish him. That is a tragic fate inherent in the struggles of ambitious people everywhere. Not only are we not in control of our lives, our very drive for control can undermine us. It was a frightening thought, enough to grab anyone by the throat.

Chapter 7

ARISTOTLE

Platonic idealism, in all its brilliant absurdity, left me up in the air. I might ridicule the theory of forms, but there was undeniably something powerful in it. When people exclaimed over "a perfect tree" or "a perfect day," they meant more than "How beautiful!" or "My needs have been fulfilled." Perhaps they meant that the happiness they felt made them think, "There must be something more, something *else,* ordering this perfection." Common sense suggested that the notion of perfection could only have been derived from many achieved beautiful days or trees—that experience and comparison were the only possible furnisher of ideals. But the impulse to understand one's supreme satisfaction in certain objects did not thereby go away. After all, common sense could not sufficiently account for the relationship between the minds that we have and a reality that is not entirely of our making, a reality that is filled with beauty and force and also extremes of evil and ugliness. Since there is considerable agreement that Gary Cooper is a handsome man, and the leopard a beautiful cat, it is not unreasonable to ask where that agreement came from. What ordered the elements of beauty, and what caused the widespread response to it? The theory of forms was not all that different from a longing for God.

It was the notion that there was a *single* ideal form of tree or car that I found hardest to swallow. Perhaps there were thousands of forms, one for each variety, such that each kind of flower or bush was not a greater or lesser approximation of a sole form of flower or bush but a physical representation of a singular form—its own special form. I warmed to this idea; unconsciously, I had always believed it. If there *were* a correspondence of material objects to their manifold ideals, that, perhaps, was the reason that some of us took such rich satisfaction in the separate integrity of each thing on earth. That a thing is itself and not another thing—a juniper bush a juniper bush and not a rose bush—is profoundly moving, perhaps the most moving circumstance in all our existence. It was also a moral fact, the beginning of ethics as well, since such a perception led inevitably to the conclusion that each person on earth was unique, too, and should be treated that way. Maybe each of us has her ideal form lodged somewhere.

The notion that each physical thing has its own integrity led me to love movies, a photographic medium which reveals the separate subjects of the world, and hate the theater, in which everything that appears—a set, a prop, a costume—gets pulled out of its relation to other things and placed in some new metaphorical arrangement that imposes meaning upon it. Not its own meaning but someone else's; whereas a juniper bush in life, and in film, remains a juniper bush. The cinema, blissfully nonsymbolic and nonmetaphoric, is moral; the theater, in which everything is freighted with meaning—too much meaning—is ambitious and desperate and immoral. So there you have it: Go to the movies and become a better person.

❖　❖　❖

A rebuke to Plato's idealism came quickly in the C.C. course—from his student Aristotle. Stephanson seized on the moment as one of the essential transactions in intellectual history. Born in Macedonia, just north of Greece, Aristotle ("not really a Greek—an outsider," as Stephanson described him) came to Athens when he was perhaps eighteen, around 366 B.C., and studied at Plato's Academy for over a decade. The brilliant student obviously entertained rebellious thoughts. In the *Nicomachean Ethics*, the first work of Aristotle's required by the C.C. syllabus, Aristotle considered and rejected the ideal form of the good, or the Idea.

> . . . even if there is some one good which is universally predicable of goods, or is capable of separate and independent existence, clearly it could not be achieved or attained by man; but we are now seeking something attainable. Perhaps, however, someone might think it worth while to have knowledge of it with a view to the goods that *are* attainable and achievable; for, having this as a sort of pattern, we shall know better the goods that are good for us, and if we know them shall attain them. This argument has some plausibility, but seems to clash with the procedure of the sciences; for all of these, though they aim at some good and seek to supply the deficiency of it, leave on one side the knowledge of *the* good. Yet that all the expo-

nents of the arts should be ignorant of, and should not even seek, so great an aid is not probable. It is hard, too, to see how a weaver or a carpenter will be benefited in regard to his own craft by knowing this "good itself," or how the man who has viewed the Idea itself will be a better doctor or general thereby. For a doctor seems not even to study health in this way, but the health of man, or perhaps rather the health of a particular man; it is individuals that he is healing. (p. 10)

On pragmatic grounds, the "idea" of the good is useless. But did Aristotle have his own notion of ideals, or the good? And did Plato know what his student thought? Perhaps not: Aristotle didn't write the words quoted above when he was a student of Plato's. The works he wrote during those years, a series of philosophical dialogues, have been lost. The *Ethics* was put together some time after Plato's death, when Aristotle had set up his own school in Athens, the Lyceum. *He* was now the teacher: the *Ethics*, like the other famous works from this period, the *Politics*, the *Poetics*, and much else, consists of written-out lecture notes, formally (though sometimes whimsically) organized with separate headings, subdivided subjects, and the like. A professor, then; one of three professors in Columbia's core reading list (Hegel and Nietzsche were the others).

If the surviving works possess little of Plato's talent for fable and metaphor, they nevertheless have a sober music of their own. Artless and plain, Aristotle's working discourse offers the pleasures of surveyorship, alertness, and I read him with a certain relief after Plato, who seemed always to be playing some elaborate joke that I wasn't quite swift or subtle enough to get. Aristotle wrote with no intent to please, concentrating only on his meaning, and reading him made me happy in a way I had not yet experienced in either course. Sitting in the living room, with the boys asleep and my wife, on the other side of the wall, reading in bed, I felt, to my amazement, a sense almost of well-being. At first, I thought it was just a flush of self-approval, and partly it was—my God, I was actually reading something besides journalism! But that wasn't all of it. The sensation came from the text itself, a small hum of pleasure, nothing great, but steady; it ranked in satisfaction somewhere near the pleasure one received from a perfectly tended garden or a newly washed car.

In my own life, order was hardly a preoccupation: I may have wanted order and civility on the streets, but I was too restless to keep a tidy desk, and I usually worked with the materials for two or three articles lying about in a pile. By normal middle-class standards, I was a mess, and planting or even tending a garden is the last thing I would want to do. But I understood the constant demand for orderliness that some people felt. The floor neatly swept, the sheets tightly tucked, the children bathed, read to, soothed into sleep and now sawing away so quietly that one had to bend over and put one's ear close to their mouths to be sure they were breathing—that was an intense happiness of a certain kind. It was contentment, and contentment was dependent on order.

Aristotle provided the satisfactions of definition and organization, of things divided, named, and placed. He sorted out the varieties of mental functioning, the nature of disparate activities—the difference, say, between the process of an activity and its purpose. He established or regularized the principles of many kinds of inquiry and the degree of precision appropriate to each. "The nature of every inquiry has to be determined by the *object* of that inquiry," as Stephanson put it. "Therefore it requires a special discourse." Obvious enough now, but revolutionary in its time. Aristotle had grasped the world by developing many discourses on how to perceive it. He had a genius for taxonomy and classification. Inquiries that he organized in the fourth century B.C. as lectures for his students became celebrated in Europe when they were revived fifteen hundred years later. For some centuries thereafter, his work maintained a remarkable authority over discussion of such theoretical and scientific subjects as metaphysics, astronomy, mathematics, biology, botany, zoology, and meteorology as well as such practical subjects as ethics, politics, rhetoric, and poetic and dramatic practice. He had an appropriating zeal: lay out the ground, set up house, and take possession. He was more than a professor; he was the Western university.

But reading Aristotle's calm classification of everything, I became obsessed with a question that never occurred to me at eighteen. Was order really possible? Is it possible outside a well-tended garden? In discourse, yes, it was possible, but in life or art? We may have longed for more civil order, more decency and responsibility, but now, after enjoying that hum of reading Aristotle, I rebelled at the complacencies of his mind. Aristotle would have disapproved of me, a modern person, rarely satisfied, always looking for contraries and irregularities, the weed that brought out the character of the rose.

At this time in Lit Hum, we were reading the Greek tragedies and also Aristotle's *Art of Poetry*, or *Poetics*, a classic of aesthetic theory based on Aristotle's experience of the plays of Aeschylus, Sophocles, and Euripides as well as many other playwrights. Aristotle was lucky; he came after a great period in art. But even though the *Poetics* was written as a descriptive theory, Aristotle's notions, I had discovered, didn't always fit the plays we were reading. For Aristotle, the tragic hero was neither perfect nor vicious but something in between, a highborn person with flaws of perception or judgment. Now this was a big advance on Plato, who so greatly feared audience identification that he would have allowed only virtuous characters on stage—a prohibition which, of course, would immediately have brought drama to a halt. Aristotle believed that sympathy, or identification, was integral to the form. Most famously:

"Through pity and fear [tragedy] achieves the purgation (catharsis) of such emotions."

But is it so? Such plays as Sophocles' *Oedipus the King* and Euripides' *Bacchae* (see Chapter Eight) were much wilder, more irrational, and more alarming than he seemed to realize. I did not feel purged after reading them but confirmed in my initial anxieties. The playwrights knew what Aristotle did not—that order was an illusion, that irrationality ruled our existence. The figures of tragedy, even brilliant Oedipus, possessed only a limited ability to understand the dangerousness of life. The universe was not a mirror of Oedipus' mind.

So even as I sat reading the *Ethics* and *Poetics*, and enjoying Aristotle's plainness and efficiency, and the well-tended-garden hum of pleasure that he gave, I sensed that order was often something imposed by power—genuine enough, but not intrinsic, not natural. I wanted to unseat Aristotle, or at least to confront him. I was bored by his shrewd, very sane advice in the *Nicomachean Ethics* that we avoid the extremes of behavior and choose the "golden mean" or middle way, a mode of existence practiced by the virtuous man as a way of taming the excesses of appetite. True enough, but so what? All this platitudinous harping on virtue was perhaps the preoccupation of the ancients that was the least invigorating to modern taste. I couldn't even finish Cicero—the philosopher as after-dinner speaker—who came along a little later in the C.C. course, and who also plucked away on the virtue harp.

So beneath the hum of contentment, another tone was playing at the same time, coming from myself—a suspicion that the weeded garden may have a skeleton buried below the hydrangeas, that the tightly tucked sheets were stained with adultery, that the sleeping children, when they stirred in the night, had dreams that took them far, far away from their peaceful beds.

We longed for order; we knew it was impossible.

❖ ❖ ❖

Stephanson launched into Aristotle at full speed, setting up the contrast. "Plato believed there was an ideal of whiteness in which all white things share; Aristotle thought we know whiteness from many white things. He's almost an empiricist, but not quite. He thought of the excellence of a thing not in terms of a transcendent ideal but in terms of its function, its end, or telos. A table was good not insofar as it partook of some ideal form of tableness but insofar as it fulfilled its inherent function as a table."

Well, this *did* make more sense. There was no single ideal of president, but one could point to Washington's probity, Lincoln's moral anguish, FDR's resourcefulness and gaiety, LBJ's pre-Vietnam persuasiveness, Nixon's guile in triangular big-power diplomacy, all aspects of greatness, all possibilities of leadership in the office. Those five men did things that presidents can do better than other presidents. Or rather, they possessed special qualities which flourished in that particular job. John Ford's film *The Searchers* was a great Western not because it came close to the ideal form of Western (Ford's earlier *Stagecoach* actually seemed more "archetypal"), but because it did certain things Westerns can do with greater power than other examples of the form. This was hardly the only reason it was great, but at least it offered a reasonable starting point for judgment. Ditto the superiority of the Nissan Maxima or the Dodge Neon to most automobiles in their class. As a middle-class man of the postindustrial age, a consumer of *goods*, I wanted things that did their job superbly well. The middle-class citizen was by nature an Aristotelian. Idealism was for aristocrats, hermits, and terrorists.

"Is Aristotle a relativist then?" Stephanson said, looking around with his handsome blue eyes and smiling rakishly at the students. They looked back at him warily. The semester was several weeks old. Crammed together in a tiny room at Mathematics Hall, they were slowly beginning to warm up. A few were intimidated by Stephanson's crashing-prow, emphatic manner; the others were getting bolder about asserting themselves. They knew well enough that relativism was a code word for the alleged sins of the modern American educated class, at least according to the late Allan Bloom, whose *Closing of the American Mind* was a huge best-seller, and a campus scandal, in 1987.

"Relativism," said Stephanson, "could be defined as the idea that there are no suprahistorical standards, that all truths are historical truths, all truths a function of *perspective*. You have to evoke the social circumstances of a given society to understand why certain things are considered true or good. Action A may be as good as Action B. There's no intrinsic value to these acts, only socially assigned or *constructed* value. Plato, on the other hand, says there is one absolute good, and either you see it or you don't."

Plato, clearly, was the opposite of a relativist. In the modern jargon, he was an "essentialist." Was Aristotle, whose notion of the good was so different from Plato's, therefore a relativist? Something more than a philosophical argument hung on this issue, though the argument was momentous in its own right. Critics of such courses as C.C. insisted that the continued existence of great-books surveys rested on some notion of "timeless" truths—presumably an extractable body of assumptions that had always and would always be true. Stephanson himself, in one of his high-tables-at-Oxford flights of irony, had asked, "Wasn't the C.C. class itself a kind of Platonic idea—the books barreling through the ages, bearing their truth for all time . . . ?"

In Stephanson's class, there were five or six students who I guessed would qualify as relativists in the Bloomian sense: They would hesitate to judge any society except by its own standards. But there were many others with very firm beliefs. There was a Jeffersonian liberal with ties to the Democratic Party—a young pol in the making who thought, as far as any of us could tell, that all truths were embedded in the Founding Fathers and *The Federalist Papers*; an Israeli-born woman now living in the States who was not about to relinquish her sense of right to anyone; some deeply religious students, including two Orthodox Jewish women, one white and one African-American; a Christian fundamentalist of Korean descent and another, a WASP, from Texas, who was one of the few Republicans. These were essentialists, sure enough, and Allan Bloom was wrong if he did not understand, in his fulminations against relativism as a student norm, that students like these existed everywhere in American universities. As for Stephanson, if he thought he was going to coax these particular men and women out of their habits, he was possibly mistaken.

Anyway, what about *him*? As a member of the cultural left, did he believe in "truths"? I would listen closely and smoke him out. I was already pretty sure that cultural leftist or not, he did not think the core-curriculum courses were a case of a Platonic ideal. If he did, he would not be teaching one of them.

Receiving no clear answer to his questions about Aristotle, he plunged ahead.

"The problem is," said Stephanson, "if we are talking about such things as *goods*, aren't we referring to something that is the same in many different contexts? We still haven't escaped the issue of an essence, a form, have we? Aristotle isn't really a relativist, is he? Aristotle believed the most fundamental cause of anything is its end—and the end is there before the beginning, inherent in the object's *nature*. The 'cause' of kids is to be grown-ups, which explains why they can't take care of themselves. The cause, or telos, of human beings is self-mastery, self-sufficiency. Happiness. Aristotle starts *inside* and goes *up*. Becoming rather than being. The universals are not an abstract ideal, as in Plato, something transcendent. They're a substance inherent in the object, but they are *there*, and there's no question what they are."

So Aristotle was no relativist either. He was just a different kind of idealist from Plato—the ideal was inscribed in the object's physical nature. It was stupid to say, as I did before, that philosophical idealism was a waste of time—that response came too fast. Without idealism, higher education wasn't really possible. Each student's ideal destiny was to become the fullest version of herself.

❖ ❖ ❖

An acorn became an oak, a caterpillar became a moth, and Aristotle, looking around Greece and observing that slaves (many of them con-

quered people) did manual work and that women did not profess philosophy, came to certain conclusions: He decided that slaves were not fit
by nature for rational thought and that girls became women in order to
procreate and take care of households. If slaves were hauling marble and
women raising children, then that's all they were meant to do—and all
their nature *was*. If their *telos* were something else, then they would *be*
something else, for you could never evolve beyond what you were meant
to be. (When you were fully developed, your purpose was clear.)
Women, he allowed, possessed the deliberative faculty, but they lacked
the ability to make choices. Slaves lacked deliberative power altogether;
they were animate objects used as instruments. In other words, whatever
exists in its observable form is natural and definitive.

This time I could not dismiss politically correct objections; nor would
I want to. No matter how you look at it—and no matter what qualify-
ing historical context you place it in—Aristotle had made a disastrous
mistake. In modern terms, Aristotle ignored the social forces, the power,
including his own, that molded people into one role or another, and he
provided a justification of that power in nature—thereby helping power
to become unconscious of itself, to see itself as a given. Aristotle's was
a way of thought common to Greek and Roman aristocrats, to slave-
owners in the American South (who justified slavery with variants of
Aristotle's arguments), to almost any hereditary elite anywhere. The cultural left would say it was a habit of thought historically common to
white males in general. Power justified itself by pointing to powerlessness in others as proof of incapacity.

Stephanson discussed the nexus of power and property in Aristotle's
thought at considerable length, but I decided it was time to go further
into the academic left. That no one was qualified by "nature" for any
particular social role—that divisions of power and property were man-
made—was perhaps the essential idea behind all radical reforms. I was
curious, therefore, to see how a radical would teach Aristotle. So I attended a C.C. section taught by Ti-Grace Atkinson, who had been well
known as a feminist theorist in the late sixties and seventies, a lesbian
separatist who wanted women to withdraw from the patriarchy. Now in
her fifties, Atkinson was getting her Ph.D. in philosophy at Columbia. "I
care for logic"—the subject of her dissertation—"more than anything,"
she said to me. In all, a strange bird to be teaching C.C., a course many
in the universities considered reactionary.

She was a tall and beautiful woman, stern, rather forbidding even;
and she stood in front of the class with Aristotle's *Politics* in her hand,
reciting long passages and expounding the text point by point. She explicated; the students listened. She began by drawing a contrast with
Plato on the issue of private property. In Plato's ideal state, "yours" and

"mine" would disappear. The guardians, after all, possessed great power but little or no property. They lived in barracks, ate together in the mess, owned no land. On the other hand, craftsmen and farmers, who had no power, would be allowed to hold property. From the point of view of the left, she said, this separation of power from property (one of the alleged goals of the revolutionary Communist state) was the most remarkable and radical element in Plato.

Aristotle's notion of property, on the other hand, was a fundament of conservative belief: The property-owning should rule. For possession was the tie of affection, the tie that protected. People took care of their own families and lands, whereas those people not part of families suffered, and those things now owned by anyone fell into disrepair. In Plato's utopia, Aristotle argued, the children would be neglected. "Exactly so," I thought to myself.

"Our society has accepted Aristotle," Atkinson said, moving across the front of the room, one hand holding the text, the other at the base of her back. "We see our possessions as extensions of ourselves; if we don't own something, we don't feel affection for it," and she mentioned the squalor of the New York subways. Americans were near-absolutists on the separation of public and private. Here the private was everything, the public a near-excremental space.

She spoke with a firm disdain, and I thought she had a point. Certainly the Greek ideal of public excellence seemed square to us. In America, the notion of public excellence reeked of PBS and liberal foundations and corporate charity. But we were possibly blind on the issue. The Greek ideal was a shaming rebuke. We made no more than nominal demands on citizens—that they pay taxes, maybe vote and serve on a jury, go to a school meeting once in a while. Despite the minimal demands, or perhaps because of them, our voting rates are the lowest in the industrial world. The spirit of civic republicanism has died. But in Aristotle's notion of the city-state, the citizens rotated in and out of office. All citizens were essentially equals: You ruled, you *were* ruled. It was all the same.

But who could be a citizen? That was the rub, the point usually forgotten in op-ed–page celebrations of "Athenian democracy." Atkinson, holding her book open in front of her, zeroed in on it. The citizens had to be men, and men who were third-generation Greeks. Women were disqualified, serving principally as producers of men. Manual workers were disqualified, too, because people should be devoted to a single activity, and if the job of citizens was reflection and public excellence, the citizens should not work manually. The life of virtue praised in the *Ethics* was available only to the few—those freed of manual labor.

"He wanted a radical democracy," she said, smiling, "but among very few people, and this was pretty close to the actual state of affairs in Athens, though in Athens some of the workers could be citizens."

Her voice was steady as a rock, but "logic" licensed scorn; for reality, as she saw it, was harsh, alien, and unjust. Aristotle's logic would meet counterlogic, *her* counterlogic, and maybe the challenge of exposing and disproving him again and again was the fuel that made her teach C.C.

"Aristotle thought that Plato made a fatal error," she went on, "in wanting to do away with the private household and male authority over women and slaves. He thought equal partnership between people leads to dissension. Hierarchy, on the other hand, leads to order. A great deal of the *Politics* is an attempt to justify unequal relations, starting with the structure of the household."

She turned to the blackboard and quickly made a diagram.

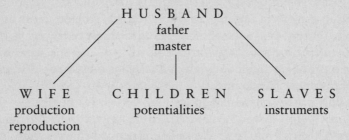

HUSBAND
father
master

WIFE
production
reproduction

CHILDREN
potentialities

SLAVES
instruments

Aristotle, she said, considered the father supreme in the household, holding sway over wife, children, and slaves, and the household provided the model by means of which the larger social structures—village, city-state—were established. She never used the word "patriarchy," but that's of course what she was talking about; she traced the ideology of male domination, and its nexus with property, back to Aristotle, and did it, I thought, with a certain grim satisfaction.

"Unfortunately," she said, "we have to face the fact that the *Politics* is alive today as an influence and is still used as a justification for such unequal partnerships as husband and wife, master and slave."

So much for modern marriage, which was just like master and slave. As she spoke about Aristotle and power, a tall, beautiful woman, pale, with a long back and red-framed glasses, a single touch of color, she stood motionless, and she smiled again.

"In Aristotle's version of the relationship of men and women," she said, "women are basically animals—more animal than human—and men are the brain."

She spoke deliberately and without wasting words. She laid out the text, point by point—Aristotle's idea of the best constitutions (monarchical or aristocratic), his distribution of voting rights (in favor of the landowning class). The students wrote in their notebooks, and spoke only at the end of the class, in a question-and-answer period. She did not ask the students, as Stephanson did, to make presentations. At the beginning of the class, she had taken attendance, and she advised the class to make an outline before writing an upcoming paper. So if she was radical in her political thinking, she also, it would seem, believed that hierarchy led to order. The austere orderliness of her speech, I thought, suited Aristotle perfectly in its diagrammatic clarity.

❖ ❖ ❖

In C.C. and Lit Hum, I realized, you are treated to "dangerous" knowledge, ideas that are now considered repugnant, models of hierarchy and oppression. That was part of the fun of the courses, particularly C.C.; you got inside the old formulations of power. Here was a radical feminist leading groups of women and people of color as well as white males through a text justifying inequality as *necessary* to civil order.

I loved it. A radical feminist and a left-wing Swede taught the core. Even if Atkinson exaggerated the continuing influence of Aristotle's ideas, she taught them clearly, without caricature, and her anger was like an electric prod. I wanted to argue with her, prove to her that she was wrong about modern marriage.

There was a very simple reason for feminists to read Aristotle: "Know your enemy." And how, I wondered, could the cultural left find fault with that? Were any of the students in danger of being indoctrinated or humiliated? Aristotle's notions about women had come up in Stephanson's class, too, and it became clear that most of the women were prepared to read Aristotle historically, as an expression of the landowning class of fourth-century Greece. They didn't "believe" anything Aristotle said about the capabilities of women. Their reading him in college was itself proof that he was wrong.

Interlude Three

I kept thinking about the black student who stormed out of the core-curriculum bitch session at Hartley Hall. It wasn't fair, I knew, to harp on a few remarks she made under pressure. In a few years, she might think differently. Like everyone else in America, she would find her own way culturally, fighting for what she wanted day by day.

Yet quite a few students and intellectuals and public figures talked as she did, and no matter how many times I heard this language, I was always amazed by it. There was "white culture" and "black culture," and the college's asking her to listen to Mozart without balancing the menu with African music was a way of imposing on her, colonizing her and making her feel inferior. It was all a matter of power and politics. The old notion that the arts were a universal language was dying fast.

But I didn't see how anyone who really loved music—any kind of music (I don't mean to fetishize classical music or my own tastes)—could possibly talk this way. People who loved music, who *needed* music, experienced it as emotion, sensation, a wave of pleasure. It was the same with jazz or rock or anything else. If she really hated Mozart or Beethoven, that was that, there was no argument—assuming she gave the music a fair chance. That was the sticking point, the fair chance. And how could you give anything in the arts a fair chance if you thought a given work was either an imposition on you or a confirmation of what you were, either a reduction or an enlargement of yourself? You couldn't feel pleasure if you wouldn't let yourself feel it, especially if the art was new and unfamiliar, in which case the pleasure had to sneak up on you, unnoticed at first, and then barely noticed, a tiny sensation of well-being, and then maybe later, after much listening, a rush of feeling that left you shaking. That kind of slow but finally overwhelming surge of emotion was of course a form of seduction, and people who thought there was something wrong with it were prigs—or simply hated art. They turned art into turf; they degraded pleasure.

Pleasure was the key, the only way of approaching the arts that wasn't false. You went from one pleasure to the next, one work to the next, and you made a chain of delight. From Bessie Smith to Billie Holiday to Dinah Washington. From Chuck Berry to Mick Jagger to Neil Young. From Billy Joel to Aerosmith to R.E.M. to Nirvana. Or whatever. (Make your own lists.) And if, at the end of one particular chain, if I was now moved by the way Mozart suddenly dropped into a minor key in the slow movement of one of his piano concertos, and my heart went *thunk* as a single instrument, a clarinet, say, settled on a phrase—because Mozart could do devastating things with woodwinds—did that happen because I was *white* and my grandparents had come to America from Europe? At a concert of the Vienna Philharmonic in New York, there were many Asians sitting around me, and they were moved, too.

But it was worse than useless to make these arguments. In the last twenty years or so, classical music had become marginal in our culture; the white students, I would bet, were no more interested in it than minority students. What left me sore, however, was the ideological decision not to experience something. From her remarks, it was clear that the student in Hartley lounge already knew about African music; Mozart and Beethoven were probably unfamiliar to her. Yet she wanted more African music, and she wanted the white students to listen to it—not a bad idea, but you can't do everything in one course, and this was an introductory course in Western classical music, which now requires a certain pushing in the universities (an opening to possible pleasure) if it is not to be swamped by pop altogether.

It was *jazz*, not African drum music, that should be added to the Music Humanities course—jazz, the great American contribution to the arts, an art of classical power, complexity, and emotional dissonance, and an art largely created by black Americans. The students needed to hear the classical tradition in jazz.

Did the requirement that all students listen to a little Mozart—or a little Armstrong, Ellington, and Charlie Parker—set up a hierarchy of values? Of course it did. It was a statement that many people in the past with intellectual equipment and social opportunities similar to the African-American student's had received extraordinarily intense pleasure from this music. You might not feel it yourself—but at least give it a chance. Give pleasure a chance. That was all such courses really said. But she thought the university should confirm what she was, not impose on her something she didn't already know. And it mattered what she thought, it mattered because anyone brave enough to stand in a room of people who mostly disagreed with her and to defy the official university policy had more grit in her than a hundred students who sheepishly went along with required courses without saying anything. When I was a student, I did not have her courage.

Chapter 8

AESCHYLUS AND EURIPIDES

~ Professor Tayler explains the origins of Greek drama
~ Greek culture and Nate Hurewitz's dream
~ Aeschylus in brief
~ Hegel's essay on tragedy: right against right
~ The leaden apples: misremembering the Greek myths
~ *The Bacchae*
~ The moviegoer and the cowardice (or was it courage?) of voyeurism

"See . . . look, look," said Professor Tayler.

He was in his lecturing mode, which rarely lasted more than ten minutes or so. "I'm going to tell you lies for a while," he said, by which he meant he was slipping into English-teacher talk rather than holding a conversation with students. Standing at a lectern in the small room in Hamilton, he squinted at notes on cards and spoke slowly in his gravedigger's baritone. The students smiled: they liked these little talks, which frequently went off in odd directions. Each of them had settled into a fixed relation to Tayler. A number of them were good at finding passages in the text to elucidate specific points but then balked at going beyond rudimentary interpretation. There were emotional but inarticulate men who spoke in fragments, and women who were more confident, more precise, but less expansive. Tayler tried to pull them out of their rut, sometimes successfully, sometimes not. He had an affectionate little tag line for many of them: He seized on a successful response (sometimes just a sentence or two) and referred to the student as an expert in that kind of reading, and then urged them to go beyond their expertise. It was all part of the business of "creating selves." He controlled them, but to a benevolent end, building up a reading ego in the students, brick by brick, and the students tried to live up to his expectation. Some of them, I thought, might have preferred to subvert Tayler's idea of who they were, but he was powerful and tricky in his friendly, small-professor way. He went on:

"Before Homer, it was an oral culture, a mnemonic culture—right?—

131

but then the Greeks take over this script from their trading partners, the Phoenicians, and in the reign of the tyrant Pisistratus, in the sixth century B.C., a proper Homeric text is established on Pisistratus' orders and Homer gets written down. So look—here you've got Athens, and it's about the size of Plainfield, New Jersey, maybe thirty thousand citizens—no, it's smaller than Plainfield, New Jersey—and in the fifth century B.C. they start producing philosophy and history. And also drama. Greek poetry moves from epic to lyric, and epic and lyric both end up in what the city-states do. When Athenians want to do something, they have a debate. There was an extraordinary level of social intercourse. They talked in the street, at the market, in the courts. Drama is a form of debate."

He looked up, and cast his gaze around the room, as if he expected students to begin debating like Athenians. But they sat listening, expectantly. In this room, it was Tayler who licensed the talking, as he well knew.

"Probably," he went on, "probably it was also Pisistratus who instituted a kind of festival in Athens, the Pan-Athenic Games, in which people came from other city-states to compete. He needed prestige, commerce with other city-states, so he establishes a theater, the Theater of Dionysus—Dionysus, the god of intoxication, sex, and revelry. And they decided, We will have an agon, a contest, between the bards. We'll have a tragedy, a comedy, and a satyr play—a kind of burlesque, as a relief from the tragedies. In the satyr plays, people whack each other over the heads with phalluses.

"From the three geniuses, thirty-three plays survive, starting with Aeschylus' *Persians* about 472 B.C., and ending around seventy or so years later with Sophocles' and Euripides' last plays—Sophocles' *Philoctetes* and Euripides' *Bacchae*. They still produced drama in Athens after that, but the high period is only about seventy years."

He stopped for a second, and I thought, Well, *there* was an idea to give one pause as one shambled into a routine play or passed the sweetly gelid popcorn stand at the sixplex at Eighty-fourth and Broadway. Quite an idea to knock around as one sat at home, numbed, before some noisy sitcom with people sitting in a San Fernando Valley kitchen. *Narrative entertainment on a stage, at least in the West, developed out of ritual and worship—singing and dancing for Dionysus—and perhaps out of drunkenness and revelry, too.*

Tayler didn't mention Nietzsche, but that night I wandered to my bookcase, and reread parts of the hair-raising book Nietzsche wrote in his middle twenties, *The Birth of Tragedy*, published in 1871. The young professor of classical philology at the University of Basel traced the development of tragedy from its source in Dionysian ritual, in which "the individual forgets himself completely," often in a display of "sexual promiscuity overriding every form of tribal law." This frenzy required the taming hand of Apollo—the spirit of rationality—and the development of the dramatic medium of the chorus before it could issue, transformed, in the ordered and devastating art of the tragedies. But the origin in frenzy is the primal stuff, the first cause.

In old Hamilton Hall, the theater was about to be born. Tayler continued telling lies:

"Look," he said. "Earlier they were singing, they were chanting hymns and prayers to make the cows come home and the sun come up. And Thespis said, 'Let's pretend the singing place is Persia or Sparta, and let's pretend the singers are Greek women.' It's a big invention, really a staggering development. You have an actor representing someone, and you're watching actors play wives killing their husbands and kings blinding themselves—all this horrific legendary stuff. Why?"

Delores Merton, a tough Texas woman with a very plain manner, raised her hand. "It's entertainment, it's fun, it's kicks."

"Yeah," said Tayler. "It's a very peculiar situation when you come to think of it. In drama, you go from being a participant in prayers and rituals to being a spectator. The actor is born, and the spectator is born. Someone who sees and hears but is not seen or heard. Look, for a long time Athens was a naval and commercial center. All you've got is *pots*. But when the Athenians took up drama and philosophy, the city becomes a cosmopolitan culture, the hub of the world. What did they do? Why has it lasted? Hurewitz, what was that dream you had about your mother and father?"

Nate Hurewitz—the guy who had trouble, in Tayler's *Iliad* class, telling a rat from a pig—was a quiet young man of mixed Chinese and Jewish background; he had a round, serious face, spectacles and short hair. Tayler was asking him about a dream he had reported earlier, a dream about his parents.

"Umm . . . my mom was cooking my dad."

"Yeah. Cooking him whole?"

"No, he wouldn't fit in that way"—sounds of repressed hilarity escape in the corners of the room—"but I didn't see her cut him up."

"Yeah," said Tayler. "Yeah. Good."

❖ ❖ ❖

The violent and erotic acts of the gods, the "history" of the Trojan War—such was the matter of the tragedies, which reformulated and electrified the moral significance of the sacred and legendary material. Everyone who went to the theater (i.e., everyone) was expected to know these stories and myths. The playwrights didn't have to explain anything; they could interpret, interrupt, recast, invert the obvious meanings.

In the first play of Aeschylus' trilogy, the *Oresteia*, which initiates the tragic tradition for us, the victorious Agamemnon returns home from Troy, and there's a sense in the choral utterances that the Greeks may have gone too far in the mayhem, that the sacking of Troy was less a fulfillment than a desecration, that the Greeks corrupted themselves in the process of defeating their enemies. The war, an act of revenge, was attended by obscenities at its birth (Agamemnon sacrificed his daughter Iphigenia in order to mollify the gods) and by atrocities at its moment of triumph. The legend that Homer accepted as tragic, but tragically glorious, now appears dark and depraved. So here at the beginning of what later became identified as the Western "core," the leading spirits were not simply celebrating or building on earlier glories, but revising, criticizing, deepening, darkening.

Aeschylus constructed the *Oresteia* out of two intersecting legends, that of Troy and the dreadful House of Atreus. Murder, adultery, sacrifice of children—dream on, Nate Hurewitz! All goes back to the primal crime, the infamous banquet when Atreus, father of Agamemnon, became so enraged with his own brother Thyestes that he hacked up Thyestes' children and served them to him in a stew. In the legend, one child escaped the banquet—Aegisthus, who, years later, seduces Clytemnestra, Agamemnon's wife, while the king is at Troy, and usurps his throne. As Agamemnon returns home in the first play of the trilogy, Clytemnestra induces him to step down from his triumphal chariot and onto a barbarically splendid crimson tapestry. The path of blood. A few minutes later, Clytemnestra and the waiting Aegisthus throw a net over the king and kill him in his bath.

Aeschylus offers not the glare of righteous vengeance but the anguish of wounded men and women in conflict. In the remainder of the trilogy, Agamemnon's children take their revenge against their murderous mother and her lover, and the Furies, the loathsome harpies of retribution, then hound the avengers—until at last the goddess Athena calls a jury of Athenians to decide the case. Orestes, Agamemnon's son, is freed, the Furies packed off; the city-state triumphs, law triumphs, the dark dream fades away. The *Oresteia* can be understood, though not complacently (it's too bloody for that), as a fable chronicling the passage from barbarism to civilization, from blood feud to law, from vengeance to justice—from the primitive past, in other words, to fifth-century Athens.

I didn't say so out loud, but I was glad when we got past the *Oresteia*. Great it is, but I don't actually like it. Of all the Greek dramas we read, Aeschylus' trilogy shows most clearly the origins of the form in ritual: the dark talk of sacrifices in the early speeches of the chorus leads to the sacrificial revenge murder of Agamemnon, and so on, a grand, and (to me) oppressive train of crimes and suffering, dramatized with all the hyperbolic flamboyance of the high, premonitory style.

> Get out, I tell you, go and leave this house. Away
> in haste, from your presence set the mantic chamber free,
> else you may feel the flash and bite of a flying snake
> launched from the twisted thong of gold that spans my bow
> to make you in your pain spew out the black and foaming
> blood of men, vomit the clots sucked from their veins.
> (*Eumenides*, 179–184)

Not even the redoubtable translator Richmond Lattimore can make this gibberish—Homer having a seizure—sound anything more than funny.

The animals destroy their young, the snakes bite their mothers. . . . But leaving aside the constant violence of style, which left me cold, what an amazing violence of conception! Nietzsche may have cleared away the more genteel Victorian notions about Greek culture, but even now the commonplace op-ed–page talk of the "miracle" of Athens elides too smoothly over the irrational and barbaric strength of Greek art. People longing for an idyllic antidote to the chaotic twentieth century may sometimes forget that the real miracle was not "Greek serenity" but Greek fearlessness—the evident possibility that these immensely sophisticated people were in touch with the savage beginnings of their own civilization. Both Tayler and Shapiro made it clear that rituals necessary to purge fears of drought—the rituals, say, that provide the background to the "Hymn to Demeter"—were still emotionally important to the people who invented democracy, built the Parthenon, and asked questions about how we know what we know. They were civilized men and women with access to their unconscious.

Since they weren't afraid, they had no need to simplify things, and they made drama, not melodrama, the struggle of right against right rather than right against wrong. When we read Sophocles, Professor Shapiro, bored with the placid theories of Aristotle, had asked us to read Hegel's great essay on Greek tragedy from his *Philosophy of Fine Art*. Most of the essay—one of the few things by Hegel that freshmen can possibly understand—centered on another of Sophocles' dramas, *Antigone*, which we also read in Lit Hum. Before turning to Oedipus, Sophocles had written a remarkable play about Oedipus' daughter. This is confusing, so take a deep breath: Chronologically, the events of *Antigone* take place *after* the events of *Oedipus the King*. Oedipus is dead; Creon, his brother-in-law, is in power and has just defeated an uprising in which Antigone's brother Polyneices has died. No one shall bury the corpse of this traitor, Creon decrees. But Antigone, a harshly lucid, paradoxical young woman (she will "dare the crime of piety" by burying the body), goes to her death rather than let the body lie on the ground. Hegel asserted that the essence of such plays as *Antigone* lay in the clash between two individuals embodying opposing ethical principles—a personal or social duty of overwhelming force. The conflict must end in the death of one or the other, or the death of both, leading to a new synthesis on the ethical plane. Right against right.

The Coach started in on his rhetorical questions again. Break the frozen sea! Hack away at it! Antigone risks her life to bury her brother and Shapiro's question was: What personal bonds, what obligations are the most important in life? "In a burning building," he demanded, "who are you going to pull out, child or parent or wife?"

The women say "child," but Henry said, "I wouldn't go in." He implied that a black man had to face too serious a struggle for self-realization to spend time committing acts of altruism, and some of the students sighed at this—he was pulling rank on them, and they didn't like it. But a second later, he changed his mind, and said, "I'm gonna get my mom."

"What about Creon's choices?" asked Shapiro. "Polyneices was trying to overthrow the government. If he wins, Creon and the others will be carried off as slaves. But he has lost. Polyneices is a rotting corpse lying on the ground. That's what Creon ordered. Is Creon right?"

Creon and Antigone are both right. Creon, in Hegel's terms, embodies the law of the state and the power of kingship as guaranteed by Zeus, and Antigone embodies the private loyalties, family love, and worship of the nether gods who abhor an unburied corpse. They are both right, and they are both destroyed. Hegel, I thought, was a more reliable—and more moving—analyst of Greek tragedy than Aristotle.

❖   ❖   ❖

Sophocles dropped the terrifying mystifications, the incantations and near-lunatic grandeur that stalled my pleasure in Aeschylus. He was the greatest, the most powerful of the Greeks. Reading *Oedipus* and *Antigone* again, I was stirred in the same way I was stirred by Beethoven, Tolstoy, and Verdi, the great "ethical" artists, solid all the way through, who faced in their art the most overwhelming difficulties and accepted suffering as the price of knowledge. Euripides, on the other hand, introduces sarcasm and subversion—he was perhaps the first master of dissonance in Western literature. Euripides never won a prize. He questioned the gods, made fun of the Trojan War, parodied Aeschylus' elevated manner. In *Electra*, *his* version of the revenge murder of Clytemnestra by her children, Electra, the daughter of the queen, is a competitive, hostile girl—a pushy, neurotic martyr. After *Electra*, we read a very late Euripides play, *The Bacchae*, which, without doubt, is one of the most devious, antagonistic, and confounding works of art I have ever confronted. In 1961, Lit Hum assigned *The Bacchants*—same play, different translation—but I must not have read it (oh, *no*!). Reading it now for the first time, I fought it off violently, and I knew why: It came and found me out; it discovered where I lived and shook the house like an earthquake. In *The Bacchae*, it's not just family members who are killed, it's the spectator—in my mind, the moviegoer. Myself. And perhaps you, too.

❖ ❖ ❖

In high school, I forgot what was in Pandora's box; I couldn't keep the muses straight and remained unclear on how the dead were supposed to get across that river. If I were one of the departed, I might have petted the three-headed dog rather than paid the ferryman. In brief, I could never remember the Greek myths. When Americans bought books about myth by the hundred thousand, I looked on in amazement. I couldn't remember the myths even after I had read poems or seen operas or ballets based on them. I was a big-city boy who thought animals were to be either pampered or feared, who longed to see the stars without the glare of city lights, whose profoundest happiness was to experience nature for what it was, a storm in one's face, hot sand under one's toes—and who therefore did not believe in the gods as embodied forces of nature. Don't give me metaphor; give me the cold water of an Adirondack mountain lake.

But let me try. Ah, yes. Zeus raped . . . Leda, who escaped in a cloud to . . . the underworld, where she gave birth to twins, Paris and Narcissus, both of whom emerged from her head eating golden apples and were so beautiful that Sisyphus, yes!, Sisyphus stared at them in wonder and took off his magic girdle and refused to row his boat across the river Styx, at whose banks, stung by a gadfly, he died. But then Orpheus—of course!—trying to win back Persephone, played his flute so beautifully that Sisyphus was reborn as a bull. And that is why bulls have horns. Yes, that was it. Now I had it.

Yet I know that, whatever my confusions, from this time on I will remember at least one myth: I will remember the birth of Dionysus, for I will recall the sinister way Euripides drew on it in his vicious late masterpiece *The Bacchae*. Traditional Lit-Hum wisdom was, "With *Oedipus*, teach the play and not the myth." But *The Bacchae* is *about* the myth, the myth of Dionysus, the patron of the theater in which all these plays were put on. And its significance for the moral life of the theater, the moral nature of our relationship to movies and television—our whole existence in Plato's cave—is incalculable and incalculably nasty. As I read, I searched for my own myth, the myth of the spectator.

He is born in an explosion of violence. Zeus, straying from Olympus, impregnates a mortal woman, an act that arouses the wrath of Hera, his jealous wife. The gentle Hera commands the Titans—the giants—to tear apart the newborn child and eat him raw. Which they do. But Zeus destroys the Titans with lightning and reconstitutes the child, and this child, restored to life, is Dionysus—Zeus's son, Dionysus the twice-born, a half-human god who dies and is restored, the celebration of whose divinity may include the tearing apart of a living creature. Got it? The symbolic destruction and ingestion of the god (in the form of a goat, say), followed by rebirth in the worshipers. Sound slightly familiar? This part of the ritual bears a clear relationship to Christianity and the rituals of transubstantiation, in which the blood and body of Christ enter the body of believers. In either religion, it is an affirmation.

But now let us see what Euripides does with this affirmation. In *The Bacchae*, Dionysus, or Bacchus, appears right at the beginning, in the guise of a man with long, blond, curling hair. A new god, not fully established, a conquering, jealous, youthful god, Dionysus has traveled all over Persia and Arabia initiating men and women into his mysteries; he now arrives in Thebes, his birthplace, with a host of Asian bacchae— women devoted to his cult—trailing in his wake. In Thebes, the women have been mocking his dead mother, refusing to believe that she was impregnated by Zeus, and he has taken his revenge on them, driving them mad and sending them up into the hills, where they are devoted to . . . to . . . to *what*? Drinking? Dancing? Gathering flowers? Fornicating with shepherds? We don't know at first. The rites are secret. We hear only that the celebrants are dressed in fawn skin and that they hold aloft a thyrsus—a stalk of fennel tipped with ivy leaves, which, in the first of many bewildering gender shifts, can be taken as representative of the male genitalia. The women hold aloft the male genitalia. Already there are hints of the sexual hierarchy thrown into confusion.

Dionysus is furious at those who will not believe, but not in the manner of the severe and majestic Old Testament deity; he is, in fact, something of a rogue. Vindictive and tricky, he finds his perfect antagonist—his patsy, really—in the untested king of Thebes, Pentheus. The young king has been away, and when he returns, summoned by odd reports, all the women are gone, including his mother, Agave. Enraged, he complains of "mock ecstasies" and "obscene disorder"—he thinks the women are pretending to worship, or that they're really followers of Aphrodite, sleeping around up there in the hills.

Pentheus is perhaps sixteen or seventeen, even younger than the first-year students at Columbia, beardless, athletic, a stubborn and inflexible boy given power far too early in life and fatally unprepared for it. He locks up some of the women and tries to take control of everything. In Shapiro's class, Henry had taken his measure. He gave the king some hard-nosed advice. "Dionysus is the irrational and appetitive sport, and you wouldn't expect that kind of power to make sense," said Henry.

"Make a deal, have a feast, worship for a few days. Give the god what he wants."

That's what everyone in the play tells Pentheus. Give *over*. It's what the modern, tolerant reader wants him to do. *Worship the god, and then mind your own business. Stop resisting. Stop punishing the worshipers.* But Pentheus is sure the god is a fake. Ignorant, priggish, and violent, he has the dirty mind of a teenager who's never been to bed with anyone. The fear of unharnessed female sexuality has him spooked. He's afraid of losing control of the women—and of himself, perhaps.

For a member of the audience in the Theater of Dionysus, and for the reader, the trap has been sprung. At first, the play seems to be a warning: Never mock another person's god! Yes, we tell ourselves, it's a warning against the stupidity of disdaining religious enthusiasm, the stupidity of fighting the will of god. Intolerance breeds violence. Look at Pentheus— he wants to control everybody. But Euripides is just playing with us. Malice and parody trouble the air. The meanings are unstable. And, as readers, we share some of the instability: The young king may be a prig, but as much as Pentheus, we want to know what's going on in the hills outside the city. I read on uneasily, sensing that I was being baited.

Pentheus meets Dionysus (in his golden-haired disguise), and they loathe each other. The god is soft and fleshy, and Pentheus finds him effeminate, at which point Dionysus turns on the young king savagely. "You do not know the limits of your strength. You do not know what you do. You do not know who you are."

The last line, of course, offers a menacing echo of *Oedipus*, but with new sexual overtones. The two men are tearing at each other again when a messenger—a shepherd—arrives from the country with a report of the women's activities in the hills. And so we hear it at last.

> About that hour
> when the sun lets loose its light to warm the earth,
> our grazing herds of cows had just begun to climb
> the path along the mountain ridge. Suddenly
> I saw three companies of dancing women,
> one led by Autonoë, the second captained
> by your mother Agave, while Ino led the third.
> There they lay in the deep sleep of exhaustion,
> some resting on boughs of fir, others sleeping
> where they fell, here and there among the oak leaves—
> but all modestly and soberly, not, as you think,
> drunk with wine, nor wandering, led astray
> by the music of the flute, to hunt their Aphrodite
> through the woods.
> But your mother heard the lowing

of our hornèd herds, and springing to her feet,
gave a great cry to waken them from sleep.
And they too, rubbing the bloom of soft sleep
from their eyes, rose up lightly and straight—
a lovely sight to see: all as one,
the old women and the young and the unmarried girls.
First they let their hair fall loose, down
over their shoulders, and those whose straps had slipped
fastened their skins of fawn with writhing snakes
that licked their cheeks. Breasts swollen with milk,
new mothers who had left their babies behind at home
nestled gazelles and young wolves in their arms,
suckling them. Then they crowned their hair with leaves,
ivy and oak and flowering bryony. One woman
struck her thyrsus against a rock and a fountain
of cool water came bubbling up. Another drove
her fennel in the ground, and where it struck the earth,
at the touch of god, a spring of wine poured out.
Those who wanted milk scratched at the soil
with bare fingers and the white milk came welling up.
Pure honey spurted, streaming, from their wands.
If you had been there and seen the wonders for yourself,
you would have gone down on your knees and prayed
to the god you now deny.   (677–714)

I don't know that I've ever read anything that more powerfully evokes the strangeness, the almost uncomfortable freedom and beauty of pagan culture than does this astounding passage of poetry. Even in translation—by the great scholar-critic William Arrowsmith—it is overwhelming. Here is Dionysian worship as a celebration of the bursting powers of life. Male and female sexual energies alternate in liquid profusion, which is certainly too much moisture for the dry young king. What a religion! Dionysus is vain and ruthless, yet he liberates the life force in people. One understands the anxiety Pentheus must feel—the miracles in the hills presage a breakdown of order, hierarchy, gender. But oh, it's wild and sweet!

Now hold on, because I have played a nasty trick on you (quite in the spirit of the play). I have quoted only the first part of the messenger's speech. The shepherd and his friends, hoping to pick up some points with the king, try to capture Pentheus' mother, Agave, and bring her back to the city. But Agave and the other women turn on them.

At this we fled
and barely missed being torn to pieces by the women.
Unarmed, they swooped down upon the herds of cattle

grazing there on the green of the meadow. And then
you could have seen a single woman with bare hands
tear a fat calf, still bellowing with fright,
in two, while others clawed the heifers to pieces.
There were ribs and cloven hooves scattered everywhere,
and scraps smeared with blood hung from the fir trees.
And bulls, their raging fury gathered in their horns,
lowered their heads to charge, then fell, stumbling
to the earth, pulled down by hordes of women
and stripped of flesh and skin more quickly, sire,
than you could blink your royal eyes. Then,
carried up by their own speed, they flew like birds
across the spreading fields along Asopus' stream
where most of all the ground is good for harvesting.
Like invaders they swooped on Hysiae
and on Erythrae in the foothills of Cithaeron.
Everything in sight they pillaged and destroyed.
They snatched the children from their homes. And when
they piled their plunder on their backs, it stayed in place,
untied. Nothing, neither bronze nor iron,
fell to the dark earth. Flames flickered
in their curls and did not burn them. Then the villagers,
furious at what the women did, took to arms.
And *there*, sire, was something terrible to see.
For the men's spears were pointed and sharp, and yet
drew no blood, whereas the wands the women threw
inflicted wounds. And then the men *ran*,
routed by women! Some god, I say, was with them.
The Bacchae then returned where they had started,
by the springs the god had made, and washed their hands
while the snakes licked away the drops of blood
that dabbled their cheeks.   (733–768)

The animals are rent to pieces, the wands that only an instant earlier were spouting honey now tear human flesh—and thus the rug is rudely pulled from beneath the spectator in the Theater of Dionysus and twenty-four hundred years later from beneath the reader, too. After accepting that the rites were nothing less than the gushing forth of creative ecstasy, a necessary overwhelming release that only Pentheus' terrified prurient imagination could construe as harmful or noxious, we're suddenly faced with this raging destructiveness, the wolves suckled but the children stolen. Here we were just congratulating ourselves on our broad-mindedness—never mock another person's religion!—and the rites turn out to be even more dangerous than Pentheus had thought. Some religious affirmation! The person who wants tolerance for new forms of worship turns out to be the butt of Euripides' joke. And the joke was just beginning.

❖   ❖   ❖

"Mr. Huggins," said Professor Tayler, "do you dance for Dionysus?"

"I'm not much of a dancer," said Huggins. He was large and heavy-shouldered, a football player from California with short blond hair combed straight up. Earlier, he had sat with his legs thrust way out, but now he was gathering himself in, hunkering over his notes. He had lost the cap-backward, doofus look of the first few weeks. He was intrigued by Tayler, though today he had a smile on his face, as if something a little too weird were going on.

Tayler went around the room asking various students about their dancing habits. "There's no way you can avoid dancing for Dionysus unless you want to remain Calypsoed—cloaked—the rest of your lives," he said.

Oh God, he was after them again.

"Look," he said suddenly, "this is just a small professor telling you this is one of the great masterpieces of literature. Now clear out your beautiful minds and go to work on this thing. If you don't talk about 'tragic flaws,' or the 'hubris of excessive rationality,' and all that Aristotle stuff, you can see something exciting. Instead of that stuff, do the parts, the hermeneutic circle—you cannot see the whole without the parts and you can't see the parts without the whole."

And so he was off, dividing the play into sections, and they were good at it, he had trained them that way, and they could do it, but the violent and antagonistic core of *The Bacchae* kept breaking into the conversation, and if Aristotle's dignified theory seemed wildly irrelevant, Tayler's New Critical structural analysis seemed a bit beside the point, too. Miller could not dance for Dionysus because he thought he was clumsy. Did he also fear what his big body could do to himself or someone else if he ever unleashed it?

❖   ❖   ❖

The drama of self-transformation and self-immolation reaches an unspeakably destructive climax. Dionysus, still disguised, convinces Pentheus that he can see the mountain rites for himself, but only if he wears women's clothes, for as a man, he will be torn apart by the celebrants. The god casts a spell and dresses Pentheus in a fawn skin and dress, and gives him a wig of long blond curls. Suddenly, Euripides turns to sinister burlesque: the young Pentheus, dazed, enjoys himself as a girl and even begins primping, checking to see if his hem is straight. Has he become what he fears, what he secretly wants to be? In Shapiro's class, debate broke out between those students reveling in the cruel irrationality of the play and those trying to hold it to some standard of moral equilibrium. "What bothers me," said Rebecca, grinding her hands, "is that there's no one to hate." She was still looking for accountability, a world that made moral sense. She wanted a villain. And Fareed, an Indian-born rationalist who had grown up in the Middle East (in Abu Dhabi), and who was often contemptuous of the muddy-headedness of the Americans, thought he had found the play's meaning. "If you remove all the socially imposed constructs, men and women would be more alike. It's an argument for the equality of the sexes."

"Or is it the enmity of the sexes?" asked Shapiro. "After all, they tear each other apart."

The end arrives with cataclysmic ruthlessness. Dionysus bends down the upper branches of a tree and lets the king climb on, and then betrays the helpless boy, loudly denouncing him as a voyeur; the women, frothing at the mouth, eyes crazed in frenzy, pull the tree down and tear Pentheus apart. Too intoxicated to know what she has done, Agave brings her son's head back to the city on the end of her wand.

"When you eat the porridge," Tayler had told us, looking at Hurewitz, who had those mucky dreams, "you ingest the gods."

The malevolent brilliance of it was stunning. In the standard religious rites for Dionysus, the god incarnated as a goat or bull was dismembered and consumed by the celebrants (a memory of the way Dionysus was first consumed by the Titans), and here, in a ferociously ironic displacement of the myth, Pentheus is substituted for the god. *The Bacchae* has sadistic overtones: The young man is first emasculated and then destroyed; his mother, Agave, initially proud of her brave deed in the hills (she is still intoxicated), at last realizes what she has done. She is ruined—cast adrift by Dionysus to expiate her "crime." The entire royal family is ruined. Dionysus's triumph is complete—so complete that no one from Pentheus' family is left to learn the lesson. What seems at first to be a warning against excessive rationality, against disdain for the gods or disdain for "religious affirmation," turns into its opposite, a warning against the excesses of religious enthusiasm and (perhaps) a protest against the arbitrariness of the gods. Pentheus was right: Dirty stuff *was* going on up there in the hills.

But even putting it that way seems stuffily proper. No such formulation can capture the sheer antagonistic bitterness of *The Bacchae*. Consider: We need holidays, we need release, we need transgressions, rituals of role reversal, cross-dressing, the overthrow of hierarchies of power, at least for a while, and in this play people embrace all that and they are destroyed. You're damned if you resist the god and damned if you go too far in worshiping him.

A masterpiece, but is the play tragedy or obscenity? And don't think I missed the stinging attack on people like myself. Don't think that I was not hurt deep in my soul and my vanity by this play, for obviously *The Bacchae* was a kind of allegory of the theatrical experience, the peculiar new relation between spectator and spectacle. It's as if Euripides were saying to his audience: "You who want to watch without participating, hiding in your tree; you who think you *know* more than mighty Oedipus or fierce Clytemnestra—what are you but cowards?" As much as Pentheus, the spectator gets pulled out of his hiding place. The play entices him with comforting thoughts (one should respect the gods) and then punishes him for his goodwill and prurience (don't get too close— you may tear someone apart or get torn apart yourself).

Moviegoing, of course, even more than theatergoing, was a case of spying from the dark. And TV-watching, done in the bedroom or the kitchen, was even safer than moviegoing. And playing computer games, which the player controlled, shooting at Hitler from point-blank range, was safer still. Modern life was all about watching without danger. We were in the tree, in the cave, trying to be safe. Realizing this, I was aghast. I had devoted a good part of my life to one form or another of this activity. No wonder I had no story to tell. No wonder I couldn't see any distance between myself and the media, between myself and the shadows of representation.

But was it all weakness? At the movies, we voyeurs profited from being alone in the dark, and not just because it was safe. For it was precisely that cowardly removal into the audience (so we would respond to Euripides) that made art possible—and that made a new kind of moral response to art possible, too. Instead of participating directly, we identified with one character and then another, we were manipulated by the play of dramatic forces, and we were forced to sort things out. Being a voyeur was no easy responsibility. After all, narrative itself is a kind of ritual, a secular ritual: The way the story "comes out"—the representation, either realistic or symbolic, of certain actions—embodies some truth or falsehood of social and personal life. We can withdraw our sympathy, or hold certain possibilities in mind, relishing criminals and failures as well as warriors, lovers, and saints. Spectatorship was irresponsible and morally queasy to a degree, but finally it was not. We had to sift and weigh, and if the work possessed some measure of truthfulness to the complexity of experience, the sorting out was a tough slog through uncertainties, reversals, and misfortunes. We became critics. Not just me, but everyone.

Yet no one, I thought, could quite sort out *The Bacchae*. With a sigh of relief, I stumbled out of Greek tragedy, a hegemonic white male fully empowered into a state of shock.

Interlude Four

I could not suppress paradoxical thoughts about the left-academic critique of Western classics and the famous hegemony of the West. The *Iliad* and the *Odyssey* were both bitterly and unresolvably split in their meanings; Aristotle severely corrected Plato; Sophocles, in *Oedipus the King,* suggested that the drive for dominance—hegemony, if you like— necessarily entailed a condition of blindness; the playwrights darkened the old violent legends. . . . What was the academic left talking about? Even in its earliest stages, the central line of this tradition offered less a triumphant code of mastery than a tormented ideal of obligation and self-knowledge.

Was Columbia's—or anyone's—version of the Western classics a monolith that simply crushed or "empowered"? Or would the books appear to the students as a porous, unstable tradition, in which the works turned out to be at odds with one another or even at odds with themselves—less a devouring beast than a snake that twists, writhes, folds back on itself and occasionally bites its own tail? And those who read such embattled books in the middle of our media culture—would they inherit a series of easy privileges and prejudices? Or would they inherit self-critical habits of mind that were as much an ordeal as a strength?

Chapter 9

VIRGIL

~ Fall at Columbia
~ The *Aeneid* as a "hegemonic" work
~ Shapiro's women students disapprove of tragic Queen Dido
~ I grant the critics of the canon a point

It was early November and Columbia's leaves were just about gone. The city campus was bare, with too much exposed cement and brick, and the wind came off the Hudson, rushing uphill through the wide corridor of 116th Street, and ripped across College Walk, which bisected the great open space between Low and Butler. As the river wind hit my face, I thought of chilly days thirty years earlier, when it wasn't the style to be warm (President Kennedy rarely wore an overcoat). I had walked around campus shivering in a tweed jacket and a muffler or at best a pea coat. Rushing back to the dorm, I would make hot tea and wrap my hands around the cup. Now I wore a Nautica down parka and nestled inside the hood; I was swathed in goose feathers, and I told myself that Kennedy had worn long johns. There was no benefit in being cold.

November was certainly the right time of year to read a long poem about loss; or let us say a long poem that was ambiguously—oh so cryptically and enigmatically—about loss. Virgil's *Aeneid*, the great epic poem of the Roman era, chronicled the fall of Troy and the founding of Rome. It was a paradoxical, uneasy work, a magnificent celebration of duty, which is certainly the least exciting of virtues; at the same time, it mourned everything sacrificed to duty. Who knew what to make of the *Aeneid*? One heard of people at Columbia who had been reading it for years and did not claim to understand it. Surpassingly beautiful, superbly composed, the poem was clear enough from line to line but elusive in its overall meaning. It was full of feelings—tears, at any rate—and yet, despite some unsurpassable sections, it felt calculated and coldly ambitious at its heart. In some ways, the *Aeneid* confirmed the most antagonistic assumptions about the true purpose of canon formation and the entire core curriculum. For here was an official poem of hegemony, a conscious poem of hegemony.

Virgil composed it between 29 B.C. and 19 B.C., mostly during the reign of Caesar Augustus—the great Augustus, who brutally restored order after the assassination of Julius Caesar. The empire now stretched from Britain to Syria; the epoch of administration and law—the Pax Romana—was at hand. Virgil the court poet, writing for a highly sophisticated and powerful circle, created a legendary past for Rome, a great myth that would seem to predict, ordain, and bless the new imperial state. He turned to Homer. Educated Romans, Professor Tayler told us, knew their Homer almost as well as the Greeks did, and so, even though Virgil lived some 750 years after Homer—as many years after Homer as we are living after Eleanor of Aquitaine—he set his long poem in the mythical period of Homer's heroes. However you look at it, he performed an outrageous act of appropriation. He recounted, from the Trojan side, the sacking of Troy and the escape of the Trojan warrior Aeneas, and then the founding of a new civilization in Italy. And he put both of Homer's epics in *his* epic, though in reverse order. The first half of the *Aeneid* is a kind of retelling of the *Odyssey*; a homecoming poem, with sea adventures. (The "home" that Aeneas arrives at—Italy—will be his only in the future, but it is home nevertheless.) The second half of the *Aeneid* is Virgil's version of the *Iliad*; a war poem, with much pain and slaughter. In brief, Homer and the Trojan legends were swept into Rome's past and deployed, from the fictional vantage of the past, toward the present glory. Homer was made to predict and bless the new Roman power.

Power creates a special kind of cruelty, the cruelty of indifference. Early in the poem, Aeneas, having escaped from the burning city of Troy, wanders like Odysseus on the sea, suffering storms and disasters. He washes ashore in Libya, where he beaches his ships, walks inland, and gazes in wonder on a great city in the making. The city is Carthage, and Queen Dido, also in exile (from Tyre), is ruler here. An industrious and brilliant woman, she is putting up walls, temples, a theater. Dido welcomes the lordly survivor and almost immediately falls in love. Virgil is quite explicit about this: She is a widow, and she's aroused in the way that a woman whose sexual emotions have long been dormant can be aroused—feverishly, obsessively, without protection or limit. In Robert Fitzgerald's translation:

> The queen, for her part, all that evening ached
> With longing that her heart's blood fed, a wound
> Or inward fire eating her away.
> The manhood of the man, his pride of birth,
> Came home to her time and again; his looks,
> His words remained with her to haunt her mind,
> And desire for him gave her no rest.
>
> (IV, 1–7)

Her ardor, however, is disastrously misplaced. For Aeneas is making no more than a provisional visit. Earlier, as the Greeks were setting fire to Troy, the great Trojan hero Hector appeared to Aeneas as he slept and exhorted him to leave the burning city and set up a new Troy elsewhere. By the time Aeneas arrives in Libya, he knows it is his destiny to go to Italy with the survivors of Troy and found a great race. "Pious," Virgil calls him, and "dedicated." He makes love, in other words, with the future always in his thoughts. He closes his eyes and thinks of Rome.

The audacity of Virgil's scheme is amazing. Collapsing time and space, he summoned old myths, old prophecies, and wild tales of the gods; he mixed legend and history, or, rather, swept legend *into* history in order to create divine sanction and the glamour of inevitability for both Julius Caesar and the empire of Caesar's adoptive grandson, Augustus. At one point in the poem, in a vision of the imperial future, conquered peoples—Africans and Indians—are paraded through the streets of Rome. In recent years, in the academy at any rate, a certain suspicion if not outright contempt has attached itself to Virgil's motives. Was not the poem, however great, a gigantic propaganda piece, written to flatter Augustus, Virgil's patron? To use Stephanson's words, it is not an innocent text.

Poor Dido! Completely in love, she does not know that she is being manipulated by history. Heedlessly, she falls into disaster.

> Unlucky Dido, burning, in her madness
> Roamed through all the city, like a doe
> Hit by an arrow shot from far away
> By a shepherd hunting in the Cretan woods—
> Hit by surprise, nor could the hunter see
> His flying steel had fixed itself in her;
> But though she runs for life through copse and glade
> The fatal shaft clings to her side.
>
>   Now Dido
> Took Aeneas with her among her buildings,
> Showed her Sidonian wealth, her walls prepared,
> And tried to speak, but in mid-speech grew still.
> When the day waned she wanted to repeat
> The banquet as before, to hear once more
> In her wild need the throes of Ilium,
> And once more hung on the narrator's words.
> Afterward, when all the guests were gone,
> And the dim moon in turn had quenched her light,
> And setting stars weighed weariness to sleep,
> Alone she mourned in the great empty hall
> And pressed her body on the couch he left:

She heard him still, though absent—heard and saw him.
Or she would hold Ascanius in her lap,
Enthralled by him, the image of his father,
As though by this ruse to appease a love
Beyond all telling.   (IV, 95–120)

This was something marvelous and new. Homer could not have done it—would not have wanted to. In the works we had read so far in Lit Hum, only Sappho had suggested anything like this delicacy and inwardness, this sense of the body as a vibrating instrument, suffering pleasure and pain. Dido is a fully created female character, intelligent, loving, scornful. Aeneas, by comparison, is a cold fish, and finally a cad. He has no self, only his destiny, his heroic function ("pious Aeneas"); he's far less interesting than the prideful and troubled Achilles, the devious Odysseus, the weak, self-justifying bully Agamemnon. The question that was unfathomable was this: What did Virgil expect us to make of Aeneas' duty-bound stoicism? The man who made Dido so fully alive could not have been oblivious to Aeneas' unattractive remoteness. Destiny had made his hero a dummy. Was Virgil offering some kind of covert admission of the hollowness of his grand poetic enterprise? Or did he simply fail, a victim of the enterprise himself?

Who *is* this cipher Aeneas? He makes a minor appearance in the *Iliad* as a Trojan warrior who survives battle with Achilles. The gods have some unnamed future in store for him: He is, like Achilles, the son of a goddess, and even though Troy is doomed, he will rule over future Trojans. Virgil took off from this fragmentary notation of Homer's. In Virgil's extraordinary account of the downfall of Troy (Book II)—one of the greatest things I have ever read—Aeneas escapes the burning city, somehow losing his wife in the flames and confusion but not his father, whom he carries out on his back, nor his little son, whom he leads out by the hand. The male lineage is intact, the way to the past and future secure. But as a character, Aeneas never lives up to the gigantic events created around him. In the second half of the poem, fighting the Latins for dominance of Italy, he wages a war he cannot possibly lose (Rome must be founded), and he disappears into his heroic role.

"He's unappealing," said Shapiro's student Joseph, a well-mannered, pale-faced schoolboy from the Washington, D.C., area. And Joseph said, "He doesn't risk death," a casually profound remark that moved me a great deal when I thought about it. Aeneas will die, but not in Virgil's poem. Aeneas is answered for, he cannot fail—that's what Joseph meant, I thought. He's not vulnerable in the same way that Hector or Achilles is. He doesn't risk death in love either. Other men in Shapiro's class made similarly dismissive remarks. Aeneas' dutiful temperament meant

little to them. Perhaps it repelled them, as a contraction of the freedom
they wanted for themselves; or frightened them, since Virgil associated
duty with loss of friends, family, and love.

It meant something to the women, however. To my amazement, they
warmed to Aeneas more than to Dido. In the great Book IV, the lovers
retire to a cave, and for a while the activity of the world is suspended:
The walls do not go higher; Carthage ceases to be built. Finally, Jove (the
Latin Zeus) sends the messenger Mercury to give Aeneas a prod. "The
man should sail: that is the whole point." Jove, it turned out, had another messenger in Shapiro's class. "Aeneas has a higher purpose," said
Sally, a beautiful young woman with auburn hair, Sally who was born in
a Pennsylvania coal town and who took a hard line about everything.
"That's the way it goes."

O mockery of a woman's hopes! When Dido realizes Aeneas is about
to sneak away, she is enraged and heartbroken ("Can our love not hold
you, can the pledge we gave not hold you? . . . Oh, heartless!"); she begs
and threatens, and later, when it becomes clear he cannot be moved, she
resolves to commit suicide. Her final curses summon up the savage
Greek past: she imagines how she could have killed Aeneas' father and
Ascanius, his son, and served them up to him in a Thyestian banquet;
she calls for a blood feud lasting for ages (the feud that will become the
future rivalry of Rome and Carthage), and demands the early death of
Ascanius.

> ". . . If by necessity that impious wretch
> Must find his haven and come safe to land,
> If so Jove's destinies require, and this,
> His end in view, must stand, yet all the same
> When hard beset in war by a brave people,
> Forced to go outside his boundaries
> And torn from Iulus, let him beg assistance,
> Let him see the unmerited deaths of those
> Around and with him, and accepting peace
> On unjust terms, let him not, even so,
> Enjoy his kingdom or the life he longs for,
> But fall in battle before his time and lie
> Unburied on the sand! . . ."   (IV, 851–63)

> "I die unavenged," she said, "but let me die.
> This way, this way, a blessed relief to go
> Into the undergloom. Let the cold Trojan,
> Far at sea, drink in this conflagration
> And take with him the omen of my death!"
>   (IV, 915–19)

Dido falls on her sword. Escaping at sea, Aeneas is disturbed by the flames of the mysterious funeral pyre but continues his voyage.

The grandeur and emotional violence of this is incomparable, yet the women in Shapiro's class were unmoved. At least publicly. Did their disdain for Dido and approval of Aeneas reflect their own sense of duty? Women had to gear up; they were expected now, no less than men, to enter large-scale careers. Or were they too much moved—truly frightened in a way that I could not be? And was it their fear that made some of them openly contemptuous of Dido? As they talked, I remembered that a few of them had had trouble with that other extraordinary woman, Sophocles' Antigone, who buries the corpse of her brother (a traitor to the king) and dies for it; some had not understood her giving up her life for a principle. Like Antigone, Dido goes too far in her actions and emotions; she cannot come back. And Dido does it for love.

"Look," said Sally, renewing the attack, "if someone commits suicide, it's their own fault."

And others spoke in the same way. The woman dying for love repelled them. *It was her own fault.* You were supposed to pull yourself out of despair. "Why did she have to kill herself?" said Fran, a Midwesterner who sat quietly for long periods, saying little, and then burst out with things. She was exasperated now. "Not all people who love can get together. Other people have overcome these things in the past."

Shapiro grinned and shook his head. "That's the first time I ever heard love go undefended in Lit Hum class," he said.

Fran turned red; she was angry now. She may not have liked the way her remark sounded in the classroom (a couple of the men made scornful noises). But embarrassed or not, she was a true child of the age. Tragedy, she knew, was not possible except by accident. And Shapiro had probably put his finger on a sore spot. They were eighteen or nineteen, and maybe they had never been passionately in love. It was an awkward thought, and I didn't want to pursue it any further than this: Perhaps they simply couldn't imagine falling in love as Dido does, falling so hard they would not want to live. If that was it, their anger made more sense, but I was still amazed by it. Late adolescents were supposed to be romantic, weren't they? Thirty years earlier, soaked in D. H. Lawrence and Lawrence Durrell, we were all of us, men and women alike, rather solemn about passion. Even if we hadn't felt it, we believed in it, we were awed by it. But these young women were mainly embarrassed by great Dido. They thought she was ridiculous.

In all, the women's response was baffling. It seemed both prefeminist and postfeminist at the same time. Prefeminist because their comments on Antigone suggested they thought it dangerous for women to assert themselves so openly; and postfeminist, because their disdain for Dido suggested that a woman who fell that deeply in love was foolish. *She had lost herself to a man.* What I had noticed during Shapiro's *Oedipus* class seemed true again: The students came to literature with their media-based sense of irony and role-playing, their sense that anything could be mediated by therapy, and true decisiveness of character irritated and possibly frightened them.

Lit Hum was a stretch; some of these classical works no longer easily made sense. But by reading them, maybe the students, male or female, were jarred, made conscious of some larger life, some grander principle of personal force. It's the nature of being a student, after all, to be "wrong." Error was the path to knowledge, and Shapiro, as always, nodded gravely, accepted the students' naïve remarks, and then went to work, turning what the students said against them, forcing their innocence into a conflict with the literature that inevitably challenged it, and sometimes overturned it.

❖   ❖   ❖

Reading the *Aeneid* again after thirty years, and knowing now what I couldn't have known earlier—how difficult it is to write anything well, even a thousand-word movie review, a short essay, a decent letter—I was amazed by Virgil's skill. What a surprise! Journalist discovers that the most famous poet of classical Rome can write! In fact, it was quite clear from Robert Fitzgerald's translation that Virgil was a perfect writer, supremely equal to every occasion. Battles, storms, love affairs, wild creatures—he did all of it better than anyone. But as I said this to myself, I realized that my admiration was narrowly based and even grudging. Something was wrong: The second half of the work, Books VI through XII (the *Iliad* part, in which Aeneas fights the Latins) was strangely uninvolving. Since Aeneas, as Joseph suggested, cannot lose, the war seems unnecessary, almost absurd, and therefore more brutal, bitter, and exhausting than anything in the *Iliad*. The war scenes aren't boring, exactly, but they feel distant and willed; and after a while, I didn't care who killed whom or why. Homer makes you feel the pain of battle; Virgil leads you to admire his virtuosity in rendering the pain of battle.

In the shadows of my frustration with the book, some of the ideological arguments against the core began to make a little more sense.

Virgil loaded both the *Iliad* and the *Odyssey* into the *Aeneid*, letting them settle in as foundation, as reference, as a theme demanding a variation. There was something knowing, almost creepy about this, an appropriating ruthlessness. Behind it lay a political reality: the Romans had taken over Greece. Aeneas, at one point in his wanderings, encounters one of Odysseus' men, a dazed survivor of the encounter with the

Cyclops; he's been left behind, out there in the Aegean, and he's in a state of terror. This, I assumed, was a kind of classical-lit inside joke, an ancient-world version of Brian De Palma's "quoting" a famous passage in Hitchcock, only across a span of 750 years. But even though it was funny, it also made one uneasy, almost as if Virgil were rewriting the old guy, straightening him out, removing the crude spots in Homer's genius and reusing him. What we get in the *Aeneid* is conscious mythmaking rather than Homer's spontaneous embodiment of myth; intentional manipulation of fantasy rather than Homer's working in the grip of the fantastic.

The *Aeneid* is the epitome of what opponents of the canon hate: a self-empowering myth of origins, a celebration of empire as a divinely sanctioned and predestined triumph. No doubt about it—the poem asserts the centrality of Rome in such a way that renders other people besides the Greek-Trojan-Roman line marginal. Virgil is very explicit about this. When Aeneas visits Anchises, his father, in the underworld, Anchises lays out for him all of Roman history right through Julius Caesar and Augustus. Virgil trafficked in power and majesty; he justified conquest. And it is no surprise that in the years after Augustus, the *Aeneid* became, in the words of one scholar, "enshrined as Rome's national epic and as the ideological prop for one-man rule of the Empire."* In the twentieth century, T. S. Eliot, no hater of empires, took the enshrinement a lot further: "The Roman Empire and the latin language were not any empire and any language, but an empire and a language with a unique destiny in relation to ourselves; and the poet in whom the Empire and that language came to consciousness and expression is a poet of unique destiny," and so on. Well! That was hegemony with a vengeance: Eliot's rhyming syntax was like a set of iron bars shutting out disagreement. Virgil, Eliot thought, was *the* classic for all of European civilization. After reading Eliot, dull Aeneas, in my mind, came to embody the culture of the West itself, marching grimly but purposefully into the future. He brought his father and son, but he left his women behind. Yet when Dido dies, Aeneas' epic almost dies as well.

Shapiro made passing reference to the political way of reading the *Aeneid*. But then he argued that Virgil subverted the glorification of empire at every turn, making it clear that the splendors of rule were not worth the effort. Aeneas loses everything: not just Dido, but his friends, his happiness, his sense of mercy—what we would call his soul. The work was profoundly ambiguous. "You can't say that it's a pro-imperialist or anti-imperialist poem," said Shapiro. "It's both." And Tayler,

---

* David Quint, *Epic and Empire: Politics and Generic Form from Virgil to Milton* (Princeton: Princeton University Press, 1993).

working, as always, on the structure, also emphasized loss. He pulled the poem apart and then put it together again with many encouraging cries to his troops ("You can do this!"); he got the class to read the *Aeneid* as a poem about walls going up and down, a poem about fathers and sons, about gaining an empire and losing everything else that mattered. "Now you can brush it off," he said, summing up in his out-of-the-sepulcher tones. "But don't read this poem when you get older. Look, each book of the *Aeneid* ends with someone dead. You run out of the past, but you have to keep going."

A melancholy epic, then; a depressed celebration, magnificent but haunting in its mixture of vainglory and sadness. And in some ways mute. Virgil does not comment on Aeneas' sufferings, his extraordinary personal diminution, at least not explicitly. He writes with an imperviousness that is almost frightening in its oddly blinkered strength. At the very end, Aeneas has his rival, Turnus, at the point of his sword. Turnus expects to be killed, but he asks that his body be returned to his father, an echo of the beautiful ending of the *Iliad*, when Achilles agrees to return Hector's body to Priam. But Aeneas remembers a young warrior that Turnus has slain in battle, and the spirit of mercy dies in him. The poem ends as follows:

> Fierce under arms, Aeneas
> Looked to and fro, and towered, and stayed his hand
> Upon the sword-hilt. Moment by moment now
> What Turnus said began to bring him round
> From indecision. Then to his glance appeared
> The accurst swordbelt surmounting Turnus' shoulder,
> Shining with its familiar studs—the strap
> Young Pallas wore when Turnus wounded him
> And left him dead upon the field; now Turnus
> Bore that enemy token on his shoulder—
> Enemy still. For when the sight came home to him,
> Aeneas raged at the relic of his anguish
> Worn by this man as trophy. Blazing up
> And terrible in his anger, he called out:
>
> "You in your plunder, torn from one of mine,
> Shall I be robbed of you? This wound will come
> From Pallas: Pallas makes this offering
> And from your criminal blood exacts his due."
>
> He sank his blade in fury in Turnus' chest.
> Then all the body slackened in death's chill,
> And with a groan for that indignity
> His spirit fled into the gloom below.
>
> (XII, 1277–98)

Aeneas feels "rage," but these lines are permeated less by rage than a frozen sadness, a grief for the spiritual death of Aeneas as much as the physical death of Turnus. So distant! As a modern reader, I wanted transparency and accountability, and what I got was an uneasy sense from the poem that Virgil was fighting against his own purpose, separating himself from what he had set himself to do. No wonder people who had been reading the poem for years did not understand it. Virgil himself may not have understood it.

Stymied, I realized that I could not brush aside the political attacks on the *Aeneid* as philistine and merely politically correct. There is a clear artistic and emotional failure in the second half of the poem, and since a political purpose—Virgil's—may account for that failure, a political critique of the poem becomes plausible. That Virgil's attitudes were "wrong" should not bother anyone. That his poem is hurt as art by those attitudes is something to grieve over and deplore.

Virgil locked himself into a grandiose scheme that justified power, and then receded into his work. The mood of loss extended to my reading: I lost a good part of the *Aeneid*, though I could never argue against undergraduates reading it. Nothing in literature is greater than Books II and IV, and a student who stretched to understand duty or overpowering love learned what she was and what she was not; she learned of courage and fear, of self-sacrifice in death and also of a self diminished through duty.

Chapter 10

THE OLD TESTAMENT

~ The strangeness of Genesis
~ Leora Cohen does a presentation: feminism and orthodoxy
~ Recognizing myself
~ Professor Stephanson intervenes
~ Who has read the Bible?
~ Exodus and monotheism
~ Cecil B. DeMille's *Ten Commandments*
~ The Book of Job
~ I have a small crisis, and Shapiro's students show me the way

How could a book so defining and inescapable turn out to be so unfamiliar? And so adverse, too: abrupt, imposing, and terrible. And not explanatory and comprehensive but baffling and fragmentary. The history of a single people offering itself as the authoritative, universal history, the Book of Genesis was as much about power as about spirit; or rather, the mystery of power relenting into favor. Power grants life and takes it away, grants it again, and, still threatening to extinguish life, makes instead a special compact, a covenant that is renewed and repeated in its essential mystery by the arbitrary blessing of sons—some sons—by their fathers.

In the early pages of Genesis, power asserted itself without reason, without justification. Power did not "make sense." By definition, it was that thing which compelled you to obey without making sense. Later, power subsides into law and mercy. An ethics of mutual obligation emerges. Ethics allows the Hebrews to exist. But in the beginning, power cares only to impose itself: God.

I had read Genesis before (as a child, and in Lit Hum when I was a freshman, and various times as an adult), but never closely, and as I read it now, it had the taunting oddity, even the hostile oddity, of one's own city encountered in a dream. Each of the buildings, signposts, and monuments stood in the right place but not quite as I had remembered them. I knew the Bible; I knew nothing of the Bible. My puzzlement and dismay, I quickly realized, was no different from that of any modern person who did not live with this book. Did Lot's daughters really sleep with their father after their husbands were killed at Sodom, and did the narrator really approve this act as a necessary means of propagating the line? So it seemed. Perhaps the strange sensations one had from reading Genesis were produced by the awkward effort to reconcile the text with one's memory, or rather, with memory's parody, the aureole of second-handedness that gathers around memory in the late twentieth century and finally replaces it—in this case, references to Genesis encountered throughout a lifetime in newsmagazines, in children's books, in movies, in inscriptions, in every place but the Bible itself. As a young man, I had seen many of the cinematic "biblical spectaculars," and they now lay wet and heavy, like strips of fat, across my recollection of the Bible. The most central of all books now seemed a startling correction of its echoes.

Why does God create man first "in his own image" and then create him again, only eleven verses later, "of the dust of the ground"? Is man a mirror of God or a shapely vessel crafted on the potter's wheel? Essentially spirit or inevitably clay? Yes, a mixture of the two, but in what proportion? Why is knowledge, the knowledge of good and evil that men and women assume by eating the forbidden fruit, punished by shame and death? Could God value obedience offered *without* knowledge? Why would He want the obedience of the innocent?

I was all agog. Why does God favor Abel over Cain, Jacob over Esau, Joseph over all his brothers? Always, as it turns out, the younger or youngest brother, which, as a father of two sons, I found disturbing, since of course the older son, by the very fact of his primacy, must feel some stirrings of fury in his heart at the brothers who interrupt the paradise of mother, father, and himself. How, he wonders, has he failed to satisfy? God's blessing on the younger brother was almost cruel—or should it be taken as a symbolic confirmation of the misery of the older?

Questions from a secular age, in which sacred books are read in college courses.

❖   ❖   ❖

"From the Orthodox point of view, the Hebrew Bible stands by itself, a sacred text, an instructional text, a historical text. There is also the Christian Bible, but that is something else."

Leora Cohen, one of Stephanson's students, a sophomore, was doing a presentation—analyzing the text, identifying problems and areas of discussion. Up to that point, the presentations had not gone as well as Stephanson had hoped. In the first class of the year, he had asked for an intellectual engagement with the books, a critique perhaps, even a hostile critique. But the students, understandably abashed, were not eager to "problematize" (Stephanson's word) their relations to Plato or Aristotle, and had merely summarized, sometimes fluently, sometimes halt-

ingly, what they had read. Leora, however, was not summarizing but expounding. She was a believer, an Orthodox Jew. Short, pale, with a mass
of dark curls hanging over her forehead, she had been quiet most of the
year, often taking notes with her face low to the desk. But now she gathered herself together over her Bible and her notes and spoke with great
clarity. The Bible, she said, was literally true. In her own life, she followed all the dietary laws. She was persistent and stubborn, and the students were fascinated by her. She actually believed something.

"Was the flood a mistake by God?" someone burst out impishly.

"No, the Jews deserved punishment," she said. "Human beings have
free will. When they choose wrong, they are punished."

Tough love.

It was no surprise that many of them disagreed. They were middle-
class Americans, most of them, and perhaps the fruit of gentle love; they
had been given a second chance, and then a third. Rob Lilienthal, the
self-confident student who challenged Stephanson about the calendar on
opening day, complained that the love in the Old Testament was too
hard—abusive and punitive. As a child, he was never struck. When he
did something wrong, he was told it was wrong. If he committed the
same nuisance, he was told again that it was wrong. Well, fine, I
thought, and that is the way I was brought up, and it's the way I bring
up my sons, too, except on those occasions when I lose my temper and
scream at them. But how great could Lilienthal's crimes have been?
(Mine were piddling.) The comfortable American liberalism of his remark annoyed me. What did he know of rage, hunger, exclusion? He did
not bear the mark of Cain. I couldn't repress myself: "Did you ever stick
a knife into your brother?" I asked, interrupting him. But he only
grinned at me.

There were at least six students in the class (out of twenty-four) who
were openly and intensely religious, and several of them nodded and
smiled as Leora spoke. Her words were manna from heaven, the words
of belief miraculously appearing in the secular atmosphere of the modern university. And she had courage: Interpreting the Bible, especially the
Torah, was an area of contest and turmoil, where Jewish women—ruled
out of the game by most Orthodox congregations—ventured at their
risk.

Leora used the words "Hebrew Bible." At Columbia, the book was
known in reading lists by its usual title, the Old Testament. Which was
the right name? Parts of the Old Testament may have been composed as
early as 950 B.C.—that is, before Homer. But the college, like almost
everyone else, went along with the custom of placing the book just before the New Testament, which was written, of course, in the century after the death of Jesus. So the Old Testament had been wrenched out of

its chronological place, and not entirely innocently. Christians considered it a prelude. Professor Tayler, in a rare burst of political correctness, complained about the placement of the book just before the New Testament. He considered it a denigration of the Jewish tradition, which was something fully capable of standing on its own.

Well . . . I couldn't agree. Okay, yes, it was striking that liberal American universities, generally so sensitive to the concerns of African-American and other ethnic-minority cultures, were holding to Christian tradition on this issue and cold-shouldering the Jews. But was this a point worth making a stink about? I was one secular Jew perfectly content to abide by hegemonic usage in this case, since reading the Old Testament, as Tayler apparently wanted to, before Homer in Lit Hum and before Plato in C.C., would have left the book hanging at the beginning of each course. The students would then read the Greeks and Romans before coming back to the New Testament. No, the Old and New Testament belonged together. History had placed them together. Students needed to understand the difference, say, between Jewish and Christian ethics. In this case, as in many others, political correctness just missed the point.

For Leora, I gathered, the New Testament was simply irrelevant. There was only the book of books, "the Hebrew Bible." She began by saying she would be supplementing her remarks with material from the oral tradition—words given to Moses by God and not set down but passed along and woven into the endless commentary on the Bible, a practice that has constituted the principal intellectual exercise of religious Jews for well over two thousand years.

Thus, she said, even though God did indeed create the world in six days, as it says in Genesis, the first day covered an indeterminate period of time—in fact, the formless "void" of uncreated earth existed before the concept of time had any meaning, and so could hardly be considered a single "day" as we knew it. And later she said that the oral tradition authorized the view that God created woman not as an afterthought, from Adam's rib ("It is not good that the man should be alone; I will make him an help meet for him"), but as an equal to man: Man and woman were initially joined at the rib, and were then separated—one creature being separated by God into two.

As she spoke, I looked around me and struggled to take in what was happening. Not just Jews and Christians but also Muslims, who recognized the Old Testament prophets as their ancestors, had long contended with this ornery, ungovernable text. Suddenly, I was extraordinarily happy. We were just a single class on the Bible in a featureless small seminar room on the ground floor of Mathematics Hall. A few leafless trees stood outside in the square appended to the bulky rear of Low Library.

We were in this place, at this moment, with one another. We were also part of an endless chain of such discussions, a link of immortality. The core curriculum was a secular manifestation, but it had become, this day, part of that endless chain. Leora spoke, and as Stephanson remained quiet, the students asked questions. They were aloft, flying on their own.

"The binding of Isaac," Leora said, looking up and pushing a few curls away. "Why? The answer based on the oral tradition is that a man of exceptional belief like Abraham knew from God that he was to be father of nations, and so Isaac couldn't die. The passage should be read as a demonstration by God of Abraham's greatness as a human being."

This was suggestive (and answered one of my puzzlements), though it left me uneasy. If you believed that Genesis was the word of God as rendered by his servant Moses, then you were unlikely to believe that God spoke in ironies, saying one thing and meaning another—sending signals to the knowing while confusing the literal-minded. Why would God confuse people? If one proceeded in this way, one could reverse almost any meaning by "interpretation."

As it happened, some of my initial confusion receded as I read deeper into Genesis. The murderous hostility between brothers, for instance, ends in the magnificent reconciliation of Jacob and Esau, and Joseph, the great Joseph, the most astounding success in literature, an early version of Jesus mixed with the temperament of a supremely successful and confident manager, Joseph forgives his brothers for their offenses against him. The father of two sons, reading these passages, breathed more easily.

I was relieved, but I also knew that not every question needs to be answered. To ask people to give up interpretation was hopeless, yet I preferred mysteries to anything that would reduce the power of the words. The weight and rhythm of the King James Version, just the sound and sequence of the words, carried their own significance. For millions of people, the Bible *was* the sound of those words. And all of English and American literature carried those sounds and their attendant meanings, too—meanings that would vanish if people refused to read the Bible or read only toneless new translations that turned the words into something more literal and comprehensible. Jacob wrestling with the angel through the night before he seeks forgiveness from his brother Esau is just a few lines, but the idea of a contest that settles one's personal destiny and the destiny of one's people is so extraordinary that it is taken up again and again, and resonates through Jewish history and Jewish literature and even modern Jewish selfhood—the tussle with God becomes the tussle with alternate selves, with doubt, with fear.

I was moved without belief; or rather, I believed in the greatness of the Bible. As the narrative moves past the early generations of the Hebrews,

God remains wrathful but He is no longer arbitrary. He is educated by the hope that he can make sense. God teaches man; man teaches God. The wrestling with the angel continues forever.

But as Leora spoke, the atmosphere in the room began to change. If the students were initially fascinated by her because she was rooted, formed, encumbered—she *believed* something—they now became angry that she used the oral tradition as she did. She was removing from the Old Testament much that was primitive and irrational about it. She was gentling it, they thought, in order to believe in it.

She hung in there, and it became clear how difficult her task was, for she launched into a feminist interpretation of God's punishment of Eve. "The verse 'And thy desire shall be to thy husband, and he shall rule over thee' has a sexual meaning," she said. "This is the explanation that is given: The verse is meant in a sexual sense. The main action is from men to women. It's not meant as a political statement or as the nature of a person. The man initiates sex."

"Can you make that distinction?" said Stephanson, breaking the embarrassed silence. "Can you talk about sexual dominance without other kinds of dominance?"

"Yeah, and are we talking of the missionary position?" said one of the women. "Because otherwise . . ."

"Let's not get technical," Stephanson interrupted. The conversation was becoming a bit strange. Leora was trying to reconcile the Old Testament, one of the fountainheads of patriarchy, with contemporary feminism, a task most people would say was almost impossible—an attempt to square the circle. We were watching, I suddenly realized, something like a struggle for faith. She must have had questions, too—fundamental questions. How could she *not*? It didn't matter whether she was wrong. She struggled, she was great. How many of my family and friends so struggled? I couldn't think of any.

As for myself, I had never read the Bible for guidance or comfort—not when either of my parents died, not when one of my best friends, Steven Harvey, a film scholar and critic, died young of AIDS, though when Steven died, I may have cursed God once or twice. I had never read it for inspiration, or for ethical training, except long ago, in Sunday school, but only as I was reading it now, for pleasure as literature. Yet I was certainly a Jew, as obviously a Jew in my fears and pleasures as many an observant man, and now, poring over the first two books of the Old Testament, I felt as if I were confronting the hidden pattern of my being. It was a violent, clenched, generative text that offered a powerful sense of right, of obligation wrenched from barbarism. What had any of that to do with movie criticism? The Jewish tradition, as I had absorbed it from family, and from New York teachers and intellectuals, insisted on

the essential things, and the right things. These men and women separated what was lasting and serious from what was temporary and unworthy; they wanted a book or a movie to have a plot, a joke to have a
point, a life to have direction. The Jewish demand for getting to the
point of something and sticking to it could (and did) lead to humorless
self-importance and hypocrisy but not (without great guilt) to triviality
and time-wasting. Criticism was an occupation suited to so wearying a
demand for focus; perhaps no critic of whatever religion could be worth
reading for very long without a little of Jeremiah in him.

The conversation in Stephanson's class had become testy. Leora talked
about the history of the Jews and the changing interpretation of the
Bible, and as far as the nonbelieving students could see, she was trying
to have it both ways, trying to make the Bible immutable and eternal
and placing it within history and commentary at the same time. Noah
Martz, the best-informed and most fair-minded of the students—he was
the type of liberal Jew who wanted to understand the Palestinian side in
the conflict with Israel and read many books about it—Noah suddenly
looked at her coldly and said, "I thought Orthodoxy wouldn't allow this
kind of relativistic interpretation."

Leora lifted her face from the text. The two pale-faced Jews confronted each other. "The more people lose touch with their religion . . ."
Leora said, an accusation forming on her lips, the ancient rage of the Orthodox at the assimilated suddenly boiling to the surface. But she never
finished her sentence, because Stephanson was suddenly riding in to the
rescue.

"Now hold on," he fairly shouted. "Despite the fact that you recognize the historicity of the text, you can always claim that *this*, and this
alone, is what it originally meant. Despite the fact that I exist in history,
it doesn't make the text relativistic. There still can be a right meaning."

I felt as if I were seeing Stephanson for the first time. Underneath his
bluster, he was truly fair and delicate in feeling. He didn't believe a word
that Leora said (he confirmed this for me, privately, later); he didn't believe that there was any meaning outside history, and he was, I would
guess, an atheist, yet he made a case for seeking an absolute truth. *He
said it was legitimate to seek it.* That Leora was "wrong" was not the
point; he wanted to teach his students to frame an argument, to stick to
it, and defend it.

"You say, 'How can you make an argument that's not relative after allowing history in?'" Stephanson said. "The answer is: There is no release from interpretation."

❖ ❖ ❖

The Bible was one of those few works read in both Lit Hum and C.C.,
and when Shapiro got to it, later in the fall semester, he began by polling

the students. How familiar were the twenty-four men and women with the Old Testament? Many said they had read parts of it, but only five had had extensive religious training (two Orthodox Jews, two Catholics, one Baptist), and only two of these students—the Orthodox Jews, both women again—admitted to finding it important in the conduct of their lives at that point. Henry, the African-American student who was the Baptist, said he read it for its "socioeconomic-philosophical interest," which seemed to me quite a lot of interest indeed. But for most of the others who had read the Bible, it was something from their childhood, something arbitrary and quaint, a collection of stories that had been unaccountably and improperly governing their lives. They regarded it with a mixture of chagrin and amusement.

And a fair number *had never read it at all*. Not only the five Asian students, who shrugged their shoulders and seemed diverted by it, but several of the Americans and an Italian woman who spoke accentless English announced that they had opened the book for the first time the night before the class. They found themselves amazed that anyone could have taken the Old Testament seriously as a guide to conduct.

The students were living with the effects of the Bible everywhere, institutionally, politically, in art and literature, yet nothing in their lives or education had impelled them to look into it. And without someone's requiring them to read the Bible in a literature course, it might be lost to them forever, dissolving into its farcical media echoes. The core-curriculum courses amounted to remedial work on their own existence.

Shapiro worked hard with them, getting them to see the moral sense (and occasionally the perversity) in the primitive tales. We went through the wrenching stories of God's blessings and God's forgiveness. If so many of the stories in Genesis are about barrenness and fruitfulness, the Hebrews' obsession may have been derived from no lesser force than the determination to survive—to perpetuate their line so they could achieve the fate that God had promised them. The book was grounded in fear. And in Exodus, fear rendered the notion of the covenant rather paradoxical. The Hebrews were favored and protected, they were destined for the promised land, but the destiny was revocable. Were they worthy? Would God destroy them in their unworthiness? In Exodus, these questions never quite disappear. And the Hebrews are scornful and skeptical and easily discouraged. Man and God seem to have made a covenant to be unsure of each other.

When Moses is in Midian, and God appears to him out of a burning bush, lord and servant have a tense little conference. How shall God's authority be recognized? And how shall Moses' authority, as His agent and servant, also be recognized?

> And Moses said unto God, Behold, when I come unto the children
> of Israel, and shall say unto them, The God of your fathers hath sent
> me unto you; and they shall say to me, What is his name? what shall
> I say unto them?
>
> And God said unto Moses, I AM THAT I AM: and he said, Thus
> shalt thou say unto the children of Israel, I AM hath sent me unto
> you. (Exod. 3:13–14)

Idiot! You do not ask God his *name*, though it turns out He has one, YHWH, or Yahweh, which He uses in reference to Himself (in the Hebrew text) immediately after. Yahweh, which the King James scholars translated simply as "Lord," means (literally) "he lets be." I AM THAT I AM—perhaps the most awesome sentence in any language—is God's annunciation of the principle of being. He is existence itself.

I had lived within monotheism my whole life. But coming on it this way, just after reading the Greeks and Romans, I felt the intellectual and emotional force of it as if for the first time. (Thirty years earlier I had read right past this moment.) Here is one of the shifts in consciousness that change everything. In Genesis and Exodus, there are not the many roistering, malicious, unreliable gods of the Greek religion but only the one awesome faceless unincarnated immaterial absolute God who is the very principle of existence on earth, without whom nothing would exist and life would end. As much as the students, I needed remedial work on my own existence.

Was monotheism still considered "an advance" on paganism? Professor Tayler had said in passing that Lit Hum was designed (in the late 1930s) by Columbia's Christian humanists, who thought of paganism as a fascinating indiscretion in the moral history of the West, an indiscretion that had to be overcome. No one at Columbia talked that way anymore; no one wanted to be caught "privileging" the Judeo-Christian tradition. But I had promised myself not to shrink from the naïve questions. I knew I missed the Greek union of seriousness and frivolity, the devotion to reason and virtue that somehow did not preclude a love of pleasure, sex, and art nor a thrilling and terrifying access to the irrational. Monotheism, by contrast, was a notion that had done little for laughter. A new solemnity and strenuousness came into Western literature, an ethical ardency. Judged by the standard of vivacity and brilliance, monotheism was not an advance but a simplification. But what power lay in the idea! God may have created man in his own image, but, according to the ancient Hebrews, man could not create an image of God. He had to be imagined, not imaged. Through that effort, men and women begot themselves as conceivers of the laws and forms of things. They became dedicated to purposeful activity, and they were not alone; they were accompanied by an idea that imposed a specific destiny and an implacable sense of right, a light whose sternly directed and focused beam both illuminated the distance ahead and cast the areas outside it into a profounder darkness.

❖ ❖ ❖

Pleasure was the teacher; not blasphemy but pleasure. I had to see it again. How could I not? I was a movie critic reading the Bible, and now I had to revisit one of its most familiar echoes. *The Ten Commandments*, the 1956 "biblical spectacular," was the crowning work of Cecil B. De-Mille's long career as a mountebank. Some sober and good movies had been made from biblical stories, and even a few exciting ones, but this giant efflorescence of kitsch was lovable in its violent absurdity. I had always adored it.

In the beginning, some words appear on the screen: THOSE WHO SEE THIS MOVIE PRODUCED AND DIRECTED BY CECIL B. DEMILLE WILL MAKE A PIL-GRIMAGE OVER THE VERY GROUND THAT MOSES TROD OVER 3000 YEARS AGO, it says, and then he, almost He, comes out before a curtain, De-Mille himself, confronting the faithful, and he speaks in his orotund lisp: "The shtory takes three hours and thirty-nine minutesh to unfold. There will be an intermission." Well, I thought, give the old faker his due. At least in those days a story *unfolded*, unlike now, in the MTV age, when movie stories jump ahead in fragments and charged little spurts.

But silence, God is about to speak. There are asses and goats, many asses and goats, and vast deserts surrounded by great cliffs rising straight up, and, at the edge of the desert, Mt. Sinai, a reddish volcano continuously erupting—erupting God, who speaks, when He speaks, in a basso droning whoosh, as if a wind tunnel were embedded in his nose. One was awed all right, by the audacity of DeMille's foolishness, which was the foolishness of the movies. Just as I remembered, Charlton Heston, as Moses, was as dull as concrete. But my God, Yul Brynner as Ramses! Concupiscent shining baldness, quivering nipples and flaring nostrils, hooded onyx voice—he was sublime, he was preposterous, his performance was a convulsively erotic piece of camp. Yet in some way he was sincere, too, just as Bela Lugosi was said to have been sincere when he acted unhappy, thirsty Dracula. Brynner, born a Russian gypsy, one of Marlene Dietrich's many lovers, played a violently narcissistic man of evil, a Man Without God. Anne Baxter as Nefertiti, his bride, despises him, and moaning "Mohh-ses, Mohhhh-ses . . ." throws herself in masochistic frenzies on his rival. A hot, scheming woman, she wants her own promised land even more than the Jews want theirs, and it seems ungallant of Moses not to give it to her. She sustains for years a sexual competition between the two men, one of whom is hairy, the other smooth—yes, it was now the story of two chests, the hairy muscular god and the smooth, sculptural, muscular god. And the hairy god wins.

Moses' progress toward Sinai can be measured by the length and white-ness of his beard.

DeMille, hedging his bets all around, alludes to the struggles against Nazism and godless Communism; he turned Moses into a Christ figure and the deliverance of the enslaved Jews into a universal message of "dignity" and "freedom." (Slavery, of course, existed throughout the an-cient world, and the Hebrews, when free, possessed slaves of their own.) Yet what makes *The Ten Commandments* a coarse betrayal of the Old Testament is also what makes it hilariously entertaining as a movie—the lechery, the cruelty, the viperish court rivalries, the lurid miracles and painted scenic grandeur. Pharaoh's marble halls sparkle like one of Fred and Ginger's dance floors. The movie is a golden calf, idolatrous all the way through. It turns the mystery of God into painted spectacle, just the thing the Hebrews were abandoning.

So what did pleasure teach me? As much as Plato, the biblical writers hated spectacle and representation. We moderns were at odds with the profoundest moral imperatives of the ancient texts. We spent a good part of our lives attending to spectacle, and we did not expect to be pun-ished, any more than did the pathetic young king in the *Bacchae* when he was pulled from his hiding place and devoured. The world was filled with images; it was too late to cleanse the world of representation. I may have found the hidden pattern of my life in the Bible, but I found plea-sure in a work that betrayed the Bible. I would have to sort that out. We would all have to find our morality in the dark. We would have to find the morality of the spectator.

❖ ❖ ❖

Pleasure comes from many narratives, even from narratives whose meaning suggests the opposite of pleasure. It was time to go back to the Old Testament and read the Book of Job, which has sometimes been called the first novel. As I started it, however, I had a moment of dread: Would the students complain again that what happens isn't "fair"? Would Rebecca demand that God be fair? I'm not sure I could take it. Tragedy, obviously, was hard for some of Shapiro's students to deal with, and Job, despite its happy ending, was a story of unbearable painfulness. But what was happening to me? I was ready to wring their necks before they had said anything.

In Job, God makes a kind of wager with "the Adversary" (the King James version translates it as "Satan," though it is not the Satan of Christian texts). He makes a wager that his servant Job, a pious and prosperous man, will remain faithful in reverence no matter what catas-trophes he endures. With God's permission, Satan destroys Job's ani-mals, servants, and children; and then brings boils and other diseases and sufferings to Job himself; so that the baffled man, conscious of his own innocence—or at least of not having committed any sin—is reduced to sitting on the ground and scraping his body with ashes. He returns, so to speak, to the beginning of creation, when God made man out of dust.

The days turn slowly through their redundant journey, a wheel always passing back to the same point.

> When I lie down, I say, When shall I arise, and the night be gone? and I am full of tossings to and fro unto the dawning of the day. My flesh is clothed with worms and clods of dust; my skin is broken, and become loathsome. (7:4–5)

> When I say, My bed shall comfort me, my couch shall ease my complaint; Then thou scarest me with dreams, and terrifiest me through visions: So that my soul chooseth strangling, and death rather than my life. (7:13–15)

Pain so extensive throws into question the sufferer's very possession of his own body. Lepers must have felt as Job did.

> If I wash myself with snow water, and make my hands never so clean; Yet shalt thou plunge me in the ditch, and mine own clothes shall abhor me. (9:30–31)

The last phrase, in the comic extremity of its self-alienation—the clothes rejecting the person wearing them—anticipates the most grotesquely harrowing moments in Kafka. And so does the sheer hostile rationality of Job's friends, who arrive ostensibly to comfort him but who quickly turn into accusers, laying the responsibility for Job's troubles entirely on his shoulders. God does not punish the innocent, they assert; therefore you must be guilty. And, further, it is arrogant of you to say that you have done nothing, for by so saying you question God's judgment.

Shapiro took them through it, section by section, comparing the biblical poem to Greek tragedy, to the Platonic dialogues (much of Job is in dialogue form), and the class was unusually serious and purposeful. "Do you get what you deserve in this life?" Shapiro asked them, rhetorically as always, but fervently, too, with a touch of anger that I hadn't heard before.

Job's friends leave him no way out: *His suffering is proof of his guilt.* What they do to him is the original and most powerful case of "blaming the victim," and the act suggests in its unrelenting thoroughness the precise psychological basis, the need, for all such acts of blame: If the victim is not guilty, then the world no longer makes any sense. The friends blame Job to protect themselves, for they are terrified—as people are always terrified—by catastrophe without meaning. Job's troubles *must* have a meaning.

The religious students answered Shapiro's question gravely: The Book of Job was a test of faith. Sally, who always disconcerted me because she was lushly beautiful, and in dark auburn colors, like the one model in a fashion magazine who did not conform to cliché, Sally with her soft lips and lustrous head of reddish-brown hair had never said anything that was the least bit interesting—her mind had a nastily conventional turn to it—but now she said, "It's too easy to believe in God if everything's going right," which was an intelligent remark and certainly went straight to the heart of what the Book of Job was about. And she was followed up by Joseph, the proper Catholic boy from the Washington, D.C., area, conservatively dressed, very respectful, who said, "It's not enough if God is a convenience for you."

They spoke well. They had each been brought up in one of the more strenuous wards of Christianity—for them, faith was no easy ride to Disneyland. But I was annoyed, too, because they knew perfectly well the story would "come out right" in the end, and I couldn't help wondering how much they were actually tested by the book.

Some of the others answered in a comparably sober way. And I felt alienated from them, for all their seriousness. They had little sense of what Job had *lost*. Thirty years older, I thought I knew. I was reading the Book of Job after a long period not of troubles but of conventional struggle to make a good life. Unlike Job's friends, I "identified" with him all too easily—with his abandonment, the unaccountable ravaging of his family and goods as well as his body. For if you are a middle-class man, a husband, a father, you assemble a great many camels and goats around the tents. Like Job, you try to do right: You have children, though not as many as in the Bible, because you don't need them for labor, and they survive the early illnesses; you have perhaps two children or three or four, and you protect them, you do anything to protect them, and in your own life, you try to get the right job, a job that satisfies your soul and pays well; and you make investments and even, feeling like an idiot, buy some life insurance. All this wearisome dutifulness seems necessary, because few people triumph anymore by living casually and spontaneously. Not since the 1960s. No, you made a little fortress out of the assembled tents, with lots of blankets piled up inside and a big fire out front to frighten away the untethered creatures wandering about in the dark. You must *do right* and you will be rewarded—that is the modern bourgeois's version of faith, the secular faith that the system will not betray your hard work.

And of course, despite every calculation, it doesn't always work out that way. Some people fall down, the economy casts others aside. Among my own acquaintances, there was my friend Steven dead at an early age from AIDS; and Kathy Huffhines, a fellow film critic—killed when her car was hit on the parkway by a falling tree; and a young doctor, the son of close friends of my parents, who went climbing in the Himalayas, was brought down unconscious from the mountains, and died mysteriously and alone in his New York apartment a few days later; and several friends downsized out of good jobs and cast adrift. Terrible things happen, and there is no safety. So I thought: what do the students *know*? And I angrily resented their youth and their freedom from cares.

Shapiro took them deeper into the book, through the frightening pages of Job's doubt. Job goes beyond bafflement and despair and moves toward rebellion; he says what no man who fears God can easily say— that the wicked often die happy, that the good are often miserable. He questions God's judgment.

But as Shapiro talked, staring almost wrathfully at the students, and they made their mild and pious remarks, I realized with a start that I had got this thing all wrong. It was not the students who were being shallow and trivial. It was the Mature Reader, the Householder—myself. Sitting off to the side of the room, I looked down at my notes, and hoped no one would notice that I was blushing. Here I was worrying about the roof falling in on my family when actually we were doing fine. We were doing fine, just fine, and this book, of all books, should not induce fantasies of destruction. That was not the way you should read it. The religious students in Shapiro's class were quite right. The Book of Job really is about faith; Sally and Joseph may not have known how excruciating a demand faith can be, but at least they were heading in the right direction. Whereas I was merely anxious.

As Job's friends try to hold on to the covenant (the good will be rewarded, the bad punished) and Job says that life no longer seems just, God appears at last. God now speaks out of the whirlwind, in a rage, furious that Job has questioned Him. He asserts his power, his power to *create*. "Where wast thou when I laid the foundations of the earth? . . . when the morning stars sang together, and all the sons of God shouted for joy?" That Job or anyone else *exists* is due to God alone. He cites the wonders of His universe. There is the warhorse:

> Hast thou given the horse strength? hast thou clothed his neck with thunder? Canst thou make him afraid as a grasshopper? the glory of his nostrils is terrible. He paweth in the valley, and rejoiceth in his strength: he goeth on to meet the armed men. He mocketh at fear, and is not affrighted; neither turneth he back from the sword. The quiver rattleth against him, the glittering spear and the shield. He swalloweth the ground with fierceness and rage: neither believeth he it is the sound of the trumpet. He saith among the trumpets, Ha, ha. . . . (39:19–25)

And there is the leviathan:

> He maketh the deep to boil like a pot: he maketh the sea like a pot
> of ointment. He maketh a path to shine after him; one would think
> the deep to be hoary. Upon earth there is not his like, who is made
> without fear. He beholdeth all high things; he is a king over all the
> children of pride. (41:31–34)

Which is a dreadful shock. In Genesis, man is placed in dominion over
the animals, but now God in his rage goes through the entire creation
again, and this time says that man ("the children of pride") is nothing,
one of the lesser beasts. Job is aghast ("Wherefore I abhor myself, and
repent in dust and ashes") and accepts the unfathomability of God's wisdom. The covenant is laid aside. After the long climb into ethics and mutual obligation, we come back to the principle of power—you don't
question it, you simply obey it. For without God, nothing exists.

The students were right. The Book of Job was finally about faith, and
only secondarily about loss and pain. It was about the necessary irrational commitment to God as the principle of all existence, the commitment of faith that eluded people like me or such rationalist students as
Rob Lilienthal and Noah Martz, who had tried to trip up Leora Cohen.
Job must believe, even though God is incomprehensible and unjust.
When Job offers his obedience, he is redeemed and God restores his
well-being, rewarding him with greater prosperity and more children
than before.

Shapiro explained that the happy end of the story—which most scholars assume was the result of an ancient editor's collating two or more
texts—has struck many readers as unconvincing and inadequate. But the
end, however unsatisfactory as literature, makes sense enough as the consequence of a final act of obedience. Rather than finding it too pat, I found
the end alarming: God relents *this time*. If you read closely, you discover
that the overall sense of the Book of Job is that faith may be rewarded but
that the good will not necessarily triumph. Which means that for the religious, faith is rarely easy, which is exactly what Leora had demonstrated
and Sally and Joseph, in their quiet way, had said. And for secular men
and women, the equivalent to Job's belief without reason is that you live
your life fully and boldly whether it makes sense or not; and then you face
the inevitable accidents and pains of life without surprise or complaint.
Even if the students didn't understand all this, I was ashamed of my anger
at them and my melodrama about "There is no safety." Of course there is
no safety. That is exactly the point. Believer or not, you had to be strong
enough to live with that knowledge. In the end, the mighty Book of Job is
an appeal not to fear but to courage.

Chapter 11

THE NEW TESTAMENT

~ Stephanson places Christianity within history
~ Jack McKeon makes a presentation; Manuel Alon makes a
  Christian remark
~ Jesus, my Jesus
~ The Gospels
~ I have another, slightly larger, crisis, and Professor Tayler
  makes it go away

Everything was discourse for Anders Stephanson, even religious faith.
Warring notions of the divine—disagreements that for centuries had led
to loathing and murder—were now gentled into "conversation," and in
conversation what mattered to Stephanson, as I saw during Leora's presentation of Genesis, was not whether the students held the "right"
views but whether they understood that they were indeed holding *views*.
He wanted them to realize aware that they were not expressing something "natural" or "universal" or unanswerable. Such was a central doctrine of the cultural left: No purchase on truth, not even one's notion of
God, could be understood apart from the perspective of the person making it, and a perspective could never be taken for granted. Stephanson
was a historian: even revelation took place within history.

As we began our discussion of the New Testament, he spoke in his
normally cheerful and stentorian manner, and the manner made its own
kind of comment: Sacred texts were *texts* like any other. He explained
the new religion not only as an emanation of a specific time and place—
Palestine under Roman rule—but as a specialized understanding of history itself. The early Christians thought that they were living near the
end of time. Stephanson was fascinated by the thrillingly obscure and
terrifying Book of Revelation, with its notion of an apocalyptic struggle
between good and evil, followed by a millennium of Christ's rule, followed by still *another*, and final, struggle between good and evil. He
could not be indifferent to the role such thinking had actually played in
history. If the early Christians saw themselves as part of apocalyptic
events leading to the end of time, the "latter-day saints" of the Puritan

exodus to America, in the early seventeenth century, renewed these
notions, designating themselves as the newly covenanted people who
would lay claim, as a redemptive force, to the New World. The final
struggles of Armageddon and the millennium would be played out here,
in America.*

There was certainly nothing of the apocalypse, however, in the manner of Jack McKeon, the student who had volunteered for a presentation
on the New Testament. Tall and craggy, with a lantern jaw, McKeon was
a solemn young gent who already had the bearing, as a sophomore, of a
bank president or marketing director. His skin was a youthful mess, but
it didn't matter, it would clear, and he would be revealed at twenty-five
as distinguished. If Leora was troubled and restless, he was calm, even
serene.

Jack summed up the consensus among biblical scholars with admiral
briskness. He explained that there were many accounts of Jesus but only
four that the early church fathers considered authentic, those ascribed to
Matthew, Mark, Luke, and John; that most scholars thought Mark was
written first; that Matthew, the one we were discussing that day, was
written between 70 and 85 A.D. for a community of Christian believers
in Jerusalem and the surrounding area; that the text was derived from
thirty or forty years of oral tradition of narrative about Jesus and also
from a hypothetical written compilation of that oral material that scholars called Q, short for *Quelle*, or "source" in German. The disciples
Matthew, Mark, Luke, and John may have contributed, from the past,
in fragments, to the Gospels, but they had not written them. Jack easily
accepted this, but he made it clear that nothing asserted by scholars
about the material production of the Bible was inconsistent with the
view that these texts, whatever their source, were divine revelation.

Stephanson agreed, but he kept coming back to the historical circumstances, forcing the students to make the violent mental effort of laying
aside two millennia of Christian interpretation—and Christian hegemony. This was a class in social theory, not religious instruction, and he
wanted the students to see Jesus and His followers historically, as an oppositional movement within Judaism, and as an episode in the history of
ethics and of man's relation to the state and to time itself. Of the four
canonized gospels, Matthew, which presents the fullest exposition of Jesus' teachings (including the Sermon on the Mount), was the one that
most closely and consciously presented itself as a successor to the Old
Testament. "Think not that I am come to destroy the law or the

* Stephanson later elaborated on these notions in a short book called *Manifest Destiny:
American Expansion and the Empire of Right* (New York: Hill & Wang, 1995).

prophets," Jesus said. "I am not come to destroy, but to fulfill." It did not occur to Jesus that he was starting a new religion.

A hoarse-voiced student, Manuel Alon, became indignant with Stephanson's historical view. He insisted on the enormity of the philosophical break with Judaism. "You no longer have to have a symbol of your covenant with God," he said. "The ending of circumcision, the ending of animal sacrifices . . . Jesus saw that people were practicing everything but were weak in their hearts."

His voice was surprisingly husky and textured—gnarled almost—for so young a man. He was from New York, of Puerto Rican descent, and he was blind. When he spoke, he kept his eyes closed and tilted his head back and smiled, swinging back and forth in time to the words, which rolled out in endless waves. He played the drums and other instruments, and when he appeared in class with dark glasses, swaying as he spoke, he reminded me of the hipster jazz musicians of my youth, who often had a proudly preoccupied look.

Manuel was one of those eccentrically brilliant students who either hit things right on the head or wandered a long way from the subject in a fantasia of eloquence. He could be pompous, almost oracular, and he could be shockingly intimate. A couple of months earlier, in one of the classes on Plato, Stephanson had asked the students if they agreed with Socrates' remark that it was better to be the victim than the perpetrator of an injustice. Most of them shook their heads: They would rather be perpetrators; no self-accepted victimhood for them. But Manuel said, "I dunno," in his rasping voice, and swung back and forth. "It is ultimately better that a doctor didn't know what he was doing."

No one spoke, but I could feel a sense of alarm growing in the silence: He was speaking of his blindness.

"There was an operation. . . . Whether it was incompetence or negligence, I don't know, but ultimately I learned more. Peace."

The silence persisted and deepened into shock: He meant that he learned more from being blind than from being sighted. It was the kind of remark that no one in our derisive culture could easily handle, an unwanted intimacy that on the surface made little sense. Anyway, few people made large, Christian statements like that, and even fewer people meant them. Manuel's munificence (if that's what it was) embarrassed the students. Was he noble, refusing to judge a doctor who had bungled an operation? Or just a show-off? There was a pause, and Stephanson, usually so ebullient and combative, finally said (very softly) "Roight," and moved on. But Manuel's remark, and its implicit demand on us, lingered in the air for months. Manuel insisted that we either accept or reject him.

In the New Testament class, Jack the chairman of the board spoke again. "One difference between Christianity and Judaism," he said, "is that more compassion comes in through God sending his own son as a sacrifice to redeem man."

Some of the Jewish students stirred uneasily. The class remained polite, but we were getting close to the knuckle. Stephanson's notion of "conversation" was elastic—he liked to make the students stretch to the border of incivility, but not cross it. Yet in these remarks, however tentative, there was an intimation of the old, old quarrel. What had begun as a discussion of Christianity in history and then of Christian ethics had become something else, and an Israeli woman student who had lived in the United States in recent years took the bait and said, "Most of the Jews didn't believe in Jesus because there were many messiahs attempting to lead them out of bondage to the Romans."

At that, Manuel cleared his throat and renewed the attack. "The more powerful Jews sold out to the Romans," he said, and on he went. He had the voluminous, rambling fluency, the assorted bits of information and opinion of a sleepless person grabbing some time on late-night radio. He did not stick to the text; he wandered all over the place. But how could you ask a blind man to be quiet? (Eventually, Stephanson did.) Pale and fleshy, with a half-grown beard, Manuel was, as far as I could tell, a Christian Marxist humanist, Latino style. He railed against injustice and poverty.

A few weeks after the classes on the New Testament, I shared some sandwiches with him in his room. He lived on 112th Street between Broadway and Amsterdam, just down the block from the hulking neo-Gothic Cathedral of St. John the Divine, in one of the old apartment buildings Columbia had converted into dormitories. I asked him how he dealt with the reading. Sometimes people read to him, he said, but then he pointed across the small, uncomfortable room to a special kind of scanner sitting on a table. He would buy regularly printed books and lay them face down on the scanner, page by page; the scanner would then feed the pages into a computer, and out would come the words from the computer's tiny loudspeaker in bland robo-tones.

The Bible, however, presented special problems. Most Bibles are printed in double columns, of course, and since the scanner would simply read across the left-hand column and then jump to the right-hand one, the words would come out as gibberish ("Verily, verily, I say unto you, I am feast of the dedication, and it was . . .") As we ate lunch together, he told me of his quest to find a Bible printed as a normal book, in single columns stretching across the page. He made phone calls to many publishers, finally locating one near Times Square that published a single-column Bible. In a pouring rain, he took the subway from Columbia down to Forty-second Street, but after climbing the stairs to the street, he became disoriented and could not find his way to the publisher's office. A man appeared out of nowhere, a fellow Puerto Rican, and took him to the office, where the people he met were so moved by his story that they gave him the Bible, which cost fifty dollars, for nothing.

Manuel! Sitting in his room, I felt a surge of affection for him. In class, he could be a pain, but he had elements of greatness in him. He refused to judge those who had hurt him—or at least he said he did—and inspired acts of generosity. If Jack McKeon was the Church as a powerful and serene institution, established forever, then Manuel was a raw-souled early Christian, hungry for confrontation and experience, the stress and clamor of spiritual truth.

In class, Leora now jumped in to defend the Pharisees. The conversation was becoming increasingly agitated. The students seemed not to know that the Second Vatican Council, in 1965, had officially condemned anti-Semitism and had absolved the Jews of responsibility for the death of Jesus Christ. Our "conversation" came close to breaking down into rage. Placing religion *in* history, Stephanson had inadvertently summoned all of the intervening history as well, and so two millennia of bitterness entered the room and made the students quarrelsome.

❖   ❖   ❖

As I read Matthew, I felt nothing of these ancient violent controversies. At least not at first. What I felt was delight in Jesus, an unanticipated elation and excitement. Reading the Gospels at eighteen, and then picking up the New Testament now and then in the intervening years, I had noticed only ethics, preaching, miracles, and the Passion itself—the doctrinal and, so to speak, spectacular side of Christianity. I had missed most of what was so extraordinarily powerful about Jesus. How could I not have seen it? He possessed an intellectual vigor that was without parallel in literature. John Updike, a Christian writer (among many other things), characterized Jesus as he appears in Mark with these words—"a young man, a paragon of vitality and poetic assertion." *
That was the right note, I thought, the pointed emphasis on youthfulness, energy, and daring. This man heading for death was invincible—not only moving and eloquent, but supremely witty. The word "witty" may seem blasphemous, but not if you expand the definition of wit to mean quickness and aggressiveness of intellect. Wit assaulted the assumptions of the person to whom it was addressed. Seen in this way, some of the most familiar lines no longer seemed like chestnuts. They were very tough nuts indeed; they could crack your teeth.

> And when the tempter came to him, he said, If thou be the Son of God, command that these stones be made bread. But he answered

Odd Jobs (New York: Knopf, 1991), p. 233.

and said, It is written, Man shall not live by bread alone, but by every word that proceedeth out of the mouth of God. (Matt. 4:3–4)

Ye have heard that it hath been said, An eye for an eye, and a tooth for a tooth: But I say unto you, That ye resist not evil: but whosoever shall smite thee on thy right cheek, turn to him the other also. And if any man will sue thee at the law, and take away thy coat, let him have thy cloak also. And whosoever shall compel thee to go a mile, go with him twain. (Matt. 5:38–41)

Pull the ground up! Roll it up, so the listener has nowhere to stand! Jesus wanted not reform but transformation, a new person to replace the stale, unfeeling old one. Consider the famous "Judge not, that ye be not judged. For with what judgement ye judge, ye shall be judged; and with what measure ye mete, it shall be measured to you again." This was devastating: Hypocrisy would be deflected back on the person who expressed it, the will recoiling on itself like some sort of maverick catapult.

One way of reading these books was to take from them whatever part resonated in your soul and make that yours forever. And so, reading selfishly, as Professor Tayler put it, reading in order to build a self, or, at my age, rebuild a self, I had discovered what I wanted from Jesus. The man whose likeness glowed on calendars and posters in nacreous pallor, as if lit from within by dim fluorescent light; the Redeemer whose plastic body swung from taxi-drivers' dashboards and whose gaze, a column of light in old Hollywood movies, loosened the bowels of Victor Mature and struck Charlton Heston dumb, this Jesus, when encountered in his original form, was an amazing figure who laid down one challenge after another. Reading again, I was forced to put away the kitsch of Christianity, forced to touch its core, and I was stirred.

"If thine eye offend thee, pluck it out," Jesus said. No matter how metaphorically one reads that extraordinary sentence, it becomes no less exciting. You were just to *leave*, accept the call to follow Him and *leave*, walking out on your house, your wife and children, your mother and father. To reach God, you had to reject an intolerable patch of your soul. And this was no soothing and consoling message of charity and acceptance; it was as radical a demand as had ever been offered to people who thought they understood what virtue was. Even turning the other cheek to be struck, which many now considered bizarre, a weak, even masochistic act—the students, remember, except for Manuel, would rather be perpetrator than victim—even this could be seen as a kind of triumphant thwarting of the enemy. You undermined his hostility, sending it back as love. You astounded him by giving him more than he wanted, the cloak as well as the coat, and you shamed his greed.

Someone will rightly object that I am ignoring for my own convenience the spiritual and emotional power of the Gospels—the reality of Jesus' death and resurrection, the immeasurable sacrifice He made for man, the narrative of a man scourged, mocked, and crucified. Maybe so, but when someone who is not a Christian reads the Passion story, what strikes him most strongly is Jesus' extraordinary presence of mind, his strength and shrewdness as well as sweetness, and his toughness, which at times is stunning—a spiritual power that derives, in part, from intellectual high spirits and good health. Incomparable intellectual vitality overcome by the necessity of death—that was my non-Christian view of Jesus.

Oh, I loved my Jesus! And I feared him, too. The core readings, I began to see, could be arduous and demanding, all the more so if you lowered your guard and let the books hit you, and especially in middle age, when demands such as those made by Jesus threatened the protective encrustation of habit. The middle-age "success"—one of Jesus' prime targets—relied on his strengths, hid his weaknesses, and cut corners wherever he could; he observed the outward forms of the laws and wondered what was alive in his soul. I knew this person all too well, and although I was not ready to leave my family and follow anyone, I thought turning myself inside out might not be a bad idea. At least I could discover my limits, and try to push beyond them.

❖ ❖ ❖

A good part of European and American history sprang out of these books of the New Testament—wars, social organization, an immense amount of art and thought—and as I read through the Gospels, my initial elation gave way to unease.

The reason was perfectly obvious. The Gospels and the Epistles (which were composed a little earlier) were written for embattled Christian groups—the newly converted and those who might be converted. Stephanson called them the most effective organizing tools ever invented. Within a few hundred years the Roman Empire was Christian. As I sat at home reading these tracts—this electrifying, bullying movement literature—I had over and over a rather hapless fantasy. Even in the midst of my new pleasure in Jesus, I daydreamed, as I often did, but this time in the same images, again and again: I was being pulled into the rest of European history, yanked like some unwilling, flailing character in an animated film down a long corridor, on and on, past windows and doors and staircases leading in every direction. This flailing creature lost control and slid, propelled along the floor on his back, his arms raised and reaching. . . .

My daydream, I knew, was inspired by the sense that the Gospels were fashioned and then used as a weapon against me. Not me personally, but against my kind, my ancestors, the Jews. In these most central of all

Western texts, I was the enemy, the one who lacked human qualities and understanding. I was the "other." Women and blacks have complained that the classic texts of the West cast them into roles that justified exclusion; and now this became my complaint, too. Columbia's treating the Old Testament as prelude to the New had not bothered me at all, but now, though loving Jesus as never before, I was spooked.

Until about 70 A.D., the Christians understood themselves as a movement within Judaism. Out of the agony of the breakup, that bitter family quarrel or divorce, Christianity emerged as something separate, and the Gospels, written around the same time to give strength and comfort to those who might be facing persecution, turned the Jews, or at least the Pharisees, into the enemy (it wouldn't have been prudent to turn the Romans into the enemy). And so in the long corridor of European and then American history, the thrusting out from these books of institutions and wars and manners, including the rapid triumph of the new story of incarnation, death, and resurrection over the Greco-Roman god systems— in that long corridor, the Jews, now a hated minority, were dragged along, occasionally converted (and then, often, under the threat of death), but also tortured, ghettoized, scapegoated, envied, demonized, annihilated. They were as much a part of the West as the Christians, but through all of history they were made to pay for handing Jesus over to the Romans and their refusal to accept Him as the Messiah, Jesus the son of God, who of course serves his divine function for Christians precisely because he was "betrayed" and crucified.

I read the parables again, and found some of them puzzling and hostile.

> And he began again to teach by the sea side: and there was gathered unto him a great multitude, so that he entered into a ship, and sat in the sea; and the whole multitude was by the sea on the land. And he taught them many things by parables, and said unto them in his doctrine, Hearken; Behold, there went out a sower to sow: And it came to pass, as he sowed, some fell by the way side, and the fowls of the air came and devoured it up. And some fell on stony ground, where it had not much earth; and immediately it sprang up, because it had no depth of earth: But when the sun was up, it was scorched; and because it had no root, it withered away. And some fell among thorns, and the thorns grew up, and choked it, and it yielded no fruit. And other fell on good ground, and did yield fruit that sprang up and increased; and brought forth, some thirty, and some sixty, and some an hundred. And he said unto them, He that hath ears to hear, let him hear. And when he was alone, they that were about him with the twelve asked of him the parable. And he said unto them, Unto you it is given to know the mystery of the kingdom of God:

but unto them that are without, all these things are done in parables: That seeing they may see, and not perceive; and hearing they may hear, and not understand; lest at any time they should be converted, and their sins should be forgiven them. (Mark 4:1–12)

Jesus then explains the parable of the sower, and tells his listeners:

If any man have ears to hear, let him hear. And he said unto them, Take heed what ye hear: with what measure ye mete, it shall be measured to you: and unto you that hear shall more be given. For he that hath, to him shall be given: and he that hath not, from him shall be taken even that which he hath. (Mark 4:23–25)

In other words, either you get it or you don't. And since it's explicitly the Jews, or at least the Pharisees, who don't get it, they are doomed to darkness—though of course the disciples themselves often don't get it. Jesus has to explain himself even to *them*. So who does get it?

Many readers before me have found it unlikely that Jesus would wish not to be understood. After all, the passage from Mark begins by saying that he was "teaching." So what is going on here? Had Jesus given up on his fellow Jews by this time? Did he think the Pharisees in particular were not the kind of people who could understand what he had to say, and therefore there was no reason to talk straight to them?

Or had the writers of the Gospels altered what Jesus actually said? In his book *The Genesis of Secrecy: The Interpretation of Narrative,** the great English literary critic Frank Kermode, who has written widely on the Bible, remarked that "for the last century or so there has been something of a consensus among experts that parables of the kind found in the New Testament were always essentially simple, and always had the same point which would have been instantly taken by all listeners, outsiders included. Appearances to the contrary [i.e., such passages are the one from Mark] are explained as consequences of a process of meddling with the originals that began at the earliest possible moment."

From this consensus among experts, it is a short jump to my own (and not just my own) guess that the Gospels, shaped for communities of newly converted Christians surrounded by a hostile sea of Jews and Romans and Greeks, were intended to make people feel easier about the risks they were taking: "You who are persecuted must know that those who are tormenting you do not understand the word and are doomed." The parables, at least as the Gospel writers present them, are intentionally exclusionary. Obfuscation is part of their real purpose; to understand them you need not logic but a leap of faith, a commitment to Jesus. So the challenge from Jesus that had at first excited me now also

* (Cambridge: Harvard University Press, 1979), p. 25.

seemed harshly restrictive in its power. You convert or you are dropped into nonexistence.

The seeds of genuine hostility are here. The Old Testament itself was allowed into the Christian canon as a prelude only in the second century, when Christian theologians convinced themselves that it prefigured the New Testament. That the New (especially Matthew) might have been fashioned so as to conform to the Old may not have been a notion many Christians were willing to grant. History had done its amazing work, incorporating into its triumphant, indifferent sweep the less powerful traditions of earlier civilizations.

Suddenly, I felt lost. Was it possible that I was a victim of "hegemony" and had simply never admitted it?

❖   ❖   ❖

It was December, and here I was piling up presents for the boys at the base of a Christmas tree. "Just what I needed," I told myself. The tree was so large that my older son and I had to put it down on West End Avenue five or six times in the course of walking it home from nearby Broadway. In our living room, the tree scraped the ceiling and fir needles fell to the floor; the cats pawed at the needles and chewed on the ribbons around the presents. As the boxes mounted up, the children grew more excited. I was a secular Jew celebrating Christmas the way our family always did, and I was going around with an unpleasant pressure building inside my head.

Chronologically, Lit Hum was way behind C.C., so Professor Tayler took up the New Testament only in mid-January, as the initial Lit Hum reading of the second semester. Would he deal with such issues? Even if he did, I was sure his kind of formal metaphoric analysis couldn't touch what was bothering me.

Tayler wanted to discuss the connections between the Old and New Testaments. But first he went back to his opening day of the first semester, making the students pull out the sheet of quotations he had given them four months earlier. There it was again, the opening of Genesis. Adam and Eve were back in paradise, in a state of *integritas*. There was no conflict between what they wanted to do and what they ought to do. "Throughout your life," he said, looking around at the students, his baritone curling upward, "throughout your life, people have been saying to you, 'Why can't you be more like Adam in Eden?'" And by that he meant that people demanded of themselves and others an impossible consistency and simplicity and an undivided will. "But you have these splits, right?" he said, "because Adam and Eve ate the apple, and then man falls into time, and he falls into dualities," and he handed out another sheet, this time with copies of the poem "Original Sequence" by the contemporary American poet Philip Booth. The poem begins, "Time was the apple Adam ate," and ends:

> Eve held the twisted stem, the pulp;
> she heard the low snake hiss, and let fly
> blindly with a woman arm, careless
> where her new-won anger struck.
> The fodder for that two-fold flock
> fell, an old brown core, at God's
> stopped feet. He reached, and wound the clock.

"See," he said, "God wound the clock, and time starts. When you fall from the garden of Eden, as any poet can tell you, you fall into time— 'Time was the apple Adam ate'—and you fall into dualities. Everything comes in opposing pairs. Remember the opening of Genesis. Light and darkness, land and seas. God was doing a job of long division on the universe. Good and evil, too. Milton in that quotation from *Areopagitica* that I gave you on opening day said that good and evil were part of each other. 'It was from out of the rind of one apple tasted, that the knowledge of good and evil, as two twins cleaving together, leaped forth into the world. And perhaps this is the doom which Adam fell into of knowing good and evil—that is to say, of knowing good by evil.' You have to be expelled from Eden to know sin. You've got to have evil in order to have love and charity."

Tayler had been teaching Lit Hum for many years, and had built up a language, a set of references, reaching forward and backward, that held the books together, as if the course itself were a kind of epic poem with its own organic structure, its difficulties and mysteries that could be penetrated by a student alert enough to pick up the hints. In class, he could jump from one thing to another because he had his epic-poem version of the course in his head. But would his poem speak to me this time? I doubted it.

Tayler was off and winging now, and a couple of students who had shifted into his section in the middle of the year-long course looked puzzled, almost shocked, especially a student named Judith Sterngold, who was not shy about expressing her opinions. She cocked her head sideways and stared at Tayler silently.

"Look," he said, "the Greek gods screwed around, like us. They were like us. But in the Old Testament there's a gap between man and God. God says to Job, 'You weren't *there* when I created the universe, and you don't *know*.' Into that gap will step Jesus. Jesus embodies it, he is both man and God, and he explains it."

Then he started firing questions at them, and they rose to the task, making a literary structure out of the Gospels and their relation as language and metaphor to the Old Testament. They were alive to this heady talk of time and doubling, and he worked his rabbit-out-of-the-hat trick, ignoring the answers that went awry, picking one word or phrase out of a wayward answer and building something, getting the other students to respond to it.

"What is the point of the genealogy at the beginning of Matthew?" he asked. "It begins, 'The book of the generation of Jesus Christ, the son of David, the son of Abraham. Abraham begat Isaac; and Isaac begat Jacob,' and so on. The point is to establish that Jesus descended from King David, right? But why is this necessary if He's the son of God?"

Sterngold now came alive. "How can Jesus later be called the '*Lord* of David'?" she asked. "David came *earlier*. Before Jesus. This comes out of another concept than the one I know from the Hebrew Bible. I don't understand this concept of God, where things exist at two points in time."

Tayler looked delighted. Judith Sterngold was holding her head.

"Why are you holding your head?"

"Paradox," said Sterngold, irritably.

"Yes, paradox makes you hold your head. Look, Miss Sterngold, no one is trying to convert you. That's not what we do here. You may doubt that God did this, but you can't doubt that it's a description of the universe in which you live."

She smiled slightly.

"Okay, you fall into time," said Tayler. "Jesus says, in effect, 'Your time is clocks; my time is not yet; it's not my time to go to Jerusalem.' There is the appointed time and the chronological time, *kairos* and *chronos*. God dropped Jesus into time. He is the walking paradox, both God and man: He is eternity in time. So now you're messing with time; you lose life in order to gain it. Jesus is Lord of David, who came earlier, because eternity has intervened in chronological time."

Sterngold was still staring at him.

"You've all been brought up to think single, as if you were in the Garden of Eden. Think double. You've fallen into dualities. Jesus as teacher is doing what?—he's busting your head." And here he looked at Sterngold again. "He's saying you don't have eyes to see or ears to hear. He will teach you by going over the line into death, and you have to accept it."

Sterngold nodded and held her peace, and Tayler hit it again. "God drops eternity into time, and this screws up the tenses. Rhetorically, what you get is paradox. Sir Thomas Browne, in the seventeenth century, said, 'Eve miscarried of me before she conceived of Cain.' In order to *know* what time is, you have to look up vertically to God."

As I listened to him, I felt my ache fading away. He was giving us the version of time and history that Christianity brought into Western consciousness, a way of conceiving of time that had an immense influence on theology and literature at least through the Renaissance, and the scheme was dazzling. Here was an example of hegemony in operation—Sterngold's way of thinking about time had yielded to another—and one might describe it, analyze it, unmask it, but one could not do much more than that. The Christian mode of thinking had shaped literature and art and institutions, it had been woven through history and could not be shaken out. It had woven itself into me, too.

I wondered if he would come back to his old issue of the supersession of the Hebrew Bible, and in a second class, he presented the theory of type and antitype, a familiar way of reading passages in the New Testament among certain scholars. Passages of the New Testament, he said, were fashioned to look back to passages in the Old. The miraculous birth of Jesus looks back to Isaac, miraculously born to Abraham and the barren Sarah. If one reads the New Testament innocently, however, and with a view to maintaining the inevitability of Jesus, the earlier event appears to prefigure the later—though with just that measure of mystery and enigma added that made the experience uncanny, an intimation of God's single grasp holding all of life, all of history. David could be read as the type of Jesus, and Moses spreading his arms over the Red Sea doesn't know it, but he's symbolizing Jesus, too.

We were propelled into the Christian world. "Look at the beginning of John," Tayler said. "'In the Beginning was the Word, and the Word was with God.' This is a spectacular opening, a violent, scandalous revision of the opening of Genesis. The Gospels were written in Greek, and in Greek, the 'word' is *logos*, a most powerful word to the highly cultivated Greco-Roman audience that was likely to read John. Look, the entire civilization of the Greeks—logos—gets dropped into this one man. 'And the Word was made flesh.' That's the big turn from the Greco-Roman civilization.

"This is a religion that's going to take over," Tayler said, summing up. "The Emperor Constantine converts, and the Roman Empire becomes the Holy Roman Empire. They're going to take over South America, North America, and if they can't convert them, they're going to burn them. It couldn't have taken over the world without a new view of time and history."

He presented the framework of the Christian triumph. It was a double focus: He unmasked and celebrated the mask at the same time.

And, amazingly, I was soothed. My unhappiness, dimming rapidly, soon went away altogether. Anti-Semitism was a catastrophe and a disgrace, but to remain indignant over the success of Christianity—I couldn't do it, and after a while my couch fantasy of flailing down the endless corridor disappeared. One cannot reasonably fight history, the configuration of what was with the imagination of what wasn't—a futile and despairing act. History was always excluding somebody: By most definitions, it was a record of victory of one force or group over another. Which doesn't mean that one "accepts" injustice, only that one could not fashion one's being around historical memory. At least I couldn't. Even after much reading and some writing about the Holocaust, and a terrifying visit to Auschwitz, and considerable attention to the anti-Semitic remarks of Pat Robertson, Pat Buchanan, and Louis Farrakhan, I could not, without serious inauthenticity, think of myself as a victim of anti-Semitism. Not in America; not in New York. I could, and should, think of myself as a Jew, but not as a victim.

What mattered now was survival and the ability to flourish, and no one could say that the Jews, after ages of bitterness and sorrow, had not survived and flourished in America. I was lucky, I told myself, lucky, lucky, lucky, an American Jew protected by the country's traditions of tolerance and by its constitutional refusal of a state religion.

❖ ❖ ❖

This reading of sacred texts in secular courses was a bumpy ride. I had got thrown around rather harder than I wanted, and I had the bruises to show for it. But at least I felt my body, I knew it was there, and I could no longer say my identity was entirely lost in the media fog.

Chapter *12*

AUGUSTINE

~ The unwanted erection
~ *City of God* and the *Confessions*
~ Adam and Eve; perversity as the center of our nature
~ Erotic memories of an ill-run Connecticut summer camp
~ A Jew makes peace with Catholics

A common occurrence for young men sitting in a classroom: an un-wanted stirring, a vicious strain against tightly clinging jeans, followed by a quick rearrangement below the desk. . . . Such things happened frequently and without obvious cause when you were nineteen, and it was a good bet that only God knew their meaning, because a man with an erection often did not. As you got older, such things happened less often, and though hardly, at forty-eight, *old*, I was not about to look with indifference upon my manifestation of what President Kennedy called "vigah." Nor was I so proud an agnostic as to rule out the notion that God was present in the flesh, especially in the member rising of its own, during an airplane ride, in the middle of an editing session, at a concert. It was a blessing, obviously. What else could it be?

A curse, perhaps. Augustine, the great St. Augustine, who was, apart from his preeminence as a Christian theologian, an extraordinary writer, one of the heroic chroniclers of consciousness and desire, and not some-one I could ever make fun of—the great Augustine was preoccupied with his unintentional erections. He experienced them as God's reproof, a punishment for original sin. Professor Tayler was not joking on opening day when he mentioned Augustine's interest in such matters. Augustine returns to the unruly member again and again; it became one of the minor thematic keys to his theology of pride, sin, disobedience, and the divided will.

Normally, when I tried to remember things from long ago, I came away with nothing and wandered off into daydreams or movie images—the flood of desire and trivia where memory should be. I had no story to tell. But as I sat reading Augustine in both Lit Hum and C.C., a variety of unbidden scenes, remnants of my life, came rushing in. I was suddenly

185

flooded with episodes from the age of ten or twelve, memories of sin (that's what they were), and after a while I realized that the involuntary erection that so interested Augustine was neither a blessing nor a curse but simply a form of memory, a reprise of some past blessedness or crime. The body was telling the mind that the past was never entirely lost.

❖   ❖   ❖

We had arrived at the end of antiquity. Augustine, born in 354 A.D. on the fringes of the Roman Empire, in Thagaste (what would now be Algeria), was living in Hippo, near Carthage (now Tunisia), when Alaric and the Goths sacked Rome in 410. Throughout *City of God*, the vast book Augustine wrote in the years 413 to 426, one feels the tremors of an unimaginable event, the coming breakup of the Roman Empire. Was Christianity to blame? About twenty-five years before Augustine's birth, the emperor Constantine had made Christianity the dominant religion of the Empire; Christianity was well along in its conquest of Europe. Augustine, a late convert but eventually a bishop in the Church, wrote *City of God* ostensibly to combat the notion that Rome was weakened by the spread of the new faith.

But that's merely the starting point of *City of God*. It is an extraordinary work, surely one of the great efforts to tie everything together, to make all of life into radiant pattern. In hundreds of numbered paragraphs, spread over twenty sections (almost eleven hundred pages of text in the Penguin edition), the arguments move forward, recede, spring forth again in bolder and more definitive statements, on and on, lapping and overlapping, wave after wave of prose. *City of God* is a book that could go on literally forever: It moves sideways and backward as well as forward, filling up all the intellectual and conceptual space, just as Augustine said God filled all the space in creation. Augustine sums up classical culture, debating paganism and praising Plato; offers a reading of the Old and New Testaments; and speculates on such things as creation and time, the civil state, and the blessedness of God's creatures in heaven. *City of God* is a book both mazelike and lucid, for God, Augustine thought, had a comprehensible plan for man and for history. And yet (and here was the reason I loved Augustine), God's plan allowed for the irrational, the discordant, the inexplicable. Thirty years ago we read only short selections from *City of God* in C.C., and I came away with no particular impression of it. But now, reading large chunks, I lost myself in the maze and accepted Augustine's hand as the only way that led out.

Viewed narrowly and parochially, from the point of view of Columbia's C.C. class, *City of God* had the effect of consolidating the core curriculum in the fifth century A.D.—that is, it pressed Greek and Roman culture into the gathering caravan of Christian history, both as a usable past and as a projection of the caravan's progress into the future. Stephanson emphasized Plato's influence on Augustine as one of the main lines of Western thought. Augustine and the other neo-Platonists took over Plato's idealism, the hierarchy of goods in which the "forms" figure as perfection, and earthly material things as mere inferior copies. He recast Plato's idealism such that the perfection of God was now the invisible idea of pure goodness, the true reality that exists apart from us. "Plato's spirit and matter," as Stephanson put it, "becomes in Augustine the spirit and the flesh; the higher and lower are taken over as the immutable and the here-and-now. The world is an externalization of God's plan. Being—existence—is the result not of participation in the good, as in Plato, but as participation in God." The body participated, too, but disobediently, perversely. And that was the part that fascinated me and that now showed up in memory, like an old stain on faded yellow pages.

❖   ❖   ❖

I don't mean to imply that Columbia had chosen the book and stuck with it merely because it helped pull together the C.C. reading list. Augustine was one of the major shapers of European civilization. And so Columbia laid on a heavy serving. Later, in the second semester of Lit Hum, we read Augustine's *Confessions*, which was, by common consent, the first true autobiography, the first large-scale interior document, in Western literature. In the *Confessions*, begun in 397, about eleven years after his conversion to Christianity (and about sixteen years before he began *City of God*), Augustine recounts the stages of his disastrous youth: his sins and debaucheries as a teenager (Augustine had a great many voluntary erections); his earlier belief in Manicheism (the notion that good and evil are separate, equal forces in perpetual conflict with each other); and, finally, his anticipated, wished-for, much-delayed, much-feared delivery of himself to God, at the age of thirty-three, the same age as Jesus at his death. Clearly, Augustine was in no hurry; he enjoyed himself too much, though his enjoyment was shadowed by guilt and despair. This was a fleshly man, a lover of women, not some frightened person in a monk's cell. And so one tends to trust the authenticity of his struggle against himself. Yearning, wallowing, overcoming, falling again, the will often outstretching the performance—Augustine is always a man divided, and that's the exciting "modern" element in him. Even after his conversion, he must deal with the flesh going its own way.

At first, in the Garden of Eden, all was well. Adam and Eve "lived in a partnership of unalloyed felicity. . . . They were not distressed by any agitations of the mind, nor pained by any disorders of the body." They made love whenever they wanted (though somehow without lust), ate whatever they wanted; they were immortal. But pride made Eve and then Adam disobey: They ate the forbidden fruit. Astonishing act! They had everything at their disposal, all of creation, and yet, precisely when obedience would have been so simple, so easy, they disobeyed. And were punished with the aging of their flesh, with shame, and with death. Perversity, or the sin of pride—man's standing on his own ground rather than on God's—is therefore central to human life, and produces universal consequences. For we all sin with Adam, and as punishment we lose not only immortality but control of ourselves. Or, as Tayler put it in our New Testament class, we fall into dualities.

> The soul, in fact, rejoiced in its own freedom to act perversely and disdained to be God's servant; and so it was deprived of the obedient service which its body had at first rendered. . . . It did not keep its own flesh subject to it in all respects, as it could have kept it for ever if it had itself continued in subjection to God. This then was the time when the flesh began to "lust in opposition to the spirit" [Galatians 22:5, 17], which is the conflict that attends us from our birth. (*City of God,* pp. 522–23)

> . . . he who in his pride had pleased himself was by God's justice handed over to himself. But the result of this was not that he was in every way under his own control, but that he was at odds with himself, and lived a life of harsh and pitiable slavery, instead of the freedom he so ardently desired. . . . In fact, to put it briefly, in the punishment of that sin the retribution for disobedience is simply disobedience itself . . . so that because he would not do what he could, he now wills to do what he cannot. . . . For who can list all the multitude of things that a man wishes to do and cannot, while he is disobedient to himself, that is, while his very mind and even his lower element, his flesh, do not submit to his will? (p. 575)

The rebellious member was one of the unhappy consequences of this division, and another consequence (as Augustine does not fail to point out) was its opposite, the occasional flaccid member refusing the commands of desire. That such humiliating scandals did not plague women should have given Augustine pause; it should have suggested that something was seriously amiss with this part of his analysis. Women, after all, were also punished after the Fall. But the rest of the scheme fits women as well as men, for there was much more (of course) comprised by this punishment—the confusion, the despair that we all live with, never able to do exactly what we want, so often split between pleasure and duty, fantasy and reality, play and work, split down the middle, all of us, or almost all of us, the student's mind unable to settle into its book, my attention wandering from my reading when I most wanted to read. . . . We are not whole, we are not masters of ourselves.

Augustine's notions made as much sense as any other explanation of the cantankerous unpredictability of mind and will. Professor Tayler obviously thought it powerful and illuminating—as good a myth as, say, Freud's theory of the neuroses as an explanation of why people cannot do what they want to do. Millions of people had constructed their moral lives along such lines. The core curriculum was meant to be both historical and contemporary at once: It introduced students to certain frames of thought powerful enough to have lasted, with many variations, for millennia, each generation filling in the frame according to its own obsessions.

Perversity is the key to our nature. In a famous episode from the *Confessions*:

> There was a pear-tree near our vineyard, loaded with fruit that was attractive neither to look at nor to taste. Late one night a band of ruffians, myself included [Augustine was sixteen], went off to shake down the fruit and carry it away, for we had continued our games out of doors until well after dark, as was our pernicious habit. We took away an enormous quantity of pears, not to eat them ourselves, but simply to throw them to the pigs. Perhaps we ate some of them, but our real pleasure consisted in doing something that was forbidden. (p. 47)

It's the forbidden fruit all over again, the sin of pride.

> Look into my heart, O God, the same heart on which you took pity when it was in the depths of the abyss. Let my heart now tell you what prompted me to do wrong for no purpose, and why it was only my own love of mischief that made me do it. The evil in me was foul, but I loved it. I loved my own perdition and my own faults, not the things for which I committed wrong, but the wrong itself. My soul was vicious and broke away from your safe keeping to seek its own destruction, looking for no profit in disgrace but only for disgrace itself. (pp. 47–48)

"Looking for no profit in disgrace but only for disgrace itself." Augustine wrote in Latin, but even in translation (by R. S. Pine-Coffin), the phrase is almost Shakespearian in its rhythm. What did this mean to me when I was nineteen? I wracked my brain, but I could not recall whether the business of the pears had brought up any memories of my own in 1961. If I had few such thoughts as a freshman, it was doubtless because my career as a sinner had never really gotten under way.

But now, one thing did come back. . . . I now can recall one small incident. I was sitting with my cousin on a bulldozer that was parked on a beach. A beach in Atlantic Beach, not very far out on Long Island, where my parents had a summer house. I was perhaps ten, and he was eleven, and it was a cold gray day (in the fall, probably), and no one was about. The bulldozer had been left there by workmen who were building a new beach club, and my cousin, who was not at all timid, pressed the starter, put the bulldozer in gear, and without the slightest protest from me, smashed a large glass wall, maybe twenty feet wide, into bits. The noise was extraordinary, but no one came after us. I wanted to tell my parents, but I never got around to it. I remained in the house the rest of the week-end, quaking on the front porch most of the time, but the police never came, nothing ever happened.

A miniconfession at best. But surely the act, even my passive role in it, was produced by no other desire than to do something bad; and surely I wanted to live up to my cousin's daring, just as Augustine says he wanted to live up to his friends' bad impulses.

But this memory brought on another, this time from a few years later when I was at summer camp. It was a terrible camp, an ill-run place beside a lake somewhere near Willimantic, Connecticut. The junior counselors, who were sixteen or seventeen, beefy blond boys from nearby small towns, bullied the little kids, some of whom got homesick and wet their beds. As punishment, the counselors would grab the bedwetters, holding them by the arms, and swing them out over a ledge until they begged for mercy. An older counselor, an ex-marine, crouched inside a cabin and threw a knife into a wooden door, underhand, to show us how he had killed a Korean in the war—the knife coming *up*, not going down, into the Korean's belly. This was exciting, but I was the kind of kid who felt sorry for the Korean.

At lunch, flies buzzed in circles and gathered in the open pitchers of Kool-Aid left on the tables. And at night, when none of the counselors ever seemed to be around, a teenager who worked in the kitchen would hang out with the twelve-year-olds in the camp's "rec room," and every once in a while he would grab one of the boys, pull down his pants, and give him a smack or two on his naked bottom. Which amused the other little boys a great deal. *Smack! Smack!* We stood around fascinated, giggling, and no one made much of a fuss or ever reported the friendly spanker. One night, the kitchen boy slipped into my cabin and then into my bed. His hands, all over me, smelled of soap. I struggled and suddenly, without a word, he got up and left. (A counselor later told me he was waiting outside to "protect" me.) The kitchen boy, I now think, was not a sinner. Augustine would have regarded him as highly salvageable.

I'm not sure how a cautious little Jewish kid from New York wound up in that place. In fact, I was virtually the only New Yorker; most of the kids were locals, from around Willimantic, and because I was one of the "nicer" boys (i.e., my family had a little more money than the other boys' parents), I was invited by the owners, a crabby, elderly couple, to their big house at the edge of the camp. They sat me down on a floral-print couch, and complimented me for being a gentleman. They gave me more bug juice and little sandwiches with the crusts cut off. I was too young to know what snobbery was, but I certainly enjoyed my bug juice that day.

Why write down these hapless and obscure memories, these fragments of the hidden erotic life of a poorly run summer camp in north-central Connecticut in 1955? Because without those unbidden memories, fleshly proof of past experience, I no longer existed at twelve.

Involuntary memories now returned and returned.

That last year at the camp there was a boy, maybe ten, who was widely detested, a nasty little screamer named Halleck. His father owned the local company that manufactured the camp's ice cream, which was another reason to dislike him, as far as the kids were concerned. (Why, though? Because he could eat as much ice cream as he liked? Little boys are almost completely irrational and conformist in their likes and dislikes.)

The teenage counselors also hated Halleck, or enjoyed ganging up on him, which amounted to the same thing; they decided to punish him. Down the road, maybe a mile from camp, there was a haunted house—a real New England fright with a caved-in roof and crumbling walls. The house had been struck by lightning, the counselors told us. Struck and struck again. Groups of us were taken off to the haunted house every week or so, there being so little else to do at camp. On one occasion, the counselors asked for volunteers: Which camper had the guts to sleep outside the house for the night? Many volunteered, so the counselors set up a contest, which they rigged. The "winner" would sleep alone at the house, and that very night, as poor Halleck lay outside the house in his sleeping bag, the counselors and one camper—me—crept through the dark woods to the cursed site and hooted and howled and threw things until the despised ice-cream heir ran back to the camp screaming bloody murder. The next morning, he showed up at breakfast with his head wrapped in bandages, his face covered with "blood." He accused the counselors of trying to murder him. He was faking (the blood was Mercurocrome), but he had been thoroughly scared, and as the unknown conspirator, the only camper who was part of the raid, I was deliriously happy.

I remember begging to be part of the caper, but I have no idea why the counselors agreed. Obviously, I had sucked up to them, my oppressors, so they would include me. As one of the "nicer" boys, I identified with the only power around; I wanted to be part of it. Nice is as nice does.

This second reading of Augustine brought back the scene to me with rather unpleasant force. Again, the scaring of a ten-year-old Willimantic ice-cream heir is no crime to boast about (though neither, for that matter, was Augustine's raid on the pear trees), but this was sin, this was surely sin in Augustine's sense, since I barely knew Halleck and had nothing against him yet wanted to be part of the fun of terrifying him.

Augustine believed that the dishonor and squalor of an act—and the prohibition against it—increased the temptation to commit it and also the pleasure of committing it. He had an astonishingly modern understanding of the treacheries of the moral life, of the guilt that followed dishonor, and how unhappiness in sin did not stop one from sinning again. He understood the voluptuousness of guilt. And also the hell on earth that it became, for without grace, without taking Jesus Christ into your soul, you would lead your whole life this way (we're now talking of grown-ups), going to your eternal death in bitterness, unredeemed, locked in perversity, split down the middle, wanting one thing and doing another. Even if you were baptized and became a Christian, the way was not easy, because God did not necessarily punish the wicked and reward the virtuous. No, he didn't make things that easy; He didn't make His grace available to every lazy, opportunistic person. His ways were mysterious, and this, says Augustine, was exactly right, for if every person who embraced God and acted decently were quickly rewarded on earth, then sinners would believe in God and embrace goodness simply for the payoff. There would be no struggle, no *faith*.

Augustine was trying to explain and justify all the discordant elements of life—evil, death, pain, good things happening to bad people and vice versa—without simplifying anything. He would have understood our meaninglessly nasty act against Halleck and appreciated its perverse outcome: For the first time in Halleck's career at that camp, he became a popular figure. For the rest of the summer, the kids muttered ominously about the night Halleck had "almost been murdered." They gathered around him, a symbolic victim of the counselors' oppression. And I found myself held by a secret to the counselors, whom I loathed.

Augustine understood the texture of actual lives; he was more than familiar with selfishness, egotism, all the vices we take for granted as the ground of the human personality, and he understood that the desire for freedom, which he called disobedience, was so powerful that it might be the one thing in life you could never tame. He had the juice of life in him. That's why I enjoyed him, as I could not enjoy the dryly authoritarian Aquinas (also on the reading list), whose regularization of doctrine eight hundred years later solidified the power of the medieval Church. Nor did I receive much reading pleasure from the wrathful and dour Luther, stirring as he was in revolt against the corruptions of the Roman Church, or the legalistic and austere Calvin.

❖   ❖   ❖

Growing up as a Jew, I had inherited a certain disdain for Catholics. They sinned, they confessed, they sinned again, and consoled themselves with thoughts of the afterlife. This was a caricature of Catholics—a prejudice—but still, the Jewish elders were very firm about one point: Accountability came *now*. There was no putting off anything that mattered, for Jews do not really believe in an afterlife. As David Ben-Gurion, the lion of Israel, once put it, "For a Jew, hell is to be mediocre on earth." I'm quoting from memory, but I'm sure I've got the sense of Ben-Gurion's remark right. It was, of course, an insufferably chauvinistic thing to say, but it's what I believed about Jews versus other people for many years. I believed it despite the abundant evidence of many happily mediocre Jews and a variety of Catholic friends who found faith and worship no easy matter at all, but a constant, exhausting struggle. Reading Augustine again—the Christian core—I think I may have eliminated at least one prejudice forever. The divided will that Augustine described so clearly exists in everybody, and the struggle to overcome it is perhaps harder for believers than nonbelievers. The core readings could not create faith, but they had created, in me at least, faith in faith.

Chapter *13*

MACHIAVELLI

~ Students young and old; reading in New York
~ *The Prince*: unforgivable candor
~ Professor Stephanson expounds Machiavelli
~ *The Discourses*
~ Looking for a principle of social stability

I could always tell when students came to class without reading the books. Asked to speak, they would answer by stalling and blinking and finally by groggily stating the question back to the teacher. "How did Locke define . . . *property*?" They would sit in a corner, faces closed, or eyes turned down to notes. At least they showed up, I thought. In my day, if I hadn't done the reading, I just cut class. They were hard-pressed, many of them, and short of cash, so they took jobs in the university libraries and eating halls or even downtown, as bank tellers or waiters. They studied, they worked at their jobs, they played, and they went to class, where some of them nodded off. Neither laziness nor boredom was their problem, and not mine either. I still grabbed every moment, trying to read Thomas Hobbes standing up in the subway. I had no choice. Gathered like unshucked ears of corn, the books for the two courses sat next to my bed or in my study, near the computer, or on the floor of the dining room; and a familiar dread gathered in my chest, an unhappiness I had never experienced as an adult but that I remembered from long ago. At the age of forty-eight, I was behind in the reading.

At home, I would read when the children were at school, or at night, after they had gone to bed. But reading when the boys were home and awake was nearly impossible. Sometimes they would come and find me in the little study I shared with my wife. Before dinner, the TV was on, often two TVs, each boy at his station (they were allowed to watch a couple of hours a day), and as I read John Locke, the words would get mixed with the sounds, coming through the wall, of a teen sitcom and *X-Men*.

> *Nor is it so strange, as perhaps before consideration it should appear* . . . "So Zack, how are you going to ask Kelly to the prom? . . .

Nor is it so strange, as perhaps before consideration it should ap-
pear, that the property of labour should be able to over-balance . . .
Cyclops, Wolverine. Beast, get in the hovercraft! They're here! I can
smell 'em . . . *Nor is it so strange . . . Nor is it so strange. . . ."*

Sometimes the two of them, Max with his pale, high forehead and
dark brown eyes and Thomas, red hair flopping, would burst into the
living room, chasing after each other; they would duck behind chairs,
shoot, move out into the open, and when hit, they would stagger and fall
slowly, holding their chests as they crumpled to the floor. Unwilling (and
unable) to pull them out of their dream, even though they had pulled me
out of mine, I would take a deep breath and pick up my book and
notepad and move to the bedroom. From the bedroom, I would sometimes be chased back to the study, and from there to the living room, and
then back to the bedroom or even to the nanny's quarters, the narrow
room behind the kitchen, where I settled in like an adulterous husband
on a bed covered with underwear. There, amid the peach silk and
curlers, I read a few pages of Augustine. Sometimes people around the
house would shut up when I was reading, but usually not. In America, a
grown man or woman reading at home during the day is not a person to
be taken seriously.

How I longed for an extra hour to read! I would dream of it at night.
On the weekend, when I dropped one of my sons off to play at a friend's
house—that was a good time. I would settle in at a nearby coffee shop
and drink harsh, overboiled coffee, which sent a rush to my brain. I was
launched. But a few minutes later, I would get lost, because the "easy-
listening" radio station or the talk show the restaurant was piping into
the room would now attach themselves to Locke's words and dislodge
my attention. The music and talk filled every public space in America,
the coffee shops, elevators, stores, malls, lobbies, even some of the pre-
tentious "atriums" that had sprung up in mid-Manhattan corporate
headquarters, huge glass-enclosed spaces with pale green, drapelike
trees. Passing through the trees, like fog, was the sheen of electronic vi-
olins.

I loved the present-tense edginess of New York, the serious, constant
tumult, the sense that important business was always underway somewhere. But in this great business city there was virtually no public place
except a library or Central Park in which you could read anything more
demanding than a newspaper or a Grisham. If someone wanted an escape from the general din, he put on a Walkman.

I was as hard-pressed as the students. How sordid would I let my situation get? How far would I slip into the shadow world of studenthood?
I was scrambling, and not always keeping up. Would I go the rest of the

way into squalor, cutting classes, copying notes, catching up at the last minute? More than twenty-five years after finishing college, I was thinking like a harried sophomore, as if all those years of publishing words in magazines hadn't taken place. And what about the exams? Was I going to take them? It seemed a ridiculous thing to do. Yet everyone who heard about my project asked, "Are you going to take the exams?" and with a teasing smile, too. They wanted to see how I would *do*.

Receive a grade from Stephanson? From Tayler? I loved them both, but I didn't want to be graded. It was a no-win situation. If I did "better" than the students, I would feel like a cad; if worse, like an idiot. I was enjoying my time in the classroom, and not only because I was reading and talking seriously. I came in knowing something, a pro, a writer. But now everyone was proposing that I sit down and write with teenagers.

❖ ❖ ❖

Reading Machiavelli, and waiting for some devastating explosion of the famous and incomparable cynicism, I found the beginning pages of his little book *The Prince*, written in 1513–14, rather unexceptionable: First a mock-fulsome dedication to Lorenzo de' Medici, grandson of *the* Lorenzo de' Medici, whose powerful family Machiavelli needed to propitiate. (A veteran Florentine diplomat, Machiavelli was out of office, and wrote *The Prince* while living in the country.) Then some shrewd words on how to govern a colony. But then came this:

> For it must be noted, that men must either be caressed or else anni-
> hilated; they will revenge themselves for small injuries, but cannot
> do so for great ones; the injury therefore that we do to a man must
> be such that we need not fear his vengeance. (p. 9)

Now that isn't simply cynical. More than anything, it's funny. And daring. Men cannot "revenge themselves" for great injuries because, as the beginning of the sentence suggests, and the last confirms, they will be dead. The humor of it was derived as much from the balanced economy of the clauses as from the idea itself; the syntax has the finality of murder. Was Machiavelli possibly a great killing wit as well as the most notorious teacher of political realism? Was "realism" by definition witty?

The Prince might be called a guide to political power—taking it, holding it, dealing with enemies and friends, conquering hostile people and maintaining the loyalty of friendly ones, using mercenaries and regular armies, and so on. It's an utterly worldly book. In the past few weeks, we had read selections by Thomas Aquinas and Christine de Pizan, and I had been eager to run past scholastic philosophy and the Middle Ages in general. I wanted to get to the modern period. Contemporary Civilization was not a history course but a collection of key works in philosophy and political theory, and it jumped over many historical periods, leaping, for instance, almost eight hundred years from Augustine to Aquinas. Though I finally did read everything, I've done some leaping myself, leaving out of this account several extraordinarily important writers on the reading list, not just Aquinas, but also Calvin and Luther, whose writings were central to the Reformation, and Bacon, Galileo, and Descartes, creators of modern scientific reasoning. I had my own obsessions, and I was eager to feed them. I wanted to understand the social demoralization that was overtaking the United States, the fear, the crime, the class warfare, the murderous difficulties of the poor, and the consolidation of political will against them. C.C. had entered its major phase—the key texts of modern political theory and political economy. One searched for the elements of civil society and common identity. What held a society together? Crime and ethnic and interest-group antagonism seemed to be delegitimizing American society in some way. What made it legitimate in the first place?

With Machiavelli, we were thrust into modernity. The state, in Machiavelli, is something man creates with his will. Stephanson filled in the background for us. Italy in the Renaissance was a chaos of warring duchies and states, often dominated by such outside powers as France, Spain, and Austria; and Machiavelli, after years of serving Florence as an emissary to the Papal States and other powers, was looking for a unifier. The game was afoot: Victory would go to the audacious, the knowing, the strategically ruthless. Machiavelli was impatient with the endless intrigues and disgusted by men of mere goodwill. Cesare Borgia, the brilliant and ambitious bastard son of Pope Alexander VI— Machiavelli had met him a few times—was closer to his ideal.

> When he took the Romagna, it had previously been governed by weak rulers, who had rather despoiled their subjects than governed them, and given them more cause for disunion than for union, so that the province was a prey to robbery, assaults, and every kind of disorder. He, therefore, judged it necessary to give them a good government in order to make them peaceful and obedient to his rule. For this purpose he appointed Messer Remirro de Orco, a cruel and able man, to whom he gave the fullest authority. This man, in a short time, was highly successful in rendering the country orderly and united, whereupon the duke [i.e., Borgia], not deeming such excessive authority expedient, lest it should become hateful, appointed a civil court of justice in the centre of the province under an excellent president, to which each city appointed its own advocate. And as he knew that the harshness of the past had engendered some amount of hatred, in order to purge the minds of the people and to win them over completely, he resolved to show that if any cruelty

had taken place it was not by his orders, but through the harsh disposition of his minister. And having found the opportunity he had
him cut in half and placed one morning in the public square at Ce-
sena with a piece of wood and blood-stained knife by his side. The
ferocity of this spectacle caused the people both satisfaction and
amazement. (p. 27)

Yes, I bet it did. The reader, too. I loved the way the dispatching of the
vile but useful de Orco is held to the last possible second. Great comic
timing. Machiavelli was an extraordinary *writer*, something I certainly
had not noticed thirty years earlier when I first read *The Prince*. And after reading so many writers chasing virtue, so much spiritual striving
and metaphysical endeavor, I was thrilled by this our first wicked text, a
book so close in its way to the mental atmosphere of our own world.
Who would hold power? What kind of state would we live in? How
much freedom would we give up to have a stable state? Here, at least,
was a description of authority. Machiavelli would have loathed our
chaos, our confusion and sentimentality.

An ethos and a purchase on reality emerged from the startling frank-
ness, and I don't think you could call it merely cynicism or power worship. Note that the attaining of order and good government—not
holding power itself—is what Machiavelli praises in the excerpt above.
But what should be done to maintain order?

Well committed [cruelties] may be called those (if it is permissible to
use the word well of evil) which are perpetuated once for the need
of securing one's self, and which afterwards are not persisted in, but
are exchanged for measures as useful to the subjects as possible.
Cruelties ill committed are those which, although at first few, increase rather than decrease with time. . . . Whence it is to be noted,
that in taking a state the conqueror must arrange to commit all his
cruelties at once, so as not to have to recur to them every day, and
so as to be able, by not making fresh changes, to reassure people and
win them over by benefiting them. Whoever acts otherwise, either
through timidity or bad counsels, is always obliged to stand with
knife in hand, and can never depend on his subjects, because they,
owing to continually fresh injuries, are unable to depend upon him.
For injuries should be done all together, so that being less tasted,
they will give less offense. Benefits should be granted little by little,
so that they may be better enjoyed. (pp. 34–35)

This is not a passage in praise of cruelty. It's an attempt to describe the
nature of political reality. Simplicity and consistency—what most of us
would call political morality—are not possible for a prince, because his
acts invariably change the context in which subsequent acts must take

place. He continually creates his own reality. That is the nature of power
(I wish Bill Clinton understood it better). By necessity, *in order to adjust
to the changes created by his own acts*, he must dissemble, shift, appear
to be virtuous when he is not. The delayed, two-pronged wit in Machiavelli was produced by his dynamic notion of reality, in which one exercise of power always sets the ground for the next. Reality is in itself
ironic; and Machiavelli's writing is an act of malice directed at the
literal-minded, just as life is a condition of malice directed at the literal-
minded.

> . . . there is no other way of guarding one's self against flattery than
> by letting men understand that they will not offend you by speaking
> the truth; but when every one can tell you the truth, you lose their
> respect. (p. 87)

What seems to be an innocuously virtuous piece of advice—Don't
punish people for telling you the truth—becomes an acid irony. Unimportant people, it turns out, *should* flatter the prince, who need suffer
the truth only from the powerful. No wonder so many people hated
Machiavelli; he was unforgivably candid. But Machiavelli is less a cynic
than someone who understands the use of cynicism. People would not
do what they were supposed to do, or what they were told to do. The
ruler could attain their consent, but only by guile, force, wisdom, selective liberality, and a shrewd moment-to-moment assessment of the situation. Anything else was an illusion.

Stephanson, I could see, was happy. His blue eyes sparkled; he nearly
roared in joyous exposition. "There's an immense break here with the
medieval Scholastic tradition," he said, referring to Aquinas, whom we
had recently discussed. "The Scholastic tradition deals with universals.
In the world of a theologian, life is temporary. But Machiavelli's interested in the particularities of *here and now*. He doesn't participate in a
religious morality play; he's concerned with what is, not what ought to
be. History for him is about time—strategy, tactics—not about space."

Machiavelli not only avoided talk of natural law or the ideal ends of
life, he offered little evidence of what has come to be known as "essentialism"—any kind of a priori notion of an inherent quality in men or
states or goals implanted by God. Men, being alone on this earth, could
do—would do—what they willed. That is what most modern people, religious or not, actually believe, yet it was certainly new in the early sixteenth century. This brazen, unillusioned embrace of things as they are
was both immensely exciting and, in its insistence on actuality, almost
moral; it was irresponsible, Machiavelli was saying, to deny that life was
like this, irresponsible to act as if men were good in the Christian
sense—kind, loving, merciful, unselfish, forgiving.

. . . one ought to be both feared and loved, but as it is difficult for
the two to go together, it is much safer to be feared than loved, if one
of the two has to be wanting. For it may be said of men in general
that they are ungrateful, voluble, dissemblers, anxious to avoid danger, and covetous of gain; as long as you benefit them, they are entirely yours; they offer you their blood, their goods, their life, and
their children, as I have before said, when the necessity is remote;
but when it approaches, they revolt. And the prince who has relied
solely on their words, without making other preparations, is ruined;
for the friendship which is gained by purchase and not through
grandeur and nobility of spirit is bought but not secured, and at a
pinch is not to be expended in your service. And men have less scru-
ple in offending one who makes himself loved than one who makes
himself feared; for love is held by a chain of obligation which, men
being selfish, is broken whenever it serves their purpose; but fear is
maintained by a dread of punishment which never fails. (p. 61)

Which is a stunning application of reason to nasty thoughts. God, what
a mind! Unillusioned, he had attained a false reputation for callous
amorality. He outraged the dull, who thought his work a mere hand-
book for dictators. But in his immense meditation on Roman history,
The Discourses, parts of which we also read, Machiavelli spoke of republicanism and even of separate powers—people, rulers, senate—holding one another in check. And it became clear that Machiavelli, as Isaiah
Berlin has pointed out, was no amoralist at all but a man who believed
in an earlier, pagan sense of morality, the qualities of boldness, courage,
dutifulness, stoicism, and so on, shared by Pericles and the leaders of the
Roman Republic.* These qualities would lead a state to glory. Christian
morality was not wrong but generally useless in a leader and might even
lead to greater disaster—in the sense of anarchy or chaos—than outright
ruthlessness. What was paramount in the private realm might be hapless, even destructive, in the public realm. "We tend to reduce Machiavelli to a realist or power-mad tradition in which the end always
justifies the means," said Stephanson. "But this is not true of Machiavelli. Sometimes it is justified to be ruthless, sometimes to be good. It's
a pragmatic view, the opposite of a morality in which certain things are
universal—such as that killing is always bad. But Machiavelli never says
that the end justifies the means."

Stephanson was pushing us ahead to the next political thinker in C.C.,
Thomas Hobbes. "Machiavelli is at once an international and a provincial figure," said Stephanson. "The state was a prize. You could take it

* Berlin's magnificent essay, "The Originality of Machiavelli," can be found in his collection *Against the Current: Essays in the History of Ideas* (New York: Penguin, 1982).

in your hand. But he's uninterested in legitimacy, and he missed the point that the next two hundred and fifty years would be dominated by absolute sovereigns running the nation-states."

❖ ❖ ❖

Legitimacy became the key issue of the next part of the C.C. reading list. What justified the state? What justified abrogating the absolute freedom of individuals? How did there come to be civil societies and governments at all? There was no reason why Machiavelli should have addressed these issues, but the absence of any sense of stability in his work made reading him a giddy but almost nerve-wracking experience. One never came to a point of rest; power was always for the taking—and then it slipped away. Some of his examples from Roman history offer a kind of tragic cycle, in which power gives way to excesses or the degeneration of rule, leading in turn to mob democracy and disorder, followed by the assumption of power by a new leader, and so on. One searched in vain for a principle of equilibrium; instead, one got a sense of universal strife and dissatisfaction.

The issue of legitimacy was crashing in on the classroom from all sides, and the absence of any such hope in the strikingly modern Machiavelli hit hard, a reminder of the possible chaos that could envelop us in the future.

All newly appointed Columbia faculty in the humanities and in most of the social sciences were expected to teach courses in the core curriculum for a minimum of three years. But not everyone willingly did so. There were occasional dissidents and revisionists, and some outright rejectionists, professors who taught C.C. as a history of patriarchal oppression of women, or who chucked the Greeks and the Enlightenment and turned C.C. into a course about colonialism and anticolonialism, and so on.

I thought it was time to hear one of the dissenting voices. What were the objections, from within the university, to the core curriculum? Arriving in 1987 with a Ph.D. from Princeton, Assistant Professor of English and Comparative Literature Siobhan Kilfeather had taught Lit Hum for three years and had then argued loudly against continuing the course in its current form. Some of the teachers I knew who enjoyed teaching Lit Hum spoke of Kilfeather ruefully: They liked her but thought she was wrong. And now she was on her way out of Columbia—heading for a permanent lectureship at the University of Sussex, in England, a university considered more congenial to radical literary studies than Columbia. Kilfeather, obviously, had not "taken" at Columbia.

She received me in her ground-floor office at Philosophy Hall, a friendly young woman with a lilting voice who argued pleasantly but relentlessly. She began by telling me of her own interests in Irish women writers of the eighteenth century; she was angry that Irish writers had earlier been pressed into the canon of English literature, rather than seen as Irish literature written *in* English. She wanted Irish studies to be established as a separate branch of inquiry. Born a Catholic in Northern Ireland, she knew what it was like to be part of a minority.

But many of her objections to Lit Hum, it turned out, were practical rather than ideological. She focused on the students' difficulties in handling the books. "You've got people of mixed ability," she said, "many of them going into the sciences, and they're asked to take a required course. This is very difficult material to be read quickly. It's hard to absorb the *Iliad* at high speed. They're all being asked to make a very real stretch when many of them can't read a modern novel easily. When I taught Lit Hum, people had substantial difficulties reading the texts; they couldn't sort out the information and handle it: what it meant for books to come from different periods; what it meant to move from one culture to another. It was water off a duck's back."

Some of the students did indeed have difficulties with the books, and I agreed with Kilfeather that many of the freshmen were not experienced readers. But wasn't that the greatness of the course—that intelligent but untrained people hurled themselves at these gigantic works, struggled, made "errors," read parts of the books badly, learned something from their teachers and each other? They had to "stretch," which was Kilfeather's word as well as Tayler's.

I said as much, but she shook me off, and argued for a reduced reading list, with all the works in English. She thought literature lost too much in translation, and this time I partly agreed with her, since occasionally I stared at a page of translated verse and saw nothing. Aristophanes, the comic genius of the Athenian stage, hadn't worked for me at all. In translation, he seemed merely crude. But I wouldn't generalize about translation. Homer was magnificent in Richmond Lattimore's translations and Virgil in Robert Fitzgerald's, and Machiavelli was devastating in any translation, and so on. Her complaint hardly kayoed the courses.

"This is bad popularization," she went on. "You're taking things out of context. In literature, no argument is ever made in a vacuum. What happens is that students think over the most general aspects of the argument and make a vulgar paraphrase of it. Jane Austen came across as a domestic comedy of manners. The students couldn't see Austen in relation to the English novelists who came earlier like Henry Fielding, Fanny Burney, and Samuel Richardson. Also, when people don't have highly developed reading and writing skills, the pleasure of the writing isn't coming through—the pleasure of the sentences isn't coming through. In the end, the students were thrown back on their opinions, and their opinions had nowhere to go. They were stuck with the intractability of the texts."

I was tempted to describe Tayler's way of teaching, which, in part, was intended to relieve the students of mere opinion and to give them a handle on the "intractible" texts; or Shapiro's, which engaged those opinions and then turned them back on the students. Everything that she said might be true, and yet a good teacher could overcome each of these problems, providing sufficient context, introducing students to the pleasure of sentences, and so on. Anyway, this talk of context was an infuriating academic tic. How much of it did students need in order to read pleasurably? How many of these books were read three hundred years ago "in context"? When the books were first written, people just *read* them. The notion of context was an academic rather than a literary or readerly demand—an insistence on orderly exposition of influences and roots and so on, all of which had more to do with controlling the presentation of books in courses than with anyone's pleasure in reading them. People had been reading these books without any context for centuries. They read willfully, driven by pleasure or need, reading good and bad, major and minor works together.

Readers! That's what undergraduate education should be producing. Kilfeather made the classic error of the academic left: She confused literary study (and her own professional interests) with reading itself. One advantage of Lit Hum was that it avoided the procedures of graduate school—the specialized teacher working with specialized students, the depressing professionalization of literature and the subsequent deployment of books in "fields" and "conferences" and all the rest of that career-enhancing bureaucracy. In the core courses, literature and philosophy, for good or ill, remained embedded in nothing more grand than the general culture of the people teaching and reading the books. Kilfeather was a fire-breather, but her ideas led to nothing more radical than reasserting the bureaucratization of literary study. Even *one* course that escaped control offended her.

I asked her if she objected to the idea of the course itself, and a trace of mockery came into the lilt.

"I went to a pretty distinguished university [Cambridge]. Try floating that list around the high tables of Cambridge and Oxford!"

The voice climbed, then climbed higher as she spoke. " 'The canon'— it's a modern American invention. It hasn't always been fixed. The notion that you could make a shopping list of great works and be on top of them seems to me some fantasy of control. At Oxford and Cambridge, you would never get to the end of the list. You wouldn't quantify what books should be on it. It suggests insecurity. It's an American mentality."

Well, a sore point, that, though what she didn't say was that an Oxbridge undergraduate, better educated at high school than his American counterpart, would likely have read many of the books *before* arriving at university. In France, a student who got her high-school baccalaureate was required to read Rousseau and Voltaire, Racine and Molière, Hugo and Baudelaire, Stendhal and Flaubert. That's one reason there were no "lists" soiling the high tables: They weren't necessary. Americans, I was afraid, needed lists, particularly at the end of the twentieth century, or they might not read anything of great value. Later, they could dispose of lists, and read as they pleased. But when they were young, there was very little in their culture impelling them to read seriously at all. As I left Kilfeather's office, I said to myself that I couldn't see how the students' not having read the books in the past could be used as an argument for their continuing not to read them. The logic of her argument seemed to be: They haven't been educated properly; therefore let's not educate them properly.

Chapter *14*

HOBBES AND LOCKE

- Being mugged on the way to work
- *Leviathan*
- *The Second Treatise of Government*
- Cultural failure in the inner cities; what I am owed by the men who mugged me; what I owe them
- Professor Stephanson expounds Locke and I am moved

I got mugged once, on the way to work. I was sleepy, and let down my guard for an instant. In 1982 or 1983, somewhere back there before I bought a computer, I would stay up very late Sunday night, typing and retyping the last draft of a movie review, and then sleep an hour or two before taking the article to the office. On one of these dead Monday mornings, I was coming out of the subway at Forty-second Street between Park and Lexington, right near Grand Central Station, and at the base of a stairway leading to the street a young man was standing around, doing nothing. He wore running shoes—I registered that much—and he stood holding the center railing of the stairs. *Go back*, I told myself. *Go out another exit.* But I was tired, and this exit was the closest to the office, so I walked past him and started up the stairs; and at the top, at the street level, not *on* the street but within the huge arched stone entrance to Bowery Savings Bank, another young man with running shoes was waiting, and I thought, *It's my time.* The kid at the top of the stairs stepped in front of me and put a gun to my chest. Meanwhile, the first one had come up the steps behind me. There was no one else around.

They demanded my wallet. I don't know about other cities, but in New York people are trained from an early age to take their money out of their wallets when they are held up. You give the robbers your cash, and that way they don't get your credit cards, bank cards, and driver's license. I reached for my wallet, but then I just stopped and stood still and looked down at the gun. I am not a brave person, but I was outraged. I thought of refusing or running away. The rational response to armed robbery had deserted me; or perhaps I was so tired I had gone stupid.

They had no right to my cash, no right. *Stall, stall, maybe someone will come along.* The gun, just above my belly, looked fake—more like a cap pistol than a revolver. It was small, grayish, cheaply made. *It's a fake. Run, just run!*

They demanded the wallet again, this time angrily, and once more I went dead and didn't give it to them. But a few seconds later, I pulled out my wallet, removed the cash and held it up. One of the men snatched it, and they were gone. They were gone like that, right down the stairs and into the huge complex of tracks, concourses, stairways, and subway lines—three different lines in all—which gathered underground near Grand Central, and I was so tired and disgusted that I didn't run after them or tell anyone but simply ambled the rest of the way to the office. *Is that it? Is that all?*

"I was just mugged," I told everybody at *New York* magazine as I came in, and they all congratulated me because I hadn't been hurt and still had possession of my wallet. *Congratulations, you've had a successful mugging.*

Nothing had happened, really. It was quite routine. I called the transit police, but there was no point in going downtown to examine mug shots because I hadn't looked into anyone's face. The two men were tall, slender, black, young, maybe nineteen; they wore running shoes, and they carried what appeared to be a homemade revolver. It was the gun I had looked at.

In the office, sitting at my desk, I started to laugh, because I remembered the thoughts passing through my mind during the second little pause before I pulled my wallet out. This was what I had thought: I should argue with them. I should ask them *why.* Why would anyone risk five years in prison for a hundred dollars?

The folly of the American liberal! With a gun in his chest, he wants to argue with street criminals! He wants to persuade them that *crime is not in their best interests.*

I had pretty much forgotten all this. The incident was neither dramatic nor instructive, and if you dwelled on such events while living in New York or any other big American city, you would never leave home. But when reading Hobbes in C.C. class, the surly and implacable Thomas Hobbes, the experience came back. Hobbes was obsessed with what he took to be the constants in human behavior: aggressiveness and the desire for survival. The armed robbery at the subway exit was certainly an example of the first instinct. But was it in any way an example of the second—the instinct for survival? I had wanted to reason with the thieves because I was amazed. More and more, the middle-class man was afflicted with amazement, shocked that anyone would act so self-destructively. A lot of the young men in the inner cities were acting that

way. No one in the white middle-class world really understood them.
But now, reading Hobbes, I wanted to understand.

❖ ❖ ❖

Hobbes built from the ground up; he began with a notion of human nature based on the continuity of egotistical behavior, or what we would
call desire and greed. He had a fundamentally dynamic conception of
life. By the time he came to write *Leviathan*, his principal work of political theory, published in 1651, he had absorbed the influence of Galileo,
whom he knew in Florence in the 1630s. Hobbes, following Galileo's
theories, supposed that heavenly bodies were not, in their natural state,
at rest, as had been believed in the medieval sciences so heavily influenced by Aristotle. Instead, bodies, unless impeded, were constantly in
motion and hence colliding. And so with humans. We are aggressive and
acquisitive, motivated (literally) by the desire for power and the fear of
death.

> For there is no such *finis ultimus*, utmost aim, nor *summum bonum*,
> greatest good, as is spoken of in the books of the old moral philoso-
> phers [*i.e.*, Plato, Aristotle, Cicero, etc.]. Nor can a man any more
> live, whose desires are at an end, than he, whose senses and imagi-
> nations are at a stand. Felicity is a continual progress of the desire,
> from one object to another; the attaining of the former, being still
> but the way to the latter. The cause whereof is, that the object of
> man's desire, is not to enjoy once only, and for one instant of time;
> but to assure for ever, the way of his future desire. And therefore the
> voluntary actions, and inclinations of all men, tend, not only to the
> procuring, but also to the assuring of a contented life; and differ
> only in the way: which ariseth partly from the diversity of passions,
> in divers men; and partly from the difference of the knowledge, or
> opinion each one has of the causes, which produce the effect desired.
>   *A relentless desire of power in all men.* So that in the first place, I
> put for a general inclination of all mankind, a perpetual and restless
> desire of power after power, that ceaseth only in death. And the
> cause of this, is not always that a man hopes for a more intensive de-
> light, than he has already attained to; or that he cannot be content
> with a moderate power: but because he cannot assure the power and
> means to live well, which he hath present, without the acquisition of
> more. (Collier; p. 80)

All of which adds up to the most convincing account of the natural
causes of greed that I've ever read: If you don't stay on the attack, you
don't get to keep what you've already got. Greed, in Hobbes's system,
was produced by justifiable paranoia. What Hobbes has written here in

his forcefully disagreeable way was also a striking anticipation of the Freudian id: It never lets up. We are driven by desires for praise, for glory, for both riches and dignity. Hobbes minimized superiority by birth, the primacy of kings and aristocrats, and created a rudimentary ideology for a new society, a capitalist society. Men are roughly equal, in the sense that any man could kill any other man; advantages of strength and intellect could be canceled by cunning or stealth. At one point, before governments existed, we were all free and equal, and equality produces an ethos of competition and strife.

> From this equality of ability, ariseth equality of hope in the attaining of our ends. And therefore if any two men desire the same thing, which nevertheless they cannot both enjoy, they become enemies; and in the way to their end, which is principally their own conservation, and sometimes their delectation only, endeavour to destroy, or subdue one another. And from hence it comes to pass, that where an invader hath no more to fear, than another man's single power; if one plant, sow, build, or possess a convenient seat, others may probably be expected to come prepared with forces united, to dispossess, and deprive him, not only of the fruit of his labour, but also of his life, or liberty. And the invader again is in the like danger of another. (Collier; pp. 98–99)

What a grim and dislikable writer! Yet how hard he is to shake off! He has his own music—dreadful, somber, relentless—and I came to enjoy his methodically exact style of unpleasant pronouncement, his weighted and heavy-pawed seventeenth-century gait. Hobbes was the first author we had read in either course who wrote in English, and my relief in reading my own language at last, and not a translator's approximation, was overwhelming—but also shadowed with such anxiety as Hobbes always produced.*

His pessimism answered to our fears—of what we are, of what we might become. He was the bogeyman of political theory, an oversized monster almost comical in his lugubrious disenchantment. "Do we think this is what human beings are all about?" asked Stephanson. "Is this unpleasant bastard right?" Stephanson explained that Hobbes had gained his ideas of society from England during the civil wars of the 1640s. A timid man with an inveterate horror of chaos, Hobbes fled to France, and composed *Leviathan* there. His description of life in a state of na-

---

* I found, however, that Hobbes's seventeenth-century spelling, retained in the Penguin paperback edition that Columbia used, slowed me down too much, so I switched to the Collier edition, edited by Michael Oakeshott, who modernized the text.

ture—life without a powerful functioning civil government—is perhaps the single most famous passage in political theory.

> Whatsoever therefore is consequent to a time of war, where every man is enemy to every man; the same is consequent to the time, wherein men live without other security, than what their own strength, and their own invention shall furnish them withal. In such condition, there is no place for industry; because the fruit thereof is uncertain: and consequently no culture of the earth; no navigation, nor use of the commodities that may be imported by sea; no commodious building; no instruments of moving, and removing, such things as require much force; no knowledge of the face of the earth; no account of time; no arts; no letters; no society; and which is worst of all, continual fear, and danger of violent death; and the life of man, solitary, poor, nasty, brutish, and short. (Collier; p. 100)

Dread poured like sweat from the pitiless clauses, from the celebrated, climactically terrible "nasty, brutish, and short." The first state of nature, in the distant past, was not an Eden, but the contrary, a situation of scarcity, deprivation, and fear. At the current moment, says Hobbes, the state of nature exists nowhere, except during civil war; or perhaps among the savages in America; or possibly as a description of relations *among* sovereign states. The state of nature is a fiction—a theoretical construct—but because it is so awful, everyone's interest requires renouncing the possibility of it. Which means renouncing some of your freedom. Not all: You can't lay down your right to defend yourself. But you can give up, in order to have peace, the right to unlimited liberty and aggression—that is, you give up so much of your freedom in relation to others as you would have them give up in relation to you. I won't steal your property because I don't want you to steal mine. A rational calculation of self-interest sealed the compact.

And at that point, having given up your right to absolute freedom— that is, transferred your right to someone else, a sovereign—you are bound to obey. You are bound to obey even the laws that you think are unjust, because to break a law is to act against yourself, the sovereign now embodying your rights and your freedom. Since men, as we have seen, are aggressive and insatiable, desiring always to expand their dominion merely to hold on to what they've got, the sovereign should possess an absolute power to punish. Men need to be overawed: Domestic peace is based on fear. It is the conservative view *in excelsis.*

Now here is the element that has alarmed so many readers of Hobbes, including me: There is a disturbing ambiguity in Hobbes's description of a state of nature. When reading it, I did not imagine I was meant to take it as a description of an aberrant situation. No, whatever Hobbes may say, I was convinced that he meant it to be an exaggerated version of normal life. And certainly, if we didn't read Hobbes that way, as a nightmare version of our normal reality, he wouldn't have the power to haunt us. Which he does.

In Stephanson's class, Noah Martz, the most scholarly of the students, the one who had challenged Leora Cohen's reading of Jewish Orthodoxy, went on the attack. "It's a recipe for totalitarianism," he said.

"For totali-*tar*-ianism?" said Stephanson in mock disbelief. "What a bourgeois thing to say."

He was teasing Noah, one-upping him. In his language, "totalitarian" was a word that had been corrupted by too many ignorant anti-Communist tirades. He was saying, "You, as an intellectual, should not use it lightly." At the same time, I resented his use of the word "bourgeois" as an automatic insult. But I had no time to register a protest; the class swept on. "It's all or nothing," said Noah, his pale face coloring slightly as he modified his language. "The way Hobbes has set it up, it's either total control or no control. It's Manichean."

That was the central problem. There was a maddening lack of gradation in Hobbes's views. The fear of civil disorder carries the citizen along in a torrent of anxiety to the point of forever resigning his freedoms to the sovereign. "Hobbes wanted censorship," Noah said. "He opposed free political discussion in the universities." And he didn't much care, as Stephanson pointed out, whether Charles I or Oliver Cromwell ruled England, as long as one of them did so absolutely. It did not seem to have occurred to Hobbes that life under an absolute sovereign might be worse than life in a state of nature. What if the sovereign were Caligula?

❖ ❖ ❖

In Stephanson's class, almost from the beginning, I had raised my hand now and then and asked a question, sometimes proposing an issue for discussion, and Stephanson had tolerated, even welcomed, my interference—"interventions," he called my remarks, which gave them a formal and calculated sound that I knew I didn't intend. The truth was simpler: I was incapable of staying within my role of observer. Sitting off to the side, against a wall, taking notes, I would grow impatient. I wanted to shout, jump in, argue with Stephanson. Shamefully, I caught myself competing with the students. Stephanson seemed to understand my hunger, because he turned the floor over to me at one point and let me blurt out my thoughts on Machiavelli.

When Stephanson called on me, the students were surprised, but they listened quietly, gravely, and sometimes they responded. I was not the teacher, but I was something or other—a writer or something—and I could speak a little. There was Daddy, stern yet flamboyant, with his Swedish good looks, his wonderful mock-Brit strenuousness, his rather forbidding new-academic talk and his warming generosity; and then there was this other person, an eccentric uncle perhaps.

I had become friendly with a number of them, particularly with Noah, who was altogether remarkable, better informed than me about many subjects, and eager to talk about everything; and I enjoyed listening to Manuel rumbling on and on, a witch doctor without magic. They were sophomores, and much more sure of themselves than Tayler and Shapiro's freshmen. After class, continuing the discussion, we would slowly walk away from Mathematics Hall, in twos and threes, along the side of Low Library, and then down the wide steps in front of Low, descending to College Walk, a setting which—whatever I thought of the Low rotunda—lent a certain grandeur to commonplace arguments. I was a student. I may have fallen behind in the reading, but I loved this slow, meandering departure from the class—so different from normal professional life, where conversation was brief and fragmentary, and you rarely got more than an undertone of what anyone really thought.

In the Hobbes class, I burst in. Think of Wall Street and the inner cities, I said. A Hobbesian case could be made. The lessening of regulation on the Street in the Reaganite eighties, the president praising greed, telling people it's morally okay, even a good thing, and rewarding the wealthy with lower taxes. And look, one result was excessive predation, corruption, insider trading, a reversion to capitalism at its most lawlessly other-annihilating. . . . And in the inner cities, the shrinking of the police presence, the withdrawal of the cop on the beat—and hence the lessening of fear—had made it easier for kids to turn to crime. In the eighties, the fear of punishment had subsided. The war of all against all had broken out. Kids were going after one another with automatic weapons. Hobbes had written a terrific description not only of Yugoslavia after the breakup but of Wall Street, Washington, D.C., and South Central Los Angeles in the last fifteen years.

The students came back at me, insisting that many forces besides a lessening of external coercion caused insider trading and drive-by shootings. And they were right about the latter, I agreed—I knew about the postwar flight of factory jobs from cities like New York, the persistence of racism, the reduced police protection received by inner-city citizens. But couldn't they admit, I asked, that Hobbes might have something to say to them? Couldn't freedom lead to evil as well as to good?

This was nasty talk, and no one liked it. Conversation was often free-ranging in Stephanson's class, but I never heard a single generalization offered about the behavior of a given social group or human beings as a whole. The unwillingness to generalize *at all*—the desire to see absolutely everything as a very special case produced by specific historical circumstances—was the undergraduate version of political correctness.

The crime rate of inner-city black youth was extraordinarily high, and the fear of that crime as well as crime itself was clearly a threat to the society's well-being.* Yet they would not characterize the behavior of those young men. Nor could they entertain the possibility of Hobbes's notion of an essential and unchanging human nature.

If they had known the academic lingo, the students might have said something like this: The notion of a universal "rational self-interest" is a fraud. People don't necessarily act in their own interests. On the contrary, "self-interest" is a construct derived by people who already *have* power and who want to discover an allegedly inborn character trait that would justify acquiring more of it. Powerlessness is precisely the situation that prevented people like the inner-city young men from formulating "self-interest" and acting on it.

With or without the lingo, the students sensed that I was tempting them with the politically incorrect sin of social generalization, and they balked. Only certain personalities, they said, personalities who were rapacious to begin with, were attracted to the career of corporate raider, and something of the same self-selection goes on among young men vicious enough to become crack or heroin dealers and killers.

The discussion ended inconclusively, but a few days after the class I remembered my painless mugging from a decade earlier, and the way I had laughed at myself in the office afterward because I had wanted to argue with the muggers. In a way, the situation in the inner cities was even worse than Hobbes could have imagined. Hobbes assumed that however violent and aggressive, people were motivated by the desire to survive. Yet what was most frightening and baffling about the young shooters in the inner cities was that they acted at times as if their survival had become unimportant to them. Or at least less important than honor and revenge. Fear had been dissolved by something stronger: There wasn't much self-respect to go around, and the most aggressive and lawless among the young men enhanced their own self-respect by diminishing someone else's. They acted as if dignity were a zero-sum game. They committed violence against rivals, against friends, teachers, the elderly, and innocent bystanders; they got killed themselves by other young men or the police, or they wound up in prison.

It was presumptuous, I admit, for any well-fed person to speculate what someone growing up on the street might have felt. If I had been braver, I would have taken the measure of my two assailants by looking them in the eyes. Then I might have learned something. But I was mesmerized by the gun; and I knew that you did not eyeball someone holding a gun on you. I didn't see much. The muggers were dressed in black

---

* By the mid-nineties, crime rates were generally lower, but not among teenagers.

jeans, sweatshirts, and running shoes, while I wore my standard going-to-the-office rig of suit, trench coat, and briefcase. They were skinny, and I was not; they were poor, and I was not. The bourgeois and his enemies. If, as they say, a gun held to your body reveals the self that you have become, I was revealed as divided, angry, and baffled.

Street thugs steal in order to buy drugs or clothes or maybe even food; they attack the affluent far less than people in their own neighborhoods. Most black crime is committed against blacks, so it is African-Americans who suffer the most from the high crime rate among inner-city young men and from the absence of decent locks, private security forces, the money to pick up and move away and wall themselves inside suburban industrial parks and protected residential communities—everything that anxious whites have done to avoid crime. As a white victim, I was already something of an anomaly, since coming downtown to get *me* may have been a rarity for these two men. But if most criminals were acting as Hobbes said predators would, attacking their neighbors, there was this difference: They lived, it almost seemed, as if they thought they had no future, as if their lives did not amount to a "story" but only a series of random acts and improvised defenses.

The cultural left, I thought, may have a point about the socially constructed nature of a universal "rational self-interest." But how much of a point? In the end, I couldn't see why the prior possession of power was a necessary prerequisite to formulating self-interest. In the past, many powerless people in America—poor immigrants from Ireland, China, Italy, Sweden, Russia, Haiti, Korea, and Vietnam, for instance—had created some version of self-interest and acted on it. Could the desire for *survival* really be "constructed"?

No, in our postindustrial capitalist democracy something new was happening. There had been a cultural failure—the conservative usage made me wince, but there were no other words. The combination of jobs flying out of the inner cities, decades of welfare dependency, and the universality of consumerism as a way of life had destroyed the economic stability and the system of values necessary to create "rational self-interest." And the media, including *my* art form, the movies, played a part in this, though not in the way that Janet Reno and other moralists thought.

I don't, for instance, think young men simply imitate things they see in movies or hear in rap lyrics. (Other countries consume the same mass culture we do but have much lower crime rates—Japan, for instance, which receives our movies and TV shows and also makes some of the bloodiest, most violent movies in the world.) But the media spearhead of capitalism—advertising, movies, television—did help create social unrest. They stimulated envy. The media taunted the young men with the erotic allure of the prize, the many prizes, without giving them an inkling of how to attain them. Television, movies, and pop music said "pleasure, pleasure, pleasure" and virtually nothing in the surroundings of the young or in the media said "work." So here is the crunch: As a movie critic and an American man, I believe in pleasure, even in "low" pleasures, "shallow" pleasures, and yet the unrelenting hedonism of the media ethos is obviously killing us. Aroused yet dispossessed, the criminal young men have become the fools of capitalism. They want the goods. Successful people have the goods. There are few other ways of defining success and status. That longing dissolves normal self-interest. In the absence of control by fathers or external coercion, chaos ruled the inner cities.

I don't mean to imply that crime is the only force delegitimizing American society, but it is obviously having a huge effect on our wavering civility. Crime, by undermining trust between strangers, by causing businesses to close, the law-abiding to move away, public intercourse to shrivel, private rituals to grow overburdened and testy—crime corrupts everyone, not just the criminal. Physically, I had not been hurt in my encounter. But I had taken its poison into my life, becoming less adventurous in moving around the city, more wary, more suspicious, more closed in on myself and my family and friends—more tightly enveloped within the fortress of my life—and I had passed this unhappy vigilance and self-enclosure on to my children. In a variety of ways, I had lost part of my soul to the fear of crime. Perhaps if I had raised my face from the gun and looked the two muggers in the eyes, I would have seen some meaning that I now missed, some sign or emotion that would have made the entire encounter less forlorn, less empty and redundant as a social exchange. But I kept my eyes down not only because I was afraid but because I didn't want the young men to see how much I despised them.

A civil society could not exist if men and women did not trust one another on the street—that was a bottom-line gloss on Hobbes's fiction of a social contract. It sounds asinine to say that street criminals had refused the social contract, since no one had ever asked them (or us) to accept it. They had refused it nonetheless, by losing their impulse to survive.

Nothing in the C.C. readings prior to Hobbes prepared one for so dire a view of social reality. Plato and Aristotle, looking at America, would simply not have understood a society with so small a sense of common enterprise. The Old Testament speaks of vengeance, the New of mercy, but both vengeance and mercy make sense morally only as applied to *exceptions*—the rare and desperate cases that require special responses. When almost a third of a given section of the population fell afoul of the law, neither vengeance nor mercy is likely to have much effect as deterrent or as healing balm. Crime in sufficient volume creates its own momentum and alters the moral landscape, re-creating success as getting away with crime and failure as getting caught.

It was an awful thing to say of someone that he had lost the will to survive; it meant among other things that one might accept the death of that person more easily. I was aware of the antagonism in the thought, which was now widespread. In my own case, I didn't want anyone dead, including the two men who held me up. All I wanted was my liberty on the streets of New York. The criminal young men owed me my liberty. The question remained: What did I owe *them*? It was something limited. That is, I did not feel I had betrayed the two young men or failed them. I had given up on liberal guilt. With a gun pointed at a spot just above my belly, I did not care that these two young men may have been victims of historical injustice. Their failure was not my fault. But that is not the same thing as saying that I had no relation to them, no obligation to them, or that I owed the next generation nothing.

❖ ❖ ❖

C.C. was a text-based course—we jumped from masterpiece to masterpiece—but Stephanson firmly planted many of the books in their time and place. Stephanson had a talent for brief characterization of historical epochs. Holding forth, he was spontaneous and joyous. Along with his black jackets and white T-shirts, he often wore something at the neck—an ascot, say, or a scarf (never a tie)—and on one public occasion swung into a lecture hall with so much panache that my wife, who was with me that day, said, "He looks like a Swedish rock star." In his little C.C. section, he talked fluently in his cadenced Anglo-academic way, and I found myself grateful for these brief impromptu lectures on the changes in agriculture or weaponry in the sixteenth century and the military techniques of the Prussian Army in the eighteenth century.

In our classes on Hobbes, Stephanson had done some table-setting. English feudal society, he said, differed from that of continental Europe. The warrior function of the aristocracy diminished early; the anti-Catholic Henry VIII sold Church lands in the sixteenth century to the gentry in order to finance his continental adventures, thereby encouraging trade, and so on, a series of historical accidents producing an "early" version of capitalism in England and a new form of acquisitive behavior from which Hobbes may have taken his ideas about the essentially competitive nature of human personality.

And now with John Locke, we had jumped into the modern period. In fact, we were so far into the reality of modern England and the United States that I initially found Locke a little boring. He seemed mild and reasonable and highly commonsensical and even, compared to Hobbes, a little prosy and unexciting. At least at first. But then one began to feel relieved by the normalcy of his ideas, happy to be free of the awful anxiety that Hobbes induces. One regained a sense of hope about human affairs. Finally, in a rush, one realized the momentousness of what Locke had accomplished. He had laid out virtually the entire ideology of the liberal bourgeois state.

For me, the question was, Could he speak to our fears now? Could he tell us anything about our chaos, about boys risking prison or death for a few dollars?

Locke was trained as a doctor and made significant contributions to philosophy and psychology. His key political text, which we read in its entirety (it was densely written but short) was the *Second Treatise of Government*, a theoretical work that he probably composed, along with an earlier political treatise, sometime between 1679 and 1683, and for a very practical purpose. He had joined a group of conspirators looking for a way to force Charles II to give up his plan of making his Catholic brother, James, successor to the throne; Locke no doubt wanted to provide the theoretical basis for deposing a king. The conspirators failed, James ascended, and Locke fled to Holland for a while. But after the Glorious Revolution of 1688–89, in which James II was deposed, Locke returned, and published his little book, which, in the event, became a de facto justification for the revolution that had just occurred. Locke argued against the divine right of kings and in favor of limited government; he set up the theoretical basis of *rights*—not just political rights but property rights. Reading the *Treatise*, one keeps stumbling across notions (such as the right to refuse arbitrary taxation) that turned up a hundred years later in the Declaration of Independence. Locke was Thomas Jefferson's master.

We were back in the state of nature, the theoretical playpen filled with the building blocks of land, men, and goods, but this time the members of it were less feral, less belligerent. Only *some* men would threaten other men's property or lives. Most men would be ruled by reason, and reason would suggest that since we were all in the same boat, we ought to preserve one another so as to preserve ourselves. Just as in Hobbes's theoretical construct, men gave up their right to absolute freedom, and formed a civil government, but with this extraordinary difference—they could set up any kind of government they wanted and *change* it whenever they wanted. In Locke's system, there was no justification for absolutism. How could there be? If the sovereign to whom you gave your liberty then stole your property or took your life, you were back in a state of nature. So what could have been the point of leaving it?

The boring Locke! The good Locke! Even, most condescendingly, "the wise Locke," as Rousseau called him. Yet this boring theory had got the main things superlatively right and appeared, in the 1990s, to be carrying all before it. Locke established the theoretical underpinnings not only of the modern Western state, with its expanding rights, its representative bodies and popular sovereignty, but the underpinnings of capitalism, too, with all its energies and inequities.

Back in the state of nature, men not only possessed their bodies, they possessed their labor. What else do they possess? Whatever they mix their labor with.

> He that is nourished by the acorns he picked up under an oak, or the apples he gathered from the trees in the wood, has certainly appropriated them to himself. No body can deny but the nourishment is his. I ask then, when did they begin to be his? when he digested? or when he eat? or when he boiled? or when he brought them home? or when he picked them up? and it is plain, if the first gathering made them not his, nothing else could. That *labour* put a distinction between them and common: that added something to them more than nature, the common mother of all, had done; and so they became his private right. And will any one say, he had no right to those acorns or apples, he thus appropriated, because he had not the consent of all mankind to make them his? Was it a robbery thus to assume to himself that what belonged to all in common? If such a consent as that was necessary, man had starved, notwithstanding the plenty God had given him. We see in *commons*, which remain so by compact, that it is the taking any part of what is common, and removing it out of the state nature leaves it in, which *begins the property*; without which the common is of no use. And the taking of this or that part, does not depend on the express consent of all commoners. Thus the grass my horse has bit; the turfs my servant has cut; and the ore I have digged in any place, where I have a right to them in common with others, become my *property*, without the assignation or consent of any body. The *labour* that was mine, removing them out of that common state they were in, hath *fixed* my *property* in them. (pp. 19–20)

This is straightforward enough, except for that remarkable shift near the end, where the labor that fixes Locke's property in materials becomes not only his own labor but that of his servant and also whoever digs the ore out of the mine with Locke. So the property that becomes his is not simply as much as he can eat or make use of. The invention of money— or some sort of medium of exchange—changes the game. People can buy more than they can use; they can convert spoilable food into unspoilable cash. And they can buy the labor of landless men, which, when mixed with property, becomes the owner's labor, too. In sum, *Locke accepted that inequities of property were inevitably part of man's leaving a state of nature.*

Quite a trick. Capitalism with its unequal accumulations, its extremes of rich and poor, had received, in theory, the blessings of legitimacy: Accumulating large amounts of property was a natural right. Eventually such notions got fixed into American law, of which possession, as they say, is nine-tenths. For a Rousseauian, a Marxist, or any kind of radical egalitarian, it was a disastrous moment in political theory; for capitalism, it was the glorious revolution itself.

❖   ❖   ❖

But Locke left some things out, and I thought once again of my encounter at the top of the stairs. The two men who robbed me of my cash, in Locke's terms, had violated the rule of self-interest by placing me and them in a state of war. Self-interest should have protected us both, but it failed on that occasion, and Locke suggested little but rational calculation and rights as a way of holding a society together. If anything was obvious in the America of the 1990s, "rights," however central to our sense of our own place in the community, were not enough: The sense of obligation had failed; the sense of the *community's* right had withered; the sense that we were all in the same boat had collapsed.

What the nation owed the young men of the inner cities—what I owe them—is an environment that encourages work. Aristotle and Plato's notion of complete involvement in citizenship was obviously hopeless in a country as devoted as this one is to the myths of individualism, the private moment, the private pleasure, the private success. Work is our citizenship; work is the basis of the social compact in a bourgeois democracy. Welfare reform, black capitalism, investment and shopping and banking within neighborhoods—if we had the will, we could reconsecrate work. It is the only long-term solution to high crime rates.

❖   ❖   ❖

"Locke wanted to legitimate *ownership*," Stephanson boomed. "The land that can be used and the willingness to use it *confers* rights. This is a notion that looks ahead to imperialism and the displacement of the Indians in America. Andrew Jackson used variations on Locke's argument: The Indians have no rights to their land because they can't put it to productive use. Teddy Roosevelt said the same sort of thing. Whereas we have the right to it."

His voice rising, he also mentioned Israel's justification for taking over lands left uncultivated by the Palestinians. But no one wanted to follow him down *that* contentious road, and the idea was left hanging.

"I daresay," said Manuel, "that Native Americans *did* produce in the Lockean sense, and not only that, the Indians *showed* the Europeans how the land could be used."

So! Andrew Jackson's arguments for displacing the Indians from their turf provided cover for a big land grab. And these arguments were derived from Locke. Score one for political correctness. I was waiting for Stephanson to point out as well that Locke in his old age had invested in the slave trade, an act that would seem to contradict his notion of a man's inalienable right to his own labor. Was Locke not a hypocrite? A racist? But Stephanson surprised me yet again. He took the high road, and pressed on to a conclusion.

"The government keeps order and protects property—it *preserves* your rights. It's an incredibly useful line of thinking, restated in the Declaration of Independence and the Constitution. One of the ways that you assure power isn't arbitrary is by dividing authority. And if the government seizes your rights, you can rebel—it's a rebellion that claims it isn't a rebellion but a *restoration* of natural rights of someone who's being imposed on." His voice rose. " 'Our rights as proper Englishmen have been violated.' That's what the colonial revolutionaries were saying. They were restoring their inalienable rights. You are never above or beyond the constitutional framework, and if anyone oversteps this boundary, we have the right to overthrow him."

On and on he went, celebrating constitutional democracy, and by this time I was moved; I was almost in tears. It was ridiculous to get so emotional, I knew, but I loved having my own system expounded to me by a left-wing Swede. "This is a very radical argument," he suddenly said, stopping at last. The word "radical" came as a surprise, but he was right, of course—however familiar to us, the argument still hadn't been accepted by most of the world. Stephanson, in contrast to a good part of the academic left, which argued that American constitutional liberties were a sham, knew that the democratic idea would always be radical.

"Amen," I said to myself. It was the end of the fall semester. The first half of C.C. was over.

Chapter *15*

EXAMINATION

~ The Lit Hum exam: I learn what a nervous breakdown is
~ Western man attains self-knowledge

A group of nervous students from Shapiro's class stood milling about, waiting to get into the room. It was a windy, foul day in the second week of December, and a few minutes earlier, as I walked across campus, the wind had got under my parka somehow, and I felt the melancholy chill, the forlorn, dark-winter-day depression of a student who had to take an exam.

Shapiro's students were surprised to see me. Rebecca laughed, and Joseph smiled, and Henry looked at me strangely, as if I were a nut. Then a couple of them said in horror, "But you'll throw off the curve!"

"I'm not being graded."

"You came to *watch*?" said one young woman, disgusted, as if she had discovered a new form of vice.

"No, I'm *taking* it."

I had resisted the idea for a long time. But once classes ended (there was a study period of a week), I began to think it might be fun just to do it. Just go in there and take the Lit Hum exam. Stephanson was a splendid fellow, but during the semester of C.C. there had been a slight political tug of war between us, nothing at all unpleasant—he was amused, I thought, by what a stolid liberal and occasional neoconservative I was—and I wasn't ready to write an exam for him. Anyway, I was more excited, in this first semester, by the Lit Hum than the C.C. books. I would see how much I could remember. I had read everything, and enough of it would stay in my head so I could answer the questions. They always gave you a choice, didn't they?

But then, a few days before the exam, my heart began thumping heavily. What if I didn't know the answers? What would I do—smile, nod to everyone, and walk out? Write a few debonair sentences and leave the rest of the pages blank? What would I be writing in, anyway? Did they still use those little blue notebooks with the rule down the left side?

I flipped through my notes, read *The Bacchae* again, read sections of Plato again. . . . My God, I was cramming, and after a few days of this, my unease hadn't vanished. I was going to take an *exam*. I had a strange pulling in my stomach, and the muscles along the right side of my neck had become tangled and bunched, so that every time I turned my head to the left, I felt a solid line of pain from my right shoulder up along my neck and behind my right ear. This was getting serious. It was ridiculous, but it was serious. I put aside other work, stopped going to movies, and read through class notes again. Should I start reading essays on the works?

❖ ❖ ❖

We filed into the room, not our usual place in Hamilton, but a low-ceilinged classroom in the International Affairs Building with two big conference tables. Shapiro, in a jolly mood, laid out cookies and orange juice for everyone, and then gave us the exam questions and a couple of blue books, the old blue books. And the old questions:

> The theme of language—as "winged words," mere flashy rhetoric, or slippery verbal signs—appears frequently in works we have read this term . . .

> Many of the characters in the works we have read this semester suffer in different ways for different reasons and toward different ends. Consider how and what these characters gain by their suffering (and their reactions to it).

Oh, God, I should have known. The dreariness of a college exam! "Discuss the theme of self-ignorance as it is treated in three works you have read this semester, focusing upon both the similar and different ways . . ." Yes, compare and contrast. I remember them well, the Mutt and Jeff of undergraduate life. *I can't do this. I'll give them winged words and three kinds of suffering and a blast of self-ignorance, and they can shove it!*

I was sweating, and my heart was trying to leave my chest, so I looked up at Shapiro's students to see how they were doing. But none of them seemed at all troubled. No, the students, the *children*, were calmly reading the questions. This was a ritual that they knew well. Henry stretched his muscles, turning his neck this way and that like a slugger coming to bat; and Susan, who was a left-hander, put her head down on the conference table on the right side of the blue notebook and calmly set to work, almost cradling the book with her arm, her hand traveling rapidly and surely across the lines and almost touching her face.

Being examined is one of the things you become an adult to avoid. Once you pass twenty-five, you learn how to cover your weaknesses and ignorance and lead with your strengths. Every adult, by definition, is a corner-cutting phony; experience teaches you what to attend to and what to slough off, when to rest and when to go all out. But now, I had lost that advantage; I was writing in blue books.

I read the exam over and over, scribbling desperate little notes to myself. Shapiro had laid a box of Hydrox cookies at my end of the table, and I quickly ate about a third of them. After fifteen minutes or so, I began writing: "In Book VI of the *Aeneid*, Aeneas visits the underworld and encounters the shade of Dido, who . . ." Even though it violated my sense of the importance of books to treat them this way, as prisoners in cells, to be let out for a walk now and then, I still wanted to do *well*. With a ghastly groan, the rusted, ancient exam-taking machinery began to turn.

But then my writing hand went into lockup. Sharp pain attacked the joint below my thumb. I was gripping the pen too hard, one of those seventy-nine-cent BICs whose ink won't flow dark and easy but comes out only slowly, in a thin, pale line. I removed the pen, and my hand remained bent, and rigid with tension. It looked like a goddamn *claw*. I was used to writing on a computer, and this was torture. The students, to my relief, were absorbed in their work and completely ignored my mishaps. Shapiro, who had left us alone, came back into the room bearing cartons of grapefruit juice.

Taking an exam is the grown-up's classic anxiety dream, and one thing I learned about living such an event was that it may be even worse than your dream. When the three hours were over, I cabbed down from Columbia to Barocco, our favorite Italian restaurant in Tribeca, in Lower Manhattan, where I met my wife and a friend, and I quickly had a double scotch and most of a bottle of white wine. Later, at home, still quaking, I swallowed a beta blocker, a Xanax, and two fingers of Nyquil.

I slept, but not for long. At 5 A.M., I sat bolt upright in bed, pulling up so rapidly that I reached above my head as if to stop my noggin from hitting the ceiling. Cathy was sound asleep beside me. The children were asleep in their bedrooms. I walked into the living room, where I could hear an occasional car passing on West End Avenue. In the study, I worked at the computer for about an hour. That didn't do it, however. My heart was beating as heavily as ever. Gee, I said to myself, after all these years, it's nice to find out what a nervous breakdown *is*. I ran around the living room, round and round in circles, and finally, winded, the tension drained a bit, I lay on the couch, my temple of reading.

The purpose of the exam was not only to give the student a grade but to pull the course together. It imposed coherence, which meant, in practice, that any Lit Hum or C.C. exam was a function of "the hegemonic narrative." The left-academic revisionists gave exams, too, exams that enforced *their* narratives, which ran counter to the traditional ones.

Dear God, the three forms of "self-ignorance," or whatever it was. The three forms of suffering—what was it? The three forms of *what*? Why did everything come in threes? And why did the cultural left not attack the giving of exams? Maybe they did attack it. An exam was the imposition of a phallocentric dominating consciousness, the imposition of a male ethos of competitiveness through hegemonic blue books ... whose only functions was to impose ... to impose ...

... A warmth was spreading from below my belly (it was the only way to get to sleep), and forms, ideal forms, the ideal of man and woman, were eyeing each other, circling, and then removing their garments and joining together. . . .

Western man had triumphed. He had passed from self-ignorance to self-knowledge.

Winter Break

For a few days, I had no desire to read. Let the books sit there. Let them sit on the table at the side of the dining room, or stacked up in the office, or beside my bed. I busied myself around the house and took care of the children and had long, long talks with Cathy. I took my station at the sofa, but without book or notebook or even a light turned on, and I listened to the cars on West End Avenue drive through the December and January slush. Below, in the basement, the boiler revved up and gave off a slight hum (we lived on the second floor), then shut itself down. These old New York apartment buildings—ours was from 1926—had their mysteries. The heat came up through the pipes, releasing an outburst of groans, knocks, and lunatic bangs, and then made its way into the rooms in a wave so thick and hot you wanted to disconnect the radiators altogether; and I thought of overheated schoolrooms from forty-five years earlier and sloping oak desks with black metal feet, and tall streaked windows with snow clinging to the wooden frames that held the panes. For an hour at a time, I sat on the sofa doing nothing, listening to West End Avenue and trying to make music in my head out of the banging radiator, until the boys came and got me and pulled me into one of the bedrooms, and we wrestled on the bed, and Max, the older one, stood on the high brass bedstead, and jumped onto my side or back, and the pain was not pain but only the pressure of warmth; and then all of us piled in together, legs and arms stuck into necks, knees and elbows in stomachs, and I got pulled down into the mass of limbs and then rose again like a ship coming out of a deep valley, then down again, all the way to the bottom, and I knew that the knotted muscles along the right side of my neck leading to my shoulder were knotted no longer.

In C.C., there were some books to catch up to, and a general reckoning to make. I realized I could not write about everything. It was impossible, there were too many "great books"—and too many great books. And without supreme interest, without love, without confidence, I had no right to speak. So I would let Thucydides go and also Aristophanes, and Aquinas, Luther, and Calvin, and even René Descartes, stirring and central as he was. Such courses propelled one without preparation or much equipment against large, standing peaks, and sometimes one slid off without quite climbing past the middle or even getting a firm grip— Professor Kilfeather had a point about that—but there would be another peak to climb the following week, and sometimes one climbed and climbed. Kilfeather left that part out.

I was roused and happy. I had been supremely happy all through the semester despite my scrambling, my struggles to concentrate, my moments of chagrin and alarm. All day long, every day of the semester, I pressed against the frame of my life, trying to pack something into each minute. I was a reader again, and after a few days rest I wanted more— more difficulty, the more difficulty the better—and as I read, not looking for myself, but finding myself nonetheless, provoked into seeing by the books, I spied the beginnings of an edge where before there had been only an amorphous blur leading to nothing.

SECOND SEMESTER

Chapter 16

DANTE

~ Judith Sterngold complains that Dante is a hater
~ The *Inferno*
~ I cannot rise
~ Professor Shapiro's students put people in hell but miss the physicality of the poem
~ We hear some of Dante's Italian and everyone stops breathing

Judith Sterngold, the student in Tayler's class who had held her head when confronted with the paradoxes of the New Testament, was indignant again.

"Where is Dante coming from?" she asked.

Enjoying her moment of effrontery, she smiled slightly, her head cocked to the side. She had dark hair, very large eyes, and a way of staring at you when she spoke that was almost unnerving. She was a very direct woman. "Why is he so obsessed with these people? Who is he to come up with these tortures?"

She was speaking of the *Inferno*, the first part of Dante's *Divine Comedy*, the third Lit Hum reading of the new semester (after the New Testament and Augustine). As she spoke, I sighed deeply. The great Christian epic is a flabbergasting work, crazily methodical, both sublime and grotesque, cruel, dismaying, a work that bursts the usual moral and literary categories. In the *Inferno*, Dante created the topography of hell, with levels of pain and suffering appropriate to every sin, and he put into his landscape of punishment not only historical figures and characters from mythology but also his contemporaries.

"These are real people in Florence," said Tayler.

"He's getting at those people he hates," she said, "and he puts it in a religious context to make it seem like a religious work. He's covering up his hatred."

Part of me agreed with her. I was amazed by the *Inferno*. Everyone was amazed by it, by the frights, the obscenities, the filth and effluvia of a vision in which execration was often the central act of perception, and

229

suffering the central spectacle of desire. The sinners—the lustful, gluttonous, treacherous—are caught forever. *Forever.* One had to remind oneself of that. In this passage set in the Eighth Circle, serpents surround and tear at thieves, who catch fire, burn, and are then reconstituted, like the phoenix. But when they are reborn out of their own ashes, they only suffer again.

> Among this cruel and depressing swarm,
> ran people who were naked, terrified,
> with no hope of a hole or heliotrope.
>   Their hands were tied behind by serpents; these
> had thrust their head and tail right through the loins,
> and then were knotted on the other side.
>   And—there!—a serpent sprang with force at one
> who stood upon our shore, transfixing him
> just where the neck and shoulders form a knot.
>   No *o* or *i* has ever been transcribed
> so quickly as that soul caught fire and burned
> and, as he fell, completely turned to ashes;
>   and when he lay, undone, upon the ground,
> the dust of him collected by itself
> and instantly returned to what it was:
>   just so, it is asserted by great sages,
> that, when it reaches its five-hundredth year,
> the phoenix dies and is reborn again;
>   lifelong it never feeds on grass or grain,
> only on drops of incense or amomum;
> its final winding sheets are nard and myrrh.
>   And just as he who falls, and knows not how—
> by demon's force that drags him to the ground
> or by some other hindrance that binds man—
>   who, when he rises, stares about him, all
> bewildered by the heavy anguish he
> has suffered, sighing as he looks around;
>   so did this sinner stare when he arose.
> Oh, how severe it is, the power of God
> that, as its vengeance, showers down such blows!
>   (canto XXIV, 91–120)

The head and tail thrust through loins is of course an unspeakable violation, an image of permanent humiliation and entrapment. So much suffering and obscene torment! And what was Dante's relation to it? The students were shocked, for all this terror is set forth in the name of "primal love." And no matter how hard some of them tried, they could not find love in the *Inferno*. Dante, a great religious writer, outraged all their pieties. And for once, though uneasily, I thought they were right.

Like some of Dante's sinners—the schismatics, to be precise—I was split down the middle. At the beginning of my year in school, I had promised myself that my own pleasure would be the principle and motive of what I celebrated. No bowing before idols; no piety without enjoyment. Joyless appreciation was the academic curse, and I would not fall under it. I would stick to my own belief: Pleasure is the way of knowledge. Which meant I would admit when I did not enjoy something and had not learned from it. But pleasure needs cultivation; pleasure might be inadequate, and for the first time, I thought pleasure could be shaped by ignorance. My pleasures might be too limited to read Dante. In Lit Hum, you fall by not rising, or, in Professor Tayler's terms, you shrink by not stretching yourself enough to read a work that lies outside your expectations. You see not what is unique about the work but only how it differs from those expectations. In effect, you're reading yourself. O Narcissus! The book becomes your reflecting pool. I knew I was in danger of falling in.

Most serious work of the Italian Middle Ages was composed in Latin, but Dante, in a radical break, wrote in the vernacular—in Florentine Italian. Like so much revolutionary work in the arts, the poem offers a violent shift downward—down to the vernacular, the body, the common emotions and the common life. And it's the kind of shift that creates an entire new literature, and perhaps brings a new way of life into being. For T. S. Eliot and W. H. Auden, for Christian Gauss, Edmund Wilson's teacher at Princeton, and for millions of readers and scholars, *The Divine Comedy* was the central literary work of the Christian era.

At eighteen, I had accepted the *Inferno* as the expression of a fervently passionate medieval belief. In order to read it, I told myself, I didn't need to believe as a Florentine of 1300 believed. The poem was an enthralled structure of fear and hope, and Dante himself was split between terror of sin and obsession with punishment. I remember admiring Dante's mood of somber dread and even enjoying sections that were cruelly funny—so exact and detailed about the monstrous and deformed. I would read the poem as a metaphor; it had nothing to do with me. In 1961, Lit Hum students read a prose translation (by the Scot John D. Sinclair), and the *Inferno*'s stature as great poetry was never raised in class as an issue.

But now I saw that I had gotten it wrong. The way I had dealt with it as a freshman was trivial and complacent. Because you couldn't just read it metaphorically, as an allegory or as moral drama, you had to read it first of all as a poetic literalization of the unspeakable—a gigantic created reality that was at the same time a reflection of life on earth. Dante's hell was arranged by circles, concentric circles dug into the earth in the shape of a funnel. At the top of the funnel, on the surface of the earth, lay Jerusalem, the place of Jesus Christ's death; at the bottom, at mid-earth, Satan's realm, the ninth and lowest circle. One progressed downward into greater degrees of sin and punishment, a torment set aside for every vice and error, ending at the frozen pit, where even tears turned to ice. There, at the bottom, three-headed Lucifer chews on Brutus and Cassius, the betrayers of Caesar; and on Judas, who betrayed Christ. The *Inferno* was both the opening section of Dante's cosmic, geometaphysical plan (two other gigantic poems followed) and a table of ethical values. The lustful, the thieving, the treacherous. Bad, worse, worst. Circles, rings, zones. Pain, torment, agony.

What I hadn't noticed at eighteen was how much of the mass and muck of medieval life Dante had crowded into this imaginary landscape—the sewage on the streets, the muddy roads, the stinks and miasmas, the sick and deformed hobbling along. And the punitive harshness comes through as well—tortures and dungeons, plots and conspiracies and frauds and scandals. Whatever else could be found in it, the poem was a work of genius redolent of the Middle Ages in the sinister, clichéd sense. One felt the power of curses, the fear of secret pacts and long-held hatreds.

It was an amazing achievement of realism as well as of fantasy. But as I read, I felt a mounting disgust and anger. Dante himself, or rather a poetically fictionalized version of Dante, is the central character. At the beginning of the *Inferno*, the character Dante is thirty-five years old and lost in "a shadowed forest." He is suffering what we would call a midlife crisis. His soul is in danger. In order to save himself, he has to go through the experience of seeing the consequences, the embodiment, of sin. He is led through hell by none other than Virgil, the greatest poet of antiquity (the medieval Italians knew of Homer only by retellings of his works). Virgil shepherds Dante through the terraces and plateaus of vice, but he can never leave hell, where he resides (in limbo, along with other pagan worthies). Beatrice, the little girl whom the actual Dante had seen once when he was eight, and she some eight months younger, and who later died at twenty-five—Beatrice, whom Dante had long ago adopted as his muse, will take him through the next section of the Divine Comedy, purgatory (*Purgatorio*), and then through paradise (*Paradiso*), and in the end, Dante will have a beatific vision. Dante called his work *Commedia* because it progressed from darkness to light, from damnation to salvation.

The arrogance of it is stunning. Both Odysseus and Aeneas, in the course of their adventures, make frightening trips to the underworld, where they visit fallen comrades and listen to predictions of their own future. But these men are military heroes who have a certain familiarity with death. Dante the poet made *himself* the hero of his trip to the underworld, and he brought much of Florentine history and politics along with him. Dante wrote the poem in bitter exile. In 1302, during one of the endless struggles for power within Florence, he was caught on the wrong side. He had been sent to Rome and a mission to the pope, and in his absence he was condemned to exile, and later to death. He never returned to Florence, writing *The Divine Comedy* and other works while wandering from one Italian court to another. Something enraged and personal, almost a settling of scores, had fallen into the sublime plan. That is what Sterngold complained of.

What she may have missed, however, is the degree to which Dante was necessarily obsessed with public morality. If one reminds oneself that Florence was a vulnerable medieval city, often under siege, the poem's table of values makes more sense. Dante put in his hell cowardly, diffident people—people who don't "commit" themselves, as we would say—and he rated people who wasted their possessions lower than murderers. In general, private and appetitive sins were not as grave as violence against God or self; sins against the community were graver still; and political treachery the worst sin of all. In brief, the welfare of the community determines the scheme of punishment. The knave who tells secrets to the wrong person, or splits allies, or leaves the gates open so the enemy may enter creates disaster for everyone.

Sterngold didn't catch the civic passion; she saw only punishment, though I can't blame her. The fictional Dante, in Virgil's company, passes through each circle and watches as the sinners writhe up to their necks or fall head downward in slime, shit, or fire. They are stung by mosquitoes, lashed by hurricanes, horsewhipped by demons; torn apart by fiends and bitches; maimed, gutted, forced to walk on all fours with heads backward, their tears falling in the clefts of their buttocks. It is not that Dante the character holds himself apart—he doesn't. He is wounded and frightened by what he sees, fainting at one point. Nevertheless, the suffering is there for his spiritual education and improvement. And also the reader's improvement.

But what of pleasure in the suffering of others? It was not an emotion that many people in 1300 necessarily understood as sinful. But we do understand it that way. Judith Sterngold was complaining about the morally questionable experience of *fascination*, which, as moviegoers, we all know something about. (In fairness, Dante may have known about it, too: At one point, Virgil has to warn the Dante figure not to get *too* interested.) Fascination can be a state of irresponsible power: violent spectacle as entertainment. Violence in art, we moviegoers say, can only be justified by the beauty, power, or moral seriousness of the presentation. Otherwise, it's exploitation of our pleasure in cruelty. I have spoken earlier of "the morality of the spectator." Revulsion at unjustified violence is an example of it. And although the *Inferno* met every conceivable criterion for violence in art, something about its fervor still affronted and even wounded the reader.

When Sterngold made her remarks, Tayler, for once, went blank. He stared at her through his specs. "Look," he said stiffly, "you're not the alien mind; you've got to try to understand before you judge. The alternative is to put the book down and destroy it."

That was a shot to the chops. No one wanted to be responsible for *destroying* a book he didn't like. I was certainly in favor of students continuing to read the *Inferno*, if only to understand—leaving aside questions of literary greatness and influence for a second—what fanaticism in a great Western mind looks and feels like. In class, Tayler worked with the details, looking for clues to the way Dante's imagination worked, and we analyzed several episodes, which were amazingly packed with significance. The students grouchily began to respond, and some of them, at least, became convinced that the poem was a remarkably intricate yet unified work.

As I watched from my spot at the back of the room, Tayler built up a unified structure from fragments. But I was almost numb. Try as I might, I would not rise, I could not climb above a literal response. I couldn't say, as I had at eighteen, "This has nothing to do with me," and simply enjoy the *Inferno* as a somber and grotesque entertainment or as an amazing structural achievement or as a poem about the body. My role as a disconnected connoisseur of suffering would be too demeaning. Teenagers may cheer the assorted outrages and dismemberments at horror movies and then laugh them off the next day, but this was outrage and dismemberment carried out by *system*. Yes, that was the point about the violence. It was too exact, too thorough; one had to believe in it or reject the poem altogether. In this elaborated system, there were symbolic and allegorical levels of meaning—indeed, *four* levels, as Dante himself insisted (historical, allegorical, moral, anagogical)—but you could hardly ignore the ethical assumptions present in the literal ("historical") level, or treat them as purely formal elements within the poem. Not without turning formalism into idiocy, you couldn't. Tayler was the last man of my acquaintance I would call an idiot, but there were issues he ignored, just as in his discussion of the *Odyssey* he had avoided the issue of the slaughter of the suitors and the serving maids. I was picking the same bone with him. Though reconciled in the end to his view of the *Odyssey*, I remained apart this time. Certainly Dante expected his readers to take seriously his ethical system, which was strikingly idiosyncratic but consistent in its way, a personal interpretation of Church doctrine enforced by a wild, terrorizing imagination of violence.

Tayler mentioned in passing that the Romantics and the Victorians had disapproved of Dante because they believed in mercy, not judgment. As a reader of C.C. texts, I didn't see how a civil or religious order could exist without judgment. It was the idea of *eternal* judgment that I found offensive. With a heavy heart, and a vagrant sense that I might be missing the point, I agreed with Sterngold and the other students who balked.

❖   ❖   ❖

In Shapiro's class, the students were thinking along the same lines. Rebecca, who thought that literature should be fair, dug her hands into her hair and asked, "How can a religion preaching forgiveness condemn someone to hell forever?" And Christine Wong, a well-read girl from Singapore, who spoke quietly but firmly, now said that "there are mosques in hell. Dante is Turk-bashing. I don't think he's writing religiously at all." And she might have pointed out that Mohammed himself shows up, in Canto XXVIII, as one of "the schismatics," one of whom is split open from "chin to where we fart: his bowels hung between his legs, one saw his vitals and the miserable sack that makes of what we swallow excrement." No sooner are Mohammed, his nephew Ali, and the other schismatics healed than they are split open again.

Shapiro's students insisted that Dante the sin-assessor was himself guilty of the sin of cruelty; that the lawgiver was himself lawless, operating without the constraints that they, the students, operated under, the constraints of tolerance, which forbade hating anyone. They valued openness and respect more than genius and their notion of religion was naïve: Religion was simply *moral*, an area of ethical transcendence removed from the rest of life. Alone among Shapiro's students, Henry, a Baptist from Maryland, put a little steel into religion. Henry said that the militant Jesus, in his call to listeners to drop everything and follow, implied punishment of those who stayed behind.

Many of the students used "tolerance" to cover what they didn't understand. They were Americans, taught to respect all traditions, so they thought of Christianity as one religion among many. You could take it or leave it; you could choose. This may be true now, and it may be the proper attitude in a country whose constitution guarantees freedom of conscience, but in the European Middle Ages, Christianity was practically everything, good and evil, hatred and love, learning and entertainment; it was omnivorous, not something separate from life but a force stretching to the horizons, a means of seeing all the rest. In the age of faith, choice was hardly an issue. The action of the *Inferno* begins on April 7, 1300, on Good Friday, the day of Christ's Crucifixion, and ends on Easter Sunday, the day of Resurrection. Dante placed himself within the Christian cosmology; he stands between past and present, and looks to an apocalyptic future. Shapiro finally became exasperated with the students' politically correct ecumenical notions: "Everybody's a Christian, guys. It's not a sermon, but pope, politics, and religion are all bound together. It's a Christian poem written for a Christian audience in a Christian framework."

They held back; they hid. For instance, they all, as modern persons, accepted sex, accepted the body. But they accepted it only theoretically. They were too far away from an age that could hate the body by doctrine yet live *in* the body without inhibition—with a full raging acceptance of the physical as necessity. Shapiro went after them, insisting that the *Inferno* was one of the great works about physical existence. "Bodies become *unclean*," he said, lifting his head and almost crowing. "They have sex with the wrong partners, with people of the same sex. There is illicit sex, too *much* sex. They are violent; they defecate; they eat. Things are being stuck into faces. The body is a weird container from which things come out."

The students looked grim. But the Coach pressed on cheerfully. "The bodies can feel pain—pain of dismemberment, freezing, being shackled. Where does the pleasure come in? The body is conceived as the map of sin, not of pleasure."

The system of punishment was as brilliant as it was repellent. Dante's announced method of body torment was called *contrapasso*—literally, "counterpenalty." The punishment fit the crime. But the working out of *contrapasso* came closer—and this was a profound stroke—to the punishment's *becoming* the crime. The process began in life. By sinning, you gave yourself over to obsession, and obsession was disfiguring. Sin showed up in your face and limbs, a notion that expressed both primitive fears and a remarkable insight into the way the body shapes itself around the deformations of the psyche. In hell, the process goes the final step: the sinner becomes his sin; his character is fulfilled in death. You die, and become yourself, and the living poet, Dante, confronts each of the dead and sees him in essence, without worldly protection. The schismatics are split open; the avaricious and the hoarders are condemned to push weights with their chests in semicircles and shout at one another; the homosexuals (sodomites), anathema in this judgment, are connected to one another in threes.

> As soon as we stood still, they started up
> their ancient wail again; and when they reached us,
> they formed a wheel, all three of them together.
> As champions, naked, oiled, will always do,
> each studying the grip that serves him best

before the blows and wounds begin to fall,
    while wheeling so, each one made sure his face
was turned to me, so that their necks opposed
their feet in one uninterrupted flow.
                              (canto XVI, 19–27)

Fixed in a state of childless futility, homosexuals are literally spinning
their wheels. The episode has an extraordinary frozen anguish, the anguish of endless repetition. Sin makes you go round and round.

This was stunning but hard, perhaps, for young people to accept. The
physical extremity, the sense of ordeals known and experienced by many
of Dante's readers, as well as pleasures enjoyed sinfully but fully in life—
the Italianness—was so far from their anesthetized world that the students sheered away from it. Shapiro was beating upon a closed gate. He
tried an experiment, to see if he could bust it open.

"I want you to create your own circles of hell," he said, "using your
own versions of Dante's punishment." He sprung this on them without
warning, so they wouldn't have time to censor their unconscious. There
was a short pause, and then hands began to go up.

Susan (feisty, implacable): I would put in hell the Absolutes, the people who think they are always right and go about hurting other people. . . .

Henry: But what if they *are* right?

Susan (shrugging Henry off): . . . They go between the eighth and
ninth circles. Their punishment is they have to refasten the lives of the
people they had ruined; they have to rip off their own limbs and refasten
the people they have hurt.

Sally (the girl from Pennsylvania who took a hard line on social delin-
quency): People who abandon their children. The last level of the eighth
ring. Their hell was that they should be driven to insanity and guilt and
live in isolation like their children.

Henry: This is all too carnal. For people who didn't adhere to their nature, hell is the absence of good. Hell is imagining how good they could
have been if they had realized their true selves.

I was finding this fascinating as an expression of student personality
and character. Henry, for instance, had often announced his personal
practice of facing and overcoming threats to his selfhood (Nietzsche was
his favorite writer). Overcoming and self-overcoming was Henry's favored myth. He would not want to face any version of himself other
than the one he had struggled to become.

Shapiro was amused, but he was getting edgy. "You guys are resisting
the text," he declared. "The physicality of it." And he glowered at them
slightly.

Fareed (the rationalist Indian raised in Abu Dhabi): The self-righteous and ignorant. They go in the sixth circle, and they're all yelling at each other, trying to convert each other.

Alex (new student; skinny, pale, intellectual, bespectacled): People who chew gum in public. They have committed the sin of incontinence. Their punishment is that they are in hell laughing too loud. It's a misuse of jaws in life and in death.

Lucas (gent from the Deep South; speaks in a languorously bored manner): The den of the annoying: People who call at night or talk on the street without stopping. They would be placed near the heathen; their punishment is that their eyelids are removed, and they couldn't sleep.

Joseph (the polite boy from Washington, D.C.): People who reject knowledge. Their eyes itch, and they scratch them out.

Rebecca: I don't believe in hell. I would put the Nazis and Hitler in a big room with the survivors and victims of the Holocaust. They would have to listen to their sufferings. They're at the bottom of hell. They are traitors not just to people but to humanity.

Shapiro was shaking his head, and he turned and looked at me and rolled his eyes. The students were exceptionally ingenious but impossibly high-minded. Except for Susan, Alex, and Lucas—and the last two only as parody—they could not get into the uninhibited and vengeful physical life of the *Inferno*. They believed in ethics, not in sin, and so they constructed a politically correct hell in which intolerance and ignorance were the worst offenses. Christine Wong offered to put Dante himself in the circle reserved for bigots and racists, there to be chained to a monster as different from himself as possible. Most of them transformed physical into psychological torments, and they were so wary of cruelty they missed the point. Rebecca, for instance, didn't seem to realize that some of the Nazis *had* "listened to the sufferings of their victims" and hadn't been much bothered by the sound.

Shapiro kept after them, insisting on the true nature of the poem, using misunderstanding as a prelude to understanding, and some of them came around. But I groaned to myself at the end of this exercise. I was miserable, because while seeing much that was limited in their way and Sterngold's way of reading the *Inferno*, I was helpless to offer an alternative.

I got something of a reprieve, however—a moment of pleasure. One of Shapiro's students, Francesca, a tall young woman with ripely rosy lips and a head of tousled hair, spoke English so well, with so little accent, that I had hardly noticed that she was Italian. In his final class on Dante, the Coach asked her to read the opening of the *Inferno*, and as she read the first thirty lines or so of Canto I, the room fell quiet. I would ask the reader to read the lines aloud, even if, like me, he doesn't speak a word of Italian.

> Nel mezzo del cammin di nostra vita
> mi ritrovai per una selva oscura,
> ché la diritta via era smarrita.
>   Ahi quanto a dir qual era è cosa dura
> esta selva selvaggia e aspra e forte
> che nel pensier rinova la paura!
>   Tant' è amara che poco è più morte;
> ma per trattar del ben ch'i' vi trovai,
> dirò de l'altre cose ch'i' v'ho scorte.
>   Io non so ben ridir com' i' v'intrai,
> tant' era pien di sonno a quel punto
> che la verace via abbandonai. . . .

So now you've heard it, or something like it—in any case, you've heard *something*. Francesca read with no great stress or emphasis. She read in a low steady voice, lower and flatter than her normal speaking voice, but the sound was uncanny: It was like a ravishing melody on a viola, the music arising, unbidden, from the quiet, low tones. *No, this isn't happening. It can't be—it's too perfect a moment.* But it was happening; the students were silent, and as she read, her eyes facing down on the page, her high coloring rose higher, and the music of Dante's Italian, embedded in the language, effortlessly floated into the room.

Tayler and Shapiro taught us to read epic poetry for structure and significance, for symbolic energy and dramatic weight. Like most Lit Hum teachers, they talked only rarely about metrics and almost never about the sound of poetry. We were working in translation, so what would be the point? As far as Lit Hum was concerned, beginning students needed to tackle these arduous works without mourning the elements that they might be missing; a certain diminution by translation was taken for granted. But so strong was the sound of Dante's poetry that it made me feel I wasn't reading the poem at all. In Allen Mandelbaum's English, the power of the poem—the geographical and sensuous disposition of torment—came through but not the sweetness, the love of life that made Dante a "universal" writer for so many people. The beauty of his Italian must have been the greatest sign of that love.*

❖   ❖   ❖

I was lost in a shadowed forest myself. I could not rise, I was unable as a reader to give eternal damnation some sort of credence (and there were perhaps many sorts of credence short of absolute belief), so I was unable

---

* Robert Pinsky's colloquial translation of the *Inferno*, much applauded when it was published in 1994, was not available when I retook Lit Hum.

to read the poem as Tayler wanted us to read it, "in its own terms." I was trapped, as many of the students were, in *my* terms, that is, everyone's terms, the banally right-minded post-Enlightenment ethics by whose lights medieval assumptions about eternal damnation were a system of fervent and dangerous superstition.

Dante not only reproduced real horrors, I told myself, he created a great many of his own. Yes, the work was fantasy and representation, not real life, but I could not rid myself of the notion that Dante had entered into complicity with torture. In some way, he believed in torture; he justified it. In life, the torturer's lust for control yields to mortality; the victim dies. Here the torment goes on forever. A man would be tormented eternally for "barratry"—for graft. (The very thing Dante was convicted of *in absentia*.) Imagine! A New York pol caught in a parking-ticket scam buried in excrement forever! If God would do that, he must lack a sense of humor.

The emotions appropriate to the poem were not available to me. They were connected to the beliefs by which those emotions had once been generated. I could not rise. My reading of Dante was a failure, and of the most direct sort: I didn't *enjoy* it. And I was too old to tell myself that reading something I didn't enjoy was good for me.

Chapter *17*

BOCCACCIO

~ Professor Marina Van Zuylen asks her students to lighten up
~ The two disconnected sides of American temperament
~ My delusions about Boccaccio as a "ribald" bore
~ *The Decameron:* the sultan's daughter
~ Boccaccio the liberator and threat

Professor Marina Van Zuylen sat at a small, dark brown academic desk—a table, really—and faced the students grouped in front of her. "Your great question about the Bible and Augustine," she said. " 'What are we here for if not to enjoy what has been given to us?' That question has now been answered. Now we have a thirteen-hundred-page book by Boccaccio about enjoying yourself. And do I see smiles on your faces?"

The students may not have been smiling, but I was, for sure. Grinning, maybe. It was hard not to smile when Marina Van Zuylen spoke. In her early thirties, she was dark and slender and wore a purple and green blouse, a dark skirt, dark hose. Her accent was French, yet not very French; the slight foreignness of her voice was puzzling. She was either a Gallicized American or an Americanized Frenchwoman, I wasn't sure which. (Judging from her name, there was some Dutch, Flemish, or Belgian background there as well.) She had been at Columbia a couple of years, in the French Department, and she loved teaching Lit Hum. Thoroughly at home in the literature of Europe, she was candid, informal, and extremely direct.

"You've all turned into little Augustines of late," she said. "You are all very moral. But you still retain the right to rebel. You say, 'Why were we born with these bodies and these members if not to use them?' "

Well, it was about time. What had been missing in the core readings up until now was sex. Except for Sappho's sly and charming provocations, and the tormented bonds between husbands and wives in the Greek tragedies, and a few extraordinary passages in the *Aeneid* (which, all in all, was far more copious on the subject of Dido's grief than her pleasure, whereas Aeneas seemed barely capable of pleasure at all), and a *very* few wistful glances backward by the sinners in Dante's hell—ex-

241

cept for those moments, there had been little of eros, at least not in the immediate bodily sense. Eros the force of life, the builder of cities, the heroic striver—eros as metaphor of universal creative energy—had been everywhere, but the imp of lust appeared mainly as a dangerous impulse in unreliable gods or as a threat to Christian salvation. We had read several of St. Paul's searing epistles, and his loathing of the flesh echoed mightily through Augustine and Dante. The flesh had to be tamed, subdued, for it was dangerous, hell on earth, and a possible prelude to eternal damnation.

And we had seen little of joy either. Tragedy and epic, history and philosophy—the core readings, with the exceptions of the comedies of the Greek playwright Aristophanes, were grave and intense, and it would have been easy enough, I supposed, for students to assume that gravity and intensity were the exclusive qualities of greatness. Aristophanes turned the body into an exploding envelope, but where, I wondered, were the authors who saw the body as a willing vehicle of adventure and pleasure?

Not that the students balked at the gravity of the readings. They were Americans, and they came out of a culture that separated art from entertainment, a culture that encouraged its members to develop a double consciousness, the one half fueled by piety, the other by derision and irony. And they were freshmen as well, and were perhaps trying to live up to the occasion; they might not have had the self-confidence to laugh. After all, we readers of Lit Hum had a stake in seriousness. The weight of the books was part of the pleasure of taking the course—and no doubt part of the vanity of taking it as well. We *saw* ourselves reading serious books. It was no surprise, then, that few of the students had yet to realize that seriousness and fun were not opposed to one another. As they began to discuss Boccaccio, some of the students were dismissive. Not in Van Zuylen's class, but in another section I even heard several male students refer to Giovanni Boccaccio's erotic stories as "trash." A comic sexual writer! Boccaccio was a double blow to their solemnity. A few of the young men in particular were so forbidding they might have been bankers turning down a loan request; one bright young man spoke of "debauchery."

❖   ❖   ❖

A reconciliation between seriousness and fun might be one of the subtler purposes of a humanistic education. Decades earlier, the shapers of Lit Hum had established a slot, after Augustine and Dante, devoted to comedy and "the body." In 1961, when I first took the course, we had read the lusty and scatological François Rabelais, whose immense book, *Gargantua and Pantagruel,* was a riot of physical exuberance. But in 1986, Rabelais had been one of those authors bumped from the list in response to women entering the college. *Gargantua and Pantagruel* offended some readers, and anyway, it is a book filled with Renaissance lore both hard to read and hard to teach. Rabelais had been bounced for both PC and practical reasons, and Boccaccio took his place. He was new to me, and, still in a sour mood over my misadventure with Dante, I had began to read him without expecting much. One of the "minor" authors on the Lit Hum list, I thought.

Lit Hum had given us a selection from *The Decameron,* the collection of one hundred stories, mostly erotic, that Boccaccio composed in the 1530s. Boccaccio used nothing less than the bubonic plague as a frame. To escape the ravages of the disease, a small group of aristocratic young men and women withdraw from Florence to the countryside, and amuse one another by telling racy tales while living in perfect propriety. They are not prigs or hypocrites; they are keeping certain possibilities alive. The cheerfulness forges ahead against a background of terror. Boccaccio affirms the primal energies of life in the midst of universal death.

The fourth story I read in the group assigned by Lit Hum, Chapter 7 from Book II, was about a sultan's daughter with nine husbands. The sultan's daughter! I had a vision of Arabian Nights–style kitsch, a black beard tickling naked boobs and fleshy bums—something lewd but more than a little boring. Ah, yes, the sultan's daughter. Haven't I heard that one before? Yes, in *Playboy,* perhaps, where Boccaccio showed up in the "Ribald Classics" section back there in the mid-fifties. Stealing the magazine from beneath a counselor's bed at camp (I was thirteen or fourteen), I may have read a Boccaccio tale or two, finding the stories between a photo spread of Jayne Mansfield lying heavily in the grass and a stirring essay on civil liberties by William O. Douglas—God, *Playboy* was so *serious*—yes, there amid Hef's interminable "philosophy" and pages of redundant debonair balderdash (dating, food, clothes, jazz), there would be Boccaccio, in shortened form, accompanied by a cartoon. The editorial tightening, as I now discovered, killed the fluency of his style, but I didn't know that then. All I knew was that he was "bawdy," and *Playboy* thought he was a classic. And because of the words "bawdy" and "ribald" and "lusty" and "wench,"all in great favor at *Playboy* in its early days and all part of the feeble infantilism of bad erotic writing, I had gotten the impression that Boccaccio was faintly tedious, like a garrulous old sport making up stories to entertain his friends in a bar.

And so our culture reduces the reputation of a great and powerful writer to a cliché—at least in the mind of one lazy reader. My early prejudice against Boccaccio was reinforced by the movie *Boccaccio '70* (1962), with its tiresomely knowing, modern-day versions of the tales by Fellini, De Sica, and other Italian directors, and reinforced further by the handsome but resolutely unfunny Pier Paolo Pasolini movie *Decameron* (1970). Yet in fairness to the ambitious Pasolini, I do remember one ripely erotic image: A luscious naked teenage couple lie asleep on a balcony, and the girl, an angelic beauty, holds her lover's plump member in her hand. The memory of that hand reaching out should have alerted me to what was going on in the original. It turned out I had been suffering, like the students, from False Ideas.

Reading Boccaccio, I was astonished to feel, within a few pages, an immense surge of relief. In Marina Van Zuylen's terms, sensation began to waken unused limbs. I quickly revived.

Boccaccio is a joyous writer; he is also an ironic writer. There was something he believed that should be immediately obvious to the reader, and he treated it with dignified reserve, as if it were a *secret*. What he believed (that girl's hand reaching out) was as troublesome in the 1990s for some readers as it must have been for a great many readers six hundred years earlier—that women were avid, as avid for sex as men. Not all women; there were those who stayed home with their knitting. But the brave ones were as determined to have their way with their partners of choice as men were.

Of course, women weren't always free to do what they wanted, and in his gravely courteous introduction Boccaccio provides some practical instruction. Kept under the thumb of husbands, brothers, and parents, women cannot easily move about, so they must learn to manage their lives cunningly. In many of the tales, women initiate the intrigues that lead to earthly paradise. They dissemble or put on disguises; they lie in bed at night, next to inadequate husbands, with strings tied to their toes and hanging out of the window, so lovers can summon them to meetings. They hide men in chests and closets or meet them in caverns or gardens or on balconies. They create fictions and illusions, the verbal paraphernalia of sexual love. The women were great makers of fiction, in their lives as well as their speech. Restricted yet endlessly resourceful, they are the true heirs to Odysseus. They make their own stories and in some cases tell their own stories. Not *all* Boccaccio's stories are of this nature—there are plenty of randy men, too—but in general sex in Boccaccio is about will and desire, not seduction. And the women are heroines. Boccaccio is a writer of fables who wants to arouse his readers to exercise their freedom.

Even the sultan's daughter, who is, as far as we can tell, passive before her fate, enjoys a kind of freedom. Nothing roguish or coy here; the story is swift, plain, and almost viciously funny. The sultan of Babylon gives his beautiful daughter Alatiel in marriage to the king of Algarve. But on her way across the Mediterranean to meet her future husband, the lady is shipwrecked in a storm. She washes up on the shores of Majorca, where, to her relief, she's rescued from the beach by a local noble-man. He cannot understand or speak her language, but he establishes her in his castle, and one night, after getting her drunk at a banquet, he climbs into bed by her side. Earlier, she had resisted, but now she enjoys making love to him.

This happy situation is disrupted, however, by the appearance of the nobleman's handsome younger brother, who is so amazed by Alatiel's beauty that he murders his kinsman and takes Alatiel off for himself. Boccaccio presents this as another "calamity" for her (like the ship-wreck), though, again, she is consoled in bed. And so it goes, with one nobleman after another falling in love with Alatiel and killing the previ-ous "husband" and bearing her off. It is a comedy of disgrace. The men, violating every precept of morality and hospitality, prey on their broth-ers, friends, masters, and leaders; they are so inflamed by lust that they kill, and then so inflamed by killing that they immediately make love to their prize. War and chaos follow in the wake of these acts. The tale is a celebration of Eros the conqueror and destroyer.

All these scandalous and lawless goings-on are narrated without judg-ment or shock but with a brisk attention to the details of intrigue, as if murder and kidnapping were mere matters of technique.

> Being determined to move swiftly, he thrust aside all regard for rea-son and fair play, and concentrated solely on cunning. And one day, in furtherance of his evil designs, he made arrangements with one of the Prince's most trusted servants, Ciuriaci by name, to have all his horses and luggage placed secretly in readiness for a sudden depar-ture. During the night, he and a companion, both fully armed, were silently admitted by the aforesaid Ciuriaci into the Prince's bed-room. It was a very hot night, and although the woman was asleep, the Prince was standing completely naked at a window overlooking the sea, taking advantage of a breeze that was blowing from that quarter. The Duke, having told his companion beforehand what he had to do, stole quietly across the room as far as the window, drove a dagger into the Prince's back with so much force that it passed right through his body, and catching him quickly in his arms he hurled him out of the window. (p. 178)

In G. H. McWilliam's translation, Boccaccio's prose moves as rapidly as that dagger. The story turns out to be an erotic fairy tale with a dark, mischievous layer of irony. Each of these male masters of technique, showing off his beautiful "wife," treats her as a possession and is promptly dispossessed of her. A Helen of Troy whom no one can hold on to—Elizabeth Taylor in her salad days—she survives all her lovers intact in her innocence and pleasure. In this story, it is the *men* who are vio-

lated—by other men. What does Alatiel feel? That is Boccaccio's second
ironic joke. He keeps himself distant, offering nothing in the way of
"psychology," only the elaborate insistence on Alatiel's "calamities" and
"misfortunes" covering the apparent truth that she remains as indifferent to propriety as her lovers. Alatiel, we surmise, has a good time in bed
with the inflamed men; her pleasure is her revenge and her salvation, and
she enjoys a comic apotheosis. Restored to her father after years of this
strange traveling existence, she constructs a preposterous story about
living with nuns and defending her virginity, and is truly married at
last—as a "virgin"—to her original "husband," the poor, patient king of
Algarve. The story ends as follows:

> And so, despite the fact that eight separate men had made love to
> her on thousands of different occasions, she entered his bed as a vir-
> gin and convinced him that it was really so. And for many years af-
> terwards she lived a contented life as his queen. Hence the saying:
> "A kissed mouth doesn't lose its freshness, for like the moon it al-
> ways renews itself." (p. 191)

I have chosen this story from among those assigned to us precisely
because it is the most vulnerable to contemporary dismissal. Is it not
a story of repeated rape? After all, no one seeks Alatiel's consent.
Shouldn't Boccaccio, like the poor unfashionable genius Rabelais, be
thrown out of the canon of acceptable works?

But Boccaccio did not mean the tale as a chronicle of rape. We can see
from his many other stories that women who are displeased with men do
something about it—they climb down from balconies, they put on disguises, take lovers, and then they stand up in court and defend themselves against the charge of adultery. They also, at times, refuse lovers.
Presumably, Alatiel, if unhappy, would have acted as well. The unspoken assumption of Alatiel's *pleasure* is exactly what makes the story of
her "calamities" so funny. One has to read the story not in light of our
own preconceptions about sex and power but against the background of
medieval Christian society, in which well-born women were not meant
to enjoy sex.

The "saying" quoted above from the end of the story might even be
an explicit rebuke to Dante: A woman's sexual existence does *not* show
in her face; you *aren't* marked by sin for all time. Boccaccio was born
just outside Florence while Dante was still alive, and he loved Dante
greatly. A kind of proto-Renaissance humanist, he produced encyclope-
dic works in Latin and early versions of "psychological" novels, but he
also wrote the first great commentary on *The Divine Comedy* while rejecting the punitive medieval Christian fatalism of which Dante was the
poetic master. In Boccaccio's tales, the body is not betrayed by sex; nor

are flesh and spirit opposed, as in so much Christian literature. Sexuality is associated with strength, not weakness, of character: God meant you to fulfill yourself on earth, and chastity is a mere waste. Boccaccio banished the churchly division of women into virgin and whore, and in its place celebrates the fleshly woman who gets what she wants.

I had discovered a scandalous text, and the scandal had not gone away but merely changed its form. Something written 650 years ago had risen up and bitten us in a vulnerable spot. Might not Boccaccio's insistence on the sexual avidity of women be the real reason, rather than the book's alleged impiety and celebration of adultery, that had caused *The Decameron* to be banned or censored again and again, right on through the Victorian period? Boccaccio is perhaps the only great male writer who consistently celebrates women's greater sexual capacities. Did that explain why some of the young men in Lit Hum, complaining of "trash" and "debauchery," were so grumpy after reading him? Men have often been haunted by the thought that women are potentially insatiable and therefore ungovernable. The core-curriculum readings could find you out. But that was all right. At nineteen, you were supposed to be discomforted by education; you had to know what you were afraid of. A self formed itself around desire and fear. It formed around an absence as well as a presence.

Boccaccio the liberator! I called everyone I knew: They had to read these stories. They had to hear about this hitherto unknown genius Giovanni Boccaccio! In our own period, a dreary time of sexual violence and disease and (in some feminist literature) the demonization of men— as well as male fear of women's judgment—Boccaccio's good cheer is almost revolutionary. In some feminist work, the appreciation of chastity has been reborn as a recurring minor strain: Withdraw from men, and you rob the patriarchy of its power. The major strain, of course, is that sexual behavior is a "social construction" of time and place, class and gender. In the patriarchy, men dominate women. Women have only minor and limited freedoms. So now we would say that Boccaccio's view is innocent of the actual workings of power—the sexual prerogatives of money, for instance, and the incidence of rape and abuse. We might also say that he offers a male fantasy of women as totally available, a fantasy of aroused women dying for men.

But when you read the stories, they don't come off as projections of male desires; they come off as celebration of a rebellious hedonism that has escaped us. By insisting that sex was primarily about pleasure, not about power, Boccaccio subverts our most solemn pieties. In his stories, sex could level the most awesome social walls. Well-born women make love to valets and stableboys and then speak defiantly to their possessive husbands. Boccaccio was not foolish: Women in his stories keep up social appearances. But below the public social level, aristocratic position and wealth meant less than the natural aristocracy of healthy young bodies. All of nature insisted on the right matchup of sexual temperament. It was the old, normative (i.e., Mediterranean) view of relations between the sexes, the game in which everyone wins except those unwilling to play. We were back in the paradise from which, long ago, we had been expelled.

So Boccaccio was a great discovery. When reading him, I kept thinking that he was not some "ribald" early version of Fellini but dry and sparkling, closer in spirit to Mozart and Fred Astaire. He had grace and sudden power, steel springs working within the silken limbs of his lovely, grave, but swift-moving sentences. He shared with Mozart and Astaire the happiness of making art, and in his case happiness was inseparable from his love for his secret knowledge—his myth, if you like—or the way sex worked. The stories have the exhilaration of freedom, and for the first time all year, I felt giddy, as if I were getting away with something.

Van Zuylen asked the class, "Do the stories legitimize sin or resourcefulness?" They had the right answer (the second). After their initial skittishness, they had come alive. They held forth proudly and intelligently about Boccaccio as a response to Augustine, and they nodded when Van Zuylen said: *The Decameron* is about the victory of the present—whoever makes the most of the present situation. Motivation doesn't matter in Boccaccio. It's how you live your life." But they were solemn; and they were reticent, as students often are, about sex. Shifting ground slightly, Van Zuylen made them recall the passage in the introduction to the Fourth Day of *The Decameron* in which Boccaccio, defending himself against the charge that he was dwelling on women too much and exaggerating the facts, tells a story about a young man raised by his pious father in a cave. Emerging from the cave at eighteen, the newly liberated young hermit sees some beautiful women leaving a wedding party and is overwhelmed with admiration. Boccaccio then addresses the women readers of his book:

> Am I to be abused by these people, then, am I to be mauled and mangled for liking you and striving to please you, when Heaven has given me a body with which to love you and when my soul has been pledged to you since childhood because of the light that gleams in your eyes, the honeyed sounds that issue from your lips, and the flames that are kindled by your sighs of tender compassion? When you consider that even an apprentice hermit, a witless youth who was more of a wild animal than a human being, liked you better than anything he had ever seen, it is perfectly clear that those who criticize me on these grounds are people who, being ignorant of the

strength and pleasure of natural affection, neither love you nor desire your love, and they are not worth bothering about. (p. 329)

No doubt there is something in this of the sentimental cavalier, the op-
portunist, the eternal candidate, the professional lover. But there's something else as well, as there is in all of Boccaccio, a tribute to the
deep-down lovableness of women. Marina Van Zuylen read the passage,
and they discussed it, and they discussed the power of Boccaccio's liberating humor. But then, as someone made a negative remark about Augustine, Van Zuylen said in passing, not wanting to be understood too
simply, "Augustine is a great writer—the main influence on my life."
The remark startled me a great deal, but then she explained it. She had
spent some time in France under the instruction of nuns, and Augustine
had formed her perception of many things. And when she explained herself, she seemed, for a moment, both the women in Boccaccio's stories
and the young man emerging from the cave and responding to the sensual beauty of life. She had been educated by French nuns, and yet she
spoke for pleasure in literature and was eager to pass that on to her
earnest freshmen. It turned out she was both French and American. Her
mother, in an impulse, had flown to the United States in order to have a
baby there, and then had carried the baby back to France, where she had
been educated at Catholic schools and the Sorbonne before going to
Harvard. Van Zuylen had been an American student and teacher ever
since. She was teaching Lit Hum, among other reasons, to summon European humanism to the sacred cause of licensing the students' pleasure
in literature.

Lit Hum was a training in sensibility, which meant, inevitably, that
some of the books called out to aspects of the students' temperament
that had not yet been developed. I had to ease up on them. They had
been stranded by a culture that marginalized art, splitting it off from entertainment and consigning it to a small, lonely corner. But if they were
lucky, their "errors," corrected, or at least challenged, would serve as the
ground of understanding and even as an opening to a larger life. If they
were lucky, they would get a liberal education.

Chapter 18

HUME AND KANT

A familiar Columbia legend: Sidney Morgenbessser, professor of philosophy, now emeritus, was smoking in the subway. A transit cop came up to Professor Morgenbesser and demanded that he put out his pipe. "What if *everyone* smoked?" the cop said, reprovingly. "Who are you—Kant?" the irritated professor asked, whereupon the policeman, misunderstanding "Kant" as something else, hauled Sidney Morgenbesser off to the precinct house.

The transit cop, willingly or not, was applying Immanuel Kant's injunction to make up one's mind about the moral appropriateness of any particular act by using the "categorical imperative"—the demand that one act as if one were legislating for all of mankind. By that standard, if everyone smoked, the subway would be a foul, stinking mess.

In C.C., we had jumped way ahead of Lit Hum chronologically—all the way to the eighteenth century—and we had moved into laborious and difficult books. Coming home from a screening, I would help get the boys to sleep, driving the Game Boy or Doom patterns out of their heads with a story of knights and arms, a boy and a dog, a pilot breaking the sound barrier, and then I would read as much philosophy and literature as possible before falling into brain-dead fatigue. C.C. had turned its attention, for two weeks, to the treacherous subject of ethics and to works by David Hume and Kant, and I thought of Professor Morgenbesser and the reasoning policeman. The categorical imperative, or something like it, was an attempt to discover an ethical code. The absence of such codes was bothering the students in Stephanson's class a great deal.

In the first class on Hume, one of the sophomores, Charlie Kim, became rather upset. Stephanson was expounding various aspects of Enlightenment thought, and Charlie became disgusted by the philosophical and theological disposition known as deism. Certain men of the eighteenth-century Enlightenment believed that God had withdrawn from the daily affairs of the world. Having completed the work of creation, God, so to speak, had retired from the scene. He was supreme but distant. It was a creed for people unafraid of loneliness. Many of the American Founding Fathers—including Franklin and perhaps Jefferson—had held such views. But Charlie thought deism offered a hopeless prospect for morality.

"They removed the whole standard of transcendence," said Charlie Kim. "So how can there be any absolute morality?"

By forgoing a "standard of transcendence"—the active word and participation of God—deism, he thought, opened the way to relativism, by which he meant a situation of no moral standards at all. He was an ardent young man with a high, serious forehead, a sensitively molded chin, and an embarrassed smile that broke out with sudden force, completely transforming his face. His parents had married in South Korea and moved to New York, where they were part of the prosperous Korean community in the Flushing section of Queens. Charlie was a Presbyterian, a fervent believer. "I have a relationship with this man I call Jesus Christ," he told me once at lunch. "I have a relationship with him every day." Then came the smile, which was enchanting. He had been to Kenya and was determined to go again, there or elsewhere, as a Christian missionary and teacher.

Student earnestness is a necessary moment, an opening to fundamental questions that hardened grow-ups normally ignore or dissolve into the merely instrumental and practical. That opening was one of the thing C.C. was *for;* the course forced attention to the old question of how to lead a good life. Charlie received moral instruction directly from the Gospels, and though it was unlikely that many of the secular students did so, they were nevertheless ruffled by the same question as he was: Without such an absolute or transcendent code, how does one not fall into the trough of relativism, in which all ethical points of view seem equal, and "right" is up for grabs—a matter, perhaps, of mere power? For two weeks, we debated these issues, weaving Hume and Kant in and out of the debate.

Few of Stephanson's students, as I've remarked before, were in much danger of relativism. In that classroom, there was plenty of conviction—

and some absolute conviction—as well as much moral strenuousness. But one heard tell of undergraduates of a different stripe—Columbia students so fabulously tolerant that they could have been dreamed up by the late Allan Bloom, whose fulminations against relativism in *The Closing of the American Mind* had caused such a stir in the late eighties. Bloom deplored the kind of student who identified virtue with an absolute openness to all cultures and points of view. He thought such a temperament amounted not to an opening but a closing of the American mind, an abandonment of the search for the good life (which can be attained by studying Western philosophy, political theory, and literature), an unwillingness to take seriously American principles (as embodied in the Declaration of Independence and the Constitution), and a general indiscriminateness and ignorance, all of which led to the decomposition of our national morale.

Bloom would have held his head in misery, for instance, if he had heard what I heard about the students in another C.C. section who refused to make any judgment whatever of other cultures. The subject of ritual sacrifice—the Aztecs taking the life of young virgins—had come up. A woman in the class had said, "If a culture believes in ritual sacrifice, then it's all right within that culture to sacrifice people." True enough, if you took the sentence literally: "all right within that culture." But she wasn't standing within Aztec culture. Standing far outside it, could she not say that ritual sacrifice was wrong? No, she could not.

The teacher* asked the student about the Filipino women working as servants in Kuwait. After the Gulf War, some of them had run to their embassy in Kuwait City for protection from their employers, who beat them. Was beating them morally acceptable? After all, it was permissible to beat servants in Kuwait, wasn't it? Yes, it was permissible, said the student, but in such a case the Filipino women carried rights *with* them from their own culture, and therefore they should not be beaten in Kuwait. Other students in the class agreed.

Okay, said the C.C. instructor, taking a deep breath but hanging in there, "What about the *Kuwaiti* women who are beaten?" But this time the students balked. They could not form a judgment, and I found this painfully funny, since they were probably all, to a woman (and possibly to a man), feminist by instinct and conviction. Yet their instincts and convictions were overcome by their distaste for imposing moral standards on another culture. Nor could they simply say, "It is wrong to beat people anywhere," for that remark would have required elevating what

---

* Although she spoke to me copiously about her class, she chose not to let me observe, feeling it would disrupt her relation to her students, so I will guard her privacy by not stating her name.

they now considered a local construction, "Western humanism," to the status of a universal principle, and this they refused to do.

And in their refusal, the students fell into a trap. Saddam Hussein and other dictators, criticized by the West for tormenting their own people, also complained of the arrogance of "Western humanism." The West, it seems, was attempting to impose its fallacy-ridden prejudices on people who appreciated the necessity of torture and the suppression of free speech. The arrogant West! When it suited their purpose, third-world dictators spoke a language comparable to the American discourse of PC. The students, in their unwillingness to risk judgment, were foolishly aligning themselves with knowing authoritarians who would immediately limit the freedoms that the students took for granted.

In the universities, the brutalities indulged in by Islamic regimes were a particularly sore point. In his great anti-PC polemic, *Culture of Complaint* (1993), Robert Hughes pointed out that "the more politically correct among [the academics] felt it was wrong to criticize a Muslim country no matter what it did." Hughes was referring to the remarkably muted campus reaction to the Iranian mullahs pronouncing their *fatwa,* or death sentence, on Salman Rushdie, whose 1988 novel *The Satanic Verses* contained a few irreverent passages about Islam. Hughes went on:

> At home in America, such folk knew it was the height of sexist impropriety to refer to a young female as a "girl" instead of a "woman." Abroad in Teheran, however, it was more or less OK for a cabal of regressive theocratic bigots to insist on the chador, to cut off thieves' hands and put out the eyes of offenders on TV, and to murder novelists as State policy. Oppression is what we do in the West. What they do in the Middle East is "their culture." (p. 115)

So how were we to avoid this pitfall of amoral "tolerance," which would end up betraying everything we believed in? Charlie was a good student, and Stephanson was obviously fond of him and enjoyed arguing with him. He sat just to Stephanson's right and spoke quietly, in a soft voice, and Stephanson now turned his body slightly, modulating his usual trumpet blast, and said, "It doesn't follow that we have no standards just because we have no *absolute* standards."

"Absolute" was the key. Absolute standards were indeed impossible without God or what philosophers called "metaphysical truth"—something tangible, out there, something you could grasp, a truth that was everywhere true and by whose lights you would know how to order the various desires and necessities of life. The Christian or Islamic God, for instance, or Plato's forms. If one did not believe in God or Plato, that kind of truth was unknowable, Stephanson said. But saying it was unknowable or did not exist hardly ended the issue of ethics. And Stephanson began work on the text at hand. The philosopher David Hume had thought about all these issues 250 years ago.

> When a man denominates another his *enemy,* his *rival,* his *antagonist,* his *adversary,* he is understood to speak the language of self-love, and to express sentiments, peculiar to himself, and arising from his particular circumstances and situation. But when he bestows on any man the epithets of *vicious* or *odious* or *depraved,* he then speaks another language, and expresses sentiments, in which, he expects, all his audience are to concur with him. He must here, therefore, depart from his private and particular situation, and must chuse a point of view, common to him with others: He must move some universal principle of the human frame, and touch a string, to which all mankind have an accord and symphony. If he mean, therefore, to express, that this man possesses qualities, whose tendency is pernicious to society, he has chosen this common point of view, and has touched the principle of humanity, in which every man, in some degree, concurs. While the human heart is compounded of the same elements as at present, it will never be wholly indifferent to public good, nor entirely unaffected with the tendency of characters and manners. And though this affection of humanity may not generally be esteemed so strong as vanity or ambition, yet, being common to all men, it can alone be the foundation of morals, or of any general system of blame or praise. One man's ambition is not another's ambition; nor will the same event or object satisfy both: But the humanity of one man is the humanity of every one; and the same object touches this passion in all human creatures. (p. 75)

Thus Hume, writing in *An Enquiry Concerning the Principles of Morals,* a short book that I read in bursts, late at night. Hume, in his own way, answered Charlie's fear of the void. Born in Scotland in 1711, Hume was perhaps the greatest of all philosophical skeptics, an atheist who questioned every kind of absolute, even scientific absolutes. He wished to find a basis for morality not in God or "reason" but in social existence itself. Setting it up for us, Stephanson said, "Hume didn't want to talk about morality and religion in the same context. You can't ground morals in transcendental ideals, he thought. That's not how we become moral. Instead, we want to naturalize morality."

We act morally without transcendent standards, Hume thought, because we need to live in society. What is good merely for individuals—i.e., what satisfies egoistic impulses—is, by definition, particular, and therefore nothing general in morality can be based on it. But when one speaks of general virtues and vices, whose use or harm is obvious, then one speaks of values held in common. The positive and negative virtues *could* be generalized. Certain kinds of behavior (honesty, courage, benevolence, friendliness) are useful or amiable. We approve them. Other kinds of behavior (dishonesty, viciousness, adultery) are not useful or agreeable. We disapprove them. This leads to an ethics based on utility, a morality of social consensus derived not by reason but by sentiment. For nothing can be proved with reason. " 'Tis not contrary to reason," Hume said, in his most famous sentence, "to prefer the destruction of the whole world to the scratching of my finger."

At the moment a paper edge was about to cut into your finger, the rest of the world, for all you cared, might perish. Anything was better than that cut. Ethics, Hume insisted, was a matter not of reason or logic but of experience. We are motivated by expectation of pleasure or pain; our experience of such things induces us to form moral principles. Ultimate justification was not possible, but in any society, there are certain regularities, certain repetitions (certain things that are useful or that make us happy), and by observing carefully we can derive a series of general maxims about behavior. Is torture of political and criminal prisoners—a routine matter in many countries—something either useful or amiable? Useful for the ruling powers and the police perhaps, but not for anyone else.

Hume appeared eager to refute Hobbes's sour assessment of human nature. He praises men's capacity for fellow-feeling and sympathy; he praises sociability itself. He's a delightful writer, and one has the impression of an engaging man, a happy, pleasure-loving spirit, robust, witty, appreciative. Praise came naturally to him.

> We may observe, that, in displaying the praises of any humane, beneficent man, there is one circumstance which never fails to be amply insisted on, namely, the happiness and satisfaction, derived to society from his intercourse and good offices. To his parents, we are apt to say, he endears himself by his pious attachment and duteous care, still more than by connexions of nature. His children never feel his authority, but when employed for their advantage. With him, the ties of love are consolidated by beneficence and friendship. The ties of friendship approach, in a fond observance of each obliging office, to those of love and inclination. His domestics and dependants have in him a sure resource; and no longer dread the power of fortune, but so far as she exercises it over him. From him the hungry receive food, the naked cloathing, the ignorant and slothful skill and industry. Like the sun, an inferior minister of providence, he cheers, invigorates, and sustains the surrounding world. (p. 18)

Have the patriarchal virtues ever been heralded with such open affection? Reading Hume, I thought I heard echoes not only of cheerful domestic suzerainty but of fellowship in inns and taverns, the rough pleasures of the road and the city, the vigorous public social world encountered in such fictions of the middle eighteenth century as Henry Fielding's *Tom Jones*. The voice was masculine, secular, hedonistic, conservative. Good fellows act in a certain way and gather together at the end of the day for a pint or two, and let's have none of this nonsense about God and self-sacrifice. Monkishness and austerity are absurd. We are social creatures, and we enjoy virtue in others and in ourselves. For there is a "social sympathy in human nature." Even the corrupt and selfish, Hume says, would not disapprove of socially useful acts or commit random acts of violence and mayhem. . . .

And at that point in reading Hume, I began to get depressed. The cultural left might say that Hume's "social sympathy" was half nonsense to begin with, an illusion made possible by Hume's unawareness of everyone who was excluded from it. Surely you had to have money and freedom to enjoy the rich Humian sociability. Did the lower classes qualify? Probably not.

But even granting a partial truth to that critique, I was depressed even more by something else—the gap between the way Hume understood social behavior and the way many of us understand it today. He had, it would seem, little experience, or little understanding, of perversity or self-destructiveness. No dark terrors, no malice, no schadenfreude mars this immensely exuberant, positive embrace. To an amazing degree, he took benevolence as a given. Hume was hardly unaware of self-interest and self-love, but it was benevolence, he demonstrated, that best consorted with common interest. Virtue is socially useful.

He was unlikely to have foreseen anything like our derisive advanced consumerist society in which extreme selfishness is widely admired as a virtue, public duty is often mocked as a joke or a waste of time, and the sense of community has shriveled almost to nothing. Public-spiritedness, even if we don't mock it, often fails to stir us. Unless it takes a military form, we don't trust it; we think it possibly dishonest, self-serving behavior. Politics, after all, is just a career. The question "What's in it for me?" is the sign of a common human seriousness. The question "How can I help the community?" is a question asked by children and a few rare benevolent or sainted people. If asked by the adults, it may be the sign of a fraudulent personality that conceals its true wishes behind hollow grandstanding. For in a market economy, you best help the community by following your own interests. Productive individuals help the community simply by exercising their skills, by earning and consuming and by raising families.

I don't favor these attitudes, I merely cite them. Our social world is not Hume's. A number of the core-curriculum books (Plato, Aristotle,

Locke, Hume) suggested how far we have fallen from an active ideal of citizenship. The mere fact of living in society may still produce moral norms, as Hume says, but it also produces greed, insensibility, withdrawal, and a generalized malice alternating with self-pity. In our own time, what Hume called "social sympathy in human nature"—in the sense of fellow-feeling with other citizens, on the streets, in the stores, down the block—has lessened remarkably, swept away by indifference and fear and replaced by paranoia or a sinister version of itself, a nauseated fascination with "personal" stories created by the media. Empathy has dissolved into an appreciation of victims.

Despite these dismal thoughts, however, I was convinced that Hume had suggested a plausible middle way between the poles of absolutism and relativism. That moral standards change would not in itself have surprised him. Since we derive moral principles not from reason but from moral sentiment, morality varies from one society to another. But this is not the same as saying there are no standards at all. The weakening of social sympathy in America made it harder to find moral codes and harder to maintain them; it did not mean they had ceased to exist. A true moral calling, in our time, might consist in convincing widely disparate people—blacks, Hispanics, Asians, whites—that they had a stake in common standards.

Stephanson expounded Hume, yet Charlie, who was quiet, frowning, his head down, was not happy with these piecemeal solutions. And neither were the others. The students wanted consistency of behavior and judgment. No relativists here. From Charlie the missionary to Manuel the Christian Marxist, from the Orthodox Jew Leora Cohen to the rationalist-agnostic Noah, they were all looking for a firm purchase on judgment. Charlie was not the only one dissatisfied with Hume, a philosopher insufficiently dramatic for student taste; Hume's good sense hardly seemed like philosophy at all. At that moment, the students wanted sterner stuff. They wanted ethics.

And they got it, next, from Immanuel Kant.*

> . . . unless we wish to deny all truth to the concept of morality and renounce its application to any possible object, we cannot refuse to admit that the law is of such broad significance that it holds not merely for men but for all rational beings as such; we must grant that it must be valid with absolute necessity, and not merely under contingent conditions and with exceptions. For with what right could we bring into unlimited respect something that might be valid only under contingent human conditions? And how could laws of

* In referring to "law" in the following passage, Kant meant not legal statutes but the laws of morality as derived by reason and will.

the determination of our will be held to be laws of the determination
of the will of any rational being whatever and of ourselves in so far
as we are rational beings, if they were merely empirical and did not
have their origin completely a priori in pure, but practical, reason?
(*Foundations,* p. 24)

And again:

These fundamental principles [derived from pure practical reason]
must originate entirely a priori and thereby obtain their commanding authority; they can expect nothing from the inclination of men
but everything from the supremacy of the law and due respect for it.
Otherwise they condemn man to self-contempt and inner abhorrence. (pp. 42–43)

My God, what anguish lies behind these sentences! What loathing of mess
and confusion, what hatred of an existence commanded by mere circumstance or passion or anything but reason! Kant's insistence is daunting.
Only philosophy, not observation, can give us moral laws. One might say
that Kant wrote his pamphlet *Foundations of the Metaphysics of Morals*
(1785) in part to answer questions like Charlie's. He wanted to establish
a moral philosophy that was absolute yet did not depend on the word of
God. And to be absolute, it had to be free of everything contingent or con-
ditional in social existence. (Free of life, some of us would say.) For until
it was free of the social pattern, the individual stress or weakness, the special circumstance, it could not be a code that was everywhere and in all
circumstances true. It could not be a moral *law.* Instead, it would yield a
set of "imperatives" that were merely hypothetical—true in such-
and-such a case, or for such-and-such a person, and to produce such-and-
such an end. And what makes one person prosperous or happy may not
make another person prosperous or happy. Once the particular end was
achieved, the precept would vanish. And this would not do, since what we
want are precepts that are permanent.

So Kant's goal was precisely the opposite of what we now call relativism, and for the attainment of such a goal, Hume's grounding
of morality in social existence and in sentiment was anathema. Sentiments vary, and "men differ in many ways," as Stephanson said. "But
they share reason," which, of course, was the instrument by which, Hume
insisted, you could prove nothing. "Reason," Stephanson continued,
"could operate freely and in the same way in a wide condition of men.
Kant wanted to establish what could be known about morals a priori—
before observation and experience—through the free exercise of reason."

Stephanson was excited, almost exalted. He loved this laborious German difficulty; he administered the alien language to American students
as a necessary medicine. "The importance of Kant is staggering," he

said. "His whole approach to epistemology. The nature of subjectivity. What are the conditions of possibility of anything X to be X? If there is such a thing as morality, it has to look like *this*. The conditions of it are what? Not what *is* it? But if it exists, it must be this, and what *enables* it, what makes it possible? How is it possible to talk about something? What concepts allow us to talk about something?"

So Kant was interested less in the content of ethics (he accepted conventional moral codes) than in the way we talk about it. What is it that allows our moral conceptions to have the force of law? What *form* must a precept take in order to become morality?

"He was diametrically opposed to Hume," Stephanson said. "His chief targets were skepticism and antifoundationalism, the notion that since the world is secular, we can forget about guarantees, because there's nothing to depend on except perhaps ourselves. Kant thought this was nonsense. We *can* talk about secure knowledge or morality."

Was it possible? Was it sane? To derive an ethics purely from reason and will; to compose a guide to action elaborated without the pressures that every human actor feels, a rumble of indigestion, a mood, the distorting veil of hesitation and sloth and indifference? Without the obtrusive ground of actions *not* taken, the impulses not acted on? Was it even worth doing? If you achieved it, what would you do with it? Well, maybe it was worth doing. Kant wanted philosophy to go where Church teachings and common sense could no longer go. Wouldn't I give anything to hear students say—without stumbling over Saddam's sophistries about Western humanism—"No one should be beaten anywhere"?

It was impossible to exaggerate the purity of Kant's demand. As long as we act according to our inclinations, he says, we are not entirely free. We merely do what we would like to do. The will operates with true freedom and in the full exercise of reason only when it ignores inclination and acts *against* inclination, without hope of reward or happiness. A good-hearted individual who is kind by nature may deserve praise, but he does not deserve esteem.

> But assume that the mind of that friend to mankind was clouded by a sorrow of his own which extinguished all sympathy with the lot of others, and though he still had the power to benefit others in distress their need left him untouched because he was preoccupied with his own. Now suppose him to tear himself, unsolicited by inclination, out of his dead insensibility and to do this action only from duty and without any inclination—then for the first time his action has genuine moral worth. Furthermore, if nature has put little sympathy into the heart of a man, and if he, though an honest man, is by temperament cold and indifferent to the sufferings of others perhaps be-

cause he is provided with special gifts of patience and fortitude and expects and even requires that others should have them too—and such a man would certainly not be the meanest product of nature— would not he find in himself a source from which to give himself a far higher worth than he could have got by having a good-natured temperament? This is unquestionably true even though nature did not make him philanthropic, for it is just here that the worth of character is brought out, which is morally the incomparably highest of all: he is beneficent not from inclination, but from duty. (p. 14)

There is, I suppose, a certain grandeur in this portrait of the higher misery of doing good. But the passage has its loony and comical side, an excruciating pathos. It's almost as if, for Kant, enjoyment and spontaneity tainted virtue, and wretchedness and willed propriety sanctified it. Great noble booby! I thought of Ingmar Bergman's dejected pastor in *Winter Light,* bound to his duties in an empty church, his soul barely alive. Bergman did not mean this man to be an entirely admirable figure. In the modern period, we put a much higher value on authenticity than did Kant, and we perceive moral vanity where he perceives nobility. If the reasoning will is the only free part of us, Kant insists, then intentions are what matter. An action can be accorded moral worth only when it is produced by "a good will"; and that moral worth bears no relation whatever to the success or the consequences of the act. If an act is good in itself, it is good regardless of its practical success.

But I could not accept this, and neither could most of the students.

❖　❖　❖

I haven't been quite honest. So far, I have quoted passages from Kant that I could understand. But much of this little pamphlet was composed as follows:

In respect to their will, all men think of themselves as free. Hence arise all judgments of acts as being such as ought to have been done, although they were not done. But this freedom is not an empirical concept and cannot be such, for it continues to hold even though experience shows the contrary of the demands which are necessarily conceived to be consequences of the supposition of freedom. On the other hand it is equally necessary that everything that happens should be inexorably determined by natural laws, and this natural necessity is likewise no empirical concept because it implies the concept of necessity and thus of a priori knowledge. But this concept of a system of nature is confirmed by experience, and it is inevitably presupposed if experience, which is knowledge of the objects of the sense interconnected by universal laws, is to be possible. Therefore freedom is only an Idea of reason whose objective reality in itself is doubtful, while nature is a concept of the understanding which shows and must necessarily show its reality by examples of experience. (p. 73)

Imagine it in German.

I suppose that with great effort I could work out what this means, but some part of me doesn't *want* to. Repetition and more repetition, a technical vocabulary, one foot lodged in place after another—often the same foot in the same place—and then the sudden introduction, with little preparation, of a new idea. . . . As I heard someone say at Columbia, you had to read Kant backward, reading far enough so that you understood the terms, then going back with that understanding and reading again. Reading him twice, you could read him once. "Kant came out of a scholastic German tradition," said Stephanson. "He uses a nomenclature that requires a suspension of the Anglo-American requirement to write clearly." Well, that was putting it diplomatically.

I read, but only at night, when the house was nearly quiet, and only when I was physically comfortable. No lunging at *this* one in coffee shops or subway stations. The smallest itch behind my ear pulled me away. I scratched and Kant was gone, dead words on a page, and I had to begin the passage over again. For a person living in the media, his attention attracted, held, dominated, and finally released by a hundred little tricks, Kant's prose possessed a densely hostile neutrality. Reading it was like looking at a complex architectural plan in which the passageways between rooms had been left out. To understand Kant at his most difficult, you needed logical powers almost equal to his.

I sat at home, and my concentration, which I gathered with immense effort, was like a truck going up a mountain. Once I got into gear, I moved up, slowly, slowly, with an eye to the occasionally halted but finally consecutive progress of Kant's thought. He was up there ahead of me, and I had to stay in gear. I held on to the meaning, I followed it. But then he doubled back on himself, or veered this way or that, or got lost in a thicket of undefined terms—or, more likely, my attention faltered for an instant—and understanding slipped away. I fell back, and, as much as I struggled, I couldn't move forward. I felt understanding leave my body *physically,* and so I had to roll back and then get started again somewhere earlier, at a lower ridge, finding traction and beginning once more to climb. In this way, I read at the rate of six or seven pages an hour. I was a student of Kant, and the struggle with the text was fierce, close, exhausting, and not always successful.

But oddly pleasurable. That hapless difficulty of style, the awkward, cranky, hammerheaded obstinacy and rhythmless rectitude, once you got the hang of it, gave great satisfaction, perhaps because you had to fight harder for understanding than usual. Reading Kant in the 1990s required the kind of purity of intention that he demanded from moral actors. Kant was a dreadful writer. He was also a great writer, and that was the mystery of it.

❖ ❖ ❖

How do we come up with a binding moral code—a series of precepts that are true for everyone? If a moral precept or "maxim" is to be true for everyone, or at least true for all reasonable human beings—and thus to be a categorical rather than a hypothetical imperative—then you must use your will, operating freely as a reasoning agent, to construct a maxim that would necessarily *function* for everyone. You act "only according to that maxim by which you can at the same time will that it should become a universal law."

By means of the categorical imperative, you know that it is wrong (in Kant's example) to make a promise without intending to keep it. For if everyone broke promises, no promise would be worth anything; you could not assume that your future promises would be believed. Even the attempt to get away with a false promise would no longer work. For a false promise to be believed, you must will that others shall believe promises. But you cannot, at the same time, universalize the will to make false and believable promises, so deploying the categorical imperative tells you that making a false promise is wrong. Adultery is wrong because if everyone committed it, families and eventually society would fall apart. Littering: If everyone littered, we would live in sea of litter. You should not beat someone over whom you have power because then you yourself would be beaten by someone more powerful.

Obviously, the fabled policeman who reprimanded Sidney Morgenbesser understood the categorical imperative well enough. But did it stand up? In class, Charlie thought so. One of the students new in the second semester, Abel Kern, performed a detailed, passionate exposition of Kant, but at the end of his presentation only he and Charlie Kim were left defending the categorical imperative. The students may have been looking for a consistent standard of conduct, but most of them couldn't accept Kant's formulations. Suddenly, there was a good deal of anger in the room. Noah, the well-informed boy who was always willing to see the many sides of an issue, hated the way Kant stripped everything in life of its singularity in order to make the theory possible. Others balked at the idea of establishing an unvarying, "universal" law, even as a philosophical precept. Many of them thought it was absurd to separate an act from its consequences. They were too much the product of American diversity and American pragmatism to accept Kant.

Manuel Alon was the most sweepingly contemptuous. The whole idea was preposterous, he said in his husky voice. And he did what others had done before him—he tried to devise an example that would snarl a given maxim in contradictions. "If you establish that you have the right to kill a criminal holding a knife to your neck," he said, "you are also establishing the criminal's right to defend himself and kill you, too."

I thought this was clever—at first. Then I realized that there was no reason to establish your right to kill the criminal. The categorical imperative you wanted to establish was the imperative to act as if your own life were worth preserving. By that maxim—the right of self-defense—you had the right to escape the criminal but not to kill him (unless he were about to kill *you*). And by exercise of the categorical imperative, you assumed that his life was worth preserving, too. I did not want to kill the men holding a gun to my chest at the subway exit at Forty-second Street near Lexington Avenue. I wanted them to leave me alone.

But what about those young men? What was their maxim? Some of the inner-city youth were practicing a nihilistic version of the categorical imperative: I will act as if your life has no meaning. Using Kant's formulations, and turning it into a universal law, a young shooter killing without reason commissions others to act toward him as if *his* life has no meaning. The result, as Kant would have predicted, is that, increasingly, no one's life has any meaning. The desire becomes universalized: Gangs fight over tiny bits of turf; young men who sense they have nothing going for them but their reputations become inflamed over perceived insults and tiny signs of disrespect, killing each other and people passing by.

As I played this back and forth in my mind, Manuel continued his attack: "This is the first text I find reprehensible and unconscionable. This is an academician's theory," he said, smiling at Stephanson. "He never had to go out there and fight these problems, and when you flesh it out, there is only one correct choice. You have the right to make that choice or dismiss it. But there is only one *correct* choice. It's totalitarian."

Well, he was right in one respect. Kant accepted common sense and conventional ethics as a given. There is only one correct choice, and the point, precisely, of Kant's ethics was to put some logical muscle into those commonsense ethical beliefs. But conventionality is a long way from the annihilating coerciveness of what Manuel called totalitarianism. (In fact, the Nazis, knowing their enemy, burned Kant's books.) Kant's most famous maxim, the one that summarized and governed the rest, was to treat every human being as an end and not as a means. His fondest hope was to live in a "realm of ends" in which everyone respected everyone else as a free moral agent. A supporter of the French and American revolutions, Kant hated blind obedience to authority; he wanted to center moral choice in the individual will, operating autonomously, free of desire. Every man and woman his or her own moral authority! Operating in such a way, the will covered itself in glory.

But Manuel obviously had a point about parochialism. A lifelong bachelor, Kant had never gone farther than five miles from the small city of Königsberg in East Prussia. He was fifty-seven when he wrote the *Critique of Pure Reason,* his first major work, and sixty-one when he wrote the *Foundations of the Metaphysics of Morals.* Wasn't there something provincial, limited, repressed, perhaps privileged in his conception of the moral life? Was not the world right to care more about the success of an act than its purity?

I agreed with the students. The native tradition of pragmatism welled up. Consider: During the Nazi occupation of Europe, the Swedish diplomat Raoul Wallenberg as well as a variety of Danes, perhaps operating out of a Kantian sense of duty, saved some of the Jews marked for death. But the Italian people also saved Jews, perhaps out of distaste for German orders; and, as all the world now knows, the Sudeten German Catholic Oskar Schindler saved them too, out of *greed*—at least initially out of greed, and then perhaps out of personal affection. Morally, the distinctions among these acts are less important than the heroism that unites them. In defying the orders of the SS, they all risked their lives; indeed, the person among them with the purest motives, Wallenberg, enjoyed diplomatic immunity and probably took the smallest risk—smaller than the Polish Christian family that hid my friend Nechama Tec (author of *Dry Tears* and other works about the Holocaust). Nechama Tec had blue eyes and blond hair, and thus "passed" as a Christian. The family that took her in was paid in cash for what it did, but it also risked death at the hands of the SS. If we are to measure the moral worth of acts, surely risk was a more stringent measure than purity of intention.

Columbia's core curriculum itself, as well as common experience, offered a powerful critique of the categorical imperative. The toughest moral problems, after all, require not choosing duty over inclination but choosing *among* duties. What did Hegel say was the heart of Greek tragedy? The spectacle of right against right: Antigone torn between obeying the state and obeying the gods' command to bury her brother. In a case like that, the moral terrain becomes treacherous. We should tell the truth, but when I was sixteen, I spoke truthfully to my father, insulting him brutally with my low estimate of him, and he was hurt and furious. I should have been checked by a greater imperative than truth-telling—not to hurt anyone needlessly and cruelly with the truth.

I sensed a deep dissatisfaction in Stephanson's class. The students wanted firmness of judgment, and they wanted flexibility at the same time. They refused to simplify life so they could more easily handle it. They hated the kind of relativism that refused to judge the Kuwaitis for beating their Kuwaiti servants, but they could not accept an ethics that did not take at least some of the social circumstance of particular men and women into account. I was unhappy, too. Our chaos, our confusion would not be easily checked by moral judgment. In my unhappiness, I went back to what Stephanson had said about Hume.

"In the history of philosophy, Hume had earlier been seen as a prologue to Kant," he said, "because Kant had reacted so strongly to what Hume said about morality and sentiment. But the status of Hume's work in the canon has undergone change. There's a resurgence of interest in him now as a precursor of utilitarianism and Dewey-style pragmatism. He has been an influence on the American philosopher Richard Rorty and his followers."*

He turned again toward Charlie. "Once you get into a skeptical standpoint, once you assume a historical explanation of moral standards, then, yes, you might end in relativism, even in nihilism. There's no absolute standard in God, in science, or even rationality. But Hume resurrects the problem of finding standards you can recognize as community-wide. We have to look at what we applaud and don't applaud. Individuals over time undergo experience. You *learn;* there's an accumulation of instances that allows you to act within certain contexts over time. We're not judging acts in individual terms only."

So he made a case for experience, for memory, for the accumulated moral wisdom of the race, and for judgment. And he said it again: "If you're not an absolutist, you're not necessarily a relativist. If you reject that whole dichotomy, you're in a different ballgame. Hume's project is about laying contingent foundations for morals. We haven't got an essence, but we react to different appetites and desires. Human life has a kind of form."

Human life has a kind of form. It was a very modest statement, but in fact, one could go back to a condition prior to civil society, locate that form, and discover the rudiments of a fundamental code. That is, we all eat, sleep, urinate, and defecate, and most of us fornicate, and from our common physical composition there flows a considerable similarity of nature. Thus it was possible that even if we "constructed" values, there would remain certain "suprahistorical" standards—standards that didn't depend on historically derived notions of good and evil—present

---

* Both John Dewey (1859–1952) and Richard Rorty, who teaches at the University of Virginia, speak of pluralism, a notion that there is no single "end" or ultimate goal to life, but many possible ends, of which some are more useful than others in getting done the jobs that society needs to do.

everywhere or almost everywhere. Some important values in life must assume more than relative value. Every society, for instance, admires courage.

Hume offered the way people responded in the theater as proof that a common nature existed: Everyone laughed and cried in the theater at the same time. I extended this to the movies: The existence of movies, and the movie audience, are a disproof of relativism. Film as a mass medium would not be possible without the expectation that the audience would be moved to pleasure by scenes of well-deserved success and repelled by viciousness; moved to relief by the safety of the virtuous and to satisfaction by the death of the malevolent. Movies would not be possible without the morality of the spectator, which makes the drama possible. Sylvester Stallone is as much a hero in Bangkok as in Pittsburgh (that he's a hero in either place is a pity, but that's not the point). If audiences suffer when likable characters fall into danger, the suffering is produced not just by empathy but also a shared notion of how life should go. Even a criminal would weep at the death of a little child. Hume would be the first to admit that the criminal weeps because his own selfish interests are not involved; and we might add that his tears do not stop him from killing children. Yet they tell us that killing children is wrong. A movie critic *must* be a Humean. If I believe in the audience and in a group response to common emotions, then I must believe that, however many times violated, there is a moral compact in society—not just the Lockean contract or self-interest, but an agreement of sentiment. Again, the highest political calling in our time would be to derive an agreement of sentiment common to whites, blacks, Hispanics, and Asians.

Human life has a form—that was not enough, perhaps, to rouse us to solidarity, but it was far more than nothing. Stephanson did not fit my or anyone else's cliché of an academic radical. Leading us through Kant and Hume, he had repelled both relativism and rigidity at the same time.

Interlude Six

The most familiar complaint against great-books courses was that they were shallow. There's some truth to this, though I would substitute for "shallow" the words "brief in their treatment of the books." A great teacher can do remarkable work in four hours of class time. But as the year went on, I was sure that even if C.C. raced through the texts, and even if some instructors failed sufficiently to establish the background of each writer and the placement of each text in the writer's work, and so on, there were two things C.C. was not cursory about: its treatment of reading and speaking. Certain forms of intellectual activity, certain habits and associations—the struggle to read seriously, the hundred hours or so of seminar discussion—would necessarily leave their mark on the student, even after the specific matter of the texts had passed into . . . memory? prejudice? oblivion?

Of course, the critics of great-books courses did not limit themselves to the charge of shallowness. The idea of any such DWM-dominated reading list surviving in a multiethnic, multicultural country was offensive. But after spending time with students from many ethnic backgrounds, I wondered if there were not a commonsense answer to this ideological attack. After all, most of the black, Asian, and Latino minority students had grown up *here,* not in Mombasa or Kuala Lumpur or Montevideo. And most would make their lives here, not in Ulan Bator. Most were American citizens. Could not an African-American student, learning how Plato, Aristotle, and Descartes had framed an argument, use such habits of mind to analyze a problem at law or business school—or later, when starting a business in her own community?

There are many good things to do, and many useful kinds of education—the "great books" are hardly the only road to heaven. But could minority students possibly be *harmed* by understanding the ideologies that initially formed American society? How could such students be undermined by learning what the ruling intellectual powers had consti-

tuted as a civil society, as rights, as a self, as suffering, as knowledge, as
pleasure? If that was truly the "hegemonic discourse," why not learn it,
use it, and transform it? After all, the courses did not stand alone; they
were mixed with many other books and approaches and a complex play
of influences and pressures. Whatever the students did with their minds
and souls, what courses they took, how they construed their identity as
African-Americans, or Asian-Americans, would emerge from the conflict of desire and influence, personality and pressure. The courses did
not impose an identity. And if the students did rebel against the Western
tradition, they would not be the first students educated in that tradition
who learned to criticize it. The leading black intellectuals in America
had absorbed the Western classics as well as African-American literature
and African culture. Malcolm X had read everything in prison, Nietzsche and Schopenhauer as well as the Koran and Confucius, and virtually the entire academic left had been trained on the Western classics, an
indoctrination in the "hegemonic discourse" that obviously did little to
prevent them from arriving at their adversary position—if, indeed, it
were not the reason they arrived there at all. This fact alone should tell
us perhaps the most important thing about the Western tradition: It
opens almost any door that people choose to push on.

Chapter 19

MONTAIGNE

~ Professor Tayler tells us our lives are at stake
~ I can't write about Montaigne; I write about Montaigne
~ Montaigne and multiple selves: Professor Tayler reveals why our lives are at stake
~ Professor Van Zuylen overcomes her fear of vanity
~ The spirit is flesh; the flesh is spirit

"In this whole course, this whole course, your life is at stake, and particularly at this minute."

Oh, God, Professor Tayler was on his high horse again, lancing the students with threats of nonexistence and glory. It was late February, and the wind blew hard against the clouded panes high in old Hamilton Hall. Below and to the right, on the parched brown lawns in front of Butler Library, a few hardies in sweatshirts and woolen caps, indifferent to the evidence of their senses, tossed a football back and forth and shouted. The other students passed them by, heads down, ducking under the wind. It was cold, very cold, but the sky was unusually bright, and I had no idea why Tayler was telling us that our lives, our *lives,* were up for grabs. What could he mean?

Of all the authors in the core curriculum, Michel de Montaigne, whom we were reading that week, was perhaps the least imposing (at least at first glance), the most informal and likable, the most obviously and reassuringly human. Tayler loved him, and kept laughing to himself and repeating, as a mantra, such phrases (in mock-Montaignese) as "It's bad enough to piss when you walk; you shouldn't have to shit while you run." Despite our sober meditations on ethics in C.C., I was still high from Boccaccio's liberating fictions, and Montaigne, even more than Boccaccio, accepted the body in all its many activities, its fevers, digestive convolutions and evacuations as well as its enjoyment of eating, sex, and sleep. Augustine's anguish over the rebellious pride of the flesh had been put to rest at last. The body was delivered whole. Montaigne made you feel good in your own skin. So how could reading him put anyone's life at stake?

269

Montaigne might have laughed at Tayler's professorial melodrama. An aristocrat and public man, he retired to his Bordeaux estate in 1571, at thirty-eight, to read and write. Over the years (not all spent in retirement), he made notes on his reading, copying extracts from classical literature, and then adding observation and reflection. Even today, the book that he wrote and rewrote, and published and republished, the *Essays,* seems an utter original. Twelve hundred years earlier, Augustine had written his spiritual autobiography; Montaigne, who was a Catholic believer but secular and worldly in temperament, did something perhaps more daring: He made a complete inventory of his physical and mental habits, pursuing his soul, amazingly, in every limb and organ of his body, never losing personal hold of the question of how to live and how to die. Philosophy, theology, manners, the law, and a great many other things pour though his pages, but his main impulse was always autobiographical. Arrogantly, he insisted on his humility. "I set forth a humble and inglorious life," he writes in the famous opening passages of the essay "Of Repentance." "That does not matter. You can tie up all moral philosophy with a common and private life just as well as with a life of richer stuff. Each man bears the entire form of man's estate." Does he mean it? Or does he think that all men are revealed in one particular man, Michel de Montaigne? This is not humility. Nor do we want humility. Montaigne brings the ego into literature. "At least I have one thing according to the rules: that no man ever treated a subject he knew and understood better than I do the subject I have undertaken; and that in this I am the most learned man alive." Before Whitman, Montaigne made a long and glorious catalogue of himself:

> Although I was trained as much as possible for freedom and adaptability, yet it is a fact that through carelessness, and because I have lingered more in certain ways as I grow old (my age is past training and henceforth has nothing to consider except holding its own), habit, imperceptibly, has already so imprinted its character upon me in certain things that I call it excess to depart from it. And I cannot, without an effort, sleep by day, or eat between meals, or breakfast, or go to bed without a long interval, of about three full hours, after supper, or make a child except before going to sleep, or make one standing up, or endure my sweat, or quench my thirst with pure water or pure wine, or remain bareheaded for long, or have my hair cut after dinner; and I would feel as uncomfortable without my gloves as without my shirt, or without washing when I leave the table or get up in the morning, or without a canopy and curtains for my bed, as I would be without really necessary things. I could dine without a tablecloth; but very uncomfortably without a clean napkin, German

fashion; I soil napkins more than they or the Italians do, and make little use of spoon or fork. . . . ("Of Experience," p. 830)*

Nothing life-threatening here, though the tone seemed miraculously perfect. Montaigne, one feels, was a good man (not something I would dream of saying about most of the other authors in Columbia's canon). From the listing of his habits, there arises not fear and caution, and certainly not shame, but the most noble resolve. Tayler told us that Montaigne, who suffered badly from gall stones, had passed from an early stoicism to a more and more confident and joyous epicureanism—that is, his early preoccupation with pain and how to die well (a great theme of the Roman writers he admired) gave way in middle age to a greater and greater acceptance of life, especially the pleasures of life. But the stoic note never quite disappears, even in "Of Experience," his final essay before dying at age fifty-nine.

> What shall we say of the fact that even doubt and inquiry strikes our imagination and changes us? Those who yield suddenly to these propensities bring total ruin upon themselves. And I am sorry for several gentlemen who, by the stupidity of their doctors, have made prisoners of themselves, though still young and sound in health. It would still be better to endure a cold than to lose the enjoyment of social life forever through disuse by giving up so general a practice. It is a troublesome science which decries the pleasantest hours of the day. Let us extend our possession to our utmost means. Most often we toughen ourselves if we persist, and correct our constitutions, as Caesar did his epilepsy, by despising it and fighting it. We should conform to the best rules, but not enslave ourselves to them, unless to those, if any there are, to which bondage and slavery is useful.
>
> Both kings and philosophers defecate, and ladies too. ("Of Experience," p. 831)

This was extraordinary, but I was sure, when reading it, that my life was not at stake.

Listening to Tayler, I realized I had a crisis of my own, though a very small one: I loved Montaigne but would not be able to write about him. The reason was perhaps strange. He was the first writer in the core-curriculum readings to whom I felt close. I say this properly impressed by the distance between us: Montaigne, confronted by a modern bourgeois, would probably shut himself up in the tower library of his estate.

* In 1992, Columbia used the Penguin edition (since replaced with a new translator's work). Not much liking it, I used Donald Frame's translation, *The Complete Essays of Montaigne* (Stanford: Stanford University Press, 1958).

But when he says he suffers from ignorance, a poor memory, and poor attention, I know that I am not alone. Montaigne says he turns through books without reading them, and so do I. "What do I know?" was his most famous question. Now, by any standard, Montaigne, a student of classical literature, a philosopher, soldier, lawyer, twice the mayor of Bordeaux, an intimate of great men, was not ignorant at all. What he means is that he lacks specialized knowledge, and the ironic corollary, of course, is that he doesn't want such knowledge and feels superior to those who do. I loved his defiance of pedants, displayed frequently in his essays, and, like him, I knew I possessed something else besides specialized knowledge—judgment—and I sensed that this ability was my only possible salvation. Montaigne made a book by reading and looking around him, by observing himself. He is the patron saint of amateurs, a genius for nongeniuses. . . . But it is awkward to go on. Steal from him and be silent.

Well, just one other thing: I can't write about him because he is all of a piece. He is joined together body and soul, idea and image, matter and sensation, moral precept and the concrete circumstances that gave rise to it—in all, he was perhaps the least alienated personality ever to write prose. He is marvelously planted in his own life. And whether contemplating a philosophical or theological issue or sitting on his toilet—he also wrote about scratching the inside of his ears—he is the same man, the same writer, and to pull him apart would really be murder. (Not that the crime hasn't been committed, or can't be committed. It has been committed by many, sometimes magnificently. But I couldn't do it.)

One look at Montaigne made standard left-academic complaints about hegemony seem absurd. It was a literal hegemony—the tyranny of scholastic philosophy—that Montaigne disliked. In Montaigne's time, dogmatism was beginning to wane, but he went one step further than skepticism. One of the great late-Renaissance humanists, Montaigne renounced intellectual and spiritual authority, and that renunciation *became* his authority. He was interested not in scholastic proofs of this or that but in mental activity, the movement of thought, and he put such movement right into the essays themselves.

Still, I didn't know why Tayler was talking of life and death. Montaigne was an exuberant but modest flowering bush amid such oaks as Homer, Virgil, and Kant. Was Tayler trying to impress the students with mysteries to which he alone held the key? He turned to metaphor and tone, which were always central for him. At the beginning of the tiny early essay, "Of Idleness," Montaigne says that minds need to be occupied: He refers to what "we" see and know, and then he says, speaking generally of minds, that "unless you keep them busy with some definite subject that will bridle and control them, they will throw themselves in disorder hither and yon in the vague field of imagination."

At first, the notion, and the phrasing, seem conventional: A horse needs a bridle in order to become a useful domestic animal; a mind needs the discipline of subjects. Spoken just like a proper essayist, a writer of wisdom. But then, no more than a half page later, Montaigne writes as follows (quoting classical-lit extracts in the middle of the paragraph is one of his favorite habits):

> Lately, when I retired to my home, determined so far as possible to bother about nothing except spending the little life I have left in rest and seclusion, it seemed to me I could do my mind no greater favor than to let it entertain itself in full idleness and stay and settle in itself, which I hoped it might do more easily now, having become weightier and riper with time. But I find—
> Ever idle hours breed wandering thoughts (Lucan)
> —that, on the contrary, like a runaway horse, it gives itself a hundred times more trouble than it took for others, and gives birth to so many chimeras and fantastic monsters, one after another, without order or purpose, that in order to contemplate their ineptitude and strangeness at my pleasure, I have begun to put them in writing, hoping in time to make my mind ashamed of itself. ("Of Idleness," p. 21)

What's going on here? The wild horse, so recently bridled, has immediately broken free again. "Montaigne doesn't use metaphor to decorate," said Tayler. "He *thinks* in metaphor. You see, he starts with 'we' and he goes to 'I.' You start out with an orderly idea from St. Thomas Aquinas, bridling and controlling, and you wind up with Montaigne on a horse running through time in his imagination. Montaigne contradicts himself; he is like the many selves of Walt Whitman or D. H. Lawrence. And those writers are like you guys. You always cherish in your hearts that sense that you're an individual. Columbia College is not going to bully you. Some may catch the ball with surer hands than Huggins"—he looked rather cruelly at the big guy from California, the football player with heavy limbs and a brush top, who refused to dance for Dionysus—"but Huggins has got individuality going for him."

I was a little baffled by the progression of thought here, and perhaps the students looked baffled, too, because Tayler retreated into the jungle, re-formed his attack, and sent the guerrillas out again. He gave us the neo-Aristotelian way of defining a human being, the notions that prevailed in the Christian era before Montaigne. "The soul is the form of the body. The real part of you is the *form*. Boethius said there was a substance, an essence, a single central self, a rational soul, guaranteed by God; a core." Tayler looked at some of the forms before him. "Now the trouble with this sort of definition is that it can't describe anything that moves in time. It's a static position: Man is everywhere the same."

And then Tayler read the opening to Montaigne's "Of Repentance."

> Others form man; I tell of him, and portray a particular one, very ill-formed, whom I should really make very different from what he is if I had to fashion him over again. But now it is done.
>
> Now the lines of my painting do not go astray, though they change and vary. The world is but a perennial movement. All things in it are in constant motion—the earth, the rocks of the Caucasus, the pyramids of Egypt—both with the common motion and with their own. Stability itself is nothing but a more languid motion.
>
> I cannot keep my subject still. It goes along befuddled and staggering, with a natural drunkenness. I take it in this condition, just as it is at the moment I give my attention to it. I do not portray being: I portray passing. Not the passing from one age to another, or, as the people say, from seven years to seven years, but from day to day, from minute to minute. My history needs to be adapted to the moment. I may presently change, not only by chance, but also by intention. This is a record of variable and changeable occurrences, and of irresolute and, when it so befalls, contradictory ideas: whether I am different myself, or whether I take hold of my subjects in different circumstances and aspects. So, all in all, I may indeed contradict myself now and then; but truth, as Demades said, I do not contradict. If my mind could gain a firm footing, I would not make essays, I would make decisions; but it is always in apprenticeship and on trial. (pp. 610–11)

"This description moves in time," said Tayler. "It's not a definition, it's a process. Montaigne offers a sense of a self for the first time in history that isn't based on *being*. Look, all the philosophers up to Montaigne—Augustine, the rest—they were all concerned with being; God is the *big* being. But Montaigne wants to describe being in motion. 'I don't depict being,' he's saying. 'I depict becoming.' Contrast this with Dante, in which each person has an essential nature. See, man is not static; he doesn't have a fixed nature. So Montaigne moves, in that little essay, "Of Idleness," from a 'we' to an 'I.' "

The clouds parted. So *that* was the individuality that Columbia couldn't bully—the uniqueness of the "I" that emerged from the multiple selves of each student. Huggins the football player had begun contributing to the class. Something was stirring in him. He wasn't dancing, but he was moving. He spoke hesitantly, in fragments, but he was in there trying. He had been stirred by Tayler's interest in *him*. Different selves were coming to the surface, and from these selves would come a Huggins who danced for Dionysus.

Multiple selves! It's right there on the page. French schoolchildren are given Montaigne's essays at eleven, and perhaps he makes perfect sense at that age. But the older you get, the more complex and mysterious he seems, enchantingly lucid from one sentence to the next but outrageously obscure overall. He doesn't announce his plan and then fulfill it. He doesn't establish the skeleton of his subject. He moves by association and metaphor, developing complex philosophical ideas through the most material and worldly objects. Reading him is exhilarating and almost frightening. Where are the guardrails? You feel you might fall off the track and get lost.

He kept revising and reissuing the essays, and he allowed the different layers to exist side by side in the work ("I add, but I do not correct"). Reading the final versions is like peering at many geologic strata at once. Not only that, the strata are *moving*. He changes things, contradicts himself, slipping away from you as you read him. A few weeks after reading one of his essays, I had trouble remembering what he had said—his tone, which carries much of the meaning, had vanished. The regularities in his wonderful mind could surely be established, but only by exhaustive analysis. He is a quarry of meaning, like the Bible. No, he is a school of fish—the ironies glide away, flashing as they disappear into the distance. He seems, for instance, to be criticizing himself, but he's really putting down people tempted to underestimate him. Again from "Of Repentance":

> Let me here excuse what I often say, that I rarely repent and that my conscience is content with itself—not as the conscience of an angel or a horse, but as the conscience of a man; always adding this refrain, not perfunctorily but in sincere and complete submission: that I speak as an ignorant inquirer, referring the decision purely and simply to the common and authorized beliefs. I do not teach, I tell. (p. 612)

The conscience of an angel or a horse, presumably, would be simple, and clear. The conscience of a man cannot be either, so it refuses repentance in the common religious sense of denying or renouncing oneself, which, in modern terms, would be an act of bad faith. (Montaigne had an instinctive grasp of what we would call "authenticity.") Telling is a far more powerful act than reciting the accustomed moral lessons. Montaigne seems to be acceding to commonplace religious beliefs and undermining them at the same time. His writing devastates anyone who tries to understand it too quickly.

I now saw what Tayler was getting at with his portentous opening sally. Montaigne hated rote learning; he complained of his poor memory but believed in his judgment. Learning to read and to judge was what Lit Hum was about for Tayler. In Lit Hum, the student would struggle with some of the great achievements in literature, and each book would stretch a student in a different direction. The course was not a specific body of knowledge injected into students like truth serum; nor was it a way of donning the armature of "Western values." It was a struggle with difficult and faraway texts, which forced, willy-nilly, the trying on of selves; and it ended in the uniqueness of the individual student that emerged from the many selves. That's why the students' lives were at stake when they read Montaigne, for Montaigne was the supreme example of the kind of becoming that Professor Edward Tayler believed in.

❖ ❖ ❖

"My crisis of vanity," said Marina Van Zuylen to her class, smiling, her voice leaping upward. "I had a crisis of vanity yesterday. The day before I had given a public lecture, and it was well attended, everyone came, and yesterday I was glowing, just preening like a *peacock*. So I got terribly guilty. It was terrible! I wanted to flagellate myself! But finally, I said, 'Relax. We are all hubristic, we are all vain.' Montaigne saved me. Montaigne thought that the obsession with vanity is itself a form of vanity."

Driven this way and that by her scruples and counterscruples, she was very funny, and the class laughed with her as she went through the conflicting emotions. She was a cross between Joan of Arc and a French schoolgirl, a scholarly heroine yet self-critical and exasperated. She gloried in Montaigne, who acknowledged everything, high and low, vanity as well as self-doubt and self-criticism.

A couple of Van Zuylen's religious students—a born-again Christian woman who was a brilliant student, and an orthodox Jew—were made nervous by Montaigne. They missed something that they could not name, they missed authority perhaps, a hierarchy of values, the body placed within the hierarchy. But Van Z and many of her students were in a good mood, the students were more relaxed with Montaigne than with Boccaccio, and I was happy too, because I realized as she talked that Montaigne articulated something I had always felt but was never able to say.

There is no higher and lower nature in human beings. It's all one: Every act of spirit is fleshly and every physical act is formed by spirit. Dualism is absurd. Wiping the bottom of one of my little boys was as close to God as I would ever get; sitting alone and reading Boccaccio or Rousseau is a physical act. I'm reading something besides journalism, and I feel better, so my pulse rate drops; I feel relaxed and at the same time tensed, but tensed in a different way, struggling to understand, to take it all in. I respond physically. Physical and mental activity are never separate. There is so such thing as being "too cerebral" or "too physical" but only different degrees of courage, grace, intelligence, and wit.

Extrapolating from the great Montaigne, I would say that his notion of "becoming" is not just my ideal, it's an American ideal that I share. We are always in flux. The American says: My life is yet to come: it's all before me. The American never "matures"; he never grows up. He says, I am going up a hill, I am not completed, I am not finished, I will expand, I will change. Like Montaigne, though without his genius, he is always revising, laying one version of himself on top of another.

A product of the fifties and early sixties, I was brought up believing I could go anywhere, do anything, read anything. The world was my oyster. The dollar took me to Europe. Now the oyster is closed, except to the wealthy; and anyway, in middle age I know that I won't go everywhere, read everything, see everything. What I still have, however, is the American impulse to annihilate myself and be reborn. I went back to school because it was my form of becoming, which meant, in part, recovering that part of my soul that had been lost in the dismay of a media existence that blurred all distinction between myself and the atmosphere around me. And I knew I could get myself back only by the most exacting labor, slowly, one sentence of Montaigne at a time.

Chapter 20

ROUSSEAU

- ~ I throw a tomato at Ronald Reagan
- ~ The nature of great-books courses
- ~ *Discourse on the Origin of Inequality*
- ~ Northern California in the sixties: the tomato lands
- ~ *The Social Contract*
- ~ Middle-class dissatisfactions

I threw a tomato at Ronald Reagan once. I threw a tomato at Reagan while under the influence of Jean-Jacques Rousseau. I may not have acknowledged this influence at the time, but it existed nonetheless. The year was 1969, and I was a graduate student at Stanford in its brief flowers-of-radicalism period and a member, for a couple of years, of the Students for a Democratic Society. Reagan, elected governor of California in 1966, had decided that the state's extraordinary university system should charge something more than a minimal tuition fee; and SDS responded by announcing that, as minority students generally had less money than whites, the tuition increase was a racist plot. We Stanford SDSers were mustered out in support of our Cal brothers, who were traveling to Sacramento, the state capital, to bring the protest to the governor's face.

I'm not sure why I went along; the political issue I most cared about in those days was the Vietnam War, which I hated and spent much time protesting, and on the bus to Sacramento I sat morosely by myself, reading that revolutionary text, Henry James's *Portrait of a Lady*. I was an aesthete dabbling in politics, something James would have well understood. As we got off, we were handed fruits and vegetables. It was a prodigal time in American history. If I may paraphrase the reluctant revolutionist and Bonapartist (and eventual restorationist) Talleyrand: Only those who lived in California before the collapse of the defense industry can know the true sweetness of life. The land of plenty, with dazzling sunshine, and fruits and vegetables to throw at politicians. And there, standing well behind a barrier, on the steps of the state capitol, was the governor. I cocked my arm and threw; the missile arched high and then—

❖ ❖ ❖

"Rousseau!" Stephanson boomed, in perversely mispronounced Brit French. "ROU-sseau is not a conventional Enlightenment type. Many of the Enlightenment thinkers believed the means to achieve progress was intellectually *avail*able. Rationality *can* produce a society. Progress was possible. But in the first Rousseau text that we're reading, *Discourse on the Origin of Inequality,* there's no notion whatsoever of a linear progression."

Head were bent over the conference table; hair was gathered from faces and shoved behind ears; notebooks were flipped open. In C.C., we were moving into the modern period, and there was a touch of excitement in the room. Then Manuel, wearing his dark glasses, shambled in, a bit late, and settled himself. He immediately began taking notes, his fingers hitting a silent braille computer as he looked off to the side and rocked slightly. Now he suddenly exclaimed, with considerable irrelevance, "I don't know why I've become such a Marxist."

Stephanson, a little surprised by this remark, turned to him and said, "One day you're a Christian prophet, Manuel, the next you're a Marxist."

Well, exactly, I thought. That was the beauty of such survey courses as C.C. You read a persuasive argument and it filled your mind; you became an adherent of that text, swelling with it, enlarged by that implacably correct way of looking at the world—for a week. You were a rationalist, an empiricist and skeptic, a Hegelian, a Marxist. Taking on one identity after another, you were, for a while, blissfully irresponsible. No one would burn you at the stake for the wrong opinion or for false enthusiasms. One advantage of living in an era that doesn't make ideas a life-and-death matter is that you can entertain many different ideas, retaining some, discarding others, mixing together what remained. Out of this early promiscuity, if you were smart and disciplined, would come something like intellectual experience and readiness for more. At the end of the year, you unconsciously retained that version of yourself that fit most tightly around your psyche. You turned away from promiscuity.

Rousseau would have understood role-playing and the trying on of selves; he performed his own intellectually stunning version of such strategies throughout his life. Rousseau marked the beginning of a distinctly modern radicalism and (to my mind) a distinctly modern sentimentality. I had read him the first time thirty years earlier, had fallen halfheartedly under his spell in the later part of the sixties, and had fought him off ever since, merely by living in New York as a husband, a father, a householder—as a middle-class man. This time I read him with rising excitement but with violent disbelief; I *resented* him, as I would resent any superior intelligence who was determined to upset my life. He nagged at me still; his perversity spoke to the unaccommodating and dissatisfied side of any adjusted and seemingly contented citizen.

Rousseau insisted that we had expelled ourselves from the paradise we had once enjoyed and condemned ourselves to lie in the prison we had made. First, man in paradise:

> By stripping this being, thus constituted, of all the supernatural gifts he could have received and all the artificial faculties he could have acquired only by long progress, by considering him, in a word, as he must have come from the hands of nature, I see an animal less strong than some, less agile than others, but, on the whole, the most advantageously constituted of all; I see him eating his fill under an oak tree, quenching his thirst at the first stream, making his bed at the foot of the same tree which furnished his meal, with all his needs satisfied.
>
> Left to its natural fertility and covered with immense forests that the axe has never mutilated, the earth offers at every step stores of food and shelter to animals of every species. The men dispersed among them observe and imitate their industry, and thus attain the instincts of the beasts, with the advantage that, unlike any other species which has only its own instinct, man, who has none which belongs to him alone, appropriates them all, lives equally well on most of the different foods that the other animals share among themselves, and, consequently, finds his subsistence more easily than any of them. (Norton, p. 11)*

So far, straightforward enough. But then Rousseau continues:

> Nature treats them precisely as the law of Sparta treated the children of citizens; it makes strong and robust those with good constitutions and lets all the others perish, differing in that respect from our societies, in which the state, by making children burdensome to parents, kills them indiscriminately before they are born.

The last phrase, of course, is intentionally outrageous and opaque. Serious mischief—major mischief—is afoot. In this passage from *Discourse on the Origin of Inequality,* written as an entry in an academic competition in 1755, Rousseau ridicules Hobbes's insistence on the viciousness of human creatures in a state of nature. We were back to one of the great themes of C.C.: What *are* men essentially? Do they have an essential nature at all? And therefore, how should they live in civil society? Is civil society an expression of their nature or a perversion of it?

* I used the Norton edition, *Rousseau's Political Writings,* Alan Ritter and Julia Conaway Bondanella, editors, rather than the Hackett edition Columbia recommended.

Rousseau insists, against not only Hobbes but the common assumption, that man in a state of nature was happy—that is, unconscious, and therefore innocent. Man was blissfully unaware of nature as something to subdue or "appreciate." Instead, he lived *in* nature, as part of it. He hunted when he was hungry, slept when he was tired, fornicated when he felt desire and with whomever was available. Beauty was not an issue; no one yet was aware of it or responded to it. Family ties were minimal; men didn't even recognize their own children. (Feminist objections seem absolutely necessary here: Often when Rousseau says "man," he obviously means men. Could women in a state of nature, or in society, possibly be described as unable to recognize their own children? Rousseau, for the record, gave away his own children, all five of them, to an orphanage. He literally and legally didn't "recognize" them.)

The arts, hopes, knowledge, and plans of this contented creature died with him. It did not matter. He may have been cold or hungry at times, but he could not be miserable, because he lacked sufficient consciousness to be miserable. It was absurd to say he was inherently predatory and vicious, since there was no need for aggression; he lived off the fat of the land. His moral life consisted of two sentiments, the desire to preserve himself and the emotion of pity at the sight of any suffering creature.

Manuel's remark about being a Marxist was not so strange after all. He had jumped ahead from Rousseau to Marx, but it was a natural landing place, since Marx, looking for an image of an ideal society—something he might counterpose to the squalors of industrial capitalism—found himself heavily indebted to Rousseau.

And something of his anger may be found in Rousseau, too. When Rousseau, tracing man's "progress," arrives at civilization, he writes with fury:

> The extreme inequality in the manner of living, the excessive idleness of some, the excessive labor of others, the ease of exciting and satisfying our appetites and our sensual desires, the overly refined foods of the rich, which nourish them with constipating sauces and prostrate them with indigestion, the bad food of the poor, which they more often lack than not, so that they greedily overburden their stomachs whenever they can, late nights, excesses of every kind, immoderate outbursts of all the passions, hardships, spiritual exhaustion, innumerable pains and afflictions which are felt in every class, and which keep our souls in perpetual torment—this is the deadly proof that most of our ailments are of our own making, and that we could have avoided nearly all of them by preserving the simple, uniform, and solitary manner of living which was prescribed for us by nature. If nature destined us to be healthy, I venture to affirm that

> the state of reflection is contrary to nature and that the man who
> meditates is a depraved animal. (p. 13)

"The desire to walk on all fours," Voltaire wrote Rousseau, "seizes one when one reads your work." This was not a friendly joke. Jean-Jacques Rousseau offended many people. The son of a Genevan watchmaker, largely self-taught, he made himself into a philosopher, economist, sociologist, musician, and man of letters; he shuttled between Switzerland and France, never quite living easily anywhere, and made as many enemies as friends. The note of playful arrogance—a French intellectual trait ever since—irritated people like Samuel Johnson, who, according to Boswell, regarded Rousseau as both wicked and affected, a man who wrote fashionable absurdities in order to gain attention. The great radical disbelief in society begins in Rousseau's text in an almost jocular mood.

> The first man who, having fenced off a plot of land, thought of saying "This is mine" and found people simple enough to believe him was the real founder of civil society. How many crimes, wars, murders, how many miseries and horrors might the human race have been spared by the one who, upon pulling up the stakes or filling in the ditch, had shouted to his fellow men, "Beware of listening to this imposter; you are lost, if you forget that the fruits of the earth belong to all and that the earth belongs to no one." (p. 34)

Hobbes, it seems, had committed an extraordinary blunder. Hobbes had looked at Englishmen in 1650 and, noticing that many men were competitive and greedy, had projected those qualities back through history as the essential nature of man. On the contrary, says Rousseau, it was the institution of property which created what Hobbes took to be man in his natural form.

"Property comes first," said Stephanson, "before competition. That's a revolutionary idea."

It's revolutionary because it suggests that man's nature had been altered by social forces. What Hobbes called a natural state was, as Stephanson insisted, a "construction," that favorite word of the academic left. *Men and women don't have to be this way. God has not made us so. "Natural law" has not made us so. Property and social institutions have made us so.* The entire prospect of radical social criticism, right up to the orthodoxies of the cultural left in the present, opened up from this startling view.

Rousseau sends Locke spinning as well. Locke had assumed that man was a sociable animal, that cooperation was a natural and fruitful act, that dependency was inevitable, and that inequities of property, with some people controlling land and productive resources, and others merely their own labor, existed early on. For Locke, private property was the basis of civil society. For Rousseau, it was the beginning of ill-ness and of what later came to be called alienation. Looking around himself in eighteenth-century France, at the end of the aristocratic order, a time of high glory and wretchedness, he must have become possessed by an overwhelming sense that *all this was wrong.* And he used his own method of anthropological speculation to construct the stages by which we had gone from a primitive state of happiness to a cultivated state of misery. The *Discourse on the Origin of Inequality* is a moralized fable of development: The apparent upward drive to civilization was really a downward drive to barbarism. Society was sick; the individual psyche was sick from trying to conform to it. There are passages in Rousseau that seem uncannily modern. He understood one aspect of our mood; or, let us say, the mood of every rebellious adolescent, every exhausted paper-pusher fed up with the syncophancy and bullying of the office, every woman at a cocktail party who has looked around in disbelief at the people pretending so unsuccessfully to like one another. It is the great modern condition of *disgust.*

> Behold, then, all our faculties developed, memory and imagination in play, self-love aroused, reason made active, and the mind having almost reached the limit of the perfection to which it is susceptible. Behold all the natural qualities put into action, the rank and fate of each man established, not only upon the amount of his property and his power to serve or to harm, but also upon mind, beauty, strength, or skill, upon merit or talents, and since these qualities were the only ones capable of attracting consideration, it soon became necessary to possess them or to affect them; it was necessarily to one's advantage to seem to be other than what one was in fact. To be and to appear became two completely different things, and from this distinction sprang imposing ostentation, deceptive cunning, and all the vices which follow in their train. From yet another perspective, behold man as free and independent as he formerly was, subjugated, so to speak, by a multitude of new needs to all of nature, and especially to his fellowmen, whose slave he becomes, in a sense, even in becoming their master; rich, he needs their services; poor, he needs their help, and even being of average wealth does not enable him to do without them. He must, therefore, constantly seek to interest them in his fate, and make them find it profitable, either actually or apparently, to work for it. This makes him deceitful and crafty with some, imperious and harsh with the others, and makes it necessary for him to abuse all those whom he needs, when he cannot make himself feared by them, and when he does not find it in his interest to serve them in a useful way. Finally, consuming ambition, the zeal to elevate their relative fortune, less out of true need than to set

themselves above others, inspires in all men a base inclination to
harm each other, a secret jealousy, all the more dangerous as it often
assumes the mask of benevolence in order to strike its blow in
greater safety; in a word, competition and rivalry on the one hand,
conflicts of interest on the other, and always the hidden desire to
profit at the expense of others—all these evils are the first effects of
property and the inseparable consequences of nascent inequality.
(p. 42)

I don't know how that passage could be surpassed in eloquence and
power. When you read it, you can hardly find the strength to disagree
with it. Whether you are at the top, middle, or bottom, society is a trap,
and you can never escape compromise, dishonesty, loathing of others,
and vanity. "We construct these things for use, for good," said Stephanson, speaking of social institutions, "and they wind up controlling us.
Civilization is an iron cage; a quagmire."

But at the end of the class, I wondered: If civilization is an iron cage,
why get an education? So as to better rattle the bars? So it would seem.
Rousseau was the first "brilliant" author we had read in C.C., the first
to write with conscious virtuosity. (Rousseau strove to be brilliant;
Machiavelli merely was so.) We had entered modernity with all its
attendant literary and moral issues of sincerity, responsibility, role-playing, and irony. Did Rousseau really believe this stuff? Or was he just
twitting the French aristocrats and bourgeois who imagined they lived in
the best possible world? Did he want to go back to some primitive state?
He did not. Consciousness, no more than life itself, was not something
that should ever be renounced. There was no choice but to live with it
and see more and more. That was the essence of the modern condition.

❖ ❖ ❖

It was an odd class. The student who had selected Rousseau as a presentation subject hadn't made much of the job, so Stephanson, leaping
in, had expounded merrily. But not much happened. He said startling
things and got very little response. His normally voluble students sat
there dully, taking notes. Not even Noah or Manuel had much to say.
How to explain it? Were the students not passing through their own
time of disgust? Apart from clinging to my friends, I couldn't see why,
when I was nineteen or twenty, I needed to make a social existence at all.
The prospect of it daunted and depressed me. Sunk deep in my chair in
my undergrad apartment on 112th Street, I was sure it was impossible.
Why do I have to *present* myself to people? Going into business was no
more than a remote possibility; marriage remoter still; and anxieties
about status something felt only by jerks. Children? I couldn't imagine
them. Any kind of introspection inevitably led to the same realization:
Grown-up life was a crock.

A lot of college students thought that way in the sixties, especially as the war heated up, but in the nineties students were no longer as alienated (or as foolish). After watching Stephanson's students during the Rousseau discussion, I realized that they may have failed to respond for a very simple reason. American expectations had changed. In 1965, I could afford to be in a funk; they could not. Many of the students' older brothers, sisters, and friends may have had trouble finding a job. Gloomy talk of "downward mobility" was in the air. The economy was changing rapidly: entire categories of work were vanishing. Even the highly educated were vulnerable, their jobs—their functions—disappearing in a fit of corporate "downsizing." An eighteenth-century writer rejecting the very idea of society may have seemed to be playing an irritating and malicious game, taunting the students just as they felt growing anxiety about finding a way *in,* finding a *job.*

Rousseau had bombed with Columbia sophomores. But then we no longer lived in a romantic age. Back there in 1965, I had graduated from Columbia, and, a year later, from Columbia's journalism school, and I had gone out to northern California, where Rousseau's ideas, in caricatured versions, were amply watering the flowers of California's many-colored effulgence. Communalism, expanded consciousness, organic foods, home crafts—all such things could be derived from Rousseau's hatred of society, his worship of simplicity and organicism, his longing for wholeness, for unity, though what the great and haughty intellectual would have made of psychedelic drugs and cult of irrationalism and inarticulateness is easy enough to imagine.

In the sixties, worrying about jobs and careers was considered beneath the dignity of all but the neediest of college students. You were supposed to cultivate your soul, enlarge yourself, create yourself as if society and the world of work did not exist. For some people this self-exploration was thrilling and momentous—I'm not knocking it—but few of us knew, or could admit, that our indifference to the world of work was made possible by an expanding national economy, and, locally, by the incredible affluence of California. We were all intent on raising consciousness, but in some ways we were unconscious. The parental support came pouring in, and many of us could afford a modest apartment or a room in a house in Berkeley, Palo Alto, or Santa Cruz, with enough left over for a Datsun or a VW Bug. Postponing work was easy enough and even virtuous: It was called "being a graduate student." Like Rousseau's nut-gatherers, we lived off the fat of the land, i.e., parents and graduate fellowships. We weren't exactly spongers; we drifted seriously. And what a lovely time to drift in. Rock concerts were often free, and sex was everywhere, too, whether you wanted it or not. After spending a night with a woman in Palo Alto, I was sitting in her kitchen in the morning, and the door to her roommate's bedroom suddenly swung open. There sat her roommate on the floor, naked, blond hair falling on her back; she was joined by her boyfriend, also naked, a rather stocky fellow who had just opened the door. "What's going on," I whispered to my friend, trying to swallow my toast. "They want to show us that they aren't excluding us," she said.

In retrospect, the impulse seems charming, and I regret my absorption in my toast. What strikes me as bizarre was my friend's proposing a mini-orgy *on principle*. That was the sixties touch. The sixties were a great period for high moral drama but also for making moral points that no one needed to make; a great time for both self-discovery and pious time-wasting. The indifference to productive labor was inane in my case, since I had not a communal bone in my body and possessed little taste for austerity. I was fond of books, records, restaurants, travel. I needed to earn a living.

But at least I stalled in my own way, reading, making little movies and seeing classic films; and I managed to stay away from the drug culture. The sixties celebration of drugs was the worst perversion of Rousseauian rejection, the old American cult of experience in new passive and transcendental drag. In Palo Alto, or visiting some friend in Marin County, I would sit in exasperated silence as people spoke of their extraordinary trips on LSD. Solemnly, they all said the same thing, the pot- and acidheads, taking their text from the unreadable (for me) acid rag the *Berkeley Barb,* a weekly newspaper satanically decorated in purple, yellow, and green, its prose a jungle of orangutan cliché. It was the unacknowledged legislator to a generation.

I loved California, I couldn't believe my luck in being there (it took me several years to get over an Easterner's vague guilt about the daily sunshine), yet I told myself sternly, carrying my copy of the *New York Review of Books* to two-hour lunches at the Stanford coffee shop, that what one won for the spirit had to be fought for and taken an inch at a time. No one could give it to you in a chemical. Entering a party, I would head for the empty bar, there to find the only other boozer disconsolately pouring Jack Daniel's into a plastic cup. Slowly getting drunk, we would agree that drugs were a decadent mistake.

I became almost notorious as a person who never got stoned, though I did get stoned once—on the night I needed to write an application to enter Stanford's Ph.D. program. One of my housemates had invited some friends to dinner, actors at the university, and they arrived late, so late that I grabbed a dessert box out of their hands and ate three brownies. This was northern California in 1969, but I was too far out of it to know what people baked in their cookies. In a little while, I was lost in a bad trip, a nightmare partly of my own making, since I lay on my bed fighting the hash all the way. Boy, did I fight! I had my application to write. I couldn't let go, and junk came floating to the surface: I was a failure, I loved no one, no one loved me. . . .

Hours later, one of my housemates pulled me off my bed and made me sit with him in the living room. On the television, a man was dancing and laughing, his arms raised in the air. It was Anthony Quinn, doing his roaring Mediterranean-peasant thing in *Zorba the Greek*. Looking at this ruffian, his head thrown back, his big rump shaking, a man feeling good and challenging anyone to find him ridiculous, or even to feel any different than he did, I began to relax at last. I let go—and immediately got high. Which was quite pleasant, though I had no visions, not having read the *Berkeley Barb*. In all the world, I may have been the one person who accepted Anthony Quinn's bullying, excruciating performance in exactly the terms in which it was offered, as a call to personal liberation. Betrayed by actors and then saved by an actor, I'm sure I became a movie critic that very night.

"In civilization, we lose our authenticity as human beings," Stephanson said now, going through Rousseau's themes as the students sat there quietly, and I drifted out of the classroom again . . . this time to a conference of broadcasting moguls arranged by Stanford. Executives from Westinghouse, CBS, and NBC filled the room. Though normally tongue-tied on public occasions, I stood up and with temples throbbing attacked them as a bunch of phonies. They were wooden, bloody-minded corporate dummies. Inauthentic beings. We students did not want to become like them: I was only being honest in saying so. It was a very sixties speech, and it was greeted in a very sixties way: The man who was then president of CBS television, sitting in the audience that day, offered me a job at corporate headquarters in New York.

I was almost embarrassed. A job? To have a job was nothing, but to be a *student*—now *that* was something. As a member of Students for a Democratic Society, I was too involved in the excitements of student life to go to work for what was then the most distinguished broadcasting enterprise in the world. I thanked him gravely and said no.

Thus my Rousseauian sex experience; my Rousseauian drug experience; and my Rousseauian speech. I was sitting on the fence, living in the sixties and both accepting and rejecting its peculiar temper. I hated the idea of society, but only theoretically. I waited for my life to happen; I was not ready. Momentous things occurred in the country—in the spring and summer of 1968, in particular, it seemed as if America were coming unraveled—and our lives as students were infused by a weird mix of apocalypse and orgy, utmost seriousness and utmost triviality. We shifted registers very quickly; we knew it was a great time to be young, and were indifferent to everyone else.

The war was on, and like hundreds of thousands of others, I spent much time at sit-ins and on picket lines protesting American policy. I never entertained the slightest illusion of having a serious effect; mainly, I wanted to clarify things for myself. Thinking about the war, reading about it, seeing documentaries and hearing lectures, protesting, picketing, sitting in, all of this occupied draft-age college students in a way that is now hardly imaginable. The war was truly an obsession: We went to bed with it and got up with it in the morning, telephoning each other with our latest interpretations. Conservatives who now write angrily about the destructive aspects of the American antiwar movement in the late sixties and early seventies don't seem to realize that for many of us the movement was hardly a nonstop round of jeering, sloganeering, and marching, but a time of intense study. I regard the struggle to end the war in Vietnam as one of the greatest intellectual experiences of my life.

Rousseau, or at least the spirit of Rousseau, was everywhere in the radical student movement, and when Stephanson said "Rousseau puts into question what we have *here and now*," I thought of those sixties days when the desire for reform was replaced by millennial hopes of a radical revision of society. The here and now, the despicably *usual* in corporate America, had to go. It was destroying our souls. So we told ourselves. In the universities, people not otherwise stupid or fantastic spoke blithely of "the revolution," as if they lived on familiar terms with it, as if it were only a matter of time before capitalism came tumbling down. At Stanford, a Melville specialist arrived at an antiwar meeting carrying a shotgun. Was it all folly? No, of course not. Among the student left, there were privileged people who worked seriously for reform, organizing the poor, working in the civil rights movement. But most of us were preening.

"These arrangements are not for all time—they are temporal, not natural," said Stephanson, expounding Rousseau. "This system has no legitimacy. It lives by violence, so violence is justified in toppling it over."

Which was a thrilling and necessary idea in the middle of eighteenth-century France, and a thrilling but hopeless idea in sixties America. SDS, after its angelic beginnings in the early sixties, had indulged in fantasies of a violent overthrow of the government. In 1969 and 1970, part of the organization turned to bombs and bank holdups, and by 1970 I left "the movement." All I wanted to do was stop a war: I was no social revolutionary; I was a left-wing, capital-D Democrat with a strong predilection for peace and quiet.

The tomato had landed. Along with the other pieces of food thrown that day, it fell a good thirty yards short of Governor Reagan. He stood on the capitol steps and spoke sternly, facing down the pathetic band of "radicals" just as he faced down the mob (while holding a shotgun) in *Law and Order* (1953), one of the last of the fifty or so incredibly mediocre movies he made in his incredibly mediocre acting career. That was my Rousseauian act of violence. The tomato was actually less a bomb than a boomerang, striking me and others like me: Reagan was elected president years later in part because of scenes like that one in Sacramento, which he handled extraordinarily well. His voice was steady, even, authoritative, and I remember thinking, back there in 1969, "The son-of-a-bitch *has* something." In the end, one learned the prime lesson of left-wing revolutions: Never throw fruit at anyone who understands the theatrics of the situation better than you do.

❖   ❖   ❖

In class, we turned to Rousseau's most famous text, the *Social Contract,* which was quoted in the newspapers during the years of the French Revolution. It is a rousing, contradictory, but nearly incomprehensible work, perfect for selective quotation ("Man is born free, and everywhere he is in chains") but, taken as a whole, frustrating and finally of little use. Rousseau takes up the familiar question of authority and civil society. How much authority is necessary, and how much freedom should the individual have? Hobbes had answered the question with a concentration of absolute power in the sovereign, Locke with an insistence on limited sovereignty and rights. Rousseau defines the problem as follows: "To find a form of association that defends and protects the person and possessions of each associate with all the common strength, and by means of which each person, joining forces with all, nevertheless obeys only himself and remains as free as before." (p. 92)

Which would be quite a trick. What he meant, apparently, was the individuals gave their rights over to the "general will," which, according to context, is either a mystical association of everyone or a public assembly of educated and reasonable citizens—a sort of idealized Geneva composed of individuals educated along Rousseauian principles. What he does *not* mean is a representative body like the House of Commons. Rousseau, in fact, has considerable contempt for English parliamentarism. "The English people thinks it is a free people; it is greatly mistaken; it is free only during the election of the members of parliament; as soon as they are elected, it is enslaved, it is nothing." (p. 144) He wanted a republic of spirit—the people unified and expressing their will in law—not gentlemen politicians and certainly not professional politicians.

But here's the rub: What begins as a voluntary compact ends in coercion. As in Hobbes and Locke, men agree to make a civil society. Once expressed in the social contract, the general will becomes sovereign and "anyone who refuses to obey the general will shall be compelled to do so by the entire body; this means nothing else than that he will be forced to be free. . . ." In this way, and only in this way, man leaves the blessed state of nature but still improves his lot, because in forming and obeying the general will he regains the wholeness and unity he had lost. He could be sovereign and subject at the same time. He loses natural liberty and gains civil liberty; loses possession of everything and gains ownership of a few things.

It was Aristotle's old idea of active citizenship with elements of spontaneity and enthusiasm thrown in. We would participate heavily in citizenship, partaking of power; we would make laws and we must also obey, whether we want to or not. What Rousseau proposes, I thought, might describe the situation, after debate, in the town meetings of a village or commune, or in a lifeboat attempting to make it across the ocean. Something like a general will might arise, perhaps, in the early stages of a revolution, with its incessant meetings and its ecstatic rush of decision and action. Or in any compact, homogeneous society in which Rousseau's desire for unity finds expression in a community of equals ruling itself. Ross Perot, in his hapless fantasies of televised national town meetings and instant voting, revived Rousseau's hostility to representation. Skeptics called it "telefascism." Perot, like Rousseau, wants patriotism, will, excitement—an almost religious enthusiasm for the collective—not the dreary resolution of many private interests. But the dreary resolution of private interests was exactly what James Madison thought necessary if we were going to sustain a state. Madison's thinking produced the Constitution. Rousseau's produced . . . well, the issue was controversial. Some would say it produced revolutionary dictatorship, Stalinism.

"The problem," said Stephanson, summing up, "is that once you constitute a general will, there's no limit to it. You have the possibility of creating a system—I don't want to be nasty—that is totalitarian."

❖   ❖   ❖

I missed the sit-ins, communes, and police bust at Columbia in 1968, but in the spring of 1969, I sat in at a Stanford aeronautics laboratory that conducted classified research for missile guidance systems. The lab was creating weapons that conceivably could be used in the Vietnam War. We protestors had a legal as sell as a moral point: Performing classified research explicitly violated university rules. I thought then that we were right, and I still do.

We sat, and we blocked entrance to the lab, shutting it down, and eventually a few other parts of the university shut down around us as we constituted ourselves a new university, arguing, lecturing, passing around petitions, on and on, day after day. Here was "the general will" in action. Yet though I believed in the protest—the experimental collective functioning day after day—I lost my morale after a while. The endless meetings and speeches began to drain away my brain and then my spirit. After a few hours of listening to the hack language of confrontation, an indescribable restlessness would overcome me. At night, licked, I would go home and read Henry James or Walt Whitman just to clear the bad words out of my head; or I would slink off to a corner of the university where a movie-struck English teacher was showing a Hollywood film of the thirties or forties, and I would become immensely happy watching men in top hats and women in silk gowns passing in and out of white-on-white clubs with cocktails in their hands. I had had enough of the general will. I wanted the private will, the will of the artist, the will of the listener, reader, or spectator. My own will. Anyway, what would be the point of closing down the universities? Where else could we be as free? Fred Astaire saved me from the follies of the sixties.

❖ ❖ ❖

It is a commonplace to say that Rousseau initiated the two great lines of attack against the property-owning new rich, castigating the bourgeois both as exploiter (the line of criticism leading to Marxism) and as philistine (the line leading to nineteenth- and twentieth-century bohemianism). To be a bourgeois was to be alienated from your true self. Yet I knew by the end of the sixties that I was destined for the middle class, New York style. Nothing else was ever really possible.

Rousseau, however, was still powerful and stirring, and always would be. Locke's combination of property rights, legal rights, and constitutional limits of sovereignty was not enough for him. Too tame, too bland, too soulless. He wanted something for the spirit, the blood, a force as powerful as religion. And his challenge gnawed at one's peace. In bourgeois life, you chased away danger, you achieved safety, putting up the tents, filling the tents with pots and blankets and accumulating all those sheep and goats outside—all the goods that were taken from Job. But the effort to be safe, to avoid Job's fate, produced anxiety in its wake. Every once in a while, a sense of loss, even of desolation, came stealing in. Was this *it*? Wasn't there anything else? You mocked such questions, because other people were hungry and had nothing. But the question remained. Other men, suffering from the inadequacy or boredom of living within the social contract, fell from society altogether, embracing violence, the mystic brotherhood of the American outlaw spirit. Violence was not a choice open to me. But still I wondered: Where was the great thing, the transcendent moment? Where was the ease, the sustained view of the flowering hill, the beneficence of a larger, freer life? Would I even know when I had missed it?

Chapter *21*

SHAKESPEARE

- ∼ My mother at the end
- ∼ *King Lear*
- ∼ Shapiro's class: an unhappy ending
- ∼ A play that depends on emotions impossible to admit
- ∼ Professor Tayler nearly weeps
- ∼ A funeral

My mother died the way she did everything, decisively and in great haste. I had been away with my wife and two boys, visiting my wife's brother in California, and the night we returned to New York, I called my mother, as I always did when I got back from a trip. It was February 1991, and she was seventy-five. When no one answered, I knew she was in trouble, and part of me thought, *She's gone.* I knew it even though she had been fine a few days earlier when I talked to her from Los Angeles. It was not possible—it was inconceivable—that she wouldn't be home when her family came back from a trip. At times, she seemed to live for moments of reunion; they occurred every day, or almost every day, when I made my regular call. Sometimes she seemed amazed when I called, as if I had been shunning her. And if I did neglect to call for a few days, amazement was replaced by grief: It was her lot to have a son who had forgotten his mother; a rift had opened up between us that she would now, with great relief, close.

I entered her apartment, two gently murmuring New York cops at my heels, with the sense of disbelief one feels when a catastrophe actually happens, the physical life of it unaccountably not a movie or a dream but the thing itself unfolding, an accident, a fight, a body on the ground. My mother was lying in her bathtub, naked; the shower was on. Her face was black, her lips pressed together in a frown. I took her pulse and turned off the shower, which was cold. There was a small amount of dark blood in the back of the tub—from her mouth, probably. Why was the shower cold? She had had an attack while taking a shower and had fallen; a stroke, perhaps, or a cerebral thrombosis; an aneurysm. I knew it wasn't a heart attack: She had a heart like Tolstoy's. Had she collapsed before she could adjust the shower? The hot water could not have run out in a large modern apartment building in New York. Well, maybe it could have. I left the bathroom and went out into the living room and sat down on the sofa.

A doctor arrived, a small, fussy man, a Haitian in a New York public job. The cops were like angels, silent now, consoling me with moist-eyed glances in my direction—they had mothers, too—but the doctor talked a great deal, and actually rubbed his hands together and bowed. Dimly, I noticed the moment had changed; it no longer had the congealed this-can't-be-happening-but-this-*is*-happening quality. Reality was taking over; farce was talking over. The doctor and one of the policemen struggled to get the body out of the tub and onto the floor of the bathroom. Then the doctor rubbed his hands and chattered some more. There had been no foul play; he would order an autopsy. She had died the previous day, perhaps as much as twenty-four hours ago. I closed my eyes and leaned back into the sofa.

❖   ❖   ❖

When we began reading *King Lear,* in Lit Hum's spring semester, my mother had been dead a little over a year. I had, it turned out, a peculiar, unsought intimacy with this play. When my mother was ill, and at her worst, about four years before she died, I had thought about *King Lear* more than anyone would want to. "She *is* King Lear," I would say angrily to my wife after an impossible phone call or visit, the joke seeming staler and less illuminating each time. She was also my mother, Ida Denby, unhappy as hell and eager to let me know it; a flesh-and-blood worry, mine as well as her own.

The intimacy with *Lear* was not just my own. For once, the echoes knocking about in the media and our heads were not far from the truth. Everyone knows this overwhelming work, at least by reputation, as a fable of stubborn, unreasonable old age and vindictive and ungrateful youth. What people cannot know if they haven't recently read *Lear* is the play's wrenching combination of tenderness and malevolence. Gearing up to read it again, I felt something like fear. It was immense, looming, threatening; sinister and violent as well as noble, a great work that comes and finds us out. Certainly if it *doesn't* suggest something intimate to us, it risks seeming outrageous and improbable, a preposterous fable with overwrought emotions and extravagantly embittered poetry.

Much of it—details of the story and individual lines—came back readily enough, and with the force of accusation. I was unsettled, right at the beginning, by the irascible force of the opening scene—the hardness and bitterness, the sense of catastrophe unfolding as a kind of joke. Lear, a tough old bastard, intelligent but without insight, gives up the

power of the kingship but refuses to give up the precedence and trap-
pings of his royal position. We don't know why he does this. Apart from
the folly of unkinging himself, he is not in any sense failing. He describes
himself later as "every inch a king," and he is. His abdication is a mystery, a mystery compounded by vanity and wrath.

But that doesn't quite capture the strangeness of it. Look again. The
play is set in motion by an excessive parental demand for love. The demand for *love*. Could anything be more homely and banal? Before the
first scene, Lear has decided to award the largest portion of his kingdom
to Cordelia, his youngest daughter and his favorite. But then, seeking
confirmation, and promising to reward in kind, Lear asks each of his
three daughters how much she loves him. It is a kind of trial, an embarrassing command performance of affection. Disgusted, Cordelia
proudly refuses to match the effusive protestations of her sisters ("I
cannot heave my heart into my mouth"), and Lear, in a rage, immediately dispossesses her.

> LEAR
> So young, and so untender?
> CORDELIA
> So young, my lord, and true.
> LEAR
> Let it be so, thy truth then be thy dower!
> For, by the sacred radiance of the sun,
> The mysteries of Hecate and the night,
> By all the operation of the orbs
> From whom we do exist and cease to be,
> Here I disclaim all my paternal care,
> Propinquity and property of blood,
> And as a stranger to my heart and me
> Hold thee from this for ever. The barbarous Scythian,
> Or he that makes his generation messes
> To gorge his appetite, shall to my bosom
> Be as well neighbored, pitied, and relieved,
> As thou my sometime daughter.   (I, i, 106–20)

The play begins with folly and disaster and goes downhill from there.
The two flattering daughters, Goneril and Regan, divide the kingdom
and almost immediately betray their father, successively stripping him of
honor, privilege, comfort, and shelter. Little can be said in extenuation of
the way Goneril and Regan behave. They want their father dead. But
their depredations, and Cordelia's prideful silence, can both be seen as a
revolt against the humiliating demand for love.

It is an emotion most of us would find too embarrassing to talk

about. But Shakespeare was nothing if not apocalyptic at this stage of
his career (*Macbeth* came next), and once the bonds of family love are
broken, everything goes. Everything. The frame of the state, the physical universe itself cracks and splits, and the elements whirl into contention. Civilization gives way to barbarism, shelter to brutal
exposure, fellow-feeling to feral and carnivorous appetite. The imagery turns ferocious: The subordinate animal kingdom of wolves,
snakes, rats, everything that bites and eats, turns on men with fury.
Lear himself casts off his old manner, his sanity, his clothes; it is a
process, violent beyond belief, of unraveling, unhousing, and undress-
ing, until the king is out in a storm with his few remaining loyal subjects and, for the first time in his life, senses what poor and miserable
people must suffer.

> Poor naked wretches, wheresoe'er you are,
> That bide the pelting of this pitiless storm,
> How shall your houseless heads and unfed sides,
> Your looped and windowed raggedness, defend you
> From seasons such as these? O, I have ta'en
> Too little care of this! Take physic, pomp;
> Expose thyself to feel what wretches feel,
> That thou mayst shake the superflux to them
> And show the heavens more just.   (III, iv, 28–36)

Man without a house, without clothes—without civilization, laws,
forms of respect—is nothing, and Lear, now remorseful and anguished,
needs to feel the nothingness in his own skin.

> Thou wert better in the grave than to answer with thy uncovered
> body this extremity of the skies. Is man no more than this? Con-
> sider him well. Thou ow'st the worm no silk, the beast no hide, the
> sheep no wool, the cat no perfume. Ha! here's three on's are so-
> phisticated. Thou art the thing itself; unaccommodated man is no
> more but such a poor, bare, forked animal as thou art. Off, off, you
> lendings! Come, unbutton here.
> [*Begins to disrobe.*] (III, iv, 96–103)

Lear confronts his errors, harrows himself, attains a new consciousness
of himself. The forces of good rally and join, and Lear is reconciled with
Cordelia and with his old friend Gloucester, who, misjudging his own
family, has undergone a similar lacerating ordeal of betrayal and re-
newal. Redemption of a sort is possible, almost achieved, but evil has
grown perverse and extensive, and help arrives too late. The bodies pile
up, including Lear's and Cordelia's.

From its beginnings in banality and dismay, *Lear* goes right to the edge of annihilation, a myth of suffering and knowledge to rival *Oedipus the King,* with a richness of bleak imagery, an almost manic high foolishness that is no less amazing on third or fourth reading. If there's great suffering in the play, there's also a magnificent gaiety in it. Altogether it gave more pleasure and pain than any other work in either of Columbia's courses.

❖   ❖   ❖

A few years earlier, when I worried about my mother, I thought constantly of the play; now, reading *Lear* again, I thought constantly of *her.* The play is about fierce, pre-Christian aristocrats, not American Jewish mothers. But Ida Denby was the Lear of my life.

When my mother was in really bad shape, she was a fright, and I was stunned. In the past, she had been a powerful, even indomitable, figure, and I never had to worry about her. Worry about her? The idea was inconceivable. (It was myself I worried about.) She was born during the First World War, and during the Depression she became one of those women who just went out and launched a career, without benefit of education or professional training, and certainly without a theory of women's rights and capabilities. She became a businesswoman by necessity and instinct, and much later, in the sixties and seventies, she was puzzled by the emergence of a modern feminist consciousness. She couldn't see the need for it; talk of the "patriarchy" and "the oppression of women" only amused her. In truth, I don't think she could imagine anyone holding her back. She had wanted to make money—no, she *had* to make money—and so, like her two sisters, she had dropped out of school and begun working (her four brothers stayed in school and eventually went to college). She was then fourteen, and by the time she hit her early twenties, she was sailing to Europe on the *Mauritania* and buying sportswear in Paris for American department stores. She was a short Jewish girl (about five feet one) from Washington Heights, in New York, and was not especially articulate. Untutored, she *put herself together* (a favorite phrase of hers), and somehow acquired a stone-crushing self-confidence combined with an unshakable system of concealing her ignorance of everything that wasn't necessary to her work, her family, her travel, her clothes, and her table. Until the end, I never knew her to be anything but a tremendous success in her life.

And I never knew her as conscious of her effect on other people, or to be aware of when she had faked her way through something or lied. My mother was possibly the most *innocently* egotistical human being who has ever lived. In other words, she was a happy woman. She was also a heroine. I knew that when I was a very small boy.

Outside the house, I was alarmed by her. When I was thirteen or fourteen, dressed nicely in my gray flannel slacks and blue blazer, the perfect gentleman, I would accompany her on a visit to a manufacturer's plant in Pennsylvania or Long Island, and she would barge in, head for the boss's office, sit on the edge of his desk, her legs crossed and exposed (she had good legs), and say something like, "When are you going to get that fucking shipment of blouses to me?" This was around 1956, when not many women executives talked that way. Of course, she was showing off her little boy. Trembling a bit, I thought, My own movie star! Barbara Stanwyck! She was fast, spontaneous, devastating. She teased the men she worked with, and got away with things that they wouldn't have tried. As far as I could tell, they were fond of her, a prefeminist "working girl" of the thirties and forties who would join them in the shouted give-and-take of a Seventh Avenue showroom as machinery clattered in the background.

She told off salesgirls, too. She was hell to go shopping with, and I was occasionally humiliated by her high-handed ways. Having worked in the forties at McCreery's, the long-gone department store on Thirty-fourth Street near Fifth Avenue—according to family legend, she was the first Jew at McCreery's—she knew all about salesgirls. If a clerk refused to go look for something or take back a purchase, she would browbeat the girl until she broke, and I would suffer. "I saw you on Saturday at Doubleday's," a girl in my eighth-grade class said to me. "You were with your mother. You were crying."

Yet I counted myself lucky. And my father, who was awed by her and crazy about her, was lucky, too, because she was loving and easy at home. With us, she was shrewd; she would try to run everything and then, suddenly, she would pull back. Home was not business, she knew that, and she relented. In any case, she was happy with my father, a costume-jewelry manufacturer and an adroit, low-pressure salesman. He was a quiet and refined sort of man, a gentleman who dressed like Fred Astaire, not a fighter. She loved him and doted on me, the only child, her prince . . . I have a picture of her now in my living room, and she is lying in a hospital bed, her head propped up on her arm, and she is fully made up: lipstick, eyebrows, Rita Hayworth hair—the works. She is almost beautiful. And all this while lying in a hospital bed! A photographer had apparently been called to her bedside to establish that Ida Denby had put herself together. I was, I believe, born just a few days before this picture was taken. The look on her face is a cross between triumph and impatience.

The prince had no complaints. When I heard Jewish-mother jokes, or read Portnoy's Complaint, I would think that I should be the butt of the joke—but I knew that I was not. I had escaped. That wasn't me. Or her. My mother's spiritedness released people who feared her from embarrassment or anger. My mother was okay.

Until my father died. He had been ill for some years, weak from angina, and my mother by sheer willpower had kept him alive, buoying his mood and nursing him when necessary, even retiring for a while and living with him in the country. He died very abruptly, in 1980. We were in a bank on Thirty-fourth Street, he and I, looking at papers in a vault, and he had a moment's warning, a surge of pain. "Not good," he said. "Let's continue our business." And he went on looking at the papers. But a moment or so later, he leaned forward and, without a word, lost consciousness. It was over before I realized what was happening. I called for an ambulance and after that took in nothing until a paramedic, not realizing who I was, felt my father's pulse and said, "This one's a stiff." I immediately forgave him—he had seen, no doubt, several other corpses that day. And I never forgave him.

Both my parents died instantly in New York City, and if I can speak with the selfishness of a survivor, and of an only child, each death was, for me, both easy and hard, since there was no time to say anything. I had, through much of my life, taken my gentle father for granted; we both lived in the shadow of a powerful woman, and at some level I had wanted him to be as strong as my mother. I thought of him as someone who was appended to her, someone to whom she had shown mercy; I hadn't realized how much work went into being her constant companion. But after she died, I saw it clearly enough. He had absorbed much of her energy, taken her aggressiveness into himself and neutralized it. "You can wear her down," he had once confided to me with a sigh. "But you can never make her stop." Yet I don't think he wanted her to stop.

When my father died, my mother, then in her middle sixties, most astonishingly fell apart. And got worse and worse. After a few years, muttering something about taxes, she abruptly and mysteriously quit working and became, still arrayed in battle dress, a warrior without a campaign. Suddenly, she was that diminished person, an American widow; she had no arena in which to expend her desire for command and her anger. She furiously managed her apartment in New York and a house in Long Island and refused to do much else. Nothing was good enough for her. She would see no man, not even for dinner, and refused the chance to make new friends, even as she scared off many of the old ones. In a state of constant irritation, she would denounce companions of thirty years' standing. Only a few young women, loyal acolytes from her business days, retained her interest.

I suppose there was no mystery in this. She had lost her husband, her son (to marriage), and her business—a three-way diminution of power. A freewheeling big spender, a great sport, generous to a fault, my mother no longer commanded expense accounts and travel budgets; she could not invite people to her house or apartment because she didn't have the spirit to entertain them, and as a guest at someone else's house, she was restless and accusatory. If the whole day wasn't planned around her, she was in a state.

I listened and I suffered with her, and I grew embarrassed. She had been masterful for half a century, and now she couldn't seem to find herself. I made suggestions, offering to introduce her to this or that experience, but she would do nothing that I proposed, and at times my sympathy would drain away. Would she go to lectures or join in activities with other retired people at New York's YMHA? (The great "Y"— the Young Men's Hebrew Association, one of the best-run cultural institutions in the city.) She was furious. Sit with housewives? She who had been everywhere, done everything?

"You're killing me with this stuff!"

"With the suggestion that you go to the Y?"

"You're killing me."

All right, would she visit her brothers and sisters in Florida, then? No, there was nothing to do there, no one to talk to but old people. She would not go *down* there. She would die in Florida. And indeed, the one time I shamed her into visiting her kid sister and her husband, she came home accusing them of attempting to do her in.

"What am I supposed to do?" I asked my wife.

"Ask your mother."

Very funny, but my mother was telling me in her way exactly what I was supposed to do. I was supposed to love her, and that love must be unabashed, unreserved, without protection, without sight.

Now, for the first time, my mother's dropping out of school at fourteen hurt her badly. She had few interests to draw on or cultivate, and she was too proud, after years of achievement, to accept instruction. She lacked the patience to read fiction and the information and curiosity to read, say, history, so she read biographies of actresses, duchesses, and gigolos and went to the movies a great deal. For once, I could help, but there were never enough movies or the right ones, and the complaints arrived like a pelting rainstorm on my head. Tradesmen and dentists cheated her; everyone lied. She was suddenly helpless, she who had been a master of trade. For years, I had been wary of her—I had loved her, but I had been wary—and now she wanted everything done for her. She wanted to be taken care of, yet she wouldn't accept care. She would never consider visiting a shrink, and the sole meeting I was able to arrange with a psychiatric social worker turned into a comic disaster. Like mighty Oedipus, she would shatter any mirror that you held up to her. And so, unseen and unseeing, she was relentless in her woe, and there were days when I shut my heart against her.

❖ ❖ ❖

Shapiro began by insisting on the continuing primacy of Shakespeare. "His work is central to our notion of culture," he said. At times, people have thought that if they controlled Shakespeare, they controlled culture. Scholarly contention over texts and interpretation had become a heated political issue.

"Western culture," said Henry.

"All right, Anglo-American, Western—all right," said Shapiro. "But one of the beautiful things is that Shakespeare has been appropriated by the victims of imperialism. In *The Tempest,* Caliban the cannibal is taught language and curses his master."

"Caliban is still under the lash of Western culture," said Henry.

I sighed: One of *those* discussions was brewing. But Shapiro, who was certainly fearless in these matters, pulled away, and took things elsewhere. He had only wanted to establish Shakespeare's preeminence in Anglo-American literacy and the centrality, in particular, of *King Lear,* which seemed almost to recapitulate the Lit Hum course up to this point. A great deal had flowed into the play. Earlier dramatists and poets had set the story of Lear and his daughters, or had referred to it. For Shakespeare, the immediate source of the story was one of the old chronicles that he often drew on (where the story had a happy ending). Shapiro pointed out the fairy-tale nature of the plot. The king had three daughters, two bad, one good, as in *Cinderella*. And Gloucester, Lear's counselor, another foolish old man, had two sons, one good (Edgar), one bad (the bastard Edmund), as in the Cain and Abel story. There was much of the Old Testament in *Lear,* especially of Job, and Lear himself bore an obvious resemblance to Oedipus—certainly blindness rules this play as metaphor and event as much as it does *Oedipus the King*. Shakespeare probably did not know of *Oedipus,* but there *was* a reference in *Lear* to the ghastly family banquet of the Atreus legend, whose quarrels between the generations finds an echo here, as does Dante's execrations and sufferings. There was also something of Montaigne's obsession with nature and custom and the interrelation between the two (Montaigne had been translated in 1603, two years before Shakespeare began work on *Lear*), and if I can jump to C.C. for a second, Edmund, Gloucester's evil bastard son, is surely an example of Machiavellianism in the sinister sense of sheer egotistical calculation. No one at Columbia said "universal classic" or any such phrase—universalism was forbidden at the university—but *Lear* was as close to a summing up as we would get. Reading it again, I thought it was as close to a summing up of life as we would get.

I knew well enough why the play almost frightened me, and I wasn't surprised when Shapiro had to struggle with some of his freshmen to get more than a perfunctory response out of them. A play about murderous relations between parents and children could make anyone queasy—and who more so than teenagers, who were just escaping the command of mother and father and may not have escaped their emotional hold? The students couldn't describe that situation; they were *in* it. For many of them, the play seemed too violent, and quite unbelievable. The young men in particular were harsh; a few fought off *Lear* with contempt for Cordelia or with cynicism ("I would have said to Lear, 'I love you,' " said Lucas, the Southern boy with a lazily knowing manner. "To get a third of the kingdom, I would have said it"), or they read it as merely a struggle among forces of equal merit whose interests just happen to collide. There was contrarianism in this, I thought—the rebellion of young students against what they took to be the sentimental reading of a classic. Henry couldn't see the actions of the bad guys as the utter negation of social bonds that Shakespeare certainly intended; Goneril, Regan, and the rest were simply participants in a struggle for power.

But a number of the students were alive to it—the women, this time, became emotionally involved, so much so that several of them recoiled from the famously unhappy ending, in which Cordelia dies and then the chastened Lear dies, too. "It should have ended with their reconciliation," said Christine Wong. "Otherwise there's no justice in the world." Shapiro was delighted: Her response had a long history behind it. Precisely such sentiments had led to the alteration of the play in 1681 by dramatist Nahum Tate. He produced a happy-ending *Lear* that held the stage from the late seventeenth until the early nineteenth century. Even Dr. Johnson found Shakespeare's ending almost unendurable (though he retained Shakespeare's text for his own edition of the plays). In the Tate revision, the story ends in a way that justice, and especially poetic justice, seems to require: Lear gets his kingdom back and then resigns, and Cordelia marries Edgar, Gloucester's good son. Shapiro read us some of the fustian Tate: "My Edgar, Oh!"—"Truth and vertue shall at last succeed." Everyone laughed. Shapiro immediately called the students on their laughter. If they were tough enough to see that Tate was kitsch, then he would lead them into the heart of the play's tragic emotions. He turned on them relentlessly, as he had before. "What do you want literature to be in your lives?" he demanded. "What kind of resistance do you bring to this play?" He had tricked them, as it turned out, for even in Shakespeare's text there was a possible happy ending (of a sort). Cordelia has been hanged, and Lear enters with her lifeless body in his arms and holds a feather to her lips.

> This feather stirs; she lives! If it be so,
> It is a chance which does redeem all sorrows
> That ever I have felt.   (V, iii, 266–68)

And my poor fool is hanged: no, no, no life?
Why should a dog, a horse, a rat, have life,
And thou no breath at all? Thou'lt come no more,
Never, never, never, never, never.
Pray you undo this button. Thank you, sir.
Do you see this? Look on her! Look her lips,
Look there, look there—
    He dies.   (V, iii, 306–12)

Is Lear deluded? Does he die happily, thinking that Cordelia lives? (By "fool," he means, in this case, Cordelia, not the Fool.) Some of the students thought so. Or was Lear engaging in one last bitter joke? (The latter, I think.) Shapiro pursued them. "You still can't deal with the tragic weight of this? You have to have Lear died deluded? Aren't you turning away from the tragedy as much as Nahum Tate?"

He routed their bland denials, convinced that they could not face the play's dire implications. He quoted one of the play's most famous lines, "As flies to wanton boys are we to th' gods; they kill us for their sport," and took them to the edge of nihilism: "Maybe there's nothing out there, and we're only imagining gods setting out rewards and punishments." What had started as a discussion of a play's ending had turned into a discussion of whether there were *any* moral imperatives in the universe. Henry bristled at this. Imperatives, he said, were set by power. The winners write history and decide what evil is. As a black man, he said, he couldn't see it any other way.

But Shapiro didn't want to end on that note. Talk of cultural issues was, in this case, an evasion. "Shakespeare doesn't impose a philosophy on us. History is written by the winners *and* the losers." At the end of so much suffering, there was a kind of burning clarity in *Lear.*

❖ ❖ ❖

But, with my mother in mind, I thought the play—and the students' resistance to it—was also about something so obvious that everyone was loath to talk about it: the anguish that ensues when the ravages of time invert the accustomed relation between parent and child. As my mother's situation grew worse, her short-term memory began to go (this happened when she was about seventy), and she forgot appointments and addresses and even ran out into the city, a few times, in her robe and slippers. A woman who had bullied many people (though not me) had become almost abject, and once or twice I noticed in myself what I had noticed in others, a secret fascination with the scandal of her weakness. People's eyes would come alive with horrified excitement when she was late for a dinner party. Where was she—on the street? Lost in a taxi somewhere? She would eventually show up, blaming someone else for her lateness, and everyone would be relieved yet still eager to hear the *details* of it. (Her pride helped her there; she never admitted a thing.)

The layers of upper-middle-class armature, the clothes and jewels and furs and furniture that she had so happily earned and enjoyed; the New York restaurant-going and theatergoing that she had so lovingly mastered—none of this could protect her. Her condition was becoming dangerous, and I was paralyzed. I couldn't quite take it in. Suddenly, she seemed naked, and I had no idea how to clothe her. She unhoused herself, showing up at my apartment haggard and drawn, and lived with us for a while, sleeping in the living room and wandering the apartment gray-faced, her gloom relieved only by Max, my oldest son, then seven, whom she doted on.

After a while, she went home—she wanted to live in her own apartment—and we hired women to live with her and look after her, all of them trained to deal with "difficult" older people. But she couldn't bear to have anyone monitoring her and fired them all, accusing each one, after a few weeks, of incompetence or stealing. She seemed as mad as a hatter. Did she have Alzheimer's? The question became unavoidable. My wife and I took her to a well-known neurologist, who asked her such questions as "Who is the president of the United States?" Like so many doctors, he had a profound detestation of what he took to be senility. There was nothing he could do about it, and he was openly contemptuous during the examination.

I was almost ready to put my mother in a home, which would have been a defeat for all of us—almost the modern equivalent of Regan and Goneril's driving Lear out into the storm. But my wife Cathy was not. The neurologist's haughty manner so enraged her that she insisted my mother see another doctor—a young man, but one who knew something about geriatrics—and from the moment my mother entered the new doctor's office, the clouds began to lift. He quickly determined that she had an excess of calcium in her blood, a condition that her old doctor had wrongly attributed to Paget's disease, and one that can, in some cases, cause dementia. Within weeks, a benign tumor was discovered in one of her parathyroid glands, and the gland was removed. In the hospital the day after the operation, when my mother was still in pain, I noticed that she was speaking more logically than she had in years. The nurses were slow, but they were not trying to destroy her. No, they simply had problems taking care of everybody. My wife had saved my mother's life.

Ida Denby quickly regained her sense, her apartment, and some of her peace of mind, and almost enjoyed her last few years. She was better, significantly better, but she still raged against her situation and demanded more love than I could give her. The illness had exacerbated her troubles, but her fundamental nature and situation remained unchanged. She was a powerful person who had let go of the reins yet still wanted to control a team of horses.

All the people she had made feel lazy or unsuccessful in the past fastened on her troubles and then, after her operation, refused to hear that she had gotten better. Even after she was much improved, I couldn't persuade any of them to call her up. "Being weak, seem so," Regan says to Lear when the old king, no longer in office, complains about his emissary being put in the stocks. It is a vile remark. But it's almost understandable, too, because powerful people, as they age, often become obsessed with loyalty and the signs and flourishes of respect while failing to notice how much their children and friends need to maintain their *self*-respect.

Unlike Regan and Goneril, I did my parent no great harm—I took care of her in the slightly distant but steady way that wary only sons take care of mothers—but I was often in a rage. No matter, I told myself at the time. The thing required in grown-up sons was duty. What you felt was beside the point. You had obligations, and you had to fulfill them. She had never failed me, and I could not fail her. But when she died, my tears were produced as much by relief as by sorrow.

The devastating power of *King Lear*, I now realized, is derived from emotions that we barely admit. We are obsessed, so many of us, with power, with work, with money, with love, sex, and art, and meanwhile two of the most essential and unfathomable tasks in life—raising our children and lowering our parents into the earth—pull away at us steadily, unacknowledged and sometimes unattended. After all, there is a structure to professional success; once you get over the early tremors, the early opposition, you learn the way, and there are many places to pause and take stock. But no rules or guidelines, no training or expertise, really helps you take care of children or elderly parents.

The play brings you back to the inescapable struggle for power between the generations. It suggests that the basic human relations in begetting and dying can be intolerable. Maybe that, as well as the injustice of the ending, is what Dr. Johnson found so difficult to bear. For Lear is hardly the only parent to demand too much love from his children. Did I not want my sons to accept my reading, my culture, my tastes—a demand for love in its way as relentless as any other? And who hasn't had moments when he wished his parents dead, as Goneril, Regan, and Edmund did? An amazing work of art: Shakespeare begins with this humiliating, awkward stuff and splits the earth wide open with it.

❖   ❖   ❖

Tayler was wrapping up an intense ten hours—five classes—on Shakespeare. Earlier he had taken the class through a close analysis of the poetic action in a few scenes of *Richard II,* Shakespeare's early tragic history of a betrayed and discarded king. "You've finally arrived at the English language," he told them, "and the English language is pretty tough." He moved out from a few difficult metaphors to the whole play, and they had been good at it, following his lead; he demanded a lot ("More, more, please"), and when they delivered, he complimented them ("This is a very high-powered class; you've already done things that scholars can't do. Stay ahead"). His scholarly field was the English Renaissance, Shakespeare, the Metaphysical poets, and Milton, and at times he outclassed the class, and they were flabbergasted and silent, but he reassured them, and they climbed back into it. The work was all detail, highly specific, highly analytic: He had yanked the students from their freshman reading habits to graduate-school subtleties.

When we got to *King Lear,* he began in the same way, analyzing metaphor and structure, recounting the play's bounty of negatives—the many "nos" and "nothings." But suddenly he said: "Nobody can lay a glove on this play. This is the greatest thing written by anyone, anytime, anywhere, and I don't know what to do with it. In a case like this, no one else knows what to do with it, either."

He had never made a remark remotely like that one, and my wife, who had accompanied me to class that day, looked at me oddly, as if to say, "Who *is* this guy?" for Tayler, the hipster wit, normally imperturbable and allusive, was now on the verge of tears. Quickly, he returned to a notion he had developed back in the fall, when we were discussing the *Odyssey:* the difference between surface, or nominal, recognition and deep, or substance, recognition (in Aristotle's term, *anagnorisis*). Odysseus' son Telemachus, having never seen his long-missing father, voyages out from Ithaca to hear news of Odysseus; meanwhile his father breaks away from Calypso. The two meet in Ithaca, and there begins a series of tortuous recognition scenes, culminating in the mutual recognition of Odysseus and Penelope, outside the bedroom and then in bed, a meeting at first uncomfortable and then joyous.

Lear was similarly about deep recognition—an experience accompanied by pain as well as pleasure. "The play starts out bad, and gets worse and worse," Tayler said in his baritone murmur. "What we've got here is delay, protraction, until moments of supreme recognition." And we read through the scenes of the shattered Lear at the end of the play encountering his old friend, Gloucester, now blinded, and soon after, Cordelia. Tayler, following the Harvard philosopher and critic Stanley Cavell, focused on a plangent exchange between Gloucester and Lear. Gloucester says, "O, let me kiss that hand," and Lear replies, "Let me wipe it first; it smells of mortality."

"I'm sorry, this stuff gets to me," Tayler said haltingly, looking down for an instant. "Lear feels shame. Shame is one of the biggest emotions." He paused for a second, and then glared at some of the men in the class. Now he was almost shouting. "You're breaking out with pimples; your girlfriend comes upon you when you're masturbating. It's *shame!*" The men looked up, electrified but silent. "Shame, the most basic emotion. Lear wants to be *loved*. Lear says, 'Which of you shall we say doth love us most?' But what won't he give? In order to receive love, you have to be seen through and not just seen. You have to let people see your murderous impulses as well as your benevolent ones. En route to recognizing Gloucester and Cordelia, Lear has to go through a process."

And Tayler quoted the stunning speech in which Lear, for years the head of state, now questions the legal basis of authority.

> Thou rascal beadle, hold thy bloody hand!
> Why dost thou lash that whore? Strip thy own back.
> Thou hotly lusts to use her in that kind
> For which thou whip'st her. The usurer hangs the cozener.
> Through tattered clothes small vices do appear;
> Robes and furred gowns hide all.　　·　(IV, vi, 157–62)

"See," said Tayler, "Lear has recognized himself. You recognize something in yourself and you punish someone else for it. You want to fuck that whore, but instead of doing that you punish her instead. Freudian stuff. This is a play about shame and love and recognition."

Around us, the students sat dry-eyed. "I know most of you think you have no trouble recognizing love," Tayler said, "but at the deepest level, the recognition is always dearly bought. We all want love, but how much are we going to go through to get it? Will we risk being seen through? In order to be recognized and loved, you're going to have to get past this point of shame—you have to get to the point where Penelope and Odysseus recognize each other. And to get to that point, it's going to hurt. Afterward, Lear, Gloucester, Kent, and Cordelia—the good people—know the truth and die." So that's why the ending as Shakespeare wrote it is necessary and inevitable. "What you've got here is this incredible parable of human existence," Tayler had said. "It's about stuff that really matters. Love and shame, and about being willing to be seen through as well as seen."

❖　❖　❖

At my mother's funeral, a young cantor sang well, so well that he purged the regrets and ambivalence that were nearly choking me. After her young friends made eulogies, I was ready to say something. "From the beginning to last week, she was strength, my authority, my sword and shield." Which was certainly true. And then I told her story as I've told it here, but without the dismaying part about her final years.

When Lear loses everything and fears he will go insane, his loving
Fool, who continues to attend him, speaks to him in penetrable riddles:
a seeming madness to mirror Lear's madness, a manic yet utterly faithful
critique of Lear's action and state. And similarly, Edgar, Gloucester's
good son, speaks to his deluded father and to Lear in the character of
Poor Tom, a noisy addlepate who thinks that the universe has conspired
against him. Shakespeare's poetry of pretend madness is made almost
unbearably moving by the deeply loving intention behind it: The Fool
and Edgar hope to nurse the two tormented old men back to mental
health with their provocations, while hateful Goneril and Regan speak
to Lear in the tones of the coldest rationality, trying to check his anguished demands with reason. How many knights shall Lear retain
when he stays with either of them?

> LEAR
>   [*To Goneril*]   I'll go with thee.
>   Thy fifty yet doth double five-and-twenty,
>   And thou art twice her love.
> GONERIL
>   Hear me, my lord.
>   What need you five-and-twenty? ten? or five?
>   To follow in a house where twice so many
>   Have a command to tend you?
> REGAN
>   What need one?
> LEAR
>   O reason not the need! Our basest beggars
>   Are in the poorest thing superfluous.
>   Allow not nature more than nature needs,
>   Man's life is as cheap as beast's. Thou art a lady:
>   If only to go warm were gorgeous,
>   Why, nature needs not what thou gorgeous wear'st,
>   Which scarcely keeps thee warm.   (II, iv, 253–65)

The famous lines mortified me as I read the play again, because I was
forever trying to reason with my mother, trying to separate her real difficulties from her imagining of difficulty. When she went alone to her
country house for the weekend, power lines fell down on the house; the
lawn developed gaping holes; pipes burst; ants ravaged the kitchen. Catastrophe after catastrophe, the objective world a mockery of her fallen
state. Her return to the city, on Sunday night, would be capped with a
damage report on the telephone. But how much of it was true? None of
this happened when my wife and I were with her. So I would try to sort
it out, try to get *her* to sort it out.

Was I really helping her with my logical, patient questions? If only I could have let fly my fancy, any fancy that worked, and performed a cure out of love—a cure like the Fool's or Edgar's! Reading *King Lear* again, I see a bit of Goneril and Regan's stony rigor breaking through my exasperated relation to my mother. I revenged myself on her long-held strength by refusing to engage her madness. How could I not have realized that, emotionally, she needed reassurance, not reality?

My mother did not understand much of what was going on with her when she was ill, and afterward did not admit she *had* been ill. She wouldn't even credit the young doctor with saving her sanity. After a few hapless attempts, I never spoke of the matter again. My mother did not know that she possessed an unconscious. She had the noble, infuriating density of fully achieved ego, a pre-Freudian personality. That was partly the source of her strength—and of her capacity for happiness. Throughout our lives together, I struggled to get her to see herself, but she would not be my student.

HEGEL

All right, do it. Plunge in, just like a sophomore. No handrail, no buoy, no raft. Just read it. Read Hegel.

The only thought which philosophy brings with it, in regard to history, is the simple thought of Reason—the thought that Reason rules the world, and that world history has therefore been rational in its course. This conviction and insight is a *presupposition* in regard to history as such, although it is not a presupposition in philosophy itself.

In philosophy, speculative reflection has shown that Reason is the *substance* as well as the *infinite power*; that Reason is for itself the *infinite material* of all natural and spiritual life, as well as the *infinite form*, and that its actualization of itself is its content. (And we can stand by the term "Reason" here, without examining its relation and connection with "God" more closely.)

Oh, good. That last bit helps immensely.

Thus Reason is the substance [of our historic world] in the sense that it is that whereby and wherein all reality has its being and subsistence. It is the *infinite power*, since Reason is not so powerless as to arrive at nothing more than the ideal, the ought, and to remain outside reality—who knows where—as something peculiar in the heads of a few people. Reason is the *infinite content*, the very stuff of all essence and truth, which it gives to its own *activity* to be

309

> worked up. For, unlike finite activity, it does not need such conditions as an external material, or given means from which to get its nourishment and the objects of its activity. It lives on itself, and it is itself the material upon which it works.

Of course.

> Just as Reason is its own presupposition and absolute goal, so it is the activation of that goal in world history—bringing it forth from the inner source to external manifestation, not only in the natural universe but also in the spiritual. That this Idea is the True, the Eternal, simply the Power—that it reveals itself in the world, and that nothing else is revealed in the world but that Idea itself, its glory and majesty—this, as we said, is what has been shown in philosophy, and it is here presupposed as already proven. (pp. 12–13)

"Already proven," perhaps, but not already understood. Yes, reason exists in the world, not just in the heads of a few Kantian moralists. But how is reason the "infinite content"? The content of reality? The reality of wars, plague, and disaster? If so, reason must contain unreason. What about reason in a nursery full of children? Deeply serious men and women might say that the "infinite content" of life is not reason but anarchy. And how does reason "live" on itself and produce itself? Reason sounds like a silkworm suffocating in its own cocoon. In all, the passage, at first reading, seemed like a puzzle made of mud.

Thirty years ago, we had read only a few passages of the Introduction to *The Philosophy of History,* but now C.C. assigned the entire hundred pages of a text that is considered "easy" Hegel. Easy for whom? I read it even more slowly than I read Kant. I crawled through it—but not because it was dull. I wanted to read it more than any previous text in C.C. We had left ethics behind. History was now our obsession; history itself was the protagonist of Hegel's book and of our classroom discussion, and I couldn't have been more eager. But Hegel's writing was excruciatingly difficult, and I was sent reeling back to my days of misery with Kant. To read this peculiar, rolling prose, I needed to destroy so many habits that I would almost have to become a new person. Not just laziness had to be conquered, not just inattention and indiscipline; no, I would have to give up my principal vice and pleasure, daydreaming, and all its warming, voluptuous contentments, because the moment you slip away from Hegel, you lose him altogether and have to start all over again, like a child reciting the alphabet and sent back to the beginning after a mistake.

I could hardly believe it. I moved forward, backward, forward again, and at times, reading the same passage for the third time, going hand over hand on ropes leading into darkness, I thought I was blind. The journalist in me, trained in intelligibility and speed, was close to disgust: This was ridiculous, I wasn't getting anywhere. The hell with this book.

Georg Wilhelm Friedrich Hegel was an academic, a professor at various universities, including the University of Berlin, and when he died (in 1831), his associates assembled *The Philosophy of History* and a number of other volumes from his lecture notes and from notes taken by students. He was, without doubt, the all-time greatest German professor, the German professor as mad genius, and in my worst moments, I sat at home consoling myself with memories of the Marx Brothers and their incomparable German stooge, Sig Ruman (né Siegfried Albon Rumann, in Hamburg), the huge, bearded, hysterical head of the opera or great surgeon from Vienna who tried to thwart the Brothers' plans in some way. They tormented him, defeated him, sent him packing, Harpo running around Ruman's back and honking his horn up the crevasses of his morning coat. . . .

The desire to satirize dies hard in an American. I was amazed by the vagueness, the gloomy overinsistence, the episodes of sheer pomp; I went mad from the repetitions, the way the sentences stretched out and then folded back, like taffy, onto themselves ("Rome itself is the fundamental object in Roman history, and it is that which guides the consideration of all events for Roman historians. But that is because the events have proceeded from this object, and they only make sense in relation to it, for their content is in it." [p. 59]) I was accustomed to the kind of thinking in which one object or force impinged on another, bruising it, transforming it, replacing it—that was the way journalists naturally see the world—and this constant motion of forces reacting back upon *themselves* baffled me.

I took a deep breath, a great many deep breaths. I girded, I steeled, I revved; and I forced myself to read enough to get into the rhythm of it— the rhythmic use of pomposity—and after a while, though still not understanding much, I suppressed my impulse to ridicule and began to feel the surge and spontaneity of Hegel's lecturing voice, a tone of weighted but almost rhapsodic ardor. The repetitions only added to the incantatory quality, and late at night I began reading the text aloud, declaiming quietly in the living room as the cars went back and forth on West End Avenue.

The merest phrase, such as Hegel's passing remark (elsewhere) that "nothing can reveal itself in its truth, and in its intrinsic universality, except to a consciousness that is aware of itself" set off trains of reflection. For here was the essential description of the modern sense of self: To learn anything, one must not only be conscious but conscious of oneself thinking—a notion striking, I thought, in its melancholy. It produced a sense almost of dread: There was no going back; we had a history, we were cognizant of ourselves in history, and cognizant of ourselves thinking and acting. Spontaneous understanding was impossible or meaningless. Among other things, the reading lists in modern universities reflected such assumptions: Men and women would distill the elements of the past that constituted a modern awareness. Columbia's social-theory course was called Contemporary Civilization, even though most of the texts were written long ago. A conscious modern person carried history within herself; the stages were there as aspects of her personal development.

After a while, I learned to read Hegel. The backward-forward movement of my attention became less enraging, and I would understand something and then turn back to an earlier passage that I had found unintelligible, and now, understanding *that,* or at least believing that I did, I felt like a traveler in an exotic country who has learned to speak the language or an acolyte who receives an unanticipated accession of faith and clarity. I would never be a natural or excellent reader of Hegel; I lacked the temperament and the training for it. But at least I was *reading* Hegel. Caught in a profession, and a way of life, that scattered my attention and caused movie images to run through my head, unbidden, day and night, I was nevertheless reading this bizarre, thick-limbed text, and I almost hugged myself in relief. I had risen from my back: The climber loves his conquerable rock, which makes every muscle strain. It was the happiest moment of the year.

The passage of Hegel quoted above is almost on the verge of gibberish, yet everything is ripe, even the parts that are initially baffling.

So start again.

Man could not be seen in the old way, as split between mind and body, reason and passion. A new conception of man was necessary, and a new logic as well. A dynamic whole was contained in consciousness: Man was both subject and object, both self and other, the two things locked in an unending struggle, for each element contained its contrary, and the two elements clashed and merged, producing a new element, which was a synthesis of both—at which time the struggle began all over again as the synthesis developed its own contrary, and so on. History was not blind or shapeless, nor the mere collections of forces, successes, failures, and consequences. In history, Spirit [i.e., the collective human consciousness], or Reason, realizes itself through the struggle of contraries. The whole world—not just religion or the soul—was a matter of Spirit. Our reality was spiritual—an insistence on the ineffable that sent me back, unhappily at first, to Plato's "forms." As Stephanson put it, "Reason was everywhere; it was not something opposed to the body, as in Kant; no, it was *em*bodied, in human beings, who were its vehicles, and in all material things."

There was a coherent progression in what seemed random or chaotic or even catastrophic, a shape which unified everything into a single *universal* history. World history moved toward a given end. Of course, we had heard versions of this before in C.C. Christianity insisted on a gigantic plan for history, too, ending in Judgment Day and the Resurrection. But Hegel thought Jesus came late in history; He was an important part of the Hegelian plan, not its meaning.

Examined episode by episode, history might seem, as Hegel admitted, a "slaughter-bench." But Reason has "cunning"; it hid itself, sometimes hiding itself in disaster. The goals history was working for were the greater and greater enlargement of freedom. Most famously: "The history of the world is none other than the progress of the consciousness of freedom." So the essence of this universal history is not just the burgeoning experience of freedom, but the *consciousness* of it (without which the experience of it would not be possible), and that consciousness can be attained over centuries only through a series of dialectical transactions, a relentless spiraling upward. How did the progression through history actually work? And what justified the catastrophes along the way—what turned the "slaughter-bench" into a spinner's wheel? That part I did not understand yet, but still, the passage quoted earlier, now read again, made a little more sense.

Calmer now, and reading steadily, I knew I was at last beginning to break free. What had been plaguing me, not knowing where Woody Allen ended and I began, or when Michelle Pfeiffer was there speaking and wrinkling her brow and when she wasn't, when I was shooting down Nazis or just sitting in my living room; that certainty that my mind had been invaded and taken over and the movies never stopped playing, leaving me without concentration because I had abandoned the pleasures of concentration to the pleasures of fantasy; that anguish of being *lost* in the media, a part of the swamp of representation, and therefore merely another producer and consumer of images and words without identity or form of my own—all of this was beginning to fade. It had been fading all year, I realized, and now I actually felt it going, and I saw a boundary. The man reading Kant and Hegel was not part of the pulsing electronic media. Not at that moment.

❖ ❖ ❖

When reading Hegel on history (the Introduction was only the beginning of a very long work), one had the illusion of vast-ranging vistas, the long, long reach of epochs, and one felt lordly, and winged. That emotion may have been an unintended self-reward for hard work, but it was produced as well by the substance of what Hegel says—which, for Westerners, is dangerous, heady stuff. For there was a main line in history, an express train, and you were either on it or you were not.

> In the world of the ancient Orient [i.e., China, India, Egypt, Persia], people do not yet know that the Spirit—the human as such—is free. Because they do not know this, they are not free. They know only that *one* person is free [i.e., the emperor or pharaoh or king]; but for this very reason such freedom is mere arbitrariness, savagery, stupefied passion; or even a softness or tameness of passion, which is itself a mere accident of nature and therefore quite arbitrary. This *one* person is therefore only a despot, not a free man.
>
> It was among the Greeks that the consciousness of freedom first arose, and thanks to that consciousness they were free. But they, and the Romans as well, knew only that *some* persons are free, not the human as such. Even Plato and Aristotle did not know this. Not only did the Greeks have slaves, therefore—and Greek life and their splendid freedom were bound up with this—but their freedom itself was partly a matter of mere chance, a transient and limited flowering, and partly a hard servitude of the human and the humane.
>
> It was first the Germanic peoples [i.e., the Western European peoples, particularly all countries filled with Germanic tribes such as the Franks, the Saxons, etc.], through Christianity, who came to the awareness that *every* human is free by virtue of being human, and that the freedom of spirit comprises our most human nature. This awareness arose first in religion, in the innermost region of Spirit. But to introduce this principle into worldly reality as well: that was a further task, requiring long effort and civilization to bring it into being. For example, slavery did not end immediately with the acceptance of the Christian religion; freedom did not suddenly prevail in Christian states; nor were governments and constitutions organized on a rational basis, or indeed upon the principle of freedom.
>
> This application of the principle of freedom to worldly reality—the dissemination of this principle so that it permeates the worldly situation—this is the long process that makes up history itself. (p. 21)

Now we were in trouble. The description of the slowly enlarging consciousness of freedom is marvelous, but it could not be more clear that only Europe really counts. The arrogance of Hegel's assumptions took my breath away: Only Europe (and by extension, its stepchild, America) *moves* through history. The universal history is *Western* history. Apart from the "world-historical peoples" and "world-historical individuals" (Julius Caesar, Jesus, Napoleon, etc.), the great mass of humanity are not part of the advancing consciousness of freedom; they live in the back-waters. In the East, Hegel said, individuality was ground down, consciousness stifled. China and India were "stationary" societies, locked in repetition. In one crucial respect, Asian moral philosophy existed on a lesser plane than the Western varieties.

> Chinese morality has received the greatest praise and appreciative recognition from Europeans committed to Christian morality, ever since they first became acquainted with Chinese morality and with the writings of Confucius. In the same way there is recognition of the sublimity with which Indian religion and poetry (of the higher sort), and especially its philosophy, declare and demand that the sensuous must be set aside and sacrificed. Yet both these nations, it must be said, are entirely lacking in the essential consciousness of the concept of personal freedom. To the Chinese, their moral laws are like the laws of nature, expressed as external positive commands, compulsory rights and duties, or rules of courtesy toward one another. What is missing is the element of freedom, through which alone the substantive determinations of Reason become moral conviction in the individual. Morality, for them, is a matter for the state to rule on, and is handled by government officials and the courts. Their works on the topic (those which are not books of law but are rather directed at the subjective will and disposition) read like the moral writings of the Stoics: they offer a series of commandments which are necessary to the goal of happiness, so that the individual can arbitrarily decide to follow them or not; and, as in the Stoic moralists, there is the representation of the abstract subject, the sage, who stands as the culmination of Chinese moral doctrine. And in the Indian teaching about the renunciation of sensuality, the renunciation of desires and earthly interests, the aim and end is not affirmative ethical freedom, but rather the negating of consciousness—in mental and even physical lifelessness. (pp. 74–75)

There speaks Western pride, and there speaks "hegemony," too, unapologetically and heroically. Freedom was an achievement whose attainment had little to do with peace or obedience or renunciation. In the West, freedom could be attained only through the struggle of consciousness. Whatever else it did, the book offered Eurocentrism with a vengeance, Eurocentrism produced by philosophical system and ethical ardency—just what the academic left has tried to recast in recent years as prejudice, a mere rehearsing of one's own values in a mirror of self-approval.

I was alarmed, and by the time I got to the end of that passage, I knew why: Hegel's prejudice was my own. And not only my own; I would bet that many Americans and Europeans thought the same way. From the outside, at least, it appeared to some of us that Eastern cultures simplified the issue of human dignity. Obedience and conformity to the law were paramount; loyalty to the caste system, the society, the family, the group, the corporation—these were the essentials of a dignified life. One learned what was required, and one performed. *Assent* was necessary; consciousness was not, or at least not crucially.

I would remain politically incorrect in the matter, though I knew the danger inherent in such thinking—that it produced aggression, a desire to dominate other cultures. Or that it led to racism. But I was no imperialist, and the differences Hegel is speaking of are cultural, not racial. Justified pride in Western ideals is not in itself a form of imperialism or racism. Hegel, clearly, was on to something: The differences between cultures were produced essentially by deeply held religious assumptions. Even the worldwide triumph of capitalism would not bring East and West together. As everyone now said, countries like Singapore and China were modernizing but not Westernizing. Singapore, capitalist to its fingertips, was profoundly (and consciously) hostile to some of our most cherished ideals, including freedom of speech and behavior, individualism, women's rights, trial by jury, and so on. The Asians hated the American chaos; they were unimpressed by our moral glory—the insistence on freedom and selfhood even at the price of disorder. God knows it is an ideal increasingly hard to defend.

❖   ❖   ❖

Hegel, Stephanson insisted, was immensely influential in many directions. So much of modern philosophic discourse seemed to come out of his work. Again, Stephanson was in his element. His enthusiasm was challenging and contagious. He shouted, rallied, led us through the dense abstractions. He seemed almost eager to ravish the American naïveté, the American pragmatic bluntness, with this fervently complex and intoxicating German idealism. The students were happy, too. Difficult texts brought out their powers and made them eager to talk; the conversation largely stayed away from controversy and current events and remained devoted to pinning down what Hegel had *said*. The students followed the convolutions and reflexive inward turnings of Hegel's logic as closely as they had followed the matter of any text all year.

We immediately set up a contrast with Kant's idea of radical freedom—Kant's notion that an extension of will makes us free from nature and contingency, that morality was a product of rational will, quite apart from what makes us feel good, useful, or successful. "For Hegel, Kant's notion of morality was empty," Stephanson said. "*Content* will always thwart this empty notion of duty. Once you get content into the form of behavior, you get history. Things happen over time; you can't separate human beings from the rest of life."

Happy in my new success as a reader, I found this momentous. *Once you get content into the form of behavior, you get history.* That sentence alone might be definitive of what the Contemporary Civilization course was about. History, according to Hegel, fell into distinct epochs that could be characterized by the nature of Spirit in each epoch. The C.C. reading list featured some of the great texts that represented Spirit in the Greek world, the Roman world, the Renaissance, etc., all of them arrayed in a linear progression. Now, no one I heard at Columbia described the course in these terms. The great ideal of the Enlightenment, progress, had in recent years gotten a bad name. In the university (though not outside it), progress was theoretically dead as a benefit of history. In particular, no one wanted to be turned into a sucker by the twentieth century, which in some ways was the worst century. But the organization of the courses spoke louder than words or theory. There was clearly a notion of historical progress—and possibly even Hegel's notion of an advancing consciousness of freedom—implicit in the chronological procession of texts.

History moved dialectically, and Stephanson recapitulated this process. "The subject," Stephanson said, returning to the struggle of consciousness, "is both part of nature and at the same time *not*. We have an inner unity with nature, but reason struggles against this. There's a tension, a struggle. Everything is in a position of struggle or conflict. The attempt of the subject to understand necessarily entails distance: The subject is engaged in self-realization, a project which involves both identity and difference—negating ourselves at the same time that we are realizing ourselves."

Negating ourselves at the same time that we are realizing ourselves. It had a heroic sound to it. The West *in excelsis.* The self at its best was in a constant wrestling match with itself, Odysseus arriving home at last only to go away again and complete his adventures, every resolution leading to a fresh struggle, another task of consciousness. Hegel's dialectic was dynamic and relational thinking. You take that which is inwardly subjective—your essence—and make yourself objective. You *produce* yourself, and the new reality is the objectification of your subjective essence (forgive me, it's catching). You are alienated from yourself and you overcome this alienation. "We move one step ahead," Stephanson went on, "and there are new contradictions; we reach a level where Spirit has become identical to itself, a moment of self-awareness, and then there's a new gap, and on and on."

History, then, was the gap between idea, or essence, and material fact.

But Spirit constantly strives to integrate itself, to reinstate that which is opposite to it. When the gap is closed, when Spirit becomes conscious of itself, a synthesis is produced, a crystallization of values, political organization, religious practice, art, and so on (the realization of Spirit in a given era)—which, in turn, by the force of its triumph, the very one-sidedness of its victory, gives rise to internal contradictions, leading to a new gap, and so on. But Hegel cannot be summarized; he must be experienced. You must swim in the boundless sea. *Jump in again. And just keep going. Just read Hegel.* Here is a key passage, the series of dialectical transactions producing the shift from the Roman to the Christian epochs.

> The Roman world is no longer a world of individuals in the way that the Athenian polis was. Here there is no joy and cheer, but only hard and bitter work. The common interest is detached from that of individuals, although in working for it they gain an abstract, formal universality for themselves. The universal end subjugates individuals; they must surrender themselves to it. But in return they receive a universal version of themselves: the status of persons. They become legal *personae,* having a private status.
>
> In the same sense in which individuals are incorporated into the abstract concept of the person, the "individuals" that are independent nations will have to experience this fate as well: that is to say, their concrete form will be crushed by this universality, the Roman state, and they will be incorporated into the greater mass. By incorporating these different cultures, Rome becomes a pantheon of all gods and all things spiritual—although these gods and their spirituality do not retain their characteristic vitality.
>
> The development of this world has two significant sides to it. On [the] one hand, it has an express and declared antithesis within itself, an antithesis based on reflection, or upon abstract universality itself: that is, the Roman world displays within itself the struggle of that very antithesis [i.e., between universality and individuality]. The necessary outcome of all this is that an arbitrary individuality eventually gets the upper hand over the abstract universality. Rome passes into the utterly contingent and thoroughly worldly power of *one overlord,* the emperor. Originally there is the antithesis between the common good of the state (as the abstract universal) and the abstract person. But then, in the course of history, the element of personality becomes predominant; the community then begins to break up into its component atoms, so that it is only held together by means of external power. And then the subjective force of sovereign domination comes forward, as though summoned to this task. For abstract legality cannot be concretely real in the individual, and his

life is not genuinely organized around compliance with the law; and inasmuch as abstract legality has come to power, this power is merely arbitrary, as the contingent subjectivity of one mover, one ruler. And then the individual subject seeks consolation for his lost freedom through the development of private right. This is the purely *worldly* reconciliation of the antithesis.

There is also a *spiritual* reconciliation (which is the second side to the development of the Roman world). With the fragmentation of the outer political world, held together only by external force, the pain of the despotism begins to be felt. And the spirit, driven back into its innermost depths, abandons the world that has lost its gods. Spirit then looks to itself for the reconciliation that it needs. Now there begins the life of its inwardness, a fulfilled concrete inwardness, which at the same time possesses a substantiality that is not rooted in outer experience. In the inwardness of the soul, therefore, there arises that spiritual reconciliation, in the fact that the individual personality is purified and transfigured into universality, or into its own implicitly universal subjectivity—transfigured into divine personality. Now the merely secular world is more readily opposed by the spiritual; it is the world of those who know themselves in their own subjectivity, and know that inwardness as their very essence, the world of the actual Spirit.

With this we enter the fourth [stage] of world history, that of the medieval *Germanic World*. . . . (pp. 96–97)

Okay, fine. Now read it again.

Look, it's hard, but it's not *that* hard. The Roman citizens gain a formal universality for themselves by their membership in the Empire (thesis), but there is a contradiction: They give up an aspect of freedom; they become subjugated—a great many particular existences are yoked to one "universal" existence (antithesis). The citizen, however, receives something in return, legal status, the paterfamilias now enjoying the right to pass on his estate to his son. He attains, for the first time, legal *personhood* (synthesis). What's been established in history is the separation of the public and private (thesis), which leads to new contradictions (antithesis), for in time, the notion of the universality of the Roman state devolves into the personal dictatorship of the emperor, and the individual withdraws into private right: That is, the domain of private right that had first been set up *legally* in the Empire sets the ground for an opening *spiritually,* the development of a purely inward spiritual reality, namely Christianity (synthesis).

Later Hegel will say that the immersion of the medieval Catholic Church in worldly power sets up new contradictions that are resolved by the Protestant Reformation. A new personal inwardness develops: Men form private relations with God. The dialectic moves on, an endless spiral upward, hallelujah!

But I was still troubled by the issue of violence and catastrophe, and its place in the alleged march of reason. Spirit, as it moves through history, has an unmistakably moral force: Hegel is praising a very specific historical destiny, and it is a moral one. But how could Hegel account for events that violated the moral principles that Spirit is allegedly expressing? How much disaster could be explained by—which often meant excused by—"the cunning of reason"? This was no mere academic question, since a great many atrocities—all of Stalin's crimes, for instance—had been committed in the name of a later (i.e., Marx's) version of "history" and "inevitability." Reason might have more blood on its hands than could ever be washed off.

In class, Manuel took up the Holocaust, which he discussed with a relish that made some of the students wince. "The Holocaust," he said in his raspy voice, "was the Fortunate Fall. It *drove* the founding of Israel. Nobody was going to accept the Jews in any other land but their own. The Europeans did not feel a practical necessity to acknowledge Jewish culture."

"And the Jews created a culture out of that rejection," said Noah, rather testily, his eyes flashing darkly behind his glasses.

"You can make the Hegelian argument," Stephanson said, sensing an unnecessary quarrel and rushing in, "you can make the Hegelian argument that the Holocaust can be read dialectically. When you're looking back, Hegel might say, what seem like horrendous events happened because they had to happen—they brought things forward. But this is not a justification *for* the Holocaust."

His clarification only introduced greater contention. Several students voiced their dismay, and I snarled to myself that I lacked the ingenuity to read the Holocaust dialectically as the necessary spur to Israel's creation. We had come close to endorsing the vulgar reading of Hegel, which is to use him to justify whatever has happened as inevitable and necessary. If the Holocaust were an example, however disguised, of Reason's march toward freedom, then Reason was a monster. The twentieth century, with its atavistic racial and tribal slaughters, its fanatical religious conflicts, its renewed ethnic particularism, and the degeneration of "rational" bureaucracy in Germany and the Soviet Union into systems of murder, was certainly a very treacherous time for the march of Reason. Reason's cunning must be very deep indeed if it manifested itself through all these annihilating events.

What did Hegel mean by freedom, anyway? Freely reasoning individuals, as we've heard, choose their conduct according to conscience rather than by submitting to authority. In Hegel's terms, such individuals were produced in Europe by the Protestant Reformation, which made the relationship to God, and questions of truth and morality in general, an individual matter. Such people flourished in particular in the modern nation-state—a state, that is, like Prussia after the French Revolution and the Napoleonic Wars, two events that had the effect of sweeping away feudal privilege and superstitions and establishing a rational system of administrative bureaucracy. In such a state, freedom, and the recognition of freedom, was extended to every citizen—all recognized one another as free. And since the individual, acting according to conscience, would no longer find himself in opposition to the state (as, say, he might in Rome or medieval France), the contradictions that had impelled history forward would come to an end. History would come to an end.

Which, all in all, is rather deflating and dismaying, since many of us would be loath to nominate Prussia in 1815, with its censorship, its lack of representative bodies, as our ideal of freedom. Indeed, if Prussia was Hegel's ideal, he may well have approved, despite his dismissal of the morality of the East, the paternalistic and authoritarian Singapore—approved it far more than he would modern America, with its liberty bordering at times on chaos, its commercialized hedonism, its temper split between derision and sanctimoniousness.

In the wake of Hegel, the exact meaning of history has been debated for over 150 years—by Marxists, who claimed history for the class struggle and the inevitable proletarian revolution; by capitalists, who claimed it for the marketplace and the freedoms of bourgeois democracy; and by fundamentalists, too. The future was up for grabs, and those who controlled the "meaning" of history thought they were controlling the future. But perhaps Reason's cunning would elude everyone, and those who tried to control history were left with only irony and defeat.

❖ ❖ ❖

However strange and ambivalent the view from the top, I felt happy that I had climbed the mountain. But just as I was basking in my relative success as a reader, and basking as well in the dignity that Hegel had conferred on the Western notion of consciousness, I took a tumble. Stephanson asked us to grapple with the famous, impossibly difficult nine-page passage known as "Lordship and Bondage," from Hegel's early work *Phenomenology of Mind* (1807). In Hegel's dialectic, consciousness forever contradicts and corrects itself. As I struggled with this tangled-underbrush prose, and even began to understand parts of it, a few glaring contraries in my own nature stood out rudely. So now, without intending ever to be there again, I found myself at the top of the subway stairs yet again. The encounter with the two robbers had taken on a new meaning.

"Lordship and Bondage" could be read as Hegel's version of the transactions between men in a state of nature. It was the old philosophical fiction that Hobbes and Locke had made so much of, this time with a dialectical twist. In Hegel's version, instead of an implicit contract creating a new civil society, a kind of primordial drama of self and other unfolds. Two men confront one another and become self-conscious. (Hegel means "self-conscious" not in the American sense of the word—ashamed or bashful or unspontaneous—but in the opposite sense, pridefully conscious. The men are conscious of themselves as actors.) True self-consciousness exists when each is aware of the other and aware of the other's awareness of himself. Each is *acknowledged* by the other.

> Each sees the *other* do the same as it does; each does itself what it demands of the other, and therefore also does what it does only in so far as the other does the same. Action by one side only would be useless because what is to happen can only be brought about by both. . . . They *recognize* themselves as *mutually recognizing* one another. (p. 112)

There follows a kind of explosion, a Hegelian eruption, in which two things may happen: Each may seek the death of the other; or one may refuse to risk his life, at which point he becomes the "bondsman" of the other—not literally his slave but his inferior (peasant to his lord, foot soldier to his commander, servant to his master). Francis Fukuyama discussed this transaction in endless detail in his 1992 book (which Stephanson advised we read), *The End of History and the Last Man*. In Fukuyama's interpretation of the primal conflict, which leans heavily on writings by the twentieth-century Hegel exegete Alexandre Kojève, the desire for recognition through struggle, the desire for *prestige*, was one of the mainsprings of human conduct. By prestige, Kojève intended an equivalent to Plato's "spiritedness," or what modern people mean by "pride" or the demand for "dignity." Such a force operated in work, in politics, in competitive behavior of all sorts. It is a noble demand.

So Hegel, in this account, sends Hobbes and Locke spinning. It is not the desire for self-preservation that creates society but exactly its opposite, the *refusal* of that instinct. The prideful man, by ignoring his natural instinct to preserve his life, asserts his freedom. He escapes the instinctual, which is the normal desire merely to live. He becomes the other man's superior and a social bond is formed.

My encounter on the subway steps now took a different form. I had not looked the two young men in the eyes, literally refusing them "recognition." The reason, as I said earlier, was both contempt and fear: You do not eyeball someone holding a gun on you. And yet my refusal also meant that I was unwilling to engage in a battle for "prestige." Acting to preserve myself, I obeyed what Hegel considered the baser instinct, the desire merely to survive. I would not risk my life for money or for recognition. In gross terms, the two young men "won" the encounter; I gave up my money. Yet I did not become their "bondsman" or anything close to it. For the bourgeois man, prestige, in Hegel's sense of an acknowledgment of dignity, is not at stake in a confrontation with someone holding a gun. In brief, cowardice, as a moral issue, has almost dropped out of the confrontation. Almost, but not quite.

On their side, the two young men wanted not only money, they wanted to impose themselves on me. They were angry, I now remembered, angry that I hesitated, in a moment of rebellion, withholding my wallet for an instant or two. By not giving them the money immediately, I demonstrated a lack of respect for them (people have been killed for as much). And yet, even though they won the encounter, they lost the battle for prestige. If not at first, then eventually: I didn't seek prestige because I can get it elsewhere; and their prestige, once gained, doesn't last—or rather, it is only temporary, until it is taken away by someone else. The inequality of our social positions was such that they cannot, more than momentarily, gain in prestige by forcing me to act on the mere instinct to preserve my life.

I did not need to risk my life; yet they risked *their* lives. I might have taken out a gun, like Bernhard Goetz, who shot four boys who accosted him in the subway in 1984. Running away from the robbery, they might have been shot by the police. They risked their lives in general by entering into crime.

In Hegel's fiction, the men who met at high noon had no past; they met, so to speak, as equals. The two men who faced me were probably descendants of actual slaves, and while one can't forget that, the fact doesn't, in itself, change the nature of the encounter. The difference between us was one of class. If the two young men had held up a black man in a suit on his way to work, the dynamics of the situation would have been the same.

Thinking of all this as I read "Lordship and Bondage," I was sore and unhappy—not ashamed in the way of the guilty liberal, who was convinced, or allowed himself to be convinced, that he was oppressing blacks merely by being white and privileged. That was nonsense. No, I felt uneasy because I did not have to risk anything, and they did. *They did not know that other ways to prestige were open to them.*

When I understood this, my contempt for them vanished. And was replaced by despair over their situation. People have always stolen, or plundered, but have they ever risked so much for so little? The demand for respect had been trivialized by consumerism, which perverted a noble instinct into folly.

In the Hegelian dialectic that follows the primal confrontation, the winner who becomes "lord" cannot pridefully enjoy the respect of someone who is his bondsman. But as nominal "winner," I did not want respect, I wanted only to be left alone. And on the other side, the Hegelian bondsman makes *his* demand for respect, or recognition, through work. "Work . . . is desire held in check, fleetingness staved off," Hegel writes. In work, the loser in the primal confrontation "rediscovers" himself. But work is the lost good for a sizable minority of inner-city youth, and certainly for youth who hold people up. So both parties, bourgeois and underclass criminal, lost their dialectical reward. I was left ashamed of my lack of courage, and they were trapped into scorning work as the way to recognition.

In America, at least, the dialectic had become uncoiled, yielding contraries that failed to engage their opposites. The dialectic had run aground.

Chapter 23

AUSTEN

It was early spring, and as life began to bud in Columbia's sparse bush and tree, a newborn student, like some alien creature in a horror movie, burst out from the middle-aged man. I was raising my hand more and more, "intervening" as Stephanson liked to call it (he even referred to "one of your most interesting interventions"), or "raising an interesting point," as Shapiro said. Sometimes I sat there in a flutter. I wanted to tell everyone that Hume was great stuff, that *King Lear* was overwhelming. I was full of news, and couldn't keep myself quiet. Call on me! *My* hand is up! The actual students had come to accept me as a regular participant—the Adult Who Was Not the Teacher—and the teachers had as well, though with what misgivings I could easily imagine.

In Tayler's class, however, I kept my mouth shut. For each two-hour session, Tayler carried a map of the terrain in his head, and I was fascinated by his attacks and retreats, the cagey, gracious, but dominating stratagems he used to get from one place to the other. I didn't want to interrupt him. Anyway, I couldn't. In his quiet, slow-speaking way—between his gnomic questions, he paused like Bob Newhart savoring the air—he was a teaching demon, and you had to accept his methods, or reject him altogether. He was now in the latter stages of his campaign. Teaching Jane Austen, he laid out, with considerable student help, the overall structure of *Pride and Prejudice,* but then he asked first one and then another of the students to take the role of teacher. As he remained at the front of the class, the troops took over, especially the women, who clearly loved the book and who rose to the occasion with delight. *My*

God, it's happening. He's getting them to do it. Felicia Parker, a well-drilled prep-school girl from Washington, D.C.—she had a mind as orderly as her clothes and hair and book bag—read passages aloud and asked questions of the class, and then drew together the answers into a pattern, and Tayler, who was watching intently, said, "I don't know if you can handle this, Parker, but the whole class was taking notes."

What was it he had told them way back in the fall? *They would grow in order to read the books, they would create a self, and in the end, they would make him obsolete.*

"Sterngold, get mileage out of Wu. Squeeze her dry," he urged, and when Sterngold was done squeezing Miss Wu, who was very eloquent (and accurate) about the moral limitations of Mr. Bennet, one of Jane Austen's most deceptive and alarming creations—when Sterngold and Wu had concluded, Tayler stepped away from the text and placed Jane Austen very firmly in the history of Western thought, going right back to the book of Genesis and the opening class of the year. In the organic plan for the entire course he carried in his head, Jane Austen played a major role and so did this first day of students' teaching one another.

Listening to Tayler, I felt like a freshman. But listening to the others . . . Was it just a student that I wanted to be? I talked too much, I had gone past wanting to be a student; I was competing with the teachers in some way. At home, as I sat reading, my fantasies had drifted from movies to talking with students. All year long, I continued writing my movie reviews, but my heart was elsewhere. The week before reading Jane Austen, my column began, *"Basic Instinct,* the new exploitation thriller about sex and murder, will do wonders for the sale of headboards and Hermès scarves. After tying her lover's hands to a bed, a blonde, sitting astride . . ."

Ah, the movies, God bless them! They were so innocent: They still believed in shock. The piece on *Basic Instinct* was a review I wrote with my fingers. One word after another. Once I had absorbed the movie's peculiar enticements ("At the peak of his pleasure, she kills him. With an ice pick"), I dealt with it as professionally as I could and got back to my real life as a reader. I would never "get beyond" movies; I didn't want to. But my head was filled with books, and at times I went a little out of control. I wandered around, sampling other teachers' sections (with their permission), and in one such class, taught by a young woman graduate student, I raised my hand and said a few things, a sentence or two, only to have the students glare at me with indignation. The same night the instructor called me at home and said, in a slightly tremulous voice, "Please don't come back, the students don't like it. They feel you're disrupting their relationship with me." I bit my tongue in fury. She was right.

Shapiro, who was perceptive about other people's needs, took pity. "Why don't you teach the class for a while?" he said. He would give me some space at the beginning of the first class on Jane Austen. I had to do it; I had to see what it felt like. How hard could it be?

❖ ❖ ❖

> It is a truth universally acknowledged, that a single man in posses-sion of a good fortune, must be in want of a wife.
>
> However little known the feelings or views of such a man may be on his first entering a neighbourhood, this truth is so well fixed in the minds of the surrounding families, that he is considered as the rightful property of some one or other of their daughters. (beginning of *Pride and Prejudice*)

The opening sentences—perhaps the best-known beginning in the history of the English novel—bristled with a familiar curt decisiveness. I sank into my sofa with relief. After long voyages, we were home among accustomed pleasures. Not that anyone should make the mistake of taking Jane Austen for granted. However familiar, Austen was no one's pet. As almost every reader discovers, the first sentence is a joke and a trap. Most of *Pride and Prejudice* will demonstrate the opposite of what the sentence says. It is not rich men but nearly impoverished genteel women, like the five Bennet sisters, whose father's estate is entailed away from them, who are "in want," and in want of the unmarried wealthy young men. The opening sentence represents not a truth "universally acknowl-edged" but a truth very particularly acknowledged by the mercenary Mrs. Bennet, the vulgar, tactless promoter of her daughters' prospects, who is the book's chief butt (and secret heroine—but we don't know that until much later).

This narrator can't be quite trusted; she withholds, misleads, under-mines, plays tricks on the reader's credulity. You have to come back to the opening sentence, and then, much later, you can read it still a third time and discover that it does, in a covert way, tell the truth.

We were back in English, whose supple folds yielded such intricate miracles; and I was relieved, for I had been through some tough times with the foreign gentlemen. There was my misadventure with Dante, in which my ignorance of Italian had left me with a doctrinal rather than a poetic understanding of the text, and I had got stuck in the mediocre here-and-now, the commonplace modern humanism by whose lights you did not condemn anyone to eternal burial in ordure for accepting a bribe or sleeping with a good-looking neighbor. And I had made my way grumpily though the assigned excerpts from Cervantes's enormous *Don Quixote,* thinking to myself that it was the tenderest book ever written but that excerpts would never reveal the pattern of stories and themes that made it (as the whole world insisted) a great literary experience. Columbia assigned it because it was one of the central myths of Western culture—a gigantic comic testing of the chivalric ideal in the squalid and treacherous world of reality—but it left the reader rather unhappy when encountered in pieces, even a little bored. There, I've said it.

As for Goethe's *Faust* (Part One), I knew the standard opinion that it was as central to German literature as *Hamlet* and *Lear* were to British; I was familiar with W. H. Auden's judgment that Goethe displayed in it "an amazing command of every style of poetry, from the coarse to the witty to the lyrical to the sublime." But then, after a thirty-year gap, I had read it again (in translation), and . . . dear God, the oppression of "the great books"! The boredom of the classics! Noisy, redundant, crass, overbearing, dislikable . . . I hated it, even though I obviously shared—with all due proportions kept—Faust's ambitions, dissatisfactions, and hungers, and immediately would have made a deal had any Satan been around to propose one. Disgusted with what he knows, "too old for mere amusement and still too young to be without desire," Faust makes a wager with Mephistopheles. In this arrangement, he does not, as many people think, "sell his soul." Rather, he makes a courageous bargain in which he will receive *more,* more appetite, a greater capacity for experience, greater power, and will lose his soul for all eternity should he ever reach a moment of satisfaction.

> If ever I should tell the moment:
> Oh, stay! You are so beautiful!
> Then you may cast me into chains,
> then I shall smile upon perdition!
> Then may the hour toll for me,
> then you are free to leave my service.
> The clock may halt, the clock hand fall,
> and time come to an end for me!
> (1699–1706)

Thus the great chord of Western heroism we had heard sounding again and again from the *Odyssey* to the nineteenth century. But as someone barred from enjoyment of Goethe's poetry, I was left reading the book only for its ideas, its ambition, its rhetorical heft, its anguish, and, again, its value as a great cultural myth. Well, that's reading it for quite a lot, isn't it? Perhaps. But at my age, I could make no more than a spurious connection with a great work that I did not genuinely enjoy. I would die without really "getting" Goethe's *Faust* (Part One). I was sure I had more than done my duty by twice *reading* it.

So count two more defeats, two failures of pleasure, and two more

victories for Professor Kilfeather's hostile view of survey courses largely
devoted to great works in translation. She wasn't entirely wrong.

❖   ❖   ❖

Back there in 1961, the Lit Hum reading list had not included any
women authors, but in other courses and on my own, I had read *Pride
and Prejudice* twice, maybe three times, as well as the rest of Jane
Austen's novels again and again. I was a fan, like numberless others.
Jane Austen was on the short list. Along with Shakespeare, the Brontës,
Dickens, Whitman, Tolstoy, Mark Twain, Trollope, George Eliot
(maybe), Edith Wharton, Proust, Kafka, Mann, F. Scott Fitzgerald,
Hemingway, Virginia Woolf, Nabokov, and Gabriel García Márquez,
she was one of the few unmistakably great writers who enjoyed, in
America, a large readership outside college courses. People *read* her; she
had broken free of "a-signifying elements" and "the mythopoetical
virtue of *bricolage*" and all the rest of that lovely academic attention.
She did not need to be "recuperated" like poor Henry James, whose sexual ambiguity, hesitations, and renunciations now made him a ripe subject of academic curiosity (James, the greatest—some would say the
sole—chronicler of romantic love between men and women in American
literature was being recuperated as a "queer"). Jane Austen had
shrugged off the possessive and supplanting academic literary theories
and sustained her active relation with readers; she was also, as long as I
could remember, the particular favorite of many bookish people. Among
my own acquaintances there were people who classified other people by
what novel of Jane Austen's they liked best, and others who had named
their daughters "Austen" or "Emma" or "Elizabeth."

Pride and Prejudice went like a shot. I read it without stopping, right
through meals, on the street, at home late at night, like a Grisham on the
subway, and not a single movie image interrupted the continuous pleasure. Jane Austen wrote romantic comedies, and in her books not all the
world, nor the Fates, nor God, nor hazard, nor chance could keep her
chosen men and women apart. Despite many hesitations and mishaps,
they came together like the two halves of a bridge. Instinctively, readers
know this is how the books will end, and, whatever else they get from
Jane Austen, they prize the satisfaction of man and woman joining. And
I was sure that Shapiro's students would prize it, too, and love Jane
Austen. After our experience in Lit Hum of such distant forms as epic,
tragic drama, philosophical dialogue, and so on, we had arrived at the
bourgeois age and the bourgeois art form par excellence, the novel, the
one form that all the students were familiar with. Jane Austen has many
surprises, but on the surface, at least, she is easy to read. In my teaching
gig, which now filled me with restless anticipation, I would try to or-
chestrate their enthusiasm.

❖ ❖ ❖

One of the minor characters, the desperate Charlotte Lucas, a plain young woman without fortune, accepts an offer from the obsequious clergyman Mr. Collins. The question arises of how long they should wait before the ceremony. Jane Austen tells us: "The stupidity with which [Mr. Collins] was favored by nature, must guard his courtship from any charm that could make a woman wish for its continuance; and Miss Lucas, who accepted him solely from the pure and disinterested desire of an establishment, cared not how soon that establishment were gained."

The joke has a kick to it, and then a second kick. Charlotte, who is marrying for security, not for love, can hardly be "pure." Yet, in another way, she *is*. She wants *only* an establishment; her greed and desperation remain unsullied by personal attachment. Jane Austen's wit checks the kind of conventional romantic sentimentality which assumes that people always marry for love. Only *some* people marry for love. The book will discriminate among different kinds of marriage, and even different kinds of love, and these distinctions, for all their high gaiety, will be rendered in terms that would not appear weak on the Day of Judgment.

For my generation of literature majors, the delicate, subtle, yet fiercely candid Jane Austen laid down a most insistent demand. The common (unspoken) assumption was that if you really understood Jane Austen's irony in *Emma* or *Pride and Prejudice*, you could never be the same person again. You would begin to understand the duplicitous ways in which vanity shaped your assumptions, the way that life tricked intelligent people even more than the dull. The ambitious little clergyman Mr. Collins really was "favored" by stupidity; he was impervious and therefore successful. Reading Jane Austen, you lost your moral innocence and relinquished assurance for something else—complexity, perhaps. Every force, every perception was both enriched and imperiled by doubleness: Life was not what it seemed. No, the famous irony insisted that life was treacherous; it did not necessarily collaborate with goodwill. Jane Austen was literature's answer to Kant.

This writer of marriage stories, apparently uninterested in formal ideas, had a mind as interesting as any novelist who has ever lived. In Jane Austen, the mating game assumes dimensions that Boccaccio ignored—the joining of understanding and temperament, property and taste, as well as body and body. If marriage had become the central rite of the new materialist society of Austen's England, it was also the central trial of an individual's worth, which, in *Pride and Prejudice,* became the test of his or her ability to perceive and to know. And perception and knowledge were subjected to a thousand vagaries, a thousand errors and vanities.

How limited the young people's opportunities seem to us! They encounter one another at balls, dinners, and drawing-room entertainments, and on walks, those all-important tramps through fields and gardens which assume the dangers of a spiritual journey. "This is a courtship dance," said Tayler, "immensely civilized, with wit and elegance to the ultimate degree." Civilized, yes, but not even warriors met under greater stress. The men and women must speak and look quickly, and then interpret; they look again, and reflect on what they have seen and how it connects with what they thought earlier; they make ghastly errors, and if they have the will and the judgment, they correct themselves. The world lives or dies on the strength of those corrections. *Pride and Prejudice,* I realized, was a novel perfect for students since it proposed studenthood as the essence of social existence. As much as any work in the Lit Hum syllabus, *Pride and Prejudice* belonged to the freshmen.

The best student, despite her errors, is Elizabeth Bennet, the irresistible, teasing chatterbox who attracts the notice of that great perpendicular snob, Mr. Darcy. Standing at the pinnacle of provincial society, Darcy has everything—money, property, connections—that Elizabeth lacks. She must face Darcy with only her good looks and high spirits. Despising him at first, she imagines she is using her weapons to hold him at bay, when actually, with every bit of impudence—it is the basic premise of romantic comedy—she pulls him powerfully toward her.

> "Do not you feel a great inclination, Miss Bennet, to seize such an opportunity of dancing a reel?"
>
> She smiled, but made no answer. He repeated the question, with some surprise at her silence.
>
> "Oh!" said she, "I heard you before; but I could not immediately determine what to say in reply. You wanted me, I know, to say 'Yes,' that you might have the pleasure of despising my taste; but I always delight in overthrowing those kind of schemes, and cheating a person of their premeditated contempt. I have therefore made up my mind to tell you, that I do not want to dance a reel at all—and now despise me if you dare."
>
> "Indeed I do not dare."
>
> Elizabeth, having rather expected to affront him, was amazed at his gallantry; but there was a mixture of sweetness and archness in her manner which made it difficult for her to affront anybody; and Darcy had never been so bewitched by any woman as he was by her. He really believed, that were it not for the inferiority of her connections, he should be in some danger. (p. 96)

When Darcy finally proposes, he speaks of Elizabeth's social inferiority with such insulting candor that Elizabeth not only turns him down, she accuses him of ungentlemanly conduct. Her refusal, and the boldly explicit manner of making it, is an act of extraordinary freedom, a sexual declaration of independence, the shot heard around the world. And it has an extraordinary effect. She tells Darcy he has violated his own code, which, in Darcy's world, is a serious matter. Stung, he writes a long letter of self-exculpation that reveals his true character—severe but sensitive and responsible—and Elizabeth, after much reflection, realizes that she has misjudged him.

> "How despicably have I acted!" she cried.—"I, who have prided myself on my discernment!—I, who have valued myself on my abilities! who have often disdained the generous candour of my sister, and gratified my vanity, in useless or blameable distrust.—How humiliating is this discovery!—Yet, how just a humiliation!—Had I been in love, I could not have been more wretchedly blind. But vanity, not love, has been my folly. . . . Till this moment, I never knew myself." (pp. 236–37)

St. Augustine wrote nothing in the self-harrowing line more wrenching than this. *Till this moment, I never knew myself.* Tony Tanner, the English critic and Cambridge professor who wrote the introduction to the Penguin edition of the novel, went so far as to evoke *Oedipus the King* and *King Lear,* mighty dramas of delusion and self-recognition, as precursors of *Pride and Prejudice.* I was stirred: Tanner had unwittingly made Jane Austen the logical summation of Lit Hum. This woman who rarely left her family circle, who traveled to London only a few times, who never married and was probably celibate—Jane Austen, always admired and widely read, now stood at the center of the Western canon.

❖ ❖ ❖

Shapiro began the class in his customary way. He asked the students if they liked it. He went around the room, and he quickly discovered that the girls liked it and the boys did not.

Alex (who would put people in hell for chewing gum in public): I couldn't get myself involved to the point where I got interested in any of the characters. I couldn't care whether Elizabeth married Darcy or not.

Hamilton (serious, usually genial): I can't get into the subject matter, which is these rich people in England and their little problems.

Ranjit (of Indian descent, but all-American-teen type): I couldn't figure out why this was in the course.

Their dismissals came with a frosting of contempt. Darcy himself couldn't have been any more disdainful. It was a waste of their time, this trivial girls' stuff.

Normally, in a case like this, Shapiro would turn the students' responses against them, reworking their resistance into a pattern of engagement. He would banter with the students, challenging them, and often they would come around. Instead, he made some remarks about the social structure of England in Jane Austen's time; he outlined the desire of the landed classes to perpetuate themselves amid the challenges from new money earned in trade and industry, and so on. And then he moved out of his seat and turned the class over to me.

I sat at the end of the long seminar table, with the Coach just to my right and students arrayed along the sides of the table and against the walls of the room. They looked at me curiously; a few smiled. It was an experiment of some sort, and they would put up with it for a while.

I was angry when I began. Anyone had the right not to like a book, but still! The men had to see. They all had to see that Elizabeth Bennet, so courageously facing the disapproval of her social superiors, holding her own in conversation at a ball, at the pianoforte in the drawing room after dinner—that Elizabeth is as brave and resourceful as Odysseus. Nervy, brilliant Elizabeth Bennet is our champion; she is *their* champion. She makes terrible mistakes, but that's part of her greatness, and as I paused for an instant, looking through my notes, it flashed through my mind that the men had to love this book and love Elizabeth or else they could not grow past this stage of their lives; they would remain insensible.

"My wife and I went to a dinner party recently," I began. "When we got home, we sat around talking the evening over. We examined the guests. We examined ourselves. We thought about what we had said, what we could have said. We're all looking for the right measure. To be neither too aggressive nor too retiring, too self-confident nor too self-critical, too modest or too bold. For some people, this kind of self-consciousness can become a torment. But in the modern world, there's no movement in your life without it."

The students seemed surprised. It was an odd beginning. But the smiles vanished, and when, a moment later, I spoke the ominous word "Hegel," notebooks were flung open and pens hit the page. They were taking notes. I felt a small but unmistakable tickling at the back of my neck, an erotic surge rather like the pleasure of having one's picture taken by a professional photographer. So *that* was what power felt like! I was generally unfamiliar with the sensation. Writing for *New York* magazine's good-sized audience, I addressed the reader from a distance. The reader was sitting on a commuter train or propped up in bed, an ideal in some way yet also mysterious and shockingly mute. Now I saw the effect of my words in the straightening or slump of a body, in hands fidgeting and glances shyly or boldly offered. A couple of the women smiled, the men looked interested. The reference to Hegel had come in a passage that I read to them, a quotation from a local deity, Lionel

Trilling, the great Columbia teacher and critic whose 1954 essay on Jane Austen in *The Opposing Self* I had pulled off my shelf the night before. Earlier I wasn't sure I wanted to read the passage, but when I got angry, I knew I had to.

> It was Jane Austen who first represented the specifically modern personality and the culture in which it had its being. Never before had the moral life been shown as she shows it to be, never before had it been conceived to be so complex and difficult and exhausting. Hegel speaks of the "secularization of spirituality" as a prime characteristic of the modern epoch, and Jane Austen is the first to tell us what this involves. She is the first novelist to represent society, the general culture, as playing a part in the moral life, generating the concepts of "sincerity" and "vulgarity" which no earlier time would have understood the meaning of, and which for us are so subtle that they defy definition, and so powerful that none can escape their sovereignty. She is the first to be aware of the Terror which rules our moral situation, the ubiquitous anonymous judgment to which we respond, the necessity we feel to demonstrate the purity of our secular spirituality, whose dark and dubious places are more numerous and obscure than those of religious spirituality, to put our lives and styles to the question, making sure that not only in deeds but in *décor* they exhibit the signs of our belonging to the number of the secular-spiritual elect. (p. 228)

The power of this—mixed with its slightly comical note of alarm— woke up some of the students. The women began talking. They sidestepped what Trilling said (as soon as I read it aloud, I knew the passage was a bit much for nineteen-year-olds to handle), but they expressed their admiration for Elizabeth. They saw the gallantry in her social manner; they were sympathetic to the constraints that the young women in the novel operated under, the vise that allowed them very little respectability outside marriage, and then only as a governess or spinster. To my relief, Sally, who usually took a hard line on everything, and had not a single good word for Antigone or Dido, Sally who possessed the angry self-assurance of a small-town beauty who had never in her life been contradicted (or so I imagined) now spoke generously of Elizabeth Bennet's struggle for clarity.

Marriage was no trivial matter for the women, and probably not for the men either, though they shied away from discussion of it as from a snake beneath their hooves. *Their* "terror," I guessed, was not of the self-consciousness that came with the secularization of spirit. They were frightened, I imagined, of the more immediate possibility of a social world in which women and marriage were at the center, a world in which their own freedom was restricted. But I couldn't say this, it was too awful, and when I didn't, the men took refuge by mocking the formal speaking style of Jane Austen's characters.

"Some readers will have to make a gigantic imaginative leap," Tayler had said at the beginning of *his* class on Austen. "They will have to haul themselves into a different society. No panty hose, no garter, no pill, no TV. These folks sat around at night talking and reading." So I tried a little hauling. The formalities of Jane Austen's society, I said, were molded both by a changing but still powerful class system and by the ideal of social life as performance. Despite the emphasis on manners and elegance—or perhaps because of it—the language was actually more brutal in its checks and rebukes than anything Americans were likely to be exposed to. Rudeness had the regulatory function of keeping people in their place. The manners were often bad manners.

More notes were taken. I was enjoying this. Enjoying it too much, perhaps, because I couldn't stop talking. I kept on explaining, and sometimes the students responded and sometimes not, and I began to get nervous—a bit of damp had gathered around the small of my back. I turned to Jane Austen's habits of irony, and I asked them to analyze the opening sentences. Alex, the skinny intellectual boy who had joined the class in the second semester, perked up. He had said earlier that he couldn't get "involved," but now he would play. At least for a while. Reading those sentences appealed to him as a problem in logic. He analyzed, he sorted out the permutations of expectation and surprise that flowed from the opening sentences. *Good, Alex.* The teacher was happy. A few of the men grudgingly spoke.

The women were talking well, and I had moved the men off dead center, but still, there were silences in the conversation, and some of the students looked tense and frustrated. I wasn't playing them off against each other as Tayler did, or drawing answers out of them in Shapiro's gently badgering way. If I didn't get the answer I wanted, I would blurt it out myself, and after a while, the sound of my own voice echoed off the walls. As Shapiro stirred slightly, the faces in front of me blurred. But they had to get it, and lunging at my notes, I kept going.

"You see, Mrs. Bennet is not the villain of the book after all. You have to read the opening sentences a third time. By the end, you realize that Mrs. Bennet, in pushing the marriages along, was a kind of life force. The rich young men realize that they *are* in want of wives. If the book has a villain, it's *Mr.* Bennet."

A number of the men had said earlier they admired Mr. Bennet, the retiring husband and father whose humor, at first, seems to represent Jane Austen's point of view. But it doesn't. Jane Austen's irony was directed at the reader who thought he understood irony. Mr. Bennet, it turned out, was actually an empty shell; he was merely sarcastic, which is the lowest form of irony. "You could never quite live with Jane Austen as comfortably as you wanted to," I said.

No, you couldn't. My throat was dry, and I was exhausted. Without turning in Shapiro's direction, I felt his stare. He could have been the conductor of an orchestra watching a young substitute push his musicians too hard. He called for a ten-minute break.

❖   ❖   ❖

We met in the hall.

"I enjoyed watching you," he said, his hazel eyes widening. "Do you know what you were doing wrong?"

"I was oversteering the ship."

We agreed that I was oversteering the ship. We agreed that this was a nice way of putting it. "You have to ask for the answers in the form of questions," Shapiro said. "That way they develop the ideas, and they appropriate them as their own. But if you just give it to them, they don't accept it."

He was too kind to say what he must have been thinking: I had made the error that all beginning teachers make, running to the answer too quickly out of fear of losing control.

"You have to embarrass them a little. Make them nervous. Use their bafflement as a way into the ambiguity of the work."

Make them nervous, not intimidate them. I was a critic, and I wanted to get to the right thing, the definitive statement; I wanted them to *hear*. Unless the students got there on their own, however, it was more like the wrong thing. I lacked patience, and patience was not just a manner, it was the very form of seminar teaching. Columbia's core curriculum had been designed not to enshrine the authority of the lecturing professor (that was something done at *Harvard*) but to reach understanding through discussion, however clumsy and uncertain.

Till this moment, I never knew myself. . . . Vanity, not love has been my folly! Well, yes, there you go. I had tried to hammer the students rather than teach them. I remembered my voice echoing in the room— like a car salesman's. Why couldn't I see what was wrong? As much as anyone in Lit Hum, Jane Austen had formed my generation of readers. We were taught how to read her, and how to read ourselves, by Trilling and a great many other Austen fans thirty years earlier. I did not take Jane Austen for granted, but, standing with Shapiro in the hallway, I knew that I had taken my understanding of her for granted.

Now the case had to be made all over again, it had to be built from the ground up—the case for pleasure, for comedy, for social existence as education in sensibility, for irony as the most complex pleasure. In *Pride and Prejudice,* there is irony in the very struggle to know yourself. You are not what you seem. Elizabeth Bennet realizes she had misjudged

Darcy, but she doesn't realize for a long time how much she had wanted to love him. She joshes him out of his pride and stiffness, but bit by bit, her tone ever gentler and more loving, and finally she acknowledges her own motives. The book goes from the thrust and retreat of romantic comedy to a more somber spirit of reconciliation. Self-knowledge leads each of them to an acceptance of the other. But irony doesn't come easily to anyone, not the complex kind of irony that allows you to know the tricks you play on yourself. And it could never be taken for granted. That's why it was so precious. And the absence of it so undermining.

The students were polite, but my teaching gig was a flop. In the hall, talking to Shapiro, I had a long moment of unhappiness.

But no more than a moment. Following Shapiro back into the room, I knew my sense of mortification would quickly fade. Learn, and move on! For there was work to be done. Serious work: a generation of readers to create. Shapiro turned his attention to the question of reading— how people in the novel read and write letters, how they "read" one another's character. The women were vibrant, and slowly the men joined in. But only very slowly. Clearly, the book was as difficult and as distant for some of these media-age students as was the *Iliad*. Yet that was why they should read it. The student's distance from the social world of Jane Austen, as well as their need for what the book had to say—for the daunting, unending trial of self-consciousness and self-creation—was a superior reason for its hard-won place in the core curriculum.

Chapter *24*

MARX AND MILL

~ Two "discouraged" authors
~ Leszek Kolakowski delivers a diatribe against Marx
~ Can we still read Marx?
~ *The Communist Manifesto*
~ The humanist Marx
~ The amorality of the marketplace, the "fetishism of commodities," and the endless crisis of bourgeois society
~ Mill's "platitudes," taken literally, turn out to be radical in spirit
~ Mill and "the great books"

Rushing furiously into the modern era, we arrived at Karl Marx and John Stuart Mill, two major forces in Western thought who, in altogether different ways, had fallen under a cloud. I thought of them as writers of discouraged texts. Well, partially discouraged. Within the university, Marxist thought was certainly alive, and Stephanson not only asked his students to read Marx, he asked them to read Lenin and Gramsci and other classics of the left. But in the larger world outside, Marx had become a joke—so ludicrous and damaging in his errors, and in the many failures unfolding from his theories, that it was a good question in many quarters whether he should be read at all. Mill was a different story. That Mill mattered as an influence on Anglo-American democracy was not in doubt. He was, along with Locke, Adam Smith, the Founding Fathers, the common law, and the American Supreme Court, one of the chief shapers of the ethos of the modern liberal state. But for Stephanson, Mill's very familiarity ruled him out. Modern Americans, he said, practiced, or at least thought they practiced, what Mill had advocated; and Stephanson would rather we understand notions contrary to our practice. Mill, he implied, wasn't *interesting*. He asked us to read Mill's *On Liberty* but told us we would not discuss it in class.

My suspicions were aroused. How can a classic simply die?

❖   ❖   ❖

Tall and lean, an elegantly angular man, Leszek Kolakowski loomed over the raised dais of a lecture theater and turned first to one side then the other, like some large, gray bird surveying the landscape. In his thick Polish accent, he asked, "Does Marx's theory explain anything in our world? And does Marx's theory provide any ground for prediction?"

A happy coincidence: Just as we were reading Marx in C.C., one of the leading historians of Marxism had turned up at Columbia for a public lecture. Leszek Kolakowski was an imposing figure. A member of the Polish Communist Party in his youth, he had become, during the Khrushchev "thaw" of the late fifties, one of those reformers in Eastern Europe who had dared hope that with Stalin dead a more humane version of Communism might develop. But Kolakowski, like many such people, had been defeated. Expelled from the party, he emigrated to the West and taught at Oxford for many years; and in 1978, he began issuing the three volumes of his celebrated revisionist history, *Main Currents of Marxism,* in which, amid a great many other tasks, he attacked the whole prophetic-religious side of Marxism. Kolakowski assigned blame for the catastrophes of Communism not only to the Leninist and Stalinist perversions of Marx but to Marx himself. There was sin, and there was original sin.

Now, lecturing at the Columbia Law School, he answered his initial rhetorical questions about Marx's prophetic powers. "The answer is no. Marx explains nothing."

He was entirely dismissive. Yet one had to take him seriously. This was not some talk-show blowhard gloating over Communism's failure. Kolakowski was the real thing, a philosopher and a former Communist . . . gloating over Communism's failure. A few years after the collapse, Kolakowski was in a state of high disgust. Rush Limbaugh could not have been more categorical.

"There is no clear distinction in Marx's theories between explanation and prophecy," he said, putting one hand behind his back and tilting over the lectern. "All of Marx's important prophecies turned out to be false." And he listed some of Marx's predictions of what would happen under capitalism: the growing polarization of the classes; the disappearance of the middle class; the relative and absolute misery of the working class; the inevitability of proletarian revolution. "Such a revolution has never happened anywhere," Kolakowski said. "What has come closest in the twentieth century to working-class revolution was the workers' revolution in Poland"—i.e., Solidarity—"which was carried out under the sign of the cross and with the blessing of the pope." As for those other Marxian certainties, the inevitable decline of profits and the hampering of technical progress under capitalism, they were equally false. Kolakowski's scorn came to a head. "Exactly the opposite is the truth. The market stimulated the economy. Socialism turned out to be stagnant."

As Kolakowski went on and one—he would not "turn himself into a laughingstock" by pretending that Marx had originated the notion of the class struggle—there was an uneasy stirring in the room, a painful shortening of breath, and then a few walkouts. Parts of Columbia's faculty (parts of the faculty of almost any great Western university) had cut their intellectual eyeteeth on Marx and still considered Marx's work the essential element of any serious analysis of modern society. Even if Marx's "grand narrative" had collapsed, the cultural left in the universities was committed to notions about power and ideology derived from Marx, among others. Few people in the Law School auditorium, I would guess, had expected Kolakowski's contempt to be quite so unwavering, so unmodulated in its fervor. I felt the shock myself. His mockery, I thought, was exaggeratedly bitter. He appeared to be punishing himself for his long absorption in Marxism.

But something else was going on in that talk. He was punishing us as well. Or at least trying to warn us. After all, the radicalism rejected by Kolakowski was still flourishing, at the theoretical level, in the American universities, where the cultural left frequently questioned and sometimes ridiculed democratic institutions and liberties—precisely the values and structures that Eastern Europeans like Kolakowski now struggled to construct in the formerly Communist societies. Free speech, for instance. Parts of the academic left were highly skeptical of it. Was it not a sham, a mere cover for class rule, patriarchal rule, white rule? Advocates of free speech always had *some* kind of speech that they wanted to prohibit, some kind of speech that they considered a threat to their core values or the society itself. Free speech as a value in itself did not exist; it was always politically determined. Kolakowski, I thought, was rebuking any such thoughts in his audience. He appeared to be saying something like this: You are too well protected by freedom to know what unfreedom feels like. The alternatives to free-market systems are awful beyond belief. So watch what you say about "sham" bourgeois liberties.

He brought his accusations to a conclusion: "Marx's texts are regarded with abhorrence in the former Communist countries. One should read them only as one reads many dead classics—the physics of Descartes, for instance."

In other words, Marx was not only deluded, he was simply irrelevant. And that was that.

But in C.C. class, justice needed to be rendered—and I don't meant justice to long-held illusion but justice to truth. In class, the ever-fairminded Noah insisted that Marx had not called for an authoritarian state, and Stephanson, beginning a defense, reminded us that Soviet Communism was hardly the only thing that came out of Marx. The democratic socialist parties of Europe and America and many humanizing reforms and modifications of "pure" capitalism had also been inspired, or partly inspired, by Marx's moral critique. Without the reforms forced on capitalism by the American labor movement, American capitalism would be unimaginably cruel. No one to the left of Pat Buchanan seriously imagined otherwise.

Marx had shaped the modern world and had then abruptly and bizarrely vanished, a shooting star leaving only a trail of dust in its wake. As a C.C. author, Marx was a very strange case. Along with Plato's and Aristotle's works, Marx's texts came accompanied by refutation, the refutation of history. Counterarguments and mockery rose unbidden from the page. Reading Marx, we all became ironists. The problem was this: How does one read him without *crushing* him with irony—without ironizing him out of existence?

❖ ❖ ❖

I remember the little black and red pamphlet. It was issued by a respectable American publisher, but in 1960, at the height of the Cold War, I had the feeling I was touching something forbidden and dangerous. I first read *The Manifesto of the Communist Party*, or, as everyone called it, *The Communist Manifesto*, in a high-school history course. Satan's book! I was excited, even thrilled by the violence of its denuciations of capitalism. In eleventh grade, disgusted with "conformity" and American corporate life, I told myself, this was it, Marx had got it right.

> The bourgeoisie, wherever it has got the upper hand, has put an end to all feudal, patriarchal, idyllic relations. It has pitilessly torn asunder the motley feudal ties that bound man to his "natural superiors," and has left remaining no other nexus between man and man than naked self-interest, than callous "cash payment." It has drowned the most heavenly ecstasies of religious fervour, of chivalrous enthusiasm, of philistine sentimentalism, in the icy water of egotistical calculation. It has resolved personal worth into exchange value, and in place of the numberless indefeasible chartered freedoms, has set up that single, unconscionable freedom—Free Trade. In one word, for exploitation, veiled by religious and political illusions, it has substituted naked, shameless, direct, brutal exploitation. (Tucker, p. 475)

Ah, yes, the icy waters of egotistical calculation. As opposed to the warm bath of Communist spontaneity? The old jeering and hectoring metaphorical style now made me a little sick. I greeted it without excitement or the slightest tingle of nostalgia. Even if one agreed with Marx's description of early industrial capitalism, there was nothing to do but groan. *The Communist Manifesto,* of course, was not one of Marx's scholarly or theoretical works but a pamphlet, written in 1848 in London, for the Communist League, at a time of violent social upheaval in Europe. Stephanson called it "the single most *effective* world-historical text in the whole course, with the exception of the Bible." This, I believe, was the consensus view: extraordinarily effective as a tool of persuasion.

Reading it now, one can see that the pamphlet is wildly ambiguous, that it seethes with admiration for the despised capitalist class and contempt for the beloved proletariat, that it has an unconscious, which, examined closely, might reveal Marx's buried knowledge that his own predictions were doomed to failure. But I am not generous enough to praise Marx's unconscious. I was actually shocked by the sound of his voice in the *Manifesto.* The brimming sarcasm and contumely, the pulse-raising hyperbole, the invective, the ripostes to deluded enemies, the violent slinging of historical generalization and moral indictment, all of it working together with absolute certainty. . . . I groaned because I had once warmed to the *Manifesto,* and I now knew that it was bad, bad prose. Killingly bad. Too much blood foamed in the wake of its stale metaphors. Marx didn't pull the trigger, but people who did pull it used this voice, or one like it, and the voice, which Marx regularly exercised in debate against less radical socialists or liberal reformers, licensed ruthless contempt for one's enemies. So let irony now ravage and destroy, let irony scythe away the remaining posthumous reputation of those men and women long convinced they were riding the express train of history.

Up to this point, Kolakowski was correct. In C.C., we could now read the *Manifesto* only as a historical document—or perhaps as a weird, overwrought entertainment, a symphony of bad vibes.

But this was hardly Marx's only accent. Stephanson asked us to read a number of extended excerpts from the early "humanist" Marx—from Part One of *The German Ideology,* which Marx wrote (Friedrich Engels collaborated on Part Two) in 1845–46, a book unpublished in Marx's time; and also from some of the other early papers now known as the *Economic and Philosophic Manuscripts of 1844.* In these rough drafts and early statements, unavailable to the public in Marx's lifetime, one heard not the hardened bluster and sarcasm of the professional revolutionist but the sensitivity and eloquence of a young man (around twenty-seven) in the grip of an amazing realization: In the preceding hundred years or so, everything had changed. Everything in Europe and England was different, the way men and women worked, their relations with one another, the way capital was accumulated, products manufactured and distributed, money spent. The ethical, moral, and legal systems had shifted too. Everything, everything!

Things—an immense quantity of goods—were now filling the atmosphere between people, an atmosphere regulated and controlled by cash. This new condition of life needed to be named and analyzed. We were going to see it clearly for the first time. Marx offered not just an interpretation of capitalism and a theory of history; he offered sight, the senses sharpened by outrage into a perception of paradox. A paradox was something that seemed to contradict itself. If reality had become paradoxical, reality had been dislodged and then mashed out of shape. One such reality was that industrial capitalism had created immense wealth while imprisoning the producers of wealth in hazardous factories at subsistence wages. Such a development could only be understood in philosophical terms. I will quote at length from *The German Ideology*. Irony must now lay down its arms. Listen to the young Marx.

> The worker becomes all the poorer the more wealth he produces, the more his production increases in power and range. The worker becomes an ever cheaper commodity the more commodities he creates. With the *increasing value* of the world of things proceeds in direct proportion the *devaluation* of the world of men. Labour produces not only commodities; it produces itself and the worker as a *commodity*—and does so in the proportion in which it produces commodities generally.
>
> This fact expresses merely that the object which labour produces—labour's product—confronts it as *something alien,* as a *power independent* of the producer. The product of labour is labour which has been congealed in an object, which has become material: it is the *objectification* of labour. Labour's realization is its objectification. In the conditions dealt with by political economy this realization of labour appears as *loss of reality* for the workers; objectification as *loss of the object* and *object-bondage;* appropriation as *estrangement,* as *alienation.*
>
> So much does labour's realization appear as loss of reality that the worker loses reality to the point of starving to death. So much does objectification appear as loss of the object that the worker is robbed of the objects most necessary not only for his life but for his work. Indeed, labour itself becomes an object which he can get hold of only with the greatest effort and with the most irregular interruptions. So much does the appropriation of the object appear as estrangement that the more objects the worker produces the fewer can he possess and the more he falls under the dominion of his product, capital.
>
> All these consequences are contained in the definition that the

worker is related to the *product of his labour* as to an *alien* object. For on this premise it is clear that the more the worker spends himself, the more powerful the alien objective world becomes which he creates over-against himself, the poorer he himself—his inner world—becomes, the less belongs to him as his own. It is the same in religion. The more man puts into God, the less he retains in himself. The worker puts his life into the object; but now his life no longer belongs to him but to the object. . . .

It is true that labour produces for the rich wonderful things—but for the worker it produces privation. It produces palaces—but for the worker, hovels. It produces beauty—but for the worker, deformity. It replaces labour by machines—but some of the workers it throws back to a barbarous type of labour, and the other workers it turns into machines. It produces intelligence—but for the worker idiocy, cretinism. (Tucker, pp. 71–73)

Until I came to transcribe these bumpy and repetitive sentences, I didn't quite realize how painful they were, and finally how moving in their sardonicism and outrage. Stern, logical, inexorable, implacably moral, Marx was haunted by a sense of an unspeakable disruption in the wholeness of life.

So, in the end, Kolakowski's bitterness had made him untrustworthy. In his disgust at the opéra-bouffe collapse of the ideas he had devoted his life to studying and acting on, he was denying the youthful Marx—Karl Marx, the living classic, whom American teenagers should continue to read. The students could easily ignore the prophetic drivel, the *unceasing class struggle* and *the inevitable proletarian revolution* and *the withering away of the state* and all the rest of that. But reading Marx's best work would check the students' complacency about their own system and possibly their own lives. Some of the good Marx was not just about early capitalism; it was about now.

For who was ready to say that Marx was wrong about alienation and the nature of modern labor? In the twentieth century, "alienation" has become an all-purpose word referring to many kinds of anomie, rootlessness, disaffection, distance—the hatred of the artist for a commercial society, the annoyance of the adolescent with parents and teachers—and some of that usage now borders on cant, but here, in one of its original meanings, the notion has lost none of its power. Alienation is a loss of self: We work for others, to fulfill other people's goals, and often enough we confront what we produce with an indifference bordering on disgust. And so the eternal cry of boredom and meaninglessness; the impoverishment that so many feel, the hollow exhaustion at the end of the day; the dull anger, the internal distancing of oneself, the need to escape. . . . Many of us have simply accepted as inevitable the spiritual condition that Marx considered a perversion of man's essence. Such is the nature of modern work, we assume, in factories, offices, corporations, department stores, gas stations—work that is safer than in Marx's time, but often no more engaging. Reading the early Marx is like pulling up a rock covering hidden perceptions; those feelings are still there, wriggling around in the dark. He gave them shape once again.

Americans might not express their feelings in that way, but they act on them: They divide their lives in two, work and play, earning and consuming; they drag themselves through work to reach the promised land of leisure, the ecstasy of the defining car, suit, house, or vacation that settles for all time who they are. The disgust with work makes the act of buying things an arena of anxiety and triumph. Alienation exists at all levels of American society. It is called consumerism.

❖ ❖ ❖

Reading the early Marx was no great trouble after reading Hegel, from whom Marx had taken so many modes of thinking. All that pain I had undergone boxing with the dialectic now paid off in the form of tougher skin and stronger muscle. A student for a while at the University of Berlin, Marx grew up in Hegel's intellectual shadow and became a member of a group of young intellectuals called the Young Hegelians (left division). Before long he was rewriting Hegel in ways that became momentous for Western intellectual history. Marx appropriated Hegel's mighty rhythm of struggle, reconciliation, and struggle, but, as Engels later put it, he and Marx turned Hegel, who was standing on his head, back on his feet again.

Why was Hegel standing on his head? In Hegel, Spirit in its drive to become fully conscious of itself must repeatedly overcome its alienation from itself. In its manifestation during a given epoch, Spirit realized itself in the defining art, religion, ethical formations—the consciousness—of that epoch. But Marx ended what he called the "mystification" in Hegelian thought. It was not *Spirit* that was alienated from itself, but man who was alienated from himself—and in the material world, the world we all lived and worked in. Man was alienated in his economic life.

What was all this nonsense about Spirit, anyway? How can you observe its workings or discover its regularities? Nothing scientific could emerge from the search for Spirit. People in earlier epochs formed themselves into primitive associations and then into more and more complex kinds of social organizations for reasons that had nothing to do with the working out of Spirit or Idea; they acted in ways that had nothing to do with the formation of an unwritten social contract, as Hobbes, Locke, or Rousseau had imagined. Men and women joined together because they needed, before anything else, to provide the means of their own subsistence. *Men and women* were the agents. They banded together to survive and to produce certain goods necessary for survival. In time, the division of labor allowed them to produce much more than was necessary for mere survival; leisure became possible, and rudimentary cultural activity—and also the wealth that allowed some producers, the stronger and more resourceful ones, to dominate others by hoarding the necessities of life and thereby turning the others into merely hired or dependent labor.

In each particular stage of production, the political system grew out of the divisions in property and the preponderant forces of control ("the social relations of production"). Marx provides his own version of history, from tribal ownership, which functioned without private property in a kind of primitive communism, and was led by its patriarchal family chieftains, right up to bourgeois republics dominated by industrial capitalism, with its entrepreneurs and impoverished urban-proletarian masses. No mystical Spirit was governing any of this or making history move forward; the motor, on the contrary, was human endeavor and unceasing class war. The young Marx grew exultant; the metaphysical bogeyman had been thrown from philosophy's back.

> In direct contrast to German philosophy which descends from heaven to earth, here we ascend from earth to heaven. That is to say, we do not set out from what men say, imagine, conceive, nor from men as narrated, thought of, imagined, conceived, in order to arrive at men in the flesh. We set out from real, active men, and on the basis of their real life-process we demonstrate the development of the ideological reflexes and the echoes of this life-process. The phantoms formed in the human brain are also, necessarily, sublimates of their material life-process, which is empirically verifiable and bound to material premises. Morality, religion, metaphysics, all the rest of ideology and their corresponding forms of consciousness, thus no longer retain the semblance of independence. They have no history, no development; but men, developing their material production and their material intercourse, alter, along with this their real existence, their thinking and the products of their thinking. Life is not determined by consciousness, but consciousness by life. (Tucker, pp. 154–55)

The idealist was replaced by the materialist conception of history; and a characteristically modern way of thinking about human activity was born. We are alienated, in part, because we live by myths created by others, such as the necessity of monarchical or aristocratic or priestly rule; or the alleged universal applicability and virtue of some particular economic system which actually benefits only a few. (A recent example: supply-side economics.) Such mystifications Marx called "ideology."

The ideas of the ruling class are in every epoch the ruling ideas: i.e., the class which is the ruling *material* force of society, is at the same time its ruling *intellectual* force. The class which has the means of material production at its disposal, has control at the same time over the means of mental production, so that thereby, generally speaking, the ideas of those who lack the means of mental production are subject to it. The ruling ideas are nothing more than the ideal expression of the dominant material relationships, the dominant material relationships grasped as ideas. . . . For instance, in an age and in a country where royal power, aristocracy and bourgeoisie are contending for mastery and where, therefore, mastery is shared, the doctrine of the separation of powers proves to be the dominant idea and is expressed as an "eternal law." . . . For each new class which puts itself in the place of one ruling before it, is compelled, merely in order to carry through its aim, to represent its interest as the common interest of all the members of society, that is, expressed in ideal form: it has to give its ideas the form of universality, and represent them as the only rational, universally valid ones. (Tucker, pp. 172–74)

Material life produces consciousness, not the other way around, and so Hegel gets put "back on his feet again." In this right-side upping of Hegel, one can trace the master idea of the academic left: The culture of our society is an expression of its ruling economic, racial, and gender power formations. Bringing things closer to home: One of the manifestations of that culture is reverence for "the Western classics," the centrality of which justifies the continued rule of a patriarchal white elite while marginalizing the claims to power of everyone else. The allegedly universal values derived from those books, so far from applying to everybody, merely express the values of those already in power.

But now refutation of the academic left rose up from the words. Even Marx rose up to protest the use that has been made of his ideas. Could works of art and philosophy ever merely express a single class's values? Can they not, in democratic societies, in which access to them has been opened up, become the property of anyone with the opportunity to learn from them? Would not new readers make of them something of their own, transforming their meaning, mixing them with the imperatives of their own identity? In this case, Marx and the Marxist tradition itself could be used against the academic left. The roots of the attack on "the canon" can be found in Marx, but Marx himself loved Western high culture and evinced little interest in proletarian culture or in the culture of Asia or Africa. In the socialist utopia, high culture would be available to anybody who wanted it. That was one of the reasons we should create a socialist utopia. Opponents of canon-bashing as disparate as Edward

Said and Irving Howe have pointed out that there is no tradition of such bashing in the classic left. Leon Trotsky argued against the Soviet philistines who wanted to dismiss the "reactionary culture" of the past. Trotsky praised the transcendent power of Dante; and the Italian Marxist Antonio Gramsci insisted on the centrality of Greek and Latin. More recently, E. P. Thompson, the great chronicler of the English nineteenth-century working class, has insisted on the importance of Shakespeare to working-class movements. In brief, the classic writers of the left did not attack canonical literature as "oppressive."

❖   ❖   ❖

The revolution had failed, but our classes on Marx trembled with the aftershocks of illusion. Stephanson explained that despite Marx's drastic revision of Hegel, the dialectic remained. The dialectic was still the motor of change.

"Marx means different things by the dialectic," he said. "At times—in the *Manifesto,* for instance—he means the unceasing struggle of class against class, which propels history forward. And at times he means something more specific. At certain stages in a given period, the forces of production—the way people make and distribute goods—begin to outgrow the relations of productions. The essence comes into conflict with its shell, and it bursts out. The relations change, or there's a revolution."

Did Stephanson still believe in the revolution? Now? He was not unhappy about the collapse of Soviet-style Communism, but he wouldn't let go of Marx's historical paradigm. Again and again, he turned to the magical moment of the proletariat's seizing power and the ending of alienation, and the students, though eager to understand Marx, came indignantly to life. They pooh-poohed the notion of utopia, arguing that all societies produced individuals with greater initiative than others; all societies had natural elites. There could be no perfect equality. Nor was it desirable. It was their most anti-PC moment of the year.

The mood of the class bordered on pathos. Stephanson was holding on to the old myths even as another part of his mind rejected them; on two occasions, he spoke of Stalin's policies of forced collectivization in the 1930s as if they essentially involved a *misinterpretation* of Marx—as if Stalin, paying closer attention to Marx's texts, might have been less cynical and murderous. Stephanson was as vivacious as ever, a handsome young man with blond hair, an infectious smile, and a trumpeting laugh. His raillery never flagged in its high spirits and friendliness; he was always on top of things. Yet I suspected he was in a state of intellectual crisis, and possibly despair. He spoke movingly of the abandonment of alternatives to capitalism. The market, he said, had triumphed utterly, at least for the time being.

"And what happens to ethics," he asked, "in a period in which the market itself is a transcendental signifier? The market dictates relationships, and is valorized as a good thing. The market mechanism is supposed to save everything. But the mechanism has no value in itself."

It was a good question. I would have enjoyed putting it to conservatives, especially when their blanket approval of capitalism left them incoherently criticizing the popular culture produced by capitalism. When the movies turned violent and rap music profane and nihilistic, the conservatives could do nothing but complain about low morals. But where did they think morals came from? The sky? Since conservatives couldn't, by definition, question the marketplace, in which "depravity" was often popular, they were left with a tautological critique. We have low morals because we have . . . low morals. Or because liberalism has demoralized us. Or because we lack restraint. But capitalism by its very nature is *un*-restrained—as Marx said, it was the most revolutionary force in the world. The exuberant nature of capitalism was exactly what conservatives loved about it, and in the 1990s they were eager to abolish regulation and release it even further. So their position made little sense. At the least, they should admit that capitalism was eager to sell *anything,* that it was entirely amoral; and that capitalism itself, in its normal, healthy, creative rampage through our cities and our rural communities, had produced some of the social disruption—the weakening of family ties, the replacement of reading with mass electronic culture—that led to nihilism, violence, and "depravity." Capitalism created envy and the desire to define oneself through goods. Capitalism itself, in its American version, bears part of the responsibility for low morals. But the conservatives couldn't see it. And that is precisely what Marx meant by the blinding powers of ideology.

Stephanson was right about ethics going askew when the market became the highest good. But the students did not respond to Stephanson's despondency, and the reason was obvious enough. They had no choice but to enter the market. It was *their* nightmare, and it was their task to make it not a nightmare. What could they say?

Stephanson continued, renewing the question of revolution. He wanted to provoke them, to see how far their acceptance of their own system would go. "Can we imagine, in Hegelian terms," he asked, "any determinant negation of the present system? Or is this 'the end of history,' as Francis Fukuyama has called it, with capitalism everywhere triumphant and nothing left to us but boredom and bickering over details?"

Abel Kern raised his hand. He was one of the students new to the class in the second semester. An earnest, intellectual sophomore, he was one of the best at explicating texts—he had been brilliant on Hegel—but he was awfully young, and less worldly than students not as articulate as he. "Ecological destruction," he said. "The idea of sustainable capitalist expansion is a farce. If you increase production, you run out of resources."

"Okay," said Stephanson. "Ecological disaster is the product of ever-increasing growth. But what's the social agent that succeeds in bringing about change?"

"Our resources are declining, our population increasing geometrically. The world spirit could appear in a revolution or the collapse of the system."

"Yes," said Stephanson, looking around the room, "but how is it to be decided not to continue to exploit our resources? By whom will it be decided? Are we going to tell the Chinese not to build cars but to keep to their bicycles?" And several students, speaking in the same vein, attacked the United States for hypocrisy. As we chopped down oxygen-producing trees, we warned the less developed countries—Brazil, for instance—against doing the same.

Checkmated, Abel was silent, but now Manuel spoke. "Women," he said, "*women* are the only class the revolution will come from because they have been excluded and because they have thriving internal mechanisms—" General hilarity at this. "No, the way they band together is political. They believe in negotiation. Men use violence because they have the means to; women, a disarmed population, will negotiate."

"Yes, but how will women get the power?" said Meredith, another of the new students, an imposing South African woman of mixed race. Her question hung in the air; her manner implied that women should have the power. Feminism, of course, was one of the things Marx had not foreseen (some other things were fascism, the return of nationalism and ethnic particularism, and the welfare state). Marx thought socialism would take care of women.

Stephanson reluctantly gave up the revolution as a bad job, and returned to the ills of bourgeois society and what Marx called (in *Capital*) "the fetishism of commodities." (Stephanson had asked us to read a few extended passages from the later Marx.) The commodities that workers produced with their labor, the commodities that workers were estranged from, were not, Marx insisted, the simple objects they seemed. On the contrary, commodities were "queer" things "abounding in metaphysical subtleties and theological niceties." Within its bland surface, a commodity—a blouse, a table, a can of chopped beef—hides the truth that it is a product of social labor; a commodity has the social relations of its production inscribed within it. So the actual meaning of the commodity has little to do with its physical nature. A commodity is a kind of fetish (in the religious sense); it appears to be one thing but is actually another, like a voodoo doll, and the relations between commodities take on a mystical nature. Marx was talking of ordinary commodities, made in apparent innocence. But what would he have made of American pop culture, in which commodities—shoes, shirts, insignia, everything—are consciously created as fetishes? Just before writing these paragraphs, I watched my son Max, twelve years old, wear a wool cap as he went Rollerblading in ninety-five-degree heat. No argument could dissuade him from wearing it, for the wool cap was part of his gangsta-rapper outfit. Commodity fetishism had been demystified; it is now the play style of American adolescence.

Stephanson bore in. Capitalism would not get off the hook so easily. "In bourgeois society," he said, "the relations between human beings imitate the relations between commodities. It's not the same thing as saying everything and everyone has a price. We relate to one another as if we *were* commodities; the commodity form comes to permeate every element of human life. There are no pristine relations; our relations are always filtered through the commodity form."

Was this true? It was a stunning idea. "This is still a big problem for liberal theory," Stephanson said. "If cash is the only thing connecting us, what keeps society together? What are the values we hold in common?"

I was alarmed, and my first impulse was to resist. Democratic freedoms, market freedoms, and bourgeois individualism were enough, quite enough, I thought. For I had an awful truth to tell—I didn't always *want* to be closer to my fellow man. Not in general, I mean. I wanted to be closer to this man or that woman or child, or maybe to that small group. For me, that was enough. Irritably, I thought there was an element of inappropriate high-mindedness in such yearnings for community. Those who felt as I did encountered their fellow citizens in separate spheres, at work, in leisure, at church, in professional and political groups; we got what we wanted from many different places without an organic community, and we assembled a life. We picked and chose, and many of us might not always want pristine relations with other people. Not all the time, that is. Treating some people as a commodity, and being treated as a commodity, awful as that sounds, has its own kind of low pleasure, the pleasure of artificiality, of speed, and of money. Our business civilization has produced a flowing affability in casual encounters that can be rather pleasant, even exhilarating. Anyway, cash is *not* the only thing connecting us. There were family, religion, sports, culture in all its varieties, voluntary associations and political affiliations of all sorts.

But once I had made that list, I knew I hadn't answered Stephanson's question. He was right, of course. In America, there seemed less and less holding us together. Had I not been mourning the death of civil society all year long? So many of the major writers on the C.C. list—Plato, Aristotle, Augustine, Machiavelli, Rousseau, Hegel, as well as Marx—assumed or demanded a far greater sense of social solidarity than we had in America. And whatever my needs, so many others yearned for what American capitalism and American individualism made impossible. Millions longed to be part of something larger and more nourishing than their own clan. For instance, the militia groups. Were such groups composed of anarchic individualists and right-wing libertarians, or were the members actually people clinging together for support, longing for a community they couldn't find in the pagan media and shopping-mall wastelands?

❖ ❖ ❖

"A society based on greed is better than a society based on programmed brotherhood," Leszek Kolakowski said in his Columbia talk. Well, if those were the only alternatives, most of us would agree. So render glory unto the market and the freedom that often comes with it. But still. Still! Marx's critique of capitalism and what it does to human beings cannot be simply dismissed in derision and irony. Communism's failures had not rendered into nullity every sentence that Karl Marx wrote. Kolakowski was entitled to his bitterness, but, having read a little Marx, we could say Kolakowski was extravagant, he was mistaken. Marx the failed prophet was being ridiculed and repressed not only because he was wrong but because he was right. He ruffled the pride of the triumphant capitalist order. Stephanson had seized on the elements of Marx that remained powerful, even unanswerable.

Now that the triumph of capitalism was irreversible, we should be able yet again to read Marx (selectively) on capitalism, as Westerners in search of ourselves. Marx's irrelevance in the world of power had made him supremely relevant to our souls.

❖ ❖ ❖

Before I began *On Liberty,* I thought I understood Stephanson's boredom with Mill. Victorian liberal par excellence, chief celebrant of the freedoms of speech, conscience, and conduct, an early and fervent feminist, John Stuart Mill was overwhelmingly *good.* He was noble to the point of silliness (his long platonic friendship with a married woman made a most peculiar mid-Victorian scandal), and, all in all, the least sexy great writer who still mattered. That he was indeed a great writer became clear enough as soon as I got going on Mill's extraordinary pamphlet—so clear that by the time I had reached the middle of its densely printed 113 pages, my sympathy with Stephanson's decision not to discuss Mill had evaporated. A very rich text, that pamphlet. I discovered there, among a great many other things, the key to Columbia's core curriculum—or any modern curriculum of classic texts. Its inner spirit and energies were embodied in Mill's own ardent virtue.

Expecting to encounter platitudes, I found instead an intense, muscular argument, a strenuous radicalism of spirit. Mill's whole point is that the platitudes of freedom are in fact a minority position: In world history, intolerance and persecution have been the rule, liberty the exception. No more than seventy or so years before Mill wrote *On Liberty* (in 1859), powerful people, in Europe at least, had put to death those persons whose beliefs they hated and feared. "Heresy," after a long career, was only recently dead. But it was very much alive outside of Europe and the United States, and, of course, remains alive in the 1990s, when many societies still consider freedom of speech, worship, and conduct a ridiculous and outrageous idea, a cause for arrests and trials and persecutions. Such American allies as Saudi Arabia reasoned as follows: Why should we allow women to make their own sexual and marital choices? It is an offense against God. And why should we allow other political systems and religions to be openly celebrated inside our country? Such beliefs are wrong and therefore corrupt—and dangerous to us. The strength of our country depends on unity. We do not need to collaborate in our own suicide out of deference to some foolish Western hypocrisy about "freedom."

Not that the democratic states were altogether immune to this mode of thinking. As Mill says over and over, in Victorian England (and in America, too), persecution by state and church had given way to persecution by public opinion. Democracy has a bullying and conformist spirit built into its freedoms; many people would silence their fellow citizens if they could. Allan Bloom may have imagined that relativism was sweeping America, but in fact most people respect their own opinions as self-evident. And most people, as Mill says, would like to consider such opinions universal, little realizing that most of what they believe draws on powerful institutions on all sides of them—family, church, society—or on such unmentionable forces as prejudice and superstition, envy, and, most of all, self-interest. Mill was very clear about this: Self-justification, and the blindness that it entails, is inherent in human egotism. True liberty is not comfortably supported by anyone.

So why *not* suppress other people's opinions? Mill gives two reasons. Suppressing any particular speech or opinion implies that we are infallible and could never change. After all, says Mill, the early Christians were suppressed by people as conscientious and honorable as ourselves—Marcus Aurelius, for instance, the most thoughtful of the Roman emperors—and Christianity eventually triumphed. We also need disagreement, we need to be challenged, or our doctrines dry up and become mere "received ideas"—ideas held without passion, without clarity or strength. So here is what "everyone" believes, some words from the boring Mill:

He who knows only his own side of the case knows little of that. His
reasons may be good, and no one may have been able to refute
them. But if he is equally unable to refute the reasons on the opposite side, if he does not so much as know what they are, he has no
ground for preferring either opinion. The rational position for him
would be suspension of judgment, and unless he contents himself
with that, he is either led by authority or adopts, like the generality
of the world, the side to which he feels most inclination. Nor is it
enough that he should hear the arguments of adversaries from his
own teachers, presented as they state them, and accompanied by
what they offer as refutations. That is not the way to do justice to
the arguments or bring them into real contact with his own mind.
He must be able to hear them from persons who actually believe
them, who defend them in earnest and do their very utmost for
them. He must know them in their most plausible and persuasive
form; he must feel the whole force of the difficulty which the true
view of the subject has to encounter and dispose of, else he will
never really possess himself of the portion of truth which meets and
removes that difficulty. Ninety-nine in a hundred of what are called
educated men are in this condition, even of those who can argue fluently for their opinions. (p. 35)

On Liberty was not a pleasant little pamphlet commending freedom
but a relentless attack on conformity and timidity. The health of an entire society was at stake. Courage, spirit, life were at stake. "In sober
truth, whatever homage may be professed, or even paid, to real or supposed mental superiority, the general tendency of things throughout the
world is to render mediocrity the ascendent power among mankind."
Mill would not have been happy with a merely active circulation of
opinion—an eternal Hyde Park Corner or National Public Radio. What
he wanted was a society that loathed mediocrity and timorousness and
rewarded individuality (even eccentricity) and initiative; such a society
would be exhilarating, burgeoning, progressive. True liberty of conscience and opinion would require not just laws protecting free speech
but a revolution of spirit.

How many of us could put up with the fundamental disagreement
that Mill thinks is necessary to intellectual health? As a movie critic, I
know that whatever actors and directors and writers may say, none of
them really wants criticism. What they want is praise, and then more
praise. Highly skilled and educated people are often the least likely to
live with fundamental disagreement—they've already invested a great
deal of ego in what they believe, and they don't want it shaken. Inevitably, they become contemptuous of opposing views, emptying them
of reality. They are *amused* by them. Even if you think that Mill was

fooling himself on the knowability of truth, his insistence on confrontation is alarming. In such passages as the above, one hears a fervor almost religious in its enunciation of principle, a high, anxious, driven idealism—the morally heroic side of Victorian strenuousness. Mill knows he's going against the grain of human desire, at all places and at all times.

In the United States, neither the Christian right, with its sanctimonious belittling of opposing views, nor the cultural left, with its eagerness to reduce everyone's opinions to an expression of power, was prepared to hear its fundamental assumptions debated. For people of messianic conviction, Mill's notions must be exasperating. He demands that we accept uncertainty. He wants us to live, as his great modern disciple Isaiah Berlin might say, with the assumption that life is neither stationary nor easily understood. No single idea—religious, economic, political—will organize everything, interpret everything, unify everything. We're condemned to change and complexity, and only reason and debate will produce knowledge and even progress.

How sexless, how unexciting. But what else *is* there? My disagreement with Stephanson became clear. It was important that we read Mill not only because he articulates what many of us believe about freedom in an open society but because Mill's arguments encompass the ethical condition of our believing things at all.

And as I finished Mill's defense of freedom of speech, it hit me: Mill *was* the core curriculum. That is, he had formulated the rationale for Columbia's reading—or any liberal reading—of "the great books." The books embodied not imperishable truths, and certainly not a uniformity of approach, but a radical tradition of self-questioning. In this tradition, one book challenges another, or is even at odds with itself, from Homer right up to the modern texts—Boccaccio lovingly recasting the *Divine Comedy,* Montaigne contradicting himself, Marx turning Hegel right side up again, and so on. What the books taught was not a stable body of knowledge or even consistent "values" but critical habits of mind that would never desert the student.

Marx and Mill were eternally radical. If they seemed, at the moment, less interesting or necessary than other texts, that was because they had lodged themselves like burrs in the hide of our self-approval, and certain people, left and right, would like to pluck them out.

Chapter *25*

NIETZSCHE

~ Spring breaks out quietly on the steps of Low Library
~ *On the Genealogy of Mortals:* how instinct gives way to ethics
~ Feeling strong: Nietzsche as a release from liberal dismay
~ I realize, by means of reading, that my love of movies is still alive
~ A few students try to rescue Christianity from Nietzsche's contempt
~ The end of truth
~ A conference of "radical" academics
~ Compassion restored
~ Relativism yet again

Like many another city person, I had never quite learned the names of flowers and flowering bushes, and so, early every spring, taking a bus across Central Park on some chilly afternoon, I would gaze in bewilderment at the demure appearance of color in the budded but still brownish stretches of the park. Narcissus? Hyacinth? The names went out of my head as fast as the names of the Greek and Roman gods. Urban Jewish boys growing up in the fifties never did get the hang of the natural world. A tree? It shouldn't fall on your head—what *kind* of tree it was, nobody knew, nobody cared. But now I cared, and not knowing what things were called was as maddening as seeing an old film on television and forgetting who had directed it. At Columbia, the bursts of yellow and pink, first pale, then bright and full, emerging before the brown-red brick of the central campus buildings, and around the gray sides of Low Library, softened the lines of stone, and perhaps the lines of thought, too. At Columbia, beauty had to fight for existence, and it seemed a kind of benediction.

As an undergraduate, I had never noticed these few signs of grace. Reading and thinking, I was sure, could be done anywhere—in Columbia's cramped old dormitories backing onto Amsterdam or Broadway;

in the periodicals room at Butler Library, its smoky side chamber filled with large leather chairs and "private" book-lined crannies; in the yellow light of a subway station late at night as the express roared down the center tracks. When you are twenty, you don't need beauty. You ignore it, associating it with luxury; you trust it less than squalor. But I needed it now, and I was sure that study was eased by Gothic spires, spacious academic halls, and open patches of field and woods. I felt a surge of longing for glamorous country schools. Cambridge? Duke? Dear God, had I conceived, at the age of forty-eight, a desire to go to Princeton? Study needed a setting, I told myself, as much as an opera singer needed castle ramparts or a Druid temple.

At Columbia, in early spring, the number of football and Frisbee tossers doubled and redoubled, and a great many other undergraduates, like creatures newly emerged from the sea, sat on the broad steps of Low Library with their pale faces in the sun, which hung rather low in the sky above Butler Library to the south. Climbing up the stairs to get to Mathematics Hall for C.C. class, I walked around women in black jeans, T-shirts, and leather jackets, and men in Army drab, some with long hair or a touch of beard under the chin. Undergraduates as a tribe were both sullen and polite. Proudly reserved, they would nevertheless become quite eager if anyone showed serious interest in them. (Take one out to lunch and he would tell you everything.) A vaguely parental emotion stirred within me: Let them eat; let them get some sleep, some color.

It was a happy week. Reading Nietzsche on the heels of Mill, I was wildly exhilarated: More than once, I came close to laughing out loud at how good a time I was having, how lawless and strong I felt. For the moment, at least, I was freed from the burden of respect and of *caring*. For the American liberal (and some conservatives, too), everyone must be esteemed, everyone's complaints and troubles taken seriously, every cause, every group, every problem and failure respected, understood, sympathized with, given a break. It's an exhausting and exhaustive task, producing an inevitable disgust. In the nineties, liberal faith—or at least faith in governmental solutions to the problems of poverty, crime, inequality—was crumbling rapidly, and one sign of the collapse was a little voice that muttered insistently in one's brain: *Not everyone deserves sympathy. Some people are screwing themselves up.* Say that aloud, however, and you will get killed in some quarters. If hypocrisy is the tribute that vice pays to virtue, political correctness is the tribute that virtue pays to vice. Or so I thought in my new mood of Nietzschean defiance.

Nietzsche kicked hell out of liberal dutifulness. The assigned C.C. text, *On the Genealogy of Morals,* from 1887, one of Nietzsche's last books before he fell into insanity, is a hilarious, rancorous attack on egalitarianism and democracy, on modern bourgeois civilization, on Judaism, Christianity—on everything that most Westerners would call humane and necessary. A tremendous explosion of scorn and despair, the book is unnervingly intelligent and authentically scandalous. For anyone tired of the routine shocks of movies or MTV or the farcical outrages of the New York avant-garde in recent years, this was the real thing, an untamable and unregenerate book.

The weak, it turns out, have perfected a trick of exalting themselves and making the strong feel guilty. It is called morality, and it was invented by the Jews and early Christians in revolt against the old pagan warrior elites—Greeks, Romans, Persians, Egyptians, whoever. Here is Nietzsche in mid-argument, and in the full flight of uproarious disgust:

> One will have divined already how easily the priestly mode of valuation can branch off from the knightly-aristocratic and then develop into its opposite; this is particularly likely when the priestly caste and the warrior caste are in jealous opposition to one another and are unwilling to come to terms. The knightly-aristocratic value judgments presupposed a powerful physicality, a flourishing, abundant, even overflowing health, together with that which serves to preserve it: war, adventure, hunting, dancing, war games, and in general all that involves vigorous, free, joyful activity. The priestly-noble mode of valuation presupposes, as we have seen, other things: it is disadvantageous for it when it comes to war! As is well known, the priests are the *most evil enemies*—but why? Because they are the most impotent. It is because of their impotence that in them hatred grows to monstrous and uncanny proportions, to the most spiritual and poisonous kind of hatred. The truly great haters in world history have always been priests; likewise the most ingenious haters: other kinds of spirit hardly come into consideration when compared with the spirit of priestly vengefulness. Human history would be altogether too stupid a thing without the spirit that the impotent have introduced into it— let us take at once the most notable example. All that has been done on earth against "the noble," "the powerful," "the masters," "the rulers," fades into nothing compared with what the *Jews* have done against them; the Jews, that priestly people, who in opposing their enemies and conquerors were ultimately satisfied with nothing less than a radical revaluation of their enemies' values, that is to say, an act of the *most spiritual revenge*. For this alone was appropriate to a priestly people, the people embodying the most deeply repressed priestly vengefulness. It was the Jews who, with awe-inspiring consistency, dared to invert the aristocratic value-equation (good = noble = powerful = beautiful = happy = beloved of God) and to hang on to this inversion with their teeth, the teeth of the most abysmal hatred (the hatred of impotence), saying "the wretched alone are the good; the poor, impotent, lowly alone are the good; the suffering, deprived,

sick, ugly alone are pious, alone are blessed by God, blessedness is for them alone—and you, the powerful and noble, are on the contrary the evil, the cruel, the lustful, the insatiable, the godless to all eternity; and you shall be in all eternity the unblessed, accursed, and damned!" . . . One knows *who* inherited this Jewish revaluation [i.e., the Christians] . . . In connection with the tremendous and immeasurably fateful initiative provided by the Jews through this most fundamental of all declarations of war, I recall the proposition I arrived at on a previous occasion (*Beyond Good and Evil,* section 195)— that with the Jews there begins *the slave revolt in morality:* that revolt which has a history of two thousand years behind it and which we no longer see because it—has been victorious. (pp. 33–34)

I will return to this passage, but let's get one thing out of the way fast: Nietzsche had nothing but contempt for the German national chauvinists and anti-Semites of the 1870s and 1880s; such passages as the above, though appropriated by the Nazis, have to be read with some care as an element in Nietzsche's attack on *all* modern conceptions of justice and equality. It's not only the Jews whom Nietzsche louses up (and with considerable ambiguity—the passage can be taken as *hommage*). *On the Genealogy of Morals,* which we read in its entirety, is, among many other things, a slander on the motives of any person who has tried to alleviate the sufferings of mankind. It's an attack on *pity.* The Judeo-Christian heritage, Nietzsche admits, had made man more interesting ("history would be altogether too stupid a thing without the spirit that the impotent have introduced into it"). Man acquired depth, a soul. But along the way he lost his health, his vitality, and his happiness. He had been struck down by guilt.

Some of Nietzsche's satanic laughter has, to my ears, a forced, theatrical quality, in the style of a hambone Mephistopheles singing at the Metropolitan Opera. But surely he was one of the greatest of all prose writers; an amazing writer really, spiteful, violent, rhapsodic, with a fierce psychological penetration of everything and everyone that made disagreement with him a perilous undertaking. Appealing both to malevolent pessimism and to pleasure, he drives hypocrisy right out of the reader's responses; he is the rebellious underside of equable and sociable minds, saying what many had thought at one time or another but then rejected as cruel or unpleasant. Reading him, you got high on contempt, even if you rejected half of what he wrote as too murderously funny to be true. The style, filled with repeated and italicized words, dashes, parentheses, interjections, had a speaking vehemence; it was the style of *impatience,* licensing its own excesses as Olympian play. If, at times, he rants, like some overeducated, unhinged person heard dimly on the radio in the middle of the night—Friedrich Nietzsche, the great philosopher and patron saint of cranks!—he was certainly the most subversively witty philosopher we had read since Plato. His urgency burned away the deliberate system-building of a Kant or a Hegel. After Nietzsche, all other writers seemed prissy and cautious.

How had the universities assimilated this most dangerous man? For there was no doubt Nietzsche had become a powerful influence on the academic left. In his first class on Nietzsche, Stephanson quoted Princeton (now Harvard) philosopher Cornel West to the effect that Nietzsche was the single most important influence on postmodern thought—which was pretty funny, since only fifty years earlier Nietzsche was widely reviled as the archreactionary, a sort of Nazi house philosopher. After the war, Stephanson said, Nietzsche had been pried loose from the Nazis' grip, cleaned up and revived (by translator, interpreter, and exegete Walter Kaufmann among others), the distasteful parts of him ignored. A neat trick, but what would Nietzsche have made of it? And what would he have made of American academics turning his impassioned language into the received ideas of the Modern Language Association (MLA), the professional association of college language teachers and a bastion of left-academic orthodoxy? Nietzsche the celebrator of the "superman" as patron saint of the academic *left*? There was a joke buried here somewhere.

❖ ❖ ❖

On the Genealogy of Morals was C.C.'s most decisive push into modernism—and into radical uncertainty. (We had read only excerpts from it in 1961.) A huge restlessness gathered behind the opening questions. "Under what conditions did man devise these value judgments good and evil? *and what value do they themselves possess?* Have they hitherto hindered or furthered human prosperity? Are they signs of distress, of impoverishment, of the degeneration of life? Or is there revealed in them, on the contrary, the plenitude, force, and will of life, its courage, certainty, future?" Nietzsche was trained as a philologist, so he examined the etymological significance of the words expressing "good" in the various languages, and discovered that in earlier ages "good" was associated with the self-satisfaction of noble and aristocratic men.

> . . . the concept "good" has been sought and established in the wrong place: the judgment "good" did *not* originate with those to whom "goodness" was shown! Rather it was "the good" themselves, that is to say, the noble, powerful, high-stationed and high-minded, who felt and established themselves and their actions as good, that is, of the first rank, in contradistinction to all the low, low-minded, common and plebeian. It was out of this *pathos of distance* that they first seized the right to create values and to coin names for values. . . . (pp. 25–26)

The original distinction, then, was between good and *bad*, not good and evil, and what produced the sense of good was an overflow of vitality, issuing at times in cruelty and acts of revenge, at times in generosity, joy, or piety—in any case, in careless acts, performed by instinct. *Morality had nothing to do with it.*

Which was quite an eye-opener. At the very least, Nietzsche cleared up some of the things that I, and many of the students, had found puzzling and disturbing in Homer. In the *Iliad* a lowborn character, Thersites, speaks in council, criticizing Agamemnon, the leader of the Greeks, in pretty much the same terms as anyone else, and for his troubles he gets soundly boxed on the ears by Odysseus and generally laughed at. That was bad—a lowborn person daring to speak in council. At the same time, the Greek aristocrats at war, at their feasts and fires and games, experienced themselves as justified, and felt little of what we would call pity, and nothing of what we would call guilt. (Shame, at one's own lack of success, was the negative emotion of the Greek warriors.) The absence of those guilty emotions in Homer tended to confirm Nietzsche's etymological suppositions: The words were not there, and the emotions were not there. I now understood better than ever that my dismay when Odysseus kills the suitors at the end of the *Odyssey* was an emotion Homer couldn't possibly have intended his listeners to feel. What he intended them to feel was pleasure in Odysseus's righteous anger, satisfaction in revenge.

"The upper class valorizes its notions of beauty," said Manuel Alon, nailing it down in class, "while the common people are too preoccupied with survival to create a language." A neat formulation. And for once, the new-academic "valorize" sounded almost right: The language-makers created value. For Nietzsche, the pagan warrior, despite his pleasure in cruelty, was man at his height. With slightly farcical affection, Nietzsche dubbed his superior and unconscious conqueror the "blond beast"—the *blonde Bestie*. Everything after his defeat was a falling away.

What a story! The priests (Nietzsche was speaking generally of a type), fueling their impotence, their resentment of the warrior-ruler class, engage in heroic self-denial. They commit cruelty to themselves (refusing food, sensuality, luxury) rather than to other people, an act of will that greatly impresses the poor, the weak, and the suffering. As a way of consolidating their hold on these masses, the ascetic idealists of the priestly caste then create a new system, not of good and bad but of good and *evil*, in which the sufferers are good and the strong and powerful evil. "Ethics" replaces the natural vitality of instinct. And by this sleight of hand—what Nietzsche called the "transvaluation of all values"—the forms of involuntary and resentful weakness are transformed into Christian virtues. Subjection is reborn as "obedience," cowardice as "patience," the inability to take revenge as "forgiveness," misery in this world as "eternal bliss" in the next.

So much for the Judeo-Christian tradition. So much for Jesus! Actually, the villain of the piece is less Jesus of Nazareth—who did not display "resentment," not even on the cross—than Saul the malevolent rug-weaver, later Paul the convert (later still the conquering St. Paul), whose mesmerizing eloquence and rage, and whose disgust for the body, made him the perfect "ascetic idealist." The priestly type blames the poor and weak, telling them they are sinners, the cause of their own suffering, but he also offers redemption, altering the direction of resentment.

> Admire above all the forger's skill with which the stamp of virtue, even the ring, the golden-sounding ring of virtue, is here counterfeited. They monopolize virtue, these weak, hopelessly sick people, there is no doubt of it: "we alone are the good and just," they say, "we alone are *homines bonae voluntatis*" [men of goodwill]. They walk among us as embodied reproaches, as warnings to us—as if health, well-constitutedness, strength, pride, and the sense of power were in themselves necessarily vicious things for which one must pay some day, and pay bitterly: how ready they themselves are at bottom to *make* one pay; how they crave to be *hangmen*. (p. 123)

The "will to power" was universal, Nietzsche said. Everyone felt it in one way or another, the weak as well as the strong.

What a description he had written of certain contemporary American political leaders! What a description of certain academics, feminists, and journalists! How utterly true of the Christian right and the members of the right-to-life movement, with their message of love and sanctity and their practice of revilement and hate! I reveled in Nietzsche's insight. Who would not? The country was filled with haters crying "Justice!" when they really meant "Power for me and my group!"

❖ ❖ ❖

Finishing the book, I became gaga for a few days, talking Nietzsche to anyone who would listen. I expounded on the telephone late at night; I wrote letters; I couldn't stop. I was even more worked up than I had been over Euripides, Machiavelli, and Boccaccio, my earlier "discoveries." By now, my taste in "great books" had become clear: I was drawn to energy, play, vivacity, speed, perversity, and by means of these attractions, I sensed, in a roundabout way, that my love of movies couldn't have died, and would never die, no matter how urgently literature now called, for those were among the qualities I most enjoyed in movies. There was a difference, however: After the rare great movie, like Scorsese's *Goodfellas* or Eastwood's *Unforgiven* or Tarantino's *Pulp Fiction*, I would quickly make myself busy; I would sit down and write something, the excitement over the movie generating the review as a kind of high-energy workout, a series of practical problems that needed to be solved. The movie would burn hot and then, the review finished, the flame would taper off. My responsibility to the new, daring work of art was over. My dreams might be haunted by it, but my life would not be changed. Movies, at their best, offer very complex kinds of pleasures, but they do not change your life. Nietzsche could do that.

I was beginning to relish the mixture of dread and agitation that I had been feeling all year, the alarm that came from being turned upside down, and then the struggle to right myself again. I wanted more, more! And if I tumbled around like a sneaker thrown into the dryer, bumping against the sides, that was just fine. Going around in circles, I would find the center, my center, in this time of the alleged "decentered self."

Nietzsche suggests it's a mistake to mistrust feelings of self-sufficiency and strength. What he wanted in life were flourishing, freely functioning, and creative human beings who had attained a sense of mastery. Nietzsche's writing is all about personal power: He is in favor of it. Was I also excited because I was in political trouble and Nietzsche provided a thrilling way out? No doubt this was part of it. Like many others, I was undergoing a crisis of sorts, liberal faith slipping away in a wash of distrust. We have huge problems, and government seems powerless to solve most of them. At the same time, the country is filled with "victims," some real, some imaginary, all of them pressing their claims. All of a sudden, everyone seemed to be imitating the most dubious ideological practice of the black nationalists, or the most self-dramatizing American Jews, my brothers, who brandished the Holocaust whenever anyone criticized them at all. Too many people in America were looking about for shackles to clamp on free limbs.

Nietzsche encouraged a celebration of individual will, not a mourning of collective fate. And I had days, exhilarated by Nietzsche's contempt, when I slipped into Limbaughesque rants and was willing to ignore the increasing signs of structural inequality in America, the stagnation of real wages for the middle class, the remnants of racism, the glass ceilings, and the rest; I ignored all that and I said bitterly to myself that claiming victim status for oneself or one's group was a way of avoiding the actual danger of failure by asserting defeat in advance and then promoting failure as a claim on the successful. Why do it? To make the successful feel guilty, of course. To shame power into giving up. But why not take power oneself? I was sure that those who had the steel to take power would figure out how to do so, no matter how severe their disadvantages, and that all the other "victims" should be ignored. No productive policy could come out of guilt. Not in this country; and not as long as a few doors could still be kicked open by the determined.

❖ ❖ ❖

At Columbia the new buds were filling out the cement bareness, breaking the uniformity of bleakness. Beginning his discussion of Nietzsche, Stephanson expressed his regret at presenting such an inflammatory work with so little contextual preparation. The book, like all the others, was slammed down on the table before us. And yet, eager as I was to stop and read everything Nietzsche had written, and then to go back and read Arthur Schopenhauer, his predecessor in German philosophy, I thought there was something to be said for this violent ripping of context, this naïve *reading of books*. Too much preparation might cool out the experience, making it routine, merely academic—another brick in the arch rather than what it was, a grenade.

In class, Charlie Kim, the Korean boy with the serious forehead and gentle manner, the student who wanted to be a missionary, was understandably wistful.

"Does Nietzsche's account hold true? Is the Judeo-Christian ethos like this?" Stephanson asked, and Charlie answered, "He misconstrues Christian ethics . . ." but was unable to finish. There was more, I knew, but he wasn't able to get it out yet. Nietzsche was a kick in the stomach.

"Is the Judeo-Christian tradition antilife, and all that?" asked Stephanson. He said it without his usual fierceness, softly almost. Nietzsche had insisted on the sickness of self-denial, the near criminality of it as an attack on life.

Sighs, shaking heads, a few smiles. "There is a life-affirming aspect to Jewish religion and culture," said Abel Kern at last. "But every religion has an ascetic side to it, too," meaning that he acquiesced in Nietzsche's mocking account of self-denial.

"Yes," said Charlie, "but isn't the point of asceticism not to deny life but to reach a higher form of life? It is life-affirming, isn't it?" His question trailed off and hovered. But then someone came to his aid. An intense young man of Indian descent (he was from Pennsylvania) had joined the class for the second term, and I had been staring at him for weeks, trying to remember where I had seen him before, and now as he spoke—Dinesh was his name—I remembered. He was the guy who, back in the fall, had argued with the black woman student in Hartley Hall over the core curriculum, asking her why she did not go elsewhere if she hated the Western classics so much. On that occasion, he had talked tough. But now, feeling some solidarity with a loner, perhaps, he defended asceticism. "Asceticism isn't just sitting in contemplation," he said, "it's detachment from the triviality of life."

Well, this detachment is one of the things that Nietzsche had feared (he was repelled by European interest in Buddhist thought), but the students, I thought, had kicked a few holes in his contempt, and now Charlie, finding his voice, and unfurrowing his handsome forehead, came to life.

"Jesus said, 'Follow me.' That way of following Jesus becomes the basis of your whole life." He paused for a moment. "Nietzsche misconstrues the purpose of suffering. What suffering affects—that's true life, not denial. You create a new life, a more powerful life."

He spoke slowly, as always, but strongly: Active belief was an affirmation of strength, not a consolation for the weak. Charlie had survived the great atheists Marx and Nietzsche. It was the third or fourth time in the year that a religious student, walking without many companions, had seemed braver in the midst of the secular university than the many nonreligious.

❖ ❖ ❖

Nietzsche offered still another account of the origins of civil society. In his version, cruelty, in the form of torture and punishment, forced men to remember and to renounce; cruelty forced the continuity of intent and organization that makes civil society possible. Among other things, he was surely dismissing Hobbes and Locke's fiction of a contract forming the basis of civil society. There was no contract but merely overbearing force, which caused the weak and formless nomads to gather into a society. Nor could you find much support in the *Genealogy* for Kant's notion of an absolute moral law derived by reason, nor for Hegel's insistence that the main line of history was a continuous process of Spirit tortuously realizing itself as freedom (anything but). Nor would you find a reaffirmation, going back a bit, of Aristotle's insistence on the ordering of emotions or anything of his love of moderation as the way to the good life.

Am I preparing an exam question? No, just pointing out that the core reading list features many works that revise and even overturn the earlier works on the list. If this is hegemony, it is also self-contradictory and a lot shakier on its pins than most cultural formations. Nietzsche and John Stuart Mill? They hardly agree on anything. Nietzsche may be an influence on the academic left, yet as far as such theoreticians are concerned, Nietzsche and Mill are also both members of that mysterious trampling army, the hegemonic tradition of white males; they share the discourse. But I wondered: From what distant vantage point would Mill and Nietzsche appear as anything but resolutely opposed? Apart from differences of gender, race, and class, what differences *did* matter to them? Might not left-academic talk of hegemony and logocentrism really amount to a glib way of gaining control, and even precedence, over an immense legacy of fiercely oppositional thought?

If studied with any intensity at all, Nietzsche leaves one excited, angered, and badly bruised. Charlie may have survived, but, despite my euphoria, I wasn't so sure about myself. Giddiness can make you sick as well as excited. Nietzsche is a far more radical writer than Marx, who insisted that the coming socialist utopia would end class warfare and even end alienation. Nietzsche left one with a thrilled, frightening impression of a terrific rush to the edge of something—the "abyss," he called it. The rush, frantic and laborious, took place over and over again, a peculiarly modern rhythm of restless despair, rage, and courage. "God is dead" was Nietzsche's most famous assertion (even though the remark did not originate with him), by which he meant that God no longer lived at the center of Western consciousness and that Christianity after the Enlightenment had lost its hold on the imagination; immortality and the absolute law had vanished. Values were something created by men and women, not something inherent or something you could find; not something *out there*. And this thought placed us in a situation of complete responsibility, possessed of an overwhelming opportunity to create ourselves—or lose ourselves.

In the last section of the *Genealogy*, Nietzsche makes it clear that in giving up God, one is also giving up truth—not empirical truth, something observable and measurable, such as the amount of pressure produced by steam in a closed container, but metaphysical truth, absolute truth, a set of universal norms. In a passage from the *Genealogy* that is momentous for today's academic world, Nietzsche teases the notion—derived from Descartes, perhaps—that a single mind working in a vacuum could arrive at truth.

> But precisely because we seek knowledge, let us not be ungrateful to such resolute reversals of accustomed perspectives and valuations with which the spirit has, with apparent mischievousness and futility, raged against itself for so long: to see differently in this way for once, to *want* to see differently, is no small discipline and preparation of the intellect for its future "objectivity"—the latter understood not as "contemplation without interest" (which is a nonsensical absurdity), but as the ability *to control* one's Pro and Con and to dispose of them, so that one knows how to employ a *variety* of perspectives and affective interpretations in the service of knowledge.
>
> Henceforth, my dear philosophers, let us be on guard against the dangerous old conceptual fiction that posited a "pure, will-less, painless, timeless knowing subject"; let us guard against the snares of such contradictory concepts as "pure reason," "absolute spirituality," "knowledge in itself": these always demand that we should think of an eye that is completely unthinkable, an eye turned in no

particular direction, in which the active and interpreting forces, through which alone seeing becomes seeing *something,* are supposed to be lacking; these always demand of the eye an absurdity and a nonsense. There is *only* a perspective seeing, *only* a perspective "knowing"; and the *more* affects we allow to speak about one thing, the *more* eyes, different eyes, we can use to observe one thing, the more complete will our "concept" of this thing, our "objectivity," be. (p. 119)

Knowing can only be achieved by the report of many eyes, a notion that the academic left has seized on with a passion. In the work of one of Nietzsche's modern disciples, the late Michel Foucault, whose influence over the American academy in the last twenty years has been extraordinary, truth hardly functions independently at all. Truth, or knowing, without some implication for the exercise of power is scarcely imaginable. Certain systems of knowledge—say, psychology in all that it had to say about criminality or sexual behavior—allow one to dispose of bodies, by sending them to prison or by designating them as "schizophrenic" or "homosexual" or whatever. Such "discursive practices" have functioned as forms of power, and "truth," as used within them, has served a controlling, even dominating function. So truth is hardly innocent or neutral: In making values and judgments through the means of its particular language, the discourse reinforces itself, and renders what lies outside the discourse's focus—anomalies that cannot be easily reconciled with truth as it functions within the discourse—marginal or nonexistent. Behavior gets coerced or ignored by "truth."

Foucault's American imitators, pushing his ideas in a more explicit political direction than Foucault himself, would speak as if the discourse itself constitutes the "truths" that it is supposed to be discovering. A malign paradox! Thus a Foucauldian might say that if one is talking about sex and character, sex may be fixed, but gender (in the sense of male or female temperament and roles) was something "socially constructed" by the existing language of sex as well as by economics and class and so on. There was nothing inherent, natural, or essential in gender. Its alleged characteristics were all constructed.

In certain parts of the American academy, a great many essences have bitten the dust in recent years. What once passed for truth is now impossible to assess outside the trinity of determinants—class, race, and gender—and the analysis of language as a controlling discourse. In particular, the "truth" possessed by a white male ruling class has fallen under suspicion. And this view (we are now a good way from Nietzsche) has been extended to literature itself, which, in the new politicized version of literary studies, has been seen less as an independent aesthetic experience than as a reflection of its social situation as well as the particular controlling matrix of language within which it exists. In the neutral view, all literature requires "historicization"—placement within history. In the extreme view, literature is "complicit" in the crimes of power, the crimes that literary language conceal from both writer and reader. Thus Mark Twain, an apparent critic of the swollen and corrupt American "Gilded Age," is discovered, by analysis of his language and underlying attitudes, to be as much a product of the Gilded Age as any robber baron. It is now necessary to "interrogate" literature to find such complicities.

This is a very complex subject, and I don't mean to suggest that Nietzsche is responsible for everything. His influence passed through the philosopher Martin Heidegger, and from there through Foucault and Jacques Derrida. He is one of the many currents, let us say, flowing into the current politicization of academic study of literature. The dominant current, of course, is the sense of grievance felt by women and African-Americans and others who have been left out of power in the past, and who are now part of the university population, both as teachers and students. The new academic constituencies have forced such questions as, Do we have a biased canon? Feminism, for instance, has combined elements of French theory with its own energies of revolt, and some feminists now analyze the Western classics in terms of certain modes of speech—the patriarchal modes—which render women silent or marginal. Sifting through the past, such critics perceive how women authors fought to escape. Some rejected the patriarchal language; others attempted to adapt the codes to their own purpose and were scorned for it. In brief, women were either forced to speak the master's discourse or judged trivial when speaking their own. Thus the very criteria by which we judge literary merit are themselves embedded in the male-dominated discourse. For women, in this argument, "standards" are a rigged game.

All of which is suggestive and useful as an analytic tool. But the tool can become a bludgeon, and, in the universities, reading has often enough been supplanted by the politics of reading. For the last twenty years or so, it has been open season, in some quarters, on the classics. Who is now to say that Harriet Beecher Stowe's *Uncle Tom's Cabin* or Susan B. Warner's *Wide, Wide World* are not the equal of Nathaniel Hawthorne's *Scarlet Letter*? Those criteria by which the Warner or Stowe novels might be regarded as lesser works—the books were sentimental, melodramatic, propagandistic, etc.—were themselves politically derived, were they not? If male critics said that Hawthorne was "major" and Warner "minor," weren't they merely reasserting their control in an endless tautology? All the conventional criteria for greatness—formal complexity, moral resonance, and so on—might be political or self-serving; and the common description of a classic as a work that had outlived its own age might be misleading. After all, the book regarded as a classic may be appealing to the same kind of readers and interests (male and white) in age after age. In brief, there are no purely "literary" criteria as such that define a canonical work.

In rejecting this sort of argument, I do not mean to imply that the canon is immutable. Literature is a human thing, not an idealized trajectory, and every generation of literary scholars has brought new values into judgment and "discovered" formerly neglected writers—T. S. Eliot praising John Donne and the other Metaphysical poets and denigrating Shelley, for instance. After Eliot, the canon changed; and perhaps iconoclasm flourishes in every vital literary generation. What I object to is not new values but the attempted sledgehammering of *all* prior judgment, and the inevitable attack not just on past academics but on literature itself. Among the academic left, the literature that has survived is often considered *guilty* of something. This is no harmless truism (anything that becomes part of the dominant discourse must serve some need of the powerful). At its most severe, it's a moral attack on art itself.

❖ ❖ ❖

In his insistence that truth was a matter of perspective, Nietzsche had unleased a whirlwind. And now, in the midst of these thoughts, my mind wandered back to a conference I had attended in October, early in the first semester. A small group of scholars, all from other universities, had gathered at Columbia, in a large lecture room in Schermerhorn Hall, the natural sciences building. In the university world, this was one of many such meetings. Throughout the late eighties and early nineties, big trouble was brewing: The English, Comparative Literature, and History departments had been under siege. A fusillade of books, articles, newsmagazine cover stories, and statements by public figures had attacked or at least questioned the new left-academic approach to the Western classics and Western history. The criticism had come not just from the right, but from the left and center, and now communities within the universities were hitting back. Suddenly aroused to their vulnerability, the professors complained of misrepresentation, alarmism, and hidden political agendas.

As conferences go, the Columbia gathering was small potatoes, nothing like the huge annual meeting of the Modern Language Association or the many scholarly gatherings on one aspect or another of "literature and gender" or "literature and race." The conference was no more than a handful of people pulled together by ambitious graduate students. There was one speech made in the conference that I want to argue with (later), but most of what was said on that occasion will matter little by the time this book comes out. I will not detail the standard attacks on the Western canon—by this time, you can imagine them on your own. What fascinated me, however, was the coldly disgusted tone of the remarks. I sat there silently, taking notes, thinking to myself, "They do not love literature. They do not love it."

I had one moment of sympathy, however, one moment when I felt ashamed of my hostility. A number of the professors who spoke taught at large public universities, and many of their minority students were dropping out. Their dilemma as teachers was excruciating and possibly insoluble. What could they do? Cheated by poor primary and secondary schools, many of the students weren't prepared for a college education. Once they got to college, they often needed money and therefore took jobs which drew them away from campus; and some perhaps lacked the habit, easier to build in middle- and upper-middle-class homes, of long, quiet study. Nothing, I reflected, ennobled these teachers more than their desire to reach people formerly cut off from higher education. As a journalist, I did nothing comparable to what they did, and I admired them without reservation for it.

But my moment of sympathy evaporated. Rather than identify their problems openly, the speakers attacked the curriculum and the structure of the university. If the students were bored and dropping out, then there was something wrong with the courses or the books. They turned an extraordinarily complex and deep-rooted series of social problems—the inequality of American society, the problems of poverty and race—into an attack on the Western canon.

Trying to find a way to sit comfortably in the oak-plank chair, I shifted around, sighing loud enough, I was sure, to alert everyone to the presence of a spy in their midst. But no one noticed or said anything. What was it with these people? They were radical yet weary; they lacked fire and conviction; they spoke the received truths of the cultural left in a cold rage that had nowhere to go. Iconoclasm had turned into stale orthodoxy. The graduate students spoke as well, unmemorably, in pasteboard phrases drawn from the current gods, Foucault, Jacques Lacan, and Duke University English professor Stanley Fish. The students' statements were radical in content but obsequious in tone. As *persons,* these students were as timid as mice. They sidled up apprehensively to any established professor in sight, nodding their heads in agreement. Revolutionaries? Radicals? This was a job hunt. The graduate students embracing "theory" were university careerists and inside players adapting themselves to the dominant culture of the humanities, which, at the moment, is largely feminist, neo-Marxist, multicultural, New Historicist, anticanonical, and so on. The pressures of the job hunt had enforced a desperate conformity.

I felt for them, but I did not admire them, and I knew that Mill, who wanted a true radicalism of spirit, would have looked at them in dismay. Camille Paglia, the academic antiacademic, had described them scornfully and well in her many jeremiads. The graduate students were denizens of the university world, and a good part of their radical critique of the curriculum, I now saw, was produced by nothing more earthshattering than the evident desire to claim turf, get themselves noticed, and find a job somewhere. So why get upset? They were effective only within the university. I was upset because they did not love literature, and because they would teach our children—*my* children—English, history, philosophy, sociology, anthropology, and science. My sons would take courses from these dry-souled clerics.

And there was something else: their tone. The cultural left on campus may be authorized by Nietzsche only distantly; he may be their patron saint and unholy God only through many degrees of separation, mediation, and change. Friedrich Nietzsche was not a multiculturalist. But he *has* had his influence, as Cornel West said. The notion that truth is a matter of perspective radiates in many directions, all of them subversive. Yet here's the kicker: The silliest of the academic left were precisely the kind of people Nietzsche had in mind when he described with such venomous anger the temperament of ascetic personalities. ("They walk among us as embodied reproaches, as warnings to us . . .") They exploited resentment in the name of justice and turned their anger against the strong. "The School of Resentment," critic Harold Bloom called them, thinking explicitly of Nietzsche and lumping all the theoretical and cultural-studies approaches into one.

And who, you ask, are the "strong" whom the most dreary and conformist left-academics resent? After going to that little conference at Columbia, it became clear to me that "the strong" were not just powerful white men but literature itself. The academic left had created a moralized fable of power and victimization: People were being hurt by taking courses that didn't represent them directly. Blacks and women were being weakened by reading Homer, Plato, Shakespeare, Hegel, and Freud without also reading, at the same time, female and black authors. Did the case have merit? Were people truly hurt? It was a good question, one worth looking into, but meritorious or not, these notions had successfully infected the universities with guilt and shame. So the Nietzschean comedy of ethics was complete: Some of Nietzsche's heirs had become what he despised. This was the "joke" I was looking for.

❖ ❖ ❖

By the time of Stephanson's second class on Nietzsche, I was coming down from my giddy high.

On the Genealogy of Morals is a remarkable analysis of power, culture, and morality, but it's an inhuman view, and after a few days I knew that perfectly well. Why should the freedom and magnificent health of the few noble spirits matter more than the continued suppression of the many? Nietzsche was twitting nineteenth-century utilitarianism, with its banal hope of the "greatest good for the greatest number." But in its place, he offers an essentially aesthetic view of life. The powerful old aristocratic warriors, the blond beasts or modern Napoleons, fierce, indifferent, and bold, are like works of art—sculpted spirit, magnificent and pure. Nietzsche would offer our flesh to them. But there's something both masochistic and ludicrous in the idealization of instinct. It verges on a pornography of strength. Maybe Nietzsche was a fascist after all.

Some of us might agree with his critique of Pauline Christianity without relinquishing the ideal of justice or the goal of reducing the suffering of as many people as possible. Deliberate cruelty is unforgivable, as Tennessee Williams said in *A Streetcar Named Desire*. This formulation may owe more to show business than to philosophy, but I'm fond of its simplicity and pathos. It is the starting point—perhaps the only possible starting point—of a plausible moral code. And even in the *Iliad,* I now remembered, there was a glimmer of pity. At the end of the poem, Priam, the king of Troy and Hector's father, comes to Achilles in the night, kneels at his feet, kisses his hand, and asks for the corpse of his son, so he can give it proper burial. Achilles is much moved by the suffering of the old man, who reminds him of his own father, and Lattimore translates Achilles' emotion as "pity."

> The sound of their mourning moved in the house. Then
> when great Achilleus had taken full satisfaction in sorrow
> and the passion for it had gone from his mind and body, thereafter
> he rose from his chair, and took the old man by the hand, and set
>   him
> on his feet again, in pity for the grey head and the grey beard . . .
>   (XXIV, 512–16)

Tennessee Williams's remark might be extended as follows: Allowing preventable cruelty to continue is also unforgivable. The Republican Party, in 1996, is proposing to dump a great many people with no visible means of supporting themselves off the welfare rolls (after five years) in the vague hope that such people will suddenly slap their heads and say, "Now I must be productive and become a bank teller!" Or "Now I must work at McDonald's for ten years and become a manager!" No job-training program would bring out their skills; no government or private program would teach them to be a bank teller, and, anyway, no bank would hire them, since banks, in a fit of downsizing, are closing their inner-city branches. Opportunities for unskilled labor were dwindling fast. But such was the Republican fantasy (or, even more cynically, the Republican lie): The poor would be squeezed into economically productive behavior. In time, this fantasy will be revealed as a cruel fraud, and as a new way of postponing the issue of ending welfare, and there will be a revulsion against it. All modern democratic states were founded on the premise of preventing cruelty, however faulty their efforts to do so. Liberal idealism may have failed in its institutional form, but the huge problems it is facing may not yield much to conservative "realism" either. And when conservative solutions fail, something else will be tried.

Americans could sustain compassion as a necessary emotion without giving in to false claims of victimization or denying their true feelings and turning themselves into cringing hypocrites. Charlie Kim was right. Pity could also be a form of strength, and not just vindictive strength. The relief workers in Somalia, Rwanda, and Bosnia do not fit Nietzsche's portrait of ascetic idealists; they do not resemble the terms of Nietzschean execration in the least. They seem like strong, clear-minded people, outraged that they can't do more to help people innocently suffering.

Whatever their presence in the universities, the ascetic idealists have largely disappeared elsewhere, while warrior codes survive in our worship of athletes and in the macho attitudes of working-class culture, which, in an amazing post–World War II transformation, has become mass culture for a whole society. Culturally, America can only be called neopagan, a hedonistic visual-aural carnival, devoted to popular music, the good life, and the ideals of beauty and sensual health. Fashion, movies, MTV, the local gym—the blond beasts are us.

With a sigh, I let go. Giddy no more, my exhilaration of not caring was over. I had learned much from Nietzsche; and I had rejected him.

❖ ❖ ❖

"Is Nietzsche incoherent?" Stephanson asked. He was winding up. "The philosopher Martin Heidegger's interpretation from the 1920s is very powerful. If Nietzsche gets rid of the truth, metaphysical truth, how can he evoke the will to power as the eternal recurrence? If truth is perspectival, then in whose name is he making the case that all things are a matter of the will to power? What kind of claim is that?"

"He's universalizing European norms," said Manuel. "The will to power is a European perspective: For a man to fulfill himself in power is to be human. But he doesn't think of Africans as having a will to power."

Noah, Manuel's antagonist, perked up. "There was slavery in Africa before colonialism. Why couldn't a will to power be African?"

"Is he saying anything beyond what David Hume said?" Stephanson continued, letting this pass. "Hume says morality is conventional, not transhistorical. Yes? Hume offers a sociology of norms, established in terms of what we approve or disapprove of. There's no single truth, no single set of standards."

Stephanson was coming back to the sore issue of relativism yet again. Nietzsche was said—by Allan Bloom and others—to have licensed relativism. "Our present politics," Stephanson said, "is Nietzschean: I have *mine,* you have yours. We've suffered a disintegration of the eighteenth-century ideal of politics as a place in which a community of rational wills gets together and decides what to do. *That* idea is dead. The identification of *difference* is what makes Nietzsche an intellectual for now."

But relativism, Stephanson insisted, was a false issue. He raised his voice, making it even louder than usual, and he spoke in tones almost of indignation.

"You can preserve a Nietzschean perspective," said Anders Stephanson, "and still talk about good and bad. Give up once and for all the notion that if you're not an absolutist, you're a relativist, or vice-versa. You can historicize all you want and still take the position that something is good or pernicious. Just because you can't do it in a *theoretical* sense, in an absolute sense, you can still posit a universal norm."

He stopped for a second to be sure we were getting it. And then he said, with great emphasis: "If a norm exists just between individuals, society isn't possible. You can *posit* universal norms. Say, a country should not be invaded and annihilated. Sure, you have to account, in each case, for the historical circumstances. But the idea that you can't judge is an egregious error. The Nazis created genocide as a norm. Are we saying we can't judge?"

He had said it before, but never this forcefully, and I felt immensely relieved. I had halfway restored myself politically: I would not take false claims of victimization seriously, but real claims were as pressing as ever. And now I understood that Nietzsche could not be used properly to license a shallow relativism. Like Nietzsche—and like members of the academic left—I did not believe in metaphysical truth. I was not, in the jargon, a "foundationalist." That is, I did not believe that values existed outside of human practice. On the contrary, values would exist in whatever form we give them. But still, you could judge—in life, and, by extension, in literature. You did not need some foundational notion, a "transcendent" or "universal" notion of literary value, in order to say that Jane Austen was a great writer worthy of study and emulation and Alice Walker was not. Instead, you had to make the case for pleasure from the ground up. As I discovered when trying to teach Jane Austen, the case for the most complex pleasures had to be made freshly for each generation.

By denying that case—by ruling it out as some sort of reactionary formation—members of the academic left were cutting the ground from beneath their feet, destroying the means by which we have universities and reading lists at all. By their very nature, reading lists exclude almost everything previously written—any other way of composing them would lead to sheer chaos. The canon-bashing academic left had inappropriately carried the democratic ideal of representation into the realm of culture. They had given up history, given up their own judgment, and had allowed, of all things, *market* principles—satisfy the customers' needs—into the curriculum. They began in a high-minded way, respecting everyone's culture as equal, and they were in danger of truly valuing nothing.

Our second class on Nietzsche was over, and I came out of Mathematics Hall. To my right, the religious-activities center of the campus, Earl Hall, was fronted with splendidly blooming azaleas—or hyacinths, or whatever you call them. My longing for an unseen Princeton had passed, and now, going back down the Low steps, I walked through the little mideastern bazaar that had sprung up below. Vendors had set up shop at the base of the steps, long tables and spontaneous pipe-rack boutiques filled with clothes, jewelry, and Islamic and black-nationalist literature. Rock played from loudspeakers, and the students sat in the sun, their eyes closed, faces turned upward. Columbia was blooming as much as it ever did, as much as it could.

Interlude Seven

In the last chapter, I said that I had heard one speech at the little Columbia conference that I had to take seriously. This was the talk given by Catharine Stimpson, then dean of the graduate school at Rutgers and former head of the MLA itself (and now head of the grants award program—the "genius" grants—of the MacArthur Foundation). Stimpson, a practiced academic politician and bureaucrat, and also a likable and sympathetic woman, called for "a more welcoming narrative" than the traditional core curriculum, by which she meant a new core curriculum that represented every ethnic group ("an expansive narrative that would include minorities.") I have since heard Stimpson give another speech at Columbia very similar in content. Obviously, the "more welcoming narrative" was something of an idée fixe with her, and I will quote an earlier article she wrote on the subject in order to get the words of her position exactly right.

> The dream of a "core curriculum" is, by nature, exclusionary, often destructively so. Some of the most powerful and healing work today is the recuperation of texts that the core curriculum of the earlier part of the twentieth century trivialized, marginalized, or ignored. Its authors include people of color, in the United States and elsewhere; popularizers and pleasure givers, like George Herriman, the creator of the *Krazy Kat* cartoons; and women of all races, classes, and tales. Alice Walker has read Zora Neale Hurston and rewritten Virginia Woolf. Again, and again, these acts of recuperation offer non-traditional students their traditions within the arena of a more democratic, accessible classroom. (*Change,* March–April 1988, p. 28)

Stimpson's idea, as I understand it, goes like this: Students entering a college like Columbia are presented with certain books marked canonical. Particularly if the texts are gathered in "great books" courses, they are surrounded by an aura of sanctity; they are consecrated books. In this light consider the possible emotions of a woman or an African-American student. If she does not find herself directly represented on the list, she may feel pained, or even humiliated. After all, she could be the first person in her family to go to college; she may be in a vulnerable position. In order to give such "non-traditional" students a feeling of belonging, why not make the lists more diverse? Why not include, along with canonical works, books which directly represent the experience of such students?

One bit of updating: Among those colleges that still maintain courses like Lit Hum and C.C., many include books by women; some include works by blacks. So criticism like Stimpson's has, to some degree, been heard and acted upon.

But let's leave that aside and discuss the emotional heart of her argument. It's true that some students feel pain in the way that she imagines. I have heard black students at Columbia express anger (see Interludes One and Two) at the absence of works by black authors in the core curriculum. Many students, however, do *not* feel such anger; and a number of African-American students told me they would, on the contrary, have felt patronized by the appearance of, say, one or two black authors in Lit Hum or C.C. They dismissed the idea as "tokenism"; they saw it (properly, I think) as a gesture intended to appease them. They had accepted, as did many of the women, the historical shaping of the reading lists.

For millennia, women were discouraged from heroic composition in literature, philosophy, and the arts; their work was ignored, discarded, left uncopied or unprinted. Blacks came to a written literary culture later than whites, in part because of unequal national development, in part because the slaves brought to the Americas were not taught to read and were punished if they taught themselves. Nevertheless, slaves and former slaves wrote some marvelous narratives. But could one say that Frederick Douglass or, say, a great postcolonial African writer like the Nigerian novelist and critic Chinua Achebe belong in the course with Plato, Kant, and Nietzsche? Douglass is a great writer, but he's a different kind of great writer than Hegel. He hasn't had the central influence in the West that the standard C.C. authors have had. There are ways of reading him in college (in American literature, African-American literature, and history courses) that make more sense than reading him in C.C.

In other words, the *absence* of books by blacks—and the small number of books by women—makes it own powerful statement about past oppression. But Stimpson ignored that. Behind her remarks (and her position is typical of a broad spectrum of opinion) lies the notion that university education should make people feel better about themselves. They feel better by sensing the value and power of their own cultural heritage.

When they are represented in a core curriculum course, they will be more secure in their identity and confidence.

My first response, I admit, was to laugh. What is this nonsense about feeling good, this talk of "recuperation"? You don't have to quote Nietzsche in order to find something soft and clammy in the sickroom approach to culture, the depressed scenario in which wounded books and demoralized students are ministered to by healing academics. What does any of that ostentatious *caring* have to do with art and spirit? Wouldn't any robust person denounce it as philistine? And if some students do need this kind of kid-glove treatment, should their needs determine what other people read? Don't you truly feel good about yourself by meeting high standards in school and work? Did Michael Chang become great because someone handed him, when he was young, a list of five great Chinese tennis players? Life doesn't work that way.

My second thought was a little more sober. Prodded by friends, I realized I did not have the right to ridicule the therapeutic use of literature. After all, Tayler spoke on opening day of "making a self"; Tayler obviously wanted to toughen the students for life's journey. The Lit Hum books, he implied, were uniquely the works in which the students would find themselves and shape themselves. And Shapiro, who attacked student reticence and fears, was clearly performing a rough kind of therapy, too. He was trying to summon into existence new formations of taste and sensibility. As for myself, I was seeking pleasure but also my life, and, in truth, I had begun to recover aspects of memory, temperament, and desire that I had thought lost to middle-age blahs and media amorphousness. Reading *King Lear* illuminated my mixed feelings about my mother in her final years and the strengths and weaknesses of my response to her. Couldn't I see that the books spoke to me directly because I felt at home in the tradition they were part of?

Well, yes and no. I do not seek *representation* in the narrow sense of ethnic identity that Stimpson means. In any case, if we take the notion of identity literally, I am not directly represented by anything on the lists but the Old Testament. And the Old Testament, all in all, is one of the most distant, the most "other" of all the readings. Yes, I'm a male, but that's too large a category to represent me in any way that means anything. Do I learn only from male authors? I refuse the notion. I have "male" responses but also "female" ones. I am many selves, as Montaigne might have said. I learned as much about myself—perhaps more—from reading Jane Austen as I did from reading Goethe or Cervantes. And perhaps I would learn much from Virginia Woolf, too. As for Homer, Euripides, Plato, Augustine, Kant, and Hegel, I learned from them because they were utterly different from me. The differences were far greater than our common maleness. I had to stretch to read them, just as the students had to stretch to read almost all the books. That was the real therapy—the struggle to enlarge yourself to take in a mind greater and more powerful than your own; and that task was as difficult for white males as for black, for men as for women. This stretching—not self-confirmation—was the true purpose of education in the humanities. Women and minority students, stretching constantly, would have to work hard, and they might, for a while, get stretched out of shape. But then everything else in their lives, the rest of their reading and friendship and spiritual practice would rush in to repair the stretched muscles, and they would grow. Where was the harm? College students are not that vulnerable.

The issue of ethnic and gender representation was too narrow to offer anything serious to education. It was an idea mistakenly borrowed from democratic politics, where people's material interests and rights needed to be represented in a legislative body. But representation in Congress and in a reading list are two different things. In school, even if the students are not "represented," they can still enjoy some of the books and learn from them. They can *struggle* with them. An African-American senior, on the verge of graduating, told me that "you would have to be made of stone not to be moved by at least one of the books in Lit Hum." For him, as for me, the prime mover was *Lear*. For Shapiro's student Henry, it was Nietzsche. For another African-American student I spoke with, it was Marx. They all had their favorites, and yet, in every phrase and gesture, they were African-Americans.

Chapter 26

BEAUVOIR

~ Take Back the Night and the right to say yes as well as no
~ I connect women's fear of rape to my fear of street crime
~ Public confession and the Western classics
~ Simon de Beauvoir: woman as the other; the triumph of feminism
~ Does woman have an essence? A look back to Pizan and Wollstonecraft
~ Catharine MacKinnon: sex as power
~ A decline in the sentiment of sex
~ The pressures on college women today
~ The re-creation of a private sphere

A group of us stood around, pawing the ground and glancing at each other nervously. We were waiting for the women, waiting at the gates of Barnard, Columbia's sister institution, at 117th and Broadway, across the street from the Columbia campus. The women were over there, behind the Columbia buildings and maybe a block or two south, walking around the quadrangles, and we could hear them as they marched. A strange, nasty sound, high-pitched, insistent, floated over Broadway. *Eeee ... ee ... hh! Eeee ... ee ... hh!* It was raining slightly, and the buses and speeding taxis hissed on the pavement, but the sound cut right through the street noise. A cry, a shriek—what *was* it? *Eee ... hh!* The sound was like electronic feedback. One of Shapiro's students was there, Ranjit, a handsome young man of Indian descent, and we nodded at each other grimly; he was waiting for his girlfriend, who was among the marchers.

The women—Columbia and Barnard students—now emerged from the Columbia gates at 116th Street and walked across Broadway and then north toward Barnard. The sound became clearer. Some of the women were shrieking and rapidly flapping their tongues—an evocation of Africa or perhaps Afghanistan as the mujahideen left their villages to fight the Soviet tanks—and many others were blowing whistles. Shrieks and whistles! The combination was unnerving. The antihuman quality of it, I thought, could only be intentional. Women could be as alien, hostile, and cold as crunched electrons encountering themselves in rebarbative fury. Feedback! *Women could be as inhuman as men*. That was the real meaning, wasn't it? Men were meant to be intimidated by a concentrated version of their own unpleasantness.

The marchers swept through the Barnard gates, turned right at Barnard Hall, and settled on the damp lawn in front of Lehman Hall. Ranjit met his girlfriend, and they went in together; other men joined girlfriends, or just friends, and settled on the lawn. It was late March, and Take Back the Night, a yearly event, was being held at many American campuses. The first part of the evening, the march around Columbia (men were forbidden to join), had been completed. Now, around eleven o'clock, the second part got underway. An open microphone stood on the stone terrace outside Lehman, and women lined up to speak.

"Don't go to the fraternity —— —. I was wrestled to the ground. I was overpowered and helpless. There was nothing I could do. I can't believe that I went there three times. . . ."

"My parents raped me. My parents raped me over and over. I was raped by boys and men all through school. . . ."

"It's taken me five years to say this. I was a junior in high school and I was happy; I was a virgin and I was happy. I met this boy from Georgetown, and he was cute. Not all Georgetown boys are nice. His name is John ———. If this guy runs for congressman, don't support him! He was cute and I went to a party with him and he gave me vodka to drink—only afterwards did I realize that he was pouring this much for me and this much for himself. I passed out, but the last thing I remember is saying "No." I knew he used a condom because I found it on the back of my leg. I crawled to the bathroom and threw up. . . ."

The rain had stopped, and I sat on my raincoat, in the back, near the outer edges of the crowd (perhaps five or six hundred students), and took notes, writing down as many stories as possible. Whatever else they were—and they were a great deal else—the speeches were a kind of sick joke on me. I had wanted the students to tell their stories, hadn't I? Wasn't that what I missed when we discussed the *Odyssey*—a student telling a story of herself that announces who she is, something comparable to Telemachus' tale when he leaves home? A firm sense of identity, not this American irony and tentativeness, this media-age Lettermanization of everything? Well, these were stories of who the women were, and I was chagrined, because the tellers were all victims. That was the only way women at Take Back the Night announced their identity.

I had gone out of curiosity, with no thought in mind except to see what the event was about. But as I listened, and even more so in the weeks afterward, the stories and the core-curriculum works we had been reading all year kept calling to one another in some indistinct yet clamorous way that I couldn't ignore.

In our society, sexual life is one of the worldly garments of the soul. Certainly the women's stories said much about abuse, but also about souls, about the way pain should be dealt with and life confronted. How would you make a self, a public self? Here were women grief-struck and enraged, women marked by experience as much as were the men and women in the *Aeneid* or *King Lear* or *Pride and Prejudice*. How do you handle bad times, even tragedy? The stories, and the telling of stories, connected to everything that liberal education was about, everything that the core was about. Many of the women at Lehman were from Barnard, not Columbia, and did not take core-curriculum courses, but I conceived the foolish hope that somehow they could hear something from the books; that somehow the books would enter the air and change them.

There was a more literal connection to the core curriculum. Take Back the Night could not have been conceived without the feminist movement, and feminism in the form of some of its notable texts had itself become part of the "great books." In Lit Hum, we read Sappho and Virginia Woolf; and in C.C., we read Christine de Pizan's *Book of the City of Ladies,* sections of Mary Wollstonecraft's *Vindication of the Rights of Woman* and Simone de Beauvoir's *Second Sex,* as well as an essay by the American law professor Catharine A. MacKinnon. I had wanted these texts to answer some of the silences in the Western canon about women, and they had. But a few weeks after Take Back the Night, as we started reading Beauvoir, I kept wondering how a movement that had wanted to bring full selfhood to women could possibly issue, among its many manifestations, in such an event as Take Back the Night.

How many rapes had actually taken place on the Columbia-Barnard campus? Only a few were reported. Of course, women don't easily bring charges to make complaints against men they know, so the question of how many might never receive an accurate answer. In any case, the evening was not confined to Columbia experience. A woman is under siege always—that was the point—and the stories continued for a long, long time, well into the morning hours, woman after woman, some of them clearly describing their experience for the second or third year in a row. They were a community of witness and confession, a community of "survivors." Many wept at the microphone, getting through their stories only after repeated encouragement from the audience. "It's not our fault! It's not our fault!" the audience chanted, and there were cheers and shouts of reassurance.

A man listening to such stories is like a woman overhearing tales of combat. The narratives are spectacular, mesmerizing, but distant and sometimes opaque. Outside of prison, few men are raped. As one of the protected sex, I saw that—for these women at least—the bitterest part of rape was not the experience of being overpowered and invaded against their will, awful as that was. The bitterest part was betrayal. Some of the women said they had been attacked by strangers—in parks, or at the beach. But many had been attacked by friends or family members. An uncle had abused them when they were young. Or men they had trusted—say, a man they had worked with in a summer job—has assaulted them at night somewhere, in a lonely field, in Central Park, at a fraternity party. What the women had offered to men as friendship and trust was received in seeming good faith, secretly reinterpreted, and then projected back onto the women as violence and sexual assault. *The women had been raped.* The betrayal of trust had left the women wondering: Did their offer of friendship somehow encourage the assault? And so their fury was crested with grief and guilt.

But that wasn't all of it. I heard different kinds of misery that night. Some of the stories were not quite about rape. A fair number—perhaps about a third—followed a pattern rather like this: "I went out with this guy. He seemed really nice, we went to his room [or my room] and had a few drinks and listened to music. We were kissing and fooling around, lying in bed together, but then I said no, and he continued, and I said no, and then he raped me. And now I am full of rage and shame, and I will never trust anyone again."

Having been back to Take Back the Night a second time (a year later), I've now heard many variations on this basic story—the date-rape story, the campus story. And I had the same response to it that renegade feminists Camille Paglia and Katie Roiphe have described in their books*: disbelief and ridicule; exasperation; and finally despair.

As every feminist said, the right to say no was unassailable—no was *no* and not "try again in a few minutes." But I could not understand why women should not take some responsibility, some command and control over the many stages of the evening up to the point of "no."

Responsibility and freedom were at the very heart of feminism. That's what women had taught me. For the women of my generation, women in their forties and fifties, the right to say no had become unassailable and unequivocal, but they had fought as well for the right to say yes. They had struggled for a freer sexual life: They would choose as well as reject their partners, they would sleep with someone without suffering the scorn of their parents and friends. Their revolution had been only a

* Camille Paglia, *Sex, Art, and American Culture* (New York: Vintage, 1992), and *Vamps and Tramps* (New York: Vintage, 1994); Katie Roiphe, *The Morning After: Sex, Fear, and Feminism on Campus* (Boston: Little, Brown, 1993).

partial success: At times, men exploited women's right to say yes, and women felt used. But women had ended—for good, one had thought—the old division of the female sex into virgin and whore. The two rights, yes and no, were now equal in importance and absolutely complementary. Woven together, a fabric of acceptance and rejection, attraction and indifference, they constituted the strength of sexual temperament—the taste, the living character, the mystery—of a woman in her romantic life. Isn't that what everyone but reactionaries believes? But at Take Back the Night, not a single woman in my hearing said that her right to pleasure and even love would not be compromised by the betrayal of men.

I waited in vain for that insolent note of self-assertion and ego. I waited for the "survivors" of date rape to say, "May the bastard who did this to me rot in hell. I will live my life in defiance of his evil. I deny his power over me. For he is nothing; I am everything." If the women had spoken like *that,* I would have rejoiced. But instead, many said things like this: "My emotional life has been destroyed. I am always ashamed. I'm traumatized. I cannot get close to anyone."

The horror of rape had given way to the luridly self-dramatizing culture of rape—a whole sickly system of marches, meetings, and readings that supported the moral primacy of dwelling on the act, enlarging it, feeding it, allowing it to take dominion over one's being. One gave up freedom and responsibility and reconstituted oneself as a shattered "survivor." Take Back the Night was an evening devoted not to changing men's conduct but to women's seeking solidarity with one another as a community of damaged individuals. Being damaged was the entry requirement. This tended to increase the desire to see oneself as damaged. A woman who said, "That was a disgusting night for me, a loathsome experience, but it did not destroy my life," would not have been welcome. And I did not hear any such remarks. By implication, all women were in the rape community; all women were damaged. One of the campus groups, the Rape Crisis Center Coalition, began referring, a year later, to "potential survivors."

I knew women my own age who had been forced, or persuaded, to have sex when they did not want to—what woman over thirty has not had at least one of these experiences?—and years later while expressing rage over the events they also scorned what had happened. These "survivors" really were survivors. They carried rage inside them, but they were not governed by it. The self had been reasserted, put back together again. And now, unwilling to see themselves as eternal victims, these women had no use for Take Back the Night. They were contemptuous of it.

But when I had worked myself up into a fine enough rage, I realized I was being . . . blind. I was obsessed with street crime, wasn't I? True, I rarely talked about it, I never joined a public discussion of it, and until I read Hobbes and Locke again, I lost my memory of being mugged. But the fear of crime had mugged my unconscious, altering my freedom. The women were saying something similar: The threat of rape was always there for them. From the time they were girls, they had lived with parental warnings, places not to go and times not to go there; they had lived with too-friendly looks and gestures, taunts and suggestions and invitations, and always the fear that a man would misunderstand something and move in. Take Back the Night was fighting not just rape but violence against women. Some of the students attending the event may well have disliked the atmosphere of the evening as much as I did. But they may have wanted to affirm their solidarity with a simple idea: Women should live in a society in which they were not afraid.

Were the college women literally under threat? Perhaps they exaggerated, but then my fear of crime was "subjective," too. You internalize a rational or half-rational fear and it eats away at your soul. You become less free; you cut yourself off from experience.

But then you had to fight back. In my mind (though perhaps in no one else's), Sophocles and Shakespeare stirred uneasily. The purpose of education, after all, was not just to impart knowledge and modes of thinking but to train character, which meant, in the end, the character to handle difficult or even catastrophic experience. Not to accept it, but to handle it—to be equal to it. In part, Columbia asked all its undergraduates to read such extreme works as *Oedipus the King, Antigone,* Job, and *King Lear* to acquaint them with the utmost a human being was capable of. Reading these books, you saw, and felt, the spectacle of endurance and pride; you knew that there was no soulful or heroic life without these qualities. Some of the West's greatest works yielded at least this much of pragmatic wisdom: If you lost your freedom to fear, you had to fight back. Judgment and defiance were the keys to regaining freedom. Rage, even revenge (Yes! said Nietzsche), but not self-pity and weakness.

Not that we all acted directly according to what we had read. But the books held out a possibility; they could check flagrant self-dramatization; they insisted on strength as the only true consolation.

So with the books in my head, I was half sympathetic to what I heard, half not: sympathetic to the experience of fear but not to the yielding of self to fear. For certainly confusion and defeat hung in the air at Take Back the Night. As Roiphe and Paglia said, some of the women were denying that they were sexual beings at all; they were turning back the clock to the 1950s or earlier when man was always the insensate lustful beast and woman the delicate flower; they were embracing the embarrassing rubbish of hypocritical ages past, when mendacity ruled sexual manners and women were not considered responsible for their own desires or even willing to acknowledge they *had* any. Some of the women telling the date-rape stories sounded as if they had just fallen out of Daddy's lap and were frightened not just by rape but by the danger and excitement of sex—frightened as much by their own as by men's desires. They were confused, which is a human, not a female, characteristic.

We live in a media society in which humiliation is routinely offered on afternoon TV as entertainment. At the worst moments of Take Back the Night, exhibitionists performed for voyeurs, and together they annihilated one another in waves of pity and self-pity. Of course, many of the women at Take Back the Night would say I had missed the point: The public nature of the event—the confessions, the grief, the reassurance and laying on of hands—was intended precisely as a healing experience. Pain and sorrow would not go away until they had been brought forth and shared. The women would expunge fear by expressing their anger together. But who knows if the evening worked that way? Who knows if such public avowals worked as catharsis or merely consolidated one's identity as a victim? Has anyone ever been healed by going on *Oprah*? Why were some women coming back for the second or third "confession"? Maybe they were hooked.

These were not powerless women who had been battered for years and were unable to get a response from the police. They were largely middle-class women on the way to careers in business and the professions. Yet they sounded more frightened than any women I had ever heard. The hostile banshee cry during the march—which had made me uncomfortable, as it should—had given way to a global and unappeasable sorrow, and I thought that there was more to this than I could easily understand. Something was going on below the surface; rape was not the whole story.

But while men like myself searched for understanding, we had some obligation, perhaps, to answer this question: What should be done about rape on campus? The answer, for me, is straightforward: Charges should be brought against a man who commits it. Criminal charges. The sight of a student arrested, booked, arraigned, tried, and possibly convicted and sentenced would sober up men far more effectively than a dozen Take Back the Night meetings, the real purpose of which, I could see, was not to change men's behavior at all but to politicize sexual relations and create female solidarity as an end in itself.

Rape cannot be imagined as a positive experience, but it should not be imagined as all of experience. The rest of life cried out—if not that night, then in the following weeks, when I beseeched "the great books," in my mind at least, to heal the wounds, and I wondered, in classroom discussions, what it was that male and female students wanted from one another. This public disgust, this anguish—what could a woman build on it except separatism and gender chauvinism and rage that fed on itself and justified itself? What could it produce in men, even in innocent men—especially in innocent men—but caution, guilt, and resentment? Were all relations between the sexes to be conducted, so to speak, under the curse of rape? I was amazed, and at times I felt like someone's free-thinking bachelor uncle. What about flirtation and romance? What about sex? Would no one say a word in praise of lust?

A few weeks later, we turned, in both Literature Humanities and Contemporary Civilization, to modern feminist texts. I approached these authors, as I had Pizan and Wollstonecraft earlier, eager to discover their qualities as writers but also hungry for clues. Feminism was a vast subject, and I knew I would inevitably listen and read from my narrow perspective, that of a middle-aged heterosexual white male who was baffled. Yet I had to know. Could it be possible that the most vulnerable women and the most ruthless men were suddenly threatening, in deadly combination, to ruin the eternal dialogue of sex?

❖ ❖ ❖

We were at the end of C.C., and as we entered the twentieth century, the notion of the past as a series of distinct historical epochs broke down. The recent past appeared instead as a series of warring subjects and interpretations (the syllabus called the last section of the course "Modernity and Its Discontents"). Earlier, every class had read the same books; now the individual instructors enjoyed a great deal of freedom to choose the readings. They had only to select perhaps three books from within each of two broadly defined groups, "Science and Revolution in the Twentieth Century" and "The Ambiguities of Integration: Class, Race, and Gender." For the first time, canonical works sat side by side with merely influential or even fashionable works. Stephanson, who wanted us to gain some sense of the radical tradition, chose Lenin and Gramsci. He also chose Cornel West and Malcolm X on race; and, on violence, the very much opposed Frantz Fanon, herald of Third World revolution (and now rather embarrassing to read) and Hannah Arendt, masterly analyst of totalitarianism, revolution, and violence, and certainly no radical. He had also chosen, as his principal feminist text, Simone de Beauvoir's *Second Sex*. We read only two chunks of the vast book, the introduction and the extraordinary Chapter Nine, "Dreams, Fears, Idols."

The Second Sex was issued in France in 1949, and in America in 1953, and somehow I had never looked into it. When I became aware of the book, in the sixties, I was preoccupied with the Vietnam War, and I thought, "Oh, yes. The women's issue." It wasn't important to me, and I thought of Beauvoir's work as somehow tiresome and faded. And later,

in the early seventies, when American and English feminists like Kate
Millett and Germaine Greer published their famous books (respectively,
Sexual Politics and *The Female Eunuch*), I assumed that they had "gone
beyond" Beauvoir, and so I read their books (Millett grindingly doctri-
naire; Greer funny and loose-limbed) and continued to ignore Beauvoir.
By this time, I hated the thought of her. She had snobbish views of America; she was a satellite of her longtime lover and friend, Jean-Paul Sartre,
whose philosophical views she had taken over in reduced form (a notion
I received from reading the American reviews of Beauvoir's many-
volumed autobiography, in which she said as much). Was there not
something illegitimate and cloying about her fame, something screwy
about an advocate of women's liberation attached for forty years or
more to the world's most famous male intellectual?

I write down this rubbish (some of it made worse by Beauvoir herself)
only to suggest the clouds of indifference and ignorance, the gossip and
sheer ill will that may cover the reputation of a contemporary or near-
contemporary book—and may prevent a lazy reader from opening it.
Perhaps a similar mass of envy and antagonism had initially shrouded
some of the texts in Columbia's canon. At any rate, by the early nineties,
if not earlier, *The Second Sex* had flung off its detractors, including many
of its feminist detractors.

Stephanson, starting with a bang, called it "the single most important
feminist text of the century"; and, as if answering the old dismissal of
Beauvoir as some sort of opportunistic hanger-on, he warned us against
"the common error of looking at *The Second Sex* as a mere extension of
Sartre's early existentialism." Actually, he said, Simone de Beauvoir may
have accomplished more in philosophy than Sartre. At the least, her feminist book anticipated sections of Sartre's late work, *Critique of Dialectical Reason*. "In the early phase," he said, "Sartre's position was that
we are always free to decide, even in the most extreme situation. Even
the torturer does not have the power to completely crush our ability to
choose. Sartre presupposes reciprocity and equality between ourselves
and the 'other.' No, says Beauvoir, there are situations in which my humanity may not be destroyed, but it is suppressed. And one such case in
which you can't talk of freedom is the case of the woman."

Simone de Beauvoir formulated the secondary nature of women's reality in philosophical terms, and even though her analysis is now familiar (partly from all the writers who have stolen from it, some with scant
acknowledgment), the words still have the power to startle. The book
was written almost fifty years ago. Being a man in our culture, she says,
is central. Maleness simply defines—"bestrides"—reality. The human response, as such, is male:

In the midst of an abstract discussion it is vexing to hear a man say: "You think thus and so because you are a woman"; but I know that my only defense is to reply: "I think thus and so because it is true," thereby removing my subjective self from the argument. It would be out of the question to reply: "And you think the contrary because you are a man," for it is understood that the fact of being a man is no peculiarity. A man is in the right in being a man; it is the woman who is in the wrong. It amounts to this: just as for the ancients there was an absolute vertical with reference to which the oblique was defined, so there is an absolute human type, the masculine. Woman has ovaries, a uterus; these peculiarities imprison her in her subjectivity, circumscribe her within the limits of her own nature. It is often said that she thinks with her glands. Man superbly ignores the fact that his anatomy also includes glands, such as the testicles, and that they secrete hormones. He thinks of his body as a direct and normal connection with the world, which he believes he apprehends objectively, whereas he regards the body of woman as a hindrance, a prison, weighed down by everything peculiar to it. (p. xviii)

Stephanson wanted us to read Beauvoir, in part, because she had assimilated the history of Western philosophy, making her own variants of Hegel. If the human response, as such, is male, then he is the subject, the absolute, and she is the other. But with peculiar results.

. . . following Hegel, we find in consciousness itself a fundamental hostility toward every other consciousness; the subject can be posed only in being opposed—he sets himself up as the essential, as opposed to the other, the inessential, the object.

But the other consciousness, the other ego, sets up a reciprocal claim. The native traveling abroad is shocked to find himself in turn regarded as a "stranger" by the natives of neighboring countries. As a matter of fact, wars, festivals, trading, treaties, and contests among tribes, nations, and classes tend to deprive the concept *Other* of its absolute sense and to make manifest its relativity; willy-nilly, individuals and groups are forced to realize the reciprocity of their relations. How is it, then, that this reciprocity has not been recognized between the sexes, that one of the contrasting terms is set up as the sole essential, denying any relativity in regard to its correlative and defining the latter as pure otherness? Why is it that women do not dispute male sovereignty? No subject will readily volunteer to become the object, the inessential; it is not the Other who, in defining himself as the Other, establishes the One. The Other is posed as such by the One in defining himself as the One. But if the Other is not to regain the status of being the One, he must be submissive

enough to accept this alien point of view. Whence comes this submission in the case of woman? (pp. xx–xxi)

Answering this extraordinary question, the book, like St. Augustine's
City of God, becomes an immense reasoned compendium, a passionate
summing up of the available evidence—in this case, the evidence (before
academic disciplines had quite hardened) from anthropology, biology,
medicine, history, philosophy, and literature. *The Second Sex* ranges all
over the place; it is a book both exhilarating and draining. Even though
Stephanson assigned only excerpts, I became almost overwhelmed by
facts, interpretations, theories, objections to theories, restatement of theories. I read *in* it, as one read in the Bible, savoring stories, history,
prophecy, lamentation. Simone de Beauvoir wants to tell us everything.

The Second Sex has a strong, steady intellectual flavor, and was written in a better and freer temper than many later feminist books. Millett,
Greer, and others are now falling into the background—a cruel remark,
perhaps, but irrefutable. Beauvoir remains more intelligent and comprehensive than her imitators, and part of her intelligence is to create a picture of life that men, as well as women, can recognize as true. She did
not simply write of women as victims. She wrote of life as defined by the
patriarchal system, of men and women living *together* under such a system. Men had also been shaped by the dialectic of sex; it was something
they were doing to themselves as well as to women. Wide experience,
wide sympathies, an absence of rancor or special pleading—*The Second
Sex* is a book with a generous conception of life behind it.

And there is something else, not intellectually respectable, perhaps,
but emotionally inescapable. In my movie-struck mind, there was a romantic flare to Beauvoir's attack, a warmth of sympathy as well as anger
reminiscent, temperamentally, of Jeanne Moreau and Danielle Darrieux
and other great French movie stars. The French movies of the thirties,
forties, fifties, and early sixties, with their worldly and sensual heroines,
their commingling of spirit and art, their rhetorical fervor, their romantic openness, came from an older culture than ours, a culture whose appeal, at its best, cannot be conveyed by such woefully inadequate words
as "sophisticated" and "mature." Simone de Beauvoir was part of that
culture. She avoids the abrupt and schematic resentments, the unmodulated rejections of the radical American feminists who followed and
were influenced by her. She insists that whatever the injustices of
woman's existence, life is a common enterprise.

In the immense chapter "Dreams, Fears, Idols," as Beauvoir describes
the many ways men had "constructed" female identity for their own use,
she brings an almost poetic richness to the elaboration of male folly.
Men have largely (until recently) controlled representation; since women

did not make myths of their own behavior, Beauvoir says, these male illusions, dreams, and fears were part of the way men controlled women.
A clear injustice. But what a garden of wonders! What fantasies, what
bizarre terrors and exaltations! Woman as witch, as temptress and Satan's tool, as vampire sucking out man's essence, as the scourge of nature
whose menstrual blood causes vegetables to wither and plagues to descend. And then the "positive" side! Just as mad! Woman as virgin, as
absolute purity, as earth mother, as possession. What we absorbed in
C.C. of *The Second Sex* had a kind of exotic fascination. Nothing was
alien to Simone de Beauvoir: The bourgeois marriage bed and dinner
table; the brothel, the harem, the virgin's chapel—all were encumbered
by their symbolic meanings, all were created by men (sometimes with female complicity) as a *bondage* of meaning. Woman never meant any one
thing, because she sums up all the varieties of longing in men. As Beauvoir describes it, the fecundity of male fantasy throughout history became marvelous without ceasing to be absurd and sinister.

There was a deep ambiguity in her evocations of the patriarchy that I
found fascinating and moving. Some of the ways men had imprisoned
women were touched by grace or comfort, and some of women's responses were touched by sublimity.

> Here on earth men are defenders of the law, of reason, of necessity;
> woman is aware of the original contingency of man himself and of
> this necessity in which he believes; hence come both the mysterious
> irony that flits across her lips and her pliant generosity. She heals the
> wounds of the males, she nurses the newborn, and she lays out the
> dead; she knows everything about man that attacks his pride and
> humiliates his self-will. While she inclines before him and humbles
> the flesh to the spirit, she stays on the fleshly frontiers of the spirit,
> softening, as I have said, the hard angles of man's constructions and
> bestowing upon them unforeseen luxury and grace. Woman's power
> over men comes from the fact that she gently recalls them to a mod-
> est realization of their true condition; it is the secret of her disillu-
> sioned, sorrowful, ironical, and loving wisdom. In women even
> frivolity, capriciousness, and ignorance are charming virtues be-
> cause they flourish this side of and beyond the world where man
> chooses to live but where he does not like to feel himself confined.
> Over against set meanings and tools made for useful purposes, she
> upholds the mystery of intact things; she wafts the breath of poetry
> through city streets, over cultivated fields. (pp. 204–5)

Much of this has retreated into the past. Women have fought for and
gained a degree of economic independence, and in Beauvoir's terms,
woman (at least in the more successful classes of the advanced industrial

countries) is now both subject and object, the "one," and the "other," worker and companion, professional and mother. Absolved of her magical and mythical functions, literally disenchanted, she is no longer required to bless the fields and dispense balm on all male occasions. For some women at least, liberation, power, selfhood are at hand. Looking around my health club on Manhattan's Upper West Side, I see 200-pound weightlifters meekly receiving correction on their form from 125-pound female trainers. I realize how provincial my example is: The club is no more than an overpriced yuppie gym. But what's happening there between the sexes is a social moment inconceivable even fifteen years ago.

To a considerable degree, women are no longer dependent on men physically, which is a relief for men as well as women. In the Western bourgeois democracies, many old notions have collapsed, and the balance of power has begun to shift. At their very luckiest, men and women exhibit a graciousness in their relations with one another that is something new on earth. They are trying to make equality work. However much backsliding and resistance can be counted at any one moment, however many women remain still bruised and frightened, women's liberation, as even its opponents know, is the only successful revolution of the twentieth century. C.C. and Lit Hum, allowing dead white females into its lists and thereby establishing a counterhegemonic discourse within the walls, has implicitly recognized as much.

Beauvoir announced that this change in women's estate, which was already underway in France in the 1940s, might be painful. There were elements of early existentialist thought that she had *not* rejected, and they sprang out of the text with a kind of clarion insistence.

> . . . those who are condemned to stagnation are often pronounced happy on the pretext that happiness consists in being at rest. This notion we reject, for our perspective is that of existentialist ethics. Every subject plays his part as such specifically through exploits or projects that serve as a mode of transcendence; he achieves liberty only through a continual reaching out toward other liberties. There is no justification for present existence other than its expansion into an indefinitely open future. Every time transcendence falls back into immanence [i.e., a notion of what anyone "essentially" is forever], stagnation, there is a degradation of existence into the *"en-soi"*— the brutish life of subjection to given conditions—and of liberty into constraint and contingence. This downfall represents a moral fault if the subject consents to it; if it is inflicted upon him, it spells frustration and oppression. In both cases it is an absolute evil. Every individual concerned to justify his existence feels that his existence involves an undefined need to transcend himself, to engage in freely chosen projects. (p. xxxiii)

There were feminists, I knew, who complained that Beauvoir's notion of "projects" and "transcendence" was itself a reflection of male hierarchies of achievement, and others who thought that she slighted the creativity, as well as the necessity, of motherhood. And of course, Beauvoir was setting up myths of her own. Heroic self-transcendence might not be what all women wanted; it was certainly far from a universal experience for men, many of whom work at numbingly repetitive tasks in offices, factories, or construction sites. Taking myself as I was at forty-eight, living with a wife, two children, and many obligations, I wasn't sure that the given "conditions" of my life could be overcome without betraying other people. The nobility of bourgeois life, such as it is, consists precisely in living within limiting "conditions" and finding small areas of freedom for yourself and then gradually enlarging them. With luck and extraordinary persistence, you might transform yourself. Call it piecemeal transcendence. But I'm stirred, everyone is stirred, by Simone de Beauvoir's existentialist ethics. She calls women to a heroic existence, particularly young, unmarried women. Which means life will get harder for those women.

Near the end of her introduction, in a sentence that is obviously of great moral importance for the whole book, Beauvoir asserts, "I am interested in the fortunes of the individual as defined not in terms of happiness but in terms of liberty." Simple enough. Yet, for an American, it's a daunting remark. In this country, we would like to think that liberty *leads* to happiness, and seeing the two terms opposed, with the clear implication that greater liberty might bring difficulty and pain—that's a shock. It occurred to me when reading Simone de Beauvoir that the women at Take Back the Night, who were the most empowered women undergraduates in American history, may have suspected the truth that liberty might not lead to happiness. That realization may have been part of their bitterness.

The Beauvoir excerpts were well received in class, but after Stephanson led us through a quick exposition of Beauvoir's central ideas, the conversation grew testy. The implacable Manuel weighed in.

"Here again," he rumbled, "I'm going to take the radical conservative standpoint. [Sighs from both men and women.] Most feminists are clueless as to what the society would look like if they were actually empowered. Women want equal wages, control of reproductive rights. But these are only part of the benefits of power. I don't see women wanting the right to kill or the right to exploit. Men have developed over the generations the paradoxical notion that power is not a good thing yet someone has to have it. But women don't want that kind of power."

Earlier in the year, the students had been deferential to Manuel, unwilling to argue with a blind man. But no more. Hands went up furiously. Mei Ling, one of the two Asian-American women who had joined the class the second semester, usually quiet in discussion, now looked at Manuel sourly. "What you said is so outrageous," she said. "Power is about freedom of thought, not the right to kill people," which was nobly spoken but did not answer what Manuel had said.

Her friend sitting next to her, Karen, of Korean descent, severe-looking in granny glasses but friendly as well, came in quickly before anyone else could speak. "You are defining what power is. You've read all these male texts, and now you want women to define power as you do, so then you'll say you're scared."

"Okay," said Manuel, swaying as usual. "Men now dominate women because of fear. They plow the field, so they don't get engulfed."

A deliriously mixed metaphor. But I now remembered his remark, in our class on Marx, that women would someday gather together and achieve political power. He seemed to be taunting women to put up or shut up—take power and accept the consequences of power, or stop talking about it. Manuel was also raising the old question of what women want, what women *are*. That is, do women have an inherent nature—in this case, one that is unwilling to wield power in its fiercest aspect—or is that nature defined by their political situation in a male-dominated society? Are there any temperamental differences between the sexes? *That* old question, and it never goes away.

I looked back to the earlier readings. In the late fall, we had read Christine de Pizan's strange work *The Book of the City of Ladies,* not a classic, exactly, but something of a resurrected text. By reputation, it was the most approachable production of a remarkably fluent author who is often called the first "professional woman writer." Born in 1365, in Venice, Pizan was exceptionally well educated, enjoying a rich literary culture in the wake of Dante and Boccaccio, and when her French husband died, leaving her with three small children and no inheritance, she began writing for a living, producing works on many subjects. *The Book of the City of Ladies* is an attempt to answer the slanders against women's character encountered in a lifetime of reading classical and contemporary literature. The erudite Pizan, drawing on mythology and history, creates a kind of countercanon, in which she celebrates women's dignity and prudence—a canon of exemplary deeds and nobility of character. She pleads for education for women, but she has little interest in equality. In the modern jargon, Pizan is an "essentialist"—she thought that women's nature was to serve men, and to correct their excesses with virtue and chastity. Which makes almost any modern reader groan with impatience.

Stephanson had spoken of Pizan generously, but she palled on me fast, and the classroom discussion had gotten stuck on some oddly literal points. For instance, was it right for Pizan to use mythological sources to establish the character of women? The conversation went askew, I thought, because there's an element of whimsy and prissiness in Pizan's writing—she's really a bit distant in her late–Middle Ages, educated-woman's decorum. Could not women be accounted "noble" without the solemn draperies of chastity, modesty, and virtue encumbering their movements? Power, for women in the Middle Ages, may well have depended on the appearance of chastity; even Boccaccio would have agreed with that. But I have to admit to finding very little interest in the subject, very little fascination in the nexus of power and chastity, even though it's a strain in feminist thought continuing right up to Take Back the Night.

Pizan left us all a bit grumpy. This was a tone closer to our modern appetite:

> I wish to persuade women to endeavour to acquire strength, both of mind and body, and to convince them that the soft phrases, susceptibility of heart, delicacy of sentiment, and refinement of taste, are almost synonymous with epithets of weakness, and that those beings who are only the objects of pity, and that kind of love which has been termed its sister, will soon become objects of contempt. (p. 81)

Thus Mary Wollstonecraft in 1792. At the beginning of the second semester, after Rousseau, Hume, and Kant, we had read sections of Wollstonecraft's scornfully intelligent *Vindication of the Rights of Woman*. The woman generally considered the first modern feminist, a radical egalitarian and journalist, the wife of political philosopher William Godwin and mother of Mary Shelley (author of *Frankenstein*), she reviled the social arrangements of aristocratic privilege and bourgeois marriage that encouraged women to cultivate artificial feminine graces, affectation, and weakness. Wollstonecraft is a scourge of all that is "soft" and calculating in women; she heralded the middle-class women of the future, the professional women who make their way by their wits and drive, refusing to talk nonsense to please a man. Her own prose is powerful, censorious, undismayed by ambiguity. She is a writer often witty but rarely funny.

Women, she wrote, had been undermined. For if women are created by God, they are endowed with reason; therefore, they are souls of the same kind as men. By educating them only to please, we are turning them into trivial, hapless creatures who can only receive contempt under the guise of praise. And we are setting them up for a catastrophic double betrayal. First, deprived of education, they lose the possibility of developing their minds; and second, having devoted themselves to beauty, they lose the affections of their husbands as the years go by, for the husbands have nothing to say to their empty-headed wives and go off in pursuit of younger women. Marriage should begin in passion and end in friendship, which is a higher and more long-lasting state of being.

The students who had taken Lit Hum in freshman year knew well enough what Wollstonecraft was reacting to. Any Jane Austen novel, but especially *Pride and Prejudice,* makes all too clear how limited were the options facing women in England around 1800. Either marriage, or respectable nullity as a governess—or a swift drop off the cliff to charwoman, factory worker, prostitute.

Still, agreeing with much of what Wollstonecraft said, I had found her contempt for sensuality and pleasure a little unnerving. She talks of sex as women's only power, a corrupter that in effect turns women into whores—they enjoy the triumph of an hour but no other triumph. She doesn't appear to see, or anticipate, that women can live as sexual beings and as intellectually mature beings at the same time. (Certainly she did so herself.) So here was a partial anticipation of Take Back the Night, a rage against sex as the force that disempowers women.

"What's missing between men and women, according to Wollstonecraft," Stephanson said, "is the reasonable, rational relationship. But the way in which she constructs the argument makes her marginalize sexuality." He was trying to get the class to see the oddity as well as the strength of Wollstonecraft's views. But Mei Ling was having none of it. "If you have sexual power over men," she said, "you are not relying on your powers of reason."

Well, that may have been a blow for personal honesty, but Stephanson wouldn't let go. "Is there really a dichotomy between attractiveness and reason?" he asked, his voice rising. "And isn't power a function of a given relationship, not a hammer that you use? This book is an attack on romantic love, and there are still elements of this in feminist thought today—the view that romantic life is a trap for women."

It was the inevitable male point of view, and of course I agreed with him. For me, Wollstonecraft was an encounter with an anger a long ways from my understanding. She was as much an "other" as Dante. Certainly I recognized the truth of her account of women's lives; she sets out the traps for women so incisively that one wanted to agree with her just for the pleasure and safety of being on her side. But I couldn't credit her solution. Trying to hang in there, I could go only so far before my antipathy to her censoriousness killed my pleasure in her wrathfully witty prose. When she cuts off the weedy clichés about women, she may be slashing some living roots as well.

> As for Rousseau's remarks, which have since been echoed by several writers, that [girls] have naturally, that is, from their birth, indepen-

dent of education, a fondness for dolls, dressing, and talking, they are so puerile as not to merit a serious refutation. That a girl, condemned to sit for hours together listening to the idle chat of weak nurses, or to attend at her mother's toilet, will endeavour to join the conversation, is, indeed, very natural; and that she will imitate her mother or aunts, and amuse herself by adorning her lifeless doll, as they do in dressing her, poor innocent babe! is undoubtedly a most natural consequence. . . .

In this manner, may the fondness for dress, conspicuous in woman, be easily accounted for, without supposing it the result of a desire to please the sex on which they are dependent. The absurdity, in short, of supposing that a girl is naturally a coquette, and that a desire connected with the impulse of nature to propagate the species, should appear even before an improper education has, by heating the imagination, called it forth prematurely, is so unphilosophical, that such a sagacious observer as Rousseau would not have adopted it, if he had not been accustomed to make reason give way to his desire of singularity, and truth to a favourite paradox. (p. 128)

In simpler English: The desire to please men will not be found naturally in immature girls who haven't yet been miseducated into thinking that pleasing men is their life's work. But I thought of little girls I knew with feminist-powerhouse mothers, little girls who nevertheless desired to please. Even at four, before TV images of nurturing mommies and eager bimbos had influenced them, they were a lot more charming than boys.

Something was off here, yet the students completely agreed with Wollstonecraft. One after another, men and women, they solemnly insisted that there were no gender characteristics except as society had "constructed" them. Both Karen and Meredith (the South African woman) said they had not played with dolls; Abel stepped forth bravely to say that he *had* (meaning, "and yet I became a man"). "If the girls are withdrawing into dolls," said Karen, "they sense they are in a male world," which was an interesting remark, though I wished I could have introduced her to some families I knew in which the moms wrote books or practiced law or dealt millions in bonds every day and still their daughters played with dolls and dressed up.

Girls are given Barbie, Karen said, and that's why they loved her, whereas boys were given toy guns, and were expected to play with them; and so they did, and became war-lovers and football fans and Porsche-lovers as well.

Yes, I was thinking to myself, but if a child is given a toy she doesn't want, she casts it aside. Before parental and societal hands begin mucking about, the human clay already has some shape of its own. I listened for a while but couldn't control myself. I was the only person in the room with children.

"I'm sorry, I don't mean to pull rank, but I can't take this," I began.

Annoyed smiles. They knew I did mean to pull rank. I then said what many parents knew, including a variety of feminist mothers (I had talked it over with many)—that the tempermental differences between little boys and girls could be immense. Just as the bond-dealing mothers were astounded to see their daughters playing with dolls and dressing up, I was astounded to see my boys embrace G.I. Joe toys and war movies. When they were four, they ran around the apartment hitting and poking people with whatever was handy. Few of the girls in their preschool class did that. If such behavior is merely a result of conditioning, then we are helpless, because my wife and I did not set out to condition the boys to hit people and to like war toys. Anything but: counterconditioning might be more like it, though I admit that once we saw how much they liked toy guns and swords, we gave way, not fighting it, and attempted instead the usual parental trick of beating plastic swords into plowshares. We tried to turn their interest in toy soldiers and war into an interest in history. Hannibal with his elephants, Caesar crossing the Rubicon. After a few years, when the boys got bored with running around the house hitting people, they were left with something about Alexander the Great and Napoleon. So there it was: We had "constructed" their interest in war. But we hadn't, really. We had tried to channel a disposition already there.

As I spoke, I heard a rustle of indignation, the sound of students rearranging their notebooks and pens in annoyance. The exact temperamental identity of the sexes is now a received idea among undergraduates; indeed, in the secular university, this belief is as close as the students are likely to come to a sacred doctrine. They smiled but told me with some heat that I was wrong; and I realized I had run into a modest outgrowth of political correctness. *Students will not countenance the notion of distinctions between people because they assume that all distinctions are invidious.* Thus they hate any generalizations whatsoever about gender, race, and class because they assume the point of such remarks is to put down the parties with less power. Invidious distinctions are what they hear on the street and on talk radio; invidious distinctions have oppressed people in the past; therefore all distinctions must be invidious. It is the antilogic of correctness. If you say that women are different from men, you must be saying that women are inferior to men. The idea that "different" may mean "different" had not yet gotten through. The students want to be truly tolerant and open-minded, and many of them are, but they live in a hypersensitive society, and they fall into the trap of confusing blandness and caution with tolerance.

❖ ❖ ❖

I realized I had been searching for a guilty text—something in the air, a suggestion, a tone, a perception of reality that might have contributed to that atmosphere of bitter defeat I heard at Take Back the Night. I don't mean to imply that anyone needed to read a book in order to be angry about rape. But the specific tone of the anguish, the endgame despair, the hopelessness. . . . My search, I admit, was a narrow way to address feminist texts which, after all, had many other things to offer. But if I did not pursue the logic of obsession, I would lose my hope of understanding a mood that seemed to wound so many people. Simone de Beauvoir had written a great book and was guilty of nothing (except perhaps prolixity.) She was proudly, securely defiant. And Pizan and Wollstonecraft had done what I had hoped they would do, effectively answering the silences and absurdities of earlier texts in Columbia's version of the canon—Aristotle's nonsense about women's inferior intellectual capacities, the Old Testament's patriarchal assumptions, the sexual paranoia of the Christian writers, and so on. I wasn't happy about the antierotic bent in these two writers, but no one could accuse them of a mawkish insistence on victimization.

Stephanson assigned something else, however, a 1989 essay* by the law professor and antipornography crusader Catharine A. MacKinnon titled "Sexuality, Pornography, and Method: 'Pleasure Under Patriarchy." Stephanson chose MacKinnon because he wanted us to have some sense of what a recent radical-feminist position on sexuality looked like. We had passed from the approved, the time-blessed, the classic, to a piece of academic rhetoric from the current moment.

> A theory of sexuality becomes feminist to the extent it treats sexuality as a social construct of male power: defined by men, forced on women, and constitutive in the meaning of gender. Such an approach centers feminism on the perspective of the subordination of women to men as it identifies sex—that is, the sexuality of dominance and submission—as crucial, as a fundamental, as on some level definitive, in that process. (p. 209)

> Dominance eroticized defines the imperatives of [sexuality's] masculinity, submission eroticized defines its femininity. . . . [M]ale power takes the social form of what men as a gender want sexually, which centers on power itself, as socially defined. Masculinity is having it; femininity is not having it. (p. 211)

* Revised and reprinted as chapter seven in *Toward a Feminist Theory of the State* (Cambridge: Harvard University Press, 1989).

I was quite stunned by the cement-machine prose. But let's go on. As MacKinnon notes, she is advancing a far more radical notion than did earlier feminist theorists, who generally assumed that sexuality in women, as in men, was a constant, a biological drive and necessity that had been repressed or distorted under the patriarchy. Since sexuality according to this old account was a given, its diminution or absence in women—"frigidity"—amounted to an accusation of inadequacy against the woman herself or against the society in which she lived. But who is to say, MacKinnon asks, that sexual drive in women is a given? Who is to say that "sex as such (whatever it is) is good—natural, healthy, positive, appropriate, pleasurable, wholesome, fine, one's own, and to be approved and expressed"?

MacKinnon insists that there is no female sexuality as such—nothing that exists beyond or beneath culture, a force both biological and instinctual. (So much for Darwin and Freud.) On the contrary, desire in women has been constructed by men as an element in a "script," a scenario that functions as an aspect of male social power. Female sexuality is something imposed on women. Universally approved, its hidden purpose within the social world of male power has always been to reward women for making themselves available to men. It's absurd to say that women can "express" themselves sexually, or negotiate their freedom (as they had hoped to do in the sixties sexual revolution). How can you "negotiate" with your oppressors? Women are not equal; they cannot negotiate. Indeed, all this talk about sexual freedom is just a delusionary way of women offering themselves up as victims.

What is it, then, that women are feeling, or claiming to feel? Women will experience pleasure in submission because their sexuality has been constructed by men in precisely such a way that eroticizes submission. But what if women do not feel pleasure in submission but in something else? Well, that isn't possible. Women can't feel pleasure in equality because it doesn't exist for them. In brief: If women feel anything, they've been told to feel it. "You can't argue with an orgasm," a friend of mine used to say. But apparently you can. You can try to convince it that it's incorrect.

There's a long history of this sort of thing, the savants telling women what their sexuality is. The classical mythmakers did it, the Christian writers did it, Boccaccio did it, the Renaissance poets did it, and modern psychologists still do it. The birds do it, the bees do it, they all do it. But MacKinnon may be the first to say that women's sexuality is nothing, a chimera. With equal assurance, I thought, she would tell a lioness that she should eat greens rather than gazelles.

Counterarguments sputter onto the page. Are they necessary? Perhaps not, but for the record: If all women have been conditioned by the same system of power, how does MacKinnon account for the remarkable range of sexual temperament and taste and satisfaction in women? What about a woman who has not enjoyed herself with a given man and has chosen a better? Does she really feel pleasure with the second because she is more truly submissive with him? The question is idiotic and insulting. If you take MacKinnon at all seriously, you must assume that women who receive pleasure do so in a way that is inherently destructive of their dignity as persons.

One sign, perhaps, of a text that could never last beyond the moment is that it appears to connect with nothing but its own obsessions—in this case a rigid theory that excluded experience, contradiction, variety (everything that makes Simone de Beauvoir's writing so rich). Let me note in passing a few things that MacKinnon ignores: the many varieties of sexual pleasure that women have claimed; the powers that Beauvoir evoked which women have occasionally exercised over men; the many women on all sides of us who do not appear to be submissive personalities. Neither class nor race plays any part in MacKinnon's analysis. The high-bourgeois ladies of nineteenth-century Paris; the peasant wife with a devoted brood of sons and daughters; the modern professional woman, successful as lawyer, doctor, professor, money manager—they are all equally cheated and equally deluded. But why go on? I had arrived at a canonical moment. Simone de Beauvoir would silence MacKinnon as much as Virginia Woolf had silenced the genteel popular novelists of the thirties.

Even John Stuart Mill, insisting that we should hear views contrary to our own, would be weary by now. Let us come to an end: In MacKinnon's version of relations between men and women, pornography and rape are no mere aberrant or occasional elements. On the contrary, they're at the very heart of the hetero paradigm. Pornography is the school for scoundrels in which men learn to abuse women; rape the practice of commonplace sexual relations. "Force is sex, not just sexualized; force is the desire dynamic, not just a response to the desired object when desire's expression is frustrated." The next step in the theory is obvious. If rape is the paradigm of heterosexuality, then intercourse itself is rape, or close to it. Does it not involve penetration, just like rape? MacKinnon never commits the folly of saying, in so many words, that intercourse is rape. But what other conclusion can one draw from such remarks as "Rape and intercourse are not authoritatively separated by any difference between the physical acts or amounts of force involved but only legally, by a standard that revolves around the man's interpretation of the encounter"?

For women, there is no escaping MacKinnon's peculiar tunnel of love. A woman seeking sexual pleasure must also accept her extinction as a human being.

I had found my guilty text. In Take Back the Night's utter misery, its seeming conflation (at times) of sex and rape, its luridness and obsessiveness, its expansion of rape into a universe of fear, its portrait of women as helpless losers who could retrieve their honor only by abstention, the ideology of that evening was very close to MacKinnon's writing. Not that I believed that the five hundred or so students at Take Back the Night had all read MacKinnon. I'm not claiming a direct influence, except, perhaps, in a handful of cases. But such catastrophic versions of human sexuality were certainly in the air, and they might function very powerfully, at second or third hand, as an explanation of a disastrous love affair or a loathsome experience. An extreme view had won out, at least for a significant minority.

The only escape from MacKinnon's prison house lay in chastity. MacKinnon concluded by quoting an early essay by the radical feminist Ti-Grace Atkinson, the same Ti-Grace Atkinson who was getting her Ph.D. at Columbia in the nineties and whose C.C. class I had attended in order to hear how a radical feminist would teach the patriarchal Aristotle. In 1974, Atkinson had written, "I do not know any feminist worthy of the name who, if forced to choose between freedom and sex, would choose sex. She'd choose freedom every time."

But why are these the two alternatives? How many women, even in 1974, had to "choose between freedom and sex"? Why can women not have both? Except in extreme individual cases (a woman trapped in an abusive marriage, and so on), are the two really opposites at all? What can be the point of closing down life to such mutually exclusive possibilities?

Great literature, obviously, could not rescue anyone from so grievous a foreshortening of perspective. It was naïve and false on my part to think that the students could be rescued by Western classics. I knew perfectly well that great books work on our souls only over time, as they are mixed with experience and transformed by memory and desire and many other books, great and small. At some later time, the perception of a "choice between freedom and sex" would dissolve into absurdity. But for a while, the idea worked its mischief.

❖   ❖   ❖

"Most women are alienated from their bodies," said Karen in our class on MacKinnon. She was serious-looking, with long dark hair, granny glasses, a strong voice.

"What does that mean?" asked Stephanson.

"If there's a way to look at our bodies healthfully, a lot of women get off the track. Women wind up using their bodies as tools. You yourself are instrumentalizing."

"But how?"

"You are taught that sex is good, and that you will express yourself sexually, and you get to Columbia, and you are raped—and not by the rapist in the dark alley but by Joe Guy. So you think: Was I sending false signals to him? Am I supposed to have enjoyed it? Harassment forces you to think of your body as an object. The guard at the Columbia gates calls to you, 'Hey, baby!' So you start thinking of yourself as an object. You body becomes a problem. Are you going to be angry about it the rest of your life—"

She broke off, having more than answered the question, I thought.

"A certain image of yourself," said Stephanson, "is taken away and replaced by someone else's." She nodded yes. But before we discussed how that image might possibly be replaced by a new, unalienated one, the class turned testy again. Abel said to Karen, "If you go on strike because a movement tells you to, you're not acting for yourself—you're losing your body all over again." He said it with some irritation, and his annoyance caused me to remember a moment of our class on Beauvoir, in which Dinesh, the man of Indian descent from Pennsylvania, had burst out. "It's obnoxious," he had said in his intense, staccato way. "It's obnoxious that feminists have imposed *their* idea of what woman is, what your reality is. There's an authoritarian streak in the movement. You have to create this role, or that role. Living a 'role' is itself a subjugation."

Was it a tragedy or a comedy? The men had sensed a withdrawal, or a threat to withdraw, and were trying to argue women back into the arena. The conversation about feminism was awkward, the most awkward we had had all year. "If you view sex just as penetration, you are missing the enveloping side of it," Abel said in Karen's direction, a little wanly. There was no response.

I suspected the men felt they were under a general indictment that ignored their individual qualities and their very obvious desire not to be louts. All year long, relations between men and women in the class had been respectful. Except, perhaps, for some of Manuel's speeches, the men's remarks were free of condescension to women—and even Manuel was more provoking than insulting. No man had said (as Beauvoir put it), "You think thus and so because you are a woman." The students often disagreed, but they did not insult one another on the basis of gender; they did not imprison one another in myths. But they didn't warm up to one another, either. Apart from one or two friendships that predated the

C.C. course, they all might have been colleagues at a particularly starchy biochemical lab: proper, wary, distant. They didn't seem all that *interested*. They didn't engage one another. It was a sexless class.

I looked around at the men, and I thought of myself at nineteen or twenty, a voluble admirer of women, producing words, words, nothing but words, like a confused moth attracted to the bulb but grateful for the lampshade in the way. The young college men I saw may well have been more confident than I was, but still, I thought, There are nights *they* may want to take back, too—and not always because they went too far. Who knows how sure they were of themselves?

I had stumbled into a cultural moment. I was sure of it. When Henry James wrote his great novel *The Bostonians*, in the 1880s, he said that he had discovered, in the time of the New England feminists, a "decline in the sentiment of sex," and I had found something like it, too. (Hetero sex, that is. For all I knew, some or many of the students were gay.) The students appeared becalmed, asexual. AIDS made things riskier, but that can't be the sole explanation. Something dry and sandpapery had reached the surface; the sexes were at an impasse, at least for the time.

In the wake of feminism's triumph, sex roles were spinning so rapidly that everyone was discomforted. The male students knew that women hated overbearing guys who took anything for granted; but they also knew that women hated men who held back when they *should* make a move. Either too aggressive or too passive, "rapists" or wimps—the men were in an awful bind. Unless a man possessed the looks or the charisma to transcend the situation, he had only the tiniest of margins within which to flirt, talk, court, present himself as a plausible lover. The men were damned if they did, damned if they didn't. And the women spoke as if they could not be sexually active or even interested without fear that they would be betrayed. They did not want to go out into the city of New York dependent on a male escort, but it was a dangerous place. Many of them had come from suburban or small-city backgrounds where they were relatively safer. The anguish of Take Back the Night may have been produced by fear of the big city as much as fear of rape.

"There's actually *less* looking at women in America," Stephanson was saying, as if answering Karen's earlier speech about men harassing women on the street. "Less in America than in, say, Italy. There's a de-eroticized way that men and women relate to each other in New York. For defense purposes, you have to have no eye contact, the body language has to be restricted. In Italy and France, there's a tension going on all the time, a lot of play. Looks, flirtation, it's all play, it doesn't mean a hell of a lot. In New York, you can't do it because it's dangerous. Here, Latins may engage in it, but between whites and blacks, it's risky.

"MacKinnon is an incredible prude," he went on, his voice rising in amazement. "I find nothing but repression in this text. The style, the sentences—chop, chop, chop!" and he turned his palm sideways and brought it down on the table in a slicing motion, a knife on a butcher block. "You begin with this hierarchy, and you wind up in this completely de-eroticized defense position."

But this was too much for Mei Ling. "Did we say Kant was a prude? People are freaking out on MacKinnon, and I don't think she deserves being freaked out on. We didn't do it to Kant."

Well, she was right about Kant, and she had a point about the class. At the beginning of the two hours, at Stephanson's request, I had delivered an analysis of MacKinnon's views of pornography that had turned into an attack on MacKinnon altogether. Mei Ling thought that the two of us were ganging up on MacKinnon, and we were—though not out of calculation.

Listening to the students, I was sure that radical-feminist language had colored the language of sex for everyone; if nothing else, it had helped destroy the old language of romance. In class, the students talked about sexual "roles," about "power" and "transactions." In two classes about feminism and relations between the sexes, I doubt I heard the word "love" spoken even once. Literature was about power, sex was about power—and such language was insidious, because once you talked about life and art as power, talking about it in any other terms seemed colorless or naïve. One now got the impression that for many students power was sexy but sex was not. Again I felt foolish, a liberated uncle exhorting reluctant youths to sport in the woods. What a bunch of prigs! The trouble with young people today is that they're not sleeping around enough.

I made a guess about what was going on, and I offer it here as interpretation of a cultural moment that may pass in another five or ten years.

For the last fifteen years or so, the pressures on young college women have become enormous. The very success of the women's movement has made their lives more difficult, just as Beauvoir had anticipated in the mid-forties. They are expected, when they graduate, to have major corporate, professional, or artistic careers; they are expected to be tough, disciplined, hardworking and ambitious *yet also nicer than men*; hard-driving yet nurturing; wary of male domination yet a great lay; career women yet heads of households; demythicized as earth mothers and witches yet remythicized as "total women"; and they are expected to be all these things at the same time. Men face pressures, too, and always have, but not of such contradictory nature. And for the first time in history, women have no place to hide. No place at all. Which is terrifying.

Few undergraduates would put it as I just have, but I think they feel many of these pressures by the time they reach college. And for some, their fears and difficulties focus on rape; and many of them withdraw from relations with men. Men are the one hassle they can do without. At least temporarily.

But then, at the end of the class, when I was feeling forlorn, as if a part of my own youth had vanished, Noah, my favorite student, came through.

"There's no escaping power," he said, "but power is not fixed. It can be negotiated, exchanged, modified, reversed. In sex, power is not fixed."

Well, exactly. *That* was the postfeminist paradigm, if there was one. *That* was the fruit of the one successful revolution of the twentieth century. The breaking down of the old stable sex roles was a benefit for men as well as for women. Women need not pretend they lack courage and toughness, and men need not pretend they have it all the time. That was a big change right there. The two sexes could now discard each other's myths. They could *play*. MacKinnon, on the other hand, seemed caught in a warp of her own. Outside of S and M circles, who even used the word "submission" anymore? MacKinnon's view of life—violent, lurid, and two-dimensional—was dirtier than most pornography. An equalitarian revolution between men and women was in the making—at least in the world that these students would enter—and MacKinnon's head was in pornoland.

Listening to the students talk about power, I conceived the simplest of hopes. In our media-obsessed society, in which shame had been vanquished, and humiliation was a public property, and talk of power had replaced talk of love and eros, the old idea of privacy needed to be reborn and reconsecrated. A new generation needed to reconsecrate privacy or the romantic life would die. One had to shut down the Oprah and Sally Jessy within oneself and make one's soul in communion with friends, literature, or God. One had to give oneself over to a private theater of the emotions, in which men and women assemble what is authentic in desire without the entire society and the discourse of power crowding them out of bed. Simple? Naïve? But it could be done, couldn't it? In order to achieve freedom, young men and women had to *try* to shut the door and create their own myths from the ground up. In the age of shifting power relations, which opened new possibilities for sex and for love, they had to put aside the discourse of power and let power flow spontaneously wherever it would.

Take Back the Night was not only an attack on rape; it had metamorphized, disastrously, into an attack on the possibility of happiness. The ground had to be reconsecrated. In the newly created private sphere, power would flourish—Noah was right, there was no escaping it—but it would pass back and forth, becoming playful, exploratory, spontaneous. Me Tarzan, you Jane. But tomorrow night: You Tarzan, me Jane. Let power flow where it would. Eros needed to be unchained. The Western canon told us many things, among them that it was time to take back the night.

Chapter 27

CONRAD

~ The liberal reading of *Heart of Darkness*: civilization and savagery
~ Shapiro's students become readers
~ Alex and Henry struggle, and everyone grows alarmed
~ Chinua Achebe's charge of racism
~ Professor Edward W. Said and the culture of imperialism
~ Should Conrad be thrown out of the Western canon?
~ Imperialism, modernism, and the canon
~ Amity is restored, and Professor Shapiro takes stock

We were at the end, and literature was hanging in the balance. It was time to make a reckoning.

❖ ❖ ❖

"Who here comes from a savage race?" the Coach shouted at his students.

"We all come from Africa," said the one African-American in the class, Henry, calmly referring to the supposition among many anthropologists that human life originated in sub-Saharan Africa. In other words, there are no racial hierarchies among peoples. We're all "savages."

Shapiro smiled. It was not, I thought, exactly the answer he was looking for, but it was a good answer. Then he was off again. "Are you natural?" he roared at a woman sitting quietly near him at the end of the table. "What are the constraints for you? What are the rivets? Why are you here getting civilized, reading Lit Hum?"

At the end of the year's work in Lit Hum, the mood had grown agitated, burdened, portentous. In short, we were reading Joseph Conrad. At the conclusion of Lit Hum, individual instructors are allotted a week for a free choice. Some teachers chose works by Dostoyevsky, or Mann, or Gide, or Borges. Professor Shapiro, who enjoyed trouble, had chosen Conrad. The terms of his rhetorical questions—savagery, civilization, restraint, rivets—were drawn from Conrad's great novella of colonial depredation, *Heart of Darkness*, and the students were electrified. Almost a hundred years old, and familiar to generations of readers—a masterpiece that is also a high-school classic—Conrad's little book has lost none of its power to amaze and appall. It remains, in many places, an essential starting point for discussion of modernism, imperialism, the hypocrisies of the West, the ambiguities of "civilization." Infinitely complex, it has been subjected over the years to symbolic, mythological, and psychoanalytic interpretations. T. S. Eliot put a quotation from it at the head of his poem "The Hollow Men"; Hemingway and Faulkner were much impressed by it, as were Orson Welles, who had wanted to make a movie of it, and Francis Ford Coppola, who employed it as the ground plan for his despairing epic of Americans in Vietnam, *Apocalypse Now.*

In recent years, however, Conrad—and particularly *Heart of Darkness*—had fallen under a cloud of suspicion in the academy. In the curious language of the tribe, the book has become "a site of contestation." After all, Conrad offered a nineteenth-century European's view of Africans as primitive. He attacked Belgian imperialism and in the same breath praised the British variety. In 1975, the distinguished Nigerian novelist and essayist Chinua Achebe attacked *Heart of Darkness* as racist and called for its elimination from the canon of Western classics. And recently, Edward W. Said, Columbia's most famous living critic and literary scholar, had been raising hostile and undermining questions about it (Said gathered the material together, along with a great deal else, in his 1993 book *Culture and Imperialism*). Said, certainly, was no breaker of canons, but he put the book on the defensive. And if Conrad were somehow discredited, it would be hard to imagine a more successful challenge to what the academic left has repeatedly deplored as the "hegemonic discourse" of the classic Western texts.

❖   ❖   ❖

Written in a little more than two months, the last of 1898, and the first of 1899, *Heart of Darkness* is both the story of a journey and a kind of morbid fairy tale. Marlow, Conrad's narrator and familiar alter ego, a British merchant seaman of the 1890s, travels up the Congo River in the service of a rapacious Belgian trading company, hoping to retrieve the company's brilliant representative and ivory trader, Mr. Kurtz, who has mysteriously grown silent. The great Mr. Kurtz! In Africa, everyone gossips about him, envies him, and, with rare exception, loathes him. The flower of European civilization ("all Europe contributed to the making of Kurtz"), exemplar of light and compassion, journalist, artist, humanist, Kurtz has gone way upriver and at times well into the jungle, abandoning himself to certain—practices. Rifle in hand, he has set himself up as god or devil in ascendency over the Africans. Conrad is notoriously vague about what Kurtz actually *does*, but if you said, "Kills some people, has sex with others, steals all the ivory," you would not, I believe, be far wrong. In Kurtz, the alleged benevolence of colonialism has monstrously flowered into criminality. Marlow's voyage from Europe to Africa and then upriver to Kurtz's Inner Station is a revelation of the squalors and disasters of the colonial "mission"; it is also, in Marlow's mind, a journey back to the beginning of creation, when nature reigned exuberant and unrestrained; and a trip figuratively *down* as well, through the levels of the self to repressed and unlawful desires, no longer overlaid or muffled by social existence. At death's door, Marlow and Kurtz find each other.

Rereading is often a shock, an encounter with an earlier self that has been revised, and I discovered that I was initially discomforted, as I had not been in the past, by the famous manner—the magnificent, alarmed, and (there is no other word) throbbing excitement of Conrad's laboriously mastered English. Conrad was born in czarist-occupied Poland. Though he heard English spoken as a boy (his father translated Shakespeare), English was his third language, and his prose, now and then, betrays the propensity for high intellectual melodrama and euphonious and rhymed abstraction ("the fascination of the abomination") characteristic of his second, French. Oh, inexorable, inutterable, unspeakable! Conrad's adjectives were notorious. F. R. Leavis, the influential British critic, who loved Conrad, ridiculed such sentences as "It was the stillness of an implacable force brooding over an inscrutable intention." The sound, Leavis thought, was too eloquent by half, an overwrought, thrilled embrace of strangeness. (Max Beerbohm, the great Edwardian parodist, did a terrific Joseph Conrad: "Silence, the silence murmurous and unquiet of a tropical night, brooded over the hut that, baked through by the sun, sweated a vapour beneath the cynical light of the stars. . . . Within the hut, the form of the white man, corpulent and pale, was covered with a mosquito net that was itself illusory like everything else, only more so.")

Leavis complained of style. In recent years, however, the nature of Conrad's prose has itself become an element in the political disapproval of him—the occasional abstractness now regarded by those hostile to Conrad as an example of self-serving mythmaking, the language out of contact with the realities it purports to represent.

Read in isolation, such sentences are certainly a howl, but one reads them in isolation only in criticism like Leavis's or, more recently, Chinua Achebe's. Reading the tale straight through, I lost my discomfort after twenty pages or so and fell under Conrad's spell: thereafter, even his most heavily freighted constructions dropped surely into place, summing up the many specific matters that had come before. Marlow narrates:

"Going up that river was like travelling back to the earliest beginnings of the world, when vegetation rioted on the earth and the big trees were kings. An empty stream, a great silence, an impenetrable forest. The air was warm, thick, heavy, sluggish. There was no joy in the brilliance of sunshine. The long stretches of the waterway ran on, deserted, into the gloom of overshadowed distances. On silvery sandbanks hippos and alligators sunned themselves side by side. The broadening waters flowed through a mob of wooded islands. You lost your way on that river as you would in a desert and butted all day long against shoals trying to find the channel till you thought yourself bewitched and cut off for ever from everything you had known once—somewhere—far away—in another existence perhaps. There were moments when one's past came back to one, as it will sometimes when you have not a moment to spare to yourself; but it came in the shape of an unrestful and noisy dream remembered with wonder amongst the overwhelming realities of this strange world of plants and water and silence. And this stillness of life did not in the least resemble a peace. It was the stillness of an implacable force brooding over an inscrutable intention. . . ." (pp. 35–36)*

In one sense, the writing now seemed close to the movies: it reveled in sensation, in extreme acts and grotesque violence (however indirectly presented), in shivering enigmas and richly phrased premonitions and frights. In other ways, though, *Heart of Darkness* was modernism at its most intellectually bracing, with tonalities entirely contemporary and distanced that I had also failed to notice when I was younger: immense pride, and immense contempt; a mood of barely contained revolt; and sardonic humor approaching malevolence.

". . . I don't pretend to say that steamboat floated all the time. More than once she had to wade for a bit, with twenty cannibals splashing around and pushing. We had enlisted some of these chaps on the way for a crew. Fine fellows—cannibals—in their place. They were men one could work with, and I am grateful to them. And, after all, they did not eat each other before my face: they had brought along a provision of hippo-meat which went rotten and made the mystery of the wilderness stink in my nostrils. Phoo! I can sniff it now. I had the Manager on board and three or four pilgrims [i.e., white traders] with their staves—all complete. Sometimes we came upon a station close by the bank clinging to the skirts of the unknown, and the white men rushing out of a tumble-down hovel with great gestures

*I used the Norton edition, which includes biographical and historical materials of great interest as well as the views of leading Conrad critics.

of joy and surprise and welcome seemed very strange, had the appearance of being held there captive by a spell. The word 'ivory' would ring in the air for a while—and on we went again into the silence, along empty reaches, round the still bends, between the high walls of our winding way, reverberating in hollow claps the ponderous beat of the stern-wheel. . . ." (pp. 36–7)

Out of sight of their countrymen back home, who continue to cloak the colonial "mission" in the language of Christian charity and "improvement," the "pilgrims" have become rapacious and cruel. The cannibals eating hippo-meat practice restraint; the Europeans do not. That was the point of Shapiro's taunting initial sally: "Savagery" was inherent in all of us, including the most "civilized," for we lived, according to Conrad, in a brief interlude between innumerable centuries of darkness and the darkness yet to come. Only the rivets, desperately needed to repair Marlow's pathetic steamboat, offer security and stability—the rivets and the ship itself and the codes of seamanship and duty, all holding life together in a time of moral anarchy. Marlow, meeting Kurtz at last, despises him for letting go—and at the same time, with breathtaking ambivalence, admires him for going all the way to the bottom of his soul and discovering there, at the point of death, a judgment of his own life. It is perhaps the most famous death scene written after Shakespeare:

> "Anything approaching the change that came over his features I have never seen before and hope never to see again. Oh, I wasn't touched. I was fascinated. It was as though a veil had been rent. I saw on that ivory face the expression of somber pride, of ruthless power, of craven terror—of an intense and hopeless despair. Did he live his life again in every detail of desire, temptation, and surrender during that supreme moment of complete knowledge? He cried in a whisper at some image, at some vision—he cried out twice, a cry that was no more that a breath:
>   " 'The horror! The horror!' . . ." (p. 68)

Much dispute and occasional merriment have long attended the question of what, exactly, Kurtz means by the Victorian exclamation, "The horror!" But surely one of the things he means is his long reveling in "abominations"—what he has done, the giving way, the internal collapse. Shapiro's opening questions set up a liberal reading of the novella—an interrogation of the Western civilization of which Kurtz is the supreme representative and the students, in their youthful way, representatives as well. But recently, *Heart of Darkness* as a work of art, and the liberal reading of it as a somber critique of Western civilization and selfhood, have both been questioned by critics who considered aestheticism and liberal humanism a matched pair of delusions—an unconscious body of oppression designed to convince the powerless that their situation was normal. *Heart of Darkness*, according to this way of thinking, was a guilty text. It was complicit in the imperialist depredations that it exposed and deplored.

❖   ❖   ❖

When Shapiro asked the class why they thought he had chosen the book, hands were going up before he had finished his question.

"You chose it because the whole core curriculum is embodied in Kurtz," said Henry, who had earlier answered Shapiro's question about "a savage race." "We embody this knowledge, and the book asks what do we feel in the void—do we drown or come out with a stronger sense of self?"

Well, that was a mouthful, but I knew where Henry was coming from. He had turned the book into a test of the course and of himself. Conrad had great personal significance for Henry. In his sophomore year at Columbia, he had evolved into a fervent Nietzschean, and, though Conrad claimed to hate Nietzsche, this was a Nietzschean text. The meaning of Henry's life, his personal myth, required—he had said it in class many times—challenge, struggle, self-overcoming, and self-transcendence. He was tall, strong, with a flattop "wedge" haircut and a full, coarse voice. Some months after this class, he got himself not tattooed but *branded* with the insignia of his black Columbia fraternity, an act of excruciating irony unavailable to members of the master race. Kurtz, however horrifying, was an exemplar for Henry, just as he was for Conrad's narrator, Charlie Marlow.

Christine Wong, the freshman of Chinese descent from Singapore, who was largely raised on British literature, also saw the book as a test for Western civilization. But unlike Henry, she hated the abyss. Kurtz was a seduced man, a portent of disintegration. "Can we deal with the knowledge we are seeking?" she asked. "Or will we say with Kurtz, 'The horror'?" For her, Kurtz's outburst was an admission of the failure of knowledge.

And many others made similar remarks. All of a sudden, at the end of the course, the students were quite willing to see their year of education in Western classics as problematic. Their reading of "the great books" could be affirmed only if it were simultaneously interrogated. No doubt Shapiro's rhetorical questions had shaped their responses, but still, their intensity surprised me.

"The book is a kind of test," said Joseph, the mild and polite Joseph, who now developed Christine's line. "Does its existence redeem the male hegemonic line of culture? Does it redeem education in this tradition?" By which I believe that Joseph also meant to ask, "Could the existence of such a book redeem the crimes of imperialism?" That, at least, was my question.

Shapiro's students were bolder and freer than they had been all year long, and as the class went on, they expounded points in the text, some of them holding the little paperbacks in their hands like preachers before the faithful. Over and over, Shapiro had struggled to get them to read aloud, and with some emotional commitment to the words. And all too often they had droned, as if reading a technical manual. But now they read aloud spontaneously, and their voices were up, excited, even ringing. They were becoming readers.

"For this course, it's a kind of summing up, isn't it?" Shapiro said. "We began with the journey to Troy. . . . "

"It has a resemblance to all the journeys through hell we've read," said Alex, who had been scornful and then intelligent about Jane Austen; and Alex cited the voyages to the underworld in the *Odyssey* and the *Aeneid*, and he mentioned Dante, whom Conrad, in one of his greatest moments, obviously had in mind. Marlow arrives at the trading company's Central Station, a disastrous ramshackle settlement of wrecked machinery and rusting nails, and there encounters, under the trees, dozens of exhausted African workers who have been left to die. "It seemed to me I had stepped into the gloomy circle of some Inferno," he says.

> "They were dying slowly—it was very clear. They were not enemies, they were not criminals, they were nothing earthly now, nothing but black shadows of disease and starvation lying confusedly in the greenish gloom. Brought from all the recesses of the coast in all the legality of time contracts, lost in uncongenial surroundings, fed on unfamiliar food, they sickened, became inefficient, and were then allowed to crawl away and rest. These moribund shapes were free as air—and nearly as thin. I began to distinguish the gleam of the eyes under the trees. Then glancing down I saw a face near my hand. The black bones reclined at full length with one shoulder against the tree, and slowly the eyelids rose and the sunken eyes looked up at me, enormous and vacant, a kind of blind, white flicker in the depths of the orbs which died out slowly. The man seemed young— almost a boy—but you know with them it's hard to tell. I found nothing else to do but to offer him one of my good Swede's ship's biscuits I had in my pocket. The fingers closed slowly on it and held—there was no other movement and no other glance. He had tied a bit of white worsted round his neck—Why? Where did he get it. Was it a badge—an ornament—a charm—a propitiatory act? Was there any idea at all connected with it. It looked startling round his black neck this bit of white thread from beyond the seas.

"Near the same tree two more bundles of acute angles sat with their legs drawn up. One, with his chin propped on his knees, stared at nothing in an intolerable and appalling manner. His brother phantom rested its forehead as if overcome with a great weariness; and all about others were scattered in every pose of contorted collapse, as in some picture of a massacre or a pestilence. . . ." (pp. 20–21)

Despite the final clauses, which link the grove of death to ancient and medieval catastrophes, there is a sense here, as many readers have said, of something unprecedented in horror, something new on earth—what later became known as genocide. It is one of Conrad's bitter ironies that at least some of the Europeans forcing the Congolese into labor are "liberals" devoted to the "suppression of savage customs." What they had perpetrated in the Congo was not, perhaps, planned slaughter, but it was a slaughter nonetheless, with results no different than if produced by intention, and some of the students, pointing to the passage, were abashed. Western man had done this. We had created an inferno on earth. *Heart of Darkness*, written at the end of the nineteenth century, resonates unhappily throughout the twentieth. Marlow's shock, the sheer strangeness of the ravaged human forms, anticipates what the Allied liberators of the concentration camps felt in 1945. The answer to the question "Does the book redeem the West?" could only be provisional, since no book can do that for any culture. But if some crimes are irredeemable, frank acknowledgment of crime might lead to a partial remission of sin. Conrad had written such an acknowledgment.

That was the heart of the liberal reading, and Shapiro's students rose to it willingly, gravely, ardently—and then, all of a sudden, the class fell into an acrimonious dispute. Alex was not happy with the way Shapiro and the students were talking about Kurtz and the moral self-judgment of the West. He thought it was glib. He couldn't see the book in apocalyptic terms. Kurtz was a criminal, an isolated figure. He was not representative of the West or of anything else. "Why is this a critique of the West?" he demanded. "No culture celebrates men like Kurtz. No culture condones what he did." There was general protest, even a few laughs. "Okay," he said, yielding a bit, "it can be read as a critique of the West, but not *only* of the West."

From my corner of the room, I took a hard look at him. He was tight as a drum, dry, a little supercilious. Kurtz had nothing to do with *him*— that was his unmistakable attitude. He denied the connection that the other students acknowledged. He was cut off in some way, withholding himself. Yet I knew this student. I *knew* him. I had seen him only in class, and only in the second semester, but there was something familiar in him that irked me, though exactly what it was, I couldn't say. Why was he so dense? The other students were not claiming responsibility for imperialism or luxuriating in guilt. They were merely admitting participation in an "advanced" civilization that could lose its moral bearings and collapse into viciousness. They thought it was possible.

Henry, leaning back in his chair—against the wall, behind Alex, who sat at the table—insisted on the existential reading. "Kurtz is an Everyman figure," he said. "He gets down to the soul, below the layers of parents, religion, society."

Alex disagreed. They were talking past one another, offering different angles of approach, but there was an edge to their voices that suggested an animus that went beyond mere disagreement. There was an awkward pause, and some of the students stirred uneasily. I had never seen these two quarrel in the past, and what they said presented no grounds for anger, but when each repeated his position, anger suddenly filled the room. Shapiro tried to calm things down, and the other students looked at one another in wonder and alarm. The argument between Alex and Henry wasn't about race, yet race unmistakably hovered over it. In a tangent, Henry brought up the way Conrad, reflecting European assumptions of his time, portrayed the Africans as wild and primitive. He started to make a case similar to Achebe's (whose hostile essay is included in the Norton Critical Edition of the text—some of the students had purchased it, though it wasn't required). But then Henry stopped in midsentence, abruptly abandoning his position. In our class on *King Lear* and at other times in the year, he had argued explicitly as a black man. But at this moment he wasn't interested. A greater urgency overcame him—not the racial but the existential issue, his own pressing need for identification not just as an African-American but as an embattled man. "Good and evil are conventions," he said. "They collapse under stress." And this was true for everyone.

"The book is also about the *difference* between good and evil," Alex retorted. "Everyone *judges* Kurtz." But this is not correct. Marlow judges Kurtz; Conrad judges Kurtz. But back in Brussels, Kurtz is mourned as an apostle of enlightenment.

I looked a little closer. Alex was like the fabled "wicked son" in the Passover celebration, the one who says to the others, "Why is this important to *you*?"—denying a personal connection with an event of mesmerizing significance. I knew him, all right. A pale, narrow face, a bony nose surmounted by glasses, a paucity of flesh, a general air of asexual arrogance. He was very bright and very young. Of all the students in Shapiro's class, he was—I saw it now—the closest to myself at eighteen or nineteen. He was incomparably more self-assured and articulate, but I recognized him all too well. And I was startled. All year long, hardly admitting it, I had been searching for some sign of that undergraduate of the 1960s, pale, tentative, thin, ambitious but timid, and I had come up with very little, a shadow, an imprint here and there in some corner, but nothing more. I had little expected this simulacrum to rise up as a walking ghost.

Henry sat sheathed in green turtleneck sweater, dark glasses, and a baseball cap; I couldn't see his expression. Did the quarrel between him and Alex take some of its anger from the long wrangle between blacks and Jews, the abominable bitterness that had snarled intellectual and political life in New York for years? I wasn't sure, but Shapiro was not happy. He had perhaps gone a little too far with his rhetorical questions, striking sparks that threatened to turn into a conflagration, and he quickly moved the conversation away, getting the students to explicate Conrad's use of the word "darkness." England, where Marlow sits, telling his story (on a cruising yawl docked in an estuary of the Thames)—England, Conrad says, had also been one of the dark places of the earth.

For a while, teacher and students explicated the text in a neutral way. All year long, Shapiro had gone back and forth between analyzing the structure and language of the books and attacking students' complacencies with rhetorical questions—hacking away at the frozen sea. But sober analysis wasn't what he wanted, not of this text, and he returned to the complicity of the West and even the Western universities in a policy that King Leopold II of Belgium—the man responsible for some of the worst atrocities of colonial Africa—always referred to as noble and self-sacrificing.

"How else would you guys be civilized except for 'the noble cause,' " Shapiro said. "You guys are all products of the noble cause. Columbia's slogan, translated from the Latin, is, 'In thy light shall we see light.' That's the light that's supposed to penetrate the heart of darkness, isn't it?"

"But enlightenment comes only by way of darkness," said Henry, and Alex demurred angrily again, to which Henry, his voice raised and challenging, responded, "If you don't have an opinion of what's in the darkness, Alex, you miss the point of the book. What Conrad is asking you to do is look into the void and draw a conclusion."

Alex was furious, and for a terrible moment, I thought they were actually going to come to blows. The women in the class, who were largely silent during these exchanges, were appalled and afterward muttered angrily. "It's a boy thing, macho showing off. Who's the biggest intellectual?" True, but it was also a race thing. Though Shapiro restored order, something had broken, and the class that had begun so well, with everyone joining in and expounding, had come unriveted.

❖   ❖   ❖

Is *Heart of Darkness* a depraved book? The following is one of the passages Chinua Achebe deplores as racist:

> "We were wanderers on a prehistoric earth, on an earth that wore the aspect of an unknown planet. We could have fancied ourselves the first of men taking possession of an accursed inheritance, to be subdued at the cost of profound anguish and of excessive toil. But suddenly as we struggled round a bend there would be a glimpse of rush walls, of peaked grass-roofs, a burst of yells, a whirl of black limbs, a mass of hands clapping, of feet stamping, of bodies swaying, of eyes rolling under the droop of heavy and motionless foliage. The steamer toiled along slowly on the edge of a black and incomprehensible frenzy. The prehistoric man was cursing us, praying to us, welcoming us—who could tell? We were cut off from the comprehension of our surroundings; we glided past like phantoms, wondering and secretly appalled, as sane men would be before an enthusiastic outbreak in a madhouse. We could not understand because we were too far and could not remember because we were travelling in the night of first ages, of those ages that are gone, leaving hardly a sign—and no memories.
>
> "The earth seemed unearthly. We are accustomed to look upon the shackled form of a conquered monster, but there—there you could look at a thing monstrous and free. It was unearthly and the men were. . . . No they were not inhuman. Well, you know that was the worst of it—this suspicion of their not being inhuman. It would come slowly to one. They howled and leaped and spun and made horrid faces, but what thrilled you was just the thought of their humanity—like yours—the thought of your remote kinship with this wild and passionate uproar. Ugly. Yes, it was ugly enough, but if you were man enough you would admit to yourself that there was in you just the faintest trace of a response to the terrible frankness of that noise, a dim suspicion of there being a meaning in it which you— you so remote from the night of first ages—could comprehend. . . ."
> (pp. 37–38)

Achebe believes that *Heart of Darkness* is an example of the European habit of setting up Africa "as a foil to Europe, a place of negations . . . in comparison with which Europe's own state of spiritual grace will be manifest." Conrad, obsessed with the black skin of Africans, had as his real purpose the desire to comfort Europeans in their sense of superiority: "*Heart of Darkness* projects the image of Africa as 'the other world,' the antithesis of Europe and therefore of civilization, a place where man's vaunted intelligence and refinement are finally mocked by triumphant bestiality." Achebe dismissed the grove-of-death passage and others like it as "bleeding-heart sentiments," mere decoration in a book that "parades in the most vulgar fashion prejudices and insults from which a section of mankind has suffered untold agonies and atrocities in the past and continues to do so in many ways and many places today. I am talking about a story in which the very humanity of black people is called in question."

Chinua Achebe has written at least one great novel, *Things Fall Apart* (1958), a book I love and from which I have learned a great deal. Yet this article on Conrad—originally a speech delivered at the University of Massachusetts in 1975, and revised for the third Norton edition of the novel in 1987 and reprinted as well in Achebe's 1988 collection of essays, *Hopes and Impediments**—is an act of rhetorical violence, and I recoiled from it. Achebe regards the book not as an expression of its time or the elaboration of a fictional situation, in which a white man's fears of the unknown are accurately represented, but as a general slander against Africans, a simple racial attack. As far as Achebe is concerned, Africans had struggled to free themselves from the prison of colonial discourse, and for him reading Conrad meant reentering the prison: *Heart of Darkness* is a book in which Europeans consistently have the upper hand. Conrad was a racist, and that was that.

I wanted to argue that most of the students with whom I had just read the book—not Europeans but an American elite—had seen *Heart of Darkness* as a representation of the West's infamy, and hardly as an affirmation of its "spiritual grace." And I would insist that everything in *Heart of Darkness*—not just the spectacular frights of the African jungle but everything, including the city of Brussels and Marlow's perception of every white character—is rendered sardonically and nightmarishly as an experience of estrangement and displacement.

Yes, Conrad describes the Africans gesticulating on the riverbank as a violently incomprehensible "other." But consider the fictional situation! Having arrived fresh from Europe, Marlow, surrounded by jungle, commands a small steamer traveling up the big river, en route to an unknown destiny—death, perhaps. He is a character in an adventure story, baffled by strangeness. Achebe appears to have wanted him to engage the Africans in conversation or, at least, observe them closely and come to the realization that they, too, are a people, they, too, are souls and have a destiny and spiritual struggles and triumphs and disasters of selfhood. For surely they partook of such things as much as Marlow and Kurtz. But could African selfhood be described within this brief narrative, with its ceaseless physical and philosophical momentum, and within Conrad's purpose of exposing the "pitiless folly" of the Europeans? Achebe wants another story, another hero, another conscious-

---

* Published by Vintage.

ness. As it happens, Marlow, regarding the African tribesmen as savage and incomprehensible, nevertheless feels a kinship with them. He recognizes no moral difference between himself and them. It is the Europeans who have been demoralized.

But what is the use? Although Achebe is a novelist, not a scholar, variants of his critique have appeared, in recent years, in many academic settings and in response to many classic works. Such publications as *Lingua Franca* (which reports on trends in the universities) are often filled with ads from university presses for books about literature and race, literature and gender, literature and empire, the social background of literature, "popular" genres of literature. Whatever these scholars are doing in the classroom, they are seeking to make their reputations outside the classroom with politicized views of literature. F. R. Leavis's criterion of greatness in literature—moral seriousness—has been replaced by the moral aggressiveness of the "cultural studies" or "postcolonial studies" academic who nails the author to whatever power formation existed around him. *Heart of Darkness* could indeed be read as racist by anyone sufficiently angry to ignore its fictional strategies, its palpable anguish, and the many differences between Conrad's 1890s consciousness of race and our own. It could be read as racist by anyone ruthless enough to detach its representation of life from meaning. As philosopher Richard Rorty recently complained, "Professors of cultural studies teach students to brush past heart-stopping poetry to seek out 'conditions of cultural production.'" Such readings are all part of the movement to disenchant reading. The old way of reading fiction for pleasure—my falling once again under Conrad's spell—has been declared naïve and possibly reactionary, a submission to political values whose nature is disguised, precisely, by the pleasures of the narrative. In some quarters, pleasure in reading has itself become a political error, rather like sex in Orwell's *1984*.

❖ ❖ ❖

As much as Conrad himself, Professor Edward Said is a self-created and ambiguous figure. A Palestinian Christian (from a Protestant family), Said was born in 1935 in Lebanon and was brought up in Jerusalem and Cairo—which is already an extraordinary mixture of roots and earth. Said then built a formidable career in America, where he eventually assumed the position of exiled literary man *in extremis*, an Arab critic of the West and defender of the Palestinian cause who lives and works in the West; a reader at home in Western literature who makes an active case for non-Western literature.

He is, in many ways, an admirable figure. He has attempted to bring different cultures into relation with one another; he loathes insularity,

parochialism, and national or ethnic chauvinism. While relentlessly criticizing the West, he denounces the simplicities of Third World nationalism (not as passionately or comprehensively as some of us would like,
but at least he does it); he disdains reductive Marxist and other "flatheaded" approaches to literature. In recent years, for instance, Said has
chastised some of his followers for carrying his moral and political critiques of Western literature to the point of caricature. And he has repeatedly discouraged any attempt to "level" the Western canon. I had
never heard him speak or teach (he started at Columbia just as I was
leaving as an undergraduate), but now I saw him around campus, a substantial-looking man, handsome, with a full head of hair, dark eyes, and
a gracious way of listening to whomever he talked to.

Said is perhaps the greatest and most widely read and catholic of
dissident academic critics. His most famous work is the remarkable
Orientalism (1978), a charged analysis of the Western habit of constructing an "exotic" image of the Muslim East as an aid to controlling
the Muslim East. Said wrote *Culture and Imperialism* as a sequel to that
book, and part of his intention is to bring to account the great European
nineteenth- and twentieth-century writers, as well as the many critics
and scholars devoted to such writers.* Michael Foucault provided the
model and the influence. Said was obsessed by the power of discourse
(literary, journalistic, academic) as a set of cultural attitudes that laid the
groundwork for and supported the institutions and beliefs of imperialism—particularly the Western notion, still alive today, he says, that Europeans and Americans had the right to govern subject peoples and their
successors in the Third World.

Is this true? Do Americans want to dominate or govern anyone in the
Third World? I don't think they do ("more trouble than it's worth"
would be the standard American response), but let's get to the point.
Most imaginative writers of the nineteenth century, Said writes, failed to
connect their art, their own spiritual practice, to the squalid workings of
colonialism. Such writers as Austen, Tennyson, Thomas Carlyle, Thackeray, Dickens, and Flaubert either harbored racist views of the subject
people then dominated by the English and French or simply acquiesced
in the material advantages of empire. They took empire for granted as a
space in which their characters might roam and prosper; they colluded
in evil. Here and there, one could see in their work shameless traces of
the subordinated world—a sugar plantation in Antigua whose earnings
sustain in English luxury a landed family (the Bertrams) in Austen's
Mansfield Park; a central character in Dickens's *Great Expectations* (the

* Knopf, 1993.

convict Magwitch), who enriches himself in the "white colony" of Australia and whose secret bequest turns Pip, the novel's young hero, into a "London gentleman." These novels, Said says, could not be fully understood without analyzing the connections to the imperial reality that supported them.

But how important is the source of the money to either novel? Austen mentions the Antigua plantation only a few times: Exactly *where* the Bertrams' money came from, as Said admits, clearly did not interest her. The sugar plantation is there as a means of income and as a way of getting Sir Thomas Bertram off the stage for a while, so the young people can fool around in his absence. And if the convict Magwitch had made his pile not in Australia but in, say, Scotland, by illegally cornering the market in barley or mash, how great a difference would it have made to the central thematic and metaphorical substance of *Great Expectations*? Magwitch would still be a disreputable convict whom Pip would have to reject as a scoundrel or accept as his true spiritual father. Were these novels, as literature, seriously affected by the alleged imperial nexus? Or was Said making lawyerlike points, not out of necessity but merely because they could be made?

Said admits that there's no reason for Jane Austen to have commented on the slaves on Sir Thomas Bertram's Antigua plantation, but, he says, that hardly means *we* should not be interested. Fine, but in that case, why does not Edward Said write about the slaves in Antigua? Isn't he hanging on to Jane Austen because she is a writer renowned for her acuteness and sensitivity, and he wants to shock us? "*Mansfield Park*," he asserts, "sublimates the agonies of Caribbean existence to a mere half-dozen passing references to Antigua." That tells you what Jane Austen's sensitivity comes to. Indeed, Said speaks of her as preparing the way: "[*Mansfield Park*] steadily, if unobtrusively, opens up a broad expanse of domestic imperialist culture without which Britain's subsequent acquisition of territory would not have been possible."

Such remarks caused a small furor in the British and American press when the book came out in 1993. But Said has not, I think, chosen Jane Austen carelessly. Indeed, one begins to suspect that *Mansfield Park* is useful precisely because it's so outlandish an example. For if Jane Austen, in this novel about marriage, sex, property, and role-playing, is heavily involved in the creation of imperialism, then everything is involved—every music-hall show, tearoom menu, and floral arrangement. The West's cultural innocence must be brought to the bar of justice.

In the end, isn't Said's thesis a massive tautology, an assumption that imperialism did, indeed, receive the support of a structure that produced . . . imperialism? By Said's measure, few writers would escape censure. Proust? Indifferent to French exploitation of North African native workers. (And where did the cork lining the walls of his bedroom come from? Morocco? India? The very armature of Proust's aesthetic contemplation partakes of imperial domination.) Henry James? Failed to inquire into the late-nineteenth-century industrial capitalism and overseas expansion which made possible the leisure, civilized discourse, and spiritual anguish of so many of his wealthy American characters. James's celebrated refinement was as much a product and an expression of American imperialism as Theodore Roosevelt's pugnacious jingoism. And so on. You could ravage any writer's reputation in this way, and what would be the point? *Some* sort of connection with power is part of any writer's survival.

When Said arrives at *Heart of Darkness* (a book he loves), he insists that Conrad as much as Marlow and Kurtz was enclosed within the mentality of imperial domination and therefore could not imagine any possibilities outside it; that is, Conrad could imagine Africans only as ruled by Europeans. This is fair enough. It's perfectly true that *Heart of Darkness* contains a few widely spaced and ambiguous remarks that appear to praise the British (as opposed to the Belgian or German) varieties of overseas dominion. But how much do such remarks matter against the overwhelming weight of all the rest—the awful sense of desolation produced by the represented physical chaos, the death and ravaging cruelty everywhere?

What readers remember is the *squalor* of imperialism, and it's surely misleading for Said to speak of *Heart of Darkness* as a work that was "an organic part of the 'scramble for Africa,' " a work that has functioned ever since to reassure Westerners that they had the right to rule the Third World. If we are to allow into discussion the question of the book's historical effect, shouldn't we ask, on the contrary, whether thousands of European and American readers may not have become *nauseated* by colonialism after reading *Heart of Darkness*? Said is so eager to find the hidden power structure in *Heart of Darkness*, he underestimates the power of what's right on the surface. Here is his summing up:

> Kurtz and Marlow acknowledge the darkness, the former as he is dying, the latter as he reflects retrospectively on the meaning of Kurtz's final words. They (and of course Conrad) are ahead of their time in understanding that what they call "the darkness" has an autonomy of its own, and can reinvade and reclaim what imperialism has taken for *its* own. But Marlow and Kurtz are also creatures of their time and cannot take the next step, which would be to recognize that what they saw, disablingly and disparagingly, as a non-European "darkness" was in fact a non-European world *resisting* imperialism so as one day to regain sovereignty and independence,

and not, as Conrad reductively says, to reestablish the darkness. Conrad's tragic limitation is that even though he could see clearly that on one level imperialism was essentially pure dominance and land-grabbing, he could not then conclude that imperialism had to end so that "natives" could lead lives free from European domination. As a creature of his time, Conrad could not grant the natives their freedom, despite his severe critique of the imperialism that enslaved them. (p. 30)

I have read this passage over and over, each time with increasing disbelief. It's not enough that Conrad captured the soul of imperialism, the genocidal elimination of a people forced into labor; no, his "tragic limitation" was his failure to "grant the natives their freedom." No doubt Said means something fragmentary—a tiny gesture, an implication, a few words that would suggest the liberated future. But I still found the idea bizarre as a suggested improvement of *Heart of Darkness*, and my mind was flooded with visions from terrible Hollywood movies: *Mist slowly lifts from thick, dark jungle, revealing a rainbow in the distance; Kurtz, wearing an ivory necklace, gestures to the jungle as he speaks to a magnificent-looking African chief. "Someday we will be gone. Your people will be free. . . ."*

Dear God, a vision of *freedom*? After the grove of death? Would not such a vision amount to the grossest sentimentality? And isn't Said's desire, however cautiously expressed, a slyly hostile prescription for the ruin of Conrad as an artist? Instead of doing what Said wants, Conrad says that England, too, has been one of the dark places of the earth. Throughout the book, he insists that the darkness is in all men.

Achebe indulges a similar sentimentality. Conrad, he says, was so obsessed with the savagery of the Africans that he had somehow failed to notice that Africans just north of the Congo were creating great works of art—making the masks and other artworks that only a few years later (in 1905) would astound such painters as Vlaminck, Derain, Picasso, and Matisse, thereby stimulating a new direction in European art (cubism and so on). "The point of all this," Achebe writes, "is to suggest that Conrad's picture of the people of the Congo seems grossly inadequate. . . ."

But no act of consciousness can ever be absolutely complete. Conrad did not offer *Heart of Darkness* as "a picture of the people of the Congo," any more than Achebe's *Things Fall Apart*, set in a Nigerian village, purports to be a rounded picture of the British overlords. Conrad, as much as his master, Henry James, was devoted to a ruthless notion of form. Short as it is—only about thirty-five thousand words —*Heart of Darkness* is a mordantly ironic tale of rescue enfolding a philosophical meditation on the complicity between "civilization" and savagery. Conrad practices a narrow economy and omits a great deal. Economy is also a remarkable feature of the art of Chinua Achebe; and no more than Conrad should he be required to render a judgment for all time on every aspect of African civilization.

Achebe wants the book thrown out of the Western canon. "The question is whether a novel which celebrates this dehumanization, which depersonalizes a portion of the human race, can be called a great work of art," he writes. "My answer is: No, it cannot." Said, to be sure, would never suggest dropping Conrad from the reading lists. Still, one has to wonder if blaming writers for what they *fail to write about* is not a bizarrely wrongheaded or even malicious way of reading them. Said and Achebe's complaints are all too characteristic: Among the academic left, literature now inspires restless impatience. Literature excludes; it's about one thing and not another, represents one point of view and not another, "empowers" one class or race but not another. Literature lacks the perfection of justice, in which all voices must be heard, weighed, balanced. European literature is guilty of association with power, association with the "winners" of history. Jane Austen was guilty because she failed to mention imperialism; Conrad was guilty because he *did* mention it. They are guilty by definition and by category. In the end, the complaints come down to this: Joseph Conrad lacked the consciousness of race and imperial power that we have today. Poor, stupid Conrad! Trapped in the consciousness of his own time, he could do no more than write his books.

Why am I so angry? A disagreeable essay or book does not spell the end of Western civilization, and liberal humanists, of all people, should be able—even required, Mill would say—to listen to points of view contrary to their own. But what Achebe and Said (and a number of other politicized critics) are offering is not simply a different interpretation of this or that work but something close to an attack on the moral legitimacy of literature itself. Of course, if literature were in a state of exuberant health, one might shrug off such bizarre "readings"; one might accept the anger directed at works of art as a passing academic fashion, an outbreak of conference-hall daring soon to fade away. But in a period in which literature threatens to disappear into cyberspace, or simply get pushed to the side by the omnivorousness of pop culture, the universities pretty much dominate the show. For better or worse, the future of literacy belongs to the professors; and in recent years, parts of the academic left, eager to restore the unheard voices of the past, have begun discrediting the heard voices of the past.

❖ ❖ ❖

"There is no way for me to understand your pain," Henry said the next time the class met, speaking to everyone in general but perhaps to Alex in particular. "Nor is there any way for you to understand mine. The only common ground we have is that we can glimpse at the horror."

A portentous remark for so young a man, but he backed it up, launching into a formal presentation of his ideas about *Heart of Darkness*, rising from his seat behind Alex as he spoke. At one point, shouting with excitement, he brushed past him—"Watch out, Alex"—and threw some coins in the air, first catching them and then letting them drop to the table, where they landed with a clatter and rolled this way and that. Everyone jumped. "That's what the wilderness does," he said. "It disperses what we try to hold under control. Kurtz went in and saw that chaos."

The man had a talent for melodrama. "Chaos" was another Conradian word, and I shuddered; our first class had come close to breaking apart. Today, however, Shapiro had restored civility, beginning the class with a somber speech. Hunching over the long conference table, his voice low, he said, "I had to feel a little despair the other day." He warned the students against shouting past one another. He spoke very slowly of his own ambivalence in teaching a book that challenges the very nature of Western society. "It's very hard when you teach a course like Lit Hum, which the outside world represents as the normative, or even conservative, view of social values—it's very hard to *find* yourself. As you read Conrad, are you going to say, 'I'm going to step away from this culture'? Or do you say, 'Am I going to interact with it in some way that recognizes the contradictions and lies that culture tells itself'"?

And Shapiro went on, slowly restoring the frame of his class, situating the book in the year's work, and in the elite university sitting on the hill overlooking Harlem.

❖　❖　❖

So what had pleasure learned, how had pleasure been corrected, extended, or rebuffed? Looking back on our little culture war, I realize now that however much I disliked Achebe and Said's approach—their fear of narrative pleasure, their demand for correct attitudes—they helped me to understand what went on in that room. Just as Alex fought so eagerly to keep Western civilization untouched by the stain of Kurtz's crimes, I initially wanted *Heart of Darkness* to remain impervious to political analysis. In truth, I don't think any hostile political attack can seriously hurt Conrad's novella, which is endlessly suggestive and rich. Still, I had been changed by the debate in class. To maintain that this book is not embedded in the world—to treat it innocently, as earlier academic critics did, as a garden of symbols, or as a quest for the Grail or the Father, or whatnot—is itself to diminish Conrad's achievement. And to pretend that great literature has no political component is equal folly.

So let pleasure yield this much to the academic left: However wrong or extreme in individual cases, the academic left has alerted readers to the possible hidden assumptions in language and point of view. Achebe and Said jarred me into seeing, for instance, that Shapiro's way with *Heart of Darkness* was also highly political. I will quickly add that the great value of Shapiro's "liberal" reading is that it did not depend on reductive control of the book's meanings. When the class, provoked by Shapiro's questions, broke down, it did not do so along the clichéd lines of "Conrad was a racist, an imperialist." On the contrary, an African-American student had read the book seeking not victimization through literature but self-realization through literature. And the white and Asian students, with one exception, had tried in different ways not to accuse the text but to interrogate themselves. Their responses participated in the liberal consensus of a great university, in which the act of self-criticism is itself a goal—one of the highest goals—and a fulfillment of Western education. A benevolent politics, but politics nonetheless. The core curriculum ended not in hegemony but in criticism of hegemony.

But after granting Achebe and Said their right to read politically, one has to say they have got the case backward. Conrad's precarious situation both inside and outside imperialism, both inside and outside racial consciousness, should be seen not as a weakness but as a strength. This writer had done his time as a colonial employee, working for a Belgian company in 1890, making his own trip up the river Congo. He had lived within the framework of colonial expansion. If he had not, could he have written anything like *Heart of Darkness*? Could he have captured with such devastating force the peculiar hollow triviality of the colonists' ambitions, the self-seeking, the greed, the pettiness, the lies and evasions? The ambivalence of Conrad is precisely his glory. Here was the last great Victorian, insisting on responsibility and order, and fighting, at the same time, an exhausting struggle against uncertainty and doubt, such that he cast every truth in his fictions as a mocking illusion and turned what could have been a simple, morally didactic adventure tale into an endlessly provocative battle between stoical assumption of duty and perverse complicity in evil. Conrad's sea captain Marlow loathes the monstrous Kurtz, yet feels, after Kurtz's death, an overpowering loyalty to the integrity of what Kurtz discovered in his descent into crime.

> "I have wrestled with death. It is the most unexciting contest you can imagine. It takes place in an impalpable greyness, with nothing underfoot, with nothing around, without spectators, without clamour, without glory, without the great desire of victory, without the great fear of defeat, in a sickly atmosphere of tepid scepticism, with-

out much belief in your own right, and still less in that of your adversary. If such is the form of ultimate wisdom then life is a greater
riddle than some of us think it to be. I was within a hair's-breadth of
the last opportunity for pronouncement, and I found with humiliation that probably I would have nothing to say. This is the reason
why I affirm that Kurtz was a remarkable man. He had something
to say. He said it. . . . He had summed up—he had judged. 'The horror!' He was a remarkable man. After all, this was the expression of
some sort of belief; it had candour, it had conviction, it had a vibrating note of revolt in its whisper, it had the appalling face of a
glimpsed truth—the strange commingling of desire and hate. . . . It
was an affirmation, a moral victory paid for by innumerable defeats,
by abominable terrors, by abominable satisfactions. But it was a victory. That is why I have remained loyal to Kurtz to the last. . . . "
(pp. 69–70)

"The horror" was nothing less than Conrad's burden as artist and
man—the violent contraries that possessed him. T. S. Eliot and others
understood *Heart of Darkness* to be a new kind of art, an art that pulled
together the radically disjunctive experiences of the age—utmost violence and utmost spiritual longing—into ever more complex aesthetic
forms. The great achievement of modernism was its union of the discordant and the metaphysical. Seen in that light, the daunting intricacy of
Conrad's work is unimaginable *without* his participation in imperialism.
The students seemed to understand that. The intensity of their response—even their way of reading aloud—suggested they knew that
Heart of Darkness was something special, a work of art that was
thrilling and subversive at the same time. In their zeal to prosecute,
Achebe and Said seem to have forgotten why the culture was so fascinated by Conrad in the first place. They were both locked in perverse antagonism to what they loved.

Despite his "errors," Conrad will never be dropped from the reading
lists. Achebe's and Said's anguished rejection only confirms Conrad's
centrality to the modern age—and his place as an extraordinary possible
conclusion to a core-curriculum course in Western literature.

❖   ❖   ❖

At the end of the second class, Henry spoke at length of Kurtz's progression toward death and Marlow's "privilege of watching this self encounter itself," and Alex was silent, and perhaps abashed. My
antagonism toward him eased. I had not much liked myself as a young
man, but I would try to stop blaming him for what I had been. Alex had
resisted the class consensus, which took some courage, or stubbornness.
If Henry was a hero of reading, Alex may have been a hero, too, though
of a different kind. And if he thought he was absolved of "darkness," he

had a long time to discover otherwise. Good luck to him! In this class, liberal humanism had resisted and survived, though the experience had left us all a little shaken. It was hard these days, as Shapiro said, to find yourself.

"I don't want to say that this is a work that teaches desperation," he had said at the beginning of the class, "or that the evil is something we can't deal with. In some ways, the world we live in is not as dark as Conrad's; in some ways darker. This is not a one-way slide to the apocalypse that we are witnessing. We ourselves have the ability now to recognize and even to fix and change our society even as literature reflects, embodies, and serves as an agent of change."

The students were relieved. They wanted reconciliation and peace. And one of them, it seems, had, like Marlow, arrived at the end of his journey. "We scream at the wilderness," Henry said, concluding his presentation with a flourish, "and the wilderness screams back. There's a tension, and at that point of tension we resolve our nature."

Chapter *28*

WOOLF

- ~ Recalling things that had been lost: I overcome my loathing of Virginia Woolf
- ~ Professor Tayler's students take a turn at teaching
- ~ Tayler goes through the structure of *To the Lighthouse*
- ~ Thinking of death
- ~ The male critics who formed my taste and their hatred of Woolf
- ~ Feminism and Woolf's ascendency into the canon
- ~ *A Room of One's Own* as feminist text
- ~ The issue of judgment: "The greatest release of all"
- ~ Why does one read literature? I unreel the year as a film in my head

Spring had burst Columbia's gray cement and stone, and the windows in Hamilton were raised high. The sound of birds—birds!—penetrated the New York roar. We were reading Virginia Woolf as the last assigned text (Shapiro read Conrad, after Woolf, as a free choice in his final week). The author of *To the Lighthouse* and *Mrs. Dalloway* had not been on the list when I took Lit Hum in 1961. But recently, in a fit of tardy reform (spurred in part by women joining the College), the teaching staff had added Woolf and dropped Dostoyevsky's *Crime and Punishment*. Once again, it's silly to make too much of these substitutions in an arbitrary selection of masterpieces—and just as silly to pretend that one is indifferent to the changes. A large shift in taste had touched Columbia's core curriculum: Dostoyevsky, of course, would survive, but something had been added to literature, something added to sensibility.

When I first read Woolf, as a junior, stumbling through *To the Lighthouse* in an "English Novel" survey course taken two years after Lit Hum, I had registered very little. A cloud, swellingly gracious, noble, beautiful, but shapeless, even amorphous—that's all I can bring back, and I had largely stayed away from Woolf ever since. I had been sure she wasn't worth the trouble. She was gifted, almost alarmingly gifted, and she could do anything with language. Her casual literary essays (collected in *The Common Reader*) were perfect in manner. But she was too . . . *feminine*. She wrote at the edge of her nerves all the time, and was obsessively devoted to states of feeling and sensibility. Novels, I told myself sternly, had to be about something more than *that*. It was not an original opinion; nor was it correct as a description of Woolf, though it sufficed as a reason not to read her. Virginia Woolf, the haughty yet vulnerable queen of high modernism; the regnant center of a London circle of aesthetes and privileged intellectuals; a genius but also strange and mad; a woman by reputation superior, correct, contemptuous of Americans—Virginia Woolf the writer with social clout gave me the creeps. Her aestheticism seemed inseparable from snobbery and some vaguely Victorian wilting sickness. She made me feel like a nine-year-old boy.

But now, as I went through *To the Lighthouse* again, I was stunned by Virginia Woolf's prose. I could not read those tender, pressing, inward-driving sentences without stopping, reading again, and letting the words and rhythms sink in. Unable at the beginning of the year to remember Homer, unable to find myself, stumbling over empty memories and the vanished boundary between the reader sitting at home and the media engulfing everything, I had, by degrees, recovered one thing and then another, and now I had more memories than I knew what to do with. And the oddity of it was that the most abundant flood was produced by a writer who had never meant a thing to me.

There was, for instance, an experience, everyone has had it, which was almost incommunicable precisely because it disappeared as soon as you noticed it. Virginia Woolf had gotten it down over and over. The experience was not an act, or anything that might form an anecdote or a history, but an instant of perception, a moment that clarified relations and qualities long standing in place. You are sitting or standing somewhere, and the scene composes around your attempt to take it in. You sense a kind of buzz, not an actual sound but an increased presentiment of meaning. It may happen indoors, at the dinner table, with friends or family, the fruit and cakes reduced to scraps, the napkins tossed onto the table as the conversation breaks into small exchanges; or late at night, when the house is quiet and the cats stand next to each other on the living-room carpet, alert, posed, like matched china statues; or when one of the children, unable to sleep, lies down on the sofa amid books, toys, and stuffed animals, and, with mouth open and dribbling slightly, at last drops off. But usually it happens in the open air, as you are walking across a field or that part of the beach where the surf washes up and the sand grows darker and then lighter as the ocean passes over it and then drains away. *This is what life is supposed to be.* You are overcome by a sense of sufficiency.

The feeling may be derived from memories of contentment as a child, an early experience not just of sufficiency but of *suffusion*, in which each element—air, trees, animals, people—has its own character but no more, each relation its own necessity but no more. The sensation is impersonal and nonegotistical, akin to a religious swelling out into the universe. Not: I am large enough to take all this in. But: All this immensity is happening before me.

And then you may ridicule what you're feeling as a delusion or mere self-approval. And particularly if you are a man, you say, "This is nice, but so what?" and you forget it.

As I read a writer I was sure I had always hated, I suddenly found my way to these presentiments, and to other sensations and events normally lodged below the sill of consciousness. And as these things came back, I began to read Woolf with greater and greater pleasure, rather like a starfish gaining strength as it eats its way across the bottom of the ocean. Reading Woolf made me read Woolf better. But I also read myself better, and there was something else, something about her method and style that now seemed powerful and satisfying in a way that went very deep—though I couldn't, at first, put my finger on it.

My earlier misreading was more than a personal failure; it was also, I now knew, a cultural failure. But an amazing change had taken place. Woolf's writing, beautiful, original, noble, but often considered minor, affected, insufferable—she was a feminist who nevertheless took refuge in the feminine—now seemed inevitably great and, among other things, a glorious finish to such survey courses in Western classics as Literature Humanities. The entire tradition of Western literature could be heard breathing through that book. And there was that other baffling quality, something in Woolf's work that suggested the nature of reading and remembering itself.

❖ ❖ ❖

To the Lighthouse, first published in 1927, is in fact a hard book to like as a teenager. "The characters blur into one another," I heard a student say in Marina Van Zuylen's class. "I wasn't sure who I was reading about." The book was elusive at first reading, seemingly plotless, seemingly all spirit and no muscle, and almost suffocating in its insistent delicacy.

How inconsequential the "story" seems at first. A few years before the First World War, at the end of summer, a well-known philosophy professor and his wife, Mr. and Mrs. Ramsay, and their eight children and their friends and servants are staying together in the Ramsays' summer house—shabby but large and comfortable—on the Isle of Skye. Mrs. Ramsay, after reading to James, her youngest, sits knitting at a window in the late afternoon, looking out at the lighthouse across the bay as her husband, preoccupied, and reciting Tennyson's "Charge of the Light Brigade" to himself (often aloud), walks up and down on the lawn. Mrs. Ramsay has mysterious thoughts of shrinking into herself and of peace and possibly of death. The hour has not passed without difficulty. Earlier, James, who is six, had asked to go to the lighthouse, which is well out in the bay, a considerable journey by open boat across a rough northern sea. Mrs. Ramsay had said they would go the next day if the weather was fine.

> "But," said his father, stopping in front of the drawing-room window, "it won't be fine."
>
> Had there been an axe handy, or a poker, any weapon that would have gashed a hole in his father's breast and killed him, there and then, James would have seized it. Such were the extremes of emotion that Mr. Ramsay excited in his children's breasts by his mere presence; standing, as now, lean as a knife, narrow as the blade of one, grinning sarcastically, not only with the pleasure of disillusioning his son and casting ridicule upon his wife, who was ten thousand times better in every way than he was (James thought), but also with some secret conceit at his own accuracy of judgement. What he said was true. It was always true. He was incapable of untruth; never tampered with a fact; never altered a disagreeable word to suit the pleasure or convenience of any mortal being, least of all his own children, who, sprung from his loins, should be aware from childhood that life is difficult; facts uncompromising; and the passage to that fabled land where our hopes are extinguished, our frail barks founder in darkness (here Mr. Ramsay would straighten his back and narrow his little blue eyes upon the horizon), one that needs, above all, courage, truth, and the power to endure. (p. 4)

Mr. Ramsay's fantasies take quite a satirical pounding (those "little eyes" are always searching the horizon for some inhospitable sea or ice field in which the speaker of truth may die, ever so heroically, alone). The Ramsays have an unpleasant fight about the next day's weather, after which Mr. Ramsay wordlessly apologizes for his rudeness and, wordlessly again, begs for sympathy, for some soothing of his vanity and egotism. It is a solace that Mrs. Ramsay gladly gives. Reconciled with her husband, she sits at the window knitting, like one of the Fates, and then she receives the impression I have described of fullness or sufficiency.

> How could any Lord have made this world? she asked. With her mind she had always seized the fact that there is no reason, order, justice: but suffering, death, the poor. There was no treachery too base for the world to commit; she knew that. No happiness lasted;

she knew that. She knitted with firm composure, slightly pursing her lips and, without being aware of it, so stiffened and composed the lines of her face in a habit of sternness that when her husband passed, though he was chuckling at the thought that Hume, the philosopher, grown enormously fat, had stuck in a bog, he could not help noting, as he passed, the sternness at the heart of her beauty. It saddened him, and her remoteness pained him, and he felt, as he passed, that he could not protect her, and, when he reached the hedge, he was sad. He could do nothing to help her. He must stand by and watch her. Indeed, the infernal truth was, he made things worse for her. He was irritable—he was touchy. He had lost his temper over the Lighthouse. He looked into the hedge, into its intricacy, its darkness.

Always, Mrs. Ramsay felt, one helped oneself out of solitude reluctantly by laying hold of some little odd or end, some sound, some sight. She listened, but it was all very still; cricket was over; the children were in their baths; there was only the sound of the sea. She stopped knitting; she held the long reddish-brown stocking dangling in her hands a moment. She saw the light again. With some irony in her interrogation, for when one woke at all, one's relations changed, she looked at the steady light, the pitiless, the remorseless, which was so much her, yet so little her, which had her at its beck and call (she woke in the night and saw it bent across their bed, stroking the floor), but for all that she thought, watching it with fascination, hypnotised, as if it were stroking with its silver fingers some sealed vessel in her brain whose bursting would flood her with delight, she had known happiness, exquisite happiness, intense happiness, and it silvered the rough waves a little more brightly, as daylight faded, and the blue went out of the sea and it rolled in waves of pure lemon which curved and swelled and broke upon the beach and the ecstasy burst in her eyes and waves of pure delight raced over the floor of her mind and she felt, It is enough! It is enough! (pp. 64–65)

My resistance crumbled forever. In the end, it wasn't much of a struggle. Magnificence was not something any mere mortal should attempt, and Woolf had pulled it off. First the world as suffering and disorder, the darkness of the tangled hedge, and Mr. Ramsay's sense, this time offered without satire, of isolateness, and his fear that his wife was alone and that he could not reach her; and then, after the shift back to Mrs. Ramsay's consciousness, the attempt to hold on to some small tangible thing, a sound, a household ritual; and finally the light, the affirmation of life's sufficiency; and throughout, the language gathering tension in its repetitions and short breaths and finally easing and lengthening out at the end, right into the great crescendo. It *is* enough.

Whatever else the passage meant, it was also a great moment for readers of Lit Hum. For the passage is both a fulfillment of the Western tradition and a challenge to it, and I felt a surge of emotion as I remembered the books that came before Virginia Woolf, the students struggling from within the great media bog to read and to understand. Mrs. Ramsay, knitting at her window, evokes Penelope from the *Odyssey* (Mr. Ramsay is an Odysseus who can't get past a certain point in his philosophical journeys); but more to the point, Mrs. Ramsay experiences, with such heightened delight, what might be called an anti-Faustian impulse. Faust, in Goethe's version of the legend, will lose his wager with Mephistopheles and get dragged off to hell if ever he should tell the passing moment, "Oh, stay! You are so beautiful!" And so he strives for more life, more knowledge, more power and pleasure, and that, as we've seen, is the archetypal Western impulse, the restless ambition for more. Yet Mrs. Ramsay wants to say *nothing* but "Oh, stay! You are so beautiful." Mrs. Ramsay makes things happen, creating children and marriages, causing dinner-table conversation to merge and flow, harmonizing, unifying, ordering a whole range of experience—Mrs. Ramsay, who knits things together, wants to defeat "her old antagonist, life," that is, time, and hold everything in place. But she can't do it, she can make only "a momentary stay against confusion." And the book asks the question, Is *that* enough?

Mrs. Ramsay's solitary moments of consciousness ring out like great arias of protest and celebration. There was something so tremendous in this writing—supple, cultivated, yet expansive and reckless—that my distaste for it as a young man now puzzled me the way an early fear of riding would amaze someone galloping across a meadow. The chain of pleasure lengthened and grew stronger.

❖ ❖ ❖

In Professor Tayler's final class of the year, what he had promised from the first day became true: The students made him obsolete. At least for a while. Tayler was continuing the process of student-teaching that he had begun with *Pride and Prejudice*. All year long, he had forced the students to fill in the epic organic poem of the course he kept in his head. They filled out the stanzas. But now the students were ready to roll. By prior arrangement, two freshmen—Schulberg, a balled-up, red-faced young man, the son of a Columbia professor, stammering and silent all year, perhaps feeling more than he could say, and Carter, tall and smooth, a student who had grown stronger as the year went on—led the class through *To the Lighthouse*. The men stood side by side at the lectern, while Tayler sat off to the side, smiling slightly as the conversation moved back and forth between the two-headed teacher and the class. "Where does Mrs. Ramsay sit in the beginning?" they asked. "Why is the window important?"

The two teachers were surprisingly calm and precise; and though it was the end of the term and some of the students had not finished the book (they were too busy writing papers), they nevertheless got into the spirit of the occasion. Two women did most of the talking: Marjorie Finder, matter-of-fact in manner but with clear, strong ideas, and Felicia Parker, from Washington, D.C., the prep-school girl with long straight blond hair, perhaps the most literate student in the class. Finder and Parker answered direct questions so directly—the women leading with their response for a while, and then the men with their questions—that the four of them seemed to be carrying on a conversation of strenuous formality suspended in time.

So they were doing it, at least some of them were, running on their own, reading, analyzing, "putting it together" as Tayler liked to say, attacking the hermeneutic circle; that is, simultaneously laying out the structure so they could appreciate the individual details and laying in the individual details so they could apprehend the overall structure. As Tayler had taught them, they avoided the swamp of "themes" and the tendentious waters of "character"—the high-school banalities that inevitably led one into ideological arguments—and concentrated instead on the structural and metaphoric building blocks. In the end, theme and character would come out (how could they not?) but anchored in the materials of the book rather than imposed from the outside in the hectoring current-day clichés of race, gender, class or the older clichés of "psychology." According to the spiritual logic of Tayler's method, the students would put *themselves* together, too, a self forming around the structured response to literature. They would stretch and create themselves in order to read these complicated books.

The proof was in the pudding. They had launched themselves as readers. In conversation, the two teachers and the two students plus two or three others—a minority but enough!—agreed that what unified *To the Lighthouse* was the progress of Lily Briscoe, the Ramsays' unmarried artist friend, who sits on the lawn in the early moments of the book and cannot finish her postimpressionist landscape. Mrs. Ramsay, before her ecstatic realization of life's sufficiency, withdraws into a wedge—a premonition, at the window, of death—and years later, when Mrs. Ramsay is dead, and the remaining members of the family are out on the water, at last sailing to the lighthouse, Lily tries to paint the picture again, and under stimulus of her memories of Mrs. Ramsay completes it at last. Mrs. Ramsay's view through the window becomes transformed, the students said, into Lily's vision on canvas. And there was a suggestion at the end that Lily might bend a little and offer some sympathy to that proud wreck Mr. Ramsay, now elderly and more pathetically needy than ever.

Lily Briscoe has, so to speak, absorbed what Mrs. Ramsay had to teach and has gone past her into independence.

They were launched; they were good. The two teachers asked specific questions and received specific answers, and Tayler smiled as they discussed Woolf's amazing reversal of standard sexual imagery and what it meant, and Felicia Parker read aloud the great early passage in which Mr. Ramsay stands before Mrs. Ramsay and James, wordlessly demanding sympathy.

> Mrs. Ramsay, who had been sitting loosely, folding her son in her arm, braced herself, and, half turning, seemed to raise herself with an effort, and at once to pour erect into the air a rain of energy, a column of spray, looking at the same time animated and alive as if all her energies were being fused into force, burning and illuminating (quietly though she sat, taking up her stocking again), and into this delicious fecundity, this fountain and spray of life, the fatal sterility of the male plunged itself, like a beak of brass, barren and bare. He wanted sympathy. He was a failure, he said. Mrs. Ramsay flashed her needles. Mr. Ramsay repeated, never taking his eyes from her face, that he was a failure. She blew the words back at him. "Charles Tansley [Mr. Ramsay's adoring disciple] . . ." she said. But he must have more than that. It was sympathy he wanted, to be assured of his genius, first of all, and then to be taken within the circle of life, warmed and soothed, to have his senses restored to him, his barrenness made fertile, and all the rooms of the house made full of life. . . . (p. 37)

And then Parker, as if she couldn't avoid making a few comments about character, even though it was against her better nature, said: "Ramsay feels shriveled. His sense of failure is enormous, and without her he feels he is nothing."

As Parker's remark about Mr. Ramsay hung in the air, the two men looked at Tayler and nodded. Everyone applauded, and Tayler moved back to the front, congratulating the teachers and the class. But now he had to finish up the year, pulling it together for them, taking us up to the modern period as the last element in the course he carried around in his head.

"Look," he said. "Virginia Woolf is going beyond Jane Austen, the last novelist we read, in two important ways. *Pride and Prejudice* is told by an omniscient narrator. But here you don't have omniscience. Henry James said that in fiction you're supposed to render it rather than state it, and Woolf takes that idea and moves from one center of consciousness to another. She's rendering consciousness, moving from one person to the other. And she's moving the story ahead through symbols. You're making a symbol, you're taking an ordinary element in social life and by repetition giving it more than a social meaning. The artist is playing with your expectations."

And he went to the board and put up some initials, as he had back in September.

A B C D E F

A B A B A B

He looked at the class, and then, just as he had the first day, turned back to the board and solemnly considered the alphabet, as if seeing the letters for the first time. "ABCDEF," he said slowly, in his baritone drawl. "That's your cultural baggage, what you bring to the book. You know what a lighthouse is, you know what a window is, you have ideas about marriage. And then the artist begins to use these elements and repeat— ABABAB. And she transforms what you know."

And he worked out the repeated symbolic motifs with us: the window looking out at the lighthouse; Mr. Ramsay's knifelike body cutting into the window; Lily Briscoe's incomplete picture (which resembles a window), and so on, and then he went back to the board and drew again.

"A lighthouse, with its single eye. Um, where's Nate Hurewitz today?" Nate Hurewitz was the young man who had trouble telling the difference between Tayler's drawings of a cat and a pig whose dream of his mother chopping up his father into a stew had served with such delirious appropriateness as a commentary on the more carnal messes of the Greek tragedies. Hurewitz dreamed in erotic symbols. But Hurewitz wasn't there.

"Mrs. Ramsay looks out at the lighthouse," Tayler went on, "and in the dinner-party scene, when they're all together, she sends out bits of comfort and sympathy; she makes a 'momentary stay against confusion,' as Woolf says, which is what a lighthouse does, too."

A few minutes later, as if responding to a summons, Hurewitz walked into the classroom, stopped, and stared in dismay at the "lighthouse" on the board, and everyone dissolved in laughter.

Order was restored, and Tayler said, "Work with the dichotomies, and then go beyond them."

Woolf set up certain distinctions between male and female, and then broke them down, merging the masculine and feminine characteristics—

Mrs. Ramsay the Victorian housewife a fecundating spray of life, Mr. Ramsay "a scimitar," yet, for all his eight children, "sterile" and "barren," and as Tayler went on, I realized we were in the middle of it, he was bringing character and even gender into the discussion by analyzing the metaphoric and symbolic structure of the novel.

Tayler and the class put it together, and I grew more and more excited. To the Lighthouse "amorphous"? On the contrary, it was extremely lucid. At first, Woolf seemed to be moving by association, linking one character's thoughts with the next, which is why the initial impression is of blurring, a cloud without edge, but if you looked hard and read in a different way, patiently, slowly, the steel beams and girders were clear enough. Tayler set up the structure, which, folded into the students' minds, with all its attendant eloquence and poetry and feeling, would expand again in the secret way of great books, unknown, perhaps forgotten, unacknowledged, but, I was beginning to think, always working.

A mystery, this business of memory and literature. I had been sure that Woolf had meant nothing to me all those years. But maybe it wasn't so, maybe she was there all the time, sending something drifting downward or drifting up, the ground she had laid was there, waiting until (at the least) I would read her again. Caught now, I held off for a few weeks, and then, when the term was over, read To the Lighthouse a third time, and in a state of happiness I had not known all year.

What an event! Movie reviewer discovers Virginia Woolf at the age of forty-eight! I fell in love with what everyone else had fallen in love with, the way Woolf fed the entire ordeal and ecstasy of consciousness through the simplest of domestic moments. After all, in the modern period, we know the worst: There is no common humanity, no universal view, no consciousness containing us all. We are all locked in ourselves, locked in partiality. Even the vain Mr. Ramsay knows the power of the darkness in the hedge; at that moment, his knowledge of isolation transcends vanity. Fear, admiration, egotism, loathing, the struggle to make up one's mind whether another person is good or bad, likable or detestable, a whole world of sensation and judgment goes spinning through consciousness. Our view is by necessity egostistical.

And yet, despite the isolation, little lines go out. At the end of all that thinking and weighing, Mrs. Ramsay says, at a dinner party, "Yes, there is plenty for everybody." That's all she says! And yet she is great. Just by her presence and the strength of what's floating through her mind, she overcomes egotism; she brings people *out* and together. At least for a moment. The sensations and impressions in her mind, however fleeting or fragmentary, rush out to meet what another character is thinking, joining in agreement or struggle. In Virginia Woolf's hands, the mental atmosphere of the novel had thickened and grown dramatic.

❖ ❖ ❖

I would stop and drift off as I read, just as I had at the beginning of the year, but I no longer grew exasperated with myself. I strayed, I wandered without shame, but not into fantasies of wealth or power or sex, and not into media images either. I wandered into realms I had forgotten until Woolf licensed remembering. As a small boy, I now remembered, I would often go by myself into some normally crowded and noisy place—a family dining room, a rec room at camp—when everyone was gone. I wanted to know, I think, what happened when the din of work and pleasure, the din of *use*, died away and nothing was going on at all. Sitting on the floor, I would stare at some odd bits of fluff rolled up into the corners, or at the bottom of the chair legs where the dark stain was worn away. The floor was speckled with white paint, as if ants had laid down plates for dinner; the chairs faced each other in a sociable order, like the furniture on a stage set after the curtain has gone down; and growing more and more melancholy, I would try to hear something, a remnant, an echo.

Without knowing why, children are often terribly sad. A trifle sets them off, and for a while they are inconsolable, their bafflement driving them further into grief. They feel almost a thrill of sadness, as if someone were sure to abandon them. What I did, wandering and sitting still in empty rooms, was, I think, a way of expressing childish grief. I wanted to know what absence felt like. Was absence just a variation on living, or a kind of death? When the room was empty, it was as if all the people no longer existed. I was trying to hear their sounds after they were dead. Or so I think now.

In his last year, collapsing from a stroke, Henry James thought he heard a voice, not his own, saying, "So here it is at last, the distinguished thing." James's voicing of death is both hilarious and profoundly heroic. I had forgotten my empty-room obsession for a long time, and as an adult I was incapable of thinking about "the distinguished thing." When I tried to think of death, my mind hit a wall; I did not "accept" it, as the psychologists and TV-talk-show hosts would have us do. Yet this early preoccupation with vacated rooms came back to me when I read Woolf's incomparable pages on the mortal life of the Ramsays' empty house. In "Time Passes," the second section of *To the Lighthouse*, Woolf constructs a kind of metaphysical horror movie. It is quite a scare show, every bit as frightening as Homer's quivering spear in the warrior's heart.

The Ramsays are away, off in London, and at first, the abandoned house is "innocence"; nothing penetrates the dusty silence but "the falling cries of birds, the drone and hum of the fields, a dog's bark, a man's shout." Then the house begins to crack and fade: The war intrudes, and within the house, "there came later in the summer ominous sounds like the measured blows of hammers dulled on felt, which, with their repeated shocks still further loosened the shawl and cracked the tea-cup. Now and again some glass tinkled in the cupboard as if a giant voice had shrieked so loud in its agony that tumblers stood inside a cupboard vibrated too."

The atmosphere turns sinister, even apocalyptic. And one remembers that in the prologue to this section, when the Ramsays were still in the house, one of the guests, the poet Augustus Carmichael, lies in bed reading Virgil. He blows out his candle; and now, thinking back on that moment, Lit Hum readers would recall that Virgil was Dante's guide through hell in the *Inferno*. Is this a clue? What happens in the empty house begins to seem an inferno without Virgil as guide. The candle is out. War rages outside the house and echoes are heard inside, and no one is there but the baffled novelist to give them meaning. In the Old Testament, God had frightened Job with the whales He had made, in comparison to which man was nothing, but now Woolf writes:

> Night after night, summer and winter, the torment of storms, the arrow-like stillness of fine weather, held their court without interference. Listening (had there been any one to listen) from the upper rooms of the empty house only gigantic chaos streaked with lightning could have been heard tumbling and tossing, as the winds and waves disported themselves like the amorphous bulks of leviathans whose brows are pierced by no light of reason, and mounted one on top of another, and lunged and plunged in the darkness (for night and day, month and year ran shapelessly together) in idiot games, until it seemed as if the universe were battling and tumbling, in brute confusion and wanton lust aimlessly by itself. (pp. 134–35)

So the creatures that God had said "beholdeth all high things" were now plunging the seas in meaningless violence, their "brows . . . pierced by no light of reason." The Ramsays' house, besieged by time and by God's indifference, seems to contain all of European civilization, cracking, rotting, falling into ruin ("rafters were laid bare; rats carried off this and that to gnaw behind the wainscots.)" By this point, we begin to realize that the entire book is a recapitulation and an elegy, a remembrance of the life that died in the First World War; and that each of Woolf's characters, passing everything through his mind, recapitulates the moral history of the West.

Not thinking of death, I tried to shake my dead father awake in a bank vault, and years later I reached into a bathtub to take my mother's pulse, and the touch of mortal flesh went through me. The grief-struck child is right: He will be abandoned in the end. In his 1994 book *The*

Western Canon, the critic Harold Bloom insists that the only thing great literature can do for us—besides offering pleasure—is to get us to accept death more easily. This is too grand for me: I don't think that's the only thing literature can do for us; literature may do many things for us. And why do we need to "accept" death, anyway? We need to know that it *exists*. Is that what Bloom had meant? If so, I agree with his remark. And now I was sure that death exists. Reading again Homer, Sophocles, the Bible, *Lear*, and Woolf had brought that home, by bringing back my morbid childish preoccupations and unfreezing my feelings about my parents and forcing me to care what I passed on to my children. By knowing that death exists, we know as well that certain experiences survive. Literature is survival, a gift artists make to others after learning that death exists. Lily Briscoe absorbs Mrs. Ramsay, and we absorb both of them.

So I read Woolf very slowly and gave free rein to my wanderings, swinging across the vines of association and memory and judgment and desire. Apes of thought! For many people, Virginia Woolf was irritatingly lyrical and vague. That last charge was a canard, as I now knew, but I understood the irritation with Woolf, because you must read her "deeply" or not at all. People who insist on "the story" become irritated and give up. We read literature, finally, for pleasure, and in order to know that death exists, which also means knowing how to live. A good part of living is thinking; Virginia Woolf dramatizes thinking. My "poor concentration," so enraging when I read the *Iliad*, may have been, as I had thought earlier, restlessness induced by the movie and television images chasing one another's tails across my mind, but now I knew that being unsettled has its uses, and I haltingly read Woolf and burrowed within memory and found my life.

❖   ❖   ❖

"In this novel," Tayler was saying, "the romantic image has gone into symbol. The people transcend their normal social reality, and you're going to get a symbolic picture of marriage. Mr. Ramsay wants only one thing: complete admiration, the assurance that his books are going to live. Mrs. Ramsay gives over to him. It's a great marriage, but someone has to give."

There was a stirring in the room. Sterngold did not like the idea that someone "had to give" in order to make a great marriage (I didn't like it, either; nor did I believe it). But Tayler was beginning to wind up the class, winding up the year, and he jumped ahead. "Look for the turning points, the symbolic turning points," he said, "and you'll find the meaning," and together we found one of them, a moment at the end, when the Ramsay children—the teenaged James (earlier thwarted by his father) and his sister Cam—are out there on the boat with Mr. Ramsay, at last heading toward the lighthouse, and the two of them, locked in anger at their father, are having a fierce, unspoken debate about whether to give him the sympathy he wants. Cam, who is considering forgiveness, looks at her brother and sees "James the lawgiver, with the tablets of eternal wisdom laid open on his knee." At that moment, James will not forgive, but he eventually gives way. "We're moving from the Old Testament, and justice, to the New, which insists on mercy," said Tayler. Mr. Ramsay, who would never tell anyone an untruth, not even to spare their feelings, had the sternness of the Old Testament; Mrs. Ramsay, who forgave, the spirit of the New. But in one of those transformations and reversals that rule *To the Lighthouse*, Mr. Ramsay will himself receive mercy from Lily Briscoe.

Sterngold was incensed. "Why should they give in to him?" she said. She cocked her head and glared, the way she always did when she was angry. A tough customer. Sterngold had stubbornly rejected the New Testament's notion of time; she had found Dante's revenges on his fellow Florentines unjust. Sterngold wanted justice; she was not about to give up the Old Testament. Nor was she about to agree that women had to give in to men.

❖ ❖ ❖

Gender had come in the door, as it should. The man-woman issue and questions of feminist consciousness and practice were never distant from almost any discussion of Woolf. Tayler dealt with such things in his way, and I saw the point of his method, and I admired it, but I knew there was a great deal more to say. For instance, there was an awkward truth that Tayler did not mention, and that freshmen were not likely to know: Many of the most prominent male literary critics of the century had ignored or dismissed Virginia Woolf. Her current canonical status, with which Tayler clearly agreed, is scarcely imaginable without the surge of feminist criticism in the last thirty years or so. The literary critics whom I had read over and over as a young man, and who formed a large part of my taste and taught me what a critic was, had never written so much as an essay on Woolf. Not F. R. Leavis, who hated Bloomsbury, the privileged literary circle in London (Woolf, Lytton Strachey, and so on), and who adopted as his modern master in fiction the working-class D. H. Lawrence; Leavis mentioned Virginia Woolf only to deride her pernicious influence. Not Edmund Wilson, who celebrated Gertrude Stein in his 1931 canon-making book on the moderns, *Axel's Castle*, and later wrote about Jane Austen, Edith Wharton, Edna St. Vincent Millay, Elinor Wylie, Dawn Powell, Harriet Beecher Stowe, and the diary-keeping ladies of the American Civil War, but said nothing, except in

passing, about Virginia Woolf. Not Lionel Trilling, the greatest of "the
New York intellectuals" and an immense figure at Columbia; Trilling's
modern British writers were Joyce, Lawrence, E. M. Forster, and Orwell.
Not some of the other leading literary critics among the New York intellectuals, Alfred Kazin, say, or Irving Howe, who wrote a powerful essay on Edith Wharton but turned to Virginia Woolf only in order to
defend a lesser writer, Arnold Bennett, from Woolf's attacks on him.
And John Updike, who as a critic has written about *everyone*, has mentioned Woolf only in passing.*

The one exception, at least among this list of the men in my life, was
Philip Rahv, the superbly tough-minded critic-editor who wrote a short,
negative essay in 1942, which was reprinted later in his various collections (you can find it in *Essays on Literature and Politics, 1932–1972*).
Rahv asserted that Woolf was a figure of the second rank: She had
grasped English literary tradition "one-sidedly, and perhaps in much too
feminine a fashion, not as a complete order but first and foremost as an
order of sentiments"; her idea of reality was "expressive of all the assumptions she was born to, of the safety and domestication of that
upper-class British culture to which she was so perfectly adjusted." (In
fact, Woolf was upper-middle-class.) And Rahv acknowledged an earlier
article by William Troy, from 1937, a critic now forgotten whose article
is the *locus classicus* of anti-VW complaints. Woolf's characters do not
have "that active impact . . . upon reality" that experience should have
in life or books, says Troy. "Because of this self-imposed limitation of
their experience, therefore, the characters of Mrs. Woolf are unable to
function but on a single plane of the sensibility."

These remarks have long ago withered and fallen to the ground; I
quote them only because they now appear so categorical and unexamined as to amount to outright prejudice; and because I'm ashamed that I
read them thirty years ago without seeing what was wrong with them.

Were these critics against women in general? No, they loved Jane
Austen or George Eliot or both, and some of them loved Emily Dickinson and Edith Wharton. But Woolf's writing did not fit their vitalist notion of literature. She did not write about war, finance, business,
adventure; or the great life of the urban middle classes and the urban
poor; or the follies and splendors of the aristocracy, the religious extremes, the sexual and criminal passions. Woolf stayed *inside*, and so she
struck the male critics as precious and even cloying. Admiring Virginia
Woolf must have seemed to them an embarrassingly minor aesthetic pas-

* It's possible that one of these critics has written a short article—a newspaper review,
say—that I've missed, but if so, it hasn't made the slightest ripple in the consciousness of
readers.

sion, comparable to an enthusiasm for floral arrangements or a perfectly written letter.

In recent years, however, scales have fallen from dead eyes; and the canon has creaked, cracked, and burst open. For Woolf was more worldly and hardheaded than her early male detractors or the mentioners-in-passing ever implied. (None of them told me that she could be a violent writer.) Immense amounts of experience, compressed into characterization and description, made the outer world—the great world—*there*, not directly, but distilled into the manner and thinking of its representatives. In *To the Lighthouse*, a good part of the moral and literary history of the West was there as well, and if the struggles in consciousness between one character and another lacked the brutal vitality of such moments in Homer and Shakespeare, Virginia Woolf nevertheless had her own kind of momentousness. What passed through the characters' minds stretched, despite its connection to the domestic moment—no, *because* of that connection—to the eternal questions: What was reality? What was life for? How could man and woman live together? What did women see and feel that men had no notion of?

In the years since I left college, Woolf's reputation has ascended from the modernist British-lit canon ("Joyce, Lawrence, Eliot, and Woolf") to the eternal canon. By the eighties, the small shelf of Virginia Woolf in good bookstores had expanded into a monster holding nine novels, the short fiction as well, six volumes of letters and five of diary, all the literary journalism and essays, the early journals—something like fifty volumes by last count, as well as many studies and biographies, innumerable special issues of literary quarterlies, a veritable industry, a publishing bonanza, and, at times, a joke. People with only a minor relation to Woolf, or no more than an absurd theory about her, had stepped forward to be noticed.

It was a famous victory, and in gratitude to the feminist critics, who were mainly responsible, I have tried to ignore the women in the universities who were using and misusing Woolf, claiming the most private of artists as a public possession, reading her entire work as an attack on the patriarchal family, or in terms of the childhood sexual abuse she was subjected to at the hands of her half-brother George Duckworth, and so on. I struggled to forget the mad American victim-consciousness and the separatist fantasies that have been directed onto Woolf in a manner alien to her nature as a writer and to her life as a social being. Though she disliked the word itself, Virginia Woolf was most assuredly a feminist. But to reduce her immense, varied output to a variety of current-day feminist agendas, and to marshal her iridescent metaphors as dull-edged weapons in the struggles for turf within the university, is to engage in exploitation, expropriation, and slander. If Woolf were now brought into contact with some of her academic champions, there would follow an explosion of scorn without parallel in English literature. Anyone who reads her carefully could prove as much.

So I could not altogether forget what the American academics had done to her. Praise the famous victory, but then watch out! Canonical judgment had been blind, remiss, misinformed; finally a breach had been made in the self-assurance of judgment. But how large a breach? And had the standard of judgment and the act of judging itself been compromised? Or had certain notions of the canonical been exposed as too restricted, and the old assessment of a wonderful and idiosyncratic writer revealed as false? It happened that I could turn to Woolf herself for guidance. She had addressed many of these questions, and what she said could not have pleased some of the politicized readers now laying out property with wire and fence.

❖ ❖ ❖

In 1929, two years after publishing *To the Lighthouse*, Virginia Woolf brought out *A Room of One's Own*, an explicit feminist polemic; and Professor Shapiro's class, before ending the year with Conrad, had taken it on. It's a little book, but the whole issue of the canon and its relation to social injustice is here.

Virginia Woolf had not gone to university (her brothers did, of course). She was privately tutored, and she read enormously in the library of her father, Leslie Stephen, a considerable critic and philosopher. In 1928, the women's colleges at Cambridge—Girton and Newnham— asked her to deliver some lectures on the subject of women and fiction. What she finally published as *A Room of One's Own*, an expanded and revised version of these talks, is a feminist polemic in the form of a comic novel—a novel on the subject of delivering lectures about women. At first, Woolf seems to be lost, puttering about in genteel dither, as if searching haplessly for a missing glove. Oh, dear, the subject is difficult. What shall she say? Women and literature? How tiresome. She cannot simply give a lecture. She could never "come to a conclusion." She must approach the truth roundabout; she must approach with fiction. She makes up a character, Mary Beton (the name doesn't matter, she assures us), who stands in for herself, and who studies and muses, searching the British Museum like some blue-stockinged Diogenes for the truth about women and writing.

It is all play, but with a hidden sting. The mock helplessness is a taunt, a way of provoking male impatience with female minds. Woolf joshes the rigidities of academic discourse as well; the book is a superb example of antiacademic insolence, as much so today as in 1929.

Woolf can make no argument without first grounding it in fiction, and fiction depends on the materials of life—the actual lawns of Cambridge, which Mary traverses (she is ordered off them), and its libraries, which she tries to enter (she is barred); the streets of London; and so on. Grounding everything in food and money and London coal chutes, Woolf wanders about, and touches, as if by chance, on the economic subjection of women, the male need for dominance, and the way gifted women have been confounded and defeated. In passing, finding her glove and putting it on, Woolf offers an echantingly tender yet stunningly rigorous critical history of women's imaginative writing in Britain; she lists the material requirements for a writer's life—some money and a room of one's own—and sets out the ideal qualities of a woman novelist. It is all there, the feminist case, at least for middle-class women, but stated lightly, easily, devastatingly.

Perhaps too lightly for some readers. In Shapiro's class, the discussion came around to the issue of anger, which Woolf, in a remarkable turn, described as a threat to literature. She thought it harmed literature's poise, distracting a writer from the fictional world she was creating. It was an opinion the women students, some of whom had attended Take Back the Night, found hard to accept. But then Susan, one of Shapiro's more earnest students, trying to reconcile anger and Woolf's strictures against it, said: "In the past, women were not allowed to own their anger, to express it. And now, if you express that anger in life, you won't have to express it in literature." This was an interesting remark that Woolf, I think, would have liked. Woolf did not disapprove of anger "in life." She was against it in literature when it became something obvious and didactic—as compared to her own very evident anger, which, cultivated in silken irony, was viciously exact.

Would the students understand that anger was necessary but never enough? Rebecca, who had been troubled by the tragedies of Sophocles, and who twisted her hands and wanted literature to be fair, then said, "It's hard for someone who has been oppressed not to hate," and to my surprise I felt a pang of sorrow that I would not see how she would turn out in another ten years or so. Rebecca, by the end of her freshman year, had transferred her demand for justice from literature to politics, which, of course, is where it belonged. She would be an admirable fighter for human rights. Would she also be an admirable reader? Or would she remain literal-minded and clenched, one of those restless ones searching literature for truths they could pin on their foreheads? Shapiro was fond of her because she gave him something to work with. Would others try to reclaim her? Or would she reclaim herself? She was not dull; she was a philistine, one of the rare natural ones. She would always be interesting. But I wouldn't see her, or any of the others, down the road, and I suddenly felt desolate.

The women were alive, but the men were crabby and ploddingly rational. Anger, after all, took many different forms. Fareed, the logical fellow from Abu Dhabi, claimed that he "hadn't learned anything new," which struck me as highly unlikely. And the ascetic and fleshless Alex, who was to have the angry dispute with Henry the following week about *Heart of Darkness*—and who so irritatingly reminded me of myself at nineteen—announced in his dry voice that *A Room of One's Own* was "uneven and self-indulgent, and full of tedious ideas that were misleading in relation to the book's own thesis." There was a shocked silence. He hadn't, it turned out, liked the way Woolf mixed, in one argument, the cause of women's oppression and its literary results; he thought she should keep her topics separate. He did not like indirection, levity, things mixed together or roiling below the surface.

The stinger had found its hide. Woolf knew that there would always be a priggish Alex to read her book. Hearing him, she might have said that he needed a woman's mind to fertilize his categorical nature, to broaden and soften his harsh distinctions, his either/or temperament.

"She complains of the urge to accumulate in men," he said. "She presents the urge to accumulate as a bad thing, yet the accumulative instinct has produced the beautiful universities in England that have yielded this immense stream of literature."

Nicely phrased, but there's no contradiction. It was Woolf's ironic point that accomplishment in literature has flowed in part from the male urge to conquer. The women, whose mothers mastered child-rearing rather than the rubber trade, do not have magnificent ancient colleges at Oxbridge but only rather threadbare new ones; they have rarely had education of the quality that the men have enjoyed. Taking the argument to the ground, Woolf establishes the contrast by telling the story of a magnificent lunch at a male college and a meager dinner at a female college, and she connects the richness of one meal to men's freedom to study and travel and write, and the meagerness of the other to women's limited and restricted lives. *A Room of One's Own* is a work of art whose arguments are so thoroughly intertwined with metaphor, comedy, and anecdote that the political line of the argument is inseparable from the aesthetic performance embodying it. Charmed, many of us stop seeing a political line at all. Deploring the too-virile male novel, Woolf calls for a mixing of male and female characteristics—the androgynous mind, as exemplified by Shakespeare—as the necessary intellectual soil of fiction. She wants a roundedness and sympathy of observation that goes beyond sex partisanship. By the end of the "lectures," one has a complete view of the subject. The reader says: "Here is a woman writing. What she is doing now is exactly what she is calling for."

And how could this writer who grounds everything in money and food not be deeply offended in her soul by the theoretical contemporary academic discourse? What she set up as an ideal for women has been ruled out of existence by that discourse. Follow Woolf's steps, for we are coming to the heart of the matter. First step: Just as in *To the Lighthouse*, Woolf complains in *A Room of One's Own* that the male urge to conquer everything demands of women constant support and admiration—and constant self-suppression. The men, though imposing and perhaps necessary, are also blind and sterile, and they drive women mad with rage. Yet Woolf's fictional creation "Mary Beton" (Woolf herself) has been lucky; Mary Beton has a legacy of five hundred pounds a year from her aunt. This frees her to do something extraordinary.

> I need not hate any man; he cannot hurt me. I need not flatter any man; he has nothing to give me. So imperceptibly I found myself adopting a new attitude towards the other half of the human race. It was absurd to blame any class or any sex, as a whole. Great bodies of people are never responsible for what they do. They are driven by instincts which are not within their control. They too, the patriarchs, the professors, had endless difficulties, terrible drawbacks to contend with. Their education had been in some ways as faulty as my own. It had bred in them defects as great. True, they had money and power, but only at the cost of harbouring in their breasts an eagle, a vulture, for ever tearing the liver out and plucking at the lungs—the instinct for possession, the rage for acquisition which drives them to desire other people's fields and goods perpetually; to make frontiers and flags; battleships and poison gas; to offer up their own lives and their children's lives. Walk through the Admiralty Arch (I had reached that monument), or any other avenue given up to trophies and cannon, and reflect upon the kind of glory celebrated there. Or watch in the spring sunshine the stockbroker and the great barrister going indoors to make money and more money and more money when it is a fact that five hundred pounds a year will keep one alive in the sunshine. These are unpleasant instincts to harbour, I reflected. They are bred of the conditions of life; of the lack of civilisation, I thought, looking at the statue of the Duke of Cambridge, and in particular at the feathers in his cocked hat, with a fixity that they have scarcely ever received before. And, as I realised these drawbacks, by degrees fear and bitterness modified themselves into pity and toleration; and then in a year or two, pity and toleration went, and the greatest release of all came, which is freedom to think of things in themselves. That building, for example, do I like it or not? Is that picture beautiful or not? Is that in my opinion a good book or a bad? Indeed my aunt's legacy unveiled the sky to me, and substituted for the large and imposing figure of a gentleman, which Milton recommended for my perpetual adoration, a view of the open sky. (pp. 38–39)

Now the second step. Look at that formulation near the end: *the greatest release of all . . . which is freedom to think of things in themselves*. That is, to see things in their own terms, without anger or ideology, without fear of men, or even reference to men. Particularly to see and judge works of art, which is what Virginia Woolf does through large stretches of this little book.

But isn't the "freedom to think of things in themselves" exactly the freedom that has been called illusory and impossible by the academic left? Nothing, it seems, can be seen or thought of in itself. Every judgment, every perception, we've been told, is conditioned by one's identity—by race, for instance, or by gender, or by class; by the illusion of objectivity and the trap of subjectivity; and most of all by the accumulated patterns of language, which must necessarily command much of one's thinking, and which represent in their seeming innocence long-held formations of power.

All of which is very provocative but must yield to the incomparable force of Virginia Woolf thinking of things in themselves. The name for such a desire and such a practice is "disinterestedness," which means the condition of not having a personal stake, a pecuniary or ideological interest, in the outcome of a given inquiry. Woolf believes it is not only possible but necessary. And in *A Room of One's Own*, she thinks of a great many books—especially books by women—in themselves; that is, she judges them very firmly, without thought of how the authors' sufferings might excuse the faults of their writing. She thinks that the oppression of women *produces* the bad writing. The women are angry and lose their way; they make speeches when they should be attending to the fictional situation.

So history exists, and oppression is effective; it disfigures people. These authors have strengths and talent, but they don't quite make it. Woolf writes with great tenderness of the bitter Lady Winchilsea and of the mad duchess, Margaret of Newcastle, "hare-brained and fantastical," who nevertheless had a great gift, and was mocked and ignored, until she shut herself up in her house; and of the familiar Charlotte Brontë, whose powerful novels *Jane Eyre* and *Villette* contain "an acidity which is the result of oppression, a buried suffering smouldering beneath her passion, a rancour which contracts these books, splendid as they are, with a spasm of pain." None of these women had "freedom to think of things in themselves."

Free of men, Woolf will read, she will judge, she will set standards. Jane Austen, Emily Brontë, and George Eliot are great; the others, though wonderful, and certainly worth reading, are limited, often by their anger.

So there it is: In the midst of this demand for liberation, in the full current of this passionate brief on behalf of women, Woolf affirms not only the traditional canon but the absolute necessity of unyielding literary judgment. I can think of no more stirring an expression of intellectual honesty.

Woolf said women needed money, space, and freedom—what we now call "empowerment." Scholars and critics in the university have performed their own version of empowering formerly neglected writers—women, blacks, or colonial subjects, or people who worked in "low" literary forms. They have *read* them. They have pulled a great deal of work from libraries and dusty attics, including slave narratives, diaries, fiction and poetry by subject peoples in Africa or the Caribbean. They have studied novels by eighteenth-century Irish or American women and such popular genres as Westerns, Gothic romances, and detective novels. They have made new anthologies, including forgotten works or, say, minor works by major female authors that illustrate scorned subjects or scorned experiences in the life of women. They have presented and expounded this newly revived work, which is exactly what scholars should be doing.

But the next step, the act of breathtaking intellectual honesty that Virginia Woolf performed—weighing, judging, placing, saying how writers may have been hurt as well as strengthened by their oppression—the scholar-critics have frequently ignored. On the contrary, as we've heard, they have often turned the tables on "standards," denouncing the "old narrative" of culture, casting out judgment altogether as a rigged game.

My belated "discovery" of Virginia Woolf was caused by feminist academics forcing open the canon, and I am grateful for that. The canon—thank God—is not impermeable or fixed forever. It opens now and then. And of course, hundreds of lesser writers are wonderful to read. But I have not lost my faith in the necessity of defining criteria of greatness, no matter how many people formerly without power may be hurt by such judgments. Greatness in literature is like sunshine: We receive immense pleasure from it; we take strength from it. And the books in such arbitrary selections as Columbia's reading lists have been assembled not by the exercise of class interest but by thousands of readers, over centuries, making precisely such disciminations as Virginia Woolf makes in this little book. Canon-bashing critics, by confusing their own career agendas with literary history, breed cynicism about judgment altogether and may end in destroying literature, for if their most nihilistic assumptions take hold, nothing will remain for literature but its claim on this or that injustice, this or that piece of turf, this or that formation of power. To some degree, this has already happened.

And to what end? Does anyone seriously imagine we will achieve social justice in America by reading bad or second- or third-level books and by ignoring great ones? (We will not attain it by reading great work either, but at least we will not be confused about what we are doing.) Virginia Woolf wanted rights and power for women, even the overthrow of the patriarchy, an institution which she thought led inevitably to fascism and war. But she did not seek the overthrow of literary standards; she confirmed literary standards. And now the old humanistic sense of what great literature *is* has widened, after the initial resistance, to take in Virginia Woolf. It will widen again to take in other writers, including writers recently promoted by scholars in the university. But without making the critical case in relation to the great work of the past, without making the aesthetic case—the case for more and more complex pleasures—academics are playing a con game, and in their hearts they must know it. People will not read boring books without career incentives to do so. Pleasure never lies, though pleasure requires cultivation, and complex pleasures the greatest cultivation of all: education.

❖ ❖ ❖

Professor Marina Van Zuylen, who licensed pleasure in literature for serious undergraduates, spoke fervently about Woolf in her final classes. She had dark skin and darkly beautiful eyes, and a voice that was both schoolteacherly and radiant, and when she spoke to the young men and women, she drew them into an intimacy with her.

"We began the course with Achilles' shield," she said. "Do you remember Achilles' shield?" and I remembered this time, I remembered that when Achilles returns to battle, Hephaestos, artificer and fire god, makes him new armor, especially a magnificent shield, "and upon it he elaborated many things in his skill and craftsmanship," namely the stars and the earth, and both a peaceful and warring city, and agriculture and flocks and scenes of dancing and celebration. "War, peace, life, death," Van Zuylen said. "The entire reality of Homer's epic reduced to a small space. A recognition is being elicited here, a reliving of the epic as a work of art."

But in *To the Lighthouse*, she said, there was not this recognizable monolithic reality but only the patches of light and substance on Lily Briscoe's canvas. Something evanescent. "In the modern period, we can't think of life as an epic about which we can make clear judgments. If you're looking for objectivity, for history, you're not going to get it in Woolf. You're going to get something else."

She pointed to a passage in the last section of the book where the remaining Ramsays are making their way to the lighthouse and Lily, trying to paint, sits on the lawn watching them, and Lily thinks that Mrs. Ramsay could "resolve things," bring people together; she could make moments that stayed in the mind, "affecting one almost like a work of art."

"Like a work of art," she repeated, looking from her canvas to the drawing-room steps and back again. She must rest for a moment. And, resting, looking from one to the other vaguely, the old question which traversed the sky of the soul perpetually, the vast, the general question which was apt to particularise itself at such moments as these, when she released faculties that had been on the strain, stood over her, paused over her, darkened over her. What is the meaning of life? That was all—a simple question; one that tended to close in on one with years. The great revelation had never come. The great revelation perhaps never did come. Instead there were little daily miracles, illuminations, matches struck unexpectedly in the dark; here was one. This, that, and the other; herself and Charles Tansley [whom Lily had argued with] and the breaking wave; Mrs. Ramsay bringing them together; Mrs. Ramsay saying, "Life stand still here"; Mrs. Ramsay making of the moment something permanent (as in another sphere Lily herself tried to make of the moment something permanent)—this was of the nature of a revelation. In the midst of chaos there was shape; this eternal passing and flowing (she looked at the clouds going and the leaves shaking) was struck into stability. Life stand still here, Mrs. Ramsay said. "Mrs. Ramsay! Mrs. Ramsay!" she repeated. She owed it all to her. (p. 161)

"Mrs. Ramsay makes moments," said Van Zuylen, drawing in the students more intimately. "And Mrs. Ramsay dies, and a part of you dies. But there's a resurrection of life through art. Like a dead grandparent, a part of you is lost forever, but it can be resurrected. It can be resurrected in art."

So the question receives its answer. Mrs. Ramsay's little moments survive. It is enough.

❖ ❖ ❖

Like Woolf, I could not "come to a conclusion." For the Western classics did not mean any one thing. There was no single line of significance, no "eternal truths," at least not of the type that William Bennett and Lynne Cheney thought they perceived. The Western classics were at war with one another, and there was only the experience of reading and its many shocks and comforts, its many small truths, and I thought back over my experience, my long, crowded, sofa-hugging year of concentrating and listening and drifting. I would try to unreel the year in my head as if it were a movie that I had to describe and criticize, and I began with my feeling amorphous, the sense that I was lapsing out into the media fog without boundaries or definition, that I was a person to whom nothing had ever happened except ten thousand movies, and so, beginning Homer again, I was dismayed because I didn't remember him, and I was shocked by the violence, the spear quivering in the beating heart, and by the absence of pity and also by the way Homer both gave one the physical magnificence of war and death and left one feeling, with sadness and relief, that he was far, far away; and I remembered how annoyed I had been at the students because they had no voices when they read aloud, they had no stories to tell, and I was angry at myself for having no story to tell, no story to tell the next generation. I thought of Plato and the tightly restricted education of the guardians and how, by contrast, we wanted children in a modern liberal education to experience everything, knowledge of evil as well as good, and my worrying over what part of my own culture I could give to my sons.

Shapiro's student Rebecca had wrung her hands because what happened to Oedipus was not fair, literature was not fair; she had yet to learn that fate was not something simply imposed and arbitrary, a sport of the gods, but it was your own nature and character in the face of what was irrational and unaccountable in life, and so success like Oedipus'— or even, on a much smaller scale, my own—made you blind and cut you off from knowledge of yourself. It was my lot to be a spectator, a movie critic, and so I received my comeuppance for my removal from life in *The Bacchae*, in which the young king who wants to watch the revels in the hills is pulled out of safety and torn apart, and I fought back and defended the spectator, who had to undergo his own struggle in the dark to know, to understand, to choose, and to learn.

Reading the Old Testament, I was awed and baffled by power, by God, and I panicked over Job's troubles, imagining that the roof might fall in on me and my family. But I was rescued from fear and weakness by the religious students, who saw properly that the Book of Job was a call to courage and not to self-pity. I fell in love with Jesus, my Jesus, who, whatever else he meant, was the most intelligent man in literature, supremely witty, but I became angry when I failed to comprehend the parables and I understood that as a Jew I wasn't supposed to; and so I had fantasies of flailing through a long, long corridor, the corridor of history and of the oppression of Jews, fantasies from which Tayler rescued me by expounding the New Testament's notion of time, which had triumphed, reordering the West, of which the Jews were a prominent part. And I realized it was insane to fight history if you had the means to flourish in your own life.

St. Paul introduced fear of the body, and Augustine told us we were split between what we were and what we wanted to be, the spirit hoping to love God but the unruly flesh rising on its own; we had disobeyed and now as fit punishment the flesh was in rebellion, and Dante punished that split so cruelly in his brilliant scheme of *contrapasso* (the punishment fit the crime), that I joined the students, rebelled, and refused to understand him, even though I was thrilled when Shapiro's student Francesca, her voice steady and low, read Dante's Italian aloud in the classroom. The split was healed first by Boccaccio, who believed that the sexual impulse in itself was not base but a great maker of action and of narrative; and by Professor Marina Van Zuylen, who licensed pleasure in literature; and then by Montaigne, who wrote as if the body was good, the body was life, nothing in it was higher or lower, and I wanted to steal from the great Montaigne.

And all this time, I was alarmed by thoughts that civil order in America was fading, attacked by crime, by the greed-inducing qualities of capitalism (a system I believed in) and by the deculturating attacks of the media (which I was part of), and by the failure of liberalism to provide solutions to such continuing disasters as poverty and the underclass; and my fears were increased by Hobbes, who made me remember the time two muggers put a revolver into my chest at the top of the stairs coming out of the subway at Forty-second Street near Lexington. Locke, who provided the basis in *rights* of the modern liberal state, but who offered nothing but those rights and mutual self-interest as a way of binding the state, Locke forced me to wonder what I owed the muggers (a society that encouraged work) and what they owed me (my liberty), and I thought again and again that the modern bourgeois was not much of a citizen, not what Rousseau had wanted, when, disgusted by prerevolutionary France as a corruption of spirit, he had demanded enthusiasm and spontaneity and complete participation in the collective will.

I was exposing myself to something greater than my life, stronger than my life—but also exposing my *life*—and the books called back things that I had forgotten or been afraid to face, and so I knew that I had sinned in the way Augustine said we all sinned and that I had not always served my mad and needy mother well in her final years, not as well as the Fool served Lear; for what she needed was not reason but love. By attending to the moral meaning, rather than the personal need, of her demands, I ignored my own instincts as a pragmatic American, instincts that also led me to reject Kant's laws derived from the free exercise of reason and a pure will, a morality exercised without practical success. I believed instead in Hume's notion of a social standard of morality, which was not relativism at all, as Professor Stephanson explained again and again, but a beginning code of behavior for all societies. Kant's prose was like an architectural plan with the connections between rooms left out, and I was plunged back into my unhappiness at the beginning of the year when I could not concentrate, and reading Kant, I became a truck going up a mountain, slipping often and regaining traction at a lower place. And reading Hegel, I struggled to change my habits, to give up satire and daydreaming, and when I heard at last the rhapsodic ardor of Hegel's lecturing voice, I was thrilled by the notion that there was a meaning and a shape to history and a moral destiny for the West in the expansion of freedom. Turning Hegel, who was upside down, right side up again, the young Marx knew that man in the industrial age was alienated not from Spirit, but from his own labor, and I knew that Marx the failed prophet was right about some things in our country and that young people needed to read him. He was what Mill had in mind in his heroic formulation of our duty to encounter views that directly contradicted our own—the views of Nietzsche, for instance, whose contempt for the Judeo-Christian moral heritage and dismissal of pity left me in a giddy state of indifference to everyone in our own society claiming the status of victim. But I came out of it.

I was discovering an edge, talking more and more in class, even competing with the teachers, and Professor Shapiro, sensing my need, or slyly setting me up, let me teach Jane Austen, and because she had been so important to my own literary education, I assumed she would be important to Shapiro's freshmen, too. But I tried to bully them, and I discovered, in my failure, what irony really was; and as I walked back into the room with Shapiro, I knew the case for pleasure, especially the most complex pleasures, had to be made all over again. But still, I was beginning to see the shape of desire, and now my past and my temper hove into sight, and reading still, I slipped by degrees and almost unconsciously into my own person as critic and roused myself out of neutrality and became angry at the posing academic leftists who transformed their rage at social inequality and their career agendas into an attack on the Western classics, as if art were responsible for the problems of American society. Amazed by the shriek of feedback in the night, by women telling stories of defeat, I thought I saw a decline among undergraduates in "the sentiment of sex," and I read feminist texts to see what I could learn, the blessed Beauvoir and the accusing MacKinnon, and wound up longing for the re-creation of a private theater of the emotions, which I then found, to my relief, in Virginia Woolf.

"I'm gonna miss you guys," Tayler said at the end of his class, and he had left his students with his favorite injunction, "Think double."

Thus the "old narrative." And thus the "hegemonic discourse." Dear God, the hegemonic discourse! A series of challenges, reversals, and overturnings. You are flung about like a child in an amusement park. If this be hegemony, I would not recommend it to the faint of heart. It hit me as something personal and revelatory, an electric prod to the hide of my complacence, though, in truth, by the end, I had grown stronger. Not empowered in the social way that critics of the canon meant, but personally stronger. I had followed pleasure and in so doing had recovered memory, I had recovered a good part of myself, for the Western tradition in literature, experienced as a personal adventure, questions everything and affirms everything, sloughs off and renews. At the end of it, as Tayler said, you get something, you get yourself.

The self? Like objectivity, and disinterestedness, and truth, and even reason, the self has been ruled a myth in the contemporary academy. The self, according to postmodernist theory, has been cast into fragments by contemporary life, dissolved into conflicting perspectives, constructed by language alone. The grand narratives of progress, revolution, and salvation have all collapsed, and the self could not take purchase. Without knowing the jargon, I was perhaps feeling something of this desolation myself when I began to read Homer.

But I did not feel desolate at the end of the year. The self may be a myth, but it's one of those myths, like God and objectivity, that we cannot live without. We must act as if it existed. The striving for it ennobles us; and the absence of it, as Saul Bellow has said, makes us easier to kill.

And when I had unreeled in my head the film of the year's adventure, I understood at last what had haunted me so much about Virginia Woolf's writing. It is this: The way she represents the workings of the mind parallels the workings of education. When you fail to hold any moment of supreme consciousness—the way I had failed to hold my childish exploration of death in empty rooms or my freshman reading of the *Iliad*—the moment drifts below as a buried reference, a normative check, a nutrient in the soil. Later it rises, or something rises out of it. In Woolf's writing, it rises in long arialike passages ("stream of consciousness," the usual name, doesn't seem dramatic enough) in which the many moments of registered anger, warmth, attraction, and revulsion are revived and joined to one another by association and placed into the thick mental air where they engage other people's emotions in tumultuous mute dialogue. Virginia Woolf dramatizes the habit of registering, forgetting, sorting, and retrieving. She wrote about special moments and also about what *remains*—about sensibility, the mental, thick-textured readiness that makes a person great.

And so with education. What we read as teenagers, we forget; the specific matter, detached from what concerns us in the present, falls like sediment. What remains is not so much the books themselves as a certain readiness, not formal knowledge but an imprint of the effort we made earlier to read and to understand—call it taste, temperament, judgment, whatever. "Curiously enough," Vladimir Nabokov wrote, "one cannot *read* a book; one can only reread it." Nabokov's remark is true (as well as clever) as long as one never forgets that the first sedimentary reading makes the rereading possible. And that is why it doesn't matter so much that some of us in class didn't "get" *Oedipus* or the *Aeneid* or Dante, or that I didn't get Virginia Woolf when I was twenty. What was important was that I had *read* her, and then, further advanced along the chain of pleasure, I rose up to read her again.

By the end of my year in school, I knew that the culture-ideologues, both left and right, are largely talking nonsense. Both groups simplify and caricature the Western tradition. They ignore its ornery and difficult books; they ignore its actual students, most of whom have been dispossessed. Whether white, black, Asian, or Latino, American students rarely arrive at college as habitual readers, which means that few of them have more than a nominal connection to the past. It is absurd to speak, as does the academic left, of classic Western texts dominating and silencing everyone but a ruling elite or white males. The vast majority of white students do not know the intellectual tradition that is allegedly theirs any better than black or brown ones do. They have not read its books, and when they do read them, they may respond well, but they will not respond in the way that the academic left supposes. For there is only one "hegemonic discourse" in the lives of American undergraduates, and that is the mass media. Most high schools can't begin to compete against a torrent of imagery and sound that makes every moment but the present seem quaint, bloodless, or dead.

When I began writing movie criticism in 1969, I could assume in my readers a stable background of respect (unexamined respect, perhaps) for traditional high culture against which the immediacy of pop was startling and liberating—a blow against timidity, schoolroom piety, and complacence. I was drawn to movie reviewing myself by the daring of the best movies of the late sixties and early seventies, and by the absence of a strong academic tradition in writing about them. But the only thing I can assume now is that there isn't much traditional culture left to explode. The situation has gone into reverse: The movies have declined; *pop* has become a field of conformity and complacency, while the traditional high culture, by means of its very strangeness and difficulty, strikes students as odd. They may even be shocked by it.

So the left-academic critics of the canon and of core-curriculum courses have got things comically wrong. They are eager to empower minority students and women; they want to make white male students recognize "the other"—the voices allegedly silenced by the traditional canon. But it is just such an experience as reading the canon which now forces students to confront the other. All students, not just white students, confront it when they read of Homer's pitiless warriors and of such women as Antigone or Dido who choose death as a matter of honor. They confront it in Plato's insistence on an education sanitized of representations of evil or weakness, in Aristotle's ideal of participation in government as a duty of citizenship. The students may be alarmed by the physicality of Dante's torments and, in a different way, by the sexual eagerness of women in Boccaccio. Rousseau's loathing of society and Marx's insistence that alienated labor is an unnatural state of being are both startling rebukes to our present arrangements. The style, manner, and thought of these books are all a long way from us. Yet they are part of us, too, fixed in our language and institutions, in our ideals and habits.

❖ ❖ ❖

At Columbia, the Literature Humanities course was set up in the late 1930s by humanists eager to preserve the culture of white male Christian Europe in a country increasingly populated with immigrants. These men, I suppose, may be described as hegemonists in the sense that the academic left means. But history has transformed Lit Hum (and also C.C.). After World War II, the courses were taught by intellectuals absorbed in the classics of modernism (Conrad, Yeats, Eliot, Joyce, Woolf, Kafka) and schooled by the disasters of totalitarianism and war. The teachers brought a special consciousness to their work: They taught the premodernist classics in a modernist way, emphasizing the elements of internal dissonance and conflict, the darker ironies, and the arguments between books. They saw the threats to community, the centrifugal forces that destroy human society. The way the books are taught now— and this should be true at most colleges—guarantees that no single or unitary meaning can be found in them. Reading again, I was not surprised that I loved the Western classics, but I was surprised by what they are. The books are less a conquering army than a kingdom of untamable beasts, at war with one another and with readers. Reading the books, the students receive an ethically strenuous education, a set of bracing intellectual habits, among them skepticism and self-criticism. They may be impelled to advocacy and belief as well, but they will not be impelled to any doctrine in particular—except perhaps the notion that a Western education, opening many doors at once, is an extraordinarily useful experience. In brief, the intended "hegemonic" celebration of the West became a continuing interrogation (as well as celebration) of the West.

Think double! as Professor Tayler says. To the left, I would say that reading the canon in the 1990s is unlikely to turn anyone into a chauvinist or an imperialist. The left should stop misstating the issue of elitism; it should stop confusing the literary hierarchy and the social hierarchy. The two must be disentangled. As the late Irving Howe liked to say: To believe that some books and traditions are more worthy than others is not to endorse the inequality of American society. A literary judgment may represent class prejudice, but it is naïve or dishonest to assume that it represents nothing more than class prejudice. People who deny the power of aesthetic experience or the possibility of disinterested judgment may well have cynical and careerist reasons for doing so.

And to the right, I would say that however instructive the great works might be in building the moral character of the nation's citizens, the books were more likely, in the initial brush, to mean something idiosyncratic and personal. First comes the personal reckoning, the summoning into existence of the self. A good teacher sets in motion a lifelong process of students' knowing themselves through their most complex pleasures and knowing their societies through a fundamental analysis of the principles on which they are based. I agree with William Bennett and other traditionalists to this extent: Men and women educated in the Western tradition will have the best possible shot at the daunting task of reinventing morality and community in a republic now badly tattered by fear and mistrust. These books—or any such representative selection—speak most powerfully of what a human being can be. They dramatize the utmost any of us is capable of in love, suffering, and knowledge. They offer the most direct representation of the possibilities of civil existence and the disaster of its dissolution. Reading and discussing the books, the students begin the act of repossession. They scrape away the media haze of secondhandedness.

By definition, that is an arduous and painful experience. Taking my own pulse, and watching the students struggle, fail, and succeed, I came to a conclusion that surprised me: The core-curriculum courses jar so many student habits, violate so many contemporary pieties, and challenge so many forms of laziness that so far from serving a reactionary function, they are actually the most radical courses in the undergraduate curriculum.

❖ ❖ ❖

The question of exclusion remains. Many African-American students enjoy the core-curriculum courses or at least give them grudging assent. I interviewed many students, and attended meetings on the core curriculum in which complaints were aired, and though many African-Americans wanted a more historicized consciousness around the books (what, for instance, was the role of Egypt in forming Greek culture?), few wanted a different set of texts. Yet I was haunted all year by the black student who was furious that she had been made to listen to Mozart and by other minority students I heard who insisted the courses were racist and blind and made them feel inferior.

As I listened to their complaints, I couldn't help noticing the words the students used: The West, they said, had failed in justice and equality. They employed the vocabulary and values of the West to attack the West for not living up to its own highest standards. They spoke against the courses in terms they may well have gleaned from the books. And I couldn't help noticing something else: They knew that a great culture had flourished in Europe, that the United States has inherited some of it and has been partly shaped by it. They might consider that culture their enemy, but they were not indifferent to it. They had taken its measure and they knew its power. That knowledge alone put them in a small minority of Americans.

At the risk of contradicting them, I would say that I came away with the impression that their identity as African-Americans had not been hurt or shriveled at all. People who feel inferior are not likely to stand up in public meetings and question institutional policy. (The beaten stay quiet.) Leaving college, such students would combine what they knew and what they had fought against; they would use both knowledge and resistance for their own purpose. Not the white man's purpose: their own purpose. Their identity as African-Americans would likely be strengthened by the experience.

If they refuse to consider the classics of Western culture as a "common" heritage, but use the books instead as a resource and a tool, that seems to me allegiance enough to "the West." The great thing about Western culture is that any American can stand on it, or on some small part of it. In this country, we take what we want and mix it with our own composition. No one here but the paranoid or simpleminded demands purity; no one plausibly accuses anyone else of cultural bastardy when all are truly bastards. But at the end of education, something both flexible and strong emerges from the meeting of influence and identity and takes its place in the world with a defiant freedom that no other modern culture can match.

For surely the game has changed. In the past, in the United States, we had a grave problem of access: Who writes, who reads, who composes, who publishes? Minority groups and women had no more than severely limited hold on what Marxists call "the means of cultural production." But no one can now say that women have been shut out of education, and when blacks are shut out, the reason is that they are poor and therefore suffer the dilemmas and demoralization of poverty. Inequality—power and powerlessness, the rich and the poor—remains the problem for African-Americans, not the cultural domination of white people. African-

Americans now have an abundant access to the presses, the media, the museums, the art galleries, the recording studios. What they absorb of the older "white" culture they will remake as their own; it cannot hurt them. Demagogues and ambitious academics who turn the culture of the past into a turf war are playing a diversionary game, drawing attention away from political and economic problems that can be solved only by studying, earning, voting, organizing, and taking power. None of these activities but the first can be accomplished in the English or Black Studies departments. The curriculum debate is not a tempest in a teapot but a teapot in a tempest. The storm rages outside the university.

What *can* be achieved through culture is the greatest range of pleasure and soulfulness and reasoning power that any of us is capable of. The courses in the Western classics force us to ask all those questions about self and society we no longer address without embarrassment—the questions our media-trained habits of irony have tricked us out of asking. In order to ask those questions, students need to be enchanted before they are disenchanted. They need to love the text before they attack the subtext. They need to read before they disappear into the aridities of electronic "information." They need a chance at making a self before they are told that it doesn't exist. They need a strong taste of Europe so they can become better Americans. Walt Whitman said it this way in *Leaves of Grass:*

> Dead poets, philosophs, priests,
> Martyrs, artists, inventors, governments long since,
> Language-shapers on other shores,
> Nations once powerful, now reduced, withdrawn, or desolate,
> I dare not proceed till I respectfully credit what you have left
>   wafted hither,
> I have perused it, own it is admirable, (moving awhile among it,)
> Think nothing can ever be greater, nothing can ever deserve more
>   than it deserves,
> Regarding it all intently a long while, then dismissing it,
> I stand in my place with my own day here.
>
> Here lands female and male,
> Here the heir-ship and heiress-ship of the world, here the flame
>   of materials,
> Here spirituality the translatress, the openly-avow'd,
> The ever-tending, the finalè of visible forms,
> The satisfier, after due long-waiting now advancing,
> Yes here comes my mistress the soul.

Appendix: Earlier Reading Lists

The Contemporary Civilization course has changed the nature of its reading lists so radically that printing syllabi from seventy or fifty years ago would serve little purpose. But Literature Humanities is a different story, and I thought certain changes in taste might usefully be brought out by giving a few earlier lists from the course. I have chosen the initial year of 1937–38 and then the twenty-fifth year of the course, 1961–62, which happens to be the year I first took it as a freshman.

LITERATURE HUMANITIES—1937–38

FALL SEMESTER

Homer	*Iliad*
Herodotus	*The Persian Wars*
Thucydides	*The History of the Peloponnesian War*
Aeschylus	*Oresteia*
Sophocles	*Oedipus the King*; *Antigone*
Euripides	*Electra*; *Iphigenia in Taurus*
Aristophanes	*The Frogs*; *Plutus*
Plato	*Ion*; *Apology*; *Republic*
Aristotle	*The Poetics*; *The Ethics*
Lucretius	*On the Nature of Things*
Aurelius	*Meditations*
Virgil	*Aeneid*
Augustine	*Confessions*

SPRING SEMESTER

Dante	*Inferno*
Machiavelli	*The Prince*
Rabelais	*Gargantua and Pantagruel*
Montaigne	*Essays*
Shakespeare	*Henry IV, Parts 1 and 2*

Cervantes	*Don Quixote*
Milton	*Paradise Lost*
Spinoza	*Ethics*
Molière	*Tartuffe; The Misanthrope; The Physician in Spite of Himself*
Swift	*Gulliver's Travels*
Fielding	*Tom Jones*
Rousseau	*Confessions*
Voltaire	*Candide*
Goethe	*Faust, Part 1*

LITERATURE HUMANITIES—1961–62

FALL SEMESTER

Homer	*Iliad*
Aeschylus	*Oresteia; Prometheus Bound*
Herodotus	*The Persian Wars*
Sophocles	*Oedipus the King; Antigone; Ajax; Philoctetes*
Euripides	*Hippolytus; Medea; The Bacchae*
Thucydides	*The History of the Peloponnesian War*
Aristophanes	*The Frogs; Lysistrata; The Clouds*
Plato	*Ion; Apology; Phaedo; Symposium; Republic*
Aristotle	*Ethics; The Art of Poetry*
Lucretius	*On the Nature of Things*
Virgil	*Aeneid*
The Bible	Genesis; Amos; Job

SPRING SEMESTER

The Bible	Matthew; John; Romans
Augustine	*Confessions*
Dante	*Inferno*
Rabelais	*Gargantua and Pantagruel*
Montaigne	*Essays*
Shakespeare	*Henry IV, Part 1; King Lear; Antony and Cleopatra; The Tempest*
Cervantes	*Don Quixote*
Milton	*Paradise Lost*
Spinoza	*Ethics*
Molière	*School for Wives; Tartuffe; The Misanthrope; The Physician in Spite of Himself*
Swift	*Gulliver's Travels*
Voltaire	*Candide*
Goethe	*Faust, Parts 1 and 2*
Dostoyevsky	*Crime and Punishment*

Selected Bibliography

As anyone can see, this book is not a work of scholarship. As I worked on it, I largely held to my initial intention of leaving aside the vast secondary literature devoted to the classic books studied in Columbia's core curriculum. But some works of criticism—say, Erich Auerbach's *Mimesis* or Isaiah Berlin's essays on Machiavelli and Mill—may justly be called classics in their own right, and at times, despite my resolve, affection or need drew me to these works; I also sampled, out of curiosity, the recent modes of theoretical, feminist, neohistoricist, and postcolonial criticism as well as conservative and liberal critiques of these trends. What follows is a list of such works as well as some general readings that I found useful.

Alter, Robert, and Kermode, Frank, eds. *The Literary Guide to the Bible.* Cambridge: Harvard University Press, 1987.

Anderson, Elijah. "The Code of the Streets." *Atlantic Monthly*, May 1994.

Atlas, James. *Battle of the Books: The Curriculum Debate in America.* New York: Norton, 1992.

Auerbach, Erich. *Mimesis: The Representation of Reality in Western Literature.* Princeton: Princeton University Press, 1953.

Balmer, Josephine. Introduction to *Sappho: Poems & Fragments.* Secaucus, N.J.: Meadowlands, 1984.

Bennett, William. "To Reclaim a Legacy" (1984 National Endowment for the Humanities report on education in the humanities). *Chronicle of Higher Education*, November 2, 1984.

Berlin, Isaiah. *Against the Current: Essays in the History of Ideas.* New York: Penguin, 1982; 1979.

———. *Four Essays on Liberty.* New York: Oxford University Press, 1969.

———. *Karl Marx.* Oxford University Press, 1978.

Berman, Paul, ed. *Debating P.C.: The Controversy over Political Correctness on College Campuses.* New York: Dell, 1992.

Birkerts, Sven. *The Gutenberg Elegies: The Fate of Reading in an Electronic Age*. Boston: Faber & Faber, 1994.

Bloom, Allan. *The Closing of the American Mind: How Higher Education Has Failed Democracy and Impoverished the Souls of Today's Students*. New York: Simon & Schuster, 1987.

Bloom, Harold, ed. *Joseph Conrad*. New York: Chelsea House, 1986.

———. *The Western Canon: The Books and the School of the Ages*. New York: Harcourt Brace Jovanovich, 1994.

Bromwich, David. *Politics by Other Means: Higher Education and Group Thinking*. New Haven: Yale University Press, 1992.

Cheney, Lynne. "Humanities in America: A Report to the President, the Congress, and the American People." Washington, D.C.: The National Endowment for the Humanities, 1988.

Childers, Joseph, and Hentzi, Gary, eds. *The Columbia Dictionary of Modern Literary and Cultural Criticism*. New York: Columbia University Press, 1995.

Crews, Frederick. *The Critics Bear It Away: American Fiction and the Academy*. New York: Random House, 1992.

Cross, Timothy P. *An Oasis of Order: The Core Curriculum at Columbia College*. New York: Office of the Dean, Columbia College, 1995.

Debord, Guy. *The Society of the Spectacle*. New York: Zone, 1994; 1967.

Dickstein, Morris. *Double Agent: The Critic & Society*. New York: Oxford University Press, 1992.

Diggins, John Patrick. *The Rise and Fall of the American Left*. New York: Norton, 1992.

DiIulio, John J., Jr. "The Question of Black Crime." *The Public Interest*, Fall, 1994.

D'Souza, Dinesh. *Illiberal Education: The Politics of Race and Sex on Campus*. New York: Free Press, 1991.

Eliot, T. S. *Selected Prose of T. S. Eliot*. Edited by Frank Kermode. New York: Harcourt Brace Jovanovich, 1975.

Fagles, Robert and Stanford, W. B. Introduction to *The Oresteia*. New York: Penguin, 1977.

Finley, M. I., *The World of Odysseus*. New York: Pelican, 1979.

Foucault, Michel. *Discipline and Punish: The Birth of the Prison*. New York: Vintage, 1979.

———. *A Reader*. Edited by Paul Rabinow. New York: Pantheon, 1984.

Fukuyama, Francis. *The End of History and the Last Man*. New York: Free Press, 1992.

Gates, Henry Louis, Jr. *Loose Canons: Notes on the Culture Wars*. New York: Oxford University Press, 1992.

Gless, Darryl J., and Smith, Barbara Herrnstein, eds. *The Politics of Liberal Education*. Durham, N.C.: Duke University Press, 1992.

Graff, Gerald. *Beyond the Culture Wars: How Teaching the Conflicts Can Revitalize American Education*. New York: Norton, 1992.

———. *Professing Literature: An Institutional History*. Chicago: University of Chicago Press, 1987.

Gray, Wallace. *Homer to Joyce: Interpretations of the Classic Works of Western Literature*. New York: Collier, 1985.

Himmelfarb, Gertrude. *The De-Moralization of Society: From Victorian Virtues to Modern Values*. New York: Knopf, 1995.

———. *On Looking into the Abyss: Untimely Thoughts on Culture and Society*. New York: Knopf, 1994.

Howe, Irving. *A Critic's Notebook*. New York: Harcourt Brace Jovanovich, 1994.

———. "In Defense of 'the Canon.' " *The New Republic*, February 18, 1991 (included as well in Berman anthology).

Hughes, Robert. *Culture of Complaint: The Fraying of America*. New York: Oxford University Press, 1993.

Lehman, David. *Signs of the Times: Deconstruction and the Fall of Paul de Man*. New York: Poseidon, 1991.

Kaufmann, Walter. *Nietzsche: Philosopher, Psychologist, Anti-Christ*. New York: Meridian, 1956; 1950.

Kermode, Frank. *The Genesis of Secrecy: On the Interpretation of Narrative*. Cambridge: Harvard University Press, 1979.

Kimball, Roger. *Tenured Radicals: How Politics Has Corrupted Our Higher Education*. New York: Harper & Row, 1990.

Knox, Bernard. "The Lost Lesbian" (on Sappho). *New Republic*, May 23, 1994.

Kurzweil, Edith, and Phillips, William, eds. *Our Country, Our Culture: The Politics of Political Correctness*. Boston: Partisan Review, 1994.

Leavis, F. R. *The Great Tradition*. New York: New York University Press, 1967.

Lentricchia, Frank, and McLaughlin, Thomas, eds. *Critical Terms for Literary Study*. 2nd ed. Chicago: University of Chicago Press, 1995.

MacIntyre, Alasdair. *A Short History of Ethics*. New York: Macmillan, 1966.

Malcolm X. *The Autobiography of Malcolm X*. New York: Grove, 1964.

Menand, Louis. "Lost Faculties" (review of Roger Kimball's *Tenured Radicals*). *New Republic*, July 9 and 16, 1990.

———. "The Politics of Deconstruction" (review of David Lehman's *Signs of the Times*). *New York Review of Books*, November 21, 1991.

———. "What Are Universities For? A Professor's View." *Harper's*, December 1991.

Nietzsche, Friedrich. *The Birth of Tragedy*. New York: Vintage, 1970.

Paglia, Camille. *Sex, Art, and American Culture*. New York: Vintage, 1992.

———. *Vamps and Tramps: New Essays*. New York: Vintage, 1994.

Pollitt, Katha. *Reasonable Creatures: Essays on Women and Feminism*. New York: Knopf, 1994.

————. "Why Do We Read?" *The Nation*, September 23, 1991 (also included in the Berman anthology).

Popper, Karl R. *The Open Society and Its Enemies. Vol. I, The Spell of Plato.* Princeton: Princeton University Press, 1971; 1966.

Quint, David. *Epic and Empire: Politics and Generic Form from Virgil to Milton.* Princeton: Princeton University Press, 1993.

Rahv, Philip. *Essays on Literature and Politics 1932–1972.* Boston: Houghton Mifflin, 1978.

Richter, David H., ed. *Falling into Theory: Conflicting Views on Reading Literature.* New York: Bedford, 1994.

Rorty, Richard. *Contingency, Irony, and Solidarity.* Cambridge: Cambridge University Press, 1989.

Said, Edward. *Culture and Imperialism.* New York: Knopf, 1993

————. *Orientalism.* New York: Vintage, 1978.

————. "The Politics of Knowledge." *Raritan*, Summer 1971 (also included in Berman anthology).

Schlesinger, Arthur M., Jr. *The Disuniting of America: Reflections on a Multicultural Society.* New York: Norton, 1992.

Searle, John. "The Storm over the University." *New York Review of Books*, December 6, 1990 (also included in Berman anthology).

Simons, Margaret A., ed. *Feminist Interpretations of Simone de Beauvoir.* University Park: Pennsylvania State University Press, 1995.

Smith, Barbara Herrnstein. *Contingencies of Value: Alternative Perspectives for Critical Theory.* Cambridge: Harvard University Press, 1986.

Sunstein, Cass R. "The Professor's New Clothes" (review of Stanley Fish's *There's No Such Thing as Free Speech and It's a Good Thing, Too*). *New Republic*, December 6, 1993.

Tomkins, Jane. *Sensational Designs: The Cultural Work of American Fiction 1790–1860.* Chicago: University of Chicago Press, 1989.

Trilling, Lionel. *The Last Decade: Essays and Reviews, 1965–75.* New York: Harcourt Brace Jovanovich, 1979.

————. *The Opposing Self.* New York: Viking, 1955.

Warshow, Robert. *The Immediate Experience.* New York: Atheneum, 1975 (1962).

Wieseltier, Leon. "Against Identity." *New Republic*, November 28, 1994.

Index

(continued from page 4)

For permission to reprint copyrighted material, grateful acknowledgment is made to the following publishers and translators:

Excerpts from *The Iliad of Homer* (Lattimore, trans.); *Oedipus the King* (Grene, trans.) by Sophocles, from *The Complete Greek Tragedies;* and *The Bacchae* (Arrowsmith, trans.) by Euripides, from *The Complete Greek Tragedies,* all used by permission of the University of Chicago Press.

Excerpts from *The Odyssey of Homer* (Lattimore, trans.) used by permission of Harper-Collins.

Excerpts from *The Republic* (Lee, trans.) by Plato, *The City of God* (Bettenson, trans.) and *The Confessions* (Pine-Coffin, trans.) by Augustine, and *The Decameron* (McWilliam, trans.) by Boccaccio, all used by permission of Penguin Books.

Excerpts from *The Nichomachean Ethics* (Ross, trans.) by Aristotle, used by permission of Oxford University Press.

Excerpts from *The Aeneid* (Fitzgerald, trans.) by Virgil, used by permission of Random House.

Excerpts from *The Divine Comedy of Dante: Inferno* (Mandelbaum, trans.) used by permission of Bantam Books, a division of Bantam Doubleday Dell Publishing Group.

Excerpts from *The Prince* (Ricci, trans.) by Machiavelli, used by permission of Random House.

Excerpts from *The Complete Essays of Montaigne* (Frame, trans.), used by permission of Stanford University Press.

Excerpts from *Rousseau's Political Writings* (Bondanella, trans.), Alan Ritter and Julia Conaway Bondanella, editors, and from *The Marx-Engels Reader,* Second Edition, Robert C. Tucker, editor, used by permission of W. W. Norton.

Excerpts from *Foundations of the Metaphysics of Morals* (Beck, trans.) by Kant, used by permission of Macmillan.

Excerpts from *Introduction to* The Philosophy of History (Rauch, trans.) by Hegel, used with permission of Hackett Publishing.

Excerpts from *On the Genealogy of Morals* (Kaufmann, trans.) by Nietzsche, used by permission of Random House.

Excerpts from *The Second Sex* (Parshley, trans.) by Simone de Beauvoir, used by permission of Alfred A. Knopf.

Excerpts from Lionel Trilling's essay on *Mansfield Park* from *The Opposing Self,* used by permission of the Estate of Lionel Trilling, Diana Trilling, executor.

Excerpt from *Culture and Imperialism* by Edward Said, used by permission of Alfred A. Knopf.

Excerpt from *Hopes and Impediments* by Chinua Achebe, used by permission of Vintage Books.

Excerpts from *To the Lighthouse* and *A Room of One's Own* by Virginia Woolf, used by permission of Harcourt Brace & Company.